☆ ☆ ☆ ☆

The Second Amendment on Trial

☆ ☆ ☆ ☆

The Second Amendment on Trial

Critical Essays on *District of Columbia v. Heller*

Edited by Saul Cornell & Nathan Kozuskanich

University of Massachusetts Press
AMHERST AND BOSTON

ISBN 978-1-55849-995-9 (paper); 994-2 (hardcover)

Designed by Kristina Kachele, LLC.
Set in Miller Text by House of Equations, Inc.
Printed and bound by Thomson-Shore, Inc.

Library of Congress Cataloging-in-Publication Data

The Second Amendment on trial : critical essays on District of Columbia v. Heller / edited by Saul
Cornell and Nathan Kozuskanich.
    pages   cm
Includes bibliographical references and index.
ISBN 978-1-55849-995-9 (pbk. : alk. paper) — ISBN 978-1-55849-994-2 (hardcover : alk. paper)
1. Heller, Dick Anthony—Trials, litigation, etc.   2. Washington (D.C.).—Trials, litigation, etc.
3. Firearms—Law and legislation—United States.   4. United States. Constitution. 2nd Amendment.
I. Cornell, Saul, editor of compilation.   II. Kozuskanich, Nathan, 1975– editor of compilation.
KF229.H45S43   2013
344.7305'33—dc23

                                                                        2013017812

British Library Cataloguing-in-Publication Data
A catalogue record for this book is available from the British Library.

Contents

☆ ☆ ☆ ☆

Acknowledgments

☆ ☆ ☆ ☆

THIS VOLUME WAS begun in 2006 as an effort on the part of the Second Amendment Research Center at the John Glenn School of Public Affairs at Ohio State University to bring together some of the best new scholarship on different aspects of the Second Amendment debate. The original structure of the volume included separate sections on history, law, and public policy, including some of the new work sponsored by the Center that was first presented at a series of conferences the Center organized. As the volume was taking shape, the Supreme Court agreed in November 2007 to take its first Second Amendment case in more than seventy years. Publishing a volume of scholarly essays when the Supreme Court was poised to redefine the legal meaning of the amendment did not make much sense, so plans for publication were shelved until *Heller* was decided. Before the decision had even been announced, plans and invitations for a variety of conferences on the case were in the works, so it seemed prudent to wait and see what emerged from these conferences before conceptualizing what such a volume should now include. At first it seemed that the recast volume would remain unchanged with the addition of a new section on *Heller*. After looking at the new scholarship written in response to *Heller*, we realized that the decision was sufficiently complex and important enough to warrant an entire volume. Although many of the nation's leading legal scholars had avoided the subject of the Second Amendment prior to *Heller,* the case drew some of them into the subject for the first time. The one obvious issue that the Court did not resolve in its June 2008 opinion, an issue that everyone knew would be resolved quickly, was the incorporation question. *McDonald v. City of Chicago* settled the incorporation issue in 2010, but not any of the major legal issues that *Heller* left unresolved. So once again, the volume was put on hold on the assumption that *McDonald* would generate an equally significant body of literature as *Heller.* Surprisingly, *McDonald* has not produced a comparable body of writing about the Second Amendment and gun regulation. Thus, we made the decision to focus exclusively on *Heller* as the case that redefined the way scholars, judges, and politicians talk about the Second Amendment.

The essays collected in this volume explore *Heller's* significance from a variety of different perspectives. We had hoped to include an essay by Professor Joyce Lee Malcolm in the original volume, since she is one of the few historians to support the Standard Model's individual rights conception of the amendment, but she denied us permission to republish her essay. Not wanting to lose her unique perspective, we decided to include the amicus brief she filed in *Heller* and pair it with another brief by leading early American historians. Including the amicus briefs gives the volume a unique coherence. It is possible to view the historical arguments presented to the Court and then read the scholarly reactions to how the Court used them.

This volume is the final product of the Second Amendment Research Center's efforts to bring greater historical and analytical rigor to scholarly discussion of the Second Amendment. The Supreme Court's decision in *Heller* effectively rendered new historical research on the Second Amendment moot, at least in terms of its application to current law. Although history continues to be important to the resolution of ongoing litigation on the scope of Second Amendment protections, both sides in American politics, liberals and conservatives, have embraced *Heller's* individual rights view of the Second Amendment. For the foreseeable future there is little reason to expect this to change.

We thank The Joyce Foundation for its generous support of the Second Amendment Research Center's work, which helped defray the costs of publishing this volume. Many thanks to our editor at University of Massachusetts Press, Clark Dougan, who immediately grasped the significance of the project and showed incredible patience as we tried to keep pace with the rapidly unfolding history discussed in this volume. This project has evolved significantly over the past six years and it is a much better volume thanks to his efforts. The production team at the University of Massachusetts Press was a pleasure to work with at every phase of the process. We would like to thank all of the scholars who generously agreed to allow their work to be republished here. In particular, we thank Kevin Sweeney for allowing a section from his ongoing work on guns and the militia to appear in this volume. Thanks also to Jamie Polesky and Rachel Loewen for their work preparing the manuscript for publication.

★ ★ ★ ★

Introduction

The D.C. Gun Case

Saul Cornell and Nathan Kozuskanich

★ ★ ★ ★

ON THE FINAL DAY of its 2008 term, a sharply divided U.S. Supreme Court issued a five-to-four decision in *District of Columbia v. Heller.*[1] The high court struck down the District of Columbia's stringent gun control laws as a violation of the Second Amendment, reversing almost seventy years of settled precedent that linked the meaning of the "right of the people to keep and bear arms" with the preservation of a "well regulated militia."[2] Reinterpreting the meaning of the amendment as securing an individual right to own a gun in the home for the purpose of self-defense, the Court opened up a new chapter in the contentious history of gun rights and gun control.

The Court's decision had been eagerly anticipated, and from the outset the case had a dramatic quality. *Heller* was born from *Parker v. District of Columbia*, a case that began in 2003 with a lawsuit in which Dick Anthony Heller was one of six plaintiffs to challenge the District of Columbia's gun laws (requiring all guns to be registered, but forbidding the registration of handguns) on Second Amendment grounds.[3] The District of Columbia appealed to precedent and sought to have the case dismissed because the Second Amendment protected only a collective right related to the militia. The plaintiffs then filed a motion for summary judgment. The National Rifle Association (NRA) opposed pressing *Parker* as a test case and tried to have it joined with its own recently filed gun litigation, *Seegars v. Ashcroft.*[4] The request was denied, and Heller's lawyers, a group of libertarians connected to the Cato Institute and the Institute for Justice, pushed forward. The team emulated civil rights–era legal strategy by looking for sympathetic clients who would play well before the Court and in the public eye. Heller, a District of Columbia Special Police Officer who could not legally have a gun at home but who was able to carry a firearm at his job at the Thurgood Marshall Federal Judicial Center, provided them the vehicle to bring their historic challenge to the District's law.

In 2004 the district court ruled on *Parker* and found in favor of the defendants, but that decision was reversed on appeal in early 2007. The appellate court also ruled that Heller was the only plaintiff with standing, leaving him the lone respondent when the District of Columbia appealed the reversal to the Supreme Court. Internal political bickering within the District's government led to the ouster of the lawyer who had drafted the government's brief before the oral argument.[5] In another surprise development, the pro-gun George W. Bush administration filed a brief in support of the District of Columbia, asking that the case be remanded back to the district court so that it could apply the appropriate level of judicial scrutiny. In essence, the solicitor general conceded that the Second Amendment was an individual right, but urged the Supreme Court to apply a more deferential standard of review than strict scrutiny, the most demanding standard for evaluating the constitutionality of a statute.[6] Laws subjected to the strict scrutiny test must be narrowly tailored and serve a compelling state interest. The Bush administration's brief would be the first of many ironies in the *Heller* case.

A wide assortment of politicians, academics, lawyers, and activists on both sides of the issue filed sixty-six amicus briefs and flooded the Court with over two thousand pages of reading. In addition to longtime combatants in the great gun debate like the NRA and the Brady Center to Prevent Gun Violence, smaller organizations such as Jews for the Preservation of Firearms and the gay/gun rights group the Pink Pistols also filed briefs. They were joined by contributions from professional linguists, historians, criminologists, medical doctors, lawyers, politicians, police and military personnel, and a variety of special interest groups. The scene outside the Court building on the day of the oral argument looked more like a rock concert than a typical day at the highest court in the land, with hundreds camping out in front of the Court to get a seat to watch the drama unfold.[7] The central issue in *Heller,* the meaning of the Second Amendment, had not come before the Court since 1939, when two gangsters were convicted of illegally transporting a double-barrel twelve-gauge Stevens shotgun from Oklahoma to Arkansas in violation of the 1934 National Firearms Act.[8] When the *Heller* decision was finally announced on June 26, 2008, affirming an individual right to bear arms unconnected to military service, it was hardly a surprise, given the Court's composition.[9] Though predictable, the outcome of the case did not diminish the magnitude of the Court's bold reinterpretation of the Second Amendment. Newspapers across the nation gave the *Heller* story front-page coverage, announcing the Court's new view of bearing arms and the Second Amendment.[10]

The decision in *District of Columbia v. Heller* unleashed a wave of litigation. Within hours of the decision's announcement, challenges to local gun laws were filed across America, including one from Heller's attorneys challenging Chicago's gun laws. Less than two years later, in *McDonald v. City of Chicago*, a similarly split Court once again affirmed that the Second Amendment was an individual right. This time the justices extended the right's application to states and localities, effectively incorporating the right to bear arms.[11] There have already been over six hundred challenges to gun laws or gun prosecutions filed in the wake of *District of Columbia v. Heller*.[12] Despite the significant number of challenges, apart from Chicago's comprehensive gun ban, most gun laws have survived challenge. The emerging consensus appears to be that any reasonable law short of a complete ban on handguns will likely pass constitutional muster. Literally as this introduction was being finalized in the fall of 2012, three new cases were decided: first, the Fifth U.S. Circuit Court of Appeals rejected the NRA's challenge to a 1968 federal law barring people under twenty-one from purchasing firearms from gun dealers; and second, the Second Circuit Court of Appeals upheld New York's requirement that one show "good cause" why one needs a concealed weapons permit. Finally, in *Moore* v. *Madigan*, Richard Posner, one of *Heller*'s harsh critics, concluded that an Illinois law prohibiting public carry was unconstitutional. The issue of how far *Heller*'s ruling extends outside the home has emerged as one of the most contentious issues.[13]

The two cases in which the statutes survived challenge fit the *Heller* rule that any regulation rooted in historical practice is presumptively lawful. Indeed, both laws had been on the books for just over a century. Nor is the outcome of the Illinois case all that surprising. In contrast to New York's law, the Illinois law was a complete ban similar in scope to the D.C. law at issue in *Heller*. The outcomes of these cases are not surprising if one keeps in mind that the District of Columbia's gun control law was among the strictest in the nation and was itself something of an anomaly. Indeed, the political pendulum in the mainstream debate over guns had already swung away from gun control and toward gun rights in the decade before *Heller* reached the Court.[14] Washington, D.C., and Chicago were isolated islands clinging to European-style gun regulatory schemes while the rest of America was awash in a sea of guns.

American politicians and the public had largely embraced a gun rights ideology and abandoned gun control by the end of the twentieth century, a development facilitated by a vibrant gun rights movement and a powerful gun lobby with enormous political clout. Vindicating an individual right under the Second Amendment and having it incorporated against the states has not diminished the rhetoric of the NRA or caused it to ratchet down its apocalyptic predictions about the threat of gun confiscation and domestic disarmament. In early 2012, NRA executive vice president Wayne LaPierre warned voters of a "massive Obama conspiracy . . . to destroy the Second Amendment during his second term."[15] Accordingly, the NRA spent $17 million in the 2012 general election in an attempt to defeat President Obama and Democrats in key Senate races.[16] Ironically, a dislike for Obama may be the only issue that the NRA and the Brady campaign actually share in common. While the NRA has no great love for the Obama administration, neither did the pro–gun regulation Brady Center, which awarded the Obama administration a failing F grade for its policies on gun control during its first term.[17] The basic reality in the American gun debate remains unchanged after *Heller*. The United States continues to be the most heavily armed society in world history, with an estimated 200 to 300 million firearms in private hands.[18]

The dynamics of the gun debate changed slightly in December of 2012 after the massacre of twenty small children and six adults at Sandy Hook Elementary School in Newtown, Connecticut. For the first time in well over a decade, polling data suggested that the majority of Americans believed stronger gun controls were necessary to deal with the problem of gun violence.[19] Newtown energized many voters, particularly mothers, who had never been involved in the gun control debate. Vigils and protests across the nation demanded swift and decisive action to implement stronger gun regulations. The pushback from gun rights advocates was also intense. As was true after earlier shootings, gun sales skyrocketed as gun owners rushed to purchase new assault weapons before any legislation could be enacted banning the sale or possession of such weapons.[20] The *Heller* case figured in the debate over the constitutionality of new more strict gun regulations. Democratic Senator

Charles Schumer advised gun control advocates to embrace *Heller* and work within its framework.[21] In Schumer's view, *Heller* poses no serious obstacles to effective gun regulations. Some gun rights advocates reject this view, arguing that *Heller* severely constrains the range of new regulations permissible.[22] The long-term impact of Newtown is difficult to judge. Once moribund, the subject of gun regulation has sprung back to life. Although significant change at the national level still faces serious obstacles, several states have already strengthened their existing gun laws even as other states with permissive gun regulation schemes have relaxed them even further.

GUNS AND THE CONSTITUTION: A BRIEF HISTORY

Understanding the issues in *Heller* requires some sense of the complex history of guns in America, including the tangled relationship between gun rights and gun control. For as long as there have been guns in America there have been regulations, but modern-style gun control regulations did not emerge until decades after the adoption of the Second Amendment. Founding era (1770s to 1790s) gun laws regulated the storage of firearms and gunpowder, restricted the discharge of weapons at certain times and in certain places, and limited possession to citizens judged virtuous and loyal.[23] Militia laws from the Founding era also specified the types of weapons eligible men needed to bring to muster (muskets for soldiers, horsemen's pistols for dragoons and other mounted units), and in some cases proscribed traveling with a loaded weapon to muster.[24] Militia weapons were subject to inspection by the government, and failure to maintain one's weapon or report to muster resulted in fines. States also exempted militia weapons from seizure during debt proceedings, but treated other arms as ordinary property. The goal of government firearms policy in the Founding era was to encourage ownership of military-style weapons and to regulate them closely. While modern politics offers only two real choices in the debate over guns—either pro-gun or pro-regulation—the Founders were actually both pro-gun and pro-regulation.[25]

Things changed dramatically in the opening decades of the nineteenth century. As the revolutionary world of the minuteman gave way to the rough-and-tumble individualism of the Jacksonian era and the consumerism of the market revolution, the country faced a new problem posed by cheap mass-produced handguns and knives. The republican culture of James Madison and the Second Amendment had been largely supplanted by a more democratic culture, the world of Andrew Jackson, Davy Crockett, and Jim Bowie. Indeed, the eponymous Bowie knife was only one of many new consumer products that the burgeoning market supplied in abundance. In the early 1800s, the introduction of muzzle pistols, including easily concealable pocket pistols, changed American gun culture and the calculus of individual self-defense. As pistols became cheaper, more reliable, and more available, more Americans began carrying concealable weapons. For the first time in American history, legislatures were forced to deal with a gun violence problem. In response to the growing concern over the problem of concealed weapons, states enacted new laws targeting easily concealable weapons, edged weapons, and pistols. By the time Samuel Colt applied his unparalleled marketing genius to the sale of pistols, the conditions were ripe for him to create a mythic image of the individual armed citizen as the icon of American equality and democracy. The strong link between handguns and American ideas about freedom, equality, and masculinity has been an important component of American popular culture since the marketing of Colt's pioneering revolver during the era of the Mexican-American War.[26]

The modern debate on guns in America is a product of the nineteenth-century world of the Bowie knife and the Colt revolver, not of the eighteenth-century minuteman with his musket in hand. In an attempt to curb inter-personal violence, Jacksonian-era state legislators regulated pistols and knives, passed weapons bans, and in turn helped generate the first case law on the meaning of the right to bear arms in the United States.[27] State courts, struggling to make sense of their own constitutional provisions on the right to bear arms, were divided over how to interpret the meaning of this constitutional ideal. Some courts adopted an expansive individual right, while others embraced a militia-based view. In an early case, *Bliss v. Commonwealth* (1822), the Kentucky Supreme Court reversed a lower court decision upholding a concealed weapons law.[28] Yet even in this case, there was pushback from the legislature. The court's expansive ruling prompted the legislature to amend the state constitution in order to overrule the case. The legislature concluded that the suggestion that bearing arms had anything to do with self-defense was "perfectly ridiculous."[29] In *State v. Buzzard* (1842), the Arkansas Supreme Court ruled that the right to bear arms was inextricably linked to participation in a well-regulated militia. The respected post–Civil War legal scholar Joel Prentis Bishop concluded that *Buzzard* was the dominant model for dealing with the right to bear arms. Still, Bishop acknowledged that an alternative libertarian tradition existed as well.[30]

While both sides in the modern gun debate claim to be true to the Founders' idea of the Second Amendment, the reality is that neither side would want to return to that eighteenth-century world: to do so would mean both greater militarization of American society and greater levels of regulation. Although neither side in the modern debate can legitimately trace its lineage directly back to the Founders, both can easily find their roots in the later Jacksonian debate in which identifiable gun control and gun rights ideologies appeared for the first time.[31]

MODERN SECOND AMENDMENT SCHOLARSHIP: A SHORT PRIMER

Although self-defense and militia-based views of the right to bear arms clearly emerged by the mid-nineteenth century, for most of the twentieth century the dominant scholarly and judicial view of the Second Amendment cast it as a collective right of the states to maintain a well-regulated militia. The development of this states' rights view owed much to the politics of Reconstruction, particularly the retreat from Radical Republican ideas.[32] Gun regulation became more strict in the era of Reconstruction. Although the image of the Wild West created by Hollywood glamorizes the gunfighter, the West pioneered some of the tightest gun control laws in American history.[33] By the time Maine Supreme Court justice Lucilius A. Emery summarized the state of modern thinking about the Second Amendment in a 1915 *Harvard Law Review* article, he could confidently declare that the Second Amendment protected a collective right.[34]

Gun regulation again became more stringent in the early decades of the twentieth century, but it remained primarily a matter of state regulation. The problem of organized crime, Prohibition, and the rise of "gangsters" prompted calls for a national regulatory scheme to deal with the problems posed by modern gun control. The very first issue of the journal *Law and Contemporary Problems* (1934) contained an essay discussing the necessity of a uniform federal firearms policy.[35] Modern gun control, particularly federal firearms regulation, emerged during the New Deal, a development that coincided with an enormous general growth in federal power. *U.S. v. Miller* (1939), the first Second Amendment case to reach the high court, was triggered by the expansion of federal authority into the area of firearms regulation.[36] Contemporary reactions to this case, including scholarly commentary in law reviews at the time and subsequent case law, treated the Second Amendment in exactly the way Emery's article in the *Harvard Law Review* suggested: as a collective right. This view held sway for much of the next fifty years.[37] As late as 1991, former chief justice of the Supreme Court Warren Burger categorically declared that the NRA's individual rights interpretation of the Second Amendment "has been the subject of the greatest pieces of fraud—I repeat the word 'fraud'—on the American public by special interest groups that I have ever seen in my lifetime."[38]

Burger's timing could hardly have been worse. Less than two years earlier, the liberal constitutional scholar Sanford Levinson had written an influential revisionist account of the Second Amendment in the *Yale Law Journal*, "The Embarrassing Second Amendment."[39] Levinson's article made the new individual rights view of the Second Amendment, which had previously been consigned to the margins of legal debate, respectable. In the ensuing decade, a flood of new writing on the Second Amendment, much of it with a strong libertarian streak and a passion for gun rights, inundated law reviews. Gun rights scholars proclaimed themselves victors and their interpretation the "new standard model" of the Second Amendment.[40] Many of these individuals, who were affiliated with libertarian think tanks or gun rights groups, published multiple articles on the subject, giving the appearance that a seismic shift had occurred in scholarly thinking when in reality scholars remained deeply divided. If one applied a one-author-one-vote rule, the tally was actually pretty close, with a slight edge to the new revisionist individual rights model.[41]

Professional historians were curiously absent from most of this debate, largely because constitutional history (at least constitutional history on traditional topics such as the Bill of Rights) had largely fallen out of favor among historians more interested in topics associated with the ascendant social history paradigm. All of this changed in 1999, when the journal *Constitutional Commentary* ran a historical forum on the Second Amendment, and in 2000, when *Chicago-Kent Law Review* held a symposium on the collective rights theory of the Second Amendment.[42] Unfortunately, the new historical scholarship appeared a little too late to catch the attention of the constitutional scholar Laurence Tribe, who had already revised his influential treatise on constitutional law to recognize the individual rights theory.[43]

Tribe's timing proved propitious for gun rights advocates who had mounted a new challenge to a provision of a federal law concerning gun possession that had been attached to a bill dealing with violence against women.[44] The ensuing case, *United States v. Emerson,* became the vehicle to test out the new individual rights model in federal court.[45] A divided appeals court ruled that the Second Amendment was an individual right, but upheld the government's right to regulate guns in this context. The *Emerson* decision also recognized that there were now three paradigms for the Second Amendment in modern scholarship. In addition to an individual right and a collective right, the court noted a third theory it dubbed a "sophisticated collective rights model."[46] This nomenclature, it turned out, was coined by gun rights advocates seeking to cast the traditional collective rights theory as unsophisticated—a bit like calling pro-choice proponents "pro-death."[47] A more accurate rendering of this third theory would be to cast it as a limited individual right, or an expansive collective right, or perhaps even a civic right. In essence, this new interpretation of the Second Amendment saw the right to bear arms as a right of citizens to keep and bear those arms needed to meet their civic obligation to participate in a well-regulated militia. Thus, individuals did have standing to bring Second Amendment claims, but only laws that impeded their ability to keep and bear arms related to militia service would run afoul of the Second Amendment. Rather than a simple individual/collective rights dichotomy, scholarship on the eve of *Heller* now existed along a spectrum running from an expansive individual right, to a limited militia-based individual right, and finally to a collective right of the states.[48]

The key issue before the Court in *Heller* was the original understanding of the Second Amendment: Did the Founders seek to protect the right of citizens to bear arms in a well-regulated militia controlled by the states, or did they seek to codify the common law right of self-defense, a foundational principle of Anglo-American law? Scholarship on this issue on the eve of *Heller* was deeply contested, with many legal scholars embracing the individual rights interpretation and most historians favoring some variant of the collective or civic rights model.[49]

Heller also demonstrates the power of a shadow realm of ideological think tanks that nurtured and supported much of the revisionist scholarship used by the *Heller* majority. The NRA endowed a chair at George Mason Law School devoted to advancing the individual rights view of the Second Amendment. Three of the leading gun rights activists involved in *Heller,* David Kopel, Stephen Halbrook, and David Hardy, authored over thirty articles in the 1990s and received over a million dollars to support their work on gun issues in a decade-long effort to transform legal conceptions of the amendment. Gun rights activists working outside the legal academy wrote books, articles, and amicus briefs. The NRA paid $15,000 to gun rights advocate David Hardy to write a book review critical of *A Well-Regulated Militia,* by historian Saul Cornell, a truly staggering amount of money when one considers that academic book reviews and articles are typically written without any compensation. Foundations supporting gun control showed comparatively little interest in the Second Amendment for much of the same period and entered the field only after the other side had flooded law reviews with revisionist scholarship. The Joyce Foundation spent over $500,000 to organize academic conferences, including conferences on the traditional collective rights model and conferences devoted to new paradigms and approaches to the Second Amendment.[50] The latter were organized by the Second Amendment Research Center at the John Glenn School, Ohio State University.[51] Although it is difficult to arrive at an exact figure, gun rights organizations appear to have outspent gun control organizations by something like four to one in the lead-up to the *Heller* litigation.[52]

HISTORY GOES TO COURT

Section I of this collection includes the two most important historical friend-of-the-court briefs filed in *Heller:* Joyce Lee Malcolm's amicus brief, filed in conjunction with the libertarian Cato Institute, and the early American historians' brief led by the Pulitzer Prize–winning scholar Jack Rakove. Each brief placed a wealth of historical information before the high court.[53]

Building on the premise that the U.S. Constitution cannot be understood without first understanding the British constitutional tradition, Malcolm argues that the Founders intended for the Second Amendment to extend the individual right to self-defense already protected by English law. Critical to her analysis are the 1689 Declaration of Rights, the writings of the English jurist William Blackstone, and the English common law tradition. For Malcolm there is a direct line of continuity from the Declaration of Rights' allowance that "Protestants may have arms for their defence suitable to their condition and as allowed by law," and the Second Amendment's provision that "the right of the people to keep and bear arms shall not be infringed." The Declaration's right to have arms established a personal right, and not one predicated on military service. In fact, Malcolm argues that over time, this right was expanded. Malcolm also devotes considerable attention to the thinking of early American legal treatise writers, notably St. George Tucker and William Rawle. In Malcolm's view, both authors support an individual rights reading of the Second Amendment.

There is little disagreement among scholars that an individual right of self-defense was well understood to be protected under common law. The key point of contention centers on the relationship between this right and the Second Amendment. The Rakove brief also starts in England in 1689 but concludes that the right enshrined by Parliament was extremely limited in nature. In addition to restricting the right by religion and class, the Declaration of Rights affirmed Parliament's sweeping powers to legislate in this area, including power to curtail and limit the right as it saw fit. Moreover, when the same Parliament responsible for drafting the Declaration of Rights considered a revision of the game laws that would have allowed individuals to have guns in their homes for self-protection, this idea was rejected as too radical. Such a provision would have effectively armed the mob and undermined the class-based restrictions embodied in the game laws. The bulk of the historians' brief focuses on the ratification debates of 1788–89, a debate shaped in part by the militia clause (Article I, § 8) of the Constitution. The absence of any sustained discussion of a private right to own guns for self-defense provides the essential context for understanding the debate within Congress over amendments to the Constitution. Indeed, the right to bear arms became an issue only because the Constitution had significantly changed the governance of the militia, something that deeply concerned Anti-Federalists who were worried about the abuse of federal power. Although the Federalists who dominated the first Congress did acquiesce to the Anti-Federalist demand for a Bill of Rights (Madison argued that amendments were not "essential to the federal constitution" but conceded that they would have "a salutary tendency" on government), the demand for a reallocation of power to restore greater state control over the militia was rebuffed. Finally, the Rakove brief notes that the one clear statement of a non-militia-related right, the plea of the Anti-Federalist Dissent of the Pennsylvania Minority, fell flat and had little impact on the debate or the framing of proposed amendments.[54]

Scalia's majority opinion drew on Malcolm's brief, while Stevens's dissent built on arguments developed in the Rakove brief.[55] Malcolm's emphasis on the relevance of the preexisting English right, and her stress on the importance of early American commentators such as Tucker, is mirrored in Scalia's argument about the meaning of the operative clause (i.e., "the right of the people to keep and bear arms shall not be infringed"). Following Malcolm,

Scalia dismisses the actual debates over the drafting and ratification of the Second Amendment, considering the focus on the military bearing of arms in these debate to be "unremarkable."[56] By contrast, the Stevens dissent is much more concerned with ratification and the debate over the implications of Article I, section 8. Stevens also considers the preexisting English right, and uses the Rakove brief to argue that the right adopted in 1689 actually tells us very little about the meaning of the Second Amendment.

The heated exchange between Scalia and Stevens (Scalia thinks Stevens is "dead wrong"; Stevens thinks Scalia "fundamentally fails to grasp the point" of the amendment) indicates that *Heller* did not settle the historical debate over the Second Amendment.[57] Most historians have found the Stevens dissent more persuasive than Scalia's majority opinion. Indeed, in *McDonald v. Chicago* (2010), dozens of historians contributed to historical briefs attacking virtually every historical claim made by the majority in *Heller*.[58] Relatively few historians filed briefs supporting Scalia's vision of history. Indeed, Justice Breyer has publicly underscored the irony that Scalia's originalist interpretation has little support among professional historians.[59]

Although a number of law review symposia have analyzed *Heller*, historical journals have shown little interest in exploring the case. Indeed, few historians have written about the Second Amendment or guns in the wake of the landmark decision. Given this trend, it seems likely that Second Amendment scholarship will continue to be dominated by non-historians writing in non-peer-reviewed law journals.

JUDGING THE JUDGES: SCHOLARLY RESPONSES TO *HELLER*

Although to date the practical impact of the *Heller* decision has been modest, the jurisprudential significance of Justice Scalia's majority opinion is undeniable. Indeed, *District of Columbia v. Heller* has proved to be among the most controversial cases of the Roberts Court era. Gun rights advocates, libertarians, and proponents of originalist theory have generally hailed the decision, praising its intellectual power and erudition.[60] Nevertheless, criticism of the decision has been even more sweeping and curiously cuts across an astonishingly wide swath of the contemporary ideological spectrum, as Section II of this volume shows. Some of the most trenchant critiques of the decision came from conservatives who saw Justice Scalia's decision as either a betrayal of originalism or a thinly veiled effort to wrap judicial activism in an originalist banner. Liberals also took aim at the decision, exposing its historical flaws, circular logic, and departure from established precedent. A central question in much of this critical literature was the relationship between history and constitutional meaning.

Yale Law School's Reva Siegel highlights one of the oddest features of Scalia's originalist opinion. According to the holding in *Heller,* legislatures may ban military-style assault weapons but are prohibited from banning handguns. If the first Congress had applied this rule to the Founding era, it would have meant that Congress could have prohibited the militia's muskets but not Alexander Hamilton's dueling pistols. Such an outcome seems hard to reconcile with the preamble's reference to a well-regulated militia or the era's history. Siegel notes other temporal distortions in Scalia's opinion. To justify his decision to set aside the preamble's affirmation of the need for a well-regulated militia, Scalia cites several mid-nineteenth-century treatises. Given Scalia's strong originalist theory, one would have expected him to supply evidence from eighteenth-, not nineteenth-, century authorities. Ultimately, Siegel believes the case represents a triumph for a well-funded, highly organized, and ideologically inspired gun rights movement. The modern gun rights movement was first energized by gun control victories in the 1960s under the Johnson administration. Gun rights discourse was then further radicalized in the 1990s after the Clinton administration's fiasco at Waco, Texas, where federal agents stormed David Koresh's ranch and killed several gun rights activists. This overt federal action galvanized a popular gun rights movement that, as Siegel notes, was tinged with a deeply antigovernment ethos. Of course, government action leading to an intensification of gun rights ideology was hardly a new development in American law: this dynamic first emerged in the Jacksonian era, when the first modern-style gun control measures were enacted and modern gun rights ideology was born.[61] As Siegel shows, the philosophy of originalism and gun rights became closely interwoven, perhaps never more so than in contemporary politics and law, because of the deliberate actions of an interlocking web of conservative think tanks, activists, and academics. Modern gun rights culture blended together a mythic vision of the American Revolution, an individualist libertarian ethos, and a deeply rooted suspicion of government into a potent ideology.

Nelson Lund, the Patrick Henry Professor of Constitutional Law and the Second Amendment at George Mason Law School, applauds the Court's essential holding that the Second Amendment protects an individual right unconnected to militia service. What Lund finds deeply problematic is the opinion's flight from originalist principles in its long list of presumptively constitutional gun regulations. One of the reasons why *Heller*'s impact has been so minimal is that the Court affirmed virtually all of the fairly modest regulations currently on the books. All of these measures would easily pass constitutional muster under any standard of review, from the most lax to the most stringent. Lund's critique is oddly consonant with Siegel's, despite the vast ideological gulf separating the two scholars. He too challenges *Heller*'s conclusion that handguns enjoy constitutional protection while assault weapons do not. Surely the Founders would have wished to give greater protection to the militias' muskets than to a gentleman's dueling pistols. Yet according to *Heller*'s logic, it is permissible to ban the former but not the latter. Surely the one type of weapon that ought to be protected by the Second Amendment would be the lineal descendant of the revolutionary era minuteman's musket—the modern assault weapon! Indeed, it is hard to reconcile *Heller*'s framework with the various state militia laws and the Federal Militia Act of 1792, which required citizens to own muskets, not handguns. (The notable exception was the horsemen's pistols used by dragoons.) Lund concludes that "originalism deserved better from its judicial exponents."[62]

Section III explores the relationship between *Heller* and modern constitutional doctrine. Doctrinal analysis remains one of the most important modes of constitutional reasoning and a basic tool for lawyers and judges. In this section, two leading constitutional lawyers and theorists, Cass Sunstein and J. Harvie Wilkinson III, weigh and analyze *Heller*'s relationship to earlier landmark decisions. In another ironic twist, Wilkinson, a former constitutional law professor at the University Virginia and a conservative federal judge appointed by Reagan, compares *Heller* to the Right's anathema: *Roe v. Wade*. Wilkinson concludes that *Heller* will likely go down in history as the Right's most activist decision since *Lochner v. New York* in 1905.[63] He finds the historical evidence presented in both the majority and dissenting opinions to be equally persuasive and concludes that when history cannot provide a clear direction, conservative principles require a respect for precedent and judicial modesty. Wilkinson was on the short list for Justice Alito's seat, and had he been appointed to the Court, he might well have provided a fifth vote for Stevens's or Breyer's dissent, not Scalia's majority. Wilkinson also finds the *Heller* decision hard to reconcile with other conservative values such as federalism. As he notes, the vast majority of firearms regulations are local. The virtues of federalism lay precisely in the fact that gun laws appropriate for the Bronx might well not work for Helena, Montana. Although *Heller* focuses exclusively on the District of Columbia, Wilkinson believes that the logic of the Court's opinion made incorporation of this right against the states all but inevitable. (Wilkinson was correct on this score.) The issue of federalism troubles Wilkinson on other grounds as well. The *Heller* majority not only affirmed that the Second Amendment protects an individual right but also came close to arguing that the Second Amendment had no federalism function whatsoever. The notion that the Founders would have supported federal judges' using the Second Amendment to justify striking down local gun laws seems hard to reconcile with the Anti-Federalist origins of the amendment or Madison's conception of it. Even among ardent Federalists, the notion of giving more power to the federal government, particularly judges, to define the scope of Second Amendment rights at the local level would have been unthinkable.

Heller's many ironies are even further compounded when one considers Cass Sunstein's analysis. One of the premier liberal constitutional thinkers in America, Sunstein concludes that the proper analogy to *Heller* is not *Roe*, as Wilkinson suggested, but *Griswold v. Connecticut* (1965), the case that helped establish a constitutional right of privacy by striking down a law prohibiting the sale of contraceptives.[64] He dismisses the faux-originalist history of the majority opinion, noting that Scalia's evidence and methodology are more law office history than serious historical scholarship.[65] Sunstein shares Wilkinson's conclusion that the Court erred by setting aside the view of leading historians of the period, particularly given that the Court was making new law and overruling well-established precedent. He argues that professional history is more typically characterized by "care, [and] sensitivity to context" than the "advocacy-oriented, [and] conclusion-driven" work of academic lawyers. Another way of framing Sunstein's point that avoids the suggestion that historians are completely above the ideological fray (a point that gun rights advocates would likely dispute, especially in the wake of the Bellesiles scandal, discussed later in this introduction) is to recognize that historians' primary commitments are methodological, not political. For historians, the original meaning of the Second Amendment poses a classic problem in intellectual history, a field with a long tradition, a clear methodology, and a well-established set of rules about evidence. Legal scholarship on the Second Amendment, by contrast, has largely been driven by ideological agendas, either pro-gun or pro–gun control. Indeed, the so-called new originalism favored by Justice Scalia has almost no clear rules about how various sources are to be interpreted or weighted to arrive at a genuinely historical account of their meaning.[66]

Interestingly, although Sunstein finds the Court's methodology problematic, he seems less troubled by the actual outcome of the case than his conservative counterpart Wilkinson. Sunstein concludes that the holding was not unreasonable when judged against a different standard. Although the majority opinion cast its arguments in originalist terms, Sunstein believes that the real explanation of the ruling lay in an energetic and committed popular constitutional movement for expanding gun rights. On this point he agrees with Siegel. Ironically, Scalia embraced a theory of the living Constitution but dressed it up in originalist clothing. Given this context, *Griswold*, the case that helped pave the way for the emergence of the concept of privacy as an accepted part of modern constitutional law, is a more apt analogy. One interpretation of *Griswold*, Sunstein reminds us, is that the Connecticut law banning the sale of contraceptives was out of tune with the evolving tradition of liberty as understood by most Americans. Given that polling data have consistently shown that most Americans believe the Second Amendment protects an individual right, the Court simply acted to bring the District of Columbia's law into line with mainstream American legal practice and thought.[67] Ultimately, Sunstein finds *Heller* compatible with his own philosophy of judicial minimalism. *Heller* struck down a law at odds with mainstream American thinking, and the long list of presumptively valid gun laws the Court recognized seems to preserve the gun control regime currently in place. If *Heller* hews to this line, Sunstein believes it will represent an incremental shift, effectively bringing doctrine in line with popular belief.

WHERE DO WE GO FROM HERE?

Section IV offers some pathways for future historical scholarship. While it is probably unrealistic to expect legal scholars to retool as historians, or for historians to weigh in substantively on this contentious issue on a regular basis, particularly given the growth of litigation in this area (six hundred cases already and more to come), it is not unrealistic to establish some basic methodological tools for those dealing with historical questions. In his essay, Nathan Kozuskanich turns to the newly available digital databases of Founding era printed sources and examines the typical usage of the phrase "bear arms" in American print culture during that time. If we take the most common usage of the term as the proper way to determine original public meaning, as the majority opinion did, there can be little doubt that Scalia got his history badly wrong and Stevens got it mostly right. Kozuskanich first published the results in the *University of Pennsylvania Journal of Constitutional Law.*[68] Even though this article was cited in the reply brief for the petitioners, Justice Scalia ignored it and argued that the phrase "bear arms" carried an exclusively military connotation only when accompanied by the word "against," dismissing the frequent use of "bear arms" in a military sense as "unremarkable."[69] Obviously this claim did not cover such common uses of the term as "religiously scrupulous about bearing arms" or references to those "capable of bearing arms" or individuals "able to bear arms." In the selection for this volume, an article originally published in *Journal of the Early Republic* in 2009, Kozuskanich expands his survey of the use of "bear arms" to include the years 1750 to 1800, concluding that over 95 percent of the documents use the phrase "bear arms" in a collective or military context. Indeed, his exhaustive survey should have been accorded considerable weight by the Court's originalists. Instead, Scalia ignored the relevant scholarship and relied on an impressionistic sample of cherry-picked and decontextualized quotations to support his claims about contemporary usage. Of course, it was easy for him to do so because he relied on legal scholarship that did exactly the same thing. Given the Blackstonian injunction that words are to be used in their most common signification, it is hard to understand how one could conclude that the most common use of "bear arms" encompassed both military and nonmilitary uses of weapons. The evidence to the contrary is overwhelming—evidence that once required arduous historical research in manuscript archives, now available at the click of a mouse.[70] As Kozuskanich shows, comprehensive digital databases make it possible to survey the common usage of terms quickly and effectively, and can help us move away from recycling the same (and sometimes erroneously used) quotations again and again.[71] Of course, user-friendly databases do not guarantee that those who access them understand the basic rules of historical interpretation, or that they know how to properly contextualize the sources they find. It is too early to tell if these new databases will improve the quality of research or just make it easier to churn out more bloated examples of decontextualized law office history.

The final essay in this volume focuses on the way pervasive historical myths and ideologies about early American history and guns have shaped American gun culture and the *Heller* decision. The importance of these myths was made evident in the oral argument. It may not be much of an exaggeration to say that Justice Anthony Kennedy's vote was ultimately won by Fess Parker, the star of Walt Disney's popular TV series on Davy Crockett, and not Heller's attorney, Alan Gura. Justice Kennedy embraced the frontier myth with passion, informing the court that the Founders needed their guns to defend themselves against "hostile Indian tribes and outlaws, wolves and bears and grizzlies and things like that."[72] The fact that grizzly bears are indigenous to the western United States, not the eastern, and that few reported instances of bear attacks are evident in either the Philadelphia papers or the writings of the Second Amendment's chief architect, James Madison, seemed entirely irrelevant to Kennedy's mythic conception of early American history.[73]

Kevin Sweeney's essay, appearing here for the first time, takes up an extremely controversial issue: What role did guns actually play in early American culture? This subject gained considerable attention and notoriety when the historian Michael Bellesiles published a controversial and now discredited book, *Arming America*.[74] The book earned rave reviews when it first appeared and won Columbia University's coveted Bancroft Prize. Bellesiles claimed that American culture in the era of the Second Amendment was not a gun culture. In his view, Americans neither had many guns nor were especially proficient in the use of the ones they did have. This revisionist thesis drew the ire of gun rights activists, which in turn attracted the attention of academics, who ultimately concluded not only that Bellesiles was wrong but also that his research methods had violated standard scholarly procedures.[75] As a result, Columbia University took the unprecedented step of rescinding Bellesiles's Bancroft Prize, and he lost his professorship at Emory University. Enter Kevin Sweeney, the consummate social historian, who painstakingly reconstructs the complex and diverse gun cultures of early America. His conclusions support neither Bellesiles nor his most vociferous critics. Presenting a complex account that takes due note of changes over time and diverse regional cultures in early America, Sweeney concludes that instead of there having been a single American gun culture, the possession and use of firearms was strongly influenced by differences in the regional cultures of colonial America. Politics, social conditions, and strategic considerations all influenced the pattern of gun ownership. Gun ownership and the preferences for particular weapons also reflected perceptions of internal and external threats to security and the structure of local militia establishments. Occupation and wealth also influenced an individual's ability and desire to own different types of firearms. Heavy, large-bore muskets, the type of gun ideally needed by a well-regulated militia, were neither as ubiquitous nor as lovingly maintained as the NRA's fantasy version of American history might suggest, nor as scarce and unreliable as Bellesiles's flawed revisionist account argued. The fear of disarmament that inspired the Second Amendment shared little with modern gun rights nightmares of black helicopters swooping in to take American guns. Rather, the Second Amendment was driven by a very different fear: government inaction. For most Anti-Federalists, the most likely mechanism for weakening the state militias was a failure of the government to aggressively arm them. Finally, Sweeney also notes that pistols represented a small fraction of the guns Americans owned in the Founding era. Thus, Justice Scalia's view that handguns are the particular category of weapon that ought to enjoy the greatest Second Amendment protection seems historically the most dubious proposition of all.

The outcome in *Heller* was not surprising, given the ideological composition of the Court. Nor is the Court's less than rigorous application of originalist methodology all that surprising, given that gun rights have become a core issue for the Right's legal agenda and ideology.[76] Indeed, the instrumental quality of the Court's originalism is evident if one compares the decision in *Heller* with *McDonald v. Chicago*.[77] In *Heller*, the Court's majority embraced new originalism and its focus on public meaning. In *McDonald*, the same five justices all happily relied on the original intent of the Congress responsible for drafting the Fourteenth Amendment. Had the Court applied the same methodology in *Heller*, it would have adopted Stevens's approach, not Scalia's.

McDonald and the incorporation of the Second Amendment have not inspired anything close to the same level of scholarly interest. Indeed, compared to *Heller*, the argument in *McDonald* is unremarkable. Although historians would likely quibble with the history presented by the majority in *McDonald*, the notion that incorporation follows logically from *Heller* is hard to dispute as a matter of existing legal doctrine.[78] Even among those who believed that *Heller* was incorrectly decided, there was little doubt about the outcome of *McDonald*. If the Second Amendment protected a fundamental individual right, most scholars believed that the logic of the Court's existing incorporation jurisprudence dictated that the justices would incorporate the Second Amendment. Given that many other provisions of the first eight amendments have already been applied against the states, refusing to incorporate the Second Amendment would have been remarkable.[79]

The actual impact of *Heller* and *McDonald*, apart from generating a considerable amount of business for gun rights lawyers and a host of new scholarly essays on *Heller* itself, has been limited.[80] Given that the laws at issue in both cases were written decades ago and were out of step with the current debate over guns in America, it is hardly surprising that most laws have survived court challenges in the wake of these two decisions. At least for the short term, no law capable of passing the political gauntlet is likely to run afoul of *Heller's* guidelines. Despite an avalanche of lawsuits, there are no signs that any court is likely to read *Heller* more expansively in the near future. Most courts have accepted that the core of the right protected by *Heller* extends only to the ownership and use of firearms in the home.[81] Similarly, the *Heller* Court's list of reasonable regulations that are presumptively legal, a list that the Court noted was not exhaustive, has covered virtually every existing gun law on the books. It is no less true that the decision is just as likely to remain controversial among scholars for some time to come. As the essays in this volume make clear, the *Heller* decision is rich in delicious irony: liberals embracing originalism while conservatives thumb their noses at precedent, to name two among many. Although it is too soon to predict how history will judge *Heller,* it does seem likely that future scholars will uncover additional ironies as they probe the decision further.

NOTES

1. *District of Columbia v. Heller,* 554 U.S. 570 (2008).

2. The Court had last dealt with the Second Amendment in *U.S. v. Miller,* 307 U.S. 174 (1939), in which it ruled that since shotguns with barrels less than eighteen inches in length had no relation to a well-regulated militia, the Second Amendment did not guarantee a right to keep and bear such firearms.

3. For a brief personal history of the case, see Clark Neily, "*District of Columbia v. Heller:* The Second Amendment Is Back, Baby," *Cato Supreme Court Review* (2007–8): 127–59. The Gura & Possessky, P.L.L.C., website also gives a brief history of the *Parker* case; see www.gurapossessky.com/news/parker/overview .html.

4. *Seegars v. Ashcroft,* 297 F. Supp. 2d 201 (D.D.C. 2004).

5. See Debra Cassens Weiss, "Alan Morrison Fired from DC Gun Case," *ABA Journal* (online supplement), January 2, 2008, www.abajournal.com/news /article/alan_morrison_fired_from_dc_gun_case/.

6. See Brief for the United States as Amicus Curiae, *District of Columbia v. Heller,* 554 U.S. 570 (2008) (No. 07-290), 8–10. The *Heller* Court rejected the entire modern framework of judicial scrutiny and instead seemed to adopt a categorical approach. On this, see Joseph Blocher, "Categoricalism and Balancing in First and Second Amendment Analysis," *New York University Law Review* 84 (2009): 375–439.

7. See Sterling Meyes, "Gun Fanciers, Foes Get Day in Court; Hundreds Line Up to See History Being Made," *Washington Times*, March 19, 2008, B01.

8. *U.S. v. Miller*, 307 U.S. 174.

9. The Court voted according to its well-established conservative/liberal split. Conservative justices Scalia, Roberts, Thomas, Alito, and (sometimes swing vote) Kennedy signed the majority opinion, while liberals Stevens, Souter, Ginsburg, and Breyer dissented.

10. See, e.g., Linda Greenhouse, "Justices, Ruling 5–4, Endorse Personal Right to Own Gun," *New York Times*, June 27, 2008; Bill Mears, "High Court Strikes Down Gun Ban," CNN U.S., June 26, 2008, www.cnn.com/2008/US/06/26/scotus .guns/index.html; "McCain, Obama React to Heller Decision," RealClearPolitics, June 26, 2008, http://realclearpolitics.blogs.time.com.

11. *McDonald v. City of Chicago*, 130 S.Ct. 3020 (2010).

12. See Robert Barnes, "Cases Piling Up Seeking Supreme Court's Clarification of Second Amendment Rights," *Washington Post*, August 15, 2011, A15. The six hundred figure, calculated as of the time this volume went to press, is likely to increase by the time the book appears in print. See "Post-Heller Litigation Summary," Law Center to Prevent Gun Violence, http://smartgunlaws.org/category /second-amendment/.

13. Jonathan Stempel, "U.S. Court Upholds Ban on Handgun Sales to People under 21," Reuters, October 25, 2012, http://reut.rs/TYDrFN. The cases mentioned are *National Rifle Association of America, Inc., et al. v. Bureau of Alcohol, Tobacco, Firearms, and Explosives et al.* (No. 11-10959), and *Kachalsky v. County of Westchester*, United States Court of Appeals for the Second Circuit, 2012 U.S. App. LEXIS 24363. In *Moore v. Madigan* the 7th Circuit struck down the Illinois ban on concealed carry. See Bill Mears, "Analysis: Guns and the Law; Recent Ruling Highlights Legal and Personal Stakes," CNN U.S., Monday December 17, 2012, www.cnn.com/2012/12/17/us/gun-law-court-ruling/index.html.

14. According to Gallup, 78 percent of Americans in 1991 thought that current laws covering the sale of firearms should be made more strict, compared to 43 percent in 2011. See www.gallup.com/poll/1645/guns.aspx.

15. See Sean Lengell, "NRA Official: Obama Wants to Outlaw Guns in 2nd Term," *Washington Times*, February 10, 2012; Clarence Page, "Gun Lobby Fires Up Obama Fear; NRA Targets President Despite His 'Pro-Gun' Record," *Chicago Tribune*, July 22, 2012.

16. Dan Freedman, "NRA Spent $17 Million on Election, Lost," *San Francisco Chronicle*, November 8, 2012.

17. "Weaker Gun Laws, Lack of Leadership Earn President Obama a Failing Grade," January 19, 2010, www.bradycampaign.org/media/press/view/1214/.

18. See Philip J. Cook, Jens Ludwig, and Adam M. Samaha, "Gun Control after

Heller: Threats and Sideshows from a Social Welfare Perspective," *UCLA Law Review* 56 (2009): 1045.

19. David Nakamura and Jon Cohen, "Poll: Most Americans Support New Gun-Control Measures after Newtown Massacre," *Washington Post,* January 15, 2013; Scott Clement, "How Newtown Changed Americans' Views on Guns (and How It Didn't)," *Washington Post,* December 28, 2012; Philip Rucker, "To Gun-Control Advocates, This Could Be Tipping Point," *Washington Post,* December 16, 2012.

20. Sari Horwitz and Peter Finn, "Gun Control Debate May Be Driving Higher Sales," *Washington Post,* January 18, 2013.

21. Charles Schumer, "Gun Rights, with Limits," *Washington Post,* December 20, 2012.

22. David B. Rivkin Jr. and Andrew M Grossman, "Gun Control and the Constitution," *Wall Street Journal,* February 11, 2013. There is considerable disagreement over which standard of review the courts should use when evaluating Second Amendment claims. The most common standard (particularly for regulations not burdening the core right of self-defense in the home) appears to be intermediate scrutiny. There also continues to be controversy over the definition of assault weapons. Gun-rights advocates prefer the term "modern sporting rifles." See Erica Goode, "Even Defining 'Assault Rifles' Is Complicated," *New York Times,* January 17, 2013.

23. For a discussion of various militia and storage laws, see Saul Cornell and Nathan DeDino, "A Well-Regulated Right: The Early American Origins of Gun Control," *Fordham Law Review* 73 (2004): 508–12. Pennsylvania's 1777 Test Act established that any person who refused to swear a loyalty oath "shall be disarmed." See Saul Cornell, "Commonplace or Anachronism: The Standard Model, the Second Amendment, and the Problem of History in Contemporary Constitutional Theory," *Constitutional Commentary* 16 (1999): 228 and n.30.

24. The 1792 Militia Act mandated that every eligible man procure his own gun, powder, ammunition, shot pouch, powder horn, and knapsack. See *Annals of Congress,* 2nd Cong., 1st sess., 1392.

25. See Saul Cornell, *A Well-Regulated Militia: The Founding Fathers and the Origins of Gun Control in America* (New York: Oxford University Press, 2006); and, more recently, Adam Winkler, *Gunfight: The Battle over the Right to Bear Arms in America* (New York: Norton, 2011). For additional examples of early American gun regulations, see Saul Cornell, "The Right to Carry Firearms Outside of the Home: Separating Historical Myths from Historical Realities," *Fordham Urban Law Journal* 39 (2012): 1695–1726.

26. On the evolution of gun culture in the period before the Civil War, see William N. Hosely, *Colt: The Making of an American Legend* (Amherst: Univer-

sity of Massachusetts Press, 1996). On the actual patterns of ownership, see Kevin Sweeney's essay in this volume.

27. For an overview of these early gun laws, see Cornell, *A Well-Regulated Militia*, 141–44.

28. *Bliss v. Commonwealth*, 12 Ky. 90 (1822). The other case advancing an expansive individual right was *Nunn v. State*, 1 Ga. (1 Kel.) 243 (1846).

29. Kentucky House of Representatives, *Journal of the House of Representatives of the Commonwealth of Kentucky* (Frankfort, 1837), 73.

30. *State v. Buzzard*, 4 Ark. (2 Pike) 18 (1842); and for discussion of Bishop and other nineteenth-century legal scholars who shared his view of *Buzzard*'s significance, see Cornell, *A Well-Regulated Militia*, 186–90.

31. Cornell, *A Well-Regulated Militia*, 131–57.

32. For an exploration of the origins of the modern collective rights view, see Cornell, *A Well-Regulated Militia*, 168–97.

33. Robert R. Dykstra, *The Cattle Towns* (New York: Knopf, 1968).

34. Lucilius A. Emery, "The Constitutional Right to Keep and Bear Arms," *Harvard Law Review* 28 (1915): 473.

35. John Brabner-Smith, "Firearms Regulation," *Law and Contemporary Problems* 1 (1934): 400–414.

36. *U.S. v. Miller*, 307 U.S. 174 (1939).

37. On contemporary reactions to *Miller*, see Cornell, *A Well-Regulated Militia*, 198–200. The revisionist account of *Miller* Justice Scalia adopts in *Heller* drew heavily on gun rights scholarship. See esp. Brian L. Frye, "The Peculiar Story of *United States v. Miller*," *NYU Journal of Law & Liberty* 48 (2008): 3–82. It is hard to fathom Scalia's dismissal of *Miller*'s precedential value and his claim that there was no discussion of history in the opinion. *Miller* did cite several historical sources to support its view of the militia and interpreted the Second Amendment in light of its militia purpose. Scalia ridicules Justice Stevens's argument that there was a jurisprudential orthodoxy on the meaning of *Miller*. In response to this claim, Scalia asserts a radical vision of popular constitutionalism and living constitutionalism quite out of character with his originalist views: "[Stevens's] erroneous reliance upon an uncontested and virtually unreasoned case cannot nullify the reliance of millions of Americans (as our historical analysis has shown) upon the true meaning of the right to keep and bear arms." *District of Columbia v. Heller*, at note 24, 198–200.

38. In an interview on *The MacNeil/Lehrer NewsHour*, December 16, 1991, quoted in Cass Sunstein, "The Most Mysterious Right," *New Republic*, November 18, 2007.

39. Sanford Levinson, "The Embarrassing Second Amendment," *Yale Law Journal* 99 (1989): 637–59.

40. Glenn Harlan Reynolds, "A Critical Guide to the Second Amendment," *Tennessee Law Review* 62 (1995): 461–511. This article is ironically titled; it really is an uncritical guide to pro-gun scholarship on the Second Amendment.

41. A Lexis-Nexis search for the period 1990–1999 shows three authors, Stephen Halbrook, Don Kates, and David Kopel, each publishing articles at a phenomenal rate: Halbrook published five articles, Kates seven, and Kopel authored or co-authored nineteen. See Robert J. Spitzer, "Lost and Found: Researching the Second Amendment," *Chicago-Kent Law Review* 76 (2000): 349–401.

42. "Historical Forum," *Constitutional Commentary* 16 (1999): 221–372; "Symposium on the Second Amendment: Fresh Looks," *Chicago-Kent Law Review* 76 (2000): 1–600.

43. Laurence Tribe, *American Constitutional Law*, 3rd ed. (New York: West Group, 2000).

44. See Public Safety and Recreational Firearms Use Protection Act or Violent Crime Control and Law Enforcement Act of 1994, Pub. L. No. 103-322, 108 Stat. 1796 (1994). The act became part of 18 U.S.C. § 922 (2006).

45. *United States v. Emerson*, 270 F.3d 203 (5th Cir. 2001).

46. Ibid., 219.

47. In its discussion of the sophisticated collective right, the *Emerson* decision cites Robert J. Cottrol and Raymond T. Diamond, "The Fifth Auxiliary Right," *Yale Law Journal* 104 (1995): 1003–4; and Nelson Lund, "The Ends of Second Amendment Jurisprudence: Firearms Disabilities and Domestic Violence Restraining Orders," *Texas Review of Law and Politics* 4 (1999): 184–86. Cottrol and Diamond argue that "the most simplistic variant of the collective rights theory runs into such stubborn historical and textual resistance that, at its most extreme, it can be readily dismissed as a type of result-oriented constitutional denial" (1103).

48. The category of citizen was defined more narrowly than that of individuals in the Founding era. By the era of the Fourteenth Amendment this category had expanded to include all men born or naturalized in the United States. See Rogers M. Smith, *Civic Ideals: Conflicting Visions of Citizenship in U.S. History* (New Haven: Yale University Press, 1997).

49. An obvious exception to this rule is the exchanges between historians Robert Shalhope and Lawrence Delbert Cress in the early 1980s. See Robert Shalhope and Lawrence Delbert Cress, "The Second Amendment and the Right to Bear Arms: An Exchange," *Journal of American History* 71 (1984): 587–93. By the 1990s, however, the debate had largely moved away from history journals to the pages of law reviews.

50. The vast majority of the Joyce Foundation's support is for gun control focused on public health issues, not the Second Amendment. The notable exception was

the foundation's support for the Chicago-Kent symposium on the Second Amendment, and the Second Amendment Research Center at the John Glenn School at the Ohio State University, directed by Saul Cornell. See the Joyce Foundation's Form 990s from 1999 and 2004, respectively, made available on the Economic Research Institute's website, http://207.153.189.83/EINS/366079185/366079185 _1999_00003523.pdf (at 174, showing a grant of $84,000 to Chicago-Kent College of Law "for a symposium and law review on the Second Amendment"), and http://207.153.189.83/EINS/366079185/366079185_2004_01C749A6.PDF (at 801, showing a grant of $399,967 to the Ohio State University Foundation "for the creation of a comprehensive Second Amendment Research Center").

51. The Second Amendment Research Center (SARC) did not file any brief in *Heller* and did not adopt any official position on the Second Amendment, although its director, Saul Cornell, was associated with a new paradigm for the Second Amendment, variously described as a limited individual right or civic right. In contrast to gun rights support for research, SARC academic conferences primarily focused on new approaches but did include a number of scholars supporting the individual rights view, including figures such as James Jacobs, Sanford Levinson, Brannon Denning, Raymond Diamond, Jan Dizard, and Abigail Kohn. Not all of these authors chose to contribute essays to the law review symposium generated by these conferences. Editorial control of the symposia was maintained by the student law review editors, as is the custom at most law schools. The publication of this volume, which also contains multiple perspectives on *Heller*, was subsidized by a publishing subvention from SARC before its funding ran out.

52. David Kopel, a gun rights activist at the Independence Institute, has worked on this issue nearly full-time for two decades. In the two years leading up to *Heller*, the NRA Civil Rights Legal Defense Fund provided Kopel's Independence Institute almost $300,000 in additional funding. These numbers do not include the NRA's $1 million gift to George Mason to endow the Patrick Henry Chair, almost twice the amount the Joyce Foundation spent on Second Amendment issues. See "NRA Endows Chair at George Mason U. Law School," *Chronicle of Higher Education* 49.27 (March 14, 2003): A25. When one adds additional support for *Heller* by the Cato Institute's Robert Levy, the scales tip even further in the direction of gun rights.

53. A summary of the other major briefs is provided in Appendix B.

54. *Annals of Congress*, 1st Cong., 1st sess., 1:453–54.

55. If one looks at the pattern of citation in the briefs filed in the case and in the Court's opinions, a clear pattern emerges. Scholarship was ideologically divided between supporters of an individual rights view of the amendment and those who supported the traditional collective rights or middle paradigm. Most historians

fell into these two categories. Also, the number of articles written by activists outside the academy was remarkable. The data on citation is presented in Appendixes C and D.

56. *District of Columbia v. Heller,* 554 U.S. 570 (2008), 13.

57. Ibid., 6; Stevens dissent, 14.

58. *McDonald v. Chicago,* 561 U.S. 3025 (2010).

59. The briefs on both sides are available at SCOTUSblog's excellent website, www.scotusblog.com/case-files/cases/mcdonald-v-city-of-chicago/. On Breyer's critique of Scalia, see Pauline Maier, "Justice Breyer's Sharp Aim," *New York Times,* December 21, 2010.

60. See Randy Barnett, "News Flash: The Constitution Means What It Says," *Wall Street Journal,* June 26, 2008, A13.

61. See Cornell, *A Well-Regulated Militia,* 141–50.

62. Originalists often distinguish between original meaning and originally intended application. Some originalists believe we ought to be bound by the former but not the latter. On this disagreement, see Jack M. Balkin, "Abortion and Original Meaning," *Constitutional Commentary* 24 (2007): 291–352; and John O. McGinnis and Michael Rappaport, "Original Interpretive Principles as the Core of Originalism," *Constitutional Commentary* 24 (2007): 371–82. Even if one accepts that courts are not bound by the Framers' expected application of the Second Amendment, defining what type of arms ought to enjoy constitutional protection would require establishing what the word "arms" meant in the context of the Second Amendment. Justice Scalia's approach simply took the dictionary definition of the word, which would have included handguns. For Reva Siegel and Scalia's other academic critics, such an approach makes little sense and is hard to reconcile with the amendment's clear statement of its military purpose. See Reva B. Siegel, "Dead or Alive: Originalism as Popular Constitutionalism in *Heller,*" in this volume.

63. Wilkinson writes that he hopes his "fondness for the . . . restraint of . . . Holmes is grounded in more than nostalgia for days of judicial modesty gone by." Oliver Wendell Holmes Jr. was one of two dissenting justices in *Lochner,* a case that found that the general right to make a business contract without government interference is an individual liberty protected by the Fourteenth Amendment. *Lochner v. New York,* 198 U.S. 45 (1905).

64. The majority in *Griswold v. Connecticut,* 381 U.S. 479 (1965), argued that the Constitution protected a right to privacy.

65. Law office history is a style of results-oriented history churned out by lawyers to support a particular conclusion. For a critique of lawyers' ability to produce historical scholarship because of their training in the adversarial system, and of law reviews in general, see Robert J. Spitzer, "Why History Matters: Saul Cornell's

Second Amendment and the Consequence of Law Reviews," *Albany Government Law Review* 1 (2008): 312–53.

66. For a brief methodological critique of the new originalism focusing on similar issues, see Saul Cornell, "The People's Constitution vs. The Lawyer's Constitution: Popular Constitutionalism and the Original Debate over Originalism," *Yale Journal of Law & the Humanities* 23 (2011): 295–337.

67. According to a 2012 Gallup survey, 91 percent of gun owners and 63 percent of non–gun owners believe that the Second Amendment guarantees an individual right to own firearms. See www.gallup.com/poll/1645/Guns.aspx.

68. Nathan Kozuskanich, "Originalism, History, and the Second Amendment: What Did Bearing Arms Really Mean to the Founders?" *University of Pennsylvania Journal of Constitutional Law* 10 (2008): 413–46.

69. *Heller,* 554 U.S. at 586–89.

70. On Blackstone's rules of construction, see Saul Cornell, "The Original Meaning of Original Understanding: A Neo-Blackstonian Critique," *Maryland Law Review* 67 (2007): 150–65.

71. Consider Thomas Jefferson's admission in a 1796 letter to George Washington that "one loves to possess arms," a popular quotation used to support individual gun ownership that returns 793,000 hits in a Google search (as of November 2012), appears on the NRA-ILA website, in anti-Left paraphernalia, and in published pro-gun scholarship in law journals (as late as 2009 in Don B. Kates, "A Modern Historiography of the Second Amendment," *UCLA Law Review* 56 [June 2009]: 1211). The problem is that Jefferson was not talking about guns at all, as even a cursory glance at the original source reveals. Instead, he was looking for some political ammunition against Alexander Hamilton and Henry Knox, and was asking Washington for a copy of their correspondence with the president on French policy. "Tho I do not know that it will ever be of the least importance to me," he wrote, "yet one loves to possess arms, tho they hope never to have occasion for them. They possess my paper in my own handwriting. It is just I should possess theirs." Jefferson to Washington, June 19, 1796, in *The Writings of Thomas Jefferson,* ed. H. A. Washington, vol. 4 (Washington, D.C.: Taylor & Maury, 1854), 143.

72. Transcript of oral argument, 8, www.supremecourt.gov/oral_arguments /argument_transcripts/07-290.pdf.

73. See William G. Merkel, "*The District of Columbia v. Heller* and Antonin Scalia's Perverse Sense of Originalism," *Lewis & Clark Law Review* 13 (2009): 349–81.

74. Michael Bellesiles, *Arming America: The Origins of a National Gun Culture* (New York: Knopf, 2000). Alfred A. Knopf, the original publisher, no longer publishes the book. Soft Skull Press printed a revised edition in 2003.

75. For example, in 2002 the *William and Mary Quarterly,* the premier journal of early American history, published a forum on the Bellesiles scandal. See "Forum: Historians and Guns," *William and Mary Quarterly* 59 (2002): 203–68.

76. See Jamal Greene, Nathaniel Persily, and Stephen Ansolabehere, "Profiling Originalism," *Columbia Law Review* 111 (2011): 356–418; and Robert Post and Reva Siegel, "Originalism as a Political Practice: The Right's Living Constitution," *Fordham Law Review* 75 (2006): 545–74.

77. *McDonald v. City of Chicago,* 130 S.Ct. 3020 (2010).

78. See Symposium, "Firearms, Inc., or, A Collection of Essays and Articles Discussing *McDonald v. City of Chicago,* the Second Amendment, Its Contour in Light of *District of Columbia v. Heller,* and Its Possible Incorporation through the Fourteenth Amendment," *Cardozo Law Review De Novo* (2010): 1–202.

79. After *McDonald* the incorporation of the first eight amendments was accomplished with the following exceptions: the Third Amendment was not incorporated apart from a decision in the Second Circuit limited to that jurisdiction; the Fifth Amendment was incorporated except for the clause guaranteeing criminal prosecution only on a grand jury indictment; the Seventh Amendment was not incorporated; and the Eighth Amendment was incorporated with respect to the protection against "cruel and unusual punishments," but with no specific Supreme Court ruling on the incorporation of the "excessive fines" and "excessive bail" protections.

80. Tina Mehr and Adam Winkler, "The Standardless Second Amendment," American Constitution Society Issue Brief, available at www.acslaw.org/sites /default/files/Mehr_and_Winkler_Standardless_Second_Amendment.pdf.

81. The notable exception is *Moore v. Madigan;* see note 13 above.

Section I

Historians before the Court

* * * *

Brief of the Cato Institute and History Professor Joyce Lee Malcolm as Amici Curiae in Support of Respondent

[The Right Inherited from England]

Joyce Lee Malcolm

* * * *

STATEMENT OF INTEREST[1]

THE CATO INSTITUTE is a public policy research foundation in Washington, D.C. Named after *Cato's Letters* (published in England in the 1720s), it seeks to include in public debate traditional American principles of limited government, individual liberty, free markets, and peace. Cato therefore promotes understanding of the Constitution's common law context.

Professor Joyce Lee Malcolm long has been the leading authority on the historical English right to arms. Her works include two books published by Harvard University Press: *Guns and Violence: The English Experience* (2002) (*"G&V"*) and *To Keep and Bear Arms: The Origins of an Anglo-American Right* (1994) (*"K&B"*). The latter was cited below, Pet. App. 21a n.8, and in *Printz v. United States*, 521 U.S. 898, 938 n.2 (1997) (Thomas, J., concurring); Antonin Scalia, *A Matter of Interpretation* 136–37 (1997); and *Whether the Second Amendment Secures an Individual Right*, Op. Off. Legal Counsel, passim (August 24, 2004) (*"OLC Opinion"*), available at www.usdoj.gov/olc/opinions.htm, among other places. She has a Ph.D. in comparative history from Brandeis University, is a Fellow of the Royal Historical Society, and is Professor of Legal History at George Mason University School of Law.

SUMMARY OF ARGUMENT

Over a century ago, this Court declared it "perfectly well settled" that the Bill of Rights was "not intended to lay down any novel principles of government, but simply to embody certain guaranties and immunities which we had inherited from our English ancestors," including the rights' "well-recognized exceptions." *Robertson v. Baldwin*, 165 U.S. 275, 281 (1897). Indeed, "[t]he language of the Constitution cannot be interpreted safely except by reference to the common law and to British institutions as they were when the instrument was framed and adopted." *Ex parte Grossman*, 267 U.S. 87, 108–09 (1925).

Robertson included among those inherited rights "the right of the people to keep and bear arms (art. 2)." 165 U.S. at 281–82. The Court below briefly made "reference to" the Second Amendment's foundation in English law. *See* Pet. App. 20a–21a. But Petitioners make none, citing neither the English Bill of Rights, nor any English case, nor Blackstone (yet citing him for another purpose, Pet. Br. 17), nor any other English authority—nor even the three leading early commentators on the Constitution, all of whom recognized the amendment's English foundation.

Amici therefore set out below the right to have and use arms in English law by the time of the Founding. Amici then show how early American authorities claimed and extended that right, including in interpreting the Second Amendment. The English right was a right of individuals, not conditioned on militia service; individuals might exercise the right collectively, but the unquestioned core was a broadly applicable and robust right to "keep" firearms in one's home for self-defense. Even the "well-recognized exceptions" confirmed this core right by focusing on the carrying, not the keeping, of weapons.

That core right is what the District of Columbia tramples. It bans keeping a handgun in one's home (including use there in self-defense) and keeping any functional firearm in one's home. Pet. App. 4a, 48a–55a; Resp. Br. 52–54. The Second Amendment, like the English right, may well present difficult questions concerning its outer limits. But this case does not. This Court should affirm.

ARGUMENT

I. THE ENGLISH RIGHT TO HAVE AND USE ARMS BELONGED TO INDIVIDUALS BROADLY, REGARDLESS OF MILITIA SERVICE, AND PARTICULARLY PROTECTED THEIR "KEEPING" OF GUNS FOR SELF-DEFENSE.

The English right to arms emerged in 1689, and in the century thereafter courts, Blackstone, and other authorities recognized it. They recognized a personal, individual right. It could not have been a federalism provision, and none of them conditioned it on militia service—depredations by the king's militia having provided one reason for it. Preexisting restrictions fell away as the right developed after 1689, such that by the Second Amendment's adoption, Americans had inherited a broadly applicable and robust individual right that had been settled for at least fifty years. This right of course had limits, but they did not intrude on the core right to keep firearms to defend home and family: they confirmed it.

A. The English Right Was, by Well before the Founding, a Broadly Applicable Right of Individuals, Not Depending on Militia Service.

1. The right to arms was declared in the 1689 Declaration of Rights, part of England's Glorious Revolution. A "Convention" Parliament adopted the Declaration; William and Mary accepted it before Parliament proclaimed them king and queen; and the ensuing regular Parliament enacted it as the Bill of Rights. William Blackstone, 1 *Commentaries* *128, *211–16 (*"Blackstone"*).[2]

The Declaration presented twelve indictments against King James II (Mary's father), including for having "caus[ed] several good subjects, being protestants, to be disarmed, at the same time when papists were both armed and employed, contrary to law." Then, in a parallel list of thirteen articles, it stated: "That the Subjects which are Protestants may have Arms for their Defence suitable to their Conditions and as allowed by Law." 1 W. & M., Sess. 2, c.2, § 1 (1689).

This article set out a personal right. *See* Lois G. Schwoerer, *The Declaration of Rights, 1689*, at 283 (1981) (recognizing that many articles "guaranteed rights to the individual," including the right "to bear arms (under certain restrictions)"). Neither the article nor the indictment tied having arms to militia service, which the Declaration nowhere mentioned. Rather, being "armed" and "employed" were distinct. Furthermore, the right belonged to "Subjects," allowed arms "for their Defence"; indeed, Parliament adopted such language in lieu of the House of Commons' drafts referring to "their common Defence"; *see G&V* at 58–59.

The article's two concluding clauses—"suitable to their Conditions and as allowed by Law"—were not specially expounded. Blackstone noted them without explanation, 1 *Blackstone* at *143–44, and the judge of a prominent trial in 1820 treated them as just indicating that the right was not unlimited. *King v. Dewhurst*, 1 St. Tr. 529, 597–98 (Lancaster Assize 1820).

To the extent the final clause recognized that Parliament might regulate the right's scope, it is unremarkable: in "the English constitutional experience,"

Loving v. United States, 517 U.S. 748, 766 (1996), evident with the Declaration, rights restricted the Crown's prerogative power, not "law." Federalists highlighted this—pointing to the Declaration—in opposing a bill of rights. *See Federalist No. 84*, at 578–79 (Cooke ed., 1961) (Hamilton). Yet Americans borrowed English rights as the foundation for more secure rights in a distinct constitutional structure. As James Madison conceded in proposing the Bill of Rights to Congress, although "it may not be thought necessary to provide limits for the legislative power in that country, yet a different opinion prevails in the United States." Speech of June 8, 1789, *reprinted in Creating the Bill of Rights* 80 (Veit et al. eds., 1991).

But the English experience does mean that, to determine the bearing of an English right on the Constitution, one must determine how English law regulated it and how it had grown by the Founding. This too is unremarkable: the Declaration contains no freedom of the press; it was five years later that "the press became properly free," and merely upon expiration of a licensing act, 4 *Blackstone* at *152 n.a., which Parliament could have revived "by Law." Even that freedom only set the foundation for a broader American right.

2. As explained below, by the 1700s, the English right had shed many pre-1689 restrictions, most based on "Conditions" (wealth). The one general regulation that remained "by Law" only barred carrying weapons in a threatening manner, and is explained below in Part I.C. Three preexisting restrictions particularly fell away.

First, a 1671 act had provided that anyone not among the few rich qualified to hunt game was "not allowed to have or keep" any "guns." 22 & 23 Car. II, c.25, § 3. In a 1693 game act, and again in 1706, Parliament omitted "guns" from the list of implements that those not qualified could not "keep or use." 5 Ann., c.14, § 4 (1706); *see* 4 & 5 W. & M., c.23 (1693).

The courts interpreted this omission as protecting a broadly applicable right to keep a gun so long as one did not hunt game with it. In 1704 the Devonshire Quarter Sessions, in ordering searches for hunting implements, cautioned that no Protestant subjects were to be "'disturbed in keeping arms for their own preservation.'" *K&B* at 127. The first decision of a principal court was *King v. Gardiner* in 1738. 93 Eng. Rep. 1056 (K.B.); 95 Eng. Rep. 386 (different reporter). The Court of Common Pleas six years later thought the matter "settled and determined." *Mallock v. Eastly*, 87 Eng. Rep. 1370, 1374 (1744). And in 1752 the King's Bench, citing Gardiner, thought it "not to be imagined" that Parliament had intended "to disarm all the people of England." *Wingfield v. Stratford*, 96 Eng. Rep. 787, 787–88. Richard Burn pasted *Gardiner* into his authoritative manual for local officers, first published in 1755. 2 *The Justice of the Peace, and Parish Officer*, tit. "Game," 232–33 (11th ed. 1769) (*"JP"*); *see also* 1 *Blackstone* at *354 (recommending Burn); 4 *id.* at *175 (citing Burn regarding game).

Second, a statute from 1548 had primarily outlawed shot, by which "an infinite sort of fowl" and "much Game" had been killed. 2 & 3 Edw. VI, c.14. The question arose in 1692 whether it remained in force, and the King's Bench concluded that it did. *King v. Alsop*, 87 Eng. Rep. 256. Parliament repealed it three years later, noting its desuetude. 6 & 7 Will. III, c.13, § 3 (1695).

Finally, an even older statute, from Henry VIII, had restricted ownership of crossbows and short "hand-guns" (generally those under a yard) to the rich, those earning at least £100 a year. 33 Hen. VIII, c.6, §§ 1–2 (1541). It also fined anyone who, lacking such wealth, should "carry, or have in his or their journey, going or riding in the King's highways or elsewhere," any loaded crossbow or "gun," except in war. *Id.* § 3.

This statute also fell into desuetude in the wake of the Bill of Rights and had been pronounced obsolete before the Founding. The English Reports record no successful prosecution after 1689. See *King v. Bullock*, 87 Eng. Rep. 315 (K.B. 1693); *King v. Litten*, 89 Eng. Rep. 644 (K.B. 1693); *King v. Silcot*, 87 Eng. Rep. 186 (K.B. 1691); *King v. Lewellin*, 89 Eng. Rep. 440 (K.B. 1689). They record no prosecution at all after 1693.

One reason the statute withered was that it had come to be considered a game act. After 1689, even in local courts it is "difficult to find a case in which anyone was fined for possession of a gun of any sort unless it was connected with a poaching incident or with possession of other hunting equipment." *K&B* at 127.

Burn confirmed this understanding, and the statute's obsolescence. In editions before the Founding, he placed it last in a litany of game laws, simply summarized I,; and cited no case after *Silcot. See* 2 *JP* at 240–43. In a note, he acknowledged it was "undoubtedly in force, and consequently may be put in execution," but explained, "[N]evertheless it seemeth now to be obsolete, the object thereof [primarily encouraging "the use of the long bow"] being a matter not in any use, and the effect of it with respect to the game being superseded as it were by the several subsequent statutes." *Id.* at 243 n.; *see id.* at 245 n. (object "doth not now exist"); *Sander's Case*, 85 Eng. Rep. 311, 311 n.(1) (K.B. 1671) (editor's note, 1799, describing statute as "obsolete, as the object of it is a matter no longer in any use") (footnote omitted). Beginning in 1800, the treatise dismissed the statute in one sentence as "a matter more of curiosity than of use." 2 *JP* at 439 (J. Burn ed., 19th ed.). Parliament formally repealed it in 1831, in a litany repealing twenty-seven game laws covering four hundred years. 1 & 2 Will. IV, c.32, § 1.

3. Thus, in the 1700s, English subjects of all classes possessed a broad individual right to have arms. Blackstone confirmed this in the 1760s. He delineated three "primary . . . rights of the people of England," which echo in our Constitution: "the right of personal security, the right of personal liberty, and the right of private property." 1 *Blackstone* at *129. He identified five "auxiliary subordinate rights of the subject"—"to protect and maintain" these. *Id.* at *140–41. Fourth was the right of petition, and fifth was the right to have arms, both of which, he noted, the Bill of Rights had recognized. *Id.* at *143–44. He reiterated that "the subjects of England are entitled . . . to the right of having and using arms." *Id.* at *144. A posthumous edition by Edward Christian, published in the early 1790s, added that "every one is at liberty to keep or carry a gun, if he does not use it for the destruction of game." William Blackstone, 2 *Commentaries* *412 n.8 (Lewis ed., 1900) (reprinting Christian's annotation); see St. George Tucker, 2 *Blackstone's Commentaries*, advertisement & *145 n.42 (1803) (*"Tucker's Blackstone"*) (using and discussing Christian's edition).

Jean-Louis de Lolme likewise explained before the Founding, drawing on Blackstone, that the Declaration had "expressly ensured to individuals the right of publicly preferring complaints against the abuses of government and, moreover, of being provided with arms for their own defence." 2 *The Rise and Progress of the English Constitution* 886 (Stephens ed., 1838) (1784). De Lolme was well known. See 1 *Tucker's Blackstone* at 316.

Particularly striking confirmation of the right is the 1780 opinion from London's Recorder on the legality of a private self-defense association. He was the city's legal adviser and primary criminal court judge. *See 3 Blackstone* at *80–81 n.i & *334; 4 *id.* at *404. His opinion, prompted by the Gordon Riots, was "of wide interest." Leon Radzinowicz, 4 *A History of English Criminal Law* 107 (1968); see G&V at 87–88.

Acknowledging the "difficulty" of defining the "limits" of the "rights of the people" to "bear arms, and to instruct themselves in the use of them, collectively," the Recorder began with basics:

> The right of his majesty's Protestant subjects, to have arms for their own defence, and to use them for lawful purposes, is most clear and undeniable. It seems, indeed, to be considered, by the ancient laws

of this kingdom, not only as a *right*, but as a *duty*; for all the subjects of the realm, who are able to bear arms, are bound to be ready, at all times, to assist the sheriff, and other civil magistrates, in the execution of the laws and the preservation of the public peace. And that this right, which every Protestant most unquestionably possesses *individually*, may, and in many cases must, be exercised *collectively*, is likewise a point I conceive to be most clearly established.

"Legality of the London Military Foot-Association" (1780), *reprinted* in William Blizard, *Desultory Reflections on Police* 59, 59–60 (1785) ("*Recorder*"). Forty years later the judge in *Dewhurst* asked, "Are arms suitable to the condition of people in the ordinary class of life, and are they allowed by law?" 1 St. Tr. at 601. He too answered that "people in the ordinary class of life" had a "clear right to arms." *Id.*

4. In none of the above does the right of English subjects depend on militia service. This is no surprise: the 1662 Militia Act had authorized royally appointed militia officers, on their own warrants, "to search for and seize all arms" of anyone they judged "dangerous to the peace of the kingdom." 13 & 14 Car. II, c.3, § 14.[3] Both James II and his father "made effective use" of it "to try to snuff out political and religious dissent." Schwoerer, *Declaration* at 76; see K&B at 36–38, 43–53, 85, 100, 115–16, 123 (examples). It is part of the context for the Declaration's indictment.

Thus, the right enacted in the bill partly "reflected the idea that the Militia Laws were grievous and tacitly denied the right of the government to confiscate weapons." Schwoerer, *Declaration* at 76. Blackstone later explained that any royal proclamation "for disarming any protestant subjects, will not bind." 1 *Blackstone* at *271. In discussing the right, he did not connect it to militia service, *id.* at *143–44; in discussing the militia, he did not mention the right, *id.* at *412–13.

B. The Core of the English Right, Settled by at Least the 1730s, Was the Right of Ordinary Subjects to "Keep" Firearms for Defense of Their Homes and Families.

As discussed further in Part I.C, there was room for debate as to the outer limits of the right of English subjects when bearing arms. But one thing was not open to doubt: the core of the right, especially by the Founding, was the right of ordinary individuals to "keep"—possess and own—firearms for defense of their homes and families.

The Declaration suggested this in securing subjects' right to "have Arms for their Defence." Even a contemporaneous law restricting Roman Catholics allowed such a person, with permission of a justice of the peace, to "have or keep . . . necessary weapons . . . for the defence of his house or person." 1 W. & M., Sess. 1, c.15, § 4 (1689). The restrictive class statute of Henry VIII still emphasized that a subject living in or near a town could keep a gun (of the length permitted for the non-rich) "for the defence of his person or house," and that one outside a town could "keep and have in his said house, for the only defence of the same, hand-guns" of the permitted length. 33 Hen. VIII, c.6, §§ 4 & 7.

The cases recognizing the significance of the new game laws emphasized this core of the right. In *Gardiner,* a defendant charged with "keeping a gun" noted that the 1706 act did not list guns and argued, with regard to its prohibition of "other engines," that "though there are many things for the bare keeping of which a man may be convicted; yet they are only such as can only be used for destruction of the game, whereas a gun is necessary for defence of a house, or for a farmer to shoot crows." The King's Bench agreed: "[A] gun differs from nets and dogs, which can only be kept for an ill purpose." 93 Eng. Rep. at 1056.[4] The Court of Common Pleas considered settled that "a man may keep a gun for the defence of his house and family" and "must use the gun to kill game before he can incur any penalty." *Mallock,* 87 Eng. Rep. at 1374. And the King's Bench reiterated that "a gun may be kept for the defence of a man's house and for divers other lawful purposes." *Wingfield,* 96 Eng. Rep. at 787.

Even earlier, the Quarter Sessions order noted above had protected subjects' "'keeping [of] arms for their own preservation.'" *K&B* at 172. And by 1717 most justices on the King's Bench accepted that "the keeping a gun" might be done "for the defence of [one's] house," rather than "to destroy the game." *King v. Filer,* 93 Eng. Rep. 657 (K.B. 1722); *see Gardiner,* 95 Eng. Rep. at 387.

William Hawkins in his treatise, first published in 1716, clarified that a law (discussed below) regulating being armed in public still left one free to "assembl[e] his neighbours and friends in his own house, against those who threaten to do him any violence therein, because a man's house is as his castle." 1 *Treatise on the Pleas of the Crown,* ch. 63, § 8 (Leach ed., 6th ed. 1788) ("*Hawkins*"); *see id.,* ch. 65, § 10 (same); *Payton v. New York,* 445 U.S. 573, 596 n.44 (1980) (explaining rule).

Blackstone twice connected the arms right to personal defense. He described it as "a public allowance under due restrictions, of the natural right of resistance and self-preservation," and as "for self-preservation and defence."

1 *Blackstone* at *144. A few pages earlier, he highlighted the law's not punishing homicide "*se defendendo*" or "to preserve" one's limbs, as showing the
"high value" of life and limb. *Id.* at *130; *see* 4 *id.* at *180–85 (elaborating). He
declared self-defense "the primary law of nature" and explained that a person
"forcibly attacked in his person or property" could "repel force by force." 3 *id.*
at *3–4; *cf.* 1 *id.* at *251 (distinguishing resistance to government).

The Recorder thought "clear and undeniable" the right of subjects to have
arms "for their *own* defence," and listed "immediate self-defence" as the first
lawful use of arms. *Recorder* at 59, 63 (emphasis added). And the court in
Dewhurst began with the proposition that a man "in the ordinary class of
life . . . has a clear right to arms to protect himself in his house." 1 St. Tr. at 601.

C. Rather Than Interfering with the Freedom of Individuals to Keep Firearms for Self-Defense, English Law in the 1700s Protected the Peace by Directly Punishing Belligerent Uses of Those Arms.

English law in the 1700s thus did not meddle with the ability of ordinary
English subjects to keep firearms. The law was not indifferent to keeping the
peace: it was becoming harsher, notoriously so in the Black Act, which in
1723 added innumerable felonies—punished with forfeiture and execution.
See G&V at 64–70; 4 *Blackstone* at *4, *18, *97–98, *245. Yet the law did not
restrict individuals in keeping arms (or in simply carrying them), but rather
kept the peace by punishing those who broke it, with a firearm or otherwise,
and by punishing, through one common law rule, those who carried weapons in public belligerently. That this liberal regime endured in such a context
shows how robust the English right was—particularly the core right to keep.

1. Of course one had no right to use firearms to attack others, commit other
crimes, or otherwise breach the peace or violate private property. Blackstone,
for example, while criticizing ancient game laws, approved restrictions on
trespassing. 4 *Blackstone* at *416; 2 *id.* at *411–12. He catalogued offenses
against the peace (and a quasi-nuisance) that often involved weapons. *See
OLC Opinion* at 48 n.195; 4 *Blackstone* at *125–26 (striking in palace or
courts, or injuring those under court protection); *id.* at *131 (conveying arms
to a prisoner), *176–77 (homicide), *243 (robbery with a sword).

Moreover, "the common law hath ever had a special care and regard for
the conservation of the peace." 1 *Blackstone* at *349. One way of conserv-
ing it, apart from prosecutions, was to demand a surety from persons who
posed particular risks. And one circumstance justifying a surety was if some-

one "shall go about with unusual weapons or attendants, to the terror of the people." *Hawkins*, ch. 60, § 1; *see* 4 *Blackstone* at *254–55 (same).

2. Beyond this, English law depended on one general regulation of the right: a common law rule against going about armed so as to terrify the people. Related was the medieval Statute of Northampton. It provided that "no man, great nor small," except royal officials and subjects responding to "a cry made for arms to keep the peace," could "be so hardy [1] to come before the king's justices, or other of the king's ministers doing their office, with force and arms, [2] nor bring no force in affray of peace, [3] nor to go nor ride armed by night nor by day, in fairs, markets, nor in the presence of the justices or other ministers, nor in no part elsewhere," on pain to "forfeit their armour" and be imprisoned "at the king's pleasure." 2 Edw. III, c.3 (1328), *quoted in Hawkins*, ch. 63, § 4 (numbers added).

By the 1600s, the courts had reduced this to the common law offense. *See Chune v. Piott*, 80 Eng. Rep. 1161, 1162 (K.B. 1615) (Croke, J.); *K&B* at 81 (local court example). According to Professor Malcolm, the statute "does not appear to have been enforced" then—except that men "were occasionally indicted for carrying arms to terrorize their neighbors." *K&B* at 184 n.36 & 104, respectively; *see id.* at 191–92 n.32 (similar).

This interpretation was confirmed in the agitation of the Glorious Revolution. An information charged that Sir John Knight, a torment to James II, "did walk about the streets armed with guns, and that he went into" a church, "in the time of divine service, with a gun, to terrify the King's subjects." *Sir John Knight's Case*, 87 Eng. Rep. 75, 76 (K.B. 1686); *see K&B* at 104–5. He had been carrying pistols. *King v. Knight*, 90 Eng. Rep. 330 (different reporter). The chief justice explained that the statute's "meaning" was "to punish people who go armed to terrify the king's subjects," which had been "a great offense at the common law." 87 Eng. Rep. at 76. The statute was "almost gone in desuetudinem," but "where the crime shall appear to be malo animo, it will come within the Act (tho' now there be a general connivance to gentlemen to ride armed for their security)." 90 Eng. Rep. at 330. Knight was acquitted and bound to good behavior. 87 Eng. Rep. at 76.

Hawkins thereafter discussed Northampton in a chapter on affray—fighting in public to the terror of the people. He thought it "certain," based on Northampton, "that in some cases there may be an affray where there is no actual violence; as where a man arms himself with dangerous and unusual weapons, in such a manner as will naturally cause a terror to the people." *Hawkins*, ch. 63, § 4. Blackstone tracked this formulation. 4 *Blackstone* at *149.

It followed that "no wearing of arms is within the meaning of this statute, unless it be accompanied with such circumstances as are apt to terrify the people" by causing "suspicion of an intention to commit [an] act of violence or disturbance of the peace." *Hawkins*, ch. 63, § 9. *Dewhurst* thus concluded that "[a] man has a clear right to protect himself when he is going singly or in a small party upon the road where he is traveling or going for the ordinary purpose of business." 1 St. Tr. at 601–2. Hawkins added that Northampton also did not bar arming oneself "to suppress dangerous rioters, rebels, or enemies." *Hawkins*, ch. 63, § 10. The Recorder shared this view. *See Recorder* at 62.

Hawkins did not elaborate on "dangerous and unusual" weapons. Given general usage, a firearm likely was "dangerous." See, e.g., *King v. Oneby*, 92 Eng. Rep. at 465, 467 (K.B. 1727) ("dangerous weapon" includes "a pistol, hammer, large stone &c. which in probability might kill B. or do him some great bodily harm"). Unusualness might contribute to causing a terror: "persons of quality" were "in no danger of offending against this statute by wearing common weapons." *Hawkins*, ch. 63, § 9.

Northampton, in its third subsection, did make it illegal to "go [or] ride armed" before officials or in "fairs," "markets," or any other "part," suggesting a concern with particular places. But this was subject to the judicial gloss just described. Before *Knight*, "the strict prohibition" in this subsection "had never been enforced." *K&B* at 104. *Knight* involved going armed to a "part"—a church—yet the court did not suggest this was illegal per se, apart from whether Knight was carrying pistols "malo animo," "to terrify the king's subjects." 90 Eng. Rep. at 330; 87 Eng. Rep. at 76, respectively. The location could be relevant, however, given that Hawkins approved going armed with attendants "in such places, and upon such occasions" as was common. *Hawkins*, ch. 63, § 9. And if an affray did occur, the law could punish it more, depending on "the place wherein it is committed," particularly courts or churches. *Id.* § 23. Blackstone, following Hawkins, mentioned aggravated punishment where "the particular place ought to restrain and regulate men's behavior more than in common ones." 4 *Blackstone* at *145–46.

3. The difficulties arose not from law-abiding individuals going about their business—much less keeping arms—but rather from armed groups. English law dreaded mobs, riots, and rebellions. It long had specially punished crimes by three or more persons. *See id.* at *146–47. Charles II restricted "tumultuous petitioning." *Id.* at *147. And in the 1710s, Parliament added the Riot Act, which made it a felony for twelve or more persons to disobey orders to disperse. *See id.* at *142–43, *147.

An *armed* mob would be worse, and so an armed group posed a particular risk of causing terror. The commission of justices of the peace, from 1590, charged them based on Northampton to inquire into persons who went or rode "in companies, with armed force against the peace. *Butt v. Conant*, 129 Eng. Rep. 834, 849 (C.P. 1820).

After 1689 the law wrestled with reconciling this concern and the arms right. Hawkins concluded that "persons of quality" not only could wear common weapons but also could "hav[e] their usual number of attendants with them, for their ornament or defence, in such places, and upon such occasions, in which it is the common fashion to make use of them." *Hawkins*, ch. 63, § 9. Yet "persons riding together on the road with unusual weapons, or otherwise assembling together in such a manner as is apt to raise a terror in the people," were guilty of unlawful assembly. *Id.*, ch. 65, § 4.

The London Recorder, although finding the basic individual right "clear and undeniable," wondered "[w]here, then, shall we draw the line?" on the right of private, collective bearing. *Recorder* at 59 & 61. His "best consideration" was that a private group needed to (1) have a "lawful" "purpose and object"; (2) "demean themselves in a peaceable and orderly manner" consistent with it; (3) not assemble in numbers that "manifestly and greatly exceed" that purpose; and (4) not "act without the authority of the civil magistrate" unless suppressing "sudden, violent, and felonious, breaches of the peace." *Id.* at 62 (emphases omitted).

The court in *Dewhurst* similarly had "no difficulty in saying you have no right to carry arms to a public meeting if the number of arms which are so carried are calculated to produce terror and alarm." 1 St. Tr. at 602; *see id.* (similar). The court relied on Hawkins. *Id.* at 596–97.

Unsurprisingly, when Parliament thirty years after the Founding enacted its first restrictions on the English right since before the Declaration, it was spurred by riots and the resulting "Peterloo Massacre," which in turn led to the unlawful assembly at issue in *Dewhurst. See generally King v. Hunt*, 106 Eng. Rep. 768 (K.B. 1820); *G&V* at 95–98. And Parliament restricted what the Recorder had cautiously allowed, barring unauthorized "Meetings and Assemblies" to learn "the Use of Arms" or military movement, and denouncing those who had caused "great Terror and Alarm [to] His Majesty's peaceable and loyal Subjects." 60 Geo. III, c.1, § 1 (1819).[5] Yet this difficult area was far afield from keeping arms for self-defense or simply carrying them—each of which *Dewhurst* reaffirmed as "a clear right" four months later. 1 St. Tr. at 601.

II. The Second Amendment Secures at Least the Individual Right Inherited from England, as Early American Authorities Demonstrate.

The English right was invoked in America before and soon after the Second Amendment's adoption—including in authorities interpreting that Amendment. Americans not only inherited England's individual right but also expanded it, dropping England's religious and class restrictions and coming to see it as the foundation for a citizen militia. Like the English, they confirmed the core right of keeping for self-defense by focusing regulation not on keeping but rather on belligerent bearing.

A. Authorities before the Second Amendment's Adoption Recognized the Right Inherited from England and, Owing to the Revolution, That It Facilitated Not Only Self-Defense but Also a Militia of the People.

Early Americans well knew their inheritance from England. Alexander Hamilton celebrated the Glorious Revolution, *see Federalist No. 26*, at 165–66; and the Declaration contains the foundation not only of the Second Amendment but also of the First Amendment's Petition Clause and the Eighth Amendment, among other things.

As part of this inheritance, they claimed the individual right to arms. In Boston in 1768, as tensions rose, a town meeting led by Samuel Adams, John Hancock, and others resolved that this right in the Declaration was "founded in Nature, Reason and sound Policy, and is well adapted for the necessary Defence of the Community"; praised the colony's law requiring "every listed Soldier and other Householder" to be armed; and requested that, to "be prepared in Case of Sudden Danger," any Bostonian lacking arms "observe the said Law." Boston Chronicle at 363 (September 19, 1768), *quoted in* Stephen P. Halbrook, *A Right to Bear Arms* 1–2 (1989) ("*Bear*").

British troops occupied Boston two weeks later. *Id.* at 2. The *Maryland Gazette* republished the resolution, *id.* at 61, and Boston newspapers defended it: "[I]t is certainly beyond human art and sophistry, to prove the British subjects, to whom the *privilege* of possessing arms is expressly recognized by the Bill of Rights, and, who live in a province where the law requires them to be equip'd with *arms*, &c. are guilty of an *illegal act*, in calling upon one another to be provided with them, as the *law directs*." Boston Gazette & Country J. at 2 (January 30, 1769), *quoted in Bear* at 6; *see Boston under Military Rule, 1768–1769*, at 61 (Dickerson ed., 1936) ("*Boston*") (reprinting from different paper).

A subsequent anonymous article by Adams recounted the Glorious Revolution and quoted both discussions of the right by the recently published Blackstone. Adams attacked critics of the town vote, "calling upon the inhabitants to *provide themselves with arms for their defence*," as insufficiently "attend[ing] to the rights of the constitution." Boston Gazette at 3 (February 27, 1769), *reprinted in* 1 *The Founders' Constitution* 90 (Kurland & Lerner eds., 1987).

A New York newspaper denounced the troops' "licentious and outrageous behavior" and argued: "It is a natural right which the people have reserved to themselves, confirmed by the Bill of Rights, to keep arms for their own defence; and as Mr. Blackstone observes, it is to be made use of when the sanctions of society and law are found insufficient to restrain the violence of oppression." "Boston, March 17," N.Y.J. Supp. at 1 (April 13, 1769), *reprinted in Boston* at 79; *Bear* at 7 (same).

A year later the right was reaffirmed in the "Boston Massacre" murder trial of British soldiers for firing on a harassing crowd. John Adams, their counsel, argued that they had acted in self-defense. In closing, he quoted Hawkins and conceded, "Here every private person is authorized to arm himself, and on the strength of this authority, I do not deny the inhabitants had a right to arm themselves at that time, for their defence." 3 *Legal Papers of John Adams* 247–48 (Wroth & Zodel eds., 1965). Adams also later recognized the propriety of "arms in the hands of citizens, to be used . . . in private self-defence," which he distinguished from militia service. 3 *Defence of the Constitutions of Government of the United States of America* 475 (1787).

Soon after Lexington and Concord, North Carolina's royal governor denounced those urging people "to be prepared with Arms" and train under committees of safety. North Carolina's congressional delegates, however, publicly urged the committees "to form yourselves into a Militia" in the exercise of "the Right of every *English* subject to be prepared with Weapons for his Defense." N.C. Gazette (Newbern) at 2 (July 7, 1775), *quoted in Bear* at 29–30.

Thomas Paine that year in a Pennsylvania magazine even satirized the game laws for allowing local English judges to disarm commoners on the pretext that they had hunted with guns. *Bear* at 24–25. Pennsylvania's 1776 Declaration of Rights protected hunting, and a newspaper article defended this by arguing that even though "guns are not engines appropriated to kill game," aristocrats still used the game laws to disarm commoners through false witnesses. *Id.* at 24. Noah Webster later mocked the minority of Pennsylvania's ratifying convention for proposing that the Constitution protect hunting, because America lacked the feudalism that had prompted English-style game laws. "America," Daily Advertiser (December 31, 1787), *reprinted in* 1 *Debate on the Constitution* 553, 559–60 (Bailyn ed., 1993). He had a point: an early American adaptation of Burn omitted the "Game" chapter. *Burn's Abridgement, or the American Justice* 198 (Ladd ed., 2d ed., 1792).

As the admonition of North Carolina's delegates highlights, Americans came to add to the English arms right, which was tied to individual self-defense, an affection for a citizen militia, and came to view the right as its foundation. The Boston resolution even suggests this, describing the right as "adapted for" community defense. The Revolution incubated such notions. *See OLC Opinion* at 51–55 & 24–31; Resp. Br. 20–29. This notion did not *restrict or replace* the English right but rather built on it. A similar dynamic apparently had occurred in England. Whigs' "claim that the right not only ensured individual self-defense, but served as a restraint on government," and their corresponding demand for a reformed militia, could not prevail in 1689, and only "gradually came to be accepted in the eighteenth century." *K&B* at 122; *see* Schwoerer, *Declaration* at 75–76 (similar).

B. Authorities Soon after the Second Amendment's Adoption Recognized It as Securing—and Expanding—the Right Inherited from England, with the Additional Purpose of Facilitating a Militia of the People.

The American embrace of the right inherited from England, along with the affection for militias built on it, continued in the earliest authorities after the Second Amendment's adoption. They also recognized, and praised, that the right as transplanted to America lacked England's religious and aristocratic restrictions.

1. Each of the three leading early commentators on the Constitution viewed the amendment as built on the foundation of the individual English right, and each viewed it as better because broader.

St. George Tucker set out his views in his 1803 edition of Blackstone. In an introductory essay on the Constitution, he quoted the Second Amendment and, like Blackstone, connected the right to "self defence." He noted the Declaration's "right of bearing arms," but criticized its religious limitation and qualification based on "condition," which had allowed use of game laws to undermine the right. 1 *Tucker's Blackstone, Note D*, at 300. He reiterated this criticism in discussing the Second Amendment right together with the First's right of assembly and petition, explaining that both exceeded their English antecedents. *Id.* at 315–16; *see id.* at 289 & 357 (further mention). In annotating Blackstone's descriptions of the right, Tucker praised the Second Amendment "right of the people" for omitting "any qualification as to their condition or degree, as is the case in the British government," and again criticized the game acts. 2 *Tucker's Blackstone* at *143–44 nn.40–41; *see id.* at *145 n.42 (explaining England's hunting restrictions). And in a note to one of Blackstone's critiques of the game laws, Tucker lamented that "it seems to be held" that no one but aristocrats has "any right to keep a gun in his house" or "keep a gun for their defence." But "in America we may reasonably hope that the people will never cease to regard the right of keeping and bearing arms as the surest pledge of their liberty." 3 *id.* at *414 n.3. (He here omitted Christian's clarifying note, quoted in Part I.A.3.) In none of these passages did Tucker suggest that the Second Amendment *added* a restriction—dependence on militia service.

William Rawle likewise contrasted the Second Amendment right with the English one—"secured to protestant subjects only" and "cautiously described to be that of bearing arms for their defence, 'suitable to their conditions, and as allowed by law.'" He denounced the game laws for allowing forfeiture of a gun used to kill game, and noted Blackstone's critique. *View of the Constitution of the United States of America* 126 (2d ed. 1829) ("View"). Rawle concurred in the preamble's praise of the militia, viewed the amendment's operative text as a "corollary" from this, and emphasized that the operative text's "prohibition is general," barring any "flagitious attempt" by Congress, or a State, "to disarm the people." *Id.* at 125–26; *see id.* at 153 ("In a people permitted and accustomed to bear arms, we have the rudiments of a militia.").

Joseph Story, in explaining the Second Amendment, devoted a paragraph to England's "similar provision" ("confined" to Protestants). He quoted the Declaration, cited Blackstone's descriptions, and followed Tucker's criticism of the effect of the game laws on England's "defensive privilege." 3 *Commentaries on the Constitution of the United States* § 1891 (1833). Story elsewhere noted the Declaration's "right to bear arms." *Id.* § 1858.

These three were not alone. Henry Tucker, a judge and law professor, explained that "in America" the "right of bearing arms" was "not limited and restrained by an arbitrary system of game laws as in England; but is practically enjoyed by every citizen." *Commentaries on the Laws of Virginia* 43 (1831). And Blackstone's "auxiliary" right was "secured with us by" the Second Amendment. *Id.*

The leading commentator after the Civil War, Thomas Cooley, described the Second Amendment as a "modification and enlargement from the English Bill of Rights" and "enabl[ing] the government to have a well-regulated militia." *General Principles of Constitutional Law* 271 (1880). He also explained that state constitutions' "defences to personal liberty" included "the right of the people to keep and bear arms." He recounted the Glorious Revolution, described a "well-regulated militia" as an alternative to a standing army, and observed that one "cannot exist unless the people are trained to bearing arms." He also cited two cases recognizing a broad individual right. *Treatise on the Constitutional Limitations* 350 (1868).

2. Several of the earliest cases likewise acknowledged the English foundation of the right to keep and bear arms. The leading antebellum one was *State v. Reid* in 1840. The Alabama Supreme Court upheld a ban on carrying guns or knives secretly, under the state constitution's provision that "[e]very citizen has a right to bear arms, in defence of himself and the State." 1 Ala. 612, 614–15 (1840). The court began with its origins in England's "provisions in favor of the liberty of the subject." Quoting the Declaration, the court explained, "The evil which was intended to be remedied . . . was a denial of the right of Protestants to have arms for their defense, not an inhibition to wear them secretly." *Id.* at 615. But "[a] statute which, under the pretence of regulating, amounts to a destruction of the right, or which requires arms to be so borne as to render them wholly useless for the purpose of defence, would be clearly unconstitutional." *Id.* at 616–17.

Soon after, the Tennessee Supreme Court upheld a conviction for secretly carrying a bowie knife, under the state's right of "free white men . . . to keep and bear arms for their common defence." It too recognized the English roots; although mangling them, perhaps because of "common defence" in the state provision, the court still concluded that Tennessee "citizens have the unqualified right to keep" arms. *Aymette v. State,* 21 Tenn. 154, 156–58 (1840). For analysis of *Aymette* and related Tennessee cases, *see OLC Opinion* at 87, 91–96.

In 1846 the Georgia Supreme Court in *Nunn v. State* (which Cooley cited) reversed a conviction for openly carrying a pistol. 1 Ga. 243 (1846). The court distinguished *Barron v. City of Baltimore*, 32 U.S. (7 Pet.) 243 (1833), and applied the Second Amendment. It viewed both the amendment and state protections as securing the preexisting English right: "[T]he Constitution of the United States, in declaring that the right of the people to keep and bear arms, should not be infringed, only reiterated a truth announced a century before, in the act of 1689." 1 Ga. at 249. This right was "re-established by the revolution of 1688, conveyed to this land of liberty by the colonists, and finally incorporated conspicuously in our own *Magna Charta*." In the United States, "a reason why this right shall not be infringed" was that its "free enjoyment" would "prepare and qualify a *well-regulated militia*." "The right of the whole people," "and not militia only," furthered this "important end." *Id.* at 250–51.

C. Early American Authorities Likewise Adopted the English Focus on Directly Punishing Belligerent Uses of Arms, Rather Than Interfering with the Freedom of Individuals to Keep Them for Defense of Home and Family.

Not only did American authorities recognize the foundation of the right to keep and bear arms in the English right, but also they confirmed the core of that right by focusing on directly punishing belligerent uses of those arms. As in England, the focus was on applying—and adapting—the common law rule against terrorizing the people. That is why in 1868 Cooley could "happily" note the paucity of cases on "regulat[ing] this right," making it unnecessary to determine "[h]ow far" a legislature could go. *Constitutional Limitations* at 350. There was no federal regulation of private firearms until 1934. *OLC Opinion* at 3.

1. As in England, the right did not authorize breaching the peace. The Massachusetts Supreme Court in a libel case likened the freedom of the press to the "right to keep fire arms," which did not protect "him who uses them for annoyance or destruction." *Commonwealth v. Blanding*, 20 Mass. 304, 314 (1825). The Michigan Territory's Supreme Court, also in a libel case, explained that the Constitution "grants to the citizen the right to keep and bear arms. But the grant of this privilege cannot be construed into a right in him who keeps a gun to destroy his neighbor." *United States v. Sheldon*, 5 Blume Sup. Ct. Trans. 337, 1829 WL 3021, at *12.

The three earliest suggestions for the Bill of Rights expressed this truism. Pennsylvania's convention minority proposed protecting the right to bear arms, yet allowed disarming "for crimes committed, or real danger of public injury from individuals." Bernard Schwartz, 2 *The Bill of Rights: A Documentary History* 665 (1971). Samuel Adams and other delegates urged the Massachusetts convention to recommend barring Congress from "prevent[ing] the people of the United States, who are peaceable citizens, from keeping their own arms." *Id.* at 674–75. The New Hampshire convention proposed that

"Congress shall never disarm any Citizen unless such as are or have been in Actual Rebellion." *Id*. at 761.

2. Also as in England, the main further restriction (apart from racial ones, mirroring England's on non-Protestants; *see, e.g., State v. Newsom*, 27 N.C. 250 (1844)) was the Statute of Northampton, as reduced to the common law. *See K&B* at 140 ("usual restrictions" on using firearms "to terrify" applied). Tucker, like Hawkins, implicitly treated it (as enacted in Virginia) as a species of affray, which requires terror. *See 5 Tucker's Blackstone* at *146 n.6, *149 n.14. Rawle observed that a "disturbance of the public peace" would abuse the Second Amendment right, and, citing Hawkins, that a person's "carrying of arms. . . attended with circumstances giving just reason to fear that he purposes to make an unlawful use of them" would justify a surety. *View* at 126.

The fullest antebellum judicial treatment was in *State v. Huntly*, 25 N.C. 418 (1843). Northampton was not in force, but the court, discussing Blackstone, Hawkins, Burn, *Knight,* and Coke, held that the offense was at common law. It affirmed a conviction but cautioned that the "carrying of a gun *per se* constitutes no offense. For any lawful purpose—either of business or amusement—the citizen is at perfect liberty to carry his gun." *Id*. at 422–23.

The overriding issue in antebellum cases was the constitutionality of new bans on carrying weapons secretly. Apart from the initial divided decision in *Bliss v. Commonwealth*, 12 Ky. 90 (1822), *overruled by* Ky. Const. art. XIII, § 25 (1850), every court upheld or approved them. In addition to *Reid, Aymette,* and *Nunn* (which approved them while finding keeping and openly carrying pistols protected), *see, e.g., State v. Mitchell*, 3 Blackf. 229 (Ind. 1833); *State v. Buzzard*, 4 Ark. 18 (1842); and *State v. Chandler*, 5 La. Ann. 489 (1850).

Courts implicitly extended the common law by analogy, based on an overwhelming consensus that any person carrying secretly must be planning to terrorize someone and, correspondingly, that carrying secretly did not serve self-defense. *Reid* described the law as intended "to put down lawless aggression and violence," barring carrying in "such a manner as is calculated to exert an unhappy influence upon the moral feelings of the wearer, by making him less regardful of the personal security of others." 1 Ala. at 617. Absent evidence, it was "only when carried openly" that arms could be "efficiently used for defence." *Id*. at 619. *Aymette* referred to the "terror which a wanton and unusual exhibition of arms might produce" and the danger of "desperadoes with concealed arms." It rejected any right to bear arms "merely to terrify the people or for purposes of private assassination," and thought "the manner in which they are worn and circumstances under which they are carried indicate to every man the purpose." 21 Tenn. at 159–60; *see also* Chandler, 5 La. Ann. at 489–90 (law "became absolutely necessary" to prevent surprise "assassinations"; Second Amendment protected open carrying). Thus, this court, in later declaring "laws prohibiting the carrying of concealed weapons" consistent with the Second Amendment, had cause to think them within a "well-recognized" exception, even though not one specifically "inherited from our English ancestors." *Robertson*, 165 U.S. at 281–82.

3. Laws regarding carrying in particular places seem to have been connected to fear of armed groups and in any event to have had in mind the common law. Several colonial statutes required bringing arms to church, while "[t]he usual restriction on the use of firearms in crowded areas" applied—a restriction implicit in the common law rule and no doubt barring firing without cause. *K&B* at 139–40; *cf.* Pet. Br. 3, 42. Tucker appended Northampton's first subsection (coming before judicial officers "with force and arms") to the offense of injuring persons under judicial protection, and indicated that Virginia laws regarding churches barred disturbances. *See* 5 *Tucker's Blackstone* at *126, *54 & *146; *see also Aymette*, 21 Tenn. at 159 (no right of "ruffians to enter the theatre in the midst of the performance, with drawn [weapons], or to enter the church in the same manner, during service, to the terror of the audience"). The 1776 Delaware Constitution provided that "to prevent any violence or force being used at . . . elections, no person shall come armed to any of them, and no muster of the militia shall be made on that day." *Quoted in OLC Opinion* at 55 n.225; see also Reid, 1 Ala. at 616 (stating that no right existed "to bear arms upon all occasions and in all places," but focusing on threatening carrying).

The right of assembly was less restricted. *See* 5 *Tucker's Blackstone* at *146–48. But Rawle recognized regarding the Second Amendment that "[a]n assemblage of persons with arms, for an unlawful purpose, is an indictable offense." *View* at 126. The minutemen had begun as private associations, *see OLC Opinion* at 51–53—unlawful to the British—but, after the Civil War, Americans faced struggles with such groups similar to England's. Cooley in 1880 thought the Second Amendment required a view akin to the Recorder's, while this court in 1886 briefly upheld under the Second Amendment a state restriction of private armed associations similar to the 1819 British law discussed above. *Compare General Principles* at 271 *with Presser v. Illinois,* 116 U.S. 252, 264–65. As in England, however, this area of dispute was far removed from the core right of keeping for self-defense, which neither questioned.

CONCLUSION

The District of Columbia laws violate the core of the right to arms inherited from England and secured by the Second Amendment. The Court should affirm.

Respectfully submitted,

C. Kevin Marshall
(Counsel of Record)
Jones Day
51 Louisiana Avenue, N.W.
Washington, D.C. 20001-2113
Telephone: (202) 879-3939
Facsimile: (202) 626-1700

Counsel for Amici Curiae

February 8, 2008

NOTES

1. The parties have letters on file with the clerk consenting to the filing of amicus briefs in support of either party upon seven days' written notice; amici complied with this condition. No counsel for a party authored this brief in whole or in part, and no counsel or party made a monetary contribution to fund the brief's preparation or submission. No person other than the amici, their members, or their counsel made a monetary contribution to its preparation or submission.

2. For consistency, this brief in citing *Blackstone* uses the star pagination in Tucker's edition, discussed in Parts 1.A.3 and II.B.1.

3. Persons having more than £100 per year provided "a case of pistols" for horsemen; others provided muskets of at least a yard for infantry. *Id.* at §§ 5 & 21.

4. An apparently separate case the next year was to the same effect. *King v. Gardner*, 87 Eng. Rep. 1240, 1241 (K.B. 1739) (defendant arguing that "to charge only that he kept a gun is improper, for it includes every man that keeps a gun," and that guns are kept "for the defence of a man's house"); *id.* (Lee, C.J.) (words of statute "do not extend to prohibit a man from keeping a gun for his necessary defence").

5. Another act authorized officers, in certain counties "disturbed" by riots, to search for and seize weapons kept "for any purpose dangerous to the Public Peace" (with a warrant upon the oath of one credible witness) and (with a warrant) to

arrest persons "found carrying Arms" and justly suspected of such a purpose. 1 Geo. IV, c.2, §§ 1, 3, 8 (1819). It was "hotly contested in Parliament." The government conceded it was "'not congenial with the constitution'" and infringed "'the rights and the duties of the people,'" but justified it on "'necessity.'" It expired after two years. *G&V* at 96–97.

★ ★ ★ ★

Brief of Amici Curiae Jack N. Rakove, Saul Cornell, David T. Konig, Lois G. Schwoerer et al. in Support of Petitioners

Jack Rakove et al.

★ ★ ★ ★

INTEREST OF AMICUS CURIAE[1]

AMICI CURIAE, LISTED in the Appendix, are professional historians. They have all earned Ph.D. degrees in history, hold academic appointments in university departments of history, and specialize in the American Revolution, the Early Republic, American Legal History, American Constitutional History, Anglo-American Legal History, or related areas. Amici curiae have an interest in the Court having an informed understanding of the history that led to the adoption of the Second Amendment.

INTRODUCTION AND SUMMARY OF ARGUMENT

The central question is whether the Second Amendment protects a private right to keep handguns and other firearms, independent of an individual's membership in a state-regulated militia. As a problem for constitutional historians, the question can be elaborated and restated in this way: Did the framers and ratifiers of the amendment believe they were constitutionally entrenching an individual right to keep arms for personal protection? Or did they conceive the amendment to achieve a different end by affirming that a "well-regulated militia" of citizen-soldiers would preserve "the security of a free state," principally by lessening the need for a republican government to depend on a standing army?

Historians can best assess these claims by reconstructing the context within which the adopters of the amendment acted. Recovering that context involves more than snatching a line from Blackstone's *Commentaries* or Madison's *Federalist* 46, or ringing endless changes on the references to hunting and fowling in the Dissent of the Anti-Federalist Minority in the Pennsylvania ratification convention. It instead involves explaining how a popular right to keep and bear arms figured in the ratification debates of 1787–88; how that debate was in turn shaped by the Militia Clause of Art. I, § 8; and why that clause appeared to threaten key Anglo-American political ideas dating to the Glorious Revolution of 1688–89. Setting the context for the Second Amendment also requires exploring analogous provisions in the parliamentary Bill of Rights of 1689 and the declarations of rights that accompanied the first state constitutions.

Once explored, this context establishes that the private keeping of firearms was manifestly not the right that the framers of the Bill of Rights guaranteed in 1789. Though Anglo-American political tradition did indeed value the idea of an armed populace, it never treated private ownership of firearms as an individual right. The right stated in the seminal English Bill of Rights of 1689 was vested not in individuals but in Parliament, which remained free to determine "by law" which Protestant subjects could own which weapons and how they could be used. Nor did the first American constitutions and declarations of rights include clauses protecting private use of firearms.

The right to keep and bear arms became an issue in 1787–88 only because the Constitution proposed significant changes in the governance of the militia, an institution previously regulated solely by state law. Anti-Federalists argued that Congress would abuse its proposed authority to organize, arm, and discipline the militia by allowing that venerated institution to atrophy from neglect and lack of funding. A national government that could command permanent armed forces with its own resources would gain an engine for tyranny. Republican political thinking had long regarded standing armies as a danger to liberty, and a militia of citizen soldiers as one of its greatest bulwarks. Anti-Federalists rehearsed these arguments, and several ratification conventions—notably Virginia and New York—adopted resolutions affirming that a right to keep and bear arms, when tied to service in the militia, merited constitutional protection. Nothing in the ratification debates of 1787–88, however, indicated that the exercise of this right required limiting the customary police powers of state and local government.

Federalist supporters of the Constitution dominated the First Congress that met in the spring of 1789. In framing the Second Amendment, they simultaneously sought to assuage the expressed Anti-Federalist concern about the maintenance of the militia while preserving congressional authority over its organization, arming, and discipline. They rejected language that would have modified that authority, including a qualifying provision, proposed by the House of Representatives, defining the militia as "composed of the body of the people." Acceptance of that definition would impair congressional authority to determine how extensive membership in the militia should be.

Nothing in this argument challenges the idea that eighteenth-century Americans had ready access to firearms, or that they valued the concept of a well-armed citizenry. Individuals were legally free to purchase and keep weapons as they could other property; but as with other forms of property, the keeping of firearms was subject to extensive legal regulation. What is at dispute is whether legal rights of private ownership were what the Second Amendment constitutionally entrenched. During this period, Americans were hardly shy about identifying and discussing such fundamental rights as representation, trial by jury, or freedom of conscience, or the natural rights to life, liberty, and property. The fact that references to the keeping of firearms are so few and terse, or that the modern academic controversy over the Second Amendment has been forced to squeeze so much modern interpretive blood from so few evidentiary turnips, is itself an indicator of how minor a question this was at the time. The same cannot be said about the role of the militia in the constitutional order. That was the subject that was patently in dispute in 1787–1789, and that is why the exceptional preamble to the Second Amendment is a true guide to its original meaning.

ARGUMENT

EVEN AFTER THE PARLIAMENTARY BILL OF RIGHTS OF 1689 ALLOWED CERTAIN CLASSES OF PROTESTANT SUBJECTS TO KEEP ARMS, BRITISH CONSTITUTIONAL DOCTRINE AND PRACTICE SUBJECTED THE LIMITED RIGHT THEREIN RECOGNIZED TO EXTENSIVE LEGAL REGULATION AND LIMITATION.

The closest English antecedent to the American notion of a right to bear arms appears in the Bill of Rights, the parliamentary reenactment in December 1689 of the Declaration of Rights that the new monarchs, William and Mary, accepted seven months earlier after the Glorious Revolution forced James II to vacate his throne. Knowledgeable Americans were familiar with the Bill of Rights and the circumstances of its creation. Americans saw the English document as part of a common constitutional tradition, a binding pledge by the Crown to acknowledge the legal supremacy of Parliament and thereby respect the rights of the people.

That link between parliamentary supremacy and popular rights is critical to understanding the import of Article VII of the Bill of Rights, which provided "[t]hat the Subjects which are Protestants may have Armes for their defence Suitable to their Condition and as allowed by Law." The formal grievance that Article VII answered was that James II had violated settled law "[b]y causing several good Subjects being Protestants to be disarmed at the same time when Papists were both armed and Employed contrary to Law." Bill of Rights (1689) reprinted in 5 The Founders' Constitution 1–2 (Philip Kurland and Ralph Lerner, eds., 1987). The authors of the Bill of Rights were reacting to the efforts of Charles II and James II to maintain Stuart rule through a standing army increasingly officered and manned by Irish Catholics. Commissioning Catholics as military officers did indeed violate the Test Act, which required officeholders to swear an oath denying Catholic doctrine on transubstantiation. In the paranoiac atmosphere of the 1680s, James's open practice of Catholicism and the birth of his male heir made the fear of a Catholic restoration all the more ominous.

The arms-bearing right that the bill of 1689 affirmed, then, was a response to this specific situation, tied to the belief that an armed Protestant population would safeguard the realm against a Catholic restoration. It did not establish a general right of all persons to keep weapons, and especially firearms, for purposes of individual defense. An earlier version of Article VII could be read to grant the right to all Protestants. But that expansive possibility was checked when the House of Lords added the crucial qualifying language, "Suitable to their Condition and as allowed by Law." Lois Schwoerer, *To Hold and Bear Arms: The English Perspective*, 76 Chi.-Kent L. Rev. 30–48 (2000). The first qualification tracked a long history of legislation making the possession of weapons, and again especially firearms, dependent on the holders' social and economic status. The second qualification was a reference to the Game Law of 1671, which allowed lords of manors to appoint gamekeepers to "take and seize all such guns" used by "divers disorderly persons" to hunt and trap "game intended to be preserved" for the higher classes of English society. 6 English Historical Documents 466–67 (Andrew Browning, ed., 1988). Adoption of the Bill of Rights did not affect Parliament's capacity to regulate who could or could not possess firearms. In fact, when a new Game Act was adopted in 1693, the House of Commons rejected (169–65) a proposal allowing "every Protestant to keep a musket in his House for his defence not withstanding this or any other Act." Many members voting had sat in Parliament in 1689; they evidently did not read Article VII as establishing a broad-gauged right all Protestants could claim. Schwoerer, *Hold and Bear Arms, supra* at 50–51.

The notion that Article VII made ownership of firearms a fundamental right immune to substantive regulation fails for a broader reason. The lasting constitutional significance of the Bill of Rights was not only to identify certain rights of the subject that merited protection, but also to lay down the basic premises that shaped British constitutionalism thereafter: that the monarch could not make law simply by royal edict, but that he must rule *lawfully*, with the consent of Parliaments freely elected and frequently assembled. The concept of parliamentary supremacy, as exercised through the king-in-Parliament, was the great principle the Bill of Rights vindicated. The liberty Englishmen cherished would be secured by confirming that a Parliament respectful of their rights and representative of society would have sovereign authority to make law. Article VII endorsed the idea that well-to-do Protestants might keep arms against the threat of a Catholic restoration, but as the formula "according to law" made clear, this imposed no limit on the reach of parliamentary power.

That understanding also informed a much-cited passage from Sir William Blackstone's *Commentaries* (1765): "The fifth and last auxiliary right of the subject . . . is that of having arms for their defence, suitable to their condition, and such as are allowed by law," Blackstone wrote, citing the Bill of Rights. This was "indeed, a publick allowance under due restraints, of the natural right of resistance and self-preservation, when the sanctions of society and laws are found insufficient to restrain the violence of oppression." 1 William Blackstone, Commentaries *139. Notwithstanding the reference to "self-preservation," this passage cannot be construed to assert an unregulated private right of self-defense, for two reasons. First, Blackstone's corpus of five "subordinate" or "auxiliary" rights involves the subject's relation to public authority, respectively through the constitution of Parliament; the limitation on royal prerogative; access to courts of justice; the right to petition; and, finally, the right to arms as a security against oppression. *Id.* at *136–39. Second, the phrases "suitable to their condition, and such as are allowed by law" and "under due restraints" denote the regime of parliamentary regulation

that the Bill of Rights made the fundamental principle of British constitutionalism. Blackstone was an unequivocal defender of that regime. "So long
therefore as the English constitution lasts," Blackstone wrote in the very next
chapter, "we may venture to affirm, that the power of parliament is absolute
and without control." *Id.* at 157. Whatever principle the Bill of Rights stated
always lay within the power of Parliament to apply and regulate, and thus
to modify or limit. In this sense, the Bill of Rights did not establish a catalogue of rights in the modern, positivist, constitutionally entrenched sense of
the term. Like the clauses of Magna Carta, all of its provisions were subject
to modification, control, and repeal by subsequent Parliaments. So long as
Parliament sat, Blackstone envisioned no situation under which the auxiliary
right of resistance could be invoked. *Id.*

The First American Bills of Rights Made No Mention of a Private Right to Keep Arms.

One application of parliamentary sovereignty was the program of colonial
legislation adopted after 1765. As the Declaratory Act of 1766 stated, the colonists were subject to parliamentary jurisdiction "in all cases whatsoever."
27 Danby Pickering, The Statutes at Large from Magna Carta to the End
of the Parliament of Great Britain 19–20 (London, John Archdeacon, 1767).
Americans rejected that claim by declaring independence. But in doing so
they did not repudiate the general conception of legislative supremacy, which
remained the leading principle of the new state constitutions adopted with
independence, and that principle embraced a robust conception of the reach
of legislative authority. *See generally* Gordon S. Wood, Creation of the American Republic, 1776–1787 at 162–63 (1969).

Nor did the declarations of rights that eight states concurrently adopted
effectively limit legislative power. In only two states (Pennsylvania in 1776,
Massachusetts in 1780) were they made part of the actual constitutions. These
declarations operated not as legally binding commands but rather as statements of republican principles or common law protections. They have also
been faulted for being less comprehensive than modern readers might expect
them to have been.[2]

Even so, these early declarations indicate which rights the first state constitutions deemed fundamental. It is noteworthy that none made any reference to the private ownership and personal use of firearms. There is no direct
equivalent in the American declarations to the selective Protestant "subjects"
invoked in the Bill of Rights of 1689.[3] What appear instead are statements,

either bundled together in one article or linked in successive articles, affirming the virtue of a well-regulated militia, the danger of standing armies, and the importance of maintaining civilian control over the military.

None of the modest variations among the formulae used by different states suggest that the right to bear arms vested in individual citizens for private purposes. Virginia refers to "a well-regulated Militia, composed of the body of the people, trained to arms." Delaware and Maryland simply refer to "a well regulated militia." More intriguing are the clauses stating the purposes for which arms may be borne: "for the defence of the State" (North Carolina, Art. XVII); "for the common defence" (Massachusetts, Art. XVII); and most striking, "for the defence of themselves and the state" (Pennsylvania, Art. XIII). 7 Sources and Documents of United States Constitutions 403 (William F. Swindler, ed., 1978) (N.C.) (Mass. vol. 5 at 95; Pa. vol. 8 at 279). The first two clearly have no bearing on a private right, free of legal regulation. Although the Pennsylvania clause appears open to a broader interpretation, two considerations render this reading improbable. First, the opening clause of Article XIII immediately preceded two other clauses reiterating the usual condemnation of standing armies and endorsement of civilian supremacy. The article as a whole is thus concerned with military matters. Second, and contextually more important, the Pennsylvania variant needs to be read against the colony's unique history. Since the mid-1750s, a political impasse between the proprietary governor and the assembly, and the influence of Quaker pacifism on provincial governance, effectively prevented the colonial government from maintaining a militia. Residents of frontier counties exposed to Indian attack during the Seven Years' War and Pontiac's rising of 1763 petitioned the provincial government to organize militia and provide the resources necessary to sustain it. These efforts failed, and Pennsylvania had no militia at all during the two decades preceding independence. Unlike most colonies, its legal assembly continued to meet into the spring of 1776, but without mobilizing a provincial militia against the British threat. As a result, extra legal committees arose in Philadelphia that were strongly supported by the province's voluntary militia units. These committees demanded the drafting of a new state constitution that would coerce military service from every citizen. When the constitution writers of 1776 used the phrase "for the defence of themselves," they accordingly were referring not to a personal right of self-defense but to the community's capacity to protect itself against the threats raised either by Native Americans or by the British army. Nathan Kozuskanich, *Defending Themselves: The Original Understanding of the Right to Bear Arms*, 39 Rutgers L.J. 1041 (2008).

The sole noteworthy reference to a private right to arms in 1776 appears in the draft Virginia constitution that Thomas Jefferson prepared while marooned in Philadelphia writing the Declaration of Independence. His list of Rights Private and Public included: "No freeman shall ever be debarred the use of arms [within his own lands or tenements]." The bracketed phrase did not appear in the first draft of this document, and may indicate Jefferson's uncertainty about the extent of the right. 1 Papers of Jefferson 344, 353, 363 (Julian Boyd, ed., 1950).

The lack of discussion of an individual right to firearms is unsurprising. Their ownership and use were not major issues in eighteenth-century America, as they arguably remained in contemporary Britain. There debate still raged over the revision and enforcement of game laws, with a landed aristocracy trying to protect its traditional privileges against poachers and others who could use the protein illegal hunting provided. *See* E. P. Thompson, Whigs and Hunters: The Origin of the Black Act (1975). No such aristocratic order or tradition existed in America, which was probably the most protein-rich society in the world. Americans could legally obtain and use firearms as they could other property, subject to the regulation to which all property was liable.

It is equally unsurprising that the militia remained an object of constitutional concern in 1776. The American revolutionaries were conscious heirs of a radical Whig tradition that regarded standing armies as a bane to liberty, and which celebrated the idea of a citizens' militia as the optimal form of military organization for a republic. *See generally* "No Standing Armies!" The Antiarmy Ideology in Seventeenth-Century England (1974). This was a staple theme of eighteenth-century political writing, and its lessons were reinforced when Britain sent its standing army to Boston, first to enforce the Townshend duties (1768–1770) and then to compel obedience to the Coercive Acts of 1774. The latter led to the outbreak of civil war in April 1775, when the militia organized by the Massachusetts Provincial Congress resisted the British march on Concord.

BY PROPOSING TO TRANSFER AUTHORITY OVER THE MILITIA
FROM THE STATES TO CONGRESS, THE CONSTITUTION RADICALLY
CHALLENGED CONVENTIONAL REPUBLICAN THINKING
ABOUT THE NATURE OF THE MILITIA.

Individual ownership of firearms was not an issue at the Federal Convention of 1787. The records of its deliberations contain no reference to whether the government—national, state, or local—could regulate possession of firearms.

The Framers adhered to the general concept of "internal police" that had shaped American thinking about federalism since 1776, if not earlier. Under this understanding, the states retained broad and exclusive legislative authority to regulate most facets of daily life—ownership and use of property, rules of inheritance, criminal law, and all the aspects of communal health, welfare, and safety. Pennsylvania's Declaration of Rights of 1776 expressed this value by affirming that "the people of this State have the sole, exclusive and inherent right of governing and regulating the internal police of the same." 5 Founders' Constitution *supra* at 6. The Framers no more imagined that the Constitution would abridge the states' power to regulate firearms than they thought it would impinge on their authority to control noxious substances.

The one issue addressed at the 1787 Convention that could affect citizens' access to firearms concerned the militia. Under the Articles of Confederation, its regulation remained solely under state control. But complaints about its training, discipline, and performance persisted throughout the war for independence. In a "Sketch for a Peacetime Establishment" (May 1783), Washington proposed uniform standards of training for the militia in every state and further argued that an effective militia could be formed only from a select body of young men, as opposed to the larger mass of adult males legally eligible for service. 26 Writings of George Washington 389–90 (John Fitzpatrick, ed., 1931–1944). Similar proposals were made in the Report on a Military Peace Establishment drafted by a congressional committee chaired by Alexander Hamilton. 3 Papers of Alexander Hamilton 393–96 (Harold Syrett, ed., 1962). *See* Don R. Higginbotham, *The Federalized Militia Debate: A Neglected Aspect of Second Amendment Scholarship,* 55 Wm. & Mary Q. 40–44 (1998).

Militia reform, though not the most pressing issue facing the Federal Convention of 1787, was part of the Federalist agenda for strengthening the national security powers of the Union. *Id.* at 43–44. Unlike many of the legislative powers enumerated in Article I, section 8, congressional governance of the militia sparked significant discussion at Philadelphia. An extended debate on August 18 found the Framers divided over the practicability of dividing power over the militia between national and state governments. Several delegates insisted that the states would never cede their traditional authority over training and disciplining the militia. But others, including General Charles Pinckney and James Madison, argued for the importance of "uniformity ... in the regulation of the Militia throughout the Union." 2 Records of the Federal Convention of 1787 at 330–33 (Max Farrand, ed., 1966).

The militia question was then referred to a grand committee of one member from each state. Its report of August 21 presented the clause that would finally be adopted, which empowered Congress "[t]o provide for organizing, arming, and disciplining, the Militia, and for governing such Part of them as may be employed in the Service of the United States, reserving to the States respectively, the Appointment of the Officers, and the Authority of training the Militia according to the discipline prescribed by Congress." *Id.* at 352.

When this clause was debated on August 23, several delegates again criticized the proposed scope of congressional jurisdiction over the militia. But their reservations were rebutted by other delegates, led by Rufus King, speaking for the committee, and Madison, who insisted that the only effective militia would be one ultimately controlled by Congress. This discussion included important comments on how the militia would be armed. Madison wondered whether King's initial definition of *"arming,* [as] specifying the kind size and caliber of arms" would exclude Congress's "furnishing arms" to the states. King replied that *"arming* meant not only to provide for the uniformity of arms, but included authority to regulate the modes of furnishing, either by the militia themselves, the State Governments, or the National Treasury." Several efforts to weaken the proposed clause in the interest of preserving greater state control over the militia proved futile. Madison and others argued that "[t]he states neglect their militia now," and would do no better after the Constitution gave the national government greater resources for national defense. Nine states approved the proposed change; only Connecticut and Maryland dissented. *Id.* at 384–88.

The Constitution authorized Congress "to provide for calling forth the Militia to execute the Laws of the Union, suppress Insurrections and repel Invasions." Though this clause was uncontroversial and occasioned no debate, *id.* at 390, it, too, demonstrates that the Framers contemplated converting the militia into a national institution. That commitment in turn explains why the militia question became a significant element in the public debate over ratification of the Constitution.

Anti-Federalist Objections to the Militia Clause Preponderantly Evoked the Traditional Fear of Standing Armies and Its Corollary Endorsement of the Value of the Militia.

This radical shift in jurisdiction over the militia would have been controversial by itself, but it became even more so when coupled with giving Congress independent authority to maintain an army and navy. Anti-Federalists steeped in the literature of the age knew that this amounted to the creation of a standing army, that dreaded enemy to the liberty of the people. From the start of the ratification debates, they sought to modify those clauses. Within a fortnight of the adjournment of the Federal Convention, the Virginia Anti-Federalist Richard Henry Lee urged the Continental Congress to endorse a "Bill of Rights" that would declare, *inter alia,* "[t]hat standing Armies in times of peace are dangerous to liberty" and should be raised only with a two-thirds vote in both houses of Congress. 13 DHRC at 239. Lee identified a number of fundamental rights deserving recognition, but said nothing about firearms.

The best antidote to standing armies, Anti-Federalists argued, was a militia drawn from the body of the citizenry. The survival of that venerated institution was exactly what the Constitution would threaten if Congress abused its power by failing to keep the militia well armed, by making service onerous, or by recruiting a "select militia" not drawn from the body of the people. On the other side, leading Federalists held to the Framers' view that a state-governed mass militia would lack the training and discipline needed to turn citizens into battle-ready soldiers. In *Federalist* 29, Hamilton forthrightly argued that a "well-regulated" militia must be a select one, because it would be impossibly expensive and burdensome to subject the whole body of the male citizenry to the training required.

Discussion of citizens' access to firearms during the ratification debates of 1787–88 focused nearly exclusively on the comparative merits and risks of a standing army or the militia. The hackneyed idea that standing armies were inimical to liberty was reinforced by the charge that a distant national government could rule as extensive a country as the United States only through armed force. Militia service was also treated as a matter of civic duty, for a key element in republican thinking reaching as far back as Machiavelli treated the *obligation* to bear arms in defense of one's country as one of the rights and privileges that distinguished republican *citizens* from the *subjects* of other polities that slavishly relied on hireling soldiers lacking intrinsic loyalty to the regime.[4]

As at the Federal Convention, these exchanges treated the militia not as the disembodied mass of the people but as a legal institution subject to concurrent national and state administration. That was the meaning of James Madison's oft-quoted remark in *Federalist* 46, noting that half a million armed Americans would overmatch any force a national government bent on tyranny could field. Those armed citizens would act not as a spontaneous, self-deputized force, but as members of an institutional militia "united and conducted by government possessing their affections and confidence." *Id.* at 334–35. Here, as on other issues, the dominant way in which the ratifiers constructed the danger of tyranny lurking in the Constitution was to imagine a struggle between national and state governments, and manifestly not a conflict between the people on the one hand and the combined power of the two levels of the federal system on the other. The preeminent Anti-Federalist charge against the Constitution was that it would bring about a "consolidation" of all effective power in the national government, leaving the states hollow jurisdictions. Jack Rakove, Original Meanings: Politics and Ideas in the Making of the Constitution, 148, 181–84 (1996). Federalists replied, as Madison's *Federalist* essays 45 and 46 particularly argue, by identifying all the political and structural advantages that would favor the state governments.

The central question was thus whether Congress would make the militia completely its creature, depriving the states of any residual authority over its use or even existence, and leaving it dependent on federal largesse for its arms. The fullest discussion of these concerns took place at the Virginia convention in Richmond in June 1788. Anti-Federalist Patrick Henry insisted that congressional power over the militia was plenary and exclusive. 10 DHRC 1276. George Mason similarly imagined how the militia might be disarmed: not by the federal government confiscating weapons, but rather, "[u]nder various pretences, Congress may neglect to provide for arming and disciplining the militia, and the State Governments cannot do it, for Congress has an exclusive right to arm them." *Id.* at 1270. Federalist leaders Madison, George Nicholas, and John Marshall replied strenuously that power over the militia was indeed concurrent, and that the states remained free to arm their own militias and use them for internal security. *Id.* at 1273, 1280, 1306–8. "If Congress neglect our militia," the future Chief Justice observed, "we can arm them ourselves." *Id.* at 1308. This was a critical point in a state where the militia was the first line of defense against the ever-present danger of slave rebellion. See Carl T. Bogus, *The Hidden History of the Second Amendment*, 31 U.C. Davis L. Rev. 309 (1998).

Because the Virginia convention was so evenly divided, Federalists accepted a proposal to recommend constitutional amendments to the first Congress. This was where the antecedent wording of the Second Amendment can be found, closely followed by the similar language adopted by New York two weeks later.[5] Both begin by declaring "[t]hat the people have a right to keep and bear arms"; both then declare "that a well regulated Militia [Virginia: composed of the body of the people trained to arms; New York: including the body of the People *capable of bearing arms*] is the proper, natural and safe defence of a state." The Virginia article adds further statements condemning standing armies and upholding civilian supremacy over the military. The New York declaration tracks these two provisions closely in a following article, but after first inserting an additional article declaring "[t]hat the militia should not be subject to Martial Law, except in time of War, Rebellion or Insurrection." *Id.* at 1553; Linda Grant DePauw, The Eleventh Pillar: New York State and the Federal Constitution 294 (1966).

Text and context both establish that the dominant issue throughout the period of ratification was the future status and condition of the militia, not the private rights of individuals. Even when Anti-Federalists spoke of the militia being disarmed, their expressed concern was not the specter of federal confiscation or prohibition of private weapons but rather that the national government might neglect to provide arms. They worried that militiamen might be subject to military justice, or marched to faraway locations, to their personal inconvenience and the insecurity of their own communities. Above all, Anti-Federalists worried that by allowing the traditional militia to atrophy, Congress would rely increasingly on its own permanent army, to the overall detriment of the public liberty the Revolution had been fought to establish.

EXPLICIT ANTI-FEDERALIST REFERENCES TO A PRIVATE RIGHT TO ARMS WERE CONSPICUOUSLY FEW IN NUMBER AND FAILED TO GENERATE POLITICAL SUPPORT.

In contrast to the numerous discussions of the militia during the ratification debates, explicit references to the private ownership of firearms were few and scattered. The three noteworthy statements come from the Pennsylvania, Massachusetts, and New Hampshire conventions. Only the last commanded the support of a majority of delegates, and presents a formula unique to the discussions of 1787–88. The twelfth constitutional amendment that New Hampshire recommended for future consideration read: "Congress shall never disarm any Citizen unless such as are or have been in Actual Rebellion." Neil H. Cogan, Complete Bill of Rights 181 (1997). In Massachusetts, an omnibus rights-protecting amendment that the convention *rejected* stated "that the said Constitution be never construed to authorize Congress . . . to prevent the people of the United States, who are peaceable citizens, from keeping their own arms." 6 DHRC 1453, 1469–71.

Finally, the minority Anti-Federalist delegates to the Pennsylvania ratifying convention included in their published Dissent this proposed amendment:

"7. That the people have a right to bear arms for the defense of themselves and their own state, or for the purpose of killing game; and no law shall be passed for disarming the people or any of them, unless for crimes committed, or real danger of public injury from individuals." The next proposed amendment followed section 43 of the state constitution in stating that the people "shall have liberty to fowl and hunt in seasonable times, on the lands they hold" as well as navigable waters and other unenclosed lands. 2 DHRC 597–98. *See also* Cornell, A Well-Regulated Militia, *supra* at 50–52, 55–58.

These two articles are often offered as evidence that the Founders thought of the right to bear arms as ensuring a private right to possess weapons, as did the court below. Pet. App. 27. But that reading is incorrect. First, the dissenters who endorsed this proposal comprised only a third of the Pennsylvania convention. Second, as previously noted, the reference to "the defense of themselves and their own state" had particular connotations in Pennsylvania, tied not to an individual's right to defend his home but to the colonial government's failure to organize effective militia units prior to independence. Third, the proposed formula against "disarming" leaves ample room for police-power regulation by recognizing "real danger of public injury from individuals" as a legitimate basis for public action. What constitutes a "real danger" time and circumstance must determine, but even the dissenter conceded that whatever right individuals retain must be judged against the danger of "public injury." Fourth, the dissenters appeared disinclined to push this right too far. There is no further discussion of the private use of firearms in the explanatory passages of the Dissent.

Fifth, and most important, these two clauses fell stillborn on the larger debate that continued to rage for months. One early response was witheringly sarcastic. Why not add this further clause, Noah Webster asked: "That Congress shall never restrain any inhabitant of America from eating and drinking, *at seasonable times,* or prevent his lying on his *left side,* in a long winter's night, or even on his back, when he is fatigued by lying on his *right.*" 15 DHRC at 199. Had Anti-Federalists continued to want to push for the constitutional protection of firearms, ample time remained to muster support in the nine states yet to act on the Constitution. Once published, however, these clauses of the Dissent were politically inert. If the Pennsylvania dissenters tried to place the question of a private right to arms before the body politic, their fellow Americans declined their summons. Far from being the key to a constitutional puzzle, the Dissent was an exception to the true rule: that such debate as occurred over a right to keep and bear arms always took place within the context of the future status of the militia.

James Madison's Original Draft of the Second Amendment Does Not Support an Individual Rights Interpretation.

In drafting the amendments that evolved into the Bill of Rights, James Madison had no reason to place a private right to firearms on his agenda. Madison worked from a pamphlet compiling all the amendments proposed by the states, and only New Hampshire had spoken explicitly of individuals being disarmed. Taking the Virginia and New York recommendations as his model, Madison again made the militia the urgent question to confront. In culling the amendments, Madison rejected anything that implied a structural change in the Constitution, limiting the proposals he introduced in the House of Representatives on June 8 largely to matters of rights.

Madison was primarily but not exclusively concerned with protecting individual rights, and this placed him at the leading edge of American thinking during this period. He was arguably the first major thinker to recognize how the protection of rights in a republic differed from that in a monarchy. There, the problem was to protect the people as a whole against the concentrated power of the state. In a republic, by contrast, the chief problem was to protect individuals and minorities against popular majorities wielding power through the legislature. Rakove, Original Meanings, 310–18, 330–36. But as the eventual Tenth Amendment demonstrates, Madison also intended to rebut Anti-Federalist charges of "consolidation" by affirming the reserved powers of the states and people, in a manner akin to the Second Amendment. Because he understood that the states would retain their traditional police powers, Madison would naturally have included the power to regulate firearms among those still belonging to the states.[6]

Advocates for an individual rights view of the amendment often make much of a single line in an outline of Madison's June 8 speech, to wit: "They relate 1st to private rights." Some lines later, after the fresh heading "Bill of Rights—useful not essential" and the immediately subsequent comment "fallacy on both sides—espec[iall]y as to English Decl[aratio]n of Rights," Madison made a passing reference to "arms to Protestts." 12 Papers of James Madison 193–94 (Robert Rutland, ed., 1962–1991). This elliptical material is cited as proof that Madison conceived the right "to keep and bear arms" primarily in private, individual terms. There are several difficulties with this view. One is that "1st" need not mean *exclusively* or *solely;* it may simply be a general statement identifying the first of many aspects of his amendments. Moreover, this line appears to refer to the amendments generally; it is not specifically related to the right to bear arms provision. The subsequent reference to "arms to Protestants" clearly refers to the English Bill of Rights of 1689. The passage in Madison's June 8 speech that corresponds to this portion of the outline indicates that Madison was reiterating his long-standing misgivings about the value of bills of rights as "paper" or "parchment barriers." *Compare* Speech of June 8, 1789, *id.* at 203, with Letter to Jefferson of October 17, 1788, 11 Papers of Madison 297.

In his speech, Madison did not discuss the right to bear arms. Nor was it part of the proposal he later described "as the most valuable on the whole list": to insert in Article I, section 10 a clause forbidding the states to violate "the equal rights of conscience, or the freedom of the press, or the trial by jury in criminal cases." 12 Papers of Madison, 208, 344.

Madison's original version of the Second Amendment tracked the wording of the Virginia convention, but with some changes: "The right of the people to keep and bear arms shall not be infringed; a well armed, and well regulated militia being the best security of a free country: but no person religiously scrupulous of bearing arms, shall be compelled to render military service in person." Complete Bill of Rights, *supra* at 169. Adding the phrase "well armed" responded to the concern that the militia might atrophy from joint neglect by Congress and the states. Madison omitted the references to standing armies and civilian supremacy in the Virginia and New York recommendations. The Constitution fully covered both principles with its provisions for biennial military appropriations, delegation of enumerated powers over national security to Congress, and the designation of the president as commander in chief. The final clause was derived from a similar provision recommended by the Maryland convention. *Id.* at 181. Its presence confirms that the principal subject was the militia. That clause was also the sole subject of the recorded House debate on the entire article.

THE FINAL REVISIONS OF THE SECOND AMENDMENT REFLECTED THE FEDERALISTS' DETERMINATION TO PRESERVE CONGRESSIONAL AUTHORITY OVER THE ORGANIZATION OF THE MILITIA.

The House select committee reviewing Madison's proposals revised this language in three noteworthy ways. First, it improved his syntax by turning the reference to the militia into a strong preamble rather than leaving it dangling between the "keep and bear arms" and "religiously scrupulous" sections. Second, the committee dropped the phrase "well armed." Most important, it inserted the phrase "composed of the body of the people" after "militia," thereby moving "the people" vested with the right closer to the republican ideal of the adult male citizenry. *Id.* at 169–70.

In this form, the amendment went to the Senate as Article V in the House resolutions of August 24. There three changes took place. One was minor: "best security of a free State" was altered to "being necessary to the security of a free State." *Id.* at 175–76. Two were substantive. The Senate eliminated the clause exempting religious dissenters, in effect preserving a discretionary congressional authority over the composition of the militia. More important, and to similar effect, it deleted the House-added modifier "composed of the body of the people." *Id.* at 174, 176.

Proponents of the individual right interpretation see this last alteration as sloppy editing not meant to alter the amendment's intended meaning. *E.g.,* Malcolm, To Keep and Bear Arms, *supra* at 161. That view wholly ignores the character of the Senate that did the editing. Only two Anti-Federalists sat in the inaugural Senate session, and their twenty Federalist colleagues included men like Rufus King, a shaper of the original militia clause of the Constitution, and Hamilton's father-in-law, General Philip Schuyler. These Federalists shared Washington's and Hamilton's view that the defense needs of the nation required a militia system not constitutionally yoked to the impracticable idea of keeping "the body of the people" trained to arms. The amendment, as revised, would still assuage Anti-Federalist concerns by stating a principled commitment to the value of a militia. But it would not hinder Congress in using its best judgment to determine how to organize, arm, and discipline an effective militia. The Senate had no credible motive to weaken the substantive delegation of power in Article I, section 8, which acceptance of the House language arguably might do.

On September 9 the Senate considered and rejected another substantive alteration of the article, most likely proposed by the two Anti-Federalists, William Grayson and R. H. Lee. This one would have revived the anti-standing army and civilian supremacy clauses, while requiring two-thirds votes in Congress to maintain a "standing army or regular troops" in peacetime. Complete Bill of Rights, *supra* at 173–74. The House had previously rejected a similar amendment offered by the South Carolina Anti-Federalist Aedanus Burke. *Id.* at 172. These rejected proposals again confirm that the context within which Congress considered the eventual Second Amendment was solely a military one.

On September 9 the Senate considered and rejected one other amendment: to insert "for the common defense" immediately after "keep and bear arms."

Id. at 174–75. This action has sometimes been explained as assuring that the amendment would protect an individual right by eliminating a qualification. Nelson Lund, *The Past and Future of the Individual's Right to Arms*, 31 Ga. L. Rev. 35 (1996). In the absence of recorded debate, or even knowledge of who moved the amendment, two other explanations are more compelling. One is that the phrase was superfluous, redundant with the militia's manifest purpose. Second, and more important, the adoption of such a qualification could conflict with the Militia Clauses of Article I, implying that other authorized uses of the militia, such as the suppression of insurrections, had become constitutionally suspect. Federalists intent on preserving the authority of Congress over the use of the militia would have seen this amendment as a problematic limiting qualification.

The Second Amendment Is Best Understood as an Affirmation of Federalism Values, Which Helps to Explain Why the "Insurrectionist" Theory of Its Origins Is Fallacious.

In endorsing the value of a well-regulated militia, led by officers appointed by the state governments, the framers of the Second Amendment affirmed that the militia would be a "partly federal, partly national" institution in the sense in which James Madison used that phrase in *Federalist* 39. The Militia Clause vividly illustrates the "compound" nature of the American constitutional republic. Both levels of government would have a share in controlling the militia; both would act directly on the citizens who formed it; and the line between national and state authority would be a matter for political determination. For their part, citizens had a civic duty to participate in the militia, if national and state law required them to do so. But both levels of government would have to reckon with the preferences of citizens in deciding what those duties would be. The actual history of the militia soon demonstrated that the people's aversion to serving in a well-regulated militia outweighed the Federalists' desire to turn it into a more effective combat-ready outfit. In practice Congress regularly thwarted efforts by both Federalist and Republican administrations to fulfill the nationalizing promise of the Militia Clause.

There is a second federal dimension to the origins of the Second Amendment. Outside the question of whether militia members would be armed at national, state, or personal expense, there was no credible basis on which the national government could regulate possession of firearms. Insofar as these were subject to regulation, state and local governments would be the necessary agents as they regulated all other forms of property. The existing regime of police power regulation was tolerant of private ownership of weapons, but not so lax as to prohibit states or localities from determining, for example, when the private keeping of gunpowder or the public carrying of firearms threatened public safety. Not even the most paranoid Anti-Federalist imagined that the national government would have the incentive or means to interfere with this traditional form of regulation.

Federalism also identifies a critical weakness in current academic notions of the "insurrectionist" origins of the amendment, which hold that it was conceived to preserve a right of popular resistance to tyrannical government. Here again, Madison's comparison of the authority and political resources of national and state governments in *Federalist* 45 and 46 captures an eighteenth-century reality that modern readers can easily overlook. If the national government were to act despotically, it would have to encroach upon or commandeer the residual, constitutionally recognized authority of the states. If, for example, it sought to confiscate privately owned firearms for purposes other than those associated with the militia, the states could be expected to challenge that usurpation, and a militia composed of the community and directed by the state governments would come to their support rather than be supinely dragooned into national service. The insurrectionist theory presumes what those at the time could not have fathomed: that national and state governments, both elected by the people, would collude to deny the people their fundamental rights.

An "insurrectionist" Second Amendment fails a second test of historical plausibility. As noted, the Constitution authorized Congress to mobilize the militia to "suppress Insurrections." The Republican Guarantee Clause of Article IV further empowered the national government, "on Application" by a state, to intervene within it "against domestic Violence." The clear inspiration for this provision was Shays's Rebellion in Massachusetts, which occurred only months before the Federal Convention met, an upheaval that profoundly influenced the Federalist movement. Under the Articles of Confederation, Congress lacked authority to lend military assistance to the Massachusetts government as it sought to suppress that uprising. These two clauses were the Framers' direct answer to the deficit of authority that the Massachusetts rebellion exposed. It beggars the historical imagination to think that the same Federalist congressmen who wrote the Second Amendment were intent on protecting a popular right to insurrection.

A HISTORICALLY GROUNDED ANALYSIS OF WHAT WAS ACTUALLY DEBATED IN
1787–1789 CAN ONLY CONCLUDE THAT THE STATUS OF THE MILITIA WAS ALWAYS
WHAT WAS IN DISPUTE, AND NOT THE PRIVATE RIGHTS OF INDIVIDUALS.

Historians can best contribute to the resolution of contemporary constitutional disputes by recovering and reconstructing the context within which
the adopters of particular clauses thought and acted. The process of recovering and reconstructing what the past was like must pay close attention to
the value of particular *texts,* the statements that bear most directly on the
matter in dispute. But equally important, it must also convey a sense of *context,* which requires locating particular pieces of historical evidence within
a framework that best allows us to evaluate their probative value. The historian's recurring complaint about "law office history," as it is colloquially
disparaged, is that it routinely indulges in the selective and uncritical use of
quotations, stripped from the context in which they were uttered, and given
meanings that contemporaries would have been astounded to learn they
carried. *See, e.g.,* Don Higginbotham, *The Second Amendment in Historical
Context,* 16 Const. Comment. 221 (1999). Because of the exceptional passions
surrounding the Second Amendment, this one realm of constitutional controversy appears more susceptible to this kind of misuse than any other. A vast
and sometimes vituperative literature has grown up around this subject, and
sorting out claims and counterclaims can require heroic efforts.

The central argument of this brief is that throughout the period when the
Second Amendment took shape, the status of the militia under the new Constitution indeed defined the controlling framework for discussing the people's
right to keep and bear arms. The evidence sustaining this claim is easy to find
in the voluminous records of the ratification debates, and the explanation for
its salience is equally easy to provide. The benefits of a citizens' militia and
the corresponding dangers of a hireling army were stock themes of the political literature Americans imbibed during the eighteenth century. When the
Framers applied lessons drawn from the Revolutionary War to the national
defense–related clauses of Article I, they provoked predictably critical reactions from their Anti-Federalist opponents. The idealized image of a militia
of citizen soldiers had deep roots in Anglo-American political culture, and as
the distinguished historian Bernard Bailyn has observed, on this point as on
others, the Anti-Federalists faithfully followed the radical Whig legacy that
had led the colonists to revolt a decade earlier. Bernard Bailyn, Ideological
Origins of the American Revolution 331–51 (enlarged ed., 1992).

By contrast, explicit references in the same voluminous records to the
ownership of firearms for private purposes are conspicuously few. That is one

reason why a handful of quotations figure so prominently in the modern controversy, often cited to support points at odds with their intended meaning. More important, when Pennsylvania Anti-Federalists sought to elevate the use of firearms for private purposes into a right deserving constitutional recognition, their proposal fell on deaf ears. Had Americans felt that the Constitution threatened private access to firearms, nothing would have prevented this claim from becoming another of the many persistently sustained charges that Anti-Federalists leveled against the Constitution. But that is exactly what did not happen. Instead, it was the militia question that the Virginia and New York conventions debated seven months later, endorsing the recommendations that Madison and his colleagues carefully pared. The debate, in short, was always about the militia and its public purposes, never about a private right. That is why the unique justificatory preamble to the Second Amendment is a true guide to its meaning and not rhetorical persiflage.

This brief takes no position on how well armed Americans were, something historians are still trying to gauge. It assumes that many Americans owned firearms and expected them to remain relatively easy to obtain. What this brief does argue, however, is that these private aspects of the ownership of firearms never crossed the threshold of constitutional significance in 1787–1789.

Historians are often asked what the Founders would think about various aspects of contemporary life. Such questions can be tricky to answer. But as historians of the revolutionary era, we are confident at least of this: that the authors of the Second Amendment would be flabbergasted to learn that in endorsing the republican principle of a well-regulated militia, they were also precluding restrictions on such potentially dangerous property as firearms, which governments had always regulated when there was "real danger of public injury from individuals." 2 DHRC at 624.

CONCLUSION

For all the foregoing reasons, the judgment of the United States Court of Appeals for the District of Columbia should be reversed.

Respectfully submitted,

CARL T. BOGUS
Roger Williams University
School of Law
Ten Metacom Avenue
Bristol, Rhode Island 02809

APPENDIX: AMICI CURIAE

Jack N. Rakove is the W. R. Coe Professor of History and American Studies and Professor of Political Science and (by courtesy) of Law at Stanford University. His books include *The Beginnings of National Politics: An Interpretive History of the Continental Congress* (1979); *Original Meanings: Politics and Ideas in the Making of the Constitution* (1996), which received the Pulitzer Prize in History and the Society of the Cincinnati Book Prize; and *Declaring Rights: A Brief History with Documents* (1997). His numerous essays on constitutional history include "The Second Amendment: The Highest Stage of Originalism," 76 Chi.-Kent L. Rev. 103 (2000). He is past president of the Society for the History of the Early American Republic.

Saul Cornell is Professor of History at the Ohio State University, where he also directs the Second Amendment Research Center. His first book, *The Other Founders: Anti-Federalism and the Dissenting Tradition in America, 1788–1828* (1999), received the Society of the Cincinnati Book Prize. His second, *A Well-Regulated Militia: The Founding Fathers and the Origins of Gun Control in America* (2006), was awarded the Langum Prize for Historical Literature. He has written numerous essays for law reviews and historical journals on the origins and interpretation of the Second Amendment, and edited *Whose Right to Bear Arms Did the Second Amendment Protect?* (2000).

David T. Konig is Professor of History and Law at Washington University in Saint Louis. His writings in Anglo-American legal history include *Law and Society in Puritan Massachusetts: Essex County, 1629–1692* (1979) and "The Second Amendment: A Missing Transatlantic Context for 'the right of the people to keep and bear arms,'" 22 Law & Hist. Rev. 119 (2004).

William J. Novak is Associate Professor of History at the University of Chicago. His writings in American legal history include *The People's Welfare: Law and Regulation in Nineteenth-Century America* (1996), which received the Littleton Griswold Prize of the American Historical Association for best book in American legal history.

Lois G. Schwoerer is Elmer Louis Kayser Professor of History Emerita at George Washington University, the author of *"No Standing Armies!": The Antiarmy Ideology in Seventeenth-Century England* (1974) and *The Declaration of Rights, 1689* (1981), and past president of the North American Conference for British Studies. Her article "To Hold and Bear Arms: The English Perspective" appeared at 76 Chi.-Kent L. Rev. 27 (2000)

Fred Anderson is Professor of History at the University of Colorado and author of *Crucible of War: The Seven Years' War and the Fate of Empire in British North America, 1754–1766* (2000), which received the Francis Parkman Prize of the Society of American Historians, and *A People's Army: Massachusetts Soldiers and Society in the Seven Years' War* (1984), which received the Jamestown Prize from the Institute of Early American History and Culture.

Carol Berkin is Professor of History at the Graduate Center of the City University of New York and Baruch College. Her numerous writings on the American revolutionary era include *A Brilliant Solution: Inventing the American Constitution* (2002). She recently received the rare distinction of being named Presidential Professor of Baruch College.

Paul Finkelman is President William McKinley Distinguished Professor of Law and Public Policy at Albany Law School. His extensive writings in American legal history include *An Imperfect Union: Slavery, Federalism, and Comity* (1981); *Slavery and the Founders: Race and Liberty in the Age of Jefferson* (1999); and "'A Well Regulated Militia': The Second Amendment in Historical Perspective," 76 Chi.-Kent Law Rev. 195 (2000).

R. Don Higginbotham is the Dowd Professor of History at the University of North Carolina, Chapel Hill. His writings include *The War of American Independence: Military Attitudes, Policies, and Practice, 1763–1789* (1971); *War and Society in Revolutionary America: The Wider Dimensions of Conflict* (1988); *George Washington and the American Military Tradition* (1985); and *George Washington: Uniting a Nation* (2002). He is also the author of "The Federalized Militia Debate: A Neglected Aspect of Second Amendment Scholarship," 55 Wm. & Mary Q. 39 (1998). He is past president of the Southern Historical Association and the Society for the History of the Early American Republic.

Stanley N. Katz is the 1921 Bicentennial Professor of the History of American Law and Liberty Emeritus at Princeton University, where he was also Professor of Public and International Affairs and Senior Fellow at the Woodrow Wilson School. He is past president of the American Council of Learned Societies, and was formerly Professor of Law at the University of Chicago. His writings in early American legal and political history include *Newcastle's New York: Anglo-American Politics, 1732–1753* (1968), and "Thomas Jefferson and the Right to Property in Revolutionary America," 19 J. L. & Econ. 476 (1976).

Pauline R. Maier is the William Rand Kenan Jr. Professor of American History at the Massachusetts Institute of Technology. Her first book, *From Resistance to Revolution: Colonial Radicals and the Development of American Opposition to Britain, 1765–1776* (1972), studied the tactics the colonists used to mobilize popular opposition to imperial policies. Her other books include *The Old Revolutionaries: Political Lives in the Age of Samuel Adams* (1980), and *American Scripture: Making the Declaration of Independence* (1997). She is currently completing a study of the ratification of the Constitution.

Peter S. Onuf is the Thomas Jefferson Memorial Foundation Professor at the University of Virginia. His writings in American political and constitutional history include *Origins of the Federal Republic: Jurisdictional Controversies in the United States, 1775–1787* (1983); *Statehood and Union: A History of the Northwest Ordinance* (1987); *Federal Union, Modern World: The Law of Nations in an Age of Revolution, 1776–1814* (with Nicholas Onuf, 1993); *Jefferson's Empire: The Language of American Nationhood* (2001); and essays and edited volumes on Jefferson and his legacy. He is a past president of the Society for the History of the Early American Republic.

Robert E. Shalhope is George Lynn Cross Research Professor at the University of Oklahoma. He is the author of *Bennington and the Green Mountain Boys: The Emergence of Liberal Democracy in Vermont, 1760–1850* (1996), and "The Ideological Origins of the Second Amendment," 69 J. Am. Hist. 599 (1982).

John Shy is Professor of History, Emeritus, at the University of Michigan, and the author of *Toward Lexington: The Role of the British Army in the Coming of the American Revolution* (1965), and *A People Numerous and Armed: Reflections on the Military Struggle for American Independence* (rev. ed. 1990).

Alan Taylor is Professor of History at the University of California, Davis. His extensive writings on the revolutionary and postrevolutionary frontier include *Liberty Men and Great Proprietors: The Revolutionary Settlement on the Maine Frontier, 1760–1820* (1990); *William Cooper's Town: Power and Per-*

suasion on the Frontier of the Early American Republic (1995), which received
the Pulitzer Prize in History; and *The Divided Ground: Indians, Settlers, and
the Northern Borderland of the American Revolution* (2006).

NOTES

1. No counsel for a party authored this brief in whole or in part, and no counsel or party made a monetary contribution intended to fund the preparation or
submission of this brief, other than the Roger Williams University School of
Law, which paid for the printing of this brief through Professor Bogus's research
account. This brief is filed with the written consent of the parties, reflected in
letters on file with the clerk. Amici complied with the conditions of those consents
by providing seven days' advance notice of their intention to file this brief.

2. In January 1787, to compensate for the omission of such a declaration from
its 1777 constitution, the New York legislature approved An Act Concerning the
Rights of Citizens of This State. None of its thirteen articles mentioned a right
to keep and bear arms. 19 Documentary History of the Ratification of the Constitution 504–6 (John Kaminski and Gaspare Saladino, eds., 1976–) (hereafter
DHRC). Six months later the Continental Congress adopted the Northwest Ordinance. Its supplemental six articles constituted a bill of rights but made no mention of a right to arms. 1 Founders' Constitution *supra* at 28–29.

3. Section 43 of the Pennsylvania constitution does grant "inhabitants . . .
liberty to fowl and hunt in seasonable times on the lands they hold, and on all
other lands therein not inclosed; and in like manner to fish in all boatable waters,
and others not private property."

4. This point merits far more development than it can receive here, for it illustrates how republican thinking conceived of rights not solely as something to be
protected against abuse by the state but in the very different language of the civic
duties of citizens. The right to serve on a jury was thus regarded as being at least
as important as, and arguably more so than, the right to be tried by one. The relation between this civic conception of rights and the right to keep and bear arms is
developed in Saul Cornell, A Well-Regulated Militia: The Founding Fathers and
the Origins of Gun Control in America (2006).

5. In New York, it is not part of the amendments proposed in the second part of
the instrument of ratification but rather appears in the first part, which stated the
delegates' understanding of the Constitution they were accepting.

6. Only four years earlier, he had introduced a bill, originally drafted by
Jefferson as part of the comprehensive revision of Virginia laws, to prohibit
hunters who had violated the ban on deer hunting from the "bearing of a gun [not
arms]" beyond their own lands. 2 Papers of Jefferson *supra* at 443–44.

Section II

Heller and Originalism

★ ★ ★ ★

★ ★ ★ ★

Dead or Alive

Originalism as Popular Constitutionalism in *Heller*

Reva B. Siegel

★ ★ ★ ★

We should find the lost Second Amendment, broaden its scope and determine that it affords the right to arm a state militia and also the right of the individual to keep and bear arms.—Robert Sprecher, ABA prize winner, 1965[1]

[T]he Court has taken sides in the culture war, departing from its role of assuring, as neutral observer, that the democratic rules of engagement are observed. . . . What Texas has chosen to do is well within the range of traditional democratic action, and its hand should not be stayed through the invention of a brand-new "constitutional right" by a Court that is impatient of democratic change.
—Justice Scalia, *Lawrence v. Texas*, 2003[2]

THE COURT'S ANNOUNCEMENT in 2008 that the Second Amendment,[3] ratified in 1791, protects an individual's right to bear arms against federal gun control regulation was long awaited by many, long feared by others. What produced this ruling and what might it reveal about the character of our constitutional order? For many, constitutional law changed because the Court interpreted the Second Amendment in accordance with the understandings of the Americans who ratified it: *Heller*[4] marks the "Triumph of Originalism."[5] Others saw the case very differently, observing that the Court had interpreted the Second Amendment in accordance with the convictions of the twentieth-century gun rights movement and so had demonstrated the ascendancy of the living Constitution.[6] The two accounts of the decision stand in some tension. One views *Heller*'s authority as emanating from the deliberations of eighteenth-century Americans, while the other views the constitutional debates of twentieth-century Americans as decisive.

What kind of authority did the Court exercise when it struck down the District of Columbia's handgun ban as violating the Second Amendment? On the originalism view, the Court is merely enforcing the judgments of eighteenth-century Americans who, in an epochal act of constitutional law-making, ratified a Bill of Rights that forbids handgun bans such as the District of Columbia's. On the popular constitutionalism view, the Court *itself* is deciding whether handgun bans are consistent with the best understanding of our constitutional tradition; the determination is made in the present and responds to the beliefs and values of living Americans who identify with the commitments and traditions of their forebears. In the first case, the Court stands above the fray, disinterested, merely executing the commands of Americans long deceased. In the second case, the Court is normatively engaged in matters about which living Americans passionately disagree, enforcing its own convictions about the best understanding of a living constitutional tradition to which *Heller* contributes. On this account, *Heller, through* its originalism, participates in what Justice Scalia refers to in his *Lawrence* dissent as "the culture war."[7]

Relating these two competing accounts of the opinion, this comment shows how *Heller*'s originalism enforces understandings of the Second Amendment that were forged in the late twentieth century through popular constitutionalism. It situates originalism's claim to ground judicial decision making outside of politics in the constitutional politics of the late twentieth century, and demonstrates how *Heller* respects claims and compromises forged in social movement conflict over the right to bear arms in the decades after *Brown v. Board of Education*.[8]

The comment offers this reading of the opinion in two steps. Part I begins by examining the temporal locus of authority in the *Heller* opinion itself. In *Heller*, the dissenters insist that the Second Amendment is concerned primarily with militia and military matters, whereas the majority reads the amendment as codifying an individual right of self-defense that enables citizens to protect themselves, their families, and their homes against crime. The majority presents this account as the original public meaning of the Second Amendment, yet draws upon evidence that may incorporate understandings that emerged long after the founding. This possibility becomes more pronounced as the Court explains how it will enforce the Second Amendment's right to bear arms. *Heller* holds that government cannot deprive citizens of traditional weapons of self-defense, but may ban civilian use of military weapons, even if this means that the right to bear arms may no longer be effectively exercised for the republican purpose of resisting tyranny that the "prefatory clause" discusses.[9] It is, to say the least, striking that an *originalist* interpretation of the Second Amendment would treat civic republican understandings of the amendment as antiquated and refuse to protect the arms a militia needs to defend against tyranny. What guides the majority's judgments about how to enforce the right to bear arms?

To examine more closely the authority *Heller* exercises in enforcing the right to bear arms, this comment looks beyond the text of the *Heller* opinion itself to the decades of social movement conflict that preceded the decision. This history illustrates how contest over the Constitution's meaning can endow courts with authority to change the way they interpret its provisions. The effort to persuade—and to capture institutions that can authoritatively pronounce law—can prompt mobilization, countermobilization, coalition, and compromise, a process that can forge and discipline new understandings that courts engaged in responsive interpretation recognize as the Constitution.[10] These practices of democratic constitutionalism enable mobilized citizens to contest and shape popular beliefs about the Constitution's original meaning and so confer upon courts the authority to enforce the nation's foundational commitments in new ways.[11]

To show how such processes helped shape the right *Heller* enforces, Part II of this comment examines chapters of American constitutional history not discussed in *Heller*—debates about the Second Amendment that transpired in the shadow of *Brown v. Board of Education*. Exploring this social movement history, we learn how, in the wake of *Brown*, citizens made claims on a Second Amendment concerned with law and order and self-defense; how, during the 1980s, a growing coalition of citizens came to assert their convictions about the Second Amendment as the original understanding; and why, by the 1990s, proponents of this law-and-order Second Amendment came to differentiate their claims from those of the modern militia movement, emphasizing that the Second Amendment entitled the citizen to arms needed to defend his family against crime, not against the government. The Second Amendment's twentieth-century history shows how political conflict can both motivate and discipline the claims that mobilized citizens make on the text and history of the Constitution. These contemporary struggles help explain the shape of the right *Heller* enforces. In the process, they illuminate how authority to enforce the original understanding depends on contemporary public convictions.

In analyzing the conflict leading up to *Heller,* Part III of this comment provides a positive and interpretive account of how the boundary between

constitutional law and constitutional politics has been negotiated in recent
decades. *Heller* depicts its authority as forged in one epochal act of eighteenth-century lawmaking. The twentieth-century history considered in this
comment suggests that, in important part, *Heller*'s originalist authority for
protecting weaponry popularly used for self-defense, but not for militia purposes, is responsive to contemporary constitutional deliberation—forged in
the very culture wars Justice Scalia insists should play no part in constitutional interpretation.

The result is not license of the kind Justice Scalia fears. This comment's
reading of *Heller* demonstrates that when courts apprehend the history of
constitutional lawmaking through constitutional politics, *both* guide and constrain the ways courts enforce the Constitution. If we analyze the practices of
democratic constitutionalism that help make *Heller* law, we can see forms of
discipline and discretion that narratives of originalism occlude.

I. THE TEMPORAL LOCUS OF CONSTITUTIONAL AUTHORITY IN HELLER

> *[T]he Great Divide with regard to constitutional interpretation is . . .*
> *between original meaning (whether derived from Framers' intent or not)*
> *and current meaning. The ascendant school of constitutional interpretation*
> *affirms the existence of what is called The Living Constitution, a body of*
> *law that . . . changes from age to age, in order to meet the needs of a changing*
> *society. And it is the judges who determine those needs and "find" that*
> *changing law. Seems familiar, doesn't it? Yes, it is the common law returned,*
> *but infinitely more powerful than what the old common law ever pretended*
> *to be, for now it trumps even the statutes of democratic legislatures.*
> —Justice Scalia, *A Matter of Interpretation* (1997)[12]

Justice Scalia has long advocated originalism on the grounds that it constrains judicial discretion and so enables judges to enforce the Constitution
as law, not politics. In his view, judges should interpret the Constitution to
enforce its original and "fixed meaning," without taking into consideration
"current societal values" or the judge's own preferences.[13] In *Heller,* Justice
Scalia reaffirms this account of the judge as a kind of amanuensis for those
who adopted the Constitution:

> The very enumeration of the right takes out of the hands of
> government—even the Third Branch of Government—the power to
> decide on a case-by-case basis whether the right is *really worth* insist-

ing upon. A constitutional guarantee subject to future judges' assessments of its usefulness is no constitutional guarantee at all. Constitutional rights are enshrined with the scope they were understood to have when the people adopted them, whether or not future legislatures or (yes) even future judges think that scope too broad.[14]

Justice Scalia depicts a judge interpreting the Constitution as implementing directives the judge has had no normative role in determining. This picture of constitutional interpretation is in considerable tension with the reasoning of *Heller* itself. *Heller*'s account of the Second Amendment's original public meaning invokes authorities from before and after the founding, relies on common law–like reasoning, endows judges with vast amounts of interpretive discretion, and, in these respects, resembles the practice of living constitutionalism that Justice Scalia often condemns.

In *Heller,* both the majority and dissenting opinions appeal to the Second Amendment's text and history,[15] yet offer very different accounts of the amendment's purpose and reach. The dissenting justices emphasize the Second Amendment's republican purposes,[16] depicting the amendment as a guarantee against government tyranny. They assert that the "Second Amendment . . . was a response to concerns raised during the ratification of the Constitution that the power of Congress to disarm the state militias and create a national standing army posed an intolerable threat to the sovereignty of the several States."[17] The dissenters maintain that the Second Amendment protects only "a right to use and possess arms in conjunction with service in a well-regulated militia,"[18] and not "the right to possess and use guns for nonmilitary purposes like hunting and personal self-defense."[19] The majority, however, asserts that the Second Amendment preserved the militia by codifying the common law right of self-defense,[20] and "elevates above all other interests the right of law-abiding, responsible citizens to use arms in defense of hearth and home."[21]

There are temporal oddities in the evidence the majority marshals in support of this claim about the original meaning of the Second Amendment. For example, the majority starts and finishes its argument that "bear arms" has nonmilitary meanings by citing a dissenting opinion that Justice Ginsburg wrote in 1998 that in turn cites a 1998 edition of *Black's Law Dictionary.*[22] This is perhaps the most prominent but surely not the only temporal incongruity in the evidence on which the majority's account of the original meaning relies. The majority more than once discounts evidence drawn from the amendment's drafting history, appearing to favor evidence remote in time over evidence proximate in time to the amendment's ratification. For example, the majority rejects the dissenters' claim that the military meaning of the phrase "keep and bear Arms" is elucidated by James Madison's inclusion of a conscientious objector clause in his original draft of the Second Amendment ("but no person religiously scrupulous of bearing arms, shall be compelled to render military service in person"), observing, "It is always perilous to derive the meaning of an adopted provision from another provision deleted in the drafting process."[23] In debating the amendment's purpose, the majority again discounts evidence from "the drafting history of the Second Amendment— the various proposals in the state conventions and the debates in Congress," observing, "It is dubious to rely on such history to interpret a text that was *widely understood* to codify a pre-existing right."[24] To demonstrate that it was "widely understood" that the Second Amendment codified this preexisting, individual right of self-defense, the majority opinion examines sources that range into the second half of the nineteenth century.[25] When Justice Stevens chides the majority for relying on the amendment's post-ratification history to establish its purpose and meaning,[26] the majority contemptuously explains that its reliance on these sources is "to determine *the public understanding* of a legal text in the period after its enactment or ratification."[27]

Justice Scalia has a sound basis in democratic theory for privileging the public's understanding of the amendment over its framers'—it was the public's vote that made the Constitution law[28]—but the question remains how the interpreter establishes what the public's understanding of the relevant constitutional text was. Justice Scalia himself acknowledges that the writings of the framers may be probative of the text's public meaning.[29] Given this, is there reason to favor popular views of the amendment one hundred years after its ratification?[30] Either the evidence the majority marshals to demonstrate that it was "widely understood" that the Second Amendment codified an individual right of self-defense accurately captures the understanding of those who ratified the amendment in 1791, or the majority is presenting as the original public meaning an understanding of the amendment that emerged in common law–like fashion in the decades after the amendment was ratified.

If these questions about the temporal locus of authority in *Heller* haunt the majority's account of the amendment's original understanding, they dominate its claims about the scope of the right the Second Amendment protects. The majority simply declares that the Constitution allows many familiar forms of gun control regulation: "[N]othing in our opinion should be taken to cast doubt on longstanding prohibitions on the possession of firearms by felons and the mentally ill, or laws forbidding the carrying of firearms in sensitive places such as schools and government buildings, or laws imposing conditions and qualifications on the commercial sale of arms."[31] What authority supports this claim? Does the common law right of self-defense that the Second Amendment codifies continue to evolve in history? If so, what kind of constraint on judicial interpretation does the original public understanding provide? Who decides which gun control laws are constitutionally forbidden and which ones are allowed?[32] Without answering any of these questions, the majority then announces "another important limitation on the right to keep and carry arms,"[33] which it derives from two apparently unrelated sources of constitutional authority. It notes that *United States v. Miller*[34] said that "the sorts of weapons protected [by the Second Amendment] were those 'in common use at the time,'" and then observes, "We think that limitation is fairly supported by the historical tradition of prohibiting the carrying of 'dangerous and unusual weapons.'"[35] The majority imputes a limitation on the weapons the Second Amendment protects to a passage in *Miller* that discusses arms the militia employed without imposing any such limitation;[36] it then declares this imputed limitation confirmed by Blackstone's discussion of the kinds of weapons the common law allowed individuals to carry. The resulting amalgam expresses a common law restriction on the right to bear arms (adopted in either 1769, 1791, 1939, or 2008) in the positive law language of original expected application—a restriction in some tension with the majority's earlier observation that the Second Amendment extends to arms that were not in existence at the time of the founding.[37]

More remarkably, the restriction the majority adopts renders the right the Second Amendment protects useless for its textually enumerated military purpose—*a point the majority goes out of its way to emphasize.* The majority insists that the Second Amendment doesn't protect "weapons that are most useful in military service," even if it means that the right to bear arms can no longer be exercised for the republican purpose of preventing tyranny that the text specifies:

> It may be objected that if weapons that are most useful in military service—M-16 rifles and the like—may be banned, then the Second Amendment right is completely detached from the prefatory clause. But as we have said, the conception of the militia at the time of the Second Amendment's ratification was the body of all citizens capable

of military service, who would bring the sorts of lawful weapons that they possessed at home to militia duty. It may well be true today that a militia, to be as effective as militias in the 18th century, would require sophisticated arms that are highly unusual in society at large. Indeed, it may be true that no amount of small arms could be useful against modern-day bombers and tanks. But the fact that modern developments have limited the degree of fit between the prefatory clause and the protected right cannot change our interpretation of the right.[38]

In this remarkable passage, the majority imposes restrictions on the kinds of weapons protected by the Second Amendment that the majority concedes would disable exercise of the right for the amendment's textually enunciated purposes. How could an originalist interpretation of the Second Amendment exclude from its protection the kinds of weapons necessary to resist tyranny— the republican purpose the text of the Second Amendment discusses and, on the majority's own account, "the purpose for which the right was codified"?[39] In these passages Justice Scalia seems to apply something other than an original "public understanding" analysis.

A glimpse of a different form of authority the opinion is exercising comes into view in the majority's discussion of stare decisis. The majority asserts that its account of the Second Amendment is not inconsistent with the Court's decision in *United States v. Miller*[40]—and then quickly abandons the effort to reconcile the two, breaking into a direct attack on *Miller:*

As for the "hundreds of judges" who have relied on the view of the Second Amendment Justice Stevens claims we endorsed in *Miller:* If so, they overread *Miller.* And their erroneous reliance upon an uncontested and virtually unreasoned case cannot nullify the reliance of millions of Americans (as our historical analysis has shown) upon the true meaning of the right to keep and bear arms. In any event, it should not be thought that the cases decided by these judges would necessarily have come out differently under a proper interpretation of the right.[41]

What kind of voice emerges in this attack on *Miller?* The majority seems to identify with "the reliance of millions of Americans . . . upon the true meaning of the right to keep and bear arms," dismissing the "erroneous reliance" of "hundreds of judges" on Supreme Court precedent as immaterial to a "true" understanding of the amendment. Here the Court is not dispassionately analyzing evidence of the original "public understanding," or enforcing a judicial, common law understanding of the Second Amendment, but instead declaring the amendment's "true meaning" in a full-throated populist voice. The *Heller* majority claims to derive its authority to enforce the Second Amendment solely from epochal acts of constitutional lawmaking in the eighteenth century. But as this passage makes plain, *Heller* also takes guidance from the lived experience and passionate convictions of Americans in times since the founding—convictions and experience the majority is prepared to elevate over the considered views of "hundreds of judges" in the twentieth century.

II. A SECOND AMENDMENT SOCIAL MOVEMENT HISTORY: GUN RIGHTS, ORIGINALISM, AND THE CULTURE WARS

To this point, this analysis of *Heller* has considered different kinds of constitutional authority that might be at work in the opinion—positive lawmaking associated with the Second Amendment's eighteenth-century ratification and incremental articulation of a tradition of the kind associated with common law adjudication. In fact, the state constitutions, treatises, and other evidence cited in *Heller* suggest that the temporal forms and social sources of constitutional authority are quite diverse. Judges who engage in common law reasoning about the Constitution may interpret its text in response to claims about its meaning that citizens and elected officials propose.[42]

What do we learn about the forms of authority the Court exercised in *Heller* if we look outside the opinion to the passionate national debate that preceded the Court's decision? *Heller* invites this inquiry when it appeals to popular conviction—to "the reliance of millions of Americans . . . upon the true meaning of the right to keep and bear arms"—to limit the authority of precedent on which "hundreds of judges" have relied.[43] This mode of reasoning sounds in popular constitutionalism. More precisely, it is judicial interpretation of the Constitution that is responsive to popular constitutionalism. Elsewhere I have shown how, in American constitutional culture, social movement conflict can motivate as well as discipline new claims about the Constitution's meaning, and how responsive interpretation by public officials can transmute constitutional politics into new forms of constitutional law.[44] Popular debate over the Second Amendment offers striking evidence of these dynamic features of

our constitutional order and sheds light on the forms of responsive authority
judges may exercise, even when invoking original understanding as a warrant
for judicial review.[45] The exercise illuminates relations between constitutional
politics and constitutional law otherwise not legible in *Heller.*

In these twentieth-century struggles we can learn about the meaning of the
Second Amendment to its contemporary proponents. The history provides a
different perspective on the kinds of authority the Court exercises when it con-
ceives of protecting weapons for self-defense as the core purpose of the Second
Amendment *and* when it refuses to extend the amendment's protection to
weaponry a militia might employ today. When we read the *Heller* opinion in
light of the decades of social movement conflict that preceded it, it is possible
to see how decisions enforcing the original understanding of the Constitution
can participate in a twentieth-century "culture war."

A. Great Society Advocates for Gun Control

The modern quest for gun control and the gun rights movement it triggered
were born in the shadow of *Brown.* Directly and indirectly, conflicts over civil
rights have shaped modern understandings of the Second Amendment.

Contemporary debate over gun control began in the 1960s, when President Johnson called for restrictions on firearms sales in the wake of President
Kennedy's assassination.[46] The National Rifle Association (NRA) was easily
able to spur opposition to the proposed measures.[47] In the 1950s and 1960s,
guns were popular, distributed by the government,[48] and glamorized by the
media.[49] Even so, there was significant public support for gun control.[50] And
the case for gun control grew in urgency in the next several years as the nation
was shaken by civil rights conflict, riots in the nation's cities, rising crime
rates, campus slayings, and struggles over the Vietnam war[51]—conflicts that
imbued guns with a variety of racial meanings.[52] In 1968, with the assassinations of civil rights leader Martin Luther King Jr. and presidential candidate
Senator Robert Kennedy, Congress was ready to take action on the president's
request to impose restrictions on certain classes of purchasers and to bar the
interstate mail order sale of guns.

In the 1960s it was a matter of ordinary professional reason that Congress
had power to adopt restrictions of this sort.[53] Counsel to the House Subcommittee on Postal Operations was succinct in explaining the governing
law: "The second amendment to the Constitution of the United States is only
27 words and seems plain on its face. . . . The reference to a 'well regulated

Militia' would seem to govern the phrase 'the right of the people to keep and bear Arms' which means in its context the right of the States to organize a Militia."[54] Committee reports concluded similarly.[55]

Yet, even if no court would impose Second Amendment limits on gun control legislation, the president's advisers still worried about selling a federal gun control bill to the American public. The plan they hit upon involved sending a group of Hollywood cowboys—Kirk Douglas, James Stewart, Gregory Peck, Hugh O'Brian, and Charlton Heston—to appear on the late night *Joey Bishop Show* and urge Americans to support the president's gun control bill.[56] The civil rights concerns of the bill's proponents were unmistakable. "President John F. Kennedy was murdered by a rifle. Martin Luther King was murdered by a rifle. Medgar Evers was murdered by a rifle," the cowboys emphasized, while reassuring the TV audience that the bill's purpose was "not to deprive the sportsman of his hunting gun" nor to deny to "any responsible citizen his constitutional right to own a firearm."[57] At this point even the NRA was prepared to support federal gun control laws,[58] and Congress enacted two rounds of legislation in 1968 restricting high-risk purchasers, prohibiting sale of firearms through the mail, barring import of certain guns, and creating the Bureau of Alcohol, Tobacco, and Firearms within the Treasury Department.[59]

But the 1968 gun control legislation represented at best a qualified victory for President Johnson, as it grew out of criticisms of his Great Society initiatives and was enacted encumbered with civil rights restrictions he opposed. Though willing to support gun control in 1968, many Americans—recoiling from social unrest, protests, riots, and rising crime rates—were losing confidence in the Great Society policies of gun control's liberal proponents. An administration committed to expanding opportunities for all Americans was on the defensive and had embraced gun control as part of a strategy to reduce crime by preventing crime.[60] The president's conservative critics thought the administration's gun control initiative ineffectual or insufficient and sought harsher controls on the "criminal." They opposed recent Warren Court decisions according criminal defendants constitutional rights—"de facto civil rights"[61]—and larded the 1968 bill with restrictions on them. As a result, the new gun control bill limited rights of the accused to counsel and to protections from interrogation.[62] Concerned about the bill's restrictions on civil rights and its challenge to the Court's authority, Professor Alexander Bickel publicly urged the Senate to vote against the bill.[63]

Encumbered with these restrictions on defendants' rights, the 1968 act embodied a view of the criminally accused that was anathema to gun control's civil rights supporters, who opposed Jim Crow justice and the view that there were innate and identifiable "criminal classes" that government should control.[64] A congressman protested the contradictions of the 1968 act: "Passing this legislation as a memorial to Sen. Kennedy was grimly ironic, because in life he had not supported it. He had opposed the wiretapping and confession provisions and called for strong gun controls," and observing, "There must also be a firm commitment to eliminate the root causes of crime—the sense of despair and hopelessness born of continued privation, poverty, poor education and lack of equal opportunity."[65]

But in 1968 Americans were losing confidence in this vision. Campaigning against the Great Society policies of the Johnson-Humphrey administration, Nixon deplored "the socially suicidal tendency—on the part of many public men—to excuse crime and sympathize with criminal[s] because of past grievances the criminal may have against society,"[66] and intimated "linkages between racial conflict and lawlessness."[67] "Making no effort to distinguish between street crime, political protests, and urban riots, Nixon charged that liberals had promised a Great Society but had delivered great disorder."[68] Soon thereafter, Richard Nixon swept into office on a campaign of "law and order."

B. MOVEMENT-COUNTERMOVEMENT:
THE LIBERTARIAN SECOND AMENDMENT

The political maelstrom from which the 1968 act emerged would shape the debates over gun control that exploded in its wake. The 1970s witnessed the birth of a libertarian movement for Second Amendment rights, which grew out of conservative "law and order" challenges to the Great Society.

In the early 1970s gun control initiatives continued to gather support, spurred on by the assassination attempt that crippled presidential candidate George Wallace in 1972 and two more assassination attempts against President Ford in September 1975.[69] As important, in this period gun control initiatives were supported by an uneasy coalition of law and order conservatives[70] and civil rights leadership.[71] The National Council to Control Handguns, later Handgun Control, Inc., was organized and expressed support for a national ban on handguns.[72] Washington, D.C., enacted the handgun ban at issue in *Heller* in 1976.[73]

But resistance to gun control was growing in the 1970s, both among gun rights activists and in the public at large. After a decade of protests, riots, and rising crime rates, national support for handgun bans dropped—from 60 percent in 1959 to 41 percent in 1975.[74] The NRA pointed to this shift in public support when President Ford proposed more modest restrictions on the sale of inexpensive handguns (often referred to as "Saturday night specials").[75]

With the continuing rise in crime rates,[76] a conservative insurgency in the NRA questioned the organization's willingness to support even moderate forms of gun control.[77] In 1975 Harlon Carter, head of the NRA's newly created Institute for Legislative Action (ILA), testified against a bill that would tighten federal handgun regulation. His remarks sharply differentiated "law abiding . . . gun owners" from a different group of Americans whom Carter called "criminals":

> I do not believe a man is a future criminal just because he owns, or desires to own, a firearm. . . . Law abiding people, and particularly gun owners, are tired of being blamed for crime. They are sick of being harassed with federal bureaucracy and having their freedom progressively and increasingly chipped away because of the inability or unwillingness of their government officials to deal with those responsible for crime, namely, criminals. . . . [P]eople in the media, in the Congress, in the courts seem to blame crime on everything in our society except the criminal and want to punish anyone and anything except the criminals.[78]

Opposition to gun control was now expressed in law and order frames. The argument for gun rights divided society into two classes—citizen and criminal—and demonstrated deep estrangement from Great Society government. The gun rights argument did not presume the innocence of the poor or the innocence of the accused.[79] Like law and order discourse, the gun rights claim called for individual accountability and asked government to deliver security—not social justice. Unlike law and order discourse, the gun rights claim voiced a libertarian spirit that was increasingly hostile to the government in any guise.

The same year that Harlon Carter testified before Congress, Ronald Reagan, then governor of California and a board member of Young Americans for Freedom (YAF),[80] published an article in the pages of *Guns & Ammo* that expressed these convictions in a constitutional register.[81] YAF had recently formed a Citizens Committee for the Right to Keep and Bear Arms, and an affiliated Second Amendment Foundation, with which Reagan was no doubt familiar.[82] Reagan expressed objections to gun control in law and order frames ("Criminals are not dissuaded by soft words, soft judges or easy laws. They are dissuaded by fear and they are prevented from repeating their crimes by death or by incarceration."),[83] but Reagan *also* expressed the objection to gun control in constitutional terms. At a time when the legally literate read the text of the Second Amendment as plainly allowing gun regulation,[84] Reagan read its text as—potentially—plainly prohibiting gun regulation:

> The Second Amendment is clear, or ought to be. It appears to leave little if any leeway for the gun control advocate. It reads: "A well regulated militia being necessary to the security of a free state, the right of the people to keep and bear arms shall not be infringed." . . . The second amendment gives the individual citizen a means of protection against the despotism of the state. . . . [T]he rights of the individual are pre-eminent.
>
> The founding fathers had seen, as the Declaration of Independence tells us, what a despotic government can do to its own people. Indeed, every American should read the Declaration of Independence before he reads the Constitution and he will see that the Constitution aims at preventing a recurrence of the way George III's government treated the Colonies. . . . There are those in America today who have come to depend absolutely on government for their security. And when government fails they seek to rectify that failure in the form of granting government more power. So, as government has failed to control crime and violence with the means given it by the Constitution, they seek to give it more power at the expense of the Constitution.
>
> But in doing so, in their willingness to give up their arms in the name of safety, they are really giving up their protection from what has always been the chief source of despotism—government.[85]

Harlon Carter and Ronald Reagan were harbingers of change. Within two years, conservative members of the NRA led by Carter and comrade Neal Knox conducted what insurgents called a "revolt at Cincinnati,"[86] challenging incumbent NRA leaders who supported incremental forms of gun control regulation.

As recounted by Joseph Tartaro of *Gun Week,* the conservative insurgency was "intent on reorganizing the NRA with the specific purpose of breaking a stranglehold on the ILA and its freedom to defend the Second Amendment."[87] The insurgents understood the constitutional struggle through the prism of the American Revolution. Tartaro reported: "Many pro-gun activists outside of NRA leadership were convinced that gun owners could no longer compromise on legislation designed to restrict the ownership of firearms. Indeed, some of these blamed prevailing statutes on compromises by NRA leadership in the 1930s and 1960s. . . . A classic confrontational situation developed not unlike the schism between the American colonists and the Crown in 1775."[88]

While restrictions on lobbying by the ILA were at issue, so too were questions of politics and fundraising linked to the organization's plans to move its headquarters from Washington, D.C., to Colorado Springs, where the NRA was building a complex for sports and conservation.[89] Carter's supporters had in their possession a report on fundraising feasibility that warned: "NRA must attract to its cause powerful leadership and financial support that is today either repelled or put off by NRA's image as the leader in the fight against gun control. . . . [T]he current media image of the NRA destroys its ability to raise money from foundations, especially the large ones such as Rockefeller, Ford and Mellon."[90] Distribution of this report to NRA membership helped Carter in his bid to take over the NRA in a revolt figured in constitutional terms: "As in the days preceeding [*sic*] the Declaration of Independence, the people who populated NRA's colonies felt themselves unrepresented."[91]

What the insurgents wanted was freedom for the ILA to defend "the political, civil and inalienable rights of the American people to keep and bear arms as a common law and Constitutional right both of the individual citizen and of the collective militia."[92] Thereafter, *American Rifleman* ran an article reporting on the difference between a "collective" right and an "individual" right interpretation of the Second Amendment, and insisting that reports of Supreme Court precedents to the contrary were mistaken: the collective right view could not be historically or legally substantiated.[93]

C. The Coalition Politics of the New Right: Originalism and the Republicans' Quest for Constitutional Restoration

In the revolt at Cincinnati, Harlon Carter and his compatriots had established the fundamentals of the NRA's new constitutional politics. What they needed was institutional power to embody this new constitutional understanding in law. In fact, by the time of the Cincinnati revolt, the coalition that would carry them to power was already in place. An emergent New Right movement sought restoration of the Constitution in matters concerning criminal defendants' rights, gun control, and other "social issues," including prayer, busing, and abortion.

1. "Social Issues" and the Direct Mail Strategies of the New Right. In 1974 Richard Viguerie, former executive secretary of YAF, chief fundraiser for George Wallace's 1972 presidential campaign, and a pioneer in computerized techniques of direct mail fundraising, called a meeting with Terry Dolan and Howard Phillips, formerly of YAF, and Paul Weyrich, who, with the Olin Foundation's help, had just founded the Heritage Foundation.[94] Viguerie planned to use the group's combined talents—and the mailing lists Viguerie had acquired working for YAF, for Wallace's campaign against busing,[95] and for other conservative clients[96]—to invigorate the conservative movement. At the decade's end, Viguerie's magazine, *Conservative Digest*, described their successful strategy:

> Attention to so-called social issues—abortion, busing, gun rights, pornography, crime—has also become central to the growth of the New Right. But to imagine that the New Right has a fixation on these issues misses the mark. The New Right is looking for issues that people care about, and social issues, at least for the present, fit the bill. As [Paul] Weyrich puts it, "We talk about issues that people care about, like gun control, abortion, taxes and crime. Yes they're emotional issues, but that's better than talking about capital formation."[97]

As Weyrich explained to *Time* magazine: "In the past, we conservatives have paraded all those Chamber of Commerce candidates with the Mobil Oil billboards strapped to their backs. It doesn't work in middle-class neighborhoods."[98] These conservative strategists helped draw Protestant and Catholic clergy together to intervene in politics in defense of faith and family, and a new "moral majority" was born.[99]

The emerging gun rights movement was fatefully shaped by its inclusion in this New Right coalition and by the direct mail strategies that Viguerie employed on its behalf. Direct mail strategies provided Viguerie and his clients financial independence from the Republican Party and foundation establishment and opened new communicative channels in the public sphere that would allow them to bypass the traditional media.

In the fall of 1975, Viguerie, working with California state senator H. L. Richardson, founded Gun Owners of America[100] (GOA) and soon after celebrated his direct mail fundraising success, identifying "[g]un enthusiasts [as] one of the great untapped money markets for the new right."[101] Through direct mail, GOA used law and order frames expressing fear of the "criminal element" to stimulate gun rights mobilization. A GOA solicitation letter signed by Richardson warned that "if the criminal element knew we could not legally own firearms to protect our families and our property, . . . crime would double," urging "that 'radical,' 'gun-grabbing,' 'soft on crime' politicians must not be allowed 'to destroy our Constitution and unleash what could well be the most terrifying crime wave in modern history.'"[102] Richardson would later describe direct mail's power: "Direct mail can tell your story undiluted by the media and unadulterated by your opposition. You can pinpoint your message and call people to action. You can rally an army of support from those unaccustomed to political action."[103] GOA began spending money raised by Viguerie's direct mail campaign in support of political candidates who supported gun rights.[104] At the same time, Viguerie began fundraising on an even larger scale for the NRA, and worked with Harlon Carter of the ILA to build a political donation committee for the NRA modeled on GOA.[105] The Viguerie-Carter relationship coincided with Carter's efforts to move the NRA right.[106]

The Viguerie-Carter working relationship put gun rights advocates in coalition with many other conservative single-issue groups. Together, this emergent coalition helped transform the Republican Party platform on so-called social issues, including gun control and the Second Amendment. In 1972 the Republican platform reflected Nixon's vision and charged state and federal government with responsibility for "prevent[ing] criminal access to all weapons, including special emphasis on cheap, readily-obtainable handguns," while promising to "[s]afeguard the right of responsible citizens to collect, own and use firearms for legitimate purposes, including hunting, target shooting and self-defense."[107] In 1976 Reagan narrowly lost the Republican nomination to Gerald Ford, and the party's platform adopted a different approach to gun control and the Constitution: "We support the right of citizens to keep and bear arms. We oppose federal registration of firearms. Mandatory sentences for crimes committed with a lethal weapon are the only effective solution to this problem."[108] Statist law and order talk of the Nixon era gave way to the more libertarian law and order talk of the New Right, of the kind that Reagan, Harlon Carter, and Viguerie were developing.[109]

2. Originalism and the "Social Issues" of the New Right. Reagan's election as president in 1980 raised hopes that this libertarian, law and order understanding of the Second Amendment might soon become law—despite the attempt to assassinate the president only months after his election and the

shooting murder of John Lennon.[110] In the early 1980s the town of Morton
Grove enacted a handgun ban that the Court, in a closely watched decision, let
stand.[111] In the Senate, where Reagan's election swept Republicans to power,
conservatives had their first opportunity to refashion the constitutional law
under which gun control laws would be judged. Strom Thurmond became
chair of the Senate Judiciary Committee, replacing Edward Kennedy,[112] and
Orrin Hatch assumed control of the Subcommittee on the Constitution.
The combination was ideal for Viguerie, who did direct mail fundraising for
Thurmond and Hatch;[113] Viguerie and Weyrich had helped Hatch win election to the Senate in 1976,[114] where he was now a key member of the New Right
inner circle.[115]

Upon assuming the subcommittee chairmanship, Hatch authorized
extensive historical research on the Second Amendment and, in February
1982, issued a report titled *The Right To Keep and Bear Arms*.[116] The report
announced: "What the Subcommittee on the Constitution uncovered was
clear—and long lost—proof that the second amendment to our Constitution
was intended as an individual right of the American citizen to keep and carry
arms in a peaceful manner, for protection of himself, his family, and his freedoms."[117] In 1986 Congress passed the Firearm Owners Protection Act,[118]
which specifically invoked "the rights of citizens . . . to keep and bear arms
under the second amendment" as a basis for repealing parts of the 1968 Gun
Control Act and imposing mandatory sentences for using a gun in committing
certain crimes.[119] With this act of legislative constitutionalism, principles and
policies that members of the New Right had worked out in the 1970s were now
embodied in law.

But the developments that would do most to legitimate the new Second
Amendment arguments unfolded in the Reagan Justice Department. After
his resounding reelection, President Reagan elevated Edwin Meese to attorney general in 1985. Meese was determined to translate into law the conservative movement's wide-ranging demands for constitutional restoration.[120]
Ronald Reagan made a key part of his campaign for the presidency the promise to replace the judiciary with judges who, in the words of the Republican
Party platform, "respect traditional family values and the sanctity of innocent human life."[121] As Reagan took office, Weyrich worked from the Heritage
Foundation and then the Free Congress Foundation—the conservative think
tanks he had helped found with Coors and Scaife money—to press for change
on "social issues" through the judiciary.[122] This focus on the judiciary would be
crucial: by the end of his second term, President Reagan would appoint close to

half of the lower federal court judges and three new Supreme Court justices.[123] Reagan's impact on the judiciary resulted not only from the numbers of his appointments but also from the distinctive constitutional understandings and commitments that the administration brought to the federal bench.

At the time of Reagan's election, conservative critiques of the Court had begun to shift from demands for "strict construction"—a theme of the Nixon years—to an emerging call for return to the Constitution's "original intent"—a theme sounded by Robert Bork, Raoul Berger, and *Benchmark*, a journal published by the Olin- and Scaife-funded Center for Judicial Studies.[124] The government itself began to express criticism of the Court in originalist terms in Reagan's second term, with Meese's appointment as attorney general strengthening ties between the Justice Department and the various think tank organizations of the New Right, such as Weyrich's Heritage Foundation and the Center for Judicial Studies.[125] Soon after his appointment, Meese drew fire with a series of prominent addresses embracing original intent[126] and challenging the Court's claim in *Cooper v. Aaron*[127] that its decisions were the supreme law of the land: "To confuse the Constitution with judicial pronouncements allows no standard by which to criticize and to seek the overruling of" the Court's decisions and thus was "to submit to government by judiciary."[128] As Nixon had shown, calls for "strict construction" of the Constitution that condemned the busing and criminal defendants decisions of the Warren Court helped mobilize and unite Americans;[129] Reagan demonstrated how filiopietistic appeal to the framers' Constitution could legitimate the New Right's demands for constitutional change.[130] Meese's speeches endorsing original intent and the departmental prerogative of the executive branch to challenge the Court's interpretation of the Constitution now gave the movement's constitutional politics jurisprudential form.[131]

But how would those committed to originalism achieve restoration of *their* Constitution? The Center for Judicial Studies' *Benchmark* did more than urge a jurisprudence of original intent; it helped conservatives work out a New Right approach to constitutional change. Although proponents of original intent insisted that the Constitution could be changed only through Article V amendment,[132] the director of the Center for Judicial Studies, James McClellan, penned editorials advising conservatives to "kick the habit" of relying on Article V to overturn Supreme Court decisions; the strategy had repeatedly failed in the 1960s and 1970s and tended instead to legitimate the Court.[133] "[T]here is something fundamentally wrong with our system if we are driven to amend the Constitution so as to restore its original meaning,"[134]

McClellan advised, criticizing the Reagan administration's "Prayer Amendment" and pointing out that conservatives would better achieve their aims by selectively restricting the Court's jurisdiction or filing amicus briefs in Supreme Court cases.[135] Introducing an issue of *Benchmark* in the fall of 1984 that surveyed some seven hundred decisions of the judges Reagan had appointed in his first term (a survey undertaken with the support of the Right-to-Work Foundation), McClellan was plainly impressed. McClellan predicted that the president's "careful selection of judges thus far points to the conclusion that he will succeed in protecting many of his political gains against judicial attack in the years ahead. Indeed, Reagan's reform of the Federal Judiciary, done without the benefit of legislation reducing the power of the courts, may prove to be the most enduring achievement of his presidency."[136] Thus, as conservatives took over the federal bench, they kicked their old Article V habits and began to employ new constitutional tools. Originalists might still catechistically insist that changing the Constitution required amending it,[137] but as McClellan emphasized, "to *restore* [the Constitution's] original meaning"[138] did not.

In assuming the role of attorney general in Reagan's second term, Meese approached appointments as a way "to institutionalize the Reagan revolution so it can't be set aside no matter what happens in future presidential elections."[139] Stephen Markman was named head of the Office of Legal Policy (OLP) to oversee this effort.[140] As chief counsel for Orrin Hatch's Subcommittee on the Constitution, Markman helped write *The Right to Keep and Bear Arms* and was then asked to found the D.C. chapter of the Federalist Society.[141] Reporting on Reagan's elevation of Federalist Society "favorite" Antonin Scalia to the Supreme Court in 1986, the *New York Times* quoted Markman as explaining that "[t]he Federalist Society provides a good opportunity for us to get to know people who share the constitutional conservative perspective of the Attorney General and the President."[142] By the end of his second term, Reagan had appointed nearly half of the nation's judges in a highly orchestrated and careful screening process that paid close attention to the nominees' substantive views.[143] "Reagan had certain judicial values he wanted institutionalized on the bench," Markman, now a judge on the Michigan Supreme Court," recently emphasized.[144]

In 1987, under Markman's direction, the OLP prepared an *Original Meaning Jurisprudence* sourcebook,[145] which reproduced foundational texts on original intent, including excerpts from Raoul Berger's *Government by Judiciary* and a speech by Antonin Scalia urging that claims about the original intent were better understood as claims about "original meaning"—claims based on the understandings of the Americans who ratified the document rather than those who drafted it.[146] The following year, the OLP institutionalized these views about the proper method of interpreting the Constitution in the Department of Justice's *Guidelines on Constitutional Litigation*[147] and a lengthy document titled *The Constitution in the Year 2000: Choices Ahead in Constitutional Interpretation*,[148] which singled out the areas of substantive law that judicial appointments would affect. Like the sourcebook, the *Guidelines* and *The Constitution in the Year 2000* identified favored and disfavored lines of cases that tracked "social issues" of the New Right (for example, the rights of criminal defendants, school prayer, and contraception and abortion).[149]

The OLP documents set out this New Right agenda for constitutional change as a project of restoring the original meaning of the Constitution. The OLP *Guidelines on Constitutional Litigation* explained how originalism justified changing constitutional law: "The inclusion of an original meaning section [in government briefs] will help to focus judges on the text of the Constitution and away from their personal preferences or from incorrectly reasoned court precedent as the appropriate basis for decisionmaking."[150] The originalist narrative presents change as legitimate precisely *because* it is impersonal and not responsive to the "personal preferences" of the interpreter. Markman used the same language of self-denial in explaining how the judges the administration had nominated would change constitutional law: "We've tried to appoint to the bench individuals who understand that their own policy preferences are not necessarily incorporated into the Constitution."[151]

The executive branch's project of constitutional restoration strengthened individual rights claims under the Second Amendment. President Reagan affirmed that the founders' Constitution protected an individual right to bear arms: "Our team believes that law-abiding people who want to protect their home and family have a constitutional right to own guns."[152] Similarly, the Justice Department's *Guidelines on Constitutional Litigation*, which sought changes in constitutional law that would embody the original understanding, affirmed that the "Constitution protects numerous individual liberties against government infringement," including among the rights that "the Bill of Rights expressly protects against federal government action . . . the right to keep and bear arms (Second Amendment)."[153] Even more consequentially, numerous federal judges were appointed who shared the president's constitutional vision.[154] Claims about original understanding that the Reagan

Justice Department helped forge offered a rule-of-law reason for the administration and the judges Reagan appointed to abandon Warren and Burger Court precedents addressing "social issues" of the New Right and to propose new bodies of constitutional law in their stead. Changing the Constitution required amending it, but as James McClellan had emphasized, "to *restore* [the Constitution's] original meaning"[155] did not.[156]

Commentary on the Second Amendment in the nation's law reviews changed with these movement and government activities. Discussion of the right to bear arms increased with the introduction of gun control proposals in Congress in the 1960s and 1970s, but spiked in the 1980s and after.[157] Not only were there more articles, but they were differently researched and reasoned. They focused on founding era history and appealed to the past as the repository not simply of custom and wisdom[158] but of impersonally binding law.[159]

Yet even as the New Right coalition imbued libertarian claims on the Second Amendment with originalist authority, endowing the argument with evidence, rhetorical form, and public authority, the Second Amendment claim was never wholly integrated with the other "social issues" of the New Right coalition that Viguerie and Weyrich helped build, nor was it fully integrated into the originalist constitutional vision emerging from the Meese Justice Department. The impediments may have been personal and political.[160] Or they may have stemmed from a deeper tension between the original understanding claims the New Right was making about the Second Amendment and other parts of the Constitution. In *The Constitution in the Year 2000,* originalism advanced the "social issues" agenda of the New Right by delegitimating rights recognized by the Warren and Burger Courts; originalism was a tool for criticizing *courts,* not for challenging legislatures. By contrast, the individual rights claim on the Second Amendment was a New Right right, at odds with judicial precedent and in tension with New Right complaints about judicial activism. Its recognition would require a federal bench prepared to advance original understanding as a reason for invalidating *legislative* action.

At the end of the 1980s, the bench and bar still did not see the Second Amendment as authorizing judicial intervention of that kind. In 1991 former chief justice Warren Burger appeared on *The MacNeil/Lehrer NewsHour* to call individual rights claims under the Second Amendment "the subject of one of the greatest pieces of fraud, I repeat the word 'fraud,' on the American public by special interest groups that I have ever seen in my lifetime."[161] Former solicitor general Erwin Griswold was equally sharp in chastising the

"National Rifle Association and its friends in Congress": "[T]o assert that the Constitution is a barrier to reasonable gun laws, in the face of the unanimous judgment of the federal courts to the contrary, exceeds the limits of principled advocacy."[162] These remarks disparaging the NRA's Second Amendment claims reflected what then remained the widespread view in the profession, even among conservative critics of the Warren and Burger Courts. In 1989 Robert Bork asserted that the Second Amendment operates "to guarantee the right of states to form militia, not for individuals to bear arms," and indicated his belief that all state gun control is "probably constitutional."[163] Even though the number of law review articles on the right to bear arms increased in the 1980s, at least nineteen of the twenty-seven articles written between 1970 and 1989 espousing the view that the Second Amendment protected an individual right to bear arms were "written by lawyers who had been directly employed by or represented the NRA or other gun rights organizations, although they did not always so identify themselves in the author's footnote."[164]

This was to change in the years after Sanford Levinson published his 1989 article "The Embarrassing Second Amendment,"[165] in the pages of the *Yale Law Journal*, followed by Akhil Amar's articles "The Bill of Rights as a Constitution"[166] and "The Bill of Rights and the Fourteenth Amendment,"[167] also in the *Yale Law Journal*.[168] Now prominent law professors were beginning to examine constitutional understandings of the right to bear arms as a republican strategy of the founders for resisting government tyranny[169] and as part of the liberal individual rights guarantees that emerged from Reconstruction.[170] Levinson emphasized to liberal colleagues in the academy then enamored of republicanism that republican understandings of the founders might blur the boundaries between the individualist and collectivist accounts of the Second Amendment. "[T]he implications of republicanism might push us in unexpected, even embarrassing, directions," he observed; "just as ordinary citizens should participate actively in governmental decision-making through offering their own deliberative insights . . . , so should ordinary citizens participate in the process of law enforcement and defense of liberty rather than rely on professionalized peacekeepers, whether we call them standing armies or police."[171] In 1992 the NRA responded to the favorable publicity Levinson's article generated by creating a new foundation called Academics for the Second Amendment (A2A), headed by a member of the NRA board of directors, and in 1994 it began awarding an annual "Stand Up for the Second Amendment" prize, with first place winning $25,000.[172]

D. Conflict and Compromise: Second Amendment Rights from Militias to Culture Wars

The decade in which new understandings of the Second Amendment would be taken up in the legal academy was marked by escalating political struggle over gun rights. It was an era of increasing public support for gun control, of violent countermobilization, and ultimately of unstable forms of political accommodation, affecting both the tenor of gun rights advocacy and boundaries of acceptable gun control regulation. At stake was the question of how political claims on the Second Amendment would be asserted: as an outgrowth of a republican tradition that understood the militia as defense against government tyranny, or as grounded in a more classically liberal tradition concerned with the individual's right to defend himself and his family from crime.

The newest phase of struggle over gun rights unfolded in a period of escalating crime and civilian violence.[173] Throughout the 1990s, 60 to 80 percent of the American public expressed support for the idea that "laws covering the sale of firearms should be made more strict."[174] Support for increasing gun regulation likely reflected changes in politics as well. After the drive for a national handgun ban foundered in the 1970s,[175] advocates for gun control had organized in new ways, with groups forming at the local as well as national level and advocating incremental restrictions on gun ownership, as well as local bans of the kind Morton Grove had enacted.[176]

With President Clinton's election in 1992, a supporter of gun control was now in the White House, and Democrats controlled both houses of Congress. In 1993 Congress enacted the Brady Bill,[177] named after the Reagan press secretary who had been critically injured in the attempted assassination of Ronald Reagan. The Brady Bill was incremental rather than categorical in its reach. It created a background check mechanism to enforce the provisions of the 1968 act that barred high-risk classes of persons (drug addicts, minors) from purchasing weapons.[178] The following year Congress enacted another incremental restriction on gun ownership, the 1994 assault weapons ban, which prohibited sale to civilians of certain semiautomatic "assault weapons."[179]

The passage of incremental gun control legislation early in Clinton's administration worked to provoke and mobilize the NRA,[180] first to oppose the legislation and then to press for its repeal—an aim the NRA pursued by joining forces with House Speaker Newt Gingrich and the Republican Party.[181] The Republican victory in the 1994 election was credited in significant part to the NRA's "massive effort . . . to punish Democrats who supported the Brady handgun law and the crime bill including a ban on assault weapons."[182] The NRA spent more than $3.2 million on GOP campaigns and helped win nineteen of twenty-four "priority" races the organization targeted, leading to a House with a majority of members who were "A-rated" by the NRA.[183] Thereafter, Neal Knox assured the NRA membership that, as part of its new "Contract with America," the leadership of the Republican Party had promised to attempt repeal of the assault weapons ban and adopt a "coherent Second Amendment strategy to define gun ownership as a constitutional right, not a duck-hunting right."[184]

Republicans had turned the 1994 election into a referendum on the competence of government,[185] and Gingrich appealed to gun rights to express themes about government and the body politic that had been echoing since the Johnson era. In *To Renew America,* Gingrich identified gun control as an issue that distinguished liberals and conservatives: "The Second Amendment is a political right written into our Constitution for the purpose of protecting individual citizens from their own government. . . . Generally, liberals neither understand nor believe in the constitutional right to bear arms."[186] He proudly asserted a conservative claim on the Second Amendment grounded in law and order challenges to the Great Society. "[W]e should be concerned not with legislating against weaponry but with legislating against crime," Gingrich observed, illustrating this claim by invoking in rapid succession the racially charged examples of O. J. Simpson, Willy Horton, and a serial rapist: "For some psychological reason, liberals are antigun but not anti–violent criminal."[187]

Hostility to government was even more pronounced within the NRA itself, and it was assuming new forms. In 1991 Neal Knox, who participated in the 1977 NRA takeover with Harlon Carter and was expelled in 1982 for lobbying tactics that may have alienated Edwin Meese,[188] staged a return to power in a campaign pledging opposition to all forms of gun control.[189] With Knox's return, Tanya K. Metaksa became executive director of the ILA and the NRA moved right.[190] Metaksa underscored the NRA's position of "no compromise" on gun control and drew attention to its demand for repeal of the assault weapons ban by spelling her name for reporters: "It's 'ak' as in AK-47 and 'sa' as in semi-automatic."[191]

Under Knox and Metaksa's leadership, the NRA was openly entangled with militias. A 1994 resolution declared, "Although the NRA has not been involved in the formation of any citizen militia units, neither has the NRA discouraged, nor would NRA contemplate discouraging, exercise of any constitutional right."[192] A militia movement of growing numbers understood itself in constitutional terms, arguing that "the federal government had no authority at the state and local level."[193] Bloody confrontations with the Bureau of Alcohol, Tobacco, and Firearms, first at Ruby Ridge (1992) and then at Waco (1993), had escalated the militia movement's profound mistrust of the federal government: "Gun Control is for only one thing[:] . . . people control."[194]

The militias believed themselves to be exercising their Second Amendment right to bear arms for the core purpose for which the Second Amendment was intended: resisting tyranny.[195] Calling themselves "Christian Patriots, Constitutionalists, Freemen and sovereigns,"[196] and explaining their bonds and mission in openly racial terms, the militias grew their own, violent forms of dissenting community,[197] which they explained as based in the Constitution and the Bible.[198] The militias' Second Amendment was related to the libertarian and populist Second Amendment Reagan had invoked, but more completely estranged from government—and, often, more blunt in its racial views.[199]

The militia movement's estrangement from government was enacted in graphic terms when Timothy McVeigh organized the bombing of the federal building in Oklahoma City in 1995. McVeigh, a member of the NRA, earned a living as an unlicensed dealer in paramilitary gear at gun shows, where he sold copies of *The Turner Diaries,* a key text of the militia movement that tells the tale of an ex-soldier on a "mission to blow up a federal building in the first overt act against a government 'overrun by blacks and Jews.' "[200] McVeigh "believed the federal government intended to disarm the American public gradually and take away the right to bear arms under the Second Amendment," pointing to events at Ruby Ridge as proof.[201] The Oklahoma bombing, which killed 168 people, was staged on the anniversary of the Battle of Lexington and Concord and the end of the Waco siege, and appears to have been modeled on the FBI bombing recounted in *The Turner Diaries.*[202]

The question for the NRA after Oklahoma City was how rapidly it would distance itself from the militias, and from its leadership's frequent characterization of federal agents as "jack-booted thugs." It did not act quickly, prompting the resignation of former President George H. W. Bush.[203] Thereafter, Wayne LaPierre unrepentantly asserted that the organization's description of "jack-booted thugs" applied only to Bureau of Alcohol, Tobacco, and Firearms agents, not to others in law enforcement.[204] In this same unrepentant spirit, the NRA named as its "Law Enforcement Officer of the Year" Richard

Mack, who gained notoriety for openly endorsing the militia movement.[205] "People get all upset when they hear about militias, but what's wrong with it?" Mack asked in an interview. "Paul Revere called out the militia. It's part of our history. I wouldn't hesitate for a minute to call out my posse against the federal government if it gets out of hand."[206] (The NRA selected Mack as plaintiff in its challenge to the Brady Bill, whose registration provisions the Supreme Court would declare unconstitutional in *Printz v. United States*[207] in a decision written by Justice Scalia, holding that the temporary federal registration provisions of the act "commandeer[ed]" local law enforcement officials, contrary to the original understanding of the federalist scheme.)[208]

The NRA's failure to distance itself from the militias in the wake of Oklahoma City had palpable consequences. By 1996 the organization's membership had declined by 12 percent, and its contributions to political action committees had dropped by more than a fifth.[209] Thereafter Wayne LaPierre, in an effort to save the NRA's standing in government and among voters, recruited Charlton Heston to help oust Knox and transform the organization's social profile.[210] In pursuit of the NRA's presidency, Heston appeared on radio programs where he distanced himself from the "extremist element" in the NRA, said the Brady Act wasn't worth the energy to repeal (because local police ignored it: "I don't care if they keep the Brady Act forever"),[211] and announced repeatedly that "AK-47's are entirely inappropriate for private use."[212] With Heston's takeover, the NRA began visibly to cultivate a new, more family-friendly public image. Advertisements promised that the NRA's new magazine, *American Guardian,* would feature "home & self-defense," "family recreational shooting," "women's issues," "handgun carry options," and "high-tech home security: locks, lights, alarms & more."[213] Heston gave the law-and-order Second Amendment a constitutional pedigree, emphasizing that the Second Amendment guaranteed Americans the ability to defend themselves against threats to liberty "whether it be King George's Redcoats or today's criminal predators," and spoke of gun ownership as a family "tradition" that parents had a duty to teach their children.[214] In this period, some prominently positioned interpreters of the Second Amendment emphasized the forms of gun control the Constitution allowed, while others excluded from the amendment's protection paramilitary activity.[215]

But even as Charlton Heston ceded ground on some issues, distancing the NRA from the militias and from its call for repeal of the Brady Bill and the assault weapons ban, he went on the political offensive, asserting Second Amendment rights in a populist register that recalled the claim's roots in the

New Right's challenge to the Great Society and the Warren Court. Invoking
the republican claim that the "purpose of the Bill of Rights was to protect the
people from the state," Heston told the NRA in 1996: "Our founders refused
to ratify a constitution that didn't protect individual liberties. Maybe they're
just a bunch of wise, old, dead, white guys, but they meant what they said.
The Second Amendment isn't about the National Guard or the police or any
other government entity. It is about law-abiding, private U.S. citizens, period.
You are of that same bloodline. You are sons and daughters of the Boston tea-
spillers."[216] Heston's filiopiety was unmistakably racialized. "And no amount
of oppression, no FBI, no IRS, no big government, no social engineers, no
matter what and no matter how, they cannot cleave the genes we share with
our Founding Fathers."[217]

The following year, after assuming the vice presidency of the NRA,
Heston delivered a speech at Weyrich's Free Congress Foundation, where
he announced, "I have come to realize that a cultural war is raging across
our land . . . storming our values, assaulting our freedoms, killing our self-
confidence in who we are and what we believe, where we come from."[218]
Heston identified gun owners who lacked confidence to reveal themselves as
"victim[s] of the cultural war," and equated the position of gun owners with
that of "Pentecostal Christians, or pro-lifers, or right-to-workers, or Promise
Keepers, or school voucher-ers."[219] Heston exhorted his audience at the Free
Congress Foundation to make common cause with gun owners:

> I am not really here to talk about the Second Amendment or the NRA,
> but the gun issue clearly brings into focus the war that's going on.
>   Rank-and-file Americans wake up every morning, increasingly
> bewildered and confused at why their views make them lesser citizens.
> . . . Heaven help the God-fearing, law-abiding, Caucasian, middle
> class, Protestant, or—even worse—Evangelical Christian, Midwest,
> or Southern, or—even worse—rural, apparently straight, or—even
> worse—admittedly heterosexual, gun-owning or—even worse—
> NRA-card-carrying, average working stiff, or—even worse—male
> working stiff, because not only don't you count, you're a downright
> obstacle to social progress. . . . That's why you don't raise your hand.
> That's how cultural war works. And you are losing.[220]

Again, Heston specifically appealed to white racial consciousness: "The
Constitution was handed down to guide us by a bunch of those wise old dead

white guys who invented this country." Observing that "some flinch when I say that," he asked "Why?" insisting:

> It's true . . . they were white guys. So were most of the guys who died in Lincoln's name opposing slavery in the 1860s. So why should I be ashamed of white guys? Why is "Hispanic pride" or "black pride" a good thing, while "white pride" conjures up shaved heads and white hoods? . . . I'll tell you why: Cultural warfare.[221]

In fighting the culture war, Heston defended traditional ways against equality claims of all kinds:

> Mainstream America is depending on you . . . to draw your sword and fight for them[,] . . . to battle . . . the fringe propaganda of the homo-sexual coalition, the feminists who preach that it's a divine duty for women to hate men, blacks who raise a militant fist with one hand while they seek preference with the other.[222]

He closed with an appeal for constitutional restoration: "It's the same blueprint our founding fathers left to guide us. Our enemies see it as the senile prattle of an archaic society. I still honor it as the United States Constitution."[223]

In embracing the rubric of the culture war—a theme Patrick Buchanan made notorious in a speech endorsing George Bush's nomination at the 1992 Republican National Convention[224]—Heston transmuted the NRA's affair with the militias into a different and more politically acceptable form, expressing a creed that he repeated at every opportunity.[225] He consolidated these themes in a speech, "Winning the Cultural War," delivered at Harvard Law School in 1999, which circulated widely on the Internet once it was read on air by Rush Limbaugh.[226] Warning his audience that he believed "we are again engaged in a great civil war, a cultural war that's about to hijack your birthright," Heston urged:

> As I have stood in the crosshairs of those who target Second Amend-ment freedoms, I've realized that firearms are not the only issue. No, it's much, much bigger than that.
>
> I've come to understand that a cultural war is raging across our land, in which, with Orwellian fervor, certain acceptable thoughts and speech are mandated.[227]

Heston responded to the storm of criticism his earlier remarks had generated, objecting to being called a "racist" or a "homophobe" for asserting his constitutional rights:

> For example, I marched for civil rights with Dr. King in 1963—long before Hollywood found it fashionable. But when I told an audience last year that white pride is just as valid as black pride or red pride or anyone else's pride, they called me a racist.
>
> I've worked with brilliantly talented homosexuals all my life. But when I told an audience that gay rights should extend no further than your rights or my rights, I was called a homophobe.[228]

Denouncing these complaints as if he resented the imputation, Heston instead defiantly asserted *his* constitutional identity: "But I am not afraid. If Americans believed in political correctness, we'd still be King George's boys—subjects bound to the British crown."[229]

Heston's cry for constitutional restoration touched themes that extended to the very roots of the mobilization for gun rights in the late twentieth century—a movement that grew up in the shadow of civil rights struggle. *This* Second Amendment accepted *Brown:* it renounced claims of race privilege voiced by southern conservatives in the initial years of white resistance, and was versed in forms of racial group assertion that could withstand charges of racism.[230] Yet this Second Amendment unmistakably carried the memory of civil rights struggle, and with it a deep sense of social division; it imagined society as divided into kinds—the "law-abiding citizen" and the "criminal," the deserving and the undeserving—and resented government when it identified with the undeserving other. This law-and-order Second Amendment recalled the founding as the time *before* the constitutional (un)settlements of the late twentieth century.[231]

III. *HELLER*, ORIGINALISM, AND THE CULTURE WARS

> *You see, I have my rules that confine me. I know what I'm looking*
> *for. When I find it—the original meaning of the Constitution—I am*
> *handcuffed.... Though I'm a law-and-order type, I cannot do all the*
> *mean conservative things I would like to do to this society. You got me.*
> —Justice Scalia, remarks delivered at the Woodrow Wilson International
> Center for Scholars, Washington, D.C., March 14, 2005[232]

The boundary between law and politics is forged in constitutional culture.[233] *Heller,* and most federal opinions that recognized or remarked favorably on an individual right to bear arms in the decades preceding it, were written by judges whom President Reagan appointed.[234] Originalism helps transmute their constitutional politics into constitutional law. Even as Justice Scalia changes constitutional law in ways that vindicate the values of the New Right, he presents himself as self-denying, "confine[d]" by "rules," "handcuffed."[235] Only the judge who enforces the original understanding is constrained by law, Justice Scalia claims.[236]

In dissent, where Justice Scalia speaks out most forcefully,[237] he regularly depicts his own views as fidelity to law, while denouncing his liberal colleagues for injecting their values into judging. In 1996, when the Court held that the Constitution prohibited government from expressing animus to gays, Justice Scalia famously objected, "I think it no business of the courts (as opposed to the political branches) to take sides in this culture war,"[238] in a dissent that expressed views about gays remarkably like those Charlton Heston would express in his culture war speeches for the NRA. Justice Scalia's dissents in cases concerning "social issues" (as Paul Weyrich called them)[239] or "cultural war" issues (as Pat Buchanan and Charlton Heston called them)[240] often voice resentments of the New Right as fidelity to law.[241] When the Court invalidated a law criminalizing same-sex relations in *Lawrence v. Texas,* Justice Scalia complained that "the Court has taken sides in the culture war, departing from its role of assuring, as neutral observer, that the democratic rules of engagement are observed," and objected that "[w]hat Texas has chosen to do is well within the range of traditional democratic action, and its hand should not be stayed through the invention of a brand-new 'constitutional right' by a Court that is impatient of democratic change."[242]

It might seem inconsistent for Justice Scalia to denounce his colleagues for "tak[ing] sides in the culture war" yet vote in *Heller* to strike down a law that was viewed by legally literate lawyers in the twentieth century, until the rise of the gun rights movement, as "well within the range of traditional democratic action."[243] But *Heller* recognizes a New Right right. *Heller* vindicates what Justice Scalia calls "original values" and so, in his view, requires no Article V amendment to change the law.[244] When Justice Scalia sides with a social movement, he does not present himself—and may well not understand himself—as taking sides in the culture wars. Like Heston, Justice Scalia views the gun rights movement as rescuing the founders' Constitution *from* the politics of the culture wars. Like Heston, Justice Scalia recognizes, as part of the founders' Constitution, a Second Amendment that "elevates above all other interests the right of law-abiding, responsible citizens to use arms in defense of hearth and home."[245]

This could reflect some coincidental alignment of the original understanding and the values around which the New Right has mobilized. Or this
coincidence could teach us something about the social processes that shape
interpretation of particular claims about the founding and imbue constitutional rulings with popular authority.

Consider *Heller*. The correspondence between the law-and-order Second
Amendment forged in culture wars of the New Right and the original public
meaning of the Second Amendment that *Heller* vindicates is striking. When
Justice Scalia explains that the Second Amendment protects rights of the
"law-abiding, responsible citizens to use arms in defense of hearth and home,"
he echoes Harlon Carter, Ronald Reagan, and Charlton Heston, who all claim
the Second Amendment protects rights of the "law-abiding" and invoke the
distinction between citizens and criminals to explain the Second Amendment.[246] The coincidence is deeper, manifest not only in the rhetoric of the
Heller opinion but also in its account of the Second Amendment's core purposes. Justice Scalia's Second Amendment protects the law-abiding citizen's
ability to defend himself and his family from criminals—and not the republican vision of a militia prepared to defend against government tyranny.

Twentieth-century conflict helped tutor intuitions about the Second
Amendment's core and periphery. For most of the twentieth century, literate lawyers read the Second Amendment in light of the republican purposes
enunciated in its first clause; but decades of gun rights mobilization trans-
formed the "natural" meaning of the Constitution's text so that, for increasing
numbers of Americans, a law-and-order Second Amendment simply appeared
there as the founders' Constitution: "The Second Amendment is clear, or
ought to be," Governor Reagan urged in 1975. "It appears to leave little, if
any, leeway for the gun control advocate."[247] In the ensuing decades, Congress
gathered evidence to support the New Right's reading of the amendment,[248]
the Reagan Justice Department appointed judges sympathetic to an originalist and law-and-order understanding of the Constitution,[249] academics of
note began to recognize the Second Amendment as a site of individual rights,
while others affiliated with the gun rights movement began to develop a law-
yerly case for recognizing judicially enforceable rights there. Nelson Lund, for
example, helped shift the focus of Second Amendment interpretation by characterizing its first clause as "prefatory" and its second clause as "operative"—
and received a Second Amendment chair funded by the NRA for his work.[250]
Decades of mobilization inside and outside the academy forged modes of
interpreting the Second Amendment that make libertarian, law-and-order
concerns central to its meaning and republican concerns peripheral. These

movement-tutored presumptions make plausible Justice Scalia's claim that the antecedents of the common-law right of self-defense are in the English Bill of Rights—even though the English Bill of Rights was motivated by the *abuse of political power* (the selective disarmament of Protestants by a Stuart monarch), not crime, and designed to vindicate *parliamentary supremacy,* not the rights of an individual against the legislature.[251]

The mobilization of living Americans around the text and history of the Second Amendment did more than tutor popular and professional intuitions about the amendment's core and peripheral purposes; it imbued the amendment with compelling contemporary social meaning by connecting the right to bear arms to some of the most divisive questions of late-twentieth-century constitutional politics. These debates made arguments for Second Amendment rights intelligible as arguments about guns, and much more.[252] Commonly, advocates asserted Second Amendment rights in a language of law and order that associated restoration of the constitutional order with restoration of the traditional social order.

Law-and-order critics of the Warren Court accepted the *Brown* settlement, and developed an identity and an idiom emphasizing fidelity to law that was self-consciously not racial, in part to enable Americans fighting over the reach of the *Brown* settlement to express concerns about race while fending off charges of racism. The gun rights movement employed this law-and-order idiom to defend the traditional social order in matters of race, family, and faith. Making common cause with critics of the Warren and Burger Courts as part of a New Right coalition, gun rights advocates armed for a "cultural war" to secure government's fidelity to the founders' true heirs.[253]

The New Right embraced originalism as the jurisprudential vehicle for these claims. Now that conservatives were beginning to exercise authority in the Republican Party, and from Congress, the Justice Department, and the bench, the original understanding provided authority that could legitimate their new exercises of public authority *as* the Constitution—supplying reason not only to limit judicial review but to expand it in new ways.[254]

The New Right's understanding of the original understanding was populist and popular but clearly partisan—by no means consensual, or even majoritarian. Its gun rights agenda had majority support in only the thinnest of senses. Because the leaders of the gun rights movement could deliver single-issue voters who would decide elections at the margin and punish insufficiently responsive officials, the movement was able to secure the cooperation of government and defeat gun control efforts, even on issues where the gun rights movement lacked public support.[255]

Heller enforces the original understanding in ways that are responsive to this complex mandate. After decades of gun mobilization, a large majority of Americans believe that the Second Amendment protects an individual right to bear arms.[256] But a large majority of Americans *also* believe that government can regulate gun ownership and prohibit military-style weapons through laws such as the assault weapons ban.[257] *Heller* seems to register this complex of popular beliefs when it holds that the Second Amendment protects weapons that the law-abiding citizen needs to defend himself and his family from crime—but not the military weapons citizens need to resist government tyranny.[258]

These two dimensions of *Heller*'s holding shed light on the kind of authority *Heller* exercises—the ways its originalism connects the constitutional convictions of Americans dead and living. The *Heller* Court bitterly divides over whether there is historical evidence for reading the Second Amendment as codifying a common law right of self-defense but agrees that the framers of the Second Amendment sought to prevent government tyranny.[259] Yet the majority treats weaponry traditionally used for individual self-defense as presumptively protected and military weaponry as presumptively regulable. In 2008, Americans can appeal to the law-and-order Second Amendment as the founders' Second Amendment and can make claims on others outside their normative community through it—as they could not if they were to embrace a republican Second Amendment that authorized violent insurrection and the forms of originalism the militias practiced in the 1990s. Thus, even if, on further examination of the historical sources, we continued to debate whether the founders codified a right of self-defense, we can learn from the *Heller* Court's reticence to protect arms needed to resist government tyranny that originalism implicitly depends on contemporary popular convictions for its authority.

The shape of the right *Heller* protects demonstrates how a judicial decision claiming original authority may nonetheless employ practices of responsive interpretation associated with democratic constitutionalism.[260] At the same time, it illustrates how constitutional politics can guide and discipline judicial review. As one of many factors that give shape to law,[261] movement conflict constrains, as well as motivates, the claims that mobilized Americans make on their courts.[262] After decades of argument, advocates recognize that the public responds, fitfully, to the claims of *both* the gun rights and gun control movements, and so each movement has come to incorporate, at least in part, the claims of the other. When gun control leaders could not win support for a national handgun ban, they began to argue that the category of "assault weapons"[263] could be regulated under the Second Amendment. Just as many who support gun control now, cautiously, acknowledge the Second Amendment's authority,[264] many who embrace the original understanding of the Second Amendment are prepared to renounce its republican purposes.[265] Movement conflict can create these forms of apparent consensus without securing agreement.[266] Constitutional conflict of this kind structures disagreement; it enables exercises of judicial review that can officially entrench new understandings of the Constitution as law—without immunizing them from renewed popular challenge.[267]

The Court's judgment in *Heller* will exert authority as law, to the extent that its account of the original understanding can sustain intergenerational identification. As the rift in the *Heller* Court testifies, struggle over the meaning of constitutional memory is a medium through which community in disagreement is forged. Long public struggle endowed memories of the founding with significance for living Americans and assembled a Court to recover them; but that Court and the nation to which it speaks remain, visibly, riven. In 2008, the Supreme Court, the Republican Party platform, and the Democratic Party platform all recognize that the Second Amendment confers some form of individual right. Yet at the dawn of the twenty-first century, the scope of this right and its constitutional implications remain to be decided.[268]

NOTES

Source: Reprinted from 122 Harv. L. Rev. 191. Copyright © 2008 Harvard Law Review Association; Reva B. Siegel.

1. Robert A. Sprecher, *The Lost Amendment* (pt. 2), 51 A.B.A. J. 665, 669 (1965).

2. *Lawrence v. Texas,* 539 U.S. 558, 602–03 (2003) (Scalia, J., dissenting).

3. U.S. Const. amend. II ("A well regulated Militia, being necessary to the security of a free State, the right of the people to keep and bear Arms, shall not be infringed.").

4. *District of Columbia v. Heller,* 128 S. Ct. 2783 (2008).

5. Linda Greenhouse, *Three Defining Opinions,* N.Y. Times, July 13, 2008, at WK4; *see also* Randy E. Barnett, op-ed, *News Flash: The Constitution Means What It Says,* Wall St. J., June 27, 2008, at A13 ("Justice Scalia's opinion is the finest example of what is now called 'original public meaning' jurisprudence ever adopted by the Supreme Court."); David G. Savage, *Supreme Court Finds History Is a Matter of Opinions,* L.A. Times, July 13, 2008 ("This year the Supreme Court relied more than ever on history and the original meaning of the Constitution in deciding its major cases."); Legal Theory Blog, June 26, 2008, http://lsolum.typepad.com/legaltheory/2008/06/analysis-of-hel.html ("It is difficult to

imagine a clearer or more thoroughgoing endorsement of original public meaning originalism.").

6. Posting of Jack Balkin to Balkinization, June 27, 2008, http://balkin.blogspot .com/2008/06/this-decision-will-cost-american-lives.html ("[T]he result in *Heller* would have been impossible without . . . social movement actors who, over a period of about 35 years, succeeded in changing Americans' minds about the meaning of the Second Amendment. . . . This is living constitutionalism in action."); Dave Kopel, *Conservative Activists Key to DC Handgun Decision*, HUMAN EVENTS, June 27, 2008, www.humanevents.com/article.php?id=27229 (reporting that the author—a member of the Cato Institute who helped argue *Heller*—attributes both its result and its originalist reasoning to twentieth-century social movements); posting of Adam Winkler to the Huffington Post, June 27, 2008, www.huffingtonpost.com/adam-winkler/justice-scalias-living -co_b_109728.html ("[W]hat explains the reasonable regulations that Scalia's opinion recognizes? America's living tradition of the right to bear arms.").

7. *Lawrence*, 539 U.S. at 602 (Scalia, J., dissenting) (quoted *supra*).

8. 347 U.S. 483 (1954).

9. *See* U.S. CONST. amend. II ("A well regulated Militia, being necessary to the security of a free State, the right of the people to keep and bear Arms, shall not be infringed.").

10. This comment builds on earlier work exploring how movement conflict helps guide the Constitution's development and how responsive interpretation helps sustain its democratic authority. *See* Reva B. Siegel, *Constitutional Culture, Social Movement Conflict, and Constitutional Change: The Case of the De Facto ERA*, 94 CAL. L. REV. 1323 (2006) [hereinafter Siegel, *Constitutional Culture*]; Reva B. Siegel, *The Right's Reasons: Constitutional Conflict and the Spread of Woman-Protective Antiabortion Argument*, 57 DUKE L.J. 1641–1692; Reva B. Siegel, *Text in Contest: Gender and the Constitution from a Social Movement Perspective*, 150 U. PA. L. REV. 297 (2001) [hereinafter Siegel, *Text in Contest*]; *see also* Jack M. Balkin & Reva B. Siegel, *Principles, Practices, and Social Movements*, 154 U. PA. L. REV. 927 (2006); Robert Post & Reva Siegel, *Originalism as a Political Practice: The Right's Living Constitution*, 75 FORDHAM L. REV. 545 (2006) [hereinafter Post & Siegel, *Originalism as a Political Practice*]; Robert Post & Reva Siegel, Roe *Rage: Democratic Constitutionalism and Backlash*, 42 HARV. C.R.-C.L. L. REV. 373 (2007) [hereinafter Post & Siegel, Roe *Rage*].

11. *See* Siegel, *Constitutional Culture, supra* note 10, at 1347–48; Post & Siegel, *Originalism as a Political Practice, supra* note 10.

12. Antonin Scalia, *Common-Law Courts in a Civil-Law System: The Role of United States Federal Courts in Interpreting the Constitution and Laws*, in A MATTER OF INTERPRETATION 3, 38 (Amy Gutmann ed., 1997).

13. *See* Antonin Scalia, *Originalism: The Lesser Evil*, 57 U. CIN. L. REV. 849, 854 (1989) (discussed *infra* note 137).

14. *Heller*, 128 S. Ct. at 2821 (denouncing an interest-balancing test proposed by Justice Breyer). To illustrate his claim, Justice Scalia discusses the application of the First Amendment in Skokie, Illinois—a rather odd example of the unchanging scope of rights, as the text of the First Amendment is expressly addressed to "Congress" and does not mention the states. *See id.*

15. *See, e.g., id.* at 2789–90, 2799; *id.* at 2824–25 (Stevens, J., dissenting).

16. See U.S. CONST. amend. II ("*A well regulated Militia, being necessary to the security of a free State,* the right of the people to keep and bear Arms, shall not be infringed" (emphasis added)).

17. *Heller*, 128 S. Ct. at 2822 (Stevens, J., dissenting); *see also id.* at 2823 (citing *United States v. Miller*, 307 U.S. 174 (1939)).

18. *Id.* at 2831.

19. *Id.* at 2822.

20. *Id.* at 2801 (majority opinion) ("[T]he Second Amendment's prefatory clause announces the purpose for which the right was codified: to prevent elimination of the militia.").

21. *Id.* at 2821.

22. *Id.* at 2793 (citing *Muscarello v. United States*, 524 U.S. 125, 143 (Ginsburg, J., dissenting)); *see also id.* at 2794. Sensible of the temporal discrepancy, the majority then cites state constitutional provisions it asserts "unambiguously" demonstrate that the "natural meaning" of "bear arms" is the same as its historical meaning; the sources cited do not supply unambiguous support for its claims, and a number are from a later period. *See id.* at 2793. By contrast, *Heller*'s dissenters rely on a usage study of more than one hundred texts that employed the term "bear arms" in the period between the Declaration of Independence and the adoption of the Second Amendment to establish that the term was regularly used in a military context. *See id.* at 2828 n.9 (Stevens, J., dissenting).

23. *Id.* at 2796 (majority opinion).

24. *Id.* at 2804 (emphasis added); *see also id.* (discussing "our longstanding view that the Bill of Rights codified venerable, widely understood liberties"); *id.* at 2798 (observing that the English Bill of Rights "has long been understood to be the predecessor to our Second Amendment").

25. *See, e.g., id.* at 2797 (citing *United States v. Cruikshank*, 92 U.S. 542 (1876)); *id.* at 2802 (citing *Robertson v. Baldwin*, 165 U.S. 275 (1897)).

26. *Id.* at 2837 n.28 (Stevens, J., dissenting).

27. *Id.* at 2805 (majority opinion).

28. *Cf.* Scalia, *supra* note 12, at 38 ("I will consult the writings of some men who happened to be delegates to the Constitutional Convention. . . . I do so, however,

not because they were Framers and therefore their intent is authoritative and must be the law; but rather because their writings, like those of other intelligent and informed people of the time, display how the text of the Constitution was originally understood.").

29. *Id.*

30. *See Heller*, 128 S. Ct. at 2812 (using as authority a treatise from 1891). *Cf.* Akhil Reed Amar, *The Supreme Court, 2007 Term—Comment:* Heller, HLR, *and Holistic Legal Reasoning*, 122 HARV. L. REV. 145, 173 (2008) ("But if a future twenty-third-century historian seeks to understand the 1960s, I hope she does not treat the 1980s as decisive evidence. Even if most commentators in the years after 1791 read the Second Amendment through the prism of English common law and individual rights of self-defense, this approach may well have been anachronistic and incorrect.").

31. *Heller*, 128 S. Ct. at 2816–17.

32. *Cf.* Mark Tushnet, Heller *and the Perils of Compromise*, 13 LEWIS & CLARK L. REV. 419 (2009) (arguing that in determining the scope of the right the Second Amendment protects, Justice Scalia's opinion employs as much discretion as Justice Breyer's dissent, though Justice Scalia "cannot admit the fact"); J. Harvie Wilkinson III, *Of Guns, Abortions, and the Unraveling Rule of Law*, 95 VA. L. REV. 253 (2009) ("As Justice Breyer notes, the Court does not explain why these restrictions are embedded in the Second Amendment. The Constitution's text . . . has as little to say about restrictions on firearm ownership by felons as it does about the trimesters of pregnancy" (footnote omitted); Richard A. Posner, *In Defense of Looseness: The Supreme Court and Gun Control*, NEW REPUBLIC, August 27, 2008, at 32, 34 (observing that the reach of the opinion is "up for grabs").

33. *Heller*, 128 S. Ct. at 2817.

34. 307 U.S. 174 (1939).

35. *Heller*, 128 S. Ct. at 2817 (quoting *Miller*, 307 U.S. at 179).

36. *Miller*, 307 U.S. at 179 ("These show plainly enough that the Militia comprised all males physically capable of acting in concert for the common defense. 'A body of citizens enrolled for military discipline.' And further, that ordinarily when called for service these men were expected to appear bearing arms supplied by themselves and of the kind in common use at the time.").

37. *See Heller*, 128 S. Ct. at 2791–92 ("Some have made the argument, bordering on the frivolous, that only those arms in existence in the 18th century are protected by the Second Amendment. We do not interpret constitutional rights that way. . . . [T]he Second Amendment extends, prima facie, to all instruments that constitute bearable arms, even those that were not in existence at the time of the founding.").

38. *Id.* at 2817.

39. *Id.* at 2801 ("[T]he Second Amendment's prefatory clause announces the purpose for which the right was codified: to prevent elimination of the militia. The prefatory clause does not suggest that preserving the militia was the only reason Americans valued the ancient right; most undoubtedly thought it even more important for self-defense and hunting. But the threat that the new Federal Government would destroy the citizens' militia by taking away their arms was the reason that right—unlike some other English rights—was codified in a written Constitution.").

40. *See id.* at 2815–16.

41. *Id.* at 2815 n.24 (citation omitted).

42. *See* Siegel, *Text in Contest, supra* note 10, at 299–300; *see also id.* at 314 ("Outside the courthouse, the Constitution's text plays a significant role in eliciting and focusing normative disputes among Americans about . . . rights under the Constitution—a dynamic that serves to communicate these newly crystallizing understandings and expectations about . . . rights to judges interpreting the Constitution inside the courthouse door.").

43. *Heller,* 128 S. Ct. at 2815 n.24.

44. *See* Siegel, *Constitutional Culture, supra* note 10.

45. *See* Post & Siegel, *Originalism as a Political Practice, supra* note 10.

46. Lee Kennett & James LaVerne Anderson, The Gun in America: The Origins of a National Dilemma 231 (1975) ("Within a week of President Kennedy's death a dozen firearms bills had been placed in the congressional hoppers."). A Hein Online title search for law review articles on "Second Amendment," "bear arms," or "gun control" shows that publications begin steadily to increase in the 1960s. *See infra* note 157.

47. Alexander DeConde, Gun Violence in America: The Struggle for Control 175 (2001); Kennett & Anderson, *supra* note 46, at 231–43; see also Stanley Meisler, *Get Your Gun from the Army,* 198 Nation 568, 569 (1964) (noting that members of the NRA get "a subscription to the NRA's *American Rifleman,* a chance to buy Army guns, a massive public relations campaign that included a float in the 1963 Tournament of Roses Parade saying, 'The Bill of Rights—Freedom to Keep and Bear Arms' and, most important, some lobbying on their behalf in the halls of state legislatures and Congress"); Drew Pearson & Jack Anderson, *The Washington Merry-Go-Round: Gun Industry Holds Capitol Hill at Bay,* Wash. Post, April 13, 1968, at D15 ("More moving than the memory of President John F. Kennedy and the Rev. Martin Luther King, apparently, has been the lobbying of the National Rifle Association which, for six years, has blocked every move on Capitol Hill to curb the indiscriminate sale of firearms.").

48. *See* Robert J. Spitzer, The Politics of Gun Control 102 (1995).

49. In 1956, *Life* magazine ran a story on "the western film genre, noting that 'in Hollywood eight films with "gun" in the title have been completed and actors

are learning now to shoot and be shot,'" and "each evening, a television critic in *The Nation* reported, 'twenty to thirty million American homes rock with the sound of sudden gunfire.'" KENNETT & ANDERSON, *supra* note 46, at 218; *see also* DECONDE, *supra* note 47, at 161 (reporting the depiction of gun violence in the 1950s on the "new medium of television," where "[n]ight and day with the press of a button Americans could now view programs featuring graphic firearms violence," including "*Gunsmoke, Have Gun Will Travel, The Rifleman,* and *Wanted Dead or Alive*").

50. For example, in 1959 Gallup reported 59 percent of the public in support of a handgun ban. *See* sources cited *infra* note 74 and accompanying text.

51. See DECONDE, *supra* note 47, at 173–84.

52. See Peter Bart, *Los Angeles Whites Voice Fear,* N.Y. TIMES, August 17, 1965, at 1 (reporting on "groups of white men in gas stations and stores talking about 'what they'll do if the niggers attack,'" and quoting an observer describing the "fantastic run on gun stores" as going "beyond the instinct for self protection" and the "smell of violence in the air in both the white and Negro communities"); Pearson & Anderson, *supra* note 47 (reporting that "the gun lobby has started an ugly whispering campaign that the gun control bill would prevent white people from buying weapons to defend their homes against Negro rioters"). *See generally* Vesla M. Weaver, *Frontlash: Race and the Development of Punitive Crime Policy,* 21 STUD. AM. POL. DEV. 230, 247 (2007) (discussing the ways in which conservatives reacting to different forms of violence "attached civil rights to lawlessness"). At least some gun control efforts during this period seem to have been racially motivated and were resisted by some members of the black community. See, e.g., Jane Rhodes, *Fanning the Flames of Racial Discord: The National Press and the Black Panther Party,* 4 HARV. INT'L J. PRESS/POL. 95, 95 (1999) (discussing a California bill that was motivated "in part to stifle the [Black] Panthers' open use of guns" and the Panthers' protest of that bill at the California state legislature); BLACK PANTHER PARTY, PLATFORM AND PROGRAM: WHAT WE WANT, WHAT WE BELIEVE (1966), *reprinted in* THE BLACK PANTHERS SPEAK 2, 3 (Philip S. Foner ed., 1970) ("The Second Amendment to the Constitution of the United States gives a right to bear arms. We therefore believe that all black people should arm themselves for self defense."). But racial conflict did not become entrenched in these ways. A black nationalist right to bear arms did not become the focal point of organizing in the African American community. *See* BLACK PANTHER PARTY, PLATFORM AND PROGRAM: WHAT WE WANT, WHAT WE BELIEVE (1972), www.stanford.edu/group/blackpanthers/history.shtml (omitting reference to the Second Amendment). Instead, there has been substantial support for gun control. *See* PEW RESEARCH CTR. FOR PEOPLE & THE PRESS, HANDGUNS: PUBLIC REJECTS A BAN—BUT SUPPORTS CONTROLS (2008), http://pewresearch .org/pubs/835/handgun-ban ("[F]ully three-quarters of African Americans (75%)

say controlling gun ownership is more important [than protecting] the rights of Americans to own guns."); Paul M. Barrett, *NAACP Suit Puts Race on Table in Gun Debate*, WALL ST. J., August 13, 1999, at B1 (discussing the NAACP's suit against gun manufacturers, which claimed that "African-Americans have been 'disproportionately injured' by the gun industry's 'negligent marketing'" (quoting complaint in *NAACP v. Acusport, Inc.*, 271 F. Supp. 2d 435 (E.D.N.Y. 2003))).

53. *See, e.g.*, S. REP. NO. 90-1097 (1968), *reprinted in* 1968 U.S.C.C.A.N. 2112, 2169 ("[T]he decided cases, both at the Federal and State levels, reveal no constitutional barrier to the passage of [federal gun control regulation]. To the contrary, they afford ample precedent for its validity."). The Court had sustained Congress's authority, under the Commerce Clause and the Second Amendment, to enact gun control laws during the New Deal. *See United States v. Miller*, 307 U.S. 174, 178 (1939) ("In the absence of any evidence tending to show that possession or use of a 'shotgun having a barrel of less than eighteen inches in length' at this time has some reasonable relationship to the preservation or efficiency of a well regulated militia, we cannot say that the Second Amendment guarantees the right to keep and bear such an instrument."). Lower courts understood *Miller*'s interpretation of the Second Amendment as identifying a collective right to militia-based weapons. *See, e.g., United States v. Warin*, 530 F.2d 103, 106 (6th Cir. 1976) ("It is clear that the Second Amendment guarantees a collective rather than an individual right."); *United States v. Casson*, 288 F. Supp. 86, 88 (D. Del. 1968) ("In the absence of some showing that the possession or use of the shotgun bears some reasonable relationship to the preservation or efficiency of a well regulated Militia, the Second Amendment does not guarantee defendant the right to keep and bear such a firearm."); *Galvan v. Superior Court*, 452 P.2d 930, 940 (Cal. 1969) ("The claim that legislation regulating weapons violates the Second Amendment has been rejected by every court which has ruled on the question.").

54. *Mail Order Gun Control: Hearing before the Subcomm. on Postal Operations of the H. Comm. on Post Office and Civil Serv.*, 90th Cong. 16 (1968) (reprinting legal memorandum on "The Right to Bear Arms"); *id.* at 17 (reviewing text, ratification history, and case law and concluding: "There is little or no case law on this subject. The principal case involved a sawed off shotgun which the Court held was not vital to the maintenance of a 'well regulated Militia'").

55. *See, e.g.*, S. REP. NO. 90-1097.

56. EMILIE RAYMOND, FROM MY COLD, DEAD HANDS: CHARLTON HESTON AND AMERICAN POLITICS 179 (2006).

57. *Joey Bishop Show*, ABC television broadcast, June 18, 1968 (a copy of their statement is available at www.vpc.org/nrainfo/memo.htm, as well as www .gunownersalliance.com/Lbj04.htm; original available at Lyndon Baines Johnson Library, Austin, Tex.). For correspondence between the Johnson administration and actors involved in gun control efforts, see www.vpc.org/nrainfo/doc

.htm; www.gunownersalliance.com/moses-1.htm. For Heston's perspective, *see* RAYMOND, *supra* note 56, at 178–80.

58. The executive vice president of the NRA testified before Congress that no "sane American, who calls himself an American, can object to placing in [the Gun Control Act of 1968] the instrument which killed [President Kennedy]." Keersten Heskin, *Easier Than Obtaining a Driver's License: The Federal Licensing of Gun Dealers*, 46 FLA. L. REV. 805, 819 n.123 (1994); *see also* NRA Staff, *Congress Threshes Out Gun Law Issue: Senators Defeat Four Registration and Licensing Attempts*, AM. RIFLEMAN, November 1968, at 22, 22 ("[W]hile the interstate features of the measure 'appear unduly restrictive and unjustified in their application to law-abiding citizens, the measure as a whole appears to be one that the sportsmen of America can live with and we are particularly glad to see 3 positive recommendations of the NRA become law'" (quoting NRA executive vice president Franklin L. Orth)).

59. Omnibus Crime Control and Safe Streets Act of 1968, Pub. L. No. 90-351, 82 Stat. 197 (codified in scattered sections of 5, 18, and 42 U.S.C.); Gun Control Act of 1968, Pub. L. No. 90-618, 82 Stat. 1213 (codified in scattered sections of 26 U.S.C.).

60. Weaver, *supra* note 52, at 251 ("Ultimately, liberals betrayed their early solidaristic calls for social reform and warring on poverty and, by the end of the 1960s, they began downplaying underlying causes, arguing instead for more gun control. . . . By 1968, Democrats had aligned themselves with the 'law and order' program and were trying desperately to mimic the Republicans.").

61. Yale Kamisar, *How Earl Warren's Twenty-two Years in Law Enforcement Affected His Work as Chief Justice*, 3 OHIO ST. J. CRIM. L. 11, 25 (2005) ("[T]hat so many of the coerced confession cases 'were appeals from southern courts, and so many of the defendants powerless blacks cast them as de facto civil rights cases'" (quoting ED CRAY, CHIEF JUSTICE: A BIOGRAPHY OF EARL WARREN 462 (1997))). An early draft of Chief Justice Warren's *Miranda* opinion noted that "Negro defendants were subjected to physical brutality—beatings, hanging, whipping—employed to extort confessions" and cited a 1947 report of the "President's Committee on Civil Rights [that] probed further into police violence upon minority groups." BERNARD SCHWARTZ, SUPER CHIEF: EARL WARREN AND HIS SUPREME COURT 591 (1983) (quoting an early draft of the *Miranda* opinion); *see also* A. Kenneth Pye, *The Warren Court and Criminal Procedure*, 67 MICH. L. REV. 249, 256 (1968) ("The Court's concern with criminal procedure can be understood only in the context of the struggle for civil rights. . . . If the Court's espousal of equality before the law was to be credible, it required not only that the poor Negro be permitted to vote and to attend a school with whites, but also that he and other disadvantaged individuals be able to exercise, as well as possess, the same rights as the affluent white when suspected of crime.").

62. The 1968 act was amended over the president's opposition to include war on crime provisions that restricted the rights of criminal defendants only recently recognized by the Warren Court. *See* SPITZER, *supra* note 48, at 172 n.11; ROBERT J. SPITZER, THE PRESIDENCY AND PUBLIC POLICY: THE FOUR ARENAS OF PRESIDENTIAL POWER 69–70 (1983); Weaver, *supra* note 52, at 255–58; *Crime Bill an Odd Mix of Good, Bad,* INDEP., June 24, 1968, at B-2. For example, contrary to the Court's decision in *Miranda v. Arizona,* 384 U.S. 436 (1966), "[t]he bill provided that a confession by a defendant was to be admissible in evidence if it were 'voluntary,' even if the suspect had not been warned of his constitutional rights." *Congress Passes Extensive Anticrime Legislation,* 24 CONG. Q. ALMANAC 225, 226 (1968). The bill also "provided for the admissibility in evidence of eye-witness testimony, even if the suspect had not had a lawyer when he was identified in a police lineup," *id.,* directly contradicting the Warren Court's holding in *United States v. Wade,* 388 U.S. 218 (1967), that such evidence must be excluded. For further discussion of these provisions, see Recent Case, 82 HARV. L. REV. 1392 (1969) (discussing Title II of the Omnibus Crime Control and Safe Streets Act of 1968); see also Robert A. Burt, *Miranda and Title II: A Morganatic Marriage,* 1969 SUP. CT. REV. 81.

63. See Alexander M. Bickel, *The Senate Judiciary's Abominable Crime Bill,* NEW REPUBLIC, May 25, 1968, at 13, 13 (criticizing the bill as "so mangled by the Senate Judiciary Committee as to be an abomination").

64. *See* LIVA BAKER, MIRANDA: CRIME, LAW, AND POLITICS 200–208 (1983).

65. *See* Bob Kastenmeier, *Toward a Peaceful Society,* CAP. TIMES, July 15, 1968, at 32.

66. Weaver, *supra* note 52, at 251 (quoting RICHARD M. NIXON, TOWARD FREEDOM FROM FEAR (1968), *reprinted in* 114 CONG. REC. 12936, 12936 (1968)).

67. *Id.* at 259 (describing a Nixon commercial linking protesters to "violence," which Nixon observed "hits it right on the nose. It's all about law and order and the damn Negro-Puerto Rican groups out there" (quoting PHILIP A. KLINKNER & ROGERS M. SMITH, THE UNSTEADY MARCH: THE RISE AND DECLINE OF RACIAL EQUALITY IN AMERICA 292 (1999) (internal quotation marks omitted)); *see also* BAKER, *supra* note 64, at 244 ("[A]lthough Nixon would not mention [George] Wallace by name, the Republican would appear as 'a more respectable alternative' to the Alabaman, countering his rhetoric 'with a velvet-glove version of the mailed fist'"); Steven Cann, *Politics in Brown and White: Resegregation in America,* 88 JUDICATURE 74, 76 (2004) (describing Nixon's "southern strategy" as "an electoral strategy of the Republican Party to expand its electoral base by going soft on civil rights"); *id.* ("Nixon's former presidential counsel John W. Dean argues that Rehnquist once defined 'strict constructionism' as voting against criminal defendants and civil rights plaintiffs.").

68. MICHAEL W. FLAMM, LAW AND ORDER: STREET CRIME, CIVIL UNREST, AND THE CRISIS OF LIBERALISM IN THE 1960S 173 (2005); *see also* WEAVER, *supra* note 52, at 251, 259.

69. KRISTIN A. GOSS, DISARMED: THE MISSING MOVEMENT FOR GUN CONTROL IN AMERICA 39–40 (2006).

70. For the 1972 Republican Party platform expressing support for gun control, see *infra*, note 107 and accompanying text.

71. *See* GOSS, *supra* note 69, at 166–67 ("Many early gun control leaders were inspired by the citizen movements for civil rights, women's rights, and consumer protection that unfolded in the 1950s, 1960s, and 1970s. They thought that a national victory for gun control could be next. Yet the gun control campaign was beginning to institutionalize nationally at a time when the power and moral authority of the federal government were waning. By 1974, the War on Poverty and the premises that inspired it were under attack.").

72. GOSS, *supra* note 69, at 157–62.

73. D.C. CODE ANN. § 7-2501.01 (LexisNexis 2008).

74. *Gallup's Pulse of Democracy: Gun Laws*, www.gallup.com/poll/1645/Guns .aspx; *see also* DECONDE, *supra* note 47, at 165 (reporting that in 1959 a Gallup poll found that 59 percent of Americans "wanted private ownership of handguns outlawed"); *Gun Control Bill Reported in House*, 32 CONG. Q. ALMANAC 406, 407 (1976) ("[I]n a series of lopsided votes, . . . [the House Judiciary Committee] rejected amendments to ban the sale and possession of handguns."); *Gun Control*, 28 CONG. Q. ALMANAC 524 (1972) ("Any proposal outlawing or drastically restricting the private possession of small arms would stand little chance of passage at this time" (quoting Robert McClory, H. Subcomm. on the Judiciary) (internal quotation marks omitted)).

75. Ashley Halsey Jr., *The President's Stand on Guns*, AM. RIFLEMAN, August 1975, at 23, 23 (discussing news of the Gallup polling on declining support for handgun controls and suggesting that the president was subject to "influences from within the Treasury and the Justice Departments"); *cf. supra* note 58 (describing NRA support for provisions of the 1968 Gun Control Act).

76. James Vorenberg, *The War on Crime: The First Five Years*, ATLANTIC MONTHLY, May 1972, at 63, 63 (reporting a "30 percent increase in the reported crime rate during the first three years of the Nixon Administration"); *see also* GOSS, *supra* note 69, at 40 ("By the beginning of 1975, the nation had reached the highest rate of gun violence ever recorded: 16.1 shooting deaths per 100,000.").

77. *See supra* note 58 (describing NRA support for provisions of the 1968 Gun Control Act).

78. *Firearms Legislation: Hearing before the Subcomm. on Crime of the H. Comm. on the Judiciary*, 94th Cong. 2845–47 (1975) (statement of Harlon

Carter, executive director, National Rifle Association, Institute for Legislative Action).

79. Carter continued: "There are very few victims of brutal criminality who wonder or even care about the socioeconomic conditions that may or may not have motivated their attacker. . . . [U]nder our system of justice—or at least as it was designed—the criminal who directly caused that suffering is supposed to pay the consequences. But somehow, it does not work out that way any more. . . . I do not believe that it is possible to take enough guns away from criminals to insure the safety of a disarmed public. But if the President is right, if most crime is attributable to a relatively small number of criminals, we can take them—the criminals—out of circulation." *Id.* at 2853.

80. Reagan had served on the advisory board of Young Americans for Freedom since 1962. *History,* Young Americans for Freedom, www.yaf.com/history/index .php; *see also* Gregory L. Schneider, Cadres for Conservatism: Young Americans for Freedom and the Rise of the Contemporary Right 138 (1999); *Second Amendment Foundation, in* 2 Guns in American Society: An Encyclopedia of History, Politics, Culture, and the Law 527, 527–28 (Gregg Lee Carter ed., 2002) [hereinafter Guns in American Society]; *Active National Pro-Firearms Organizations,* National Rifle Association—Institute for Legislative Action, www.nraila.org/Issues/FactSheets/Read.aspx?ID=16. For a description of the activities of the Second Amendment Foundation, see *SAF Fighting Good Fight for Constitutional Right to Keep and Bear Arms,* Conservative Dig., October 1981, at 40, 40 (describing the media activities of the foundation as created "to meet the need for an intellectual defense of freedom of gun ownership").

81. *See* Ronald Reagan, *Ronald Reagan Champions Gun Ownership,* Guns & Ammo, September 1975, at 34.

82. YAF played a key role in spearheading Reagan's drive for the presidency in 1976 and 1980. *See* Schneider, *supra* note 80, at 161.

83. Reagan, *supra* note 81, at 34.

84. *See supra* notes 53–55 and accompanying text.

85. Reagan, *supra* note 81, at 35.

86. Joseph P. Tartaro, Revolt at Cincinnati 39 (1981).

87. *Id.* at 27.

88. *Id.* at 19.

89. *Id.*

90. *Id.* at 21–22 (quoting the fundraising report by Oram International, Inc.).

91. *Id.* at 24; *see also id.* at 18 (displaying "Revolutionary War 'Don't Tread on Me' flag as the emblem of a strong pro-gun political position").

92. *Id.* at 36.

93. *Institute Reports: The Right to Keep and Bear Arms; An Analysis of the Second Amendment*, AM. RIFLEMAN, August 1977, at 37. A more circumspect account of the takeover appears in the July issue. *See* NRA Staff, *Concerned NRA Members Redirect Their Association*, AM. RIFLEMAN, July 1977, at 16.

94. Martin Durham, *Family, Morality, and the New Right*, 38 PARLIAMEN-TARY AFF. 180, 180 (1985). On Viguerie's role in the Wallace campaign, see Alan Ehrenhalt, *The "New Right" Movement Emerging in Washington*, NASHUA TELE-GRAPH, October 28, 1976, at 23.

95. In beginning his direct mail operation with the donor lists of the Wallace campaign, Viguerie was building a New Right by mobilizing Americans who were estranged from the civil rights rulings of the Warren Court. Wallace was famous for leading white resistance to *Brown. See* Michael J. Klarman, Brown v. Board: *50 Years Later*, HUMAN., March–April 2004, at 24, 28 ("Governor George Wallace of Alabama personified the post-Brown racial fanaticism of southern politics. . . . Wallace declared in his [1962] inaugural address: '. . . [S]egrega-tion now, segregation tomorrow, segregation forever'"); *see also* DAN T. CARTER, FROM GEORGE WALLACE TO NEWT GINGRICH: RACE IN THE CONSERVATIVE COUNTERREVOLUTION, 1963–1994, at 48 (1996) (quoting a radio ad for Wallace's 1970 gubernatorial campaign that observed: "Suppose your wife is driving home at 11 o'clock. She is stopped by a highway patrolman. He turns out to be black. Think about it. . . . Elect George Wallace."). In his 1972 campaign for the pres-idency, Wallace expressed these themes in more muted terms, such as through hostility to busing. *See Wallace's Showing in Primaries Kills Labor's Kingmaking Role*, HARTFORD COURANT, June 7, 1972, at 14 (reporting that Wallace told workers "that stopping busing was more important than overtime, seniority or a union shop"); Tom Wicker, *To Bus or Not to Bus*, N.Y. TIMES, February 17, 1972, at 37 ("[Wallace] entered the race, crying that a vote for him would be a vote against busing."). Viguerie continued to affiliate with racial conservatives estranged from the Warren Court after he left the Wallace campaign and began to organize the New Right. *See* RUSS BELLANT, THE COORS CONNECTION: HOW COORS FAMILY PHILANTHROPY UNDERMINES DEMOCRATIC PLURALISM 16–17 (1991) (describ-ing Viguerie's attendance at the "1976 convention of the American Independent Party (AIP) to seek a spot . . . on the national ticket. The AIP . . . was a coalition that included elements of the Ku Klux Klan, John Birchers . . . , and operatives of the Liberty Lobby.").

96. Tim Wyngaard, *On the GOP Front: New Breed Battles Old-Timers for Party Funds*, EL PASO HERALD-POST, June 17, 1977, at D-5 (observing that Viguerie started with "the mailing list of the arch-conservative Young Americans for Freedom (YAF), for which he formerly worked," and "[i]n the next decade he col-lected and codified, cross-indexed and culled the names of 10 million American

conservatives who would be willing to donate to right-wing causes on the basis of 'personalized' letters spewing from the computers"). Viguerie's clients built their own donor lists. "But they [couldn't] take the lists to another direct-mail firm. They [became] Viguerie's property as well." *Id.*; *see also* RICHARD A. VIGUERIE & DAVID FRANKE, AMERICA'S RIGHT TURN: HOW CONSERVATIVES USED NEW AND ALTERNATIVE MEDIA TO TAKE POWER 150 (2004) (recounting how "the hundreds of thousands of names of Wallace contributors [that Viguerie] amassed were later used to help conservative Republicans take over the South").

97. *The New Right: A Special Report,* CONSERVATIVE DIG., June 1979, at 9, 10.

98. *Right On for the New Right,* TIME, October 3, 1977, at 24, 26 (internal quotation marks omitted).

99. *See Mobilizing the Moral Majority,* CONSERVATIVE DIG., August 1979, at 14; *The Pro-Family Movement: A Special Report,* CONSERVATIVE DIG., May–June 1980, at 14. For an account of the role the conservative strategists of the New Right played in forging a coalition of Protestants and Catholics aroused to protest secular humanism, the Equal Rights Amendment, and abortion, see Post & Siegel, Roe *Rage, supra* note 10, at 420–23.

100. Joe Scott, *The GOA Connection,* OAKLAND TRIB., April 4, 1976, at 18. The head of GOA was State senator Bill Richardson of Sacramento, California, "a one-time field representative of the John Birch Society." ALAN CRAWFORD, THUNDER ON THE RIGHT: THE "NEW RIGHT" AND THE POLITICS OF RESENTMENT 33 (1980).

101. Paul Houston, *Foes of Gun Control Press Fund Drives,* L.A. TIMES, April 25, 1976, at 1 (internal quotation marks omitted).

102. *Id.* (quoting solicitation letter signed by H. L. Richardson, founder of Gun Owners of America) (internal quotation marks omitted).

103. H. L. Richardson, *Political Turn to the Right Would've Been Impossible without Role of Direct Mail,* CONSERVATIVE DIG., June 1981, at 23, 23.

104. Houston, *supra* note 101.

105. *Id.*; *see also* CRAWFORD, *supra* note 100, at 67–69 (reporting that in 1975 Viguerie handled fundraising for the ILA, bringing in $5.8 million at a cost of $3.2 million and building the organization's list of contributors by 600,000 names, and observing that in the late 1970s, Viguerie raised $12 million for the NRA while also doing direct mail work for the Citizens Committee for the Right to Keep and Bear Arms and Gun Owners of America).

106. *See supra* section II.B; *see also* GOSS, *supra* note 69, at 172 (describing the creation of NRA's Office of Legislative Affairs, which raised nearly $2 million in a year, and noting how "advocates dissatisfied with what they saw as the NRA's insufficiently hard-line stance created Gun Owners of America, which pulled the NRA in the direction of protecting its right flank"). Martin Durham describes

the New Right strategy: "The anti-gun-control National Rifle Association and the anti-abortion National Right to Life Committee were not so willing to give up their political independence, and the New Right was compelled to work with them as best it could. At the same time, it . . . encouraged small groups on the independent organisations' right—the Gun Owners of America in the first case, the Life Amendment Political Action Committee and the American Life Lobby in the second." Durham, *supra* note 94, at 181.

107. REPUBLICAN NAT'L CONVENTION, REPUBLICAN PARTY PLATFORM OF 1972, *available at* www.presidency.ucsb.edu/ws/index.php?pid=25842.

108. REPUBLICAN NAT'L CONVENTION, REPUBLICAN PARTY PLATFORM OF 1976, *available at* www.presidency.ucsb.edu/ws/index.php?pid=25843.

109. *See* Wyngaard, *supra* note 96 (discussing role of direct mail in changing the shape of the Republican National Party).

110. GOSS, *supra* note 69, at 45–46. *See Quilici v. Village of Morton Grove,* 464 U.S. 863 (1983) (mem.) (denying certiorari).

111. GOSS, *supra* note 69, at 162–65.

112. *Id.* at 46.

113. *He's Mail Fundraising King,* SYRACUSE HERALD-AM., January 8, 1978, at 79 (explaining that Viguerie solicits money "to fight the Panama Canal treaties, abortion, gun control, [and] the Equal Rights Amendment" and that monies are "contributed to candidates like George Wallace, Sen. Jesse Helms, R-N.C., Sen. Orin [*sic*] Hatch, R-Utah, and Sen. Strom Thurmond, R-S.C.").

114. Viguerie boasts of having helped elect Orrin Hatch. *See* RICHARD A. VIGUERIE, THE NEW RIGHT: WE'RE READY TO LEAD 38, 60 (1981). Critics charged that Viguerie's committees made loans to Hatch's Senate campaign that together exceeded the limits set by campaign finance laws. *See Panel Reports Complaint on Hatch Contributions,* SALT LAKE TRIB., October 21, 1976, at 10A. Weyrich also takes credit for helping elect Hatch. *See* Lee Edwards, *Paul Weyrich: Conscience of New Right Fighting for Conservative Victory in '82,* CONSERVATIVE DIG., July 1981, at 2, 4 (discussing how Weyrich's Committee for the Survival of a Free Congress (CSFC) helped elect Hatch in 1976).

115. *See Right On for the New Right, supra* note 98, at 24.

116. STAFF OF SUBCOMM. ON THE CONSTITUTION OF THE S. COMM. ON THE JUDICIARY, 97TH CONG., THE RIGHT TO KEEP AND BEAR ARMS vii (Comm. Print 1982) ("Immediately upon assuming chairmanship of the Subcommittee on the Constitution, I sponsored the report . . . [on] the right to keep and bear arms."). Hatch observed: "We did not guess at the purpose of the British 1689 Declaration of Rights; we located the Journals of the House of Commons and private notes of the Declaration's sponsors, now dead for two centuries. . . .We did not speculate as to the intent of the framers of the second amendment; we examined

James Madison's drafts for it, his handwritten outlines of speeches upon the Bill of Rights." *Id.* at vii–viii.

117. *Id.* at viii.

118. Pub. L. No. 99-308, 100 Stat. 449 (1986) (codified at 18 U.S.C. §§921–929 (2006)).

119. *Id.* §1(b) (codified at 18 U.S.C. §921 note).

120. *See discussion infra. See generally* Steven M. Teles, Transformative Bureaucracy: Reagan's Lawyers and the Dynamics of Political Investment, Prepared for Studies in American Development (unpublished manuscript, on file with the Harvard Law School Library).

121. REPUBLICAN NAT'L CONVENTION, REPUBLICAN PARTY PLATFORM OF 1980, *available at* www.presidency.ucsb.edu/ws/index.php?pid=25844; *see* Sheldon Goldman, *Reagan's Second Term Judicial Appointments: The Battle at Midway,* 70 JUDICATURE 324, 324–25 (1987).

122. Weyrich founded the conservative Heritage Foundation and the Free Congress Foundation with funds from Joseph Coors and Richard Scaife. By 1988 Scaife had given the Free Congress Foundation $7,014,000, making him the foundations' top lifetime donor. BELLANT, *supra* note 95, at 83. Under Weyrich's leadership, both organizations focused on judicial reform. *See* John Chamberlain, *Moral Issues Not a Good Core for Political Coalitions,* IRONWOOD DAILY GLOBE, December 1, 1981, at 4 (discussing polling by Weyrich's Heritage Foundation in the spring of 1980 reporting that "two-thirds of the people would prefer to have state rather than federal judges decide such 'social issues as abortion, busing and voluntary prayer in the schools'" and explaining that "the New Right's Paul Weyrich has decided to lead off with a call for reform of our court system"). *See generally* A BLUEPRINT FOR JUDICIAL REFORM (Patrick B. McGuigan & Randall R. Rader eds., 1981) (collecting papers of a conference sponsored by the Free Congress Research and Education Foundation).

123. David M. O'Brien, *Federal Judgeships in Retrospect,* in THE REAGAN PRESIDENCY 327, 327 (W. Elliot Brownlee & Hugh Davis Graham eds., 2003); *see also* Goldman, *supra* note 121, at 325.

124. For a history of originalism's construction in the Reagan administration, see JOHNATHAN O'NEILL, ORIGINALISM IN AMERICAN LAW AND POLITICS 111–32, 162–70 (2005). The Center for Judicial Studies connected conservatives in the foundations, government, and the academy interested in developing constitutional theory for the New Right. *See id.* at 137, 148 (observing that *Benchmark* featured articles by James McClellan and Gary McDowell, who "became associate director of the Office of Public Affairs in the Justice Department in June 1985 and helped formulate Meese's speeches on originalism"). Gary McDowell's work at the Center for Judicial Studies was reportedly funded by the Olin Foundation and

the Sarah Scaife Foundation. *See* Media Transparency, Grants to Center for Judicial Studies, www.mediatransparency.org/recipientgrantsprint.php?recipientID =1056. For more on the Center for Judicial Studies' *Benchmark* magazine, see SIDNEY BLUMENTHAL, THE RISE OF THE COUNTER-ESTABLISHMENT 301–2 (1986); Al Kamen & Howard Kurtz, *Theorists on Right Find Fertile Ground: Conservative Legal Activists Exert Influence on Justice Department*, WASH. POST, August 9, 1985, at A1.

125. *See* Kamen & Kurtz, *supra* note 124 (reporting that conservative foundations "appear to have a particularly aggressive ally in Meese" and quoting the director of the "judicial-revision project" at the Free Congress Foundation describing the foundation's relation to the Justice Department: "We're part of the team. . . . We're trying to influence the agenda. We provide some of the intellectual power.").

126. O'NEILL, *supra* note 124, at 156.

127. 358 U.S. 1 (1958).

128. Edwin Meese III, *Perspectives on the Authoritativeness of Supreme Court Decision: The Law of the Constitution*, 61 TUL. L. REV. 979, 989 (1987). In challenging the Court's authority, Meese was invoking Lincoln's challenge to *Dred Scott* and, implicitly, Raoul Berger's recent attack on the Warren and Burger Courts. *See* RAOUL BERGER, GOVERNMENT BY JUDICIARY 363 (1st ed. 1977) (criticizing proponents of a "living Constitution"); *id.* at 367 (criticizing all those who "endeavored to discredit 'original intention,' to rid us of the 'dead hand of the past'"); *id.* at 370 (stating that "[i]f the Court may substitute its own meaning for that of the Framers it may . . . rewrite the Constitution without limit").

129. *See* sources cited *supra* note 68.

130. *Cf. discussion supra.*

131. *See* Post & Siegel, *Originalism as a Political Practice, supra* note 10, at 549 ("To understand originalism's power at the dawn of the twenty-first century is to appreciate the subtle ways in which originalism connects constitutional law to a living political culture and provides its proponents a compelling language in which to seek constitutional change through adjudication and politics."); Keith E. Whittington, *The New Originalism*, 2 GEO. J.L. & PUB. POL'Y 599, 601 (2004) ("[O]riginalism was a reactive theory motivated by substantive disagreement with the recent and then-current actions of the Warren and Burger Courts; originalism was largely developed as a mode of criticism of those actions.").

132. O'NEILL, *supra* note 124, at 126 ("[Raoul] Berger . . . regularly defended . . . the reservation of basic constitutional change for the Article V amendment process."); *see also infra* note 137 (discussing an article by Justice Antonin Scalia written in 1989).

133. James McClellan, *Kicking the Amendment Habit*, BENCHMARK, January–

February 1984, at 1, 2 ("[W]e should resist efforts to add amendments to our fundamental law to correct misinterpretations rendered by the Supreme Court. At the very least, such amendments tend to wink at judicial supremacy, and color the Court's usurpations with the tint of legitimacy."); *see also* O'NEILL, *supra* note 124, at 148, 257 n.52. The New Right's assumption that constitutional change on the "social issues" agenda would come through legislative channels—statutes regulating the judiciary and Article V amendments—was visible in a conflict during the first year of Reagan's presidency. *See* John Lofton Jr., *Baker Urges Delay of Social Issues Legislative Agenda until Next Year,* CONSERVATIVE DIG., May 1981, at 2, 2–3 (reporting that the Senate would "delay until next year the so-called 'social issues' agenda—that is, legislation dealing with abortion, forced busing, voluntary school prayer, family protection, etc."—to give priority to the president's economic program, and characterizing the deferral as requiring postponement of "emotional issues and constitutional amendments").

134. McClellan, *supra* note 133, at 2.

135. *Id.* at 2–3.

136. James McClellan, *Advertisement to Our Readers,* BENCHMARK, July–October 1984, at ii.

137. As Justice Scalia analyzed the question in 1989, judges should interpret the Constitution to enforce fidelity to "original values"; it was abandoning original values that required a constitutional amendment. *See* Scalia, *supra* note 13, at 862.

138. McClellan, *supra* note 133, at 2 (emphasis added).

139. David M. O'Brien, op-ed, *Meese's Agenda for Ensuring the Reagan Legacy,* L.A. TIMES, September 28, 1986, at E3 (quoting Attorney General Edwin Meese III) (internal quotation marks omitted); *see also* Teles, *supra* note 120.

140. Press Release, Department of Justice, Markman New Head of OLP (1985), *available at* www.usdoj.gov/oip/foia_updates/Vol_VI_4/page1.htm.

141. STEVEN M. TELES, THE RISE OF THE CONSERVATIVE LEGAL MOVEMENT 145 (2008).

142. *Judge Scalia's Cheerleaders,* N.Y. TIMES, July 23, 1986, at B6 (quoting Stephen Markman, who represented the Justice Department at judicial selection meetings in the White House) (internal quotation marks omitted). In the same article, the *Times* also reported that the Federalist Society, founded in 1981, had $100,000 of its $400,000 budget in 1985 funded by the Scaife Foundation. *Id.*

143. *See* O'Brien, *supra* note 123, at 333–34 (describing the introduction of an "unprecedented screening process for potential judicial nominees" involving comparison of candidates' records in a computerized database and day-long interviews in which candidates were asked questions "about their views on abortion, affirmative action, and criminal justice").

144. T. R. Goldman, *The Flower of the Reagan Revolution*, LEGAL TIMES, August 1, 2005, at 40.

145. OFFICE OF LEGAL POLICY, U.S. DEP'T OF JUSTICE, ORIGINAL MEANING JURISPRUDENCE: A SOURCEBOOK (1987) [hereinafter OLP, SOURCEBOOK].

146. *Id.* at 101, 103–4, 139–50.

147. OFFICE OF LEGAL POLICY, U.S. DEP'T OF JUSTICE, GUIDELINES ON CONSTITUTIONAL LITIGATION 3 (1988) [hereinafter OLP, GUIDELINES] ("[C]onstitutional language should be construed as it was publicly understood at the time of its drafting and ratification and government attorneys should advance constitutional arguments based only on this 'original meaning'").

148. OFFICE OF LEGAL POLICY, U.S. DEP'T OF JUSTICE, THE CONSTITUTION IN THE YEAR 2000: CHOICES AHEAD IN CONSTITUTIONAL INTERPRETATION (1988) [hereinafter OLP, CONSTITUTION IN THE YEAR 2000]. For a fuller account, see Dawn E. Johnsen, *Ronald Reagan and the Rehnquist Court on Congressional Power: Presidential Influences on Constitutional Change*, 78 IND. L.J. 363 (2003).

149. *See* OLP, CONSTITUTION IN THE YEAR 2000, *supra* note 148; OLP, GUIDELINES, *supra* note 147, at 82 (identifying the "right of privacy cases, exemplified by *Griswold v. Connecticut*, 381 U.S. 479 (1965)," which held unconstitutional a Connecticut statute criminalizing the use of birth control, and *Roe v. Wade*, 410 U.S. 113 (1973), which held that states could not prohibit abortion, as "examples of judicial creation of 'fundamental' rights not found in the Constitution"); *id.* at 86–87 ("Neither the search and seizure exclusionary rule nor the procedural rules for custodial interrogations established by *Miranda v. Arizona*, 384 U.S. 436 (1966)," rules that protect the rights of criminal defendants, have any "constitutional or statutory basis"); *id.* at 85–86 (arguing that "no establishment of religion was involved" in a Third Circuit case where a high school refused to allow students to use school facilities for prayer meetings); OLP, SOURCEBOOK, *supra* note 145, at vi (listing the *Sourcebook's* disfavored cases "illustrating noninterpretivist jurisprudence").

150. OLP, GUIDELINES, *supra* note 147, at 10.

151. Kathryn Kahler, *Vision of a Reformed Judiciary Unlikely to Materialize*, DAILY INTELLIGENCER/MONTGOMERY COUNTY REC., January 20, 1988, at 11 (quoting Stephen Markman, assistant attorney general in the Office of Legal Policy) (internal quotation marks omitted).

152. Remarks at a Republican Campaign Rally in Mesquite, Texas, 2 PUB. PAPERS 1461, 1463 (November 5, 1988); *see also* Remarks at the Annual Members Banquet of the National Rifle Association in Phoenix, Arizona, 1 PUB. PAPERS 659, 660 (May 6, 1983) ("[T]he Constitution does not say that government shall decree the right to keep and bear arms. The Constitution says '. . . the right of the people to keep and bear Arms, shall not be infringed'").

153. OLP, GUIDELINES, *supra* note 147, at 70.

154. *See id.* (describing careful "ideological screening" of Reagan's judicial nominees). At the time Justice Scalia penned his decision in *Heller,* almost all significant opinions written by federal judges in the late twentieth century that recognize or remark favorably upon an individual right to bear arms appear to have been written by judges whom President Reagan appointed. *See infra* note 234.

155. McClellan, *supra* note 133, at 2 (emphasis added).

156. For a volume that locates the Second Amendment in a survey of the "original meaning" and "current understanding of the Bill of Rights," see THE BILL OF RIGHTS: ORIGINAL MEANING AND CURRENT UNDERSTANDING (Eugene W. Hickock Jr. ed., 1991) (compiling papers from eight separate conferences conducted by the Center for Judicial Studies between 1985 and 1987).

157. As of October 5, 2008, a Hein Online title search for "Second Amendment," "bear arms," or "gun control" in the Law Journal Library database resulted in 8 publications before 1950, 1 between 1950 and 1959, 8 between 1960 and 1969, 21 between 1970 and 1979, 59 between 1980 and 1989, 162 between 1990 and 1999, and 149 between 2000 and this writing.

158. *See, e.g.,* Sprecher, *supra* note 1, at 554 (arguing that because of "[t]he wisdom of the Founding Fathers . . . , the framework of the original document has proved durable enough to encompass great flexibility through the device of judicial interpretation"); *see also* James A. McClure, *Firearms and Federalism,* 7 IDAHO L. REV. 197, 205 (1970) ("Since the genius of the nation's founders has been the basis of our system of checks and balances and federal structure, scholars are continually attempting to interpret their words.").

159. *See, e.g.,* Bernard J. Bordenet, *The Right to Possess Arms: The Intent of the Framers of the Second Amendment,* 21 UWLA L. REV. 1, 30 (1990) ("The only proper and logical approach is to interpret the Constitution as its drafters and adopters intended. The Constitution contains provisions for amending it. Amendment through judicial fiat is both unconstitutional and illegal" (footnote omitted)); Robert Dowlut, *The Right to Arms: Does the Constitution or the Predilection of Judges Reign?* 36 OKLA. L. REV. 65, 75 (1983) ("The Americans desired a written constitution, for it was felt a constitution should contain 'a fixed and definite body of principles'" (quoting 1 R. CURRENT ET AL., AMERICAN HISTORY: A SURVEY 111 (3d ed. 1971))).

160. In the early 1980s the NRA lobbyist Neal Knox got into a conflict with Reagan's adviser Edwin Meese over plans to reorganize the Bureau of Alcohol, Tobacco, and Firearms; Knox was thereafter dismissed in what appears to have been an effort to smooth relations with the administration. *See* sources cited *infra* note 188. For a gun rights critique of Reagan's commitment to gun rights, see Keep and Bear Arms, What Do You Think of This Politician?: A Follow-Up

to the KABA Poll (June 14, 2003), www.keepandbeararms.com/NewsArchives
/XcNewsPlus.asp?cmd=view&articleid=2955.

161. *The MacNeil/Lehrer NewsHour* (PBS television broadcast, December 16,
1991) (quoting former chief justice Warren Burger); *see also* Joan Biskupic, *Guns:
A Second (Amendment) Look,* WASH. POST, May 10, 1995, at A20.

162. Erwin N. Griswold, *Phantom Second Amendment "Rights,"* WASH. POST,
November 4, 1990, at C7.

163. Claudia Luther, *Bork Says State Gun Laws Constitutional,* L.A. TIMES,
March 15, 1989, at B5; *see also* Miriam Bensimhon, *Advocates: Point and Counter-
point; Laurence Tribe and Robert Bork Debate the Framers' Spacious Terms,*
LIFE, Fall 1991 (Special Issue), at 96, 98 ("[T]he National Rifle Association is
always arguing that the Second Amendment determines the right to bear arms.
But I think it really is people's right to bear arms in a militia. The NRA thinks
that it protects their right to have Teflon-coated bullets. But that's not the original
understanding" (quoting Robert Bork)).

164. Carl T. Bogus, *The History and Politics of Second Amendment Scholarship: A Primer, in* THE SECOND AMENDMENT IN LAW AND HISTORY 1, 4 (Carl
T. Bogus ed., 2000). Sixteen were written or co-written by Stephen P. Halbrook,
Robert Dowlut, Richard Gardiner, David Hardy, or David Caplan, all current
or former lawyers for the NRA. Robert J. Spitzer, *Lost and Found: Researching
the Second Amendment,* 76 CHI.-KENT L. REV. 349, 379 n.157, app. at 387–92
(2000). Another was written by Alan Gottlieb, founder of the Citizens Committee
for the Right to Keep and Bear Arms and the Second Amendment Foundation,
GUNS IN AMERICAN SOCIETY, *supra* note 80, at 527, and two more were written
by Don Kates, a Second Amendment Foundation lawyer, *see Quilici v. Second
Amendment Foundation,* 769 F.2d 414, 415 (7th Cir. 1985). Spitzer, *supra,* app.
at 389–917.

165. Sanford Levinson, *The Embarrassing Second Amendment,* 99 YALE L.J.
637 (1989).

166. Akhil Reed Amar, *The Bill of Rights as a Constitution,* 100 YALE L.J. 1131
(1991).

167. Akhil Reed Amar, *The Bill of Rights and the Fourteenth Amendment,* 101
YALE L.J. 1193 (1992).

168. For discussion of this phase of scholarship, see Bogus, *supra* note 164, at
1, 4–13.

169. *See, e.g.,* Amar, *supra* note 166, at 1163 ("[T]he people's right to alter or abolish tyrannous government invariably required a popular appeal to arms."); Levinson, *supra* note 165, at 646–51; *id.* at 651 ("[T]he citizenry itself can be viewed as
an important third component of republican governance insofar as it stands ready
to defend republican liberty against the depredations of [the federal government
and the states], however futile that might appear as a practical matter.").

170. Amar, *supra* note 167, at 1262 (describing the transformation of the Second Amendment after Reconstruction to "an essentially 'civil' right").

171. Levinson, *supra* note 165, at 650–51.

172. *See* Bogus, *supra* note 164, at 6–7. "The N.R.A. was so delighted by Levinson's unexpected article that the group reprinted thousands of copies, which prompted a wave of fan mail for the professor." Andrea Sachs, *Why the Second Amendment Is a Loser in Court*, TIME, May 29, 1995, at 22, 22; *see also* John Ashcroft, U.S. Att'y Gen., to James Jay Baker, Exec. Dir. of NRA (May 17, 2001), available at www.nraila.org/images/Ashcroft.pdf (citing Levinson, as well as Amar, van Alstyne, and Kates, to support an individual rights interpretation of the Second Amendment).

173. Between 1987 and 1994 the firearms homicide rate rose by 40 percent and gun-related robberies by nearly 30 percent, Goss, *supra* note 69, at 46, and the media intensively covered recurrent mass shootings, *see id.*

174. Gallup Poll Editorial Staff, *Gallup Summary: Americans and Gun Control*, GALLUP, April 18, 2007, www.gallup.com/poll/27229/Gallup-Summary-Americans-Gun-Control.aspx.

175. See Goss, *supra* note 69, at 44.

176. *Id.* at 45–46.

177. Brady Handgun Violence Prevention Act, Pub. L. No. 103-159, 107 Stat. 1536 (1993) (codified at 18 U.S.C. §§921–922).

178. Goss, *supra* note 69, at 177.

179. Public Safety and Recreational Firearms Use Protection Act, Pub. L. No. 103-322, 108 Stat. 1796 (1994).

180. *See* Neal Knox, *Mr. Newt's "Second Amendment Strategy,"* AM. RIFLEMAN, March 1995, at 14, 14 (recounting promise of Republican leadership to attempt to repeal the assault weapons ban as part of the "Contract with America").

181. *Cf.* DECONDE, *supra* note 47, at 255 (noting that in August 1994 "the Republican National Committee threatened to condemn and deny campaign funds to any party representatives who voted for the ban on assault weapons," but that party members nonetheless broke ranks to enact the ban).

182. David S. Broder, *A Historic Republican Triumph*, WASH. POST, November 9, 1994, at A1, A14; *see also* Jeffrey H. Birnbaum, *Under the Gun*, FORTUNE, December 6, 1999, at 211, 214 (reporting that the NRA "played a major role in the surprising Republican takeover of the House of Representatives in 1994," helping defeat "such powerful Democrats as Speaker Thomas Foley . . . and Congressman Jack Brooks . . . , chairman of the House Judiciary Committee[,] . . . because they supported the assault weapons ban," and reporting President Clinton's observation that "[t]he NRA is the reason the Republicans control the House").

183. Michael Isikoff et al., *Of Tobacco, Torts, and Tusks*, NEWSWEEK, November 28, 1994, at 30, 30.

184. Knox, *supra* note 180, at 14 (quoting Newt Gingrich's response to President Clinton's 1995 State of the Union speech) (internal quotation marks omitted). The budget for the ILA increased from $17.7 million in 1990 to $28.3 million in 1994. Fox Butterfield, *Aggressive Strategy by N.R.A. Has Left Its Finances Reeling,* N.Y. TIMES, June 26, 1995, at A1.

185. *See* Broder, *supra* note 182, at A1.

186. NEWT GINGRICH, TO RENEW AMERICA 202 (1995).

187. *Id.* at 203.

188. *See* Paul Taylor, *Chief NRA Lobbyist's Ouster Seen, Triggered by Opposition to Meese,* WASH. POST, April 17, 1982, at A4 (recounting Neal Knox's opposition to Meese's plan to transfer responsibilities of the Bureau of Alcohol, Tobacco, and Firearms to the Secret Service); *see also* David Brock, *Wayne's World,* AM. SPECTATOR, May 1997, at 36, 39 (reporting that "Ed Meese told Harlon [Carter], 'Don't ever send me this man Knox to see me again'" (quoting Warren Cassidy, ILA director) (internal quotation marks omitted).

189. Butterfield, *supra* note 184, at A12.

190. *See id.*

191. Charles M. Sennott, *NRA Becomes Militias' Beacon,* BOSTON GLOBE, August 13, 1995, at 1 (quoting Tanya Metaksa) (internal quotation marks omitted); *see also* Birnbaum, *supra* note 182.

192. Sennott, *supra* note 191, at 15 (quoting NRA's Civilian Militia Statement of November 10, 1994) (internal quotation marks omitted).

193. DECONDE, *supra* note 47, at 257.

194. *Id.* at 258–59.

195. For an in-depth analysis of the militia movement's "theory of the Second Amendment," see DAVID C. WILLIAMS, THE MYTHIC MEANINGS OF THE SECOND AMENDMENT: TAMING POLITICAL VIOLENCE IN A CONSTITUTIONAL REPUBLIC 191–219 (2003). *See also* LANE CROTHERS, RAGE ON THE RIGHT: THE AMERICAN MILITIA MOVEMENT FROM RUBY RIDGE TO HOMELAND SECURITY 25–35 (2003).

196. MICHELE SWENSON, DEMOCRACY UNDER ASSAULT: THEOPOLITICS, INCIVILITY, AND VIOLENCE ON THE RIGHT 135 (2004)

197. *See* MORRIS DEES WITH JAMES CORCORAN, GATHERING STORM: AMERICA'S MILITIA THREAT (1996); SWENSON, supra note 196, at 130–51.

198. *See* WILLIAMS, *supra* note 195, at 217–18.

199. *See* RICHARD FELDMAN, RICOCHET: CONFESSIONS OF A GUN LOBBYIST 234–35 (2008) ("Among the more disturbing aspects of the militia movement were the anti-Semitic and white supremacist nature of several groups. . . . The BATF's gun-grabbing, black-clad storm troopers were seen as the foot soldiers of the [Zionist Occupation Government]."); Walter Goodman, *Militia Family Life, Before It Goes Undercover,* N.Y. TIMES, September 3, 1997, at C16 (quoting

members of the Rocky Mountain Militia saying, "We should celebrate the day [Martin Luther King Jr.] got shot" and "Have a white Christmas and a Jew-free New Year").

200. Charles M. Sennott, *Mainstream, Fringe Cross Paths at Gun Shows,* Boston Globe, August 13, 1995, at 14; *see also* Crothers, *supra* note 195, at 123–44; Williams, *supra* note 195, at 1–2. One must read *The Turner Diaries* to appreciate how central race is to its gun control dystopia. *See generally* Andrew Macdonald, The Turner Diaries (Barricade Books 1996) (1978).

201. Lou Michel & Dan Herbeck, American Terrorist: Timothy McVeigh & the Oklahoma City Bombing 108 (2001) (account of bombing based on interviews with McVeigh during the period of his incarceration); *see also id.* at 39 (recounting influence on McVeigh of *The Turner Diaries*).

202. *Id.* at 226–28 (recounting that McVeigh chose April 19 as the date of the Oklahoma City bombing because it was the 220th anniversary of the Battle of Lexington and Concord which began the American Revolution and because it was the second anniversary of the end of the Waco siege, and that McVeigh prepared for his capture by taking with him to the bombing a collection of documents including a pamphlet on the militia movements of 1775, a copy of the Declaration of Independence, and a quote from the protagonist of *The Turner Diaries*).

203. *See* George Bush to National Rifle Association (May 3, 1995), in N.Y. Times, May 11, 1995, at B10.

204. John Mintz, *NRA Members Take Aim at Critics,* Wash. Post, May 20, 1995, at A1, A12.

205. Mack referred to the militia movement as "the civil rights movement of the '90s." *Militia Movement Seeks Allies with Guns, Badges,* Christian Sci. Monitor, April 15, 1996, at 11 (quoting Richard Mack) (internal quotation marks omitted). This was a common refrain among militia members. *See, e.g., Militia Movement,* USA Today, March 12, 1996, at 3A; *Talk Back Live* (CNN television broadcast, April 5, 1996).

206. Sennott, *supra* note 191 (quoting Richard Mack) (internal quotation marks omitted). Mack later distanced himself from the militias, "den[ying] . . . reports in the *Los Angeles Times* and *The Boston Globe* that he . . . raised an armed citizen posse in Arizona to help enforce the law. He . . . publicly acknowledged that he organized a posse, but [claimed] that the only enforcement duties it ever took on were directing traffic." Dan Harrie, *Libertarian Throws His Hat into Utah's Governor Race,* Salt Lake Trib., November 7, 2003, at B3.

207. 521 U.S. 898 (1997).

208. *Id.* at 914.

209. Ian Brodie, *Foot Soldiers Desert the Gun Lobby,* Times (London), April 1, 1996.

210. RAYMOND, *supra* note 57, at 262–63. For Knox's account of the takeover, see Neal Knox, *The Mutiny at NRA*, URBAN ARMORY, January 1, 1999, www .urban-armory.com/nealknox010199.htm.

211. RAYMOND, *supra* note 57, at 265 (internal quotation marks omitted).

212. James N. Thurman, *NRA's New Aim: To Soften Its Edges and Re-enlist Moderates*, CHRISTIAN SCI. MONITOR, June 10, 1998, at 5. For Neal Knox's account of the positions Heston was taking in the media in the period he was seeking control of the NRA, see Knox, *supra* note 210 (discussing Heston's statements in his various TV and radio appearances). *See also* Robert W. Lee, *Heston, for the Record*, NEW AM., April 13, 1998, at 15 (reporting Heston's comments in radio interview about accepting the Brady Act and his intention "to get 'the right-wing folks off the [NRA] board and out of the picture'").

213. *The National Rifle Association Introduces American Guardian*, AM. RIFLEMAN, August 1997, at 11.

214. Charlton Heston, *The President's Column*, AM. RIFLEMAN, February 2000, at 12, 12 ("Don't let the right to keep and bear arms be forsaken or forgotten. Share these vital lessons, virtues and values with the young people in your life.").

215. *See, e.g.*, Brannon P. Denning, *Palladium of Liberty? Causes and Consequences of the Federalization of State Militias in the Twentieth Century*, 21 OKLA. CITY U. L. REV. 191, 244 (1996) ("Most regulations of firearms would remain in place, as would state prohibitions against paramilitary activity, since those are not aimed at an individual's right to bear arms. . . . [T]he exercise of Second Amendment rights would be dominated neither by the state (as is true under a collectivist interpretation of the Second Amendment) nor by wholly private entities (as urged by many in the neomilitia movement)."); Thomas B. McAffee, *Constitutional Limits on Regulating Private Militia Groups*, 58 MONT. L. REV. 45, 77 (1997) ("[T]he Second Amendment gives no protection to private armies waiting for an opportunity to confront the larger community with force."); *cf.* Laurence H. Tribe & Akhil Reed Amar, op-ed, *Well-Regulated Militias, and More*, N.Y. TIMES, October 28, 1999, at A31 ("The fact is, almost none of the proposed state or Federal weapons regulations appears to come close to offending the Second Amendment's core right to self-protection. The right to bear arms is certainly subject to reasonable regulation in the interest of public safety."). These themes carried over into the *Heller* litigation. *See infra* note 265 and accompanying text.

216. CHARLTON HESTON, THE COURAGE TO BE FREE 164, 168 (2000) (remarks before the 125th annual meeting of the NRA, March 30, 1996). For another compilation of Heston's speeches, see Varmint Al's Gun Rights & Politics, www .varmintal.com/apoli.htm#Heston.

217. HESTON, *supra* note 216, at 168.

218. Charlton Heston, First Vice President, Nat'l Rifle Assoc., Address at the Free Congress Foundation's 20th Anniversary Gala (December 7, 1997) (alteration in original), *available at* www.vpc.org/nrainfo/speech.html.

219. *Id.*

220. *Id.*

221. *Id.* (first alteration in original).

222. *Id.*

223. *Id.*

224. Although "culture war" terminology has been in use since the German *Kulturkampf* in the 1870s, it reemerged as a way of talking about contemporary American society in 1987 with the publication of *Cultural Conservatism: Toward a New National Agenda,* a survey commissioned by Paul Weyrich that advocated that conservatives take up a culture war, arguing that conservatives would be much more successful if they mobilized around social rather than economic issues. Free Congress Research & Educ. Found., Cultural Conservatism: Toward a New National Agenda 8–9 (1987); *see also* James Davison Hunter, Culture Wars: The Struggle to Define America 173 (1991) (stating that five areas in which culture war rages most intensely are the family, education, the popular media, law, and electoral politics). The culture war hit the mainstream with Patrick Buchanan's speech at the 1992 Republican National Convention, when he declared the election a "cultural war . . . for the soul of America," in which "Clinton and Clinton are on the other side, and George Bush is on our side." Patrick J. Buchanan, Speech at the 1992 Republican National Convention (August 17, 1992), *available at* www.buchanan.org/pa-92-0817-rnc.html. Buchanan's war was a moral one—to save "God's country" from "radical feminism," from "abortion on demand, a litmus test for the Supreme Court, homosexual rights, discrimination against religious schools, women in combat." *Id.* Despite Paul Weyrich's declaration in 1999 that religious conservatives had lost the culture war, *see* Dale McConkey, *Whither Hunter's Culture War? Shifts in Evangelical Morality, 1988-1998,* 62 Soc. Religion 149, 149 (2001), the 2004 election saw its resurgence, with "the left and the right mobilizing furiously around those hot-button social issues," Robin Toner, *Below the Campaign Radar, a Values War,* N.Y. Times, April 17, 2004, at A10; *see also* Robin Toner, *The Nation: To the Barricades,* N.Y. Times, February 29, 2004, at WK1.

225. See, for example, the speeches collected in the appendix of Heston, *supra* note 216. *See also NRA: "Armed with Pride,"* Am. Rifleman, March 1998, at 30, 31, 33 (interview with Charlton Heston and Wayne LaPierre) (Heston, speaking of a "cultural war," urges NRA members to "feel proud again" and warns them: "Don't run for cover when the cultural cannons roar. Remember who you are and what you believe, and . . . stand up and speak out.").

226. *See* TruthOrFiction.com, Charlton Heston's Speech at Harvard Law School, www.truthorfiction.com/rumors/h/heston-harvard.htm.

227. Charlton Heston, *Winning the Culture War,* Address at Harvard Law School (February 16, 1999), *available at* www.varmintal.com/heston3.htm.

228. *Id.*

229. *Id.*

230. Although not every advocate invoking culture war references guns, gun advocates often invoke the culture war—in terms that, like Heston's, directly or indirectly raise racial concerns. *See* Wayne LaPierre, Executive Vice President, Nat'l Rifle Assoc., Speech before the NRA Annual Meeting in Charlotte, N.C. (May 20, 2000), *available at* www.nra.org/Speech.aspx? id=6032 ("And the dirty little secret is [criminals are] overwhelmingly black and hispanic. But everybody's so scared of being called a racist they won't admit the level of killing among non-white teenaged gangbangers."); *see also* Paul Blackman, *The Federal Factoid Factory on Firearms and Violence: A Review of CDC Research and Politics,* 7 J. ON FIREARMS & PUB. POL'Y 21, 30 (1995) (arguing that violence "is epidemic only among young blacks and Hispanics"). Blackman, a research coordinator for the Institute for Legislative Action of the NRA, later argues that "studies of homicide victims," whom he has earlier identified as largely people of color, "suggest they are frequently criminals themselves and/or drug abusers. It is quite possible that their deaths, in terms of economic consequences to society, are net gains." *Id.* at 51–52; *see also infra* note 231 (lecture by assistant counsel of the NRA on guns and culture).

231. Addressing the Conservative Political Action Conference in 1997, Heston invoked "'50s-vintage movies, news clippings, . . . TV shows like Beaver and Lucy and Father Knows Best. . . . portraying traditional family units, cops who're on your side, clergy who aren't kooky, safe schools, certain punishment, manageable conflict," and urged: "America yearns to be true to itself again, to return to that warm fireside of common sense and common values. Remember how we once felt about our safety, our schools, our police, our employers, our media, our parents, our neighbors? Remember when we trusted the federal government to do the right thing? Today only one in four of us does. . . . Americans want to be American again." Charlton Heston, *Be Yourselves, O Americans,* Remarks before the Conservative Political Action Conference (January 25, 1997), *in* HESTON, *supra* note 216, 170, 172; *see also* James H. Warner, Assistant Gen. Counsel, Nat'l Rifle Assoc., Heritage Lecture: Guns, Crime, and the Culture War 6–7 (July 2, 1992), *available at* www.heritage.org/Research/Crime/upload/92266_1.pdf ("Guns do not get young girls pregnant. Guns do not create drug addiction. Guns did not create a welfare system which traps young women in dependency and keeps them in its thrall. Guns do not create music which glorifies hatred. Guns do not teach

young children that they are not part of America, and that they have no share in its culture. Guns do not cause people to urinate in the halls nor to defecate in the stairwells of public housing projects. . . . But each of these conditions can be traced back to the enemies of our culture. . . . There is no reason why the streets of Washington, D.C., could not be as safe as the streets of Lyndonville, Vermont, or Bismarck, North Dakota. But this will not happen until all Americans are assimilated into one country with one, common culture.").

232. Antonin Scalia, *Constitutional Interpretation the Old-Fashioned Way* (March 14, 2005), *available at* www.cfif.org/htdocs/freedomline/current/guest _commentary/scalia-constitutional-speech.htm.

233. *See* Siegel, *Constitutional Culture, supra* note 10, at 1327 (employing "the framework of constitutional culture to analyze the ways mobilized citizens influence officials who enforce the Constitution" and showing "how constitutional culture supplies the understandings of role and the practices of argument through which citizens and officials can propose new ways of enacting the society's defining commitments. . . . Constitutional culture preserves and perpetually destabilizes the distinction between politics and law.").

234. *See Heller*, 128 S. Ct. 2783 (Scalia, J.); *Parker v. District of Columbia*, 478 F.3d 370 (D.C. Cir. 2007) (Silberman, J.) (holding D.C.'s handgun ban unconstitutional under the Second Amendment); *United States v. Emerson*, 270 F.3d 203, 232 (5th Cir. 2001) (Garwood, J.) ("The plain meaning of the right of the people to keep arms is that it is an individual, rather than a collective, right and is not limited to keeping arms while engaged in active military service or as a member of a select militia such as the National Guard."); *see also Printz v. United States*, 521 U.S. 898 (1997) (Scalia, J.) (upholding NRA claims that background check provisions temporarily imposed by the Brady Bill amounted to federal commandeering of local law enforcement, contrary to the original understanding); *Silveira v. Lockyer*, 328 F.3d 567, 569–70 (9th Cir. 2003) (Kozinski, J., dissenting from denial of rehearing en banc); *Koog v. United States*, 79 F.3d 452 (5th Cir. 1996) (Jolly, J.) (holding unconstitutional the provision of the Brady Bill held unconstitutional in *Printz*); *United States v. Lopez*, 2 F.3d 1342, 1345, 1364 n.46 (5th Cir. 1993) (Garwood, J.) (characterizing in dicta the Second Amendment as "something of a brooding omnipresence" and noting that "some applications" of the statute at issue "might raise Second Amendment concerns."); *Printz v. United States*, 854 F. Supp. 1503 (D. Mont. 1994) (Lovell, J.). A prominent exception is Justice Thomas, appointed by President George H. W. Bush. *See Printz*, 521 U.S. at 938 n.2 (Thomas, J., concurring) ("Marshaling an impressive array of historical evidence, a growing body of scholarly commentary indicates that the 'right to keep and bear arms' is, as the Amendment's text suggests, a personal right.").

235. *See* Scalia, *supra* note 232.

236. *See id.* ("You either tell your judges, 'Look, this is a law, like all laws, give it the meaning it had when it was adopted.' Or, you tell your judges, 'Govern us'").

237. *Cf.* Jonathan Riehl, The Federalist Society and Movement Conservatism: How a Fractious Coalition on the Right Is Changing Constitutional Law and the Way We Talk and Think about It 254 (2007) (unpublished thesis, University of North Carolina at Chapel Hill) (interviewing Justice Scalia) ("'I still consider myself a teacher. That's the main reason I write my dissents,' [Justice Scalia] said. 'I think the main point of the dissent is perhaps to try to change the future, and that will occur not by persuading my colleagues, who have made their mind up, but by persuading the next generation'").

238. *Romer v. Evans,* 517 U.S. 620, 652 (1996) (Scalia, J., dissenting); *id.* at 636 ("The Court has mistaken a Kulturkampf for a fit of spite.").

239. *See discussion supra.*

240. *See supra* note 224 and accompanying text (discussing Buchanan's cultural war speech).

241. Shortly after joining the Court, Justice Scalia denounced its decision upholding affirmative action in the promotion of a road dispatcher, lamenting that "the only losers in the process are the Johnsons of the country, for whom Title VII has been not merely repealed but actually inverted. The irony is that these individuals—predominantly unknown, unaffluent, unorganized—suffer this injustice at the hands of a Court fond of thinking itself the champion of the politically impotent." *Johnson v. Transp. Agency,* 480 U.S. 616, 677 (1987) (Scalia, J., dissenting). When the Supreme Court required the Virginia Military Institute to admit women, Justice Scalia elegiacally warned of the threat to gender roles the decision posed, including in his dissent the full text of the school's traditional "Code of a Gentleman." *See United States v. Virginia,* 518 U.S. 515, 603 (1996) (Scalia, J., dissenting). When the Court reaffirmed its decision in *Miranda,* Justice Scalia denounced the Court for attempting "to write a prophylactic, extraconstitutional Constitution, binding on Congress and the States. . . . This is not the system that was established by the Framers." *Dickerson v. United States,* 530 U.S. 428, 461, 465 (2000) (Scalia, J., dissenting).

242. *Lawrence v. Texas,* 539 U.S. 558, 602–03 (2003) (Scalia, J., dissenting).

243. *See also Printz v. United States,* 521 U.S. 898 (1997) (upholding NRA claims that background check provisions temporarily imposed by the Brady Bill amounted to federal commandeering of local law enforcement, contrary to the original understanding).

244. *See supra* note 137.

245. *Heller,* 128 S. Ct. at 2821.

246. *See discussions supra* (quoting Harlon Carter in 1970s; quoting Ronald Reagan in 1975; quoting Charlton Heston in 1990s).

247. Reagan, *supra* note 81.

248. *See supra* note 116 and accompanying text.

249. *See supra* section II.C.

250. A Hein Online search for the terms "operative," "prefatory," and "Second Amendment" suggests that Nelson Lund was the first academic to introduce this terminology into the Second Amendment literature. *See* Nelson Lund, *The Past and Future of the Individual's Right to Arms*, 31 GA. L. REV. 1 (1996). Nelson Lund is the Patrick Henry Professor of Constitutional Law and the Second Amendment at the George Mason University School of Law. This position was created thanks to a $1 million commitment to GMU School of Law by the National Rifle Association Foundation announced in 2003. Press Release, $1 Million Endows Professorship at George Mason University (January 28, 2003), *available at* http://eagle.gmu.edu/newsroom/display.php? rid=399&keywords=. Justice Scalia relies on the distinction between "prefatory" and "operative" in describing the relationship of the amendment's first and second clause. *See, e.g., Heller*, 128 S. Ct. at 2789 ("The Second Amendment is naturally divided into two parts: its prefatory clause and its operative clause.").

251. *See Heller*, 128 S. Ct. at 2798 (observing of the English Bill of Rights provision guarding against disarmament of Protestants: "This right has long been understood to be the predecessor to our Second Amendment. It was clearly an individual right, having nothing whatever to do with service in a militia") (citations omitted). *But see id.* at 2837–38 & n.30 (Stevens, J., dissenting) (objecting to majority's claim that the provision of the English Bill of Rights guaranteeing arms for Protestants is appropriately understood as a predecessor to the Second Amendment). For historical accounts of the Second Amendment that emphasize its republican pedigree, see AKHIL REED AMAR, AMERICA'S CONSTITUTION: A BIOGRAPHY 324 (2005) (observing that "Founding history confirms a republican reading of the Second Amendment, whose framers generally envisioned Minutemen bearing guns, not Daniel Boone gunning bears," and noting that a military usage of arms similarly appears in state constitutions and the English Bill of Rights of 1689); SAUL CORNELL, A WELL-REGULATED MILITIA: THE FOUNDING FATHERS AND THE ORIGINS OF GUN CONTROL IN AMERICA (2006); and Jack N. Rakove, *The Second Amendment: The Highest Stage of Originalism*, 76 CHI.-KENT L. REV. 103 (2000). *See also* Brief of Amici Curiae Jack N. Rakove, Saul Cornell, David T. Konig, William J. Novak, Lois G. Schwoerer et al. in Support of Petitioners, *Heller*, 128 S. Ct. 2783 (2008) (No. 07-290), 2008 WL 157183. Historians including Jack Rakove and Saul Cornell emphasize that the Second Amendment was responsive not to the need for private self-defense but rather to a deep fear of a standing army and the debate over how control over militias would be allocated between the federal and state governments. *Id.* Indeed, the first laws

resembling contemporary gun control were not passed until after the War of 1812, well after ratification. *See* CORNELL, *supra*, at 142.

252. *See supra* sections II.A and II.D; cf. Dan M. Kahan & Donald Braman, *More Statistics, Less Persuasion: A Cultural Theory of Gun-Risk Perceptions,* 151 U. PA. L. REV. 1291, 1293–94 (2003) ("As one southern Democratic senator recently put it, the gun debate is 'about *values*'—'about *who* you are and who you aren't.' Or in the even more pithy formulation of another group of politically minded commentators, 'It's the Culture, Stupid!'") (footnotes omitted).

253. *See supra* sections II.C and II.D.

254. *See* THOMAS M. KECK, THE MOST ACTIVIST SUPREME COURT IN HISTORY: THE ROAD TO MODERN JUDICIAL CONSERVATISM 7 (2004) (presenting a political history of "the emergence of conservative activism" on the Rehnquist Court); Keith E. Whittington, *The New Originalism,* 2 GEO. J.L. & PUB. POL'Y 599, 608–9 (2004) (distinguishing traditional judicial restraint from a "new originalism" that while emphasizing "the limited authority of the judicial role in the constitutional system . . . may often require the active exercise of the power of judicial review in order to keep faith with the principled commitments of the founding.").

255. *See* BILL CLINTON, MY LIFE 630 (2004) ("After the [1994 midterm] election I had to face the fact that the law-enforcement groups and other supporters of responsible gun legislation, though they represented the majority of Americans, simply could not protect their friends in Congress from the NRA. The gun lobby outspent, outorganized, outfought, and outdemagogued them."); FELDMAN, *supra* note 199, at 229 (describing the NRA's successful campaign to unseat Jack Brooks, "the longest serving member of the House" at the time, as "payback for Jack's vote for the crime bill that contained the assault weapons ban," despite the fact that Brooks had been "one of the NRA's oldest and closest congressional allies"); Noam N. Levey, *NRA's Political Clout Is Waning,* L.A. TIMES, June 14, 2008, at A1. For polling data, see *infra* notes 256 & 257.

256. *See* Joan Biskupic, *Do You Have a Legal Right to Own a Gun?* USA TODAY, February 27, 2008, at 1A ("Nearly three out of four Americans—73%—believe the Second Amendment spells out an individual right to own a firearm."); ICR Survey Research Group Poll, August 15–19, 1997, the Roper Center at the University of Connecticut [hereinafter Roper Center Database], study no. USICR1997-933M, *available at* LEXIS, News Library, RPOLL file (reporting that 68 percent of respondents believed that the Second Amendment "guarantees individuals the right to own guns").

257. National majorities have opposed a handgun ban since the 1970s, *see Gallup's Pulse of Democracy: Gun Laws,* Gallup, www.gallup.com/poll/1645 /Guns.aspx, but a majority of Americans, and even President Bush, support an

assault weapons ban. *See Senate Defeats Gun Liability Bill*, 60 Cong. Q. Alma-nac 12–13, 12–14 (2004) (reporting that the House had passed a bill to rescind the handgun ban in Washington, D.C., while "White House officials had sig-naled President Bush's support for an extension of the [assault weapons] ban"); *Assault Weapons Ban Works: Plug Holes and Let Law Live*, editorial, USA Today, September 8, 2004, at 14A, *available at* www.usatoday.com/news/opinion /2004-09-07-assaultweapons-ourview_x.htm ("A University of Pennsylvania National Annenberg Election Survey in April found that 71% of respondents, including 64% of those in households with guns, support a renewal of the [assault weapons] ban."); Los Angeles Times Poll, March 16–17, 1989, Roper Center Data-base, *supra* note 256, study no. USLAT1989-177 (reporting that 59 percent of those polled believed that "[i]n the case of semi-automatic assault rifles . . . the interests of public safety outweigh" the Second Amendment).

258. *See supra* Part I.

259. *See, e.g., Heller*, 128 S. Ct. at 2801–2 (arguing that the Second Amendment was codified to "assure the existence of a 'citizens' militia' as a safeguard against tyranny"); *id.* at 2840 (Stevens, J., dissenting) (describing Justice Story's expla-nation of "the virtues of the militia as a bulwark against tyranny"); *see also supra* note 39 and accompanying text.

260. *See* Post & Siegel, *Originalism as a Political Practice, supra* note 10; Post & Siegel, Roe *Rage, supra* note 10.

261. There are a variety of constraints shaping *Heller*, from the historical evi-dence over which a divided Court argued to the appointments process that pro-duced the divided Court.

262. *See* Siegel, *Constitutional Culture, supra* note 10, at 1330–31 ("As move-ment and countermovement struggle to persuade (or recruit) uncommitted mem-bers of the public, each movement is forced to take account of the other's argu-ments, and in time may even begin to incorporate aspects of the other's argument into its own claims. . . . Bitter constitutional dispute can be hermeneutically con-structive, and has little noticed socially integrative effects.").

263. Josh Sugarmann, Assault Weapons and Accessories in America (1988), *available at* www.vpc.org/studies/awacont.htm.

264. For example, New York senator Charles Schumer, who in 1995 declared that "[t]he [S]econd [A]mendment does not guarantee the mythical individual right to bear arms," *Gun Laws and the Need for Self-Defense: Hearing before the H. Subcomm. on Crime of the H. Comm. of the Judiciary*, 104th Cong. 3 (1995), in 2002 articulated "the broad principle that there is an individual right to bear arms," *Reforming the FBI in the Twenty-first Century: Hearing of the S. Judiciary Comm.*, 107th Cong. 163 (2002). *See also* Democratic Nat'l Convention, Strong at Home, Respected in the World: The 2004

DEMOCRATIC NATIONAL PLATFORM FOR AMERICA 18 (2004), www.democrats
.org/pdfs/2004platform.pdf (affirming the Democrats' commitment to "protect
Americans' Second Amendment right to own firearms"); Michael Powell, *For
Obama, a Pragmatist's Shift toward the Center,* N.Y. TIMES, June 27, 2008, at
A14 (quoting Senator Barack Obama as saying, "I have always believed the Second
Amendment protects the right of individuals to bear arms."). But these shifts in
rhetoric do not necessarily indicate consensus. *See infra* note 266.

265. *See* Respondent's Brief at 30, *Heller,* 128 S. Ct. 2783 (No. 07-290), 2008
WL 336304 ("Respondent does not suggest that members of private paramilitary
organizations have a right to commit violent acts under the auspices of acting as
a citizen militia."); *cf.* Brief for the United States as Amicus Curiae, *Heller,* 128 S.
Ct. 2783 (No. 07-290), 2008 WL 157201 ("Although the court of appeals correctly
held that the Second Amendment protects an individual right, . . . the Second
Amendment, properly construed, allows for reasonable regulation of firearms.");
Brief for Amici Curiae Former Senior Officials of the Department of Justice in
Support of Respondent at 3–4, *Heller,* 128 S. Ct. 2783 (No. 07-290), 2008 WL
40551 ("The Second Amendment's protection was never understood to extend to
unfit persons or to unusual and especially dangerous firearms.").

266. Underlying the Democrats' and the NRA's increasingly similar formulations of the right remain vastly different views about its regulability. *See* Jonathan
Martin, *NRA Plans $40M Fall Blitz Targeting Obama,* Politico, June 30, 2008,
www.politico.com/news/stories/0608/11452.html (reporting the NRA's plans to
spend $15 million "portraying Barack Obama as a threat to the Second Amend-
ment rights upheld" in *Heller*); Jacob Sullum, *Isn't Self-Defense Common Sense?*
REASONONLINE, February 27, 2008, www.reason.com/news/show/125180.html
("Although [Senator Obama] has learned to pay lip service to the Second Amendment, the details of his past and present positions on gun control suggest he neither understands nor respects the right to keep and bear arms."). Progressives
who now recognize individual rights under the Second Amendment generally
believe the Constitution allows many more forms of gun control than do conservatives. *Compare The O'Reilly Factor* (Fox News Channel television broadcast,
April 23, 2007) (featuring Sen. Charles Schumer saying: "I think certain kinds
of licensing and registration is a reasonable limitation. We do it for cars."), *with*
NRA-ILA, *Fact Sheet: Licensing and Registration,* October 7, 2000, www.nraila
.org/Issues/FactSheets/Read.aspx?id=28 ("[T]hose who wonder what motivates
American gun owners should understand that perhaps only one other word in
the English language so boils their blood as 'registration,' and that word is 'con-
fiscation.' Gun owners fiercely believe those words are ominously related."). The
Democrats in 2008 adopted a party platform that provides: "We . . . will preserve
Americans' Second Amendment right to own and use firearms. We believe that

the right to own firearms is subject to reasonable regulation, . . . [and] [w]e can work together to enact and enforce commonsense laws and improvements—like closing the gun show loophole, improving our background check system, and reinstating the assault weapons ban, so that guns do not fall into the hands of terrorists or criminals." DEMOCRATIC NAT'L CONVENTION, RENEWING AMERICA'S PROMISE: THE 2008 DEMOCRATIC NATIONAL PLATFORM FOR AMERICA 50, *available at* www.democrats.org/a/party/platform.html.

267. *See* Siegel, *Constitutional Culture, supra* note 10.

268. As this comment goes to press, the Republican presidential nominee has energized his campaign by selecting an antiabortion, pro-gun, female vice presidential running mate, who, when introduced at the party's nominating convention, demonstrated her qualifications by mocking the "community organizing" experience of the first black presidential candidate ever nominated by a major political party—with apparent impunity and to great partisan acclaim. *Cf.* Erik Engquist, *Attack on Obama Carries Racial Overtones, Says Paterson,* CRAIN'S N.Y. BUSINESS.COM, September 9, 2008, http://mycrains.crainsnewyork.com /paterson/2008/09/attack-on-obama-carries-racial.html ("Gov. David Paterson this morning said that Republicans' ridiculing of Sen. Barack Obama's community organizing carries racial overtones. . . . McCain spokesman Peter Feldman [countered,] 'This is a tactic that the Obama campaign has used before, and which McCain campaign manager Rick Davis correctly called "divisive, shameful, and wrong"'"). The party's platform affirms the right to bear arms and calls for a president who will appoint judges who will interpret the Constitution as *Heller* did. REPUBLICAN NAT'L CONVENTION, 2008 REPUBLICAN PARTY PLATFORM 51 (2008), http://platform.gop.com/2008Platform.pdf ("We applaud the Supreme Court's decision in Heller affirming [the right to own firearms], and we . . . call on the next president to appoint judges who will similarly respect the Constitution.").

The Second Amendment, *Heller,* and Originalist Jurisprudence

Nelson Lund

DISTRICT OF COLUMBIA V. HELLER *gave the Supreme Court an opportunity to apply a jurisprudence of original meaning to the Second Amendment's manifestly puzzling text. Notwithstanding the chief justice's decision to assign the majority opinion to Justice Scalia, the Court squandered the opportunity.*

In a narrow sense, the Constitution was vindicated in Heller *because the Court reached an easily defensible originalist result. But the Court's reasoning is at critical points so defective—and so transparently non-originalist in some respects—that* Heller *should be seen as an embarrassment for those who joined the majority opinion. It may also be widely (though unfairly) seen as an embarrassment for the interpretive approach that the Court purported to employ. Originalism deserved better from its judicial exponents.*

INTRODUCTION

District of Columbia v. Heller[1] was a Second Amendment test case, brought by a group of libertarian lawyers on behalf of plaintiffs with respectable backgrounds and appealing reasons for seeking relief from the District of Columbia's extremely restrictive gun control regulations. The challenged statute prohibited almost all D.C. residents from possessing handguns, and required that all firearms be kept in an inoperable condition. This effort to disarm the citizenry had been in place for over thirty years, and was the most restrictive gun control law in the country. By a vote of five to four, the Court held that both the handgun ban and the safe-storage regulation violated the Second Amendment, which protects at least the right to keep a handgun in one's own home and to make it operable for purposes of immediate self-defense.

Heller turned out to be a test case in a different sense as well. With almost no relevant precedent to constrain its analysis, the Supreme Court had the opportunity to apply a jurisprudence of original meaning to the Second Amendment's manifestly puzzling text. The Chief Justice seized this opportunity when he assigned the majority opinion to Justice Scalia.

In recent decades, Antonin Scalia and other legal conservatives have used the principles of originalism as a powerful weapon for criticizing decisions that effectively amended the Constitution through judicial fiat.[2] But this has provoked counterattacks alleging that originalism gets deployed primarily as a weapon for selectively attacking decisions that political conservatives find objectionable on policy grounds.[3] This raises an important question: Can originalism truly offer a principled alternative to "living constitutionalism"— one that constrains judicial willfulness and preserves the distinction between law and politics?

In *Heller,* the lawyers who initiated the litigation won their test case, but Justice Scalia flunked his own test. This was a near perfect opportunity for the Court to demonstrate that original meaning jurisprudence is not just "living constitutionalism for conservatives," and it would have been perfectly feasible to provide that demonstration. Instead, Justice Scalia's majority opinion makes a great show of being committed to the Constitution's original meaning but fails to carry through on that commitment.

I should note at the outset that I will give the *Heller* majority opinion the respect that I think it is due by treating it as what it purports to be, namely, a legal opinion that presents the reasons for the decision. Accordingly, I will not speculate about compromises that the justices may have reached among themselves in order to achieve consensus. For all I know, some of them may have said to themselves, in the manner of a U.S. senator, "I'm joining this opinion, although it contains elements with which I disagree, because the good outweighs the bad." But none of them said so publicly. Nor did any member of the *Heller* majority follow the common practice of writing a separate opinion concurring in part and concurring in the judgment. Justice Scalia's opinion is presented as a reasoned interpretation of the law by a court, not as a political compromise, and I will leave others to speculate about logrolling and secret deals.

In a narrow sense, the Constitution was vindicated in *Heller* because the Court reached an easily defensible originalist result. But the Court's reasoning is at critical points so defective—and in some respects so transparently non-originalist—that *Heller* should be seen as an embarrassment for those who joined the majority opinion. It may also be widely (though unfairly) seen as an embarrassment for the interpretive approach that the Court purported to employ. Originalism deserved better from its judicial exponents.

I. ORIGINAL MEANING JURISPRUDENCE, IN BRIEF

All nine members of the *Heller* Court began by accepting the foundation of originalist theory: the Constitution is a written document that was publicly adopted as law, and it therefore means what its words meant to the relevant public audience at the time of its adoption. Originalist jurisprudence is the effort to use this interpretive principle to decide particular questions about what the Constitution requires and forbids.

On a large range of issues, almost everybody assumes that originalism is the proper way for courts to decide cases. Nobody claims, for example, that the minimum age requirements for the president and members of Congress should be measured by a base fifteen numbering system, even though this interpretation of the Constitution would have the salutary effect of keeping some immature people out of office; nor does anyone claim that a base nine system should be applied to the voting age rule in the Twenty-sixth Amendment, even though that would enable many mature and responsible teenagers to exercise the franchise. Similarly, nobody contends that the term "domestic violence" in Article IV refers to the infliction of physical injury on a member of one's household, even though that is the way the term is most often used today. And nobody thinks that the term "arms" in the Second Amendment should be interpreted to mean the upper limbs of the human body, even though that would forestall legal challenges to gun control regulations that are strongly favored by many as a matter of social policy.

The serious challenges for originalism involve questions about its limits as a tool for adjudication.[4] Three main difficulties arise. First, it is sometimes hard to find adequate objective evidence of how the Constitution's text would have been understood by the relevant audience at the time of adoption. Second, it is sometimes difficult to know how the commands in the text should be applied, consistent with its original meaning, to particular circumstances that the enacting public did not consider and often could not have foreseen. Third, courts will inevitably make some decisions based on mistaken interpretations of the Constitution, and later courts will have to decide how much deference to give these precedents.

The last of these difficulties is something of a confounding variable inasmuch as it does not bear directly on the original meaning of most constitutional provisions. Originalists could logically argue that precedents should be given no weight at all: the Constitution is the law, indeed the supreme law of the land, and courts are always obliged to enforce the Constitution as they understand it rather than adhere to prior judicial mistakes. Some academic commentators have taken this position,[5] but no Supreme Court justice has ever done so (at least not consistently), and there is strong evidence that the Vesting Clause of Article III implicitly incorporated a principle of stare decisis.[6]

That principle, however, does not absolutely forbid the overruling of prior decisions, and there has always been room for reasonable debate about the weight to be given to erroneous or questionable precedents in various circumstances.[7] One reason for regarding *Heller* as a particularly important test of originalism is that there were virtually no relevant Supreme Court precedents, and certainly none that could be considered dispositive.

With respect to the other two challenges for originalists, *Heller* was a good test case because the Second Amendment poses some genuine puzzles. Its text, for example, uniquely combines an explanatory preface and a command: "A well regulated Militia, being necessary to the security of a free State, the right of the people to keep and bear Arms, shall not be infringed." What does the preambular reference to the importance of a "well regulated Militia" have to do with the "right of the people" to keep and bear arms? One usually thinks of constitutional rights as obstacles, not spurs, to regulation, and it is not immediately evident (at least to typical twenty-first-century readers) why or how this right to arms would contribute to the establishment or preservation of a well-regulated militia.

A different kind of puzzle arises from changes in the circumstances to which the constitutional provision must be applied. American society is dramatically different from the world in which the Second Amendment was adopted. The militia organizations extolled by the founding generation have fallen into

desuetude, and advances in the technology of weaponry have produced arms
that are far more dangerous than those available in the founding era. Is it even
possible, let alone prudent, to apply the Second Amendment's command to a
modern society in which it could have radically different effects than would
have been expected in 1791?

II. THE THRESHOLD DISPUTE IN *HELLER*, IN BRIEF

The great threshold question in interpreting the Second Amendment concerns the relationship between the prefatory, or preambular, phrase and the
operative clause. Different interpretations of this relationship have generated
two opposing conclusions about the meaning of the text. Those who focus
on the operative clause argue that the protected right is that of individual
citizens to keep and bear their privately owned weapons. Those who focus
on the amendment's preamble argue that the protected right is the right of
state governments to maintain military organizations, or at most a right of
individuals to keep and bear arms while serving in such organizations. In
Heller, Justice Scalia's majority opinion adopts the individual, or private right,
interpretation, while Justice Stevens's dissent adopts the collective right, or
military service, interpretation.[8]

Reduced to the simplest possible summary, Justice Scalia's argument is as
follows. The term "the right of the people" in the operative clause presumptively implies a private right, just as it does in the First and Fourth amendments. The other key terms used in the operative clause—"keep and bear
Arms"—were frequently used in nonmilitary contexts, so the operative clause
does not imply that the right to arms is confined to military purposes. The
right to keep and bear arms, moreover, was already well established before the
Bill of Rights was adopted, and had never been restricted to military activities. The Second Amendment's preface, according to Justice Scalia, explains
why this preexisting right was codified in the Constitution, but does not
change the nature of the right that was thus codified.

Stripped to similarly concise essentials, Justice Stevens's argument is that
the Second Amendment's operative clause strongly suggests a military purpose, especially through its use of the term "bear arms," and certainly does
not unequivocally identify an individual right to have and use weapons for
such private purposes as self-defense. The exclusively military purpose of
the amendment is confirmed, according to Justice Stevens, by the prefatory

phrase and the legislative history, which together establish that the Second Amendment was meant to protect only "the right of the people of each of the several States to maintain a well-regulated militia."[9]

Taken as a whole, Justice Scalia's originalist arguments in favor of the private right interpretation are overwhelmingly more powerful than Justice Stevens's originalist arguments in favor of the military service interpretation. I do not agree with all of the arguments that Justice Scalia advances, and he omits some arguments that I think would have strengthened his case. I also think that Justice Stevens could have made a better argument than he did for upholding the challenged regulations. But none of this detracts from the utterly one-sided character of the dispute. In order to keep this article to a reasonable length, I will refrain from a detailed analysis of the arguments and counterarguments in the *Heller* opinions on this point, many of which I have discussed elsewhere.[10] In light of the criticisms that I will make below, however, I want to state as emphatically as I can that Justice Scalia's important threshold conclusion is correct on originalist grounds: the Second Amendment does protect a private right to keep and bear arms for the purpose of self-defense.

III. THE PURPOSE OF THE PREFACE

The strongest parts of Justice Scalia's opinion are those in which he analyzes the language of the Second Amendment's operative clause and reviews the historical evidence showing that this language was originally understood to protect an individual, private right to keep and bear arms. But very little of that evidence speaks to the scope of the right, and Justice Scalia properly assumes that the right cannot possibly be unlimited.[11] So where do we look for the limits? One obvious place to look is the prefatory phrase, if for no other reason than that this phrase and the operative clause must be interpreted so as to form a consistent whole, as Justice Scalia acknowledges.

Justice Scalia's effort to reconcile the two different statements in the text of the Second Amendment begins with his assertion that the language of the operative clause implies that it protects a preexisting right.[12] As a matter of linguistic analysis, this is fallacious. One could write a constitutional amendment, for example, that said, "The right to travel to Cuba shall not be infringed" or "The right to medical care at government expense shall not be infringed." Such language does not imply the preexistence of a right to travel to Cuba or a right to free medical care. Of course, there certainly was a pre-existing right to keep and bear arms in 1791, and the Second Amendment can be read as referring to that right. But must it be so read?

Not if you interpret the Second Amendment's prefatory phrase as defining the purpose and therefore the scope of the right. In that case, you might conclude that the right to arms is protected only to the extent that it contributes to the maintenance of a well-regulated militia. In order to invalidate the D.C. gun regulations, you would then have to show that the regulations are inconsistent with maintaining a well-regulated militia, which would not be easy to do. Justice Scalia tries to avoid this challenge by asserting that the Second Amendment's preface tells us nothing about the scope or purpose of the right to bear arms, but merely explains why the right was codified in the Constitution.[13] This may be the best reading of the text, as I think it is, but Justice Scalia merely asserts his conclusion.[14]

Justice Scalia's explanation of the purpose of the codification, moreover, makes no sense. He asserts that "the Second Amendment's prefatory clause announces the purpose for which the right was codified: to prevent elimination of the militia."[15] This is false. The text of the Second Amendment refers to "a well regulated militia," not to "the militia." It is self-evident that these are not synonymous terms, and Justice Scalia himself acknowledges as much when he distinguishes between an organized and an unorganized militia.[16] Building on his erroneous conflation of "a well regulated militia" and "the militia," Justice Scalia claims that the original Constitution and the Second Amendment both assume that "the militia" is already in existence, and that it means "all able-bodied men."[17] This is not exactly wrong,[18] but it makes nonsense of Justice Scalia's claim that the purpose of codifying the right to arms was to prevent "elimination of the militia." The nation's able-bodied men would not be eliminated if the government were to disarm them or anyone else.[19]

Justice Scalia never even addresses the most difficult, and therefore the most important, question: How could codifying the right to arms have been expected to preserve, promote, or prevent the elimination of a *well-regulated* militia? I believe there is a perfectly good answer to this question,[20] but no answer of any kind will be found in Justice Scalia's *Heller* opinion. And that is a very, very serious shortcoming in a judicial opinion that purports to rely as heavily as *Heller* does on textual analysis and originalist interpretive principles.

IV. THE PREEXISTING RIGHT

Let us assume, for the sake of argument, that Justice Scalia is right to say that the Second Amendment's preface means that the right to arms was codified in order to prevent the elimination of the militia. That does not by itself help decide the case that was before the Court. A handgun ban, let alone a handgun ban that applies only in the District of Columbia, would plainly not eliminate the militia. Even more plainly, D.C.'s safe-storage law for rifles and shotguns would not eliminate the militia, or even interfere with the ability of able-bodied men to perform militia duties. Justice Scalia tries to solve this problem by arguing that the purpose for which the right to arms was codified is completely irrelevant in determining the scope of the right. Rather, the scope or content of the constitutional right is the scope or content of the pre-existing right that the Constitution codified, and modern laws that infringe that historically determinate right are unconstitutional.

Even if Justice Scalia failed to present good reasons for treating the Second Amendment's preamble as irrelevant in defining the scope of the protected right, his decision to do so could still be right, as I believe it was.[21] And the next step in his analysis looks like the purest and most faithful kind of originalism. All we need to do is check the historical sources to find out what the preexisting right was, much as Justice Scalia ably checked the historical sources to determine the meaning of various words and phrases used in the constitutional text. If a modern gun control statute would have infringed the historically identified preexisting right, it is unconstitutional, period.

That approach promises to eliminate the need for policy-driven interest balancing and easily manipulated multifactor tests, and it rules out flighty living constitutionalizing. As Justice Scalia puts it: "Constitutional rights are enshrined with the scope they were understood to have when the people adopted them, whether or not future legislatures or (yes) even future judges think that scope too broad. . . . Like the First, [the Second Amendment] is the very *product* of an interest-balancing by the people—which Justice Breyer would now conduct for them anew."[22]

This passage is almost enough to make an originalist stand up and cheer. But perhaps the cheering should be postponed until we examine how Justice Scalia's historical approach resolves the case before the Court. His discussion has two main elements. First, he makes a good historical case that the preexisting right to arms was considered important because it protected the ability of people to exercise their natural right of self-defense. That natural right extends both to the people's right to oppose tyrannical governments and to the right of individuals to respond with force against threats from which the government fails to protect them, such as violent criminals. Second, Justice Scalia shows that none of the statutory limitations on the right to arms prior to 1791, of which there are not many examples, was remotely as restrictive as the D.C. statutes at issue in *Heller*.[23]

Because Justice Scalia successfully demonstrated that self-defense was the purpose of the preexisting right, D.C.'s safe-storage regulation presented an easy case. A requirement that all firearms be disabled at all times constitutes an almost complete deprivation of the right to have firearms for self-defense, and is therefore clearly unconstitutional.[24] But what about the handgun ban? Evaluating that regulation requires a more precise description of the scope of the preexisting right.

The most obviously originalist approach would ask what kind of gun regulations were accepted, or acceptable, in the late eighteenth century. These would include, presumably, those that were actually adopted (at least if they were widespread and noncontroversial) and those that would have been permissible according to well-accepted legal principles at the time. But how can we determine which laws that were never even considered would have been acceptable if they had been proposed?

One possibility, easily ruled out, is that the scope of the Second Amendment is coextensive with the constitutional right enshrined in the English Bill of Rights.[25] That right was expressly subject to abridgement by the legislature, and it belonged by its terms only to Protestants.[26]

A somewhat more plausible alternative might be the preexisting right that Americans enjoyed under their state constitutions. But most state constitutions did not include right-to-arms provisions.[27] And in the states that did have such constitutional provisions, how could we now determine the scope of the right they protected? The paucity of eighteenth-century gun control laws might have reflected a lack of political demand rather than constitutional limitations. Since American legislatures had enacted scarcely any gun control statutes, there was little reason to wonder how far they could constitutionally go in restricting access to firearms, let alone reason for anyone to determine those limits with the legal precision needed to assess specific modern regulations like the D.C. handgun ban.

The remaining historical source that might define the scope of the preexisting right to arms is the common law as it was understood at the time, and as it had been modified by statutes before 1791. If the scope of the preexisting right to arms is to be determined solely by a historical inquiry, this is the most plausible place to look. The Second Amendment might have incorporated that law, much as the Seventh Amendment has been held to have "frozen" the law/equity distinction as it existed in 1791.[28] Modern gun control regulations would then be upheld only if they had close analogues in identifiable common law or statutory restrictions in place at that time, just as modern causes of action are covered by the Seventh Amendment only if they are more like cases that in 1791 would have been tried at law rather than in equity.[29]

Whatever the merits of this line of analysis (to which I will return below), the *Heller* Court did not conduct this historical inquiry, or any other, in evaluating D.C.'s handgun ban. Instead, Justice Scalia announced the following conclusion:

> The handgun ban amounts to a prohibition of an entire class of "arms" that *is* overwhelmingly chosen by American society for that lawful purpose [*viz.* self-defense]. The prohibition extends, moreover, to the home, where the need for defense of self, family, and property is most acute. Under any of the standards of scrutiny that we have applied to enumerated constitutional rights, banning from the home "the most preferred firearm in the nation to 'keep' and use for protection of one's home and family," would fail constitutional muster. . . .
>
> It is no answer to say, as petitioners do, that it is permissible to ban the possession of handguns so long as the possession of other firearms (i.e., long guns) is allowed. It is enough to note, as we have observed, that the American people have considered the handgun to be the quintessential self-defense weapon. There are many reasons that a citizen may prefer a handgun for home defense: It is easier to store in a location that is readily accessible in an emergency; it cannot easily be redirected or wrestled away by an attacker; it is easier to use for those without the upper-body strength to lift and aim a long gun; it can be pointed at a burglar with one hand while the other hand dials the police. Whatever the reason, handguns *are* the most popular weapon chosen by Americans for self-defense in the home, and a complete prohibition of their use is invalid.[30]

This does not even purport to be a historical analysis. It consists entirely of a report (or supposition) about what arms Americans *today* prefer to keep for self-defense, along with a few of the reasons that may make these preferences sensible. Is this a form of living constitutionalism, in which the scope of a constitutional right is defined largely by judicial perceptions of current social mores? Or is it the result of a covertly Breyer-esque judicial interest balancing, in which the Court has concluded that Americans should be allowed to keep handguns because their advantages over long guns outweigh their disadvantages? Whatever it is, this is not the result of a historical study of the scope of the preexisting eighteenth-century right to arms. And if Justice Scalia's explanation of the Court's handgun holding rests on any kind of originalist analysis at all, it is pretty well disguised.

V. ACTIVIST DICTA

Originalism can face some tough challenges in resolving specific cases. If tough challenges can be met only with a quick and unacknowledged transition to living constitutionalism, or with a self-confident ipse dixit, this approach to constitutional adjudication deserves much of the scorn it has received from sophisticated academic critics.

Had Justice Scalia's *Heller* opinion done no more than feed these critics with its insouciant analysis of the D.C. handgun ban, that would be bad enough. Unfortunately, the Court compounded this sin with an astounding series of dubious obiter dicta pronouncing on the constitutionality of a wide range of gun control regulations that were not before the Court. Justice Scalia seems to promise an "exhaustive historical analysis" supporting these conclusions in future cases.[31] If that turns out to be anything like the analysis he used in ruling on the D.C. handgun ban, it will not be exhaustive and it will not be historical. In any event, one should not hold one's breath while waiting for these cases—lower courts routinely treat Supreme Court dicta as though they were holdings, and the Court routinely declines to review such decisions.

Because the *Heller* dicta will likely be treated as law for all practical purposes, it is worth asking how much basis they have in the original meaning of the Second Amendment. These dicta, moreover, throw some revealing light on Justice Scalia's failure to present a historical or originalist argument for striking down the D.C. handgun ban.

A. POTENTIAL ABUSERS

"[N]othing in our opinion should be taken to cast doubt on longstanding prohibitions on the possession of firearms by felons and the mentally ill."[32] This certainly sounds unobjectionable, at least at first. But how "longstanding" are these prohibitions? Justice Scalia either doesn't know or chose not to tell us. Apparently, however, the first general ban on the possession of firearms by felons was enacted in 1968.[33] Longstanding? This was 177 years after the adoption of the Second Amendment, and less than a decade before the D.C. handgun ban was enacted.

Aside from the absence of historical support for the claim that such prohibitions are consistent with the preexisting right to arms, they are inconsistent with what Justice Scalia himself calls its "core," namely, self-defense.[34] On what understanding of that core does it make any sense to leave American citizens defenseless in their own homes for the rest of their lives on the basis of nothing more than a nonviolent felony like tax evasion or insider trading? It would make more sense to say that the government may *silence* these felons for the rest of their lives—regulatory crimes, after all, usually involve an abuse of speech, such as making false statements to the government or negotiating contracts that the government forbids. Such regulatory crimes have nothing at all to do with violence or the use of firearms.

It might have been possible for the *Heller* Court to elaborate a plausible historical analysis addressing the issue that Justice Scalia gratuitously raised. C. Kevin Marshall, for example, has examined the history of regulations restricting access to weapons by those convicted of crimes, both before and after the Bill of Rights was adopted. While acknowledging that this history cannot solve all line-drawing problems, Marshall makes a powerful case that the traditional understanding of the right to arms did not authorize much more than laws forbidding those convicted of *crimes of violence* to carry firearms *outside* their homes, and possibly also forbidding them to possess easily concealable weapons, at least for as long as the offender continued to present a credible threat of recidivism.[35]

Imputing this understanding of the right to the Second Amendment might not be unreasonable, but Justice Scalia's casual and sweeping dictum is a very long way from Marshall's analysis, both in method and in result.[36]

B. Gun-Free Zones

Heller next endorses prohibitions on "the carrying of firearms in sensitive places such as schools and government buildings."[37] Were Americans forbidden to carry firearms in schools and government buildings prior to 1791? Justice Scalia does not even pretend to make such a claim. Nor does he explain what makes these places "sensitive," or how courts are supposed to go about determining the scope of this newly announced exception to the right to arms. Is a university campus more "sensitive" than a shopping mall across the street? Is a government-owned cabin in a national forest more "sensitive" than a public road or a privately owned hotel? Why or why not? Did the whole city of New Orleans become a "sensitive" place after Hurricane Katrina, thus justifying the government in forcibly disarming law-abiding citizens whom the government was unable to protect from roving bands of criminals?[38]

Maybe this dictum about sensitive places simply means that judges will decide whether the costs of allowing citizens to take their guns to certain places exceed the benefits. If so, it is not easy to see the difference between this approach and the Breyer analysis that Justice Scalia ridicules with the following observation: "The very enumeration of the right takes out of the hands of government—even the Third Branch of Government—the power to decide on a case-by-case basis whether the right is *really worth* insisting upon. A constitutional guarantee subject to future judges' assessments of its usefulness is no constitutional guarantee at all."[39] Well, there is one difference between Justice Scalia's approach and Justice Breyer's: Justice Breyer goes to the trouble of actually conducting a cost-benefit analysis.

C. Commercial Transactions

The *Heller* majority next endorses "laws imposing conditions and qualifications on the commercial sale of arms."[40] Once again, Justice Scalia presents no historical evidence about the nature or even existence of pre-1791 commercial regulations. Nor does he suggest any limit on the government's power to impose "conditions and qualifications" on these commercial transactions. For all we are told here, Congress could place a prohibitively high tax on the sale of firearms, or create burdensome regulatory obstacles that would make it impractical for a commercial market to exist. If the Court means that it would approve only reasonable conditions and qualifications, it failed to say so, and it suggested no criteria by which reasonable restrictions could be distinguished from unreasonable restrictions.

D. Concealed Carry

The Court introduces the three Second Amendment exceptions just discussed with the unimpeachable observation that the right protected by the Second Amendment is not unlimited, and with the historical claim that "the majority of the 19th-century courts to consider the question held that prohibitions on carrying concealed weapons were lawful under the Second Amendment or state analogues."[41] This appears to be an endorsement of yet another exception to the constitutional right.

Justice Scalia provides no evidence of any such prohibitions prior to 1791, and the nineteenth-century cases do not provide direct evidence of the scope of the preexisting right. Nor does Justice Scalia explain why or to what extent judicial decisions under state analogues of the Second Amendment would be relevant to the original meaning of the Second Amendment. Nor does he provide arguments to support his apparent assumption that the majority of nineteenth-century state cases were correctly decided.

Perhaps the "exhaustive historical analysis" alluded to by Justice Scalia will someday provide good answers to some of these questions.[42] A cursory look at the early leading cases, however, suggests that an exhaustive analysis is more likely to undermine his conclusion than to support it. The first court to consider the issue, for example, held that restrictions on concealed carry were unconstitutional, contrary to Justice Scalia's suggested interpretation of the Second Amendment.[43] This decision is especially significant both because it is nearest in time to the founding era[44] and because the state court assumed (just as Justice Scalia does) that the constitutional provision at issue codified a preexisting right. Later cases did uphold such laws, but they did not purport to adopt precodification understandings of the scope of a preexisting right to arms, and they rested on interpretive principles and conclusions that *Heller* itself rejects.[45]

The two state cases actually cited by Justice Scalia, moreover, offer little support for his conclusion. The first was an 1850 decision that involved the validity of an 1813 Louisiana statute making it a misdemeanor to carry a concealed weapon. The Louisiana court concluded:

> This law became absolutely necessary to counteract a vicious state of society, growing out of the habit of carrying concealed weapons, and to prevent bloodshed and assassinations committed upon unsuspecting persons. It interfered with no man's right to carry arms (to use its words) "in full open view," which places men upon an equality. This is the right guaranteed by the Constitution of the United States, and which is calculated to incite men to a manly and noble defence of themselves, if necessary, and of their country, without any tendency to secret advantages and unmanly assassinations.[46]

In 1846 the Georgia Supreme Court declared that the Second Amendment was violated by an ambiguously worded statute that appeared to make it a misdemeanor to sell or use any handgun except a "horseman's pistol."[47] The court concluded: "We are of the opinion, then, that so far as the act of 1837 seeks to suppress the practice of carrying certain weapons *secretly*, that it is valid, inasmuch as it does not deprive the citizen of his *natural* right of self-defence, or of his constitutional right to keep and bear arms. But that so much of it, as contains a prohibition against bearing arms *openly*, is in conflict with the Constitution, and *void*."[48] These decisions reflected a belief that there would seldom be reason to conceal a weapon on one's person unless one had a criminal intent. The presumption of criminal intent may well have been sensible in a world where the open carry of weapons was common and socially accepted, as it may have been in Georgia in 1846 and Louisiana in 1850. But the world of 1791 may have been different, and America today is certainly very different.

It is far from evident that these two state courts would have approved concealed carry prohibitions in other circumstances, in which a presumption of criminal intent would be much less deserving of credence and in which a prohibition on concealed carry might operate to "deprive the citizen of his natural right of self-defence."[49] In some American jurisdictions today, for example, openly carrying a firearm might plausibly be thought to violate the ancient common law prohibition against "terrifying the good people of the land" by going about with dangerous and unusual weapons.[50] If courts were to conclude that open carry violates this common law prohibition (and thus is not within the preexisting right protected by the Second Amendment), after *Heller* has decreed that bans on concealed carry are per se valid, the constitutional right to bear arms would effectively cease to exist.

E. Dangerous and Unusual Weapons

"[We] read *Miller* to say only that the Second Amendment does not protect those weapons not typically possessed by law-abiding citizens for lawful purposes, such as short-barreled shotguns. That accords with the historical understanding of the scope of the right, see Part III, *infra*."[51] The claims in both these sentences verge on the risible.

Beginning with the second of Justice Scalia's two claims, the historical discussion in Part III of the *Heller* opinion asserts that the conclusion attributed to *Miller* "is fairly supported by the historical tradition of prohibiting the carrying of 'dangerous and unusual weapons.' "[52] Note that Justice Scalia can claim at most that there is a tradition of prohibitions on the *carrying* of certain arms, not on their possession. That is quite different from his more general claim (attributed to *Miller*) that these weapons are not protected by the Second Amendment at all. But even the narrower point is wrong, or at best exceedingly misleading, as one can see by looking at the sources referenced in the long string cite that Justice Scalia offers in support of his assertion.[53]

- His first authority, William Blackstone, does use the term "dangerous or unusual weapons," but Blackstone does not say that there is a general prohibition on carrying them: "The offence of *riding* or *going armed*, with dangerous or unusual weapons, is a crime against the public peace, by terrifying the good people of the land."[54] Blackstone goes on to say that this practice was particularly prohibited by the fourteenth-century statute of Northampton, which Blackstone cites but does not quote.

  That statute was worded more broadly than Blackstone's summary of the common law, as it purported to command that no one go armed "by night nor by day, in fairs, markets, nor in the presence of the justices or other ministers, nor in no part elsewhere."[55] The statute does not appear ever to have been enforced except in accordance with the "terrifying" limitation articulated by Blackstone. When James II, for example, used the statute to prosecute a political opponent in a famous case, he was careful to charge the defendant with carrying a gun into church "to terrifie the King's Subjects."[56] In any event, King's Bench recognized in that case a "general Connivance to Gentlemen to ride armed for their security," and the jury acquitted the defendant.[57] Justice Scalia should have been aware of all this information, which was presented in one of the *Heller* briefs.[58]

- Justice Scalia's next cite is to James Wilson's *Lectures on Law*. Wilson essentially repeats Blackstone's definition of the common law crime, noting that "there may be an affray, where there is no actual violence; as where a man arms himself with dangerous and unusual weapons, *in such a manner,* as will naturally diffuse a terrour among the people."[59]

- The same limited exception to the right to bear arms appears in Justice Scalia's next authority, an 1815 New York treatise, which reports, "It is likewise said to be an affray, at common law, for a man to arm himself with dangerous and unusual weapons, *in such manner as will naturally cause terror to the people.*"[60]

- Justice Scalia's next source is even more emphatic about the limited nature of this exception to the right to bear arms. An 1822 Kentucky treatise reports: "Riding or going armed with dangerous or unusual weapons, is a crime against the public peace, by terrifying the people of the land . . . . But here it should be remembered, that in this country the constitution guarranties to all persons the right to bear arms; then it can only be a crime to exercise this right in such a manner, as to terrify the people unnecessarily."[61]

- The next treatise, from 1831, repeats the standard, limited definition of a nonviolent affray, and adds a discussion of both the fourteenth-century statute of Northampton and the narrowing constructions that statute had received in England.[62]

- An 1840 treatise reports, without further elaboration, that the statute of Northampton made it a misdemeanor to ride or go armed with dangerous or unusual weapons.[63]

- Finally, an 1852 treatise repeats the usual definition of an affray, adds a citation to the statute of Northampton, and concludes by reviewing a handful of apparently conflicting state decisions on the constitutionality of restrictions on the right to bear arms in public.[64]

- To the list of these treatises, Justice Scalia adds citations to four nineteenth-century state cases, introduced with a "see also" signal.[65] All four of these cases repeat the familiar definition of an affray, including the qualification involving terror to the people.

  Only one of the four cases adds anything relevant to Justice Scalia's claim, but that case affirmatively undermines his contention that the Second Amendment covers only weapons that are "typically possessed by law-abiding citizens for lawful purposes."[66] In 1871 the Supreme Court of Texas interpreted the Second Amendment to cover only "the arms of a militiaman or soldier," but this included all such weapons, including even "the field piece, siege gun, and mortar."[67]

In sum, Justice Scalia educes exactly zero historical support for his claim that the original meaning of the Second Amendment covers only those arms that are in common civilian use at any given time.

That brings us to *Miller*, whose holding resembles that of the 1871 Texas court and is by its terms directly contrary to Justice Scalia's claim:

> In the absence of any evidence tending to show that possession or use
> of a "shotgun having a barrel of less than eighteen inches in length"
> at this time has some reasonable relationship to the preservation or
> efficiency of a well regulated militia, we cannot say that the Second
> Amendment guarantees the right to keep and bear such an instru-
> ment. Certainly it is not within judicial notice that this weapon is any
> part of the ordinary military equipment or that its use could contrib-
> ute to the common defense.[68]

Justice Scalia claims that reading this holding to mean that short-barreled
shotguns are protected by the Second Amendment if they have military utility
would involve "a startling reading of the opinion, since it would mean that the
[1934] National Firearms Act's restrictions on machineguns (not challenged
in *Miller*) might be unconstitutional, machineguns being useful in warfare in
1939."[69] Not very startling at all, once you recognize that *Miller* nowhere says
or implies that the government is forbidden to place restrictions on protected
weapons. And that *Miller* says nothing about what restrictions might be permissible. And that *Miller* does not foreclose the possibility that the government might be permitted to put more restrictions on some protected weapons than on others. Justice Scalia must have been startled by something that
Miller did not say, which hardly justifies the Court in ignoring what *Miller*
did say.

Rather than focusing on the obvious narrowness of the *Miller* holding,
Justice Scalia argues that *Miller* implies that the Second Amendment does
not protect arms unless they are typically possessed by civilians for lawful
civilian purposes. He attempts to derive this implication from a statement
of historical fact that appears later in the *Miller* opinion, and in a different
context. Commenting on the meaning of the term "militia" at the time the
Bill of Rights was adopted, *Miller* says, "[O]rdinarily when called for service
these men [i.e., members of the militia] were expected to appear bearing arms
supplied by themselves and of the kind in common use at the time."[70] This is
perfectly consistent with *Miller*'s plain insistence that the Second Amendment covers only weapons with military utility. It would not make much sense
to expect men to appear for military service armed with weapons that have no
military utility or are not commonly used for military purposes.

In an acrobatic but unexplained leap, however, Justice Scalia concludes that
Miller's holding refers only to weapons that are in common *civilian* use at the
time. As a matter of historical fact, it may well be true that eighteenth-century

civilians commonly kept for private purposes the same kinds of weapons that they were expected to bring with them when called for service in the militia. That is why the *Miller* Court could reasonably have thought this historical fact relevant to its conclusion that the Second Amendment does protect weapons that have military utility. But it cannot support Justice Scalia's bizarre conclusion that *Miller*'s reference to weapons that are "part of the ordinary military equipment or [whose] use could contribute to the common defense" is actually a reference to weapons typically possessed by law-abiding citizens only for lawful *civilian* purposes.

It is possible that this weird and untenable reading of *Miller* was driven at least in part by Justice Scalia's mistaken belief that "[t]he judgment in the case upheld against a Second Amendment challenge two men's federal convictions for transporting an unregistered short-barreled shotgun in interstate commerce, in violation of the National Firearms Act."[71] If *Miller* had upheld convictions for violating these regulations, it might colorably be argued that the Court did so because short-barreled shotguns are outside the scope of the Second Amendment. In fact, the extremely concise *Miller* opinion plainly stated that *there had been no convictions,* and the Court remanded the case for further proceedings in which the defendants might well have established that short-barreled shotguns meet the legal test set out in its holding.

The notion that *Miller* concluded that short-barreled shotguns, let alone machine guns, are unprotected by the Second Amendment is an indefensible canard.[72] Justice Scalia's claim that there is an exception from the Second Amendment for weapons that are not in common civilian use was neither dictated nor supported by judicial precedent, and it has no basis in the historical sources he cites.

Justice Scalia's baseless assertion also makes no sense under originalist principles. Under the rule that he conjured from his misreadings of history and precedent, short-barreled shotguns and machine guns are per se excluded from protection by the Second Amendment. Why? Because they are not "typically possessed by law-abiding citizens for lawful purposes" today. Congress assured that this test could not be met when it imposed oppressive tax and regulatory burdens, beginning in 1934, that guaranteed such weapons would not be in common use. But for that congressional action, these arms might be quite common today.[73] Thus, Justice Scalia's test empowers Congress to create its own exceptions to the Second Amendment, so long as the Supreme Court waits a while before it asks whether particular weapons are in common civilian use.

Suppose, for example, that the federal handgun ban imposed in the District of Columbia in 1976 had been applied by Congress to the entire nation that same year. If a case challenging the ban had not reached the Supreme Court until 2008, the ban would presumably have been upheld under the test that Justice Scalia invented in order to justify bans on machine guns and short-barreled shotguns. This result would also have been supported by Justice Scalia's use of the term "longstanding" to characterize felon-in-possession laws that did not exist until 1968.

Alternatively, suppose Congress decides now or in the future to adopt "laws imposing conditions and qualifications on the commercial sale"[74] of handguns, perhaps along the lines of the conditions and qualifications that have been used to suppress the market for short-barreled shotguns and machine guns. Given the large number of handguns already owned by civilians, it might take some time for handguns to become as rare as machine guns or short-barreled shotguns. But the government could presumably accelerate that process by purchasing handguns from their current owners, especially if onerous burdens (such as high taxes on ammunition) were placed on those who were reluctant to sell. Presto! A handgun ban would no longer be an unconstitutional law that "amounts to a prohibition of an entire class of 'arms' that is overwhelmingly chosen by American society for [the] lawful purpose [of self-defense]."[75]

Before composing a dictum that impliedly permits Congress to decide which arms are protected by the Second Amendment, Justice Scalia might have reflected on his own pointed comment earlier in the opinion: "Constitutional rights are enshrined with the scope they were understood to have when the people adopted them, whether or not future legislatures or (yes) even future judges think that scope too broad."[76]

The Court should have refrained from issuing dicta on an array of issues to which it had apparently devoted little thought and less research. One might have expected Chief Justice Roberts, at least, to insist on what he has called "the cardinal principle of judicial restraint—if it is not necessary to decide more, it is necessary not to decide more."[77]

It is possible, of course, that *Heller*'s wide-ranging and unsupported dicta will someday be disavowed (or, in typical judicial fashion, "clarified"). *Heller* itself provides a model for doing so. Dismissing a comment about the Second Amendment in an earlier case, Justice Scalia says, "It is inconceivable that we would rest our interpretation of the basic meaning of any guarantee of the

Bill of Rights upon such a footnoted dictum in a case where the point was not at issue and was not argued."[78] The *Heller* dicta deserve the same dismissive treatment.

VI. WHAT MIGHT A GENUINELY ORIGINALIST COURT HAVE DONE?

Perhaps the Court will someday provide an originalist rationale for *Heller's* invalidation of the D.C. handgun ban—a rationale that *Heller* promised but did not deliver. Meanwhile, this case will stand as a monument to a peculiar kind of jurisprudence, which might charitably be called half-hearted originalism.[79]

Was there a better alternative? *Heller's* successful effort at originalism begins and ends with its persuasive demonstration that the Second Amendment protects an individual and private right to keep and bear arms, at least for the legitimate purpose of self-defense. The fundamental problem with the *Heller* opinion is its failure to admit that some questions about the original meaning of the Constitution cannot be answered on the basis of a bare textual and historical inquiry. The logic of Justice Scalia's theory that the Second Amendment codified a preexisting right would render virtually all modern gun control regulations unconstitutional because few regulations existed in 1791 (leaving everyone with the right to do anything that was not forbidden), and there is no historical record indicating what kinds of regulations that were not then adopted would have been considered permissible.

This interpretation of the original understanding of the Second Amendment is not altogether implausible. The Bill of Rights was originally understood to apply only to the federal government, and the states were left completely free to adopt new gun control laws in light of changed circumstances or changes in public opinion. Oddly, however, nobody at the time appears to have asked whether the federal government would be restrained by the Bill of Rights in governing the territories or the federal seat of government. The D.C. handgun ban, of course, raises exactly this question.

It is now settled that the Bill of Rights applies in the District of Columbia, and the courts have little choice but to fashion a jurisprudence that answers new questions that went unasked at the time of the framing.[80] Justice Scalia's historical, preexisting-right approach cannot provide useful or reliable guidance on all these issues, and it is hardly surprising that he resolved the handgun issue without performing the historical analysis he promised.

This forces one to ask what courts should do instead. The alternatives can be roughly grouped into four main categories.

Living Constitutionalism. In its purest form, this approach simply replaces the written Constitution with the political preferences of contemporary judges, at least on matters that the judges consider sufficiently important. *Roe v. Wade*[81] is the most frequently cited example, but another excellent specimen is *Home Building & Loan Ass'n v. Blaisdell*,[82] in which the Court declared the original meaning of the Contracts Clause irrelevant. The dissenting opinion in that case advanced unrebutted historical evidence that the clause was adopted primarily to prevent the state governments from adopting exactly the sort of debtor relief law that was challenged in *Blaisdell* itself.[83] The majority simply declared that times had changed, and that the Court was free to change the Constitution to fit the times.[84] This decision was especially egregious because there was not even a plausible argument that times had changed in a way that created a need for judges to amend the Constitution. The *Blaisdell* case arose as a result of a nationwide economic depression, and the Court did not even pause to consider that the Contracts Clause left unimpaired the power of Congress to adopt debtor relief laws pursuant to the Bankruptcy Clause.

Judicial Deferentialism. An alternative possibility is that courts might refuse to strike down any statute unless it is indubitably inconsistent with the Constitution. This approach—defended more than a century ago by James Bradley Thayer and more recently by Lino Graglia[85]—seems to have been followed by the Supreme Court, in substance if not always in form, in some areas of the law during some periods of our history. This might explain, at least in part, the absence of pre-twentieth-century decisions invalidating any statutes under the Free Speech and Free Exercise of Religion Clauses,[86] as well as some modern decisions that reject strong constitutional challenges to exceedingly questionable exercises of congressional power.[87]

This approach is like living constitutionalism to the extent that it does not treat the Constitution as binding law. The main difference is that it puts the power to amend the Constitution in the legislature rather than in the judiciary.

Living Constitutionalism in Originalist Clothes. A different approach is to read various vague and ambiguous constitutional provisions as warrants for courts to vindicate broad principles of justice and convenience. Taken to an extreme, this might authorize courts to treat the Constitution's Preamble as the critical text (much in the way that Justice Stevens treated the Second Amendment's preambular language). Thus, for example, if judges thought that legislative restrictions on abortion, bestiality, or the distribution of recreational drugs were unjust, they could strike them down on the basis of that text. Similarly, if judges thought that the general welfare required a president to be allowed a third term in office, or required that an important treaty be treated as valid without Senate ratification, they could rest such decisions on the text of the Constitution's Preamble. This would be practically indistinguishable from pure living constitutionalism.

A related variant is exemplified by Professor Jack Balkin's recent effort to argue, on originalist grounds, that the Fourteenth Amendment protects a right to abortion.[88] Abortion restrictions were commonplace in 1868, and Professor Balkin offers no evidence that the words of the Fourteenth Amendment would have been understood at the time to make these restrictions unconstitutional. Instead, he invokes select passages in the legislative history to support his conclusion that the Fourteenth Amendment stands for a general principle of "equal citizenship."[89] With this elastic principle in hand, Professor Balkin argues that a broad right to abortion is necessary to vindicate women's right to equal citizenship. The scope of that right turns out to be almost the same as the one generated through pure living constitutionalism in the *Roe-Casey* line of decisions.

Using Professor Balkin's interpretive technique, one could just as easily argue that state laws *permitting* abortions (except perhaps to save the life of the mother) are unconstitutional. Unborn children are a vulnerable and politically powerless minority, and laws allowing them to be selectively killed deprives them of the "equal protection of the laws" in a much more obvious way than abortion restrictions deprive women (an electoral majority) of equal citizenship. It may be true, as Professor Balkin argues, that the words of the Fourteenth Amendment would not have been thought applicable to the unborn when the Fourteenth Amendment was adopted, but it is no less true that those words would not have been thought to create a right to abortion.

An interpretive approach that can so readily produce such diametrically opposite results dissolves the distinction between originalism and living constitutionalism. A moderately clever and determined practitioner of such "originalism" should be able to get just about any result that a living constitutionalist might desire. And Professor Balkin's own presentation of his version of originalism comes asymptotically close to pure living constitutionalism: "[I]t follows from my [i.e., Professor Balkin's] arguments that there could be other constitutional principles [i.e., other than "equal citizenship"] embodied by the Equal Protection Clause that no particular person living in 1868 intended but that we come to recognize through our country's historical experience."[90]

Conscientious Originalism. Professor Balkin's essay, misguided though I think it is, recognizes an important truth that Justice Scalia refused to acknowledge in *Heller.* The core of originalism is the proposition that text and history impose meaningful, binding constraints on interpretive discretion, but this does not mean that every legal question can be answered by identifying (or guessing at) what Professor Balkin calls the "original expectations" of the lawmakers. Unless one rejects originalism in favor of living constitutionalism or judicial deferentialism, some recourse to the purposes or principles of the Constitution's provisions is unavoidable.

That means that there will often be room for reasonable disagreements about the right way to resolve particular disputes about the original meaning of the document. The challenge for originalist theory, and for originalist jurisprudence, is to distinguish genuinely originalist interpretations from those that amount to living constitutionalism or judicial deferentialism dressed up in originalist clothing.

Without pretending to present an adequately elaborated interpretive theory, I would describe the approach that courts ought to follow as "conscientious originalism." When the Constitution's text—understood as the historical sources tell us it was or would have been originally understood—provides an answer to a legal question, that answer should be treated as binding (subject to whatever qualifications are imposed by an appropriately originalist doctrine of stare decisis). This will answer a great many constitutional questions, as, for example, whether the Second Amendment protects an individual and private right to arms or a state's right to maintain militia organizations. When there is such an answer, that is the end of the analysis.

When the text does not supply an adequately precise answer, a conscientiously originalist court has no choice but to decide the issue in light of the purpose of the provision as that purpose was understood by those who adopted it. This is not an algorithm, and it does not sufficiently describe what kinds of evidence should be considered or the relative weights that various kinds of arguments and evidence deserve. Nor is it enough to establish that any particular interpretation, like the Fourteenth Amendment abortion argument offered by Professor Balkin, is wrong. I offer it here only as a broad and crude indication of the approach that I think the *Heller* Court could have and should have employed in evaluating the constitutionality of the D.C. handgun ban.[91]

Unlike section 1 of the Fourteenth Amendment, whose original purpose is quite difficult to identify with the precision needed for legal analysis, the Second Amendment was adopted for a distinct and easily intelligible reason. *Heller* accurately identified its purpose: to facilitate the right of the people to exercise their natural right of self-defense. That includes the right to defend oneself against all forms of illegitimate violence, whether from criminals, foreign invaders, or tyranny. When the Second Amendment was adopted, the danger most to be feared from the new and untried federal government was that it would disarm the citizenry in order to pursue illegitimate political goals. That fear has now justifiably diminished, and changes in military technology have in any case vastly reduced the power of an armed citizenry to resist a modern army. For these reasons, the relative importance of the anti-tyranny and anti-invader functions of the Second Amendment have dramatically diminished as a practical matter in comparison with the importance of the anti-criminal function.

That does not imply that the purpose or meaning of the Second Amendment has changed, but only that the likeliest significant threats have changed. While an armed citizenry continues to create some deterrent to federal tyranny,[92] it is no longer possible for it to create as effective a deterrent as it could have created in the eighteenth century. No one could reasonably think that the Second Amendment requires that the ratio of federal military power to civilian (or state militia) military power remain fixed at its 1791 level, and no court could possibly impose such a requirement.

In 1791 a citizenry armed with weapons typically kept for ordinary civilian purposes might fairly rapidly have organized itself into a reasonably credible military force. Today, very few citizens would have both the money and the inclination to keep the extremely expensive weaponry employed by modern armies, even if the Second Amendment gave them the right to do so. Widespread ownership of anti-tank rockets and Stinger missiles, let alone tanks, fighter planes, and nuclear weapons, is simply not going to happen, no matter how the Second Amendment is interpreted. For that reason, granting citizens a right to have such devices would merely empower a tiny minority of the population to inflict unthinkable carnage on everybody else, and to seriously undermine the exercise of perfectly legitimate government authority. Such a result would be affirmatively inconsistent with the Constitution, which specifically authorizes the federal government to execute the laws of the Union and to suppress insurrections.[93] Nothing in the text or purpose of the Second Amendment requires or permits this result.

Nor does the Second Amendment require the virtual absence of regulatory restrictions on ordinary civilian firearms that existed in 1791. New regulations do not violate the Constitution just because they are new. In order to apply the Second Amendment faithfully to contemporary circumstances, the courts must instead evaluate restrictions on the right to arms in light of the purpose of the constitutional provision, which is to protect what its enactors considered the inherent or natural right of self-defense. And contrary to the position Justice Scalia tried to take in *Heller,* that cannot be done without comparing the burdens of a challenged regulation on the individual's right to self-defense with the regulation's public safety benefits. This balancing of burdens and benefits can be done overtly or covertly, but it cannot be avoided.

Justice Scalia showed one way to do it in *Heller:* simply announce the result. Or, what may be worse, announce that a handgun ban is unconstitutional because a large number of contemporary Americans have weighed the costs and benefits of keeping handguns in their homes and decided to keep them. I think this approach is self-evidently wrong, at least in the sense that it is indistinguishable from living constitutionalism.

Justice Breyer's approach in *Heller* also seems manifestly wrong to me, at least to the extent that it amounts to judicial deferentialism. He performs an explicit cost-benefit analysis, but one that is dominated by deference to the judgments of elected officials.[94] The entire analysis is thus conducted in the shadow of a strong presumption of constitutionality, and one that could easily become effectively irrebuttable. This is how judges repeal constitutional provisions they dislike.[95]

The approach most consistent with the original meaning of the Constitution would reverse Justice Breyer's presumption and require the government to provide an extremely strong public safety justification for any gun control law that significantly diminishes the ability of individuals to defend themselves against criminal violence. In performing this analysis, doctrinal labels like "strict scrutiny" or "reasonable regulation" would be less important than judicial respect for the value of the inherent right of self-defense and a correlative judicial skepticism about the wisdom of government officials who want to restrict the people's ability to exercise that right.[96]

Under this approach, it does not seem to me that the D.C. handgun ban presents an especially close question. The *Heller* parties and their many amici discussed the benefits and burdens of the handgun ban in considerable detail.

The most plausible point made in support of the ban was that criminals prefer handguns over long guns because they are concealable, and criminals will have more opportunities to steal handguns if law-abiding citizens are permitted to keep them in their homes.[97] On the other side, the Court was provided with a great deal of theoretical and empirical evidence showing both that such bans do not (and cannot be expected to) affect significantly the supply of weapons available to criminals, and that many law-abiding people have good reasons to prefer handguns as instruments of self-defense in their homes.[98]

Even without considering the effects that a handgun ban would have on the constitutional right to bear arms outside the home, the balance of constitutionally cognizable costs and benefits in *Heller* essentially boiled down to the government's interest in illusory or wildly speculative public safety effects versus a substantial reduction in the ability of many citizens to defend themselves against criminal violence.

In light of the arguments and evidence presented in the briefs, Justice Scalia is right to say that the handgun ban would (or at least should) be struck down under "any of the standards of scrutiny that [the Court has] applied to enumerated constitutional rights."[99] While I agree with this conclusion, I also believe that the Court was obliged to provide a legal analysis, rather than an ipse dixit, and to do so in a way that could lay the foundation for a coherent and robust constitutional jurisprudence.

This would not have been very difficult. As Justice Scalia's reference to the conventional standards of scrutiny suggests, the Court has done just this with respect to other provisions of the Bill of Rights. The case law dealing with free speech and the free exercise of religion provides a particularly good analogue.[100] In that area, the modern Court has conscientiously sought to respect the purposes of the First Amendment by defining the scope of the rights (both of which have a textual breadth comparable to that of the Second Amendment) in a way that permits the government to advance legitimate public interests without unduly compromising the rights at issue or unduly trusting legislative wisdom. No doubt there have been significant mistakes along the way, sometimes in construing First Amendment rights too broadly and sometimes too narrowly. Some of the Court's opinions have been badly reasoned, and some of the mistakes may never be corrected. Nevertheless, the Court has exhibited a sustained commitment to the importance of these enumerated rights and a sustained resistance to governmental efforts to squelch them in the name of the general welfare.

Until it is repealed or amended through Article V, the Second Amendment requires courts to treat the right it protects with at least the same vigorous care that courts have exhibited in these First Amendment cases. With its generally sound analysis of the basic nature of the Second Amendment right, *Heller* took an important first step in that direction. The elaboration of a genuinely originalist jurisprudence, however, will require a majority of justices who are willing to take the Second Amendment as seriously as they take the First, and to do so with respect to the specific issues that arise in particular cases. To judge from the *Heller* opinions, not a single member of the current Court takes originalism, or the purpose of the Second Amendment, quite that seriously.

NOTES

Source: Reprinted from 56 UCLA L. Rev. 1343. Copyright © 2009 Regents of the University of California; Nelson Lund.

1. 128 S. Ct. 2783 (2008).

2. One response to these critiques has been that such judicial amendments are justified by the good results they produce. *See, e.g.,* CASS R. SUNSTEIN, RADICALS IN ROBES: WHY EXTREME RIGHT-WING COURTS ARE WRONG FOR AMERICA 73 (2005). I deny that judges are authorized to amend the Constitution, whether or not they are right to think an amendment is needed. Nor is it clear that judges can be expected to make amendments that are on the whole beneficial. *See, e.g.,* John O. McGinnis & Michael B. Rappaport, *A Pragmatic Defense of Originalism,* 31 HARV. J.L. & PUB. POL'Y 917 (2008).

3. *See, e.g.,* Erwin Chemerinsky, *The Jurisprudence of Justice Scalia: A Critical Appraisal,* 22 U. HAW. L. REV. 385, 385 (2000) ("Justice Scalia uses [original meaning jurisprudence] selectively when it leads to the conservative results he wants, but ignores [it] when it does not generate the outcomes he desires."); Christopher L. Eisgruber, *Birthright Citizenship and the Constitution,* 72 N.Y.U. L. REV. 54, 89 (1997) ("Scalia prefers a Constitution that authorizes the judiciary to protect certain libertarian rights."); Gene R. Nichol, *Justice Scalia and the* Printz *Case: The Trials of an Occasional Originalist,* 70 U. COLO. L. REV. 953, 968 (1999) ("[Originalism's] principal advocates relentlessly refuse to stick by it. Originalism works if they agree with the outcome dictated by history. If history does not lead them where they want to go, they simply reject it."); *see also* David M. Zlotnick, *Justice Scalia and His Critics: An Exploration of Scalia's Fidelity to His Constitutional Methodology,* 48 EMORY L.J. 1377, 1423 (1999) ("Occasionally

reaching 'liberal' results such as [invalidating bans on flag burning] has proven very useful to Scalia. He holds up the contrarian cases as proof that his methodology is politically neutral and constrains judicial discretion.").

4. Recent decades have seen an outpouring of scholarly debate about the merits of various versions of originalism and non-originalism. A review of that debate is beyond the scope of this article.

5. *See, e.g.,* Gary Lawson, *The Constitutional Case against Precedent,* 17 HARV. J.L. & PUB. POL'Y 23 (1994); Michael Stokes Paulsen, *The Intrinsically Corrupting Influence of Precedent,* 22 CONST. COMMENT. 289 (2005).

6. *See, e.g.,* THE FEDERALIST NO. 37, at 269 (James Madison) (Benjamin Fletcher Wright ed., 1961) ("All new laws . . . are considered as more or less obscure and equivocal, until their meaning be liquidated and ascertained by a series of particular discussions and adjudications."); THE FEDERALIST NO. 78, at 496 (Alexander Hamilton) (Benjamin Fletcher Wright ed., 1961) ("To avoid an arbitrary discretion in the courts, it is indispensable that they should be bound down by strict rules and precedents which serve to define and point out their duty in every particular case that comes before them.").

7. This need not lead to the conclusion that stare decisis is inconsistent with originalism or that originalists necessarily deploy stare decisis opportunistically, as a rhetorical device to defend decisions reached on other grounds. For somewhat different efforts to articulate an originalist theory of stare decisis, see, for example, Caleb Nelson, *Stare Decisis and Demonstrably Erroneous Precedents,* 87 VA. L. REV. 1 (2001); and John O. McGinnis & Michael B. Rappaport, *Reconciling Originalism and Precedent,* 103 Nw. U. L. Rev. 803 (2009).

8. Ordinarily, the Stevens position is called the collective or states' right interpretation. He rejects this label in the first paragraph of his dissent, agreeing that individuals have legal standing to vindicate the right. The insignificance of the label is shown by Justice Stevens's description of this nominally individual right as "the right of the people of each of the several States to maintain a well-regulated militia." *District of Columbia v. Heller,* 128 S. Ct. 2783, 2822 (2008) (Stevens, J., dissenting).

9. *Id.*

10. The arguments and evidence that I have advanced in support of the conclusion reached by Justice Scalia are summarized in Nelson Lund, *D.C.'s Handgun Ban and the Constitutional Right to Arms: One Hard Question?* 18 GEO. MASON U. CIV. RTS. L.J. 229 (2008), and set forth in more detail in the articles cited therein at 229, note *.

11. *See Heller,* 128 S. Ct. at 2799.

12. *Id.* at 2797 ("The very text of the Second Amendment implicitly recognizes the pre-existence of the right and declares only that it 'shall not be infringed.'").

13. *Id.* at 2801 (stating that the Second Amendment's prefatory phrase "can only show that self-defense had little to do with the right's *codification;* it was the *central component* of the right itself").

14. For an argument supporting this conclusion, see Lund, *supra* note 10, at 236–45.

15. *Heller,* 128 S. Ct. at 2801.

16. *Id.* at 2800 ("Although the militia consists of all able-bodied men, the federally organized militia may consist of a subset of them.").

17. *See id.* at 2799–2800.

18. The text of the Constitution does appear to assume that there will be a militia that can be called upon when needed. It is also true that there was considerable sentiment at the time of the founding favoring a militia comprising most able-bodied men, and it is true that the preexisting state militia laws of the time generally assigned militia duties accordingly. Beginning only a year after the adoption of the Second Amendment, however, Congress assumed that Article I gave it the authority to exempt many able-bodied men from militia duties. *See* Act of May 8, 1792, ch. 33, 1 Stat. 271. Moreover, Congress has now included some women in the militia. *See* 10 U.S.C. §311 (2006). Whatever truth there may be in the proposition, both abstract and imprecise, that the Constitution assumed the existence of a militia consisting of all able-bodied men, the Constitution also gave Congress virtually plenary authority to define the militia differently for all practical purposes. U.S. CONST. art. I, §8, cl. 16.

The imprecision of Justice Scalia's definition is illustrated by the founding era sources that he cites in its support. *See Heller,* 128 S. Ct. at 2799. One of the cited sources, a quote from a letter that Thomas Jefferson wrote in 1811, says just what Justice Scalia says: "[T]he militia of the State, that is to say, of every man in it able to bear arms." *Id.* (citing Thomas Jefferson to Destutt de Tracy (January 26, 1811), in THE PORTABLE THOMAS JEFFERSON 520, 524 (Merrill D. Peterson ed., 1975)). Justice Scalia also offers a Madison quotation from the *Federalist Papers:* "near half a million of citizens with arms in their hands." *Id.* (citing THE FEDERALIST NO. 46, *supra* note 6, at 334). This, however, is not a definition at all, but a description of the militia as it then existed and was organized, as the context clearly indicates. Madison is claiming that oppression by federal armies is little to be feared because they would be opposed by "a militia amounting to near half a million of citizens with arms in their hands, officered by men chosen from among themselves . . . and conducted by governments possessing their affections and confidence." THE FEDERALIST NO. 46, *supra* note 6, at 334. The third source, Webster's 1828 dictionary, gives a definition that on its face is significantly different from Justice Scalia's: "the able bodied men organized into companies, regiments and brigades . . . and required by law to attend military exercises on certain

days only, but at other times left to pursue their usual occupations." 2 NOAH WEB-
STER, AN AMERICAN DICTIONARY OF THE ENGLISH LANGUAGE 15 (New York, S.
Converse, 1828). This last definition, moreover, is the most relevant because it is a
deliberate effort by a lexicographer to capture the generally accepted usage of the
term. Thus, while it is was widely agreed that the militia should, and at that time
did, include most able-bodied men, it is at best misleading to say that "the militia"
means "all able-bodied men."

19. One might try to save Justice Scalia's opinion from absurdity by interpreting it to mean that the right to arms was codified in the Constitution in order to
prevent the elimination of a "self-armed militia." But that is not what he says,
and more important, it is not what the Constitution says. The constitutional text
refers to a "well regulated Militia," which does not necessarily mean "all able bodied men owning and/or bearing their privately-owned arms." Justice Scalia's only
comment on this part of the constitutional text is his assertion that "the adjective
'well-regulated' implies nothing more than the imposition of proper discipline and
training." *Heller*, 128 S. Ct. at 2800 (citations omitted). This is accurate enough,
but it simply makes more conspicuous Justice Scalia's complete failure to explain
how the codification of a private right to arms could contribute to the preservation
of a *well-regulated* militia.

20. Stated as concisely as possible: A well-regulated militia is one that is, among
other things, *not inappropriately regulated*. The codification of the people's right
to keep and bear arms in the Constitution served to prevent Congress from using
its Article I authority to adopt inappropriate militia regulations that infringed on
that right. For more detailed presentations of the arguments leading to this conclusion, see Brief of the Second Amendment Foundation as Amicus Curiae Supporting Respondent at 6–28, *Heller*, 128 S. Ct. 2783 (2008) (No. 07-290); Lund,
supra note 10, at 235–45; Nelson Lund, *The Past and Future of the Individual's
Right to Arms*, 31 GA. L. REV. 1, 20–26 (1996).

21. I have explained why I think this conclusion is correct in the sources cited
supra note 20.

22. *Heller*, 128 S. Ct. at 2821. Justice Breyer's opinion, joined by all four of the
Heller dissenters, assumes for the sake of argument that the Second Amendment
protects an individual right to have weapons for self-defense. *See id.* at 2847
(Breyer, J., dissenting). Justice Breyer then balances the individual's interest in
self-defense against the government's interest in public safety, and concludes that
D.C.'s regulations should be upheld. *See id.* at 2854–70 (Breyer, J., dissenting).

23. *See id.* at 2819–20 (majority opinion).

24. Even a court that was extremely deferential to the legislature recognized
that this kind of regulation would go too far. *See State v. Reid*, 1 Ala. 612, 616–17
(1840) ("A statute which, under the pretence of regulating, amounts to a destruc-

tion of the right, or which requires arms to be so borne as to render them wholly useless for the purpose of defence, would be clearly unconstitutional.").

25. The English Bill of Rights provided that "the Subjects which are Protestants may have Arms for their Defence suitable to their Conditions and as allowed by Law." Bill of Rights, 1 W. & M., 2d Sess., c. 2 (1689) (Eng.).

26. Americans would have been familiar with the English constitutional right primarily through Blackstone's description of it: "[T]hat of having arms for their defence, suitable to their condition and degree, and such as are allowed by law. Which is also declared by the [English Bill of Rights] and is indeed a public allowance, under due restrictions, of the natural right of resistance and self-preservation, when the sanctions of society and laws are found insufficient to restrain the violence of oppression." WILLIAM BLACKSTONE, 1 COMMENTARIES *143–44. Although this passage might be read as a hint that the constitutional right was broader than the one described in the English Bill of Rights, it need not be so read. Even if there is such a hint, the passage does not indicate how or how much any such broader right might have differed from the right as it was described in 1689.

27. Only four of the fourteen states in the Union in 1791 had right-to-arms provisions in their constitutions: Massachusetts, North Carolina, Pennsylvania, and Vermont. *See Heller,* 128 S. Ct. at 2802–3.

28. *See, e.g., Markman v. Westview Instruments, Inc.,* 517 U.S. 370, 376 (1996).

29. *See, e.g., Granfinanciera, S.A. v. Nordberg,* 492 U.S. 33, 42 (1989).

30. *Heller,* 128 S. Ct. at 2817–18 (footnote and citation to opinion of the court below omitted) (emphasis added).

31. *Id.* at 2816–17.

32. *Id.* In a footnote to the sentence containing this dictum and the dicta about sensitive places and commercial sales discussed below, the Court says, "We identify these presumptively lawful regulatory measures only as examples; our list does not purport to be exhaustive." *Id.* at 2817 n.26. The Court does not say how strong the presumption is, but the opinion later refers to these restrictions as "regulations of the right that we describe as permissible," and calls them "the exceptions we have mentioned." *Id.* at 2821. And, at the very end of the opinion, the Court flatly declares, "The Constitution leaves the District of Columbia a variety of tools for combating [the problem of handgun violence], including some measures regulating handguns." *Id.* at 2822 (citing the page on which the Court had earlier endorsed the three Second Amendment exceptions). All of this suggests that the presumption is very strong indeed, if it can be overcome at all.

33. *See* C. Kevin Marshall, *Why Can't Martha Stewart Have a Gun?* 32 HARV. J.L. & PUB. POL'Y 695, 698–99, 735 (2009). Even limited bans on the possession of concealable weapons by violent felons were apparently not adopted until well

into the twentieth century. *See id.* at 707–8. It might be possible to interpret the sentence from *Heller* quoted in the text to refer only to those felon-in-possession laws that are in fact "longstanding," and perhaps a court determined to read the dictum narrowly might adopt such an interpretation. That is, however, a highly unnatural reading of the sentence, and such a court would still be left to wonder how long a particular felon-in-possession law has to have been in existence to be "longstanding."

34. *Heller,* 128 S. Ct. at 2818.

35. *See* Marshall, *supra* note 33, at 728–35.

36. Unlike Justice Scalia, Marshall provides a great deal of historical evidence to support his conclusions. The result of his analysis of the evidence is that Justice Scalia's broad endorsement of bans on firearms possession by all felons is unsupported. *Id.* at 696–98.

37. *Heller,* 128 S. Ct. at 2816–17.

38. *See generally* Stephen P. Halbrook, *"Only Law Enforcement Will Be Allowed to Have Guns": Hurricane Katrina and the New Orleans Firearm Confiscations,* 18 GEO. MASON U. CIV. RTS. L.J. 339 (2008).

39. *Heller,* 128 S. Ct. at 2821.

40. *Id.* at 2817.

41. *Id.* at 2816 (citations omitted).

42. *Id.*

43. *Bliss v. Commonwealth,* 12 Ky. (2 Litt.) 90 (1822), invalidated restrictions on the carrying of concealed weapons under a 1792 state constitutional provision commanding "that 'the right of the citizens to bear arms in defense of themselves and the state, shall not be questioned.'" *Id.* at 90 (citation omitted). Justice Scalia was presumably familiar with this case, which he cited for a different point elsewhere in his opinion. *See Heller,* 128 S. Ct. at 2794 n.9.

44. Justice Scalia acknowledges that discussions long after the ratification of the Second Amendment "do not provide as much insight into its original meaning as earlier sources." *Heller,* 128 S. Ct. at 2810.

45. The entire opinion in *State v. Mitchell,* 3 Blackf. 229, 229 (Ind. 1833), for example, reads as follows: "It was held in this case, that the statute of 1831, prohibiting all persons, except travelers, from wearing or carrying concealed weapons, is not unconstitutional." This unexplained conclusion reveals nothing about the pre-1791 right to arms. *State v. Reid,* 1 Ala. 612 (1840), upheld restrictions on concealed carry under a state constitution that provided "Every citizen has a right to bear arms, in defence of himself and the State." *Id.* at 614–15. The court rested its decision on the principle that "[b]efore the judiciary can with propriety declare an act of the Legislature unconstitutional, a case should be presented in which there is no

rational doubt." *Id.* at 621 (citation omitted). *Heller* rejects this interpretive principle. 128 S. Ct. at 2817 n.27. *Aymette v. State,* 21 Tenn. (2 Hum.) 154 (1840), upheld a ban on the concealed carry of certain kinds of knives, which was challenged under an 1834 state constitutional provision that declared "the free white men of this State have a right to keep and bear arms for their common defence." *Id.* at 156. The qualifying terminology at the end of the provision ("for their common defence") is absent from the Second Amendment, and the Tennessee court rested its conclusion on the ground that these knives were not "such as are usually employed in civilized warfare, and that constitute the ordinary military equipment." *Id.* at 158. *Heller* rejects a similar interpretation of the Second Amendment. 128 S. Ct. at 2815–16. *State v. Buzzard,* 4 Ark. 18 (1842), upheld restrictions on concealed carry against challenges under the Second Amendment and an 1836 state constitutional provision that protected citizens' right to keep and bear arms "for their common defense." *Id.* at 26. One member of the court treated the state and federal provisions as though they were identical, and concluded that their purpose was only to enable the citizenry to resist would-be tyrants. *See id.* at 26–27. Another member of the court argued that the Second Amendment does not protect an individual right. *See id.* at 32 (Dickinson, J., concurring). A dissenting member of the court argued that the majority had effectively rendered the Second Amendment a nullity. *See id.* at 41–43 (Lacy, J., dissenting). *Heller* rejects the interpretations of the Second Amendment adopted by the *Buzzard* majority. 128 S. Ct. at 2797–99.

46. *State v. Chandler,* 5 La. Ann. 489, 489–90 (1850).

47. *Nunn v. State,* 1 Ga. 243 (1846).

48. *Id.* at 251. The court appeared to imply that the ban on the sale of certain weapons was also invalid, although their sale was not at issue in the case and the court did not explicitly address that question.

49. *Id.*

50. WILLIAM BLACKSTONE, 4 COMMENTARIES *148. For a discussion of the common law rule, *see infra* notes 54–64 and accompanying text.

51. *District of Columbia v. Heller,* 128 S. Ct. 2783, 2815–16 (2008) (footnote omitted). The case referenced here is *United States v. Miller,* 307 U.S. 174 (1939), which I discuss below.

52. *Heller,* 128 S. Ct. at 2817.

53. *Id.*

54. BLACKSTONE, *supra* note 50, at *148–49.

55. *See* JOYCE LEE MALCOLM, TO KEEP AND BEAR ARMS: THE ORIGINS OF AN ANGLO-AMERICAN RIGHT 104, 184 n.36 (1994).

56. *Id.* at 104–5.

57. *Id.* at 105.

58. *See* Brief of the Cato Institute and History Professor Joyce Lee Malcolm as Amici Curiae in Support of Respondent at 15–19, *District of Columbia v. Heller*, 128 S. Ct. 2783 (2008) (No. 07-290).

59. 3 JAMES WILSON, WORKS OF THE HONOURABLE JAMES WILSON 79 (Bird Wilson ed., Philadelphia, Bronson and Chauncey 1804) (footnote omitted) (emphasis added).

60. JOHN A. DUNLAP, THE NEW-YORK JUSTICE 8 (New York, Isaac Riley 1815) (emphasis added).

61. CHARLES HUMPHREYS, A COMPENDIUM OF THE COMMON LAW IN FORCE IN KENTUCKY 482 (Lexington, Ky., William Gibbes Hunt 1822). Justice Scalia knew about the second sentence in this quotation, which he quoted elsewhere in the Court's opinion. *See District of Columbia v. Heller*, 128 S. Ct. 2783, 2795 n.10 (2008).

62. 1 WILLIAM OLDNALL RUSSELL, A TREATISE ON CRIMES AND INDICTABLE MISDEMEANORS 271–72 (Philadelphia, P. B. Nicklin and T. Johnson, Boston, Lilly and Wait 1831).

63. HENRY J. STEPHEN, SUMMARY OF THE CRIMINAL LAW 48 (Philadelphia, John S. Littell, New York, Halsted and Voorhies 1840).

64. FRANCIS WHARTON, A TREATISE ON THE CRIMINAL LAW OF THE UNITED STATES 726–27 (Philadelphia, James Kay, Jun. & Brother, 2d ed. 1852). Justice Scalia cites only the first page of Wharton's discussion, which presents the standard definition of an affray, including the qualification "in such a manner as will naturally cause a terror to the people." *District of Columbia v. Heller*, 128 S. Ct. 2783, 2817 (2008).

65. *Heller*, 128 S. Ct. at 2817 (citing *O'Neill v. State*, 16 Ala. 65, 67 (1849); *State v. Lanier*, 71 N.C. 288, 289 (1874); *State v. Langford*, 10 N.C. (3 Hawks) 381, 383–384 (1824); *English v. State*, 35 Tex. 473, 476 (1871)).

66. *Heller*, 128 S. Ct. at 2816.

67. *English*, 35 Tex. at 476.

68. *United States v. Miller*, 307 U.S. 174, 178 (1939) (citation omitted).

69. *Heller*, 128 S. Ct. at 2815.

70. 307 U.S. at 179.

71. *Heller*, 128 S. Ct. at 2814. Even if the Court alters this sentence when it publishes the opinion in the U.S. Reports, it won't be able to alter the fact that the mistake was made in the slip opinion that issued on the day of decision.

72. For a more detailed analysis of Justice Scalia's misrepresentations of *Miller*, and an argument that the *Heller* Court was not obliged to embrace *Miller*'s interpretation of the Second Amendment, see Nelson Lund, Heller *and Second Amendment Precedent*, 13 LEWIS & CLARK L. REV. 335 (2009).

73. Properly configured and loaded with appropriate ammunition, short-barreled shotguns may be optimal weapons for home defense in many circumstances. If the government stopped suppressing them, they might become very popular.

74. *Heller,* 128 S. Ct. at 2817.

75. *Id.*

76. *Id.* at 2821.

77. *PDK Labs. Inc. v. U.S. Drug Enforcement Admin.,* 362 F.3d 786, 799 (D.C. Cir. 2004) (Roberts, J., concurring in part and concurring in the judgment).

78. *Heller,* 128 S. Ct. at 2816 n.25 (discussing *Lewis v. United States,* 445 U.S. 55 (1980)).

79. Compare Justice Scalia's well-known discussion of "faint-hearted originalism," in which he suggests that most originalists would strike down laws providing for public flogging, even in the face of unequivocal evidence that such a punishment was not considered "cruel and unusual" in 1791. Antonin Scalia, *Originalism: The Lesser Evil,* 57 U. Cin. L. Rev. 849, 861–62 (1989).

80. This point will assume even greater importance if the Court makes the Second Amendment applicable to the states under substantive due process, which is a likely outcome, given the existing incorporation precedents. For more detail, see Nelson Lund, *Anticipating the Second Amendment Incorporation: The Role of the Inferior Courts,* 59 Syracuse L. Rev. 185 (2008) and Lund, *supra* note 20, at 46–55. One court has already reached this conclusion. *See Nordyke v. King,* 563 F.3d 439 (9th Cir. 2009).

81. 410 U.S. 113 (1973).

82. 290 U.S. 398 (1934).

83. *See id.* at 453–82 (Sutherland, J., dissenting).

84. The majority stated: "It is no answer to say that this public need was not apprehended a century ago, or to insist that what the provision of the Constitution meant to the vision of that day it must mean to the vision of our time. If by the statement that what the Constitution meant at the time of its adoption it means to-day, it is intended to say that the great clauses of the Constitution must be confined to the interpretation which the framers, with the conditions and outlook of their time, would have placed upon them, the statement carries its own refutation." *Blaisdell,* 290 U.S. at 44–43.

85. *See, e.g.,* James Bradley Thayer, *The Origin and Scope of the American Doctrine of Constitutional Law,* 7 Harv. L. Rev. 129 (1893); Lino A. Graglia, *Constitutional Interpretation,* 44 Syracuse L. Rev. 631 (1993).

86. *See, e.g., Gompers v. Buck's Stove & Range Co.,* 221 U.S. 418, 439 (1911) (explaining that joining with others to call for a boycott is not speech but a "verbal

act"); *Davis v. Beason*, 133 U.S. 333 (1890) (approving an Idaho territorial statute denying Mormons, polygamists, and advocates of polygamy the right to vote and to hold office); *Late Corp. of the Church of Jesus Christ of Latter-Day Saints v. United States*, 136 U.S. 1 (1890) (upholding federal statute dissolving the Mormon church and providing for the seizure of all its property); *Ex parte Jackson*, 96 U.S. 727, 736–37 (1878) (upholding a federal statute that banned lottery material from the mail because Congress may deny access "for the distribution of matter deemed injurious to the public morals").

87. *See, e.g., Garcia v. San Antonio Metro. Transit Auth.*, 469 U.S. 528 (1985) (holding that the Interstate Commerce Clause authorizes Congress to regulate wages and hours of employees of local, municipally operated mass transit system); *Buckley v. Valeo*, 424 U.S. 1 (1976) (upholding limits on contributions to political campaigns); *Red Lion Broad. Co. v. FCC*, 395 U.S. 367 (1969) (upholding regulatory control over editorial decisions by broadcasters); *Wickard v. Filburn*, 317 U.S. 111 (1942) (permitting Congress to forbid the consumption of homegrown wheat on the ground that such consumption may affect interstate commerce).

88. *See* Jack M. Balkin, *Abortion and Original Meaning*, 24 CONST. COMMENT. 291 (2007).

89. This principle is composed of three sub-principles: prohibitions against class legislation, caste legislation, and subordinating legislation. *Id.* at 319–20.

90. Jack M. Balkin, *Original Meaning and Constitutional Redemption*, 24 CONST. COMMENT. 427, 498 (2007).

91. Eugene Volokh's excellent contribution to the 2009 *UCLA Law Review* symposium on the Second Amendment adopts an approach that I think is generally consistent with conscientious originalism. *See* Eugene Volokh, *Implementing the Right to Keep and Bear Arms: An Analytical Framework and a Research Agenda*, 56 UCLA L. REV. 1443 (2009).

92. For further detail, see Lund, *supra* note 20, at 56–58; Nelson Lund, *The Second Amendment, Political Liberty, and the Right to Self-Preservation*, 39 ALA. L. REV. 103, 114–15 (1987).

93. U.S. CONST. art. 1, §8, cl. 15; art. 2, §2, cl. 1, §3.

94. *See, e.g., District of Columbia v. Heller*, 128 S. Ct. 2783, 2852 (2008) (Breyer, J., dissenting) (advocating a standard of scrutiny in which "the Court normally defers to a legislature's empirical judgment in matters where a legislature is likely to have greater expertise and greater institutional factfinding capacity"); *id.* at 2859 ("[T]he question here is whether [empirically based arguments against the handgun ban] are strong enough to destroy judicial confidence in the reasonableness of a legislature that rejects them."); *id.* at 2860 ("[L]egislators, not judges, have primary responsibility for drawing policy conclusions from empirical fact."); *id.* ("[D]eference to legislative judgment seems particularly appropriate

here, where the judgment has been made by a local legislature, with particular knowledge of local problems and insight into appropriate local solutions.").

95. Neither Breyer nor any other justice consistently applies this presumption of constitutionality to individual rights that are enumerated in the Constitution. Ironically, Justice Breyer and the other *Heller* dissenters reject such a presumption of constitutionality when considering *unenumerated* rights that they like, such as the right to abortion. For an extremely vivid example, see *Stenberg v. Carhart,* 530 U.S. 914 (2000).

96. If any proof of the inefficacy of doctrinal labels on the standard of review were needed, one could simply read *Grutter v. Bollinger,* 539 U.S. 306 (2003), in which the Court applied strict scrutiny in a manner that is indistinguishable from rational basis review.

97. *See* Brief for Petitioners at 49, 51, 53, *District of Columbia v. Heller,* 128 S. Ct. 2783 (2008) (No. 07-290).

98. *See, e.g.,* Brief of Criminologists, Social Scientists, Other Distinguished Scholars, and the Claremont Institute as Amici Curiae in Support of Respondent, *District of Columbia v. Heller,* 128 S. Ct. 2783 (2008) (No. 07-290); Brief of Int'l Law Enforcement Educators and Trainers Ass'n. et al. as Amici Curiae in Support of Respondent, *District of Columbia v. Heller,* 128 S. Ct. 2783 (2008) (No. 07-290); Brief of Amici Curiae Southeastern Legal Foundation, Inc., et al. in Support of Respondent, *District of Columbia v. Heller,* 128 S. Ct. 2783 (2008) (No. 07-290).

99. *Heller,* 128 S. Ct. at 2817–18.

100. Justice Scalia repeatedly recognized that these provisions of the Constitution require similar treatment. *See, e.g., id.* at 2791–92, 2797, 2799, 2821. For an early judicial recognition of this point, *see United States v. Sheldon,* 5 Blume Sup. Ct. Trans. 337, 346 (Mich. 1829).

Section III

Heller and Constitutional Doctrine

Of Guns, Abortions, and the Unraveling Rule of Law

J. Harvie Wilkinson III

INTRODUCTION

CONSERVATIVES ACROSS THE NATION are celebrating. This past term, in *District of Columbia v. Heller,*[1] the Supreme Court held for the first time in the nation's history that the Second Amendment protects an individual right, unrelated to military service, to keep and bear arms. I am unable to join in the jubilation. *Heller* represents a triumph for conservative lawyers. But it also represents a failure—the Court's failure to adhere to a conservative judicial methodology in reaching its decision. In fact, *Heller* encourages Americans to do what conservative jurists warned for years they should not do: bypass the ballot and seek to press their political agenda in the courts.

In this article, I compare *Heller* to another Supreme Court opinion, *Roe v. Wade.*[2] The analogy seems unlikely; *Roe* is the opinion perhaps most disliked by conservatives, while many of those same critics are roundly praising *Heller.* And yet the comparison is apt. In a number of important ways, the *Roe* and *Heller* Courts are guilty of the same sins.

Both decisions share four major shortcomings: an absence of a commitment to textualism; a willingness to embark on a complex endeavor that will require fine-tuning over many years of litigation; a failure to respect legislative judgments; and a rejection of the principles of federalism. These failings have two things in common. First, each represents a rejection of neutral principles that counseled restraint and deference to others regardless of the issues involved. Second, each represents an act of judicial aggrandizement: a transfer of power to judges from the political branches of government—and thus, ultimately, from the people themselves.

The tale of the judiciary in American history is a story with high and low points from which it is difficult to draw a consistent lesson. There have been moments where the Court has heroically rejected judgments by the elected branches of government,[3] and moments where the Court shamefully refused to do so.[4] But if any one theme emerges when looking at the role of the courts in American history, it is this: when the channels of democracy are functioning properly, judges should be modest in their ambitions and overrule the results of the democratic process only where the Constitution unambiguously commands it.

These principles should be uncontroversial. Many of the most respected jurists in our nation's history have written against judicial imperialism. Consider Justice Brandeis's warning to judges that "we must be ever on our guard, lest we erect our prejudices into legal principles."[5] Or Justice Cardozo's admonition that the judge "is not a knight-errant, roaming at will in pursuit of his own ideal of beauty or of goodness."[6] Or Justice Holmes's warning that a constitution "is made for people of fundamentally differing views, and the accident of our finding certain opinions natural and familiar or novel and even shocking ought not to conclude our judgment upon the question whether statutes embodying them conflict with the Constitution of the United States."[7]

It does no good to recount the Court's misadventures when it failed to heed these fundamental maxims of modesty, deference, and restraint. Suffice it to say the caution befitting the judiciary's interpretive task and unelected station is periodically forgotten—often to the accompaniment of short-term applause but at the expense of long-term institutional respect. In both *Roe* and *Heller* the Court claimed to find in the Constitution the authority to overrule the wishes of the people's representatives. In both cases the constitutional text did not clearly mandate the result, and the Court had discretion to decide the case either way. And in both cases the majority was challenged for exercising its discretion to promote the justices' own policy preferences.

It is the solemn duty of judges on the inferior federal courts to follow, both in letter and in spirit, rules and decisions with which we may not agree. Our oath demands it, and our respect for the Supreme Court as an institution and for the able and dedicated individuals who serve on it requires no less. But esteem can likewise be manifest in the respectful expression of difference—that too is the essence of the judicial craft. *Roe* and *Heller* are by any measure two of the most important decisions of the modern judicial era. They now together cast a long shadow over contemporary constitutional law. Law's power to shape human conduct depends on its perceived legitimacy as much as on the threat of force that stands behind its commands.[8] Law is seen as legitimate only if it lays down rules applicable to all, rules that are enforced day in and day out, in good times and bad, for conservative and liberal ends, for policies the justices like and for those they do not. *Roe* and *Heller* do not meet this basic requirement. Each decision discarded the tenets of restraint that alone make the application of neutral principles possible, and *Heller* found the justices in both camps at odds with positions they had earlier and passionately espoused.

The dilemma is an especially acute one for Justice Antonin Scalia. No one has more consistently or eloquently exposed the flaws of the *Roe* decision. In his opposition, the justice did far more than mount a challenge to the constitutional law of abortion. Rather, he took to task the whole methodology for which *Roe* stands. His is a powerful legacy—if, that is, *Heller* does not detract. To his credit, the justice undertook the inquiry into the Framers' original intentions that was missing in *Roe*. While *Heller* can be hailed as a triumph of originalism, it can just as easily be seen as the opposite—an exposé of original intent as a theory no less subject to judicial subjectivity and endless argumentation as any other. *Roe*'s flaw was not just that it was anti-originalist, but that it was inimical to the values of textualism, self-restraint, separation of powers, and federalism as well. These values too were central to the Framers' design and intent. These values too are the solid foundation of conservative thought. Unlike the aggressive brand of originalism practiced in *Heller*, these values alone guarantee that the judiciary will resist the lasting temptation to enshrine its own preferences in law.

Heller has swept away these counsels of caution. It has left only originalism as the foundation of conservative jurisprudence. A set of reasonable tenets, each providing a separate check on judicial activism, has now been replaced by a singular focus on original understanding. Whereas once legal conservatism demanded that judges justify decisions by reference to a number of restraining principles, *Heller* requires that they only make originalist arguments supporting their preferred view. Yet originalism cannot bear the weight that the *Heller* majority would place upon it. Originalism, though important, is not determinate enough to constrain judges' discretion to decide cases based on outcomes they prefer. Some may see *Heller*'s originalism as the answer to the judicial legislation practiced in *Roe*, but as I will show in this article, the two approaches lead to the same bad consequences.

It is astonishing that two decisions supported by such different majorities would share so many of the same infirmities. Part I critiques *Roe* and *Heller* for recognizing a substantive right grounded in an ambiguous constitutional text. Part II argues that *Roe* did, and *Heller* will, lead the Court into a dense political thicket that it would do best to avoid. Part III discusses legislative and judicial competence, and argues that legislatures are better positioned to address the tough issues surrounding gun and abortion rights. Part IV contends that both *Heller* and *Roe* rejected the principles of federalism that conservatives ought to cherish.

Above all, I write in the hope that there are more important values at stake here than even rights to guns and choice. It may no longer be possible to judge a Supreme Court ruling by anything other than result. The time may have passed when judicial process matters. It may all be bottom line: gun rights enthusiasts rush to hail *Heller* as pro-choice advocates hailed *Roe*. Who can blame them? Many gun regulations may be quite ill-advised; many restrictions on abortion may be most intrusive. But before popping the champagne on the Supreme Court's latest edict, maybe someone should wonder whether we purchase today's victory at the cost of tomorrow's freedom. The largest threat to liberty still lies in handing our democratic destiny to the courts.

I. FASHIONING NOVEL SUBSTANTIVE RIGHTS

Roe and *Heller* share a significant flaw: both cases found judicially enforceable substantive rights only ambiguously rooted in the Constitution's text. I will first document some of the criticisms of Roe on this point. I will then show that these same criticisms can be made of the *Heller* decision.

A. *ROE*

In 1973 the Supreme Court in *Roe v. Wade* and *Doe v. Bolton*[9] held that a woman's right to end her pregnancy was a fundamental one under the Fourteenth Amendment's Due Process Clause. In doing so, the Court set forth a rigid set of constitutional rules restricting the state's regulation of abortion. During the first trimester of pregnancy, "the abortion decision and its effectuation must be left to the medical judgment of the pregnant woman's attending physician"; after the first trimester and prior to viability of the fetus, "the State . . . may, if it chooses, regulate the abortion procedure in ways that are reasonably related to maternal health"; while after viability, "the State . . . may, if it chooses, regulate, and even proscribe, abortion except where it is necessary, in appropriate medical judgment, for the preservation of the life or health of the mother."[10]

Roe has been criticized because of the absence of any relationship between this newly discovered right to abortion and the text or structure of the Constitution. While the Court declared a right to personal privacy as the basis of its decision, it is a long trek from the liberty protected by due process to a general right of privacy; a longer journey still from a general privacy right to a specific right to induce an abortion; and a longer distance still from a right to abort a fetus to the elaborate trimester framework set forth in the Court's decision. Without some way to point to some evidence that the Constitution has anything at all to say about abortion, *Roe* was subject to the criticism that the justices in the majority had simply enacted their policy preferences into constitutional law.

The justices should never have attempted to find substantive rights in what was at best an ambiguous constitutional provision. The difference between substantive and procedural due process is an important one in Fourteenth Amendment law. To be sure, the point should not be pushed to extremes, as salutary substantive decisions like *Loving v. Virginia*,[11] *Pierce v. Society of Sisters*,[12] and *Meyer v. Nebraska*[13] make clear.[14] But the dichotomy is there. When the concept of due process—which most naturally suggests procedure—is deployed to limit substantive political options, judges begin to assume a legislative mien. When the Constitution clearly and unequivocally enunciates an issue of substantive right, judges explicating those rights are at their most judicial.

The creation of *new* substantive constitutional rights is one of the biggest steps the Supreme Court can take. Society is a defined balance between individual and community. When rights are enumerated, courts are empowered to strike the balance; when they are not enumerated, or only ambiguously so, the balance is set by democracy. To confuse the two is to slight communal claims to shared values. Because the history of substantive due process rights is so laden with land mines,[15] the ground beneath the judicial foot in *Roe* should have been absolutely firm. *Roe* was a flawed decision because the Court found in the Due Process Clause a set of complex rules governing the substantive right to abortion that are not even remotely suggested by the text or history of the Fourteenth Amendment—or any other source that should bear on legal interpretation, as opposed to the legislative craft.

Quite apart from the Fourteenth Amendment, there is a broader point to be made about the judiciary's creation of substantive rights not explicit, or at best ambiguously indicated, in the constitutional text. Inasmuch as Article III does not provide the judiciary with prescriptive authority in the manner that Article I, section 8, for example, provides the Congress, it behooves the judiciary to be cautious in creating for itself new substantive—and hence prescriptive—power that the Constitution did not clearly envision.

The justices should thus never have divined a complicated set of directives regarding abortion in the sparsely worded Due Process Clause. On the Court itself, the dissenters in *Roe* and *Bolton* emphasized the anti-textual nature of the decision. Finding "nothing in the language or history of the Constitution to support the Court's judgment," Justice White accused the majority of "simply fashion[ing] and announc[ing] a new constitutional right" and called the decision "an exercise of raw judicial power."[16] Then-Justice Rehnquist questioned whether a right of privacy forbade the Texas law at issue in *Roe*, arguing that "the 'privacy' that the Court finds here [is not] even a distant relative of the freedom from searches and seizures protected by the Fourth Amendment."[17]

The original dissenters reiterated these and other critiques in subsequent abortion cases. In *Thornburg v. American College of Obstetricians & Gynecologists*,[18] Justice White argued that the principle of stare decisis did not justify continued adherence to *Roe*, for "decisions that find in the Constitution *principles or values that cannot fairly be read into that document* usurp the people's authority, for such decisions represent choices that the people have never made and that they cannot disavow through corrective legislation."[19] White noted that "the [Constitution's] text obviously contains no references to abortion, nor, indeed, to pregnancy or reproduction generally; and, of course, it is highly doubtful that the authors of any of the provisions of the Constitution believed that they were giving protection to abortion."[20] Justice White set forth his approach to constitutional interpretation, arguing that it is appropriate for the Court to safeguard specifically enumerated constitutional rights, but that "[w]hen the Court . . . defines as "fundamental" liberties that are nowhere mentioned in the Constitution . . . it must, of necessity, act with more caution, lest it open itself to the accusation that, in the name of identifying constitutional principles to which the people have consented in framing their Constitution, the Court has done nothing more than impose its own controversial choices of value upon the people."[21]

In his dissent in *Planned Parenthood of Southeastern Pennsylvania v. Casey*,[22] Chief Justice Rehnquist elaborated upon his earlier critique of the holding in *Roe*. Neither the Court's precedent nor "the historical traditions of the American people support the view that the right to terminate one's pregnancy is 'fundamental,'" the Chief Justice argued.[23] *Roe* was wrongly decided because "the sort of constitutionally imposed abortion code of the type illustrated by our decisions following *Roe* is inconsistent 'with the notion of a Constitution cast in general terms, as ours is, and usually speaking in general principles, as ours does.'"[24]

Justice Scalia was not on the Court when *Roe* was decided, but he has criticized it unreservedly in the abortion decisions in which he has participated. The absence of any textual basis for *Roe* continued to be the flash point. In his concurrence in *Ohio v. Akron Center for Reproductive Health*,[25] Justice Scalia contended that "[the] right to abortion . . . is not to be found in the longstanding traditions of our society, nor can it be logically deduced from the text of the Constitution."[26] In his separate opinion in *Webster v. Reproductive Health Services*,[27] Justice Scalia argued for reversal of *Roe*, contending that "our retaining control, through Roe, of what I believe to be, and many of our citizens recognize to be, a political issue, continuously distorts the public perception of the role of this Court."[28] In his separate opinion in *Hodgson v. Minnesota*,[29] Justice Scalia insisted that he would continue dissenting from what he described as "this enterprise of devising an Abortion Code, and from the illusion that we have authority to do so."[30] In his dissent in *Casey*, in which the Court famously upheld the core holding in *Roe*, Justice Scalia reaffirmed his view that *Roe* was wrongly decided: "The issue [in this case] is whether [abortion] is a liberty protected by the Constitution of the United States. I am sure it is not. I reach that conclusion . . . because of two simple facts: (1) the Constitution says absolutely nothing about it, and (2) the longstanding traditions of American society have permitted it to be legally proscribed."[31]

While *Roe* has had many defenders, to be sure,[32] criticism from outside the Court has been fierce. Some commentators were outraged that the Court did not hold that fetuses were persons under the Fourteenth Amendment, thus making legalized abortion unconstitutional.[33] The most common reaction, however, has been discomfort with the shaky legal foundation of the Court's judgment. Gerald Gunther professed his inability to find "a satisfying rationale to justify *Roe* . . . on the basis of modes of constitutional interpretation I consider legitimate."[34] According to Alexander Bickel, the Court "refused the discipline to which its function is properly subject. It simply asserted the result it reached. This is all the Court could do because moral philosophy, logic, reason, or other materials of law" could not resolve the question of whether abortion should be permitted.[35] Richard Epstein criticized "the comprehensive legislation which Mr. Justice Blackmun (with the concurrence of six brethren) has enacted in the name of the Due Process Clause of the Constitution."[36] John Hart Ely chastised the Justices for issuing an opinion that "is *not* constitutional law and gives almost no sense of an obligation to try to be."[37] Ely deplored the Court for announcing a "super-protected right . . . not inferable from the language of the Constitution, the framers' thinking respecting the specific problem in issue, any general value derivable from the provisions they included, or the nation's governmental structure."[38] Before her elevation to the Supreme Court, then-Judge Ruth Bader Ginsburg—a passionate defender of legal equality for women—argued that "*Roe* ventured too far in the change it ordered"[39] and that the Court's justification was "incomplete."[40]

Remarkably, the criticism continues from all quarters and has not abated with the passage of time. The result in *Roe* remains without any rationale that its defenders could comfortably call home. Even defenders of *Roe* have admitted that the holding should have been reached on a different basis, though on what basis remains unclear. The recent and revealingly titled book *What* Roe v. Wade *Should Have Said* contained a number of pieces by legal scholars, most of which were attempts by supporters of the outcome in *Roe* to put the Court's judgment on surer constitutional ground.[41] Erwin Chemerinsky has argued that the opinion would have been better justified if it had protected the right to abortion as a "private moral judgment."[42] Donald Regan,[43] Justice Ginsburg,[44] and others[45] have suggested that *Roe* should have been written as an equal protection case. For many observers, the decision "symbolized, more than any other case, the risk that constitutional law might be nothing more than judicial value judgments"; these critics consider the case "our generation's *Lochner* . . . the preeminent symbol of judicial overreaching."[46]

The stakes of this debate can hardly be overstated. It is no exaggeration to say that *Roe* gave rise to the modern conservative legal movement. The decision came to stand for the worst kind of judicial overreaching; a generation of conservative lawyers came of age in its shadow. Conservatism was all those things that *Roe* was not, the movement's virtues illumined by *Roe*'s vices. It became all the more crucial therefore that the conservative denunciation of

Roe be accompanied by the principled application of those neutral principles that *Roe* had violated: textualism, structuralism, federalism, historicism, and plain old modesty and restraint. For the attack on *Roe* would appear over time to be hollow if its assailants were to practice an unprincipled activism of their own. So the challenge to conservatism was clearly to transcend the parties or interests or even the results involved, and to lead the way back to a rule of law whose distinct and separate nobility would discredit the stark forays into policy practiced by the judiciary in some of the more questionable periods of its history. Unfortunately, as I discuss in the next section, conservatism has not met this challenge.

B. *HELLER*

There is now a real risk that the Second Amendment will damage conservative judicial philosophy as much as the Due Process Clause damaged its liberal counterpart. The Second Amendment reads: "A well regulated Militia, being necessary to the security of a free State, the right of the people to keep and bear Arms, shall not be infringed."[47] In those twenty-seven words, the Court found an individual, judicially enforceable right—unconnected to military service—to keep and bear handguns, at least for self-defense in the home.[48]

This has placed the very basis of the conservative attack on *Roe* at risk. After decades of criticizing activist judges for this or that defalcation, conservatives have now committed many of the same sins. In *Heller,* the majority read an ambiguous constitutional provision as creating a substantive right that the Court had never acknowledged in the more than two hundred years since the amendment's enactment. The majority then used that same right to strike down a law passed by elected officials acting, rightly or wrongly, to preserve the safety of the citizenry. To be sure, the *Heller* dissenters' claims of dedication to democratic processes can hardly be squared with decades of overturning legislative restrictions on abortion. Indeed, the new activism of the majority and new restraint of the dissents might cause both the advocates of gun activism and abortion activism from the bench to blush. The setback to conservative legal theory is, however, unique, because the vociferous opposition to *Roe* placed upon conservatives a special obligation to avoid the pitfalls that the search for congenial results presents.

It can, of course, be readily agreed that of the two decisions, *Roe* involved the more brazen assertion of judicial authority. *Heller* differs from *Roe* in important respects. Most strikingly, the text of the Constitution alludes to a right "to keep and bear arms," but it does not so much as mention a right to abortion. There is a big difference between when the text says something (whatever that something may be), and when it says absolutely nothing.

Second, the cases use history in markedly different ways. *Heller* made an extended inquiry into history to determine the "[n]ormal meaning" of the amendment as understood by people at the time it was written.[49] In contrast, *Roe* did not look to history to interpret an ambiguous textual phrase. Nor did it look to history for a tradition of protection for abortion—no such history exists. Instead, the Court's discussion of history was mostly spent explaining away ancient, common law, and statutory prohibitions on abortion to prove that this history did not preclude finding a constitutional right to abortion.[50]

Next, *Heller* struck down a draconian law, one that completely banned handgun possession at home. That law was one of the strictest in the nation.[51] In contrast, the *Roe* Court struck down Texas's prohibition on abortion *and* the much more moderate Georgia law that merely regulated abortion. The Court in *Roe* and *Doe* cut a wide swath through all sorts of state laws, while *Heller*, at least initially, cut down only the most extreme variety.

Finally, *Heller*'s actual holding is narrower than *Roe*'s. The rationale of its holding—that the Second Amendment embodies an individual right to bear arms—is sure to call many gun restrictions into question, but the application of that rationale, invalidating a statute forbidding handguns in the home for self-protection, is much narrower.[52] *Roe*, in contrast, established from the start a detailed trimester framework.[53] Unlike *Roe*, no page in *Heller* reads like a statute.

So *Heller* is not *Roe*. But to say that *Heller* was marginally more justified than *Roe* is not saying much—surely the bar of justification for judicial intervention has not been set so low. It would be a sad mistake for defenders of *Heller* to treat *Roe* as a floor, such that all decisions less egregious in their methods are in some way acceptable. This cannot be. The requirements of the rule of law are not so relative. Fidelity to true judicial values requires that judges impartially apply neutral principles of law, not merely be *more* principled than the other side.

Thus, despite a difference in the magnitude of judicial overreaching, the methodological similarities between *Roe* and *Heller* are large. Both cases interpreted ambiguous constitutional provisions, and both claimed to find in them mandates that put to rest an extremely controversial issue of social policy, in the process overturning decisions by popularly elected officials. If there is a reasonable case for the majority's interpretation of the Second Amendment, there is also a reasonable case for the position taken by the dissenters. Stuart Taylor, for example, noted that he found Justice Scalia's argument for striking down the District of Columbia's handgun ban "persuasive. But then I studied the dissents by liberal Justices John Paul Stevens and Stephen Breyer and found them pretty persuasive, too."[54] Taylor found himself on the fence for an obvious reason: namely that "the justices' exhaustive analyses of the text and relevant history do not definitively resolve the ambiguity inherent in the amendment's curious wording."[55]

When a constitutional question is so close, when conventional interpretive methods do not begin to resolve the issue decisively, the tie for many reasons should go to the side of deference to democratic processes. For a court that decides to strike down legislation based on an interpretation of the Constitution that is only plausible and not incontrovertible will appear to the public to be exercising discretion. And when a court appears to be exercising that discretion in a way that arguably accords with the political preferences of the judges in the majority—as was the case in *Heller*—more members of the public lose faith in the idea that justice is blind. For as Taylor continues, "even though all nine justices claimed to be following original meaning, they split angrily along liberal-conservative lines perfectly matching their apparent policy preferences, with the four conservatives (plus swing-voting Justice Anthony Kennedy) voting for gun rights and the four liberals against."[56] The upshot of all this argumentation is that both sides fought into overtime to a draw. And the argumentative exchange, even under the guise of an originalist inquiry, came perilously close to re-creating *Roe*'s fundamental misapprehension—namely, that law is politics pursued by other means.

What is lacking in *Heller* is what was lacking in *Roe:* the sort of firm constitutional foundation from which to announce a novel substantive constitutional right. Consider the text of the Second Amendment. Does the amendment's prefatory clause limit the scope of the right found in the operative clause, or merely explain its justification? Justice Scalia, rejecting the arguments made by professors of linguistics and English to the contrary,[57] dismissed quickly the possibility that the prefatory clause could restrict the operative clause,[58] and concluded that the right in the operative clause need only be "consistent with the announced purpose" in the prefatory clause.[59] Justice Stevens in his dissent called this approach "novel" and not in keeping with conventional interpretive methods.[60] He argued that rather than attempting to determine the meaning of the operative clause independently of the prefatory clause, and then checking to make sure that the meaning of the operative clause is "consistent with the announced purpose," the Court should have read the two clauses together.[61] Both sides cite support for their vigorously defended positions.[62]

Is "keep and bear arms" a construction that refers specifically to military uses, or does it mean the personal right to possess and carry firearms? Justice Scalia brings forth founding era dictionaries and treatises, English and colonial laws, and legal scholarship supporting his claim that the phrase is not restricted to military uses,[63] while to buttress his opposing claim, Justice Stevens marshals an amicus brief by linguistics professors, an eighteenth-century treatise on synonymous words, and a different edition of one of the same dictionaries on which Justice Scalia relies.[64]

As to pre-enactment history, the two sides went at it again. Each, not surprisingly, found the history to support its own view of the text. The majority looked to the British and American historical background of the Second Amendment, and determined that it confirms the conclusion that the amendment "guarantee[s] the individual right to possess and carry weapons in case of confrontation."[65] Englishmen were "extremely wary of concentrated military forces run by the state" and "jealous of their arms" in light of Charles II's and James II's attempts to disarm their political opponents,[66] while the colonists had bad memories of George III's attempts to disarm them.[67] The founders must indeed have thought the right to bear arms unconnected with military service fundamental, the majority stated.[68] Further, the Court argued that similar state constitutional amendments before (and after) the drafting of the Second Amendment reinforced its interpretation of the right at stake.[69] Justice Stevens countered by arguing that these state constitutional provisions each "embedded the phrase ['keep and bear arms'] within a group of principles that are distinctly military in meaning."[70] Focusing on the drafting history of the amendment, Justice Stevens found in it support for the claim that the Framers meant to limit the amendment to military uses of weapons.[71] Some pre–Bill of Rights amendments proposed by several states deliberating ratification of the Constitution "focused on the importance of preserving the state militias and reiterated the dangers posed by standing armies," while others were worded more broadly, and would have protected a right to bear arms unconnected to military service.[72] "Faced with all of these options, it is telling that James Madison chose to craft the Second Amendment as he did. . . . [I]t is clear," Justice Stevens argued, "that he considered and rejected formulations that would have unambiguously protected civilian uses of firearms."[73] The amendment was motivated by "an overriding concern about the potential threat to state sovereignty that a federal standing army would pose, and a desire to protect the States' militias as the means by which to guard against that danger."[74]

The debate over post-enactment developments was every bit as lively. The majority cited post-enactment commentary on the Second Amendment,[75] post–Civil War legislative history,[76] as well as a number of nineteenth-century cases[77] all suggesting that the amendment established an individual right to bear arms unconnected to military service. But the very range of sources consulted by the majority carries with it the danger of selectivity, that is, picking and choosing from a vast array of materials those that appear to support the preferred result. Justice Stevens criticized the sources as "shed[ding] only indirect light on the question before us, and in any event offer[ing] little support for the Court's conclusion."[78] Further, Justice Stevens argued that such sources were equivalent to "postenactment legislative history,"[79] against which Justice Scalia had inveighed in earlier cases, calling it a "contradiction in terms."[80] Justice Scalia defended "the examination of a variety of legal and other sources to determine the public understanding of a legal text in the period after its enactment or ratification" as "a critical tool of constitutional interpretation" necessary to a thorough and exhaustive inquiry into originalist meaning.[81]

With respect to precedent, Justice Scalia distinguished the cases—notably *United States v. Cruikshank*,[82] *Presser v. Illinois*,[83] and *United States v. Miller*[84]—appearing to view the Second Amendment right as a collective one,[85] while Justice Stevens contended that they foreclosed the Court's interpretation.[86] And so on. I need not completely rehash the debate about the right at stake in *Heller;* the story is simple. For every persuasive thrust by one side, the other has an equally convincing parry.[87] The argumentative style of the debate would not be unfit for opposing advocates in a trial. Just as a plaintiff and a defendant each brings forth its expert witnesses who unequivocally testify in favor of their side's view of the facts, so does each set of justices marshal its authorities to cite for its preferred position on the Second Amendment's meaning.

What is a neutral observer left with? Each of the points on which the two sides take issue ends inconclusively. It is hard to look at all this evidence and come away thinking that one side is clearly right on the law. After a careful analysis, Mark Tushnet has concluded that "the arguments about the Second Amendment's meaning are in reasonably close balance,"[88] and that given this indeterminacy, people's positions on the Second Amendment's meaning will have more to do with their ideas about policy than with legal principle.[89] Tushnet's thesis is borne out by the opinions in *Heller*. Each side seems to have—as Justice Scalia accused the majority of doing by relying on sociological studies in *Roper v. Simmons*[90]—"look[ed] over the heads of the crowd and pick[ed] out its friends."[91]

In this freewheeling enterprise, each side travels through time and across the ocean assembling its eclectic array of support for its position. While originalism has many virtues—chiefly an encouragement of historical inquiry and an emphasis on the lawmakers' meaning—it was hardly intended to sanction such untethered inquiries into contradictory signals extending up to a century after the operative event. In the face of such equivocal evidence, plausibly supporting both the majority and dissenting positions, the choice before the Court was a discretionary one. *Heller* was wrong because the majority exercised its discretion to assert judicial supremacy in a manner, I will argue, that will place the courts in the same position envisioned by the judicial supremacists in *Roe*. Justice Stevens and his fellow dissenters should have prevailed—not because Justice Stevens's analysis of the Second Amendment was more persuasive, but simply because it was equally so: "Even if the textual and historical arguments on both sides of the issue were evenly balanced, respect for the well-settled views of all of our predecessors on this Court, and for the rule of law itself, would prevent most jurists from endorsing such a dramatic upheaval in the law."[92]

Heller was not a case of statutory interpretation, where the Court is obliged to weigh close arguments and find the better answer. And even in the statutory arena, there exist interpretive maxims that accord the benefit of the doubt on the most difficult questions to Congress[93] and the states.[94] If *Heller* now stands for the opposite proposition—that ties in constitutional adjudication are to go to the interventionist—then *Roe*'s vision of judicial primacy will be well on its way. For, like *Roe, Heller* is not just a run-of-the-mill constitutional case defining the contours of a long-recognized right. Rather, the textual ambiguity in *Heller* goes to the very existence of an individual right, not its scope; the case involved the creation of a new substantive constitutional right that had not been recognized in over two hundred years.

If further evidence that *Heller* veered toward judicial lawmaking is needed, one can find it in the majority's statement: "[N]othing in our opinion should be taken to cast doubt on longstanding prohibitions on the possession of firearms by felons and the mentally ill, or laws forbidding the carrying of firearms in sensitive places such as schools and government buildings, or laws imposing conditions and qualifications on the commercial sale of arms."[95]

As Justice Breyer notes, the Court does not explain why these restrictions are embedded in the Second Amendment.[96] The Constitution's text, at least, has as little to say about restrictions on firearm ownership by felons as it does about the trimesters of pregnancy. The *Heller* majority seems to want to have its cake and eat it, too—to recognize a right to bear arms without having to deal with any of the more unpleasant consequences of such a right. In short, the Court wishes to preempt democracy up to a point. But up to what point, and why? Justice Scalia eloquently warned the majority in *Casey* that

> the American people love democracy and the American people are not fools. As long as this Court thought (and the people thought) that we Justices were doing essentially lawyers' work up here—reading text and discerning our society's traditional understanding of that text—the public pretty much left us alone. Texts and traditions are facts to study, not convictions to demonstrate about. But if in reality our process of constitutional adjudication consists primarily of making value judgments; if we can ignore a long and clear tradition clarifying an ambiguous text, . . . then a free and intelligent people's attitude towards us can be expected to be (ought to be) quite different. The people know that their value judgments are quite as good as those taught in any law school—maybe better.[97]

Thus the dangers of letting "value judgments" drive constitutional interpretation. *Roe* was rightfully criticized not simply because it was an anti-originalist opinion, but because it was anti-democratic, allowing the justices to make "value judgments" that belonged to the people themselves.

Some observers may be tempted to view *Heller* as a revenge of sorts for *Roe*. One substantive constitutional right deserves another: a sort of judicial tit for tat.[98] Without *Heller*, the course of constitutional law may seem a one-way ratchet, where one side creates a succession of new rights, and the other has no counter. But payback is no solution to what ails constitutional law. For the game of dueling activist Constitutions will become too painful to watch, and the reputational loss to law from the programmatic assumption of political authority will become too great to bear.

To sum up: *Heller* represents a form of judicial activism that is new, yet familiar. The novelty results from *Heller*'s basis in originalism. But this new activism cannot be justified as an exercise in originalism because originalism did not dictate the outcome in *Heller*. To pretend otherwise is to close one's eyes to the subjective choices that originalism allows. Like the choice to consult sources that extend one century after the amendment's enactment in order to discover a meaning that was not apparent to the Court for over two centuries. Or the choice to cut loose from the Constitution a preamble that also reflected the Framers' views and that set the context in which the amendment was to be read. Or the choice to toss overboard like tea in Boston Harbor the Framers' insight of federalism and to ship the Framers' design of separation of powers out to sea. It was only by making these choices—so familiar in their pliability to substantive ends—that the majority in *Heller* found its originalist case to be conclusive.

For a time, conservatives offered a different way: a republican virtue of restraint that held in check the strongest of judicial wills. Now, both sides are playing the same game. The majority won the battle in *Heller;* the dissenters will win battles in the future, as judicial appointments become ever more shaped by the ebb and flow of politics and the sense that many of the great issues of the age, now including gun control, will be settled not by the ballot but in the courts. For when the fog of battle clears, it will be plain that the true casualty of *Heller* was the same casualty as in *Roe:* the right of the American people to decide the laws by which they shall be governed.

II. DESCENDING INTO THE POLITICAL THICKET

Heller is similar to *Roe* for another reason: both decisions placed courts in the middle of political thickets. By finding an individual right to bear arms in the Second Amendment, the Court called into question the whole complex maze of federal, state, and local gun control regulations. As courts get drawn farther into the gun control thicket, they will be forced, as they were by *Roe*, to decide contentious questions without clear constitutional guidance.

A. *ROE*

The notion of the thicket has a venerable lineage. Justice Frankfurter first cautioned the Court about the dangers of the thicket in the context of legislative apportionment.[99] He warned against delving into issues of "extraordinary complexity" that judges are not "equipped to adjudicate by legal training or experience or native wit," and where the "contending forces of partisan politics" often meet.[100] Because of this, Justices Frankfurter and Harlan warned that the issue of apportionment was better left to the legislative branches, as it had been for hundreds of years.[101] Justice Scalia, too, warned against the dangers of the thicket in his plurality opinion rejecting intervention into the treacherous area of political gerrymandering.[102]

The political process was badly unrepresentative, however, before the Warren Court's reapportionment decisions. No such malfunction was identified to justify the prospect of cascading litigation and the difficulties of extraction in the area of abortion law. Thus prescient warnings of the thicket have reverberated through conservative criticism of the Court's abortion jurisprudence since *Roe* was decided in 1973.

The full extent of *Roe*'s infirmities only became apparent with the passage of time, as courts were drawn further and further into an array of subsidiary technical questions regarding abortion. The Supreme Court alone has decided more than twenty-five cases involving abortion.[103] Lower courts have decided many more.[104] Courts have decided cases involving the constitutionality of informed consent requirements from the woman undergoing an abortion,[105] mandatory waiting periods,[106] parental notification and consent requirements,[107] spousal notification and consent requirements,[108] judicial bypass procedures for notification requirements,[109] a lack of funding for nontherapeutic abortions,[110] zoning ordinances excluding abortion clinics,[111] medical requirements for abortion procedures,[112] partial-birth abortion procedures,[113] and regulations regarding the disposal of fetal remains.[114] As one critic put it, "Every new round of abortion cases draws the federal judiciary more deeply into the morass of detail-regulation involving increasingly strained applications of the abortion privacy doctrine."[115]

The Court's entanglement is perhaps best exemplified by its decision in *Casey*. This decision is startling for the number of issues presented and their technical nature. The Court considered the constitutionality of the Pennsylvania spousal notification requirement, informed consent requirement, parental notification requirement and judicial bypass procedure, a medical emergency exception to these requirements, and requirements that facilities report various information about the woman, her medical history, and the physician performing the procedure.[116] The Court's analysis of these issues was detailed, debatable, and inescapably arbitrary. The decision also demonstrates how far the Court had come since *Roe*. As the Court delved into subsidiary issues, the constitutional standard mutated to accommodate the broad array of issues and the need for judicial discretion in resolving them: it went from what was to have been the authoritative trimester framework in *Roe* to an eye-of-the-beholder "undue burden" test applied in *Casey*.[117]

It is almost inevitable that courts will get caught up in the thicket when ruling on issues such as these without clear constitutional guidance. Consider just one of the subsidiary questions cast up by *Roe*—that of parental consent. The Court considered parental consent requirements and judicial bypass procedures no fewer than eight times in sixteen years.[118] Initially in *Danforth*, the Court held that under the *Roe* framework, a "blanket provision" requiring written consent of a parent is unconstitutional during the first trimester because it gives a third party an "absolute, and possibly arbitrary, veto" over the abortion decision without a sufficient state interest to justify the requirement.[119] Three years later the Court confronted a parental consent requirement that provided a judicial bypass procedure.[120] The Court held that such a requirement could be constitutional if the judicial bypass procedure provides the minor an opportunity to show that she is mature enough to make the abortion decision independently or that receiving an abortion is in her best interests.[121] States responded to these constitutional directives from the Court by amending their statutes and thereby presenting the Court with even more choices. For example, in *Hodgson*, the justices disagreed over whether there was a different *constitutional* standard for one-parent versus two-parent notification requirements.[122] As Justice Scalia noted, "One will search in vain the document we are supposed to be construing for text that provides the basis for the argument over these distinctions."[123] Finally, in *Casey*, the Court further refined the constitutional test by holding that it is constitutional for the state to require that parents give *informed* consent after a mandatory twenty-four-hour waiting period because these requirements have "particular force with respect to minors."[124]

The struggle over parental consent requirements shows how courts creating landmark rights inevitably become ensnared in subsidiary questions. As states reacted to Supreme Court rulings and amended their abortion statutes, the Court was forced to draw finer and finer distinctions in order to determine the constitutionality of these provisions. Ultimately, and inevitably, the Court had created a detailed set of regulations resembling an abortion code. Whether the Court was acting more like a legislature or an agency may be unclear, but it was not performing as a court.

The dangers of entering such a morass are exceeded only by the difficulties of extrication from it. Repudiating *Roe* at this late date would leave egg on lots of faces. No one breathlessly anticipates the renunciation of decisions and doctrines in which the justices over time have become deeply invested. But continuing to fine-tune abortion law is not a happy prospect either.

The volume and complexity of *Roe*'s progeny have consumed judicial resources. The technicality of the issues has forced courts to draw arbitrary lines. The volatility of the questions has made courts look value-laden and political. And many of the issues presented have forced courts to make decisions outside the realm of judicial competency.[125] Justice Scalia once described the Court's abortion jurisprudence as "wanderings in [a] forsaken wilderness" that the Court should "get out of"—an area "where we have no right to be, and where we do neither ourselves nor the country any good by remaining."[126] The potential now exists for the same to be said about the Court's new fling with the Second Amendment.

B. *HELLER*

Perhaps in some odd sense, the decision to create a new blockbuster constitutional right can be compared to the decision to launch an invasion. The landmark decision is the easy part; the difficulty comes in the aftermath. The flags flutter at the initial constitutional foray, and then the conflict settles down into a prolonged and politicized trench warfare, with the courts as the generals of both lines.

Just as in *Roe*, the Court in *Heller* is now facing a thicket of subsidiary issues that will thoroughly ensnare it if it applies anything but the most deferential standard of review.[127] The Court has invited future challenges by not defining the scope of the right to bear arms, by not providing a standard of review for firearms regulation, and by creating a list of exceptions to the newfound personal Second Amendment right. The cases filed since *Heller* and the multitude of federal, state, and municipal gun control regulations threaten to suck the courts into a quagmire.

Some have praised *Heller* as a minimalist ruling,[128] for the Court purported to decide only two narrow issues: whether an "absolute prohibition of handguns held and used for self-defense in the home" is constitutional,[129] and whether a requirement that any lawful firearm in the home be disassembled or trigger locked, and thereby "kept inoperable at all times," is constitutional.[130] The Court held that these prohibitions struck at the core of the newly personalized Second Amendment right, and therefore are unconstitutional "[u]nder any of the standards of scrutiny that we have applied to enumerated constitutional rights."[131] Because the District of Columbia laws at issue were some of the strictest in the country,[132] and in the Court's mind clearly unconstitutional, the actual holding of the opinion does not provide much guidance for future cases. The Court did not even provide a standard of review.[133] Instead, by simply rejecting rational-basis review and describing a robust right to self-defense,[134] the Court created "an open invitation to challenge every gun law."[135]

The Court did provide some guidance to lower courts by addressing potential limits on the right to bear arms, but what those limits are and what rationale now justifies them remain open—and litigious—questions. The Court suggested that laws prohibiting the carrying of concealed weapons would be constitutional because these laws had historically been lawful under analogous state constitutional provisions.[136] The Court also stated that "nothing in our opinion should be taken to cast doubt on longstanding prohibitions on the possession of firearms by felons and the mentally ill, or laws forbidding the carrying of firearms in sensitive places such as schools and government buildings, or laws imposing conditions and qualifications on the commercial sale of arms."[137]

Just how these regulatory exceptions came to be "presumptively lawful" and what other exceptions exist await future litigation. Perhaps the list of exceptions was an attempt to offer guidance and forestall future cases, similar to the Court's attempt in *Roe* to tidy the landscape with a "clear" trimester framework. But just as the trimester framework did not fulfill this promise and save the Court from resolving complex medical and legislative issues, the Court's guidance in *Heller* cannot possibly anticipate even a tiny fraction of the questions lurking in the complex array of firearms regulation across the United States.

The Court also recognized one important across-the-board limit on the right to bear arms: it only protects the types of weapons that are commonly used for "lawful purposes like self-defense" and allows the prohibition of "dangerous and unusual weapons."[138] This limit was not at issue in *Heller* because it involved a handgun prohibition. The Court reasoned that handguns were clearly within the types of weapons covered by the Second Amendment because they are the "most popular weapon chosen by Americans for self-defense in the home."[139]

Although the limits that the Court announced were not directly at issue in *Heller*, they were quickly tested in the courts—the "avalanche of Second Amendment claims" has already begun.[140] The day that *Heller* was decided, suit was filed against the City of Chicago challenging its ban on handgun registration and its re-registration requirement for other firearms.[141] The next day, the National Rifle Association filed five lawsuits challenging handgun prohibitions in Chicago, in the suburbs of Chicago, and in public housing in San Francisco.[142] Many motions based on *Heller* were also filed in preexisting criminal cases.[143] Some of these motions have already been denied by courts that have upheld the constitutionality of various gun control regulations, including a prohibition on the possession of firearms by felons,[144] a prohibition on the possession of firearms on post office property,[145] and a prohibition on the possession of machine guns.[146]

The cases and motions filed almost immediately after *Heller* may seem to have clear answers. In some, plaintiffs challenged handgun prohibitions that were similar to those at issue in *Heller* and are likely to be struck down. In others, criminal defendants challenged gun control regulations that were explicitly listed as "presumptively lawful" in *Heller* and are likely to be upheld. But even simple cases foreshadow complicated questions. For example, if the Second Amendment only protects a right to bear arms for the purpose of self-defense, what type of proof suffices that someone sought the weapon for some other purpose? What classes of persons may be presumed to possess a weapon for other than self-defensive purposes, and what classes of weapons may be presumed non-self-protective? Can a municipality that wants strict gun control regulations simply ban the possession of weapons outside the home—for example, in the car? Does the right to bear arms protect the possession of weapons for purposes other than purely self-defense—for recreational pursuits, for the protection of property, or for the protection of others?

Similar issues are raised by the "presumptively lawful" regulations. The Court stated that "prohibitions on the possession of firearms by felons and the mentally ill, or laws forbidding the carrying of firearms in sensitive places such as schools and government buildings, or laws imposing conditions and qualifications on the commercial sale of arms" are "presumptively lawful."[147] What are the scope and rationale of these exceptions to the Second Amendment? Can a nonviolent felon be prohibited from owning firearms? What procedures must be followed before someone is constitutionally classified as "mentally ill" and thereby stripped of his Second Amendment rights? Would a park qualify as a "sensitive place" where guns could be banned in order to protect children even if it left other users of the park defenseless? Even the *Heller* majority confessed that the "presumptively lawful" regulations leave scores of questions. In response to the criticism that *Heller* would create uncertainty, the Court reassured us that "there will be time enough to expound upon the historical justifications for those exceptions we have mentioned if and when those exceptions come before us." But the Court's statement is not reassuring at all; instead, it is an admission that there is a long, hard slog ahead. Even if *Heller* itself sought to be simple, it has simply opened the door.

Just a few weeks after *Heller* was decided, the plaintiff in *Heller* filed a second lawsuit that tests the boundaries of the new individual right to bear arms and presents highly contestable issues.[148] While some of the questions were mooted when the D.C. Council repealed certain gun restrictions in an effort to head off congressional action,[149] the initial suit in *Heller II* is illustrative of the types of issues that are likely to arise. The plaintiffs challenged three main aspects of the amended D.C. statute: the prohibition of machine guns,[150] the requirements for registering guns,[151] and the restrictions on gun storage in the home.[152] This would have immediately drawn courts into ancillary issues left unanswered by *Heller*.

Although the Court in *Heller* suggested that the Second Amendment only protects weapons "in common use" and allows the prohibition of "dangerous and unusual weapons," including machine guns, the plaintiffs argued that the D.C. statute's ban on machine guns was too broad.[153] The definition of "machine gun" included any semiautomatic weapon "which shoots, is designed to shoot, or can be readily converted or restored to shoot . . . more than 12 shots without manual reloading," even if the owner did not have a magazine with the capacity to shoot more than 12 shots without manual reloading.[154] The plaintiffs, who had six-cartridge and ten-cartridge magazines, argued that this interpretation of "machine gun" included guns that were protected by the Second Amendment because they were "in common use" for lawful purposes.[155] The plaintiffs argued further that semiautomatic pistols made up the majority of handguns possessed in the United States and, therefore, just as the handgun ban was unconstitutional in Heller because it prohibited an "entire class" of weapons lawfully used for self-defense, the D.C. machine gun ban also infringed on the core Second Amendment right.[156] This assertion would require the courts to decide *how many shots* a gun must be able to fire without manual reloading before it is too uncommon, and therefore no longer protected by the Second Amendment. Such a line will, to say the very least, be arbitrary, but it is inevitable when dealing with detailed gun control regulations designed to test the constitutional limits of the Second Amendment. The constitutional standard could also require further refinements based on the ability of a semiautomatic weapon to be modified and converted into a validly prohibited weapon—a highly technical determination that is hardly answered by the Constitution or within most judges' competence. As *Heller II* illustrates, the "in common use" standard is so vague as to provide an invitation to litigate. And because the weapons in common use for lawful purposes will inevitably change over time, even the answers provided by litigation will be inherently unstable.

The other allegations in the complaint presented similar types of issues. The plaintiffs argued that the gun registration requirements were onerous and the imposition of a fee for ballistic identification testing was unconstitutional.[157] They pointed to the requirements that gun owners take a written test, pass a vision test, have their fingerprints taken, undergo a background check, and pay a fee, that pistols be submitted for ballistics identification tests, and the potential delay these requirements would cause in issuing registrations.[158] The court was asked to decide whether each of these requirements infringed on the right to bear arms for self-defense, even though they did not approach the complete ban at issue in *Heller*. All this sounds dangerously like the subsidiary issues considered in *Casey* under the "undue burden" test.

The other main allegation was that it was unconstitutional to require that guns be disassembled or secured by a trigger lock unless the gun was being used for self-defense against a "reasonably perceived threat."[159] The addition of the self-defense exception was clearly in response to the Court's decision in *Heller*, and it provoked a new set of questions about the effectiveness of trigger locks in preventing serious accidents in the home and the costs they impose on self-defense.[160] While the battle royal over the D.C. gun regulations was postponed because threatened congressional action caused the D.C. Council to repeal many of the restrictions,[161] the issues are bound to arise in other jurisdictions lacking the District's special relationship with Congress. The echoes of *Roe* are eerie: legislative responses to judicial decisions posed more and more intricate questions to the courts. And similar to what happened in the abortion context, it is easy to see how answers to these questions will quickly turn into a constitutional gun control code, drafted by none other than the judiciary.

Heller II only begins to express the difficulty of the questions on the horizon. There are roughly six main types of gun control regulations: laws regulating classes of weapons, the sale of weapons, gun dealers, gun ownership, mandated safety precautions, and crime detection measures.[162] The specific laws are much more complex and vary widely between federal, state, and local regulations. They include laws regulating assault weapons, large-capacity ammunition magazines, handguns, types of ammunition, restrictions on who can purchase weapons including mental health, minimum age, and domestic violence restrictions, background check requirements, mandatory waiting periods, restrictions on bulk purchases, licensing requirements for gun dealers, licensing for gun owners, registration requirements, restrictions on carrying concealed weapons, safety requirements such as trigger locks and minimum design specifications, crime detection measures such as ballistic identification requirements and retention of background check records, and prohibitions of guns in government buildings and universities.[163] This array of issues rivals and may exceed the number and complexity of subsidiary issues that were eventually decided by courts in the aftermath of *Roe*. Furthermore, these issues are apparent just on the face of current gun control regulations, but it is likely that states will adjust their laws as Second Amendment cases are decided and will further test the constitutional limits. Just as in the abortion context, this will force courts to devise progressively narrower distinctions between permissible and impermissible regulations, thereby drawing them further into the quagmire.

Take the area of restrictions on firearm possession by perpetrators of domestic violence, where we would expect courts to show the most deference because of the obvious state interest in protecting potential victims of domestic violence abuse. Even in this area of greatest deference, questions abound and provide fodder for multiple lawsuits, no matter their likelihood of success. Can a legislature constitutionally prohibit persons who have been convicted of a "misdemeanor crime of domestic violence" from possessing firearms?[164] What if the offender did not use a firearm and only attempted to use physical force?[165] What if the offender has moved to a different state from the former victim? What if the offender has undergone extensive counseling and never committed a second offense? What if the offense was over twenty-five years ago? Is it constitutional for a state to strip all of these offenders of their Second Amendment right to self-defense in the home forever? Questions arise even in seemingly clear areas.

It is not as if the justices in *Heller* were not warned. The problems the thicket presents—consuming judicial resources and forcing unending arbitrary decisions outside the realm of judicial competency—came to the forefront in the aftermath of *Roe* as courts got drawn into deciding complex abortion issues. It is astonishing that the Court has entered the gun control thicket, given the recency of its experience with *Roe*. Many of the justices currently on the Court criticized the Court's immersion in abortion—a similarly contentious, technical, value-laden field—but seem content to replicate the difficulties the abortion quagmire created. It would be heartening to think the Court was chastened by its misadventure and determined not to repeat it. Perhaps the dissenters have been chastened, for they have sounded Scalia-like alarums about "the Court's unjustified entry into *this* thicket."[166] But the majority has disregarded its own long decades of red flags. Rather than emulating *Roe,* *Heller* should have provided the corrective.

So now, predictably and inevitably, the litigation will take off. Courts across the country will face detailed questions about firearms regulations and will provide varied and often inconsistent answers. Circuit splits and open questions will persist for our lifetimes. And for what purpose? What justifies the judiciary asserting its primacy in yet another new arena? Surely not its greater expertise. Surely not, as in apportionment, a dysfunctional political process. As Justice Stevens observed in *Heller,* "no one has suggested that the political process is not working exactly as it should" in firearms regulation.[167] Accordingly, the Court should honor the structure of our Constitution, stay out of the thicket, and leave the highly motivated contestants in this field to press their agendas in the political process where the issue properly belongs and where for centuries it has remained.

III. IGNORING THE LEGISLATURE'S STRENGTHS

In addition to involving courts in complex inquiries best left to the political process, *Heller* and *Roe* are alike for a similar reason: the rights involved in both cases depend on judgments that legislatures are far better equipped than courts to make.

A. *Roe*

Roe's problems began with how it read: more like a statute than a judicial opinion. In 1973 John Hart Ely called *Roe*'s detailed trimester framework a guideline "one generally associates with a commissioner's regulations."[168] Ely was no pro-lifer—he admitted that he agreed with *Roe*'s outcome and would "vote for a statute very much like the one the Court ends up drafting."[169] But as a constitutional lawyer, he could not abide the Court's approach. "[O]rdinarily," he wrote, "the court claims no mandate to second-guess legislative balances."[170] Justice Rehnquist's verdict was succinct. *Roe* was, he said, "judicial legislation."[171]

Later commentators have echoed this critique, noting several unfavorable consequences of *Roe*'s legislative character. First, by usurping the legislative role, the Court ignored the legislature's comparative expertise in assessing empirical claims and adjusting to changes in science and technology. Second, *Roe* shut down the political process by foreclosing legislative compromise and ignoring the lessons of community experience. Finally, the Court's legislative foray has had sociological and institutional effects—emboldening the pro-life movement and radicalizing public positions on abortion, while weakening the Court's legitimacy as an interpretative arbiter on sensitive cultural issues.

1. Separation of Powers and Comparative Expertise

Many scholars have noted that *Roe* was uncommonly aggressive, establishing a framework far beyond the issues presented by the *Roe* plaintiff. Lynn Wardle writes that the result is "a legal doctrine that reads like a set of hospital regulations," and that "[t]he legality of abortion is precisely the kind of policy issue that legislatures are well-suited to address, and that courts are not."[172] This is because legislatures can assess competing factual claims, unconstrained by judicial rules on standing and evidence. Committee reports, expert testimony, and public debate all help legislatures sift through complicated facts to shape informed policy. As Ely wrote, it is "precisely because the claims involved are difficult to evaluate" that we should not trust courts "to guess about them."[173]

In his *Roe* dissent, Justice Rehnquist foresaw that adopting a heightened standard of scrutiny would require courts to continually examine state laws and engage in a "conscious weighing of competing factors" to determine which restrictions on abortions are permissible.[174] These issues have included whether a state law definition of fetal viability conflicts with *Roe*,[175] whether states may prohibit saline amniocentesis abortions after the first trimester,[176] and what types of partial-birth abortion procedures are part of the abortion right.[177] Each of these issues involves complicated science and conflicting medical opinions: *Danforth,* for instance, required the Court to assess the risks and benefits of saline amniocentesis versus the abortifacient prostaglandin. In support of its law banning saline amniocentesis, Missouri presented evidence on the medical risks of the saline method, including rates of tissue destruction in the uterine cavity, bleeding coagulopathies, and maternal mortality rates.[178] The state noted that Japan (and the Yale–New Haven hospital, to boot) had banned this method because of health risks.[179] In response, Planned Parenthood presented evidence from the HEW Center for Disease Control that analyzed the mortality rate per 100,000 legal abortions from 1972–73 and showed that two other methods of abortion (which Missouri had not banned) were more dangerous than the saline method.[180] Further, the amici wrote that amniocentesis, a test to detect birth defects, is best given after the twelfth week of pregnancy, and that women seeking late-term saline abortions tend to have fewer financial and social resources than women who have their abortions earlier.[181]

What did the Court do with these thorny medical and social science questions? The district court deferred to the Missouri state legislature. But the Supreme Court swan-dived into the medical morass, deciding that the saline method is an accepted medical procedure and that the statute's language could ban future, safe abortion methods and the intra-amniotic injection of prostaglandin.[182] Therefore, the Court found the ban "unreasonable or arbitrary" and unconstitutional.[183]

Justice White dissented in part, urging that the Court uphold the saline ban "unless [the Court] purport[s] to be . . . the country's . . . *ex officio* medical board with powers to approve or disapprove medical and operative practices and standards throughout the United States."[184] Later justices have echoed this critique. In *City of Akron,* the Court held that a state could no longer require that all second-term abortions be performed in hospitals; although this regulation was reasonable to protect maternal health in 1973, it was not reasonable for this purpose in 1983.[185] Justice O'Connor objected to the Court's interference with Akron's city government and doubted that the Court was competent to make such calls without the resources of a legislature.[186]

Akron shows that not only is the science complicated, but it constantly advances, leaving courts scrambling in its wake. Ten years after *Roe,* one scholar noted that "[c]hanges in medical technology [had] already necessitated modification of [*Roe's*] model."[187] Legislatures can amend laws when medicine or social conditions change, while courts must wait for the right plaintiff and for direction from superior courts. Abortion is one area where "dramatic changes of circumstances are not only expected but common," and where we want to preserve the ability to tinker with regulations as our knowledge increases.[188] But because legislatures must act within *Roe's* and *Casey's* limits, governments cannot meaningfully debate policy even as science and social conditions change. The country is thus in a state of "willful blindness to evolving knowledge."[189] For example, recent studies suggest that abortion may have more lasting physical and emotional effects on women than previously thought.[190] And although *Roe* assumed a close relationship between women and their doctors,[191] abortion clinic staff members have testified that women rarely receive counseling at their clinics.[192] Neonatal studies now pinpoint when fetuses develop sensitivity to pain and other stimuli.[193] Finally, an uptick in government support may ease the burden of unwanted pregnancies; for example, since 1999, at least forty states have enacted "Baby Moses" laws that let parents leave a newborn anonymously in state care.[194]

Of course, legislatures need not accept these studies. In fact, they are perfectly free to reject them as flawed on any number of grounds. The point is to keep open the debate. Yet the Court in *Casey* moved in exactly the opposite direction, holding that controversial opinions—*even if wrongly decided*—have super–stare decisis power. In *Casey*, the Court implied that the *Roe* rule should be upheld "whether or not mistaken."[195] Because social forces will push back on divisive decisions, the Court should grant such cases "rare precedential force."[196] So the Court is not only institutionally impaired but also institutionally *committed* to maintaining the same rules as facts change on the ground.

2. Political Process and Compromise

When the Court acts legislatively, it interferes with the political process. Although judicial review requires some such interference, it is justified only when a legislature threatens a fundamental right or when the political process is broken. But *Roe* was not a "discrete and insular minority" case.[197] As Ely points out, women are underrepresented in legislatures, but not more than fetuses, and both sides of the abortion debate had been politically active before 1973, each side trading gains and losses and accommodations.[198] For example, Georgia passed a law in 1968 that permitted abortions for a broader range of reasons, but required that the abortion be performed in an accredited hospital and approved by a hospital committee.[199] Polls from the early 1970s to early 1980s show that about 20 percent of the public identified itself as pro-life, while 25 percent identified as pro-choice, with the rest somewhere in between.[200] It is generally recognized that state legislatures were liberalizing abortion rights when *Roe* was decided[201]—there was no political process defect that justified interference from on high.

Moreover, *Roe* shut down this process of legislative accommodation, polarizing the debate and making future compromise more difficult. In 1973 Ely doubted that *Roe* would generate much protest; in fact, he guessed that legislatures were happy to be free of the abortion problem.[202] But a decade later, one scholar observed that "[n]o other case . . . caused such a loud and sustained public outcry" and that "[t]he abortion debate has become an area of impasse, not argument."[203] Public debate typically serves the important democratic function of educating people about an issue, but *Roe* changed the terms of the debate from fetal and maternal health, viability, and medical techniques to the proper role of courts in our society.[204]

Many scholars have commented on *"Roe* backlash"—how the pro-life movement was emboldened by the Court's decision. As Robert Post and Reva Siegel argue, progressives were "[s]tunned by the ferocity of the conservative counterattack" that followed *Roe.*[205] Some people suggest that Roe might have led to increased violence at abortion clinics,[206] and to executive actions such as Nixon's and Reagan's decisions to cut U.S. funding for overseas programs that provided information on abortion.[207] When people feel they have no avenue through the democratic process, they may use much less desirable means to make their voices heard. Looking at polling data in the early 1990s, Michael McConnell predicted that if the abortion issue were returned to state legislatures, many people would support making abortion freely available early in a pregnancy or in cases of rape or incest, but would restrict later abortions and provide waiting periods, counseling, and parental notification.[208] Legislators would be expected to consider dangers to maternal health, the financial and emotional burdens of unwanted pregnancies, and the importance of protecting choice in intimate decisions, and to weigh such things against the need to protect innocent and vulnerable unborn life. These are the kinds of compromises that legislatures, not courts, can and should craft.

Finally, these political and institutional consequences illustrate that separation of powers is not a nicety—it is the basis of our constitutional system. Alexander Bickel wrote that the Court undermines its own power when it strikes down legislation without a strong basis in principle.[209] Others have urged that the Court act with humility and avoid striking down democratically enacted laws when the laws have robust public support and there is a strong risk that the Court is wrong.[210] The result of judges-as-legislators, in Blackstone's words, is "equity without law," where rules come from nothing but each judge's varying sentiments.[211] In the *Federalist Papers,* Alexander Hamilton warned that entangling the judicial, legislative, and executive powers would undermine democratic control of law and portend the end of liberty.[212]

B. *Heller*

Justice Breyer's dissent in *Heller* sounds familiar. He criticized the majority for acting like a legislature. He noted that courts typically defer to legislatures' empirical judgments, and that legislatures are better than courts at analyzing facts. He acknowledged there is a right at stake, but finds that the D.C. regulation is reasonable. This sounds all too much like Justice Rehnquist in *Roe,* who would have upheld Texas's law as a reasonable regulation of the Fourteenth Amendment's due process right.[213] Justice Rehnquist's dissent weighed in heavily on the defects of the judicial perspective and the virtues of the legislative craft. But in *Heller,* the calculus has not changed one whit. Every one of the infirmities that Justice Rehnquist identified in *Roe*—the superior capacity of legislatures to evaluate facts, the narrow perspective that judges bring to contested social issues, and the straitjacket that a constitutional rule places on legislative compromise and changing information—is also present in *Heller.*

1. Separation of Powers and Comparative Expertise

Both *Roe* and *Heller* turn on complicated facts. Under the Court's new *Heller* rule, whether a state regulation passes constitutional muster depends on whether that regulation interferes with the Second Amendment's right to bear arms. Therefore, *Heller* (like *Roe*) has given birth to a balancing test that will force courts into the "conscious weighing of competing factors" as they decide which state interests are sufficiently strong and which regulations unduly burden the new right.[214]

Ironically, Justice Scalia deplores this sort of balancing. In *Heller,* he rebutted Justice Breyer's dissent by chiding that judges cannot balance away the core of an enumerated right. In the Second Amendment context, this core is the "lawful purpose of self-defense."[215] But the Court's dicta on the likely constitutionality of commercial sale regulations and felon possession bans sure looks like balancing: because the history is ambiguous, the opinion seems to announce that some state interests in safety outweigh some personal interest in gun possession. In this way, *Heller* reads like *Roe,* deciding issues not before the Court and making casual empirical assumptions to justify those decisions.

State courts that have ruled on state rights to bear arms have traditionally underenforced the right by deferring to legislative regulations on guns. Adam Winkler, who has studied these decisions, suggests that state courts defer because courts are ill-suited to "'prescrib[ing] workable standards of state conduct and devis[ing] measures to enforce them.'"[216] Winkler suggests that heightened judicial scrutiny in this area would raise "[p]rofound questions of institutional competence" because "[t]he debates over the effectiveness of various forms of gun control are dense, and the empirical data often conflicting, leaving courts understandably reluctant to engage with them."[217] Winkler argues that judicial interference in complicated issues of social science may have particularly dangerous consequences where forcing states to ease gun restrictions could lead to more violent deaths.[218] And deference in the area of gun control should mirror judicial deference in areas like prison regulations, where complex security problems require that local officials have maximum flexibility to adapt to changing information and new threats.[219]

Two specific issues—trigger locks and concealed carry laws—illustrate the inability of courts to decide issues of gun policy. First, the D.C. law at issue in *Heller* required residents to keep lawfully owned firearms "unloaded and disassembled or bound by trigger lock or similar device," with some exceptions.[220] The Court concluded that the trigger lock requirement rendered guns inoperable, and impossible to use for the core right of self-defense. Therefore, the requirement was unconstitutional.[221] But the Court wrote that laws regulating the storage of guns (presumably to keep them beyond the reach of thieves and children) would likely be upheld.[222] The Court never explains why exactly safe storage laws are constitutional, or how they intrude less on Second Amendment rights than trigger locks do.

It is not even clear that trigger locks *do* render guns inoperable. During oral argument, the justices asked about the details of trigger lock technology and how quickly gun users can disable the locks:

CHIEF JUSTICE ROBERTS: So how long does it take? If your interpretation is correct, how long does it take to remove the trigger lock and make the gun operable.

MR. DELLINGER: You—you place a trigger lock on and it has—the version I have, a few—you can buy them at 17th Street Hardware—has a code, like a three-digit code. You turn to the code and you pull it apart. That's all it takes. Even—it took me 3 seconds. . . .

CHIEF JUSTICE ROBERTS: . . . I'd like some idea about how long it takes.

MR. DELLINGER: It took me 3 seconds. I'm not kidding. It's—it's not that difficult to do it. That was in daylight. The other version is just a loop that goes through the chamber with a simple key. You have the key and put it together.[223]

In response, Justice Breyer made the sensible point that we may not want judges all over the country deciding how well trigger locks work.[224] Heller's attorney conceded that legislatures can look to facts such as crime statistics

and murder rates when regulating guns—for instance, presumably, deciding whether a university can ban handguns from dorms will require some
fact-finding.[225] Presumably, courts will be assessing these factual findings
too.[226]

Courts will also confront contested data on concealed carry laws. In *Heller,*
the Court noted that many nineteenth-century courts had upheld concealed
carry bans under the Second Amendment or state analogues.[227] This statement implies that concealed carry bans are safe under *Heller.* But it is not
clear why: preventing someone from carrying a handgun limits the Second
Amendment's core right of self-defense. Once courts are in the business of
second-guessing gun regulations, it makes sense to ask whether concealed
carry bans are reasonable, and the facts are highly disputed. Most prominently, research scientist John Lott argues that banning concealed weapons
increases violent crime, and that "shall-issue" laws, which require states to
issue concealed carry permits to most people who ask, are associated with
decreased violence.[228]

Several scholars have challenged Lott's results in great detail. Ian Ayres and
John Donohue criticize Lott's research with twenty figures and thirty-four
tables designed to challenge Lott's statistical methodology and basic empirical claims.[229] Stephen Teret, a professor at the Johns Hopkins University
School of Public Health, argues that Lott's study "uses incorrect and discredited methodology." He criticizes Lott for using arrest rates to predict crime
rates; for not accounting for general downward trends in violent crime; for
failing to explain why criminals would substitute property crimes for violent
crimes like rape and murder; and for ignoring the possible effects of other gun
laws, such as mandatory waiting periods and background checks.[230] Although
the Court did not dive into this debate in *Heller,* future courts will have to.

A few weeks after *Heller,* the *New England Journal of Medicine* warned
that "[t]he Supreme Court has launched the country on a risky epidemiologic
experiment."[231] For instance, the *Journal* noted that increased access to guns
may increase rates of adolescent suicide.[232] I can imagine future courts analyzing contested empirical studies on gun ownership and suicide to decide
whether state gun regulations are reasonable. As in the abortion context,
courts may be able to find an unreasonable limitation on gun ownership "simply by selectively string-citing the right social science articles."[233] The inca-
pacity of courts to sift through complicated data is exactly what justices have
lamented about *Roe*—for instance, Justice O'Connor noted that *Roe* requires
courts, "[w]ithout the necessary expertise or ability, [to] pretend to act as

science review boards."[234] But no one has explained why judges would be any more suited to assessing data about gun control than they would about abortion. Indeed, the trigger lock and concealed carry examples show that gun technology and crime data, just like the social and scientific data surrounding abortion, will constantly evolve and engender highly technical debate even among experts in the field.

With *Heller,* the Court shut down some of this debate. Regardless of the thicket problem, *Heller* takes legislative options off the table—options that empirical evidence may justify and constituent concerns and fears may warrant. According to the Court, state and local governments cannot require that handguns be disassembled or trigger-locked inside the home, but can restrict to a much greater extent whether and where gun owners carry their guns in public. So imagine a hypothetical city confronting the following crime data: high rates of accidental gun deaths and injuries in the home, high levels of domestic violence and suicide, and a high rate of street crime involving handguns purchased assertedly for home use. The city might want to restrict access to handguns in this case. A city government or state legislature could weigh the costs and benefits of this approach, take testimony, assess the latest studies, and reach some compromise to best address the city's problems. The resulting law might still be poor policy, but a representative government has a right to make that call. Instead, the state or locality would have to follow *Heller,* which would keep it from considering new evidence and require that guns be readily available at home. As with abortion, the Court has thrust the nation into a state of willful blindness to evolving facts. And as with *Roe,* the Court has repositioned the debate from one centered on facts and policy to one focused on surviving multiple layers of judicial scrutiny.[235] The debate will thus become one in which lawyers will play an ever more prominent role, while ordinary citizens and many with practical experience concerning the merits and demerits of firearms legislation will see their role diminished.

2. Political Process and Compromise

Next, as with abortion, there is no political process problem when it comes to gun control—in fact, debate over guns has been quite vigorous. The National Rifle Association currently has over 4 million members,[236] and advocacy groups for gun control, such as the Brady Campaign and the Coalition to Stop Gun Violence, are also strong. The latter group is comprised of forty-five national organizations that include child welfare advocates, religious associations, and public health professionals who work at the grass-roots level to oppose gun violence.[237] These interest groups reflect the strong and varying views held by the public on this issue: polls taken just after *Heller* show that about 54 percent of Americans support stricter gun control laws, while 40 percent oppose them;[238] 27 percent think that stricter laws would reduce violent crime a lot, 21 percent think more laws would reduce violence somewhat, and 50 percent think stricter laws would not reduce violent crime at all.[239] This issue is clearly one that has engaged the electorate's attention, engendered intense feeling, and spawned muscular interest group participation. There is no reason to remove it from what is plainly a highly energized electorate and place it in the lap of the courts.

Instead, the Court should have left these and other decisions to elected bodies. This is partly because legislatures are responsive; they can adjust gun regulations as social conditions change, as trigger lock technology improves, and as studies show more clearly whether gun control increases or decreases violent crime. Legislatures can also capture community experiences not easily expressed in empirical studies—for instance, local concerns about domestic violence, a desire to get guns off the streets, or parents' worries about adolescent suicide or childhood accidents. Legislators are funnels for lots of information, and—perhaps most importantly—they are periodically elected and democratically accountable. Finally, legislators represent a broader cross-section of society than judges do: a teacher is not disqualified from serving in a legislature, but he is effectively disqualified from serving on a court. As Justice Scalia has argued, the Court "has no business imposing upon all Americans the resolution favored by the elite class from which the Members of [the Court] are selected."[240] This is not only because judges bring to the Court a relatively narrow set of life experiences, but also because judges, like most people, talk primarily to people within their own social and professional set. Their political decisions generally "[reflect] the views and values of the lawyer class."[241]

Moreover, it is patently wrong to have an issue that will not only affect people's lives, but could literally *cost* them their lives, decided by courts that are not accountable to them. Some studies suggest that restrictions on handguns reduce violent crime, and that overturning these laws may lead to increased rates of murder and suicide.[242] Absent the clearest sort of textual mandate, we should not entrust courts with such life-and-death decisions. As noted above, the sheer hubris of unelected and unaccountable judges taking over the legislative function on a sensitive political issue was at the core of conservative criticism of *Roe.* Justice Scalia, for instance, has criticized the Court for employing an "ad hoc nullification machine" that prevents one part of our democratic society—those morally opposed to abortion—from persuading the majority that its views are correct.[243] But no one has explained why either the Court's hubris or its takeover is any more justified when gun regulation is at issue. Gun owners are hardly lacking for passionate advocacy in the political process. Legislatures can be expected to register this sentiment and to balance the legitimate desires of citizens to own guns with the legitimate concerns of citizens for their personal and family safety. Federal judges have no business striking down laws whenever they perceive a growing "national consensus"[244]—whether on abortions, guns, or any other hot-button social issue—and thereby disabling all other political viewpoints. Like citizens who oppose abortion, gun control advocates are now increasingly "deprived . . . of the political right to persuade the electorate" that their views are correct.[245]

This final point has nothing to do with empirical studies but everything to do with the central point of the *Roe* dissenters' lament. The dissenters in *Doe* and *Roe* made clear that trust and faith in our democratic system runs at its highest when broad participation throughout the body politic is permitted, and that there is a strong independent value—quite apart from any competence in dealing with facts—in having compromises that reflect people's opinions.[246] The answers to some empirical questions may never be definitively known. But a great part of the value of leaving these questions to a legislature is simply the feeling of empowerment and satisfaction that people enjoy when they live under laws they have had some hand in producing. As with abortion, gun control is one area where "the answers to most of the cruel questions posed are political and not juridical."[247] By removing this issue from the political process, the Court has short-circuited one of the primary benefits of our democratic system—ensuring that "all participants, even the losers, [have] the satisfaction of a fair hearing and an honest fight."[248] This exact infirmity in *Roe,* identified by conservatives again and again since the case was decided, is present in full force in *Heller.*

Finally, given that *Roe* and *Heller* employ such strikingly similar methodologies—relying on contested premises to create a new substantive right and to strike down a legislative act on a sensitive social issue—it is remarkable that no justice in *Heller* even mentions *Roe.* Why, given the parallels between the two cases, is *Heller* so silent on *Roe*? I believe it is because once the comparisons to *Roe* begin, the inconsistencies in the approach of both conservatives and liberals on the Court become undeniable. For decades, conservatives and liberals have held just the opposite view on the relative capacities of courts and legislatures; in *Heller*, both contingents wheeled about to march in the opposite direction, with no explanation for the change in course. Conservatives may argue that turnabout is fair play. But their role as judges requires them to explain why guns and abortions belong in separate boxes, and why a methodology so unacceptable in one context is so appealing in another. There is no good answer to these questions. Once the similarities between *Roe* and *Heller* become apparent, the Court's silence on *Roe* becomes deafening.

IV. DISREGARDING FEDERALISM'S VIRTUES

The Court's impersonation of a legislature in *Heller* was not the decision's final similarity to *Roe*. Both *Roe* and *Heller* also demonstrated a lack of respect for the constitutional division of powers between the federal government and the states. By raising the controversy over guns to the constitutional level, *Heller* continued *Roe*'s troublesome course of arrogating to the Court the power to override laws at the core of the residual police powers the Framers plainly allocated to the states.

A. *ROE*

It is important to remember just how sharp the criticism of *Roe* on federalism grounds actually was. The federalism-based critiques took two basic forms. First, conservatives denounced *Roe* for uprooting traditional state authority over abortion regulations. And second, conservatives faulted *Roe* for improvising a nationwide set of rules for abortions and thus extinguishing the many salutary benefits inherent in our federal structure: adaptation of local policies to local preferences, assimilation of actual experience within the content of the law, the protection of individual liberty through mobility and competition between the states, and the fostering of compromise and unity on divisive policy issues by avoiding a single constitutional approach.

Although much of this federalism-based opposition to *Roe* came from conservatives, the opposition was not necessarily to abortion as such. Instead, critiques of *Roe* from a federalist perspective can be seen as taking a more moderate position, arguing that the states were the proper forum for airing the admittedly powerful arguments on both sides of the abortion debate— arguments deserving of toleration and respect. That said, these critics were far from moderate in their attacks on *Roe* for casting aside the principles of federalism. It is the depth and intensity of this opposition that makes *Heller's* abandonment of federalism so very difficult to comprehend.

1. Traditional State Authority

Roe drew sharp criticism—and charges of judicial activism—for overriding the traditional police power of the states. There is no question that the regulation of abortions historically had fallen within the states' police power over the health, welfare, safety, and morals of the people.[249] Indeed, most states had regulated abortions from the mid-nineteenth century onward.[250] And until *Roe* was decided in 1973, the states' authority over abortion regulations remained plenary.[251] *Roe* washed away that settled landscape, nationalizing the abortion issue and invalidating existing legislation in nearly every state.[252] And while one might have expected *Roe* "to take account of [its] potential intrusiveness in areas of traditional state concern," the Court revamped the federal-state balance on abortion without so much as mentioning the demise of federalism that its decision portended.[253]

The *Roe* decision invited charges of activism—that is, that *Roe* had "'usurped' decisionmaking authority constitutionally vested in the state governments."[254] Justice Rehnquist's dissent in *Roe* questioned how a fundamental right to abortion could be squared with the states' long-standing restrictions on the practice.[255] Justice White echoed those sentiments, observing that the Court's own recognition of historical abortion regulations in *Roe* "convincingly refute[d]" the traditional or fundamental nature of the abortion right in the United States.[256] Thus, *Roe's* abandonment of the historical division of powers between state and federal governments made it appear that the Court had engaged "not in constitutional interpretation, but in the unrestrained imposition of its own, extraconstitutional value preferences" to the detriment of "state electoral majorities."[257]

2. The Federal Design

Roe's conservative critics did not stop at denouncing the decision for disrupting the traditional authority of the states over abortion policy. They went on to assail *Roe* for ignoring the advantages of leaving the abortion issue to the states as well. One common critique was that *Roe* neglected an obvious benefit of the Framers' federal design: the states' ability to tailor their policies to local preferences and conditions, thereby tending to please more constituents than could be done with a single national rule.[258] Critics pointed out that abortion policy was particularly suited to reap the benefits of decentralized decision making. For example, abortion involves controversial and fundamental moral value judgments on which reasonable people can differ from place to place.[259] And the issue does not fly under the radar. Whereas many issues decided below the national level may be too humdrum to excite civic participation, the salience of the abortion debate ensures that citizens will take advantage of their proximity to state political processes and promote localized abortion policies that satisfy their preferences.[260] As Justice Scalia observed, "[T]he division of sentiment within each state [on abortion] was not as closely balanced as it was among the population of the Nation as a whole [prior to *Roe*], meaning not only that more people would [have been] satisfied with the results of state-by-state resolution, but also that those results would [have been] more stable."[261]

Thus, sensitivity to federalism should have counseled respect for local preferences. Instead, *Roe* foreclosed variation and "adopted an extraordinarily detailed set of restrictions on state power."[262] In fact, by "imposing on all states a policy of unrestricted previability abortion, the Court obliterated the genius of structural pluralism."[263]

Roe also generated substantial criticism for ignoring a second "happy incident" of our federal system, recognized famously by Justice Brandeis: experimentation and innovation in the natural laboratories of the states.[264] The issue is particularly fitting for experimentation in the states because it is a complex, multifaceted one involving, inter alia, elements of both medicine and morality.[265] If left to themselves, states could weigh innumerable variables in their abortion policies, beginning with the fundamental questions of how much to restrict abortions, at what stages of the pregnancy to do so, and what sorts of exceptions to allow.

Only the allowance of policy variations permits the assemblage of critical data, the comparisons of different laws and approaches, and the improved decision making by state legislatures. Moreover, prior to *Roe,* the states affirmatively *were* exercising their power to innovate on abortion. The Court itself recognized that Georgia's abortion statute—along with recent reforms in a number of other states—represented "new thinking about an old issue."[266] In short, the prospect of different approaches to abortion was powerful in theory and was occurring in practice. The *Roe* decision significantly narrowed the scope of possible experimentation in the states. Of course, no one contends that *Roe* eliminated state-by-state improvisation entirely. For example, the

Court subsequently permitted Connecticut to limit its Medicaid benefits for nontherapeutic abortions,[267] and it allowed Pennsylvania to try coupling an informed consent requirement with a twenty-four-hour waiting period.[268] But these examples themselves demonstrate that *Roe* limited the states' experimentation on abortion policy to the margins. The "undue burden" test in *Casey* reaffirmed the impotence of states to address the core of the abortion issue—whether and how to limit previability abortions.[269] Innovation was further limited because the states operated under the constant threat of litigation after *Roe*. And facial challenges ensured that many state regulations never became operative, thus preventing any possibility of gleaning useful experiential data from them.[270]

Critics went on to fault *Roe* for overlooking a third benefit of federalism with respect to abortion, namely, the inherent protection of fundamental liberties within our federal structure. Dividing power between the federal and state governments was intended to create "a double security" for "the rights of the people"[271]—to enable each level of government to check the other's ability to encroach upon individual liberties and rights.[272] And by allowing for mobility between the states, our federal system secures a second form of liberty—a democratic or common liberty.[273] This democratic liberty is the familiar right of persons to live, to go to work, and to raise their families in communities that reflect their own deepest moral and personal views. Prior to *Roe*, democratic liberty through mobility was particularly salient to the abortion issue because, for example, Pennsylvania could choose to restrict abortions, whereas neighboring New York could choose to allow abortions, even for Pennsylvanians.[274] But the Court in *Roe* renounced the benefits of democratic liberty by establishing a constitutional rule that was considerably harder to escape through mobility than a comparable rule at the state level.[275]

Roe also was harshly criticized for neglecting a fourth and final benefit of federalism: the ability to achieve compromise, and even national unity, on a divisive issue like abortion. As discussed above in the context of separation of powers, compromise between stark policy choices can often occur more easily within a legislature than within a court. But federalism fosters a different sort of compromise as well, in which citizens of different states can effectively agree to disagree by achieving their own policy objectives within their own jurisdictions. *Roe* effectively obliterated this possibility of compromise between states on matters of abortion policy. In fact, by ignoring state differences and elevating abortion policy to the national level, *Roe* cultivated divisiveness. Both opponents and proponents of abortion rights criticized the decision because it snuffed out a moderate position on abortion, one in which persons in each state could have tolerated and respected the thoughtful positions of persons in other states, despite their disagreements.[276] Instead, citizens of Oklahoma and Massachusetts, of Alabama and California, were forced to swear fealty to the national rule. That *Roe* produced persistent and intense controversy is ironic because *Roe* and its progeny declared their mission as one of promoting an amicable truce on the abortion issue.[277] History quickly contradicted those assertions. No one put it better than Justice Scalia:

> Not only did *Roe* not, as the Court suggests, *resolve* the deeply divisive issue of abortion; it did more than anything else to nourish it, by elevating it to the national level where it is infinitely more difficult to resolve. . . . Pre-*Roe*, moreover, political compromise was possible. . . . *Roe*'s mandate for abortion on demand destroyed the compromises of the past, rendered compromise impossible for the future, and required the entire issue to be resolved uniformly, at the national level. . . . [T]o portray *Roe* as the statesmanlike "settlement" of a divisive issue, a jurisprudential Peace of Westphalia that is worth preserving, is nothing less than Orwellian.[278]

B. *Heller*

Several members of the *Heller* majority have been among the most outspoken critics of *Roe*'s abandonment of federalist principles. Yet the *Heller* decision threatens to subvert federalism in precisely the same manner as *Roe*. The Court's nascent Second Amendment jurisprudence will inevitably upset the states' long-standing authority over gun regulations. *Heller*'s renunciation of federalist principles in the context of the Second Amendment is problematic for a number of reasons, not least of which is that gun regulations are so tied to regional preferences and local concerns. Constitutionalizing the issue of firearms regulation will erode the diversity that geography and demography would otherwise produce. And the extent of that erosion will be entirely up to the Court. By contrast, the interventions of the Rehnquist Court marginally curtailed the powers of Congress under the Commerce Clause and Section 5 of the Fourteenth Amendment, but those interventions had the virtue of simultaneously opening up options for the individual states.[279] Put another way, the Rehnquist Court acted to protect the authority of one democratic institution from the overreaching of another. *Heller* cannot claim that advantage. Like *Roe, Heller* threatens to restrict both federal and state initiatives, thereby cementing the authority of the Court alone to decide the proper scope of gun restrictions throughout the country.

Of course, *Heller* itself invalidated only the firearm regulations operating in the District of Columbia, which is under the control of Congress and thus not subject to the same federalist concerns as the states. But the Court would hardly have gone to such great lengths to recognize a robust Second Amendment right if it did not plan to incorporate that right against the states as well.[280] *Heller* plainly signaled as much: the Court first noted that its 1875 decision in *United States v. Cruikshank* failed to incorporate the Second Amendment against the states. The Court then proceeded to all but label *Cruikshank*'s holding erroneous, observing that *Cruikshank* "did not engage in the sort of Fourteenth Amendment inquiry required by our later cases" and was decided at a time when the Court had not yet applied even the First Amendment to the states.[281] The Court in *Heller* also hinted broadly at its expectation of a future Second Amendment docket. The Court volunteered (less than subtly), "We may as well consider at this point (for we will have to consider eventually) what types of weapons [*United States v.*] *Miller* permits."[282] It is difficult to imagine that the referenced future decisions will not focus on state regulations. Moreover, the majority drafted a list of "presumptively lawful regulatory measures," many—if not all—of which are in place at the state level.[283] But enumeration presupposes something not enumerated,[284] so the Court's list suggests that there are other state regulatory measures that it will find to be unlawful when, to the surprise of no one, it incorporates the Second Amendment against the states.

1. Traditional State Authority

So the shadow is cast over the traditional authority of the states in the same manner that drew such heated criticism in *Roe*. *Heller* acknowledged that the regulation of firearms has historically fallen within the states' police power over public safety;[285] indeed, the Court discussed both state constitutional provisions and state and local regulations dealing with firearms that were contemporaneous with the nation's founding.[286] Congress has mostly respected states' control of gun regulations in the years since the founding,[287] and the Court itself has previously been jealous of any such congressional interference.[288] But *Heller* gave us several reasons to suspect that the Court will show no more respect than *Roe* did to a long tradition of state legislative primacy.

First, the Court read early state constitutional provisions and local regulations to support the majority's own preferred reading of the Second Amendment. Consider for a moment the Court's treatment of founding era state constitutions. It seems reasonable that provisions in those constitutions that expressly referred to a right of self-defense might have meant something different from the Second Amendment, which included no such express reference.[289] But the *Heller* majority summarily dismissed that sensible, textual theory as "worthy of the mad hatter."[290] Instead, the Court chose to read the different texts to mean the same thing.[291] If the Court is willing to deride its opponents for suggesting that texts with different words have different meanings when comparing state and federal gun provisions, can we not expect the Court to continue to override differences between state and federal policies in subsequent decisions? Consider also *Heller*'s treatment of founding era gun regulations. While *Heller* conceded the existence of a ban in colonial Boston against keeping loaded guns indoors, the Court effectively rewrote the text of that prohibition—as well as laws penalizing with a fine the firing of weapons in colonial cities like Philadelphia and New York—by reading a non-textual self-defense exception into the statute.[292] Again, does this signal anything less than the Court's determination to curtail the states' authority to enact their own policies controlling firearms?

Second, *Heller* failed to appreciate the traditional power of the states over firearm regulations because the Second Amendment itself can be seen to embody federalist principles. Under this view, the amendment was drafted as a means of protecting the sovereignty of the states by safeguarding the states' militias against federal disarmament (but of course leaving the states to regulate the arms of their militias as they pleased).[293] But the majority dismissed that historical, federalism-based interpretation through sheer ipse dixit: "The Second Amendment right, protecting only individuals' liberty to keep and carry arms, did nothing to assuage Antifederalists' concerns about federal control of the militia."[294] Thus, while the Court may conceivably give more consideration to federalism in future cases extending beyond the District, *Heller* has already announced the majority's lack of respect for traditional principles of federalism in connection with the Second Amendment. All the anguish over *Roe*'s displacement of traditional state prerogatives was forgotten. By the time the Court finishes explicating the full scope of its new Second Amendment right, the states' power over guns may resemble little more than the fading grin of the Cheshire cat.

2. The Federal Design

The Court's apparent willingness to constitutionalize the field of firearms also threatens to sacrifice—as in *Roe*—the many prospective benefits produced by different policies in different places under our federal structure. For one, *Heller* diminished the benefits of decentralized decision making in adapting gun policies to local opinions and concerns. In particular, establishing a more uniform national gun policy through the Second Amendment would be particularly improvident because gun regulations are so uniquely tied to the different views and conditions among regions, individual states, and even smaller units of government.[295]

It should go without saying that preferences for gun regulations vary widely among regions within the United States. Even a cursory review reveals that firearm regulations tend to be stricter in coastal, northeastern, and a few midwestern states than in the mountain West and southern states, where antipathy to gun control runs deep and wide. For example, only seven states currently ban assault weapons: California, Connecticut, Hawaii, Massachusetts, Maryland, New Jersey, and New York.[296] The regional distribution of those states is readily apparent. And when the Brady Campaign to Prevent Gun Violence recently ranked the states based on the overall restrictiveness of their firearm regulations, the ten most restrictive states exhibited a similarly striking regional concentration: California, New Jersey, Connecticut, Massachusetts, Maryland, New York, Rhode Island, Hawaii, Illinois, and Pennsylvania.[297] These examples provide a flavor of the regional differences in gun laws throughout the nation and the corresponding benefits of decentralized firearm policies.

The marked differences among gun regulations in individual states also demonstrate the utility of allowing states to tailor their policies to local preferences. California, for instance, has enacted the following laws, among others: bans on assault weapons, large-capacity ammunition magazines, and fifty-caliber rifles; regulations of ammunition and non-powder guns; waiting periods for gun purchases; a limit of one handgun purchase per person per month; regulations of firearm dealers and gun shows; universal background checks for all firearm transfers; licensing requirements for handguns; and locking device requirements.[298] Montana and Arkansas, on the other hand, have enacted *none* of those policies.[299] And North Carolina, for example, operates somewhere in between: it regulates ammunition, non-powder guns, and gun dealers, and it also requires licenses for handguns, but it shares none of California's additional restrictions.[300]

Important distinctions also exist between policies at the statewide and local levels, suggesting even further benefits of localized decision making. For example, no state bans all types of handguns.[301] But some cities have enacted complete handgun bans, including Chicago (and some of its suburbs), San Francisco, and, of course, the District of Columbia.[302] Similarly, nearly every state issues permits to allow concealed carrying of weapons.[303] But a number of cities—including Chicago, Cleveland, Columbus, Hartford, New York City, and Omaha—restrict concealed carrying much more strictly than their respective states; some of those cities prohibit concealed carrying altogether, while others bar the practice with limited exceptions.[304] These local policies are undoubtedly premised on the perceived dangers associated with guns in urban environments, namely, higher rates of violent crime (particularly homicides) involving firearms (particularly handguns).[305] Conversely, the absence of such restrictions in other localities may reflect the central place of firearms in the life of more rural communities.

Indeed, the connection between gun policy and local conditions was quite apparent in *Heller*. As Justice Breyer stressed in dissent, the District enacted its handgun ban to counteract the specific problems of gun violence in the "District's exclusively urban environment."[306] Thus, deference to the District's judgment would have seemed "particularly appropriate" because that judgment was based on "particular knowledge of local problems and insight into appropriate local solutions."[307] But the majority in *Heller* rejected such deference without even appearing to consider the important federalism interests that informed criticism of *Roe*. The variation in views that made a state-by-state approach seem desirable in the area of abortion law somehow became irrelevant to the majority in *Heller*.

The *Heller* decision emphasized instead the severity of the District's handgun ban in comparison to other historical examples of statewide gun regulations.[308] But that emphasis completely failed to appreciate the distinctions between the local conditions faced by the District today and those faced by Georgia and Tennessee in the mid-nineteenth century. Thus, *Heller* set the Court on the path of ignoring and abandoning the benevolent effects of decentralized policymaking on gun regulations—just as the Court did with respect to abortions in *Roe*.

Heller also endangers, like *Roe* before it, another fundamental benefit of federalism: experimentation and innovation in the natural laboratories of the states. Experimentation among states and cities is critical to producing effective gun regulations. The persistence of gun violence in the schools, offices,

malls, and fast-food restaurants of our country demonstrates that some creative thought is necessary. And state and local governments need the freedom
to improvise and innovate and, in particular, to adapt their solutions to the
unique circumstances in their own community.[309] Furthermore, innovative
policies in one jurisdiction benefit not only that jurisdiction but also, through
the sharing of information and results, the nation as a whole. As discussed
above, legislatures are in a better position than courts to weigh empirical
evidence with respect to gun policies.[310] But that empirical data must come
from somewhere. And that somewhere is the natural laboratory of federalism.
Variations in policy between state and local governments provide results that
legislatures can compare, thereby pushing the entire nation toward more effi-
cacious solutions. One important example is the prickly issue of causation: Do
gun restrictions cause more or fewer gun crimes?[311] More guns may equate
to more violence or to more mutual deterrence, and judges, as noted, are in
the least advantageous position to answer such thorny questions. Innovative
policies could help to resolve the causation issue by showing how violence
changes when regulations change in various settings.[312]

As was the case with abortion policies before *Roe,* states and cities were
exercising their prerogative to innovate prior to the *Heller* decision. The
District's handgun ban—no matter how unwise in the eyes of a majority of
the Court—is a ready example of such an experiment. Richmond, Virginia,
presents an alternative, innovative technique for combating gun violence.
Beginning in the late 1990s, Richmond "reduced firearm-related violence
dramatically . . . not by making gun purchases more difficult—Virginia is one
of the easiest places to legally buy a handgun—but by severely punishing all
gun crimes, including those as minor as illegal possession."[313] As expected, the
results of those efforts have been shared with representatives from other cities
who have visited Richmond to learn about its enforcement program.[314] Furthermore, in states like California, innovations at the local level have continuously spawned reforms at the state level.[315] And at the state level, for example,
twenty-nine states have enacted legislation permitting concealed carrying of
firearms since 1990.[316]

Heller threatens to curb this experimentation and its benefits. As with *Roe,*
innovation now faces almost certain litigation. While the Court in *Heller*
insisted that numerous policy options are still available to the District,[317] the
lessons of *Roe* are clear: as the Court establishes a national set of restrictions
on gun regulations, it will limit the space in which states and cities can innovate. Although Justice Kennedy was in the majority in *Heller,* he previously

observed in *Lopez* the specific danger that a mere federal statute poses to beneficent local experimentation on gun regulations.[318] The threat of litigation under a federal constitutional rule increases that danger exponentially.[319] And as was the case after *Roe,* many jurisdictions are likely to respond to the *Heller* decision not with new and thoughtful solutions for the problems of gun violence, but with legislation aimed at evading the Court's decision. In fact, the District of Columbia revised its regulations after *Heller* in what appears to be the narrowest manner possible—and a manner that may still conflict with *Heller*'s announcement of a vigorous right to self-defense in the home.[320] Such efforts—provoked by the Court's overreaching—reposition resources that could be devoted to useful thinking into how to avoid lawsuits. *Heller* thus repeated the mistake of *Roe* and courts the same sad consequences.

The *Heller* decision also repeated *Roe*'s mistake of underestimating federalism's inherent capacity to protect liberty. Like the Court's recognition of a fundamental right to abortion in *Roe,* the Court's recognition of a robust Second Amendment individual right appeared to presume that states and cities cannot adequately protect the liberty to keep and bear arms. But that presumption ignored the protection of liberties in our federal system through diffusion of power, as well as mobility and competition between the states. Residents of the District who were unhappy with the handgun ban, for example, remain free to move to other localities more protective of gun rights. To be sure, moving anywhere is no small inconvenience, but staying put does not confer the right to have the law comply with one's own preferences. Under the Court's rigid national rule, moreover, no one will be able to exercise the liberty to live in a city in which handguns are prohibited. Because the Second Amendment is at best ambiguous in establishing a fundamental right to self-defense in the home, I have little doubt that Madison and Hamilton would describe the Court's rule, not the District's, as the greater infringement on liberty.

Finally, the *Heller* decision abandoned a fourth benefit of our federal structure: the possibility of state-by-state compromise on the controversial issue of gun control and the fostering of national unity around the positive principle of federalism. Just as *Roe* made the abortion issue significantly more divisive by taking the possibility of its resolution away from the states, *Heller* elevated the review of gun regulations to the national level, "where it is infinitely more difficult to resolve."[321] These efforts will serve only to make the debate over gun laws more intractable. Others have reacted to *Heller* by proposing that the decision may actually lessen divisiveness. Their theory is that *Heller* will encourage reasonable debate because the decision took the polarizing policy of handgun prohibitions off the table.[322] But those arguments merely replicate the failed predictions that *Roe* would resolve the abortion issue. As the Court blueprints its Second Amendment jurisprudence and subjects every state and local regulation to federal court review, the national controversy over gun policy will intensify. Placing issues in the courts is no safety valve, and it builds frustration in those whom judicial decisions disenfranchise.

So, *Heller* jettisoned the many benefits of federalism, and it did so despite the lessons of *Roe*. This course is both troubling and perilous. Federalism must remain more than a pliable means to substantive ends—treated as either a rhetorical device to be employed when convenient or a nuisance to be ignored when less so. It is disheartening that Justices who deplored decisions like *Roe* on federalism grounds ignore the constraints of federalism when the substantive terrain shifts to firearms. It is disheartening that the dissenting Justices in *Heller* decline to apply their federalism-based critiques across the board, even on issues like abortion. The shoe must be worn when it pinches as well as when it comforts.[323] Uneven treatment denies dual sovereignty the respect it deserves and will fuel accusations of a policy-driven Court.

CONCLUSION

Law entrusts judges with responsibilities and society accords them its respect. In return, the social order asks of judges one basic thing—that they respect the parameters of those tasks the Constitution assigns them and observe the need for self-imposed restraint. All persons, be they teachers or carpenters, ministers or congressmen, gain stature within prescribed roles and are over time diminished by departures. A judge's view of law may be esteemed; a judge's view on policy is worth no more than any other. It is that simple compact that the rule of law embodies—we have been given much, but it comes with a warning. It is that warning *Roe* and *Heller* failed to heed.

In closing, I cannot help but recall Justice Scalia's lament in *Casey:* "[B]y foreclosing all democratic outlet for the deep passions this issue arouses, by banishing the issue from the political forum that gives all participants, even the losers, the satisfaction of a fair hearing and an honest fight, by continuing the imposition of a rigid national rule instead of allowing for regional differences, the Court merely prolongs and intensifies the anguish."[324]

Yet, sixteen years later, the Court now takes an issue about which the nation is deeply divided and narrows democratic outlets, overlooks regional differences, and imposes a rigid national rule. *Heller* thus represents the worst of missed opportunities—the chance to ground conservative jurisprudence in enduring and consistent principles of restraint. The Constitution expresses the need for judicial restraint in many different ways—separation of powers, federalism, and the grant of life tenure to unelected judges among them. It is an irony that *Heller* would in the name of originalism abandon insights so central to the Framers' designs. The losers in *Heller*—those who supported the D.C. handgun law, or, more accurately, supported the D.C. voters' right to enact it—have cause to feel they have been denied the satisfaction of a fair hearing and an honest fight. I hope only that my fondness for the Scalia of *Casey* and the restraint of Hand[325] and Holmes is grounded in more than nostalgia for days of judicial modesty gone by.

NOTES

Source: Reprinted from 95 Va. L. Rev. 253 Copyright © 2009 Virginia Law Review Association; J. Harvie Wilkinson III.

1. 128 S.Ct. 2783 (2008).

2. 410 U.S. 113 (1973).

3. See, e.g., *Brown v. Bd. of Educ.*, 347 U.S. 483 (1954).

4. See, e.g., *Plessy v. Ferguson*, 163 U.S. 537 (1896).

5. *New State Ice Co. v. Liebmann*, 285 U.S. 262, 311 (1932) (Brandeis, J., dissenting).

6. Benjamin N. Cardozo, The Nature of the Judicial Process 141 (1921), *quoted in* Robert A. Sedler, The Constitution, the Courts and the Common Law, 53 Wayne L. Rev. 153, 157 n.11 (2007).

7. *Lochner v. New York*, 198 U.S. 45, 76 (1905) (Holmes, J., dissenting).

8. See generally Tom R. Tyler, Why People Obey the Law (2006).

9. 410 U.S. 179 (1973).

10. *Roe*, 410 U.S. at 164–65.

11. 388 U.S. 1 (1967).

12. 268 U.S. 510 (1925).

13. 262 U.S. 390 (1923).

14. The cases all overturned laws that represented the worst sort of bias toward racial (*Loving*), religious (*Pierce*), or ethnic (*Meyer*) minorities. It would be odd for defenders of *Heller* or *Roe* to use them as a basis for substantive rights creation. I am also not persuaded by the argument that because the Court prior to *Roe* announced certain non-textual rights—see, for example, *Skinner v. Oklahoma*, 316 U.S. 535 (1942)—that the Court in *Roe* and thereafter was free to embark upon a course of loose substantive rights recognition.

15. *Lochner v. New York,* 198 U.S. 45 (1905).

16. *Doe v. Bolton,* 410 U.S. 179, 221–22 (1973) (White, J., dissenting).

17. *Roe,* 410 U.S. at 172 (Rehnquist, J., dissenting).

18. 476 U.S. 747 (1986).

19. Id. at 787 (White, J., dissenting) (emphasis added).

20. Id. at 789.

21. Id. at 790.

22. 505 U.S. 833 (1992).

23. Id. at 951–52 (Rehnquist, C.J., concurring in the judgment in part and dissenting in part).

24. Id. at 953 (quoting *Webster v. Reprod. Health Servs.,* 492 U.S. 490, 518 (1989) (plurality opinion)).

25. 497 U.S. 502 (1990).

26. Id. at 520 (Scalia, J., concurring).

27. 492 U.S. 490 (1989).

28. Id. at 535 (Scalia, J., concurring in part and concurring in the judgment).

29. 497 U.S. 417 (1990).

30. Id. at 480 (Scalia, J., concurring in the judgment in part and dissenting in part).

31. *Planned Parenthood of S.E. Pa. v. Casey,* 505 U.S. 833, 980 (1992) (Scalia, J., concurring in the judgment in part and dissenting in part).

32. See, e.g., Walter Dellinger & Gene B. Sperling, Abortion and the Supreme Court: The Retreat from *Roe v. Wade,* 138 U. Pa. L. Rev. 83 (1989); Ronald Dworkin, Unenumerated Rights: Whether and How *Roe* Should Be Overruled, 59 U. Chi. L. Rev. 381 (1992); Philip B. Heymann & Douglas E. Barzelay, The Forest and the Trees: *Roe v. Wade* and Its Critics, 53 B.U. L. Rev. 765 (1973).

33. See, e.g., Robert M. Byrn, An American Tragedy: The Supreme Court on Abortion, 41 Fordham L. Rev. 807 (1973); Charles E. Rice, The Dred Scott Case of the Twentieth Century, 10 Hous. L. Rev. 1059 (1973).

34. Gerald Gunther, Commentary, Some Reflections on the Judicial Role: Distinctions, Roots, and Prospects, 1979 Wash. U. L.Q. 817, 819.

35. Alexander M. Bickel, The Morality of Consent 28 (1975).

36. Richard A. Epstein, Substantive Due Process by Any Other Name: The Abortion Cases, 1973 Sup. Ct. Rev. 159, 180.

37. John Hart Ely, The Wages of Crying Wolf: A Comment on *Roe v. Wade,* 82 Yale L.J. 920, 947 (1973).

38. Id. at 935–36 (footnote omitted).

39. Ruth Bader Ginsburg, Essay, Some Thoughts on Autonomy and Equality in Relation to *Roe v. Wade,* 63 N.C. L. Rev. 375, 381 (1985).

40. Id. at 382.

41. See What *Roe v. Wade* Should Have Said (Jack M. Balkin ed., 2005).

42. Erwin Chemerinsky, Rationalizing the Abortion Debate: Legal Rhetoric and the Abortion Controversy, 31 Buff. L. Rev. 107, 126–28 (1982).

43. See Donald H. Regan, Rewriting *Roe v. Wade*, 77 Mich. L. Rev. 1569 (1979).

44. See Ruth Bader Ginsburg, Speaking in a Judicial Voice, 67 N.Y.U. L. Rev. 1185, 1199–200 (1992).

45. See, e.g., Robin West, Concurring in the Judgment, *in* What *Roe v. Wade* Should Have Said, supra note 41, at 121, 121–35.

46. Cass R. Sunstein, Comment, *in* What *Roe v. Wade* Should Have Said, supra note 41, at 248, 249.

47. U.S. Const. amend. II.

48. See *Heller*, 128 S.Ct. at 2817–18.

49. Id. at 2788.

50. See *Roe*, 410 U.S. at 129–41 (concluding that recent regulations on abortion were more restrictive than historical regulations).

51. See D.C. Code §7-2507.02 (2001); *Heller*, 128 S.Ct. at 2817–18.

52. Specifically, the Court only held that citizens have the right to keep an operable handgun at home for self-defense. *Heller*, 128 S.Ct. at 2818–19.

53. See *Roe*, 410 U.S. at 164–65.

54. Stuart Taylor Jr., Torn by the Past: D.C. Gun Case Shows Shortcomings of Originalism, Legal Times, July 7, 2008, at 44, 44.

55. Id. at 45.

56. Id. at 44.

57. See Brief for Professors of Linguistics and English Dennis E. Baron, Ph.D., Richard W. Bailey, Ph.D. and Jeffrey P. Kaplan, Ph.D. in Support of Petitioners, *District of Columbia v. Heller*, 128 S.Ct. 2783 (No. 07-290) [hereinafter Linguists' Brief].

58. *Heller*, 128 S.Ct. at 2789.

59. Id. at 2790.

60. Id. at 2826 (Stevens, J., dissenting) ("That is not how this Court ordinarily reads such texts, and it is not how the preamble would have been viewed at the time the Amendment was adopted.").

61. Id. (quoting *Heller*, 128 S.Ct. at 2790 (majority opinion)).

62. See id. at 2789–90 (majority opinion) (citing Fortunatus Dwarris, A General Treatise on Statutes 268–69 (Platt Potter ed., 1871); Theodore Sedgwick, A Treatise on the Rules Which Govern the Interpretation and Construction of Statutory and Constitutional Law 42–45 (2d ed. 1874); Eugene Volokh, The Commonplace Second Amendment, 73 N.Y.U. L. Rev. 793, 814–21 (1998)); *Heller*, 128 S.Ct. at 2826 n.7 (Stevens, J., dissenting) (citing Dwarris, supra, at 268, 269; 2A Norman J. Singer, Sutherland on Statutes and Statutory Construction §47.04, at 146 (rev. 5th ed. 1992)).

63. Id. at 2791–97 (majority opinion) (citing, inter alia, An Act for the Trial of Negroes, 1797 Del. Laws ch. XLIII, §6, in 1 The First Laws of the State of Delaware 102, 104 (John D. Cushing ed., 1981 (pt. 1)); Pa. Declaration of Rights §XIII, *in* 5 The Federal and State Constitutions, Colonial Charters, and Other Organic Laws 3082, 3083 (Francis Newton Thorpe ed., 1909); 4 William Blackstone, Commentaries on the Laws of England 55 (3d ed. 1769); 1 Timothy Cunningham, A New and Complete Law Dictionary (1771); 1 William Hawkins, A Treatise of the Pleas of the Crown 26 (1771); 1 Samuel Johnson, A Dictionary of the English Language 107 (5th ed. 1773); 30 Journals of the Continental Congress 349–51 (John C. Fitzpatrick ed., 1934); Randy E. Barnett, Was the Right to Keep and Bear Arms Conditioned on Service in an Organized Militia? 83 Tex. L. Rev. 237, 261 (2004)).

64. Id. at 2827–30 (Stevens, J., dissenting) (citing, inter alia, Linguists' Brief, supra note 57, at 19; 1 Samuel Johnson, A Dictionary of the English Language (2d ed. 1755); 1 John Trusler, The Distinction between Words Esteemed Synonymous in the English Language 37 (3d ed. 1794)).

65. Id. at 2797 (majority opinion).

66. Id. at 2798.

67. Id. at 2799.

68. Id. at 2798.

69. Id. at 2802–3.

70. Id. at 2834 (Stevens, J., dissenting).

71. Id. at 2833–37.

72. Id. at 2833.

73. Id. at 2833–35.

74. Id. at 2836.

75. Id. at 2805–7 (majority opinion) (citing, inter alia, 2 Blackstone's Commentaries 143 (St. George Tucker ed., 1803); William Rawle, A View of the Constitution of the United States of America 122 (1825); 3 Joseph Story, Commentaries on the Constitution of the United States §1891, at 747 (1833); Joel Tiffany, A Treatise on the Unconstitutionality of American Slavery 117–18 (1849)).

76. Id. at 2809–11 (citing, inter alia, H.R. Rep. No. 41–37, at 7–8 (3d Sess. 1871) (statement of Rep. Butler); Joint Comm. on Reconstruction, H.R. Rep. No. 39–30, pt. 2, at 229 (1st Sess. 1866) (Proposed Circular of Brigadier General R. Saxton); Cong. Globe, 39th Cong., 1st Sess. 1182 (1866) (statement of Sen. Pomeroy); id. at 1073 (statement of Rep. Nye)).

77. See id. at 2807–9 (citing *Nunn v. State*, 1 Ga. 243, 251 (1846); *State v. Chandler*, 5. La. Ann. 489, 490–91 (1850); *United States v. Sheldon* (Mich. 1829), *in* 5 Transactions of the Supreme Court of the Territory of Michigan 1825–1836, at 337, 346 (William Wirt Blume ed., 1940); *Aldridge v. Commonwealth*, 4 Va. 447, 2 Va. Cas. 447, 449 (Gen. Ct. 1824)).

78. Id. at 2837 (Stevens, J., dissenting).

79. Id. at 2837 n.28.

80. Id. (quoting *Sullivan v. Finkelstein*, 496 U.S. 617, 631–32 (1990) (Scalia, J., concurring in part)).

81. Id. at 2805 (majority opinion) (emphasis omitted).

82. 92 U.S. 542 (1875).

83. 116 U.S. 252 (1886).

84. 307 U.S. 174 (1939).

85. *Heller*, 128 S.Ct. at 2812–16.

86. Id. at 2842–46 (Stevens, J., dissenting).

87. Cf. Karl N. Llewellyn, The Common Law Tradition: Deciding Appeals 521–35 (1960) (describing contradictory canons of statutory interpretation as "thrusts" and "parries").

88. Mark V. Tushnet, Out of Range: Why the Constitution Can't End the Battle over Guns xvi (2007).

89. Id. at 116–17.

90. 543 U.S. 551 (2005).

91. Id. at 617 (Scalia, J., dissenting).

92. *Heller*, 128 S.Ct. at 2824 (Stevens, J., dissenting) (citations omitted).

93. See, e.g., *Chevron U.S.A. Inc. v. Natural Res. Def. Council Inc.*, 467 U.S. 837, 843–45 (1984) (explaining that, in cases of ambiguity, deference is given to the interpretation of the agency with which Congress has entrusted enforcement of the statute).

94. See, e.g., *Gregory v. Ashcroft*, 501 U.S. 452, 470 (1991) (finding that the clear statement rule requires that the federal government speak with clarity if it intends to override the traditional prerogative of the states when acting pursuant to the Commerce Clause in addition to section 5 of the Fourteenth Amendment).

95. *Heller*, 128 S.Ct. at 2816–17 (majority opinion).

96. Id. at 2869–70 (Breyer, J., dissenting).

97. *Planned Parenthood of S.E. Pa. v. Casey*, 505 U.S. 833, 1000–1001 (1992) (Scalia, J., concurring in the judgment in part and dissenting in part) (emphasis omitted).

98. See Richard A. Posner, In Defense of Looseness, The New Republic, August 27, 2008, at 32, 33 ("The idea behind the decision . . . may simply be that turnabout is fair play. Liberal judges have used loose construction to expand constitutional prohibitions beyond any reasonable construal of original meaning; and now it is the conservatives' turn.").

99. *Colegrove v. Green*, 328 U.S. 549, 556 (1946).

100. *Baker v. Carr*, 369 U.S. 186, 323–24 (1962) (Frankfurter, J., dissenting).

101. Id. at 268 (Frankfurter, J., dissenting); id. at 337 (Harlan, J., dissenting); see also *Reynolds v. Sims*, 377 U.S. 533, 624 (1964) (Harlan, J., dissenting) ("What

is done today deepens my conviction that judicial entry into this realm is profoundly ill-advised and constitutionally impermissible.").

102. See *Vieth v. Jubelirer*, 541 U.S. 267, 278–91 (2004) (plurality opinion).

103. See, e.g., *Gonzales v. Carhart*, 550 U.S. 124 (2007); *Ayotte v. Planned Parenthood of N. New Eng.*, 546 U.S. 320 (2006); *Stenberg v. Carhart*, 530 U.S. 914 (2000); *Mazurek v. Armstrong*, 520 U.S. 968 (1997); *Lambert v. Wicklund*, 520 U.S. 292 (1997); *Planned Parenthood of S.E. Pa. v. Casey*, 505 U.S. 833, 833 (1992); *Rust v. Sullivan*, 500 U.S. 173 (1991); *Ohio v. Akron Ctr. for Reprod. Health* (*Akron II*), 497 U.S. 502 (1990); *Hodgson v. Minnesota*, 497 U.S. 417 (1990); *Webster v. Reprod. Health Servs.*, 492 U.S. 490 (1989); *Thornburgh v. Am. Coll. of Obstetricians and Gynecologists*, 476 U.S. 747 (1986); *Simopoulos v. Virginia*, 462 U.S. 506 (1983); *Planned Parenthood Ass'n of Kan. City, Mo. v. Ashcroft*, 462 U.S. 476 (1983); *City of Akron v. Akron Ctr. for Reprod. Health* (*Akron I*), 462 U.S. 416 (1983); *H.L. v. Matheson*, 450 U.S. 398 (1981); *Williams v. Zbaraz*, 448 U.S. 358 (1980); *Harris v. McRae*, 448 U.S. 297 (1980); *Bellotti v. Baird* (*Bellotti II*), 443 U.S. 622 (1979); *Colautti v. Franklin*, 439 U.S. 379 (1979); *Poelker v. Doe*, 432 U.S. 519 (1977); *Maher v. Roe*, 432 U.S. 464 (1977); *Beal v. Doe*, 432 U.S. 438 (1977); *Planned Parenthood of Cent. Mo. v. Danforth*, 428 U.S. 52 (1976); *Doe v. Bolton*, 410 U.S. 179 (1973); *Roe v. Wade*, 410 U.S. 113 (1973); see also NARAL Pro-Choice Am. Found., U.S. Supreme Court Decisions Concerning Reproductive Rights 1965–2007, www.prochoiceamerica.org/assets/files/Courts-SCOTUS -Choice-Cases.pdf (listing cases).

104. See Lynn D. Wardle, Rethinking *Roe v. Wade*, 1985 BYU L. Rev. 231, 238 & n.41 (1985) (noting that lower federal courts decided over 250 cases involving abortion between 1973 and 1985 alone).

105. See, e.g., *Akron I*, 462 U.S. at 444.

106. See, e.g., id. at 449–51.

107. See, e.g., *Hodgson*, 497 U.S. at 422–23.

108. See, e.g., *Casey*, 505 U.S. at 887–98.

109. See, e.g., *Bellotti v. Baird* (*Bellotti II*), 443 U.S. 622, 643–44 (1979).

110. See, e.g., *Maher v. Roe*, 432 U.S. 464, 466 (1977).

111. See, e.g., *W. Side Women's Servs. v. City of Cleveland*, 573 F.Supp. 504, 506, 523–24 (N.D. Ohio 1983).

112. See, e.g., *Planned Parenthood Ass'n of Kan. City, Mo. v. Ashcroft*, 462 U.S. 476, 494 (1983).

113. See, e.g., *Gonzales v. Carhart*, 550 U.S. 124, 132 (2007).

114. See, e.g., *Akron Ctr. for Reprod. Health v. City of Akron*, 651 F.2d 1198, 1211 (6th Cir. 1981).

115. Wardle, supra note 104, at 249.

116. *Planned Parenthood of S.E. Pa. v. Casey*, 505 U.S. 833, 844, 900 (1992).

117. Id. at 876.

118. Id. at 899–900; *Ohio v. Akron Ctr. for Reprod. Health (Akron II)*, 497 U.S. 502, 510–19 (1990); *Hodgson v. Minnesota (Hodgson)*, 497 U.S. 417, 461, 497–501; *City of Akron v. Akron Ctr. for Reprod. Health (Akron I)*, 462 U.S. 416, 440 (1983); *Planned Parenthood Ass'n of Kan. City, Mo. v. Ashcroft*, 462 U.S. 476, 490–94 (1983); *H.L. v. Matheson*, 450 U.S. 398, 406–11 (1981); *Bellotti v. Baird (Bellotti II)*, 443 U.S. 622, 643–51 (1979); *Planned Parenthood of Cent. Mo. v. Danforth*, 428 U.S. 52, 72–75 (1976).

119. *Danforth*, 428 U.S. at 74.

120. *Bellotti II*, 443 U.S. at 643–51.

121. Id. (striking down parental consent requirement because judicial bypass procedure did not satisfy this standard).

122. *Hodgson*, 497 U.S. at 420, 423 (upholding two-parent consent requirement with judicial bypass procedure).

123. Id. at 480 (Scalia, J., concurring in the judgment in part and dissenting in part).

124. *Planned Parenthood of S.E. Pa. v. Casey*, 505 U.S. 833, 899–900 (1992).

125. For example, in the Court's most recent abortion decision, the Court decided whether a certain type of partial-birth abortion procedure is ever safer than other types of partial-birth abortion and, therefore, medically necessary to preserve the health of the mother. *Gonzales v. Carhart*, 550 U.S. 124, 161–67 (2007).

126. *Casey*, 505 U.S. at 986 n.4, 1002 (Scalia, J., concurring in the judgment in part and dissenting in part).

127. This also assumes that the Second Amendment will be incorporated against the states. For a full discussion of this assumption, see Section IV, infra.

128. Cass Sunstein has suggested that *Heller*, like *Griswold v. Connecticut*, 381 U.S. 479 (1965), "is a narrow ruling with strong minimalist features." See Cass R. Sunstein, Second Amendment Minimalism: *Heller* as *Griswold*, 122 Harv. L. Rev. (forthcoming) 3, 14, 20–21, available at http://ssrn.com/abstract=1204942. The whole point, however, is that *Griswold* did not remain confined to a right to use birth control in the bedroom, but foreshadowed the rise of *Roe* itself.

129. *Heller*, 128 S.Ct. at 2822.

130. Id. at 2817–18. The statute did not include a self-defense exception.

131. Id.

132. Id. at 2818. The Court emphasized the restrictiveness of the ban: "[H]andguns are the most popular weapon chosen by Americans for self-defense in the home, and a *complete prohibition* of their use is invalid" (emphasis added).

133. Id. at 2817–18 (holding that the D.C. law would be unconstitutional under any standard for enumerated rights and therefore not specifying the appropriate standard).

134. Id. at 2817–18 n.27 (rejecting rational basis). The Court also rejected Justice Breyer's interest-balancing approach. Id. at 2821.

135. Posting of Erwin Chemerinsky to CATO Unbound, The *Heller* Decision: Conservative Activism and Its Aftermath; Reaction Essay, www.cato-unbound .org/2008/07/25/erwin-chemerinsky/the-heller-decision-conservative-activism -and-its-aftermath/ (July 25, 2008, 11:31); see also Glenn H. Reynolds & Brannon P. Denning, *Heller*'s Future in the Lower Courts, 102 Nw. U. L. Rev. Colloquy 406, 406 (2008) (noting that *Heller* did not specify a standard of review and therefore "litigants have a rare opportunity to write on a *tabula* much more *rasa* than is ordinarily the case in constitutional litigation").

136. *Heller*, 128 S.Ct. at 2816.

137. Id. at 2816–17.

138. Id. at 2815–17.

139. Id. at 2818; see also id. at 2817 (noting that handguns are the type of weapon "that is overwhelmingly chosen by American society for [self-defense]").

140. See posting of Dennis A. Henigan to CATO Unbound, The *Heller* Paradox: A Response to Robert Levy; Reaction Essay, www.cato-unbound.org/2008/07/16 /dennis-henigan/the-heller-paradox-a-response-to-robert-levy/ (July 16, 2008, 10:01).

141. Complaint, *McDonald v. City of Chicago*, No. 08-3645 (N.D. Ill. June 26, 2008); see also posting of Lyle Denniston to SCOTUSblog, www.scotusblog.com /wp/new-case-tests-second-amendments-reach/ (June 27, 2008, 11:37).

142. Complaint, *Nat'l Rifle Ass'n v. S.F. Housing Auth.*, No. 08-3112 (N.D. Cal. June 27, 2008); Complaint, *Nat'l Rifle Ass'n v. City of Chicago*, No. 08-3697 (N.D. Ill. June 27, 2008); Complaint, *Nat'l Rifle Ass'n v. City of Evanston*, No. 08-3693 (N.D. Ill. June 27, 2008); Complaint, *Nat'l Rifle Ass'n v. Village of Morton Grove*, No. 08-3694 (N.D. Ill. June 27, 2008); Complaint, *Nat'l Rifle Ass'n v. Village of Oak Park*, No. 08-3696 (N.D. Ill. June 27, 2008); see also posting of Lyle Denniston to SCOTUSblog, www.scotusblog.com/wp/links-to-new-gun-rights-lawsuits/ (July 1, 2008, 17:52); NRA Press Release, NRA Files Second Amendment Lawsuits in Illinois and California Following Supreme Court Ruling (June 27, 2008), www .nraila.org/Legislation/Read.aspx?ID=4053.

143. See postings of Eugene Volokh to The Volokh Conspiracy, www.volokh .com/posts/chain_1215395769.shtml (July 7–August 5, 2008) (listing post-*Heller* court orders and decisions).

144. See, e.g., *U.S. v. Robinson*, No. 07-CR-202, at *1 (E.D. Wis. July23, 2008) (denying motion to dismiss and upholding 18 U.S.C. §922(g)(1) ban on possession of firearms by a felon).

145. See, e.g., *U.S. v. Dorosan*, No. 08-042, at *6 (E.D. La. June 30, 2008) (denying motion to dismiss and holding that *Heller* does not invalidate ban on firearms on U.S. Post Office property).

146. See, e.g., *U.S. v. Fincher*, 538 F.3d 868, 874 (8th Cir. August13, 2008) (holding that Second Amendment does not protect right to possess machine guns).

147. *Heller*, 128 S.Ct. at 2816–17 & n.26.

148. There were two other plaintiffs to the suit as well. See Complaint, *Heller v. District of Columbia* (*Heller II*), No. 08-1289 (D.D.C. July 28, 2008). See also posting of Lyle Denniston to SCOTUSblog, New Second Amendment case in D.C., www.scotusblog.com/wp/new-second-amendment-case-in-dc/ (July 28, 2008, 17:31).

149. See Local Rule 16.3 Report at 2, *Heller II*, No. 08-1289 (October 2, 2008) (reflecting the parties' agreement that the Second Firearms Control Emergency Amendment Act of 2008, if enacted permanently, moots Counts I and III of the Complaint).

150. Complaint at 4–5, 8–9, *Heller II*, No. 08-1289.

151. Id. at 5–6, 9.

152. Id. at 6, 9–10.

153. *Heller*, 128 S.Ct. at 2815–17 (discussing *United States v. Miller*, 307 U.S. 174 (1939)).

154. D.C. Code §7-2501.01(10) (2001); see also Complaint at 4, *Heller II*, No. 08-1289.

155. Complaint at 3, *Heller II*, No. 08-1289.

156. Id. at 3, 4–5, 8.

157. Id. at 5–6, 9.

158. Id. at 5–6, 7, 9.

159. Id. at 6, 9–10. See also D.C. Code §7-2507.02 (as amended July 16, 2008, by the Firearms Control Emergency Amendment Act of 2008).

160. See Part III infra.

161. See D.C. Code §7-2501.01 *et seq.* ("Second Firearms Control Emergency Amendment Act of 2008").

162. See Legal Community against Violence, Regulating Guns in America: An Evaluation and Comparative Analysis of Federal, State, and Selected Local Gun Laws ii (2008), available at www.firearmslawcenter.org/library/reports_ analyses /RegGuns.entire.report.pdf [hereinafter Regulating Guns in America].

163. See id., ii–xvii, 206 (summarizing gun control regulations by type and level of government); see also NRA Institute for Legislative Action, Firearms Laws for [State] (various dates), available at http://2www.nraila.org/GunLaws/ (summarizing gun control regulations by state).

164. See 18 U.S.C. §922(g)(8), (9) (2008). See also Regulating Guns in America, supra note 162, at 88–89.

165. Federal law currently prohibits firearm possession by someone convicted of any offense that is a misdemeanor and involves "the use or attempted use of physical force" against a current or former spouse, child, or person with whom

the offender has a child. 18 U.S.C. §921(a)(33)(A) (2008). Some state and local laws provide broader prohibitions. See Regulating Guns in America, supra note 162, at 89–104.

166. *Heller*, 128 S.Ct. at 2846 n.39 (Stevens, J., dissenting).

167. Id.

168. Ely, supra note 37, at 922 (citing *Doe v. Bolton*, 410 U.S. 179 (1973)).

169. Id. at 926.

170. Id. at 923.

171. *Roe*, 410 U.S. at 174 (Rehnquist, J., dissenting).

172. Wardle, supra note 104, at 261–62.

173. Ely, supra note 37, at 935 n.89.

174. *Roe*, 410 U.S. at 173–74 (Rehnquist, J., dissenting).

175. *Planned Parenthood of Cent. Mo. v. Danforth*, 428 U.S. 52, 64 (1976) (upholding a Missouri state law because it defined viability flexibly).

176. Id. at 75–79 (striking down a state law that prohibited abortion by saline amniocentesis after the twelfth week of pregnancy).

177. E.g., *Stenberg*, 530 U.S. at 930–932 (2000) (holding in part that a state statute was unconstitutional because it applied to dilation and evacuation and to dilation and extraction procedures).

178. Motion and Brief, Amicus Curiae of Dr. Eugene Diamond and Americans United for Life, Inc., in Support of [John C. Danforth, Attorney General of Missouri] at 126, *Danforth*, 428 U.S. 52 (1976) (No. 74-1151).

179. Id. at 126–27.

180. Brief for Dr. David Acker et al., as Amici Curiae for Planned Parenthood of Central Missouri at 24–25, *Danforth*, 428 U.S. 52 (1976) (No. 74-1151).

181. Id. at 30, 35.

182. *Danforth*, 428 U.S. at 77–79.

183. Id. at 79.

184. Id. at 99 (White, J., concurring in part and dissenting in part).

185. *City of Akron v. Akron Ctr. Reprod. Health (Akron I)*, 462 U.S. 416, 435–46 (1983).

186. Id. at 455–56 (O'Connor, J., dissenting).

187. Wardle, supra note 104, at 263 (citing *Akron I*, 462 U.S. at 431, 434).

188. Id. at 262.

189. *McCorvey v. Hill*, 385 F.3d 846, 853 (5th Cir. 2004) (Jones, J., concurring).

190. Id. at 850–51 (citing Affidavits of More Than One Thousand Post-Abortive Women; Affidavit of David Reardon, Ph.D.) (reporting clinical findings that link abortion to physical and emotional problems for women).

191. *Roe*, 410 U.S. at 163 ("[T]he attending physician, in consultation with his patient, is free to determine, without regulation by the State, that, in his medical judgment, the patient's pregnancy should be terminated.").

192. *McCorvey*, 385 F.3d at 851 (Jones. J., concurring) (citing Affidavit of David Reardon, Ph.D.) (reporting that women receive little counseling at abortion clinics, and that counseling is heavily biased toward encouraging abortions).

193. Id. at 852 (citing David H. Munn et al., Prevention of Allogeneic Fetal Rejection by Tryptophan Catabolism, 281 Science 1191 (1998)).

194. E.g., Tex. Fam. Code Ann. §262.301–07 (Vernon 2002). See also *McCorvey*, 385 F.3d at 851–52 n.5 (collecting statutes).

195. *Planned Parenthood of S.E. Pa. v. Casey*, 505 U.S. 833, 857 (1992).

196. Id. at 867.

197. See *United States v. Carolene Products Co.*, 304 U.S. 144, 152 n.4 (1938).

198. Ely, supra note 37, at 933–34.

199. See *Doe v. Bolton*, 410 U.S. 179, 192 (1973) (describing the Georgia statute). The Court struck down these requirements.

200. Michael W. McConnell, How Not to Promote Serious Deliberation about Abortion, 58 U. Chi. L. Rev. 1181, 1200 n.43 (1991) (book review) (citing Mary Ann Lamanna, Social Science and Ethical Issues: The Policy Implications of Poll Data on Abortion, in Abortion: Understanding Differences 1, 4 (Sidney Callahan & Daniel Callahan eds., 1984)).

201. Ely, supra note 37, at 946.

202. Id. at 946–47.

203. Chemerinsky, supra note 42, at 107, 109.

204. See Lynn D. Wardle, The Quandary of Pro-Life Free Speech: A Lesson from the Abolitionists, 62 Alb. L. Rev. 853, 876 (1999) ("The vice of judicial supremacy . . . has been its progressive closing of the avenues to peaceful and democratic conciliation of our social and economic conflicts" (quoting *Fullilove v. Klutznick*, 448 U.S. 448, 491 (1980) (quoting Robert H. Jackson, The Struggle for Judicial Supremacy 321 (1941)))).

205. Robert Post & Reva Siegel, *Roe* Rage: Democratic Constitutionalism and Backlash, 42 Harv. C.R.-C.L. L. Rev. 373, 374 (2007).

206. See Wardle, supra note 104, at 261.

207. See Scott L. Cummings, The Internationalization of Public Interest Law, 57 Duke L.J. 891, 961 (2008).

208. McConnell, supra note 200, at 1201–2.

209. See Cass R. Sunstein, Backlash's Travels, 42 Harv. C.R.-C.L. L. Rev. 435, 439 (2007) (quoting Alexander Bickel, The Least Dangerous Branch: The Supreme Court at the Bar of Politics 69 (2d ed., Yale Univ. Press 1986) (1962)).

210. Id. at 448.

211. William Blackstone, Commentaries on the Laws of England 62 (1765).

212. See The Federalist No. 78 (Alexander Hamilton) (quoting Baron de Montesquieu, The Spirit of the Laws 152 (Thomas Nugent Trans., Hafner Publ'g Co. 1949) (1748)).

213. See *Roe*, 410 U.S. at 173 (Rehnquist, J., dissenting) ("The Due Process Clause of the Fourteenth Amendment undoubtedly does place a limit, albeit a broad one, on legislative power to enact laws such as this.").

214. Id. at 173–74 (Rehnquist, J., dissenting).

215. *Heller*, 128 S.Ct. at 2818. Justice Scalia later crafts a more specific explanation of the core right: "the right of law-abiding, responsible citizens to use arms in defense of hearth and home." Id. at 2821.

216. Adam Winkler, Scrutinizing the Second Amendment, 105 Mich. L. Rev. 683, 713 (2007) (quoting Lawrence Gene Sager, Fair Measure: The Legal Status of Underenforced Constitutional Norms, 91 Harv. L. Rev. 1212, 1217 (1978)).

217. Id. at 713–14 ("Judges do not want, and are not especially competent, to sort out such disputes and settle intensely debated issues of social science.").

218. Id. at 714 (citing Jeffrey Monks, Comment, The End of Gun Control or Protection Against Tyranny? The Impact of the New Wisconsin Constitutional Right to Bear Arms on State Gun Control Laws, 2001 Wis. L. Rev. 249, 264 n.94).

219. Id.

220. D.C. Code §7-2507.02 (2001).

221. *Heller*, 128 S.Ct. at 2817–18.

222. Id. at 2820.

223. Transcript of Oral Argument at 83–84, *Heller*, 128 S.Ct. 2783 (No. 07-290). See also Brief for American Public Health Ass'n et al. as Amici Curiae in Support of Petitioners at 26–27, *Heller*, 128 S.Ct. 2783 (No. 07-290) (discussing trigger locks that can be removed in one to three seconds).

224. Transcript of Oral Argument, supra note 223, at 73–74.

225. Id. at 81 (Alan Gura, Esq., speaking).

226. Id. at 79.

227. See *Heller*, 128 S.Ct. at 2794, n.9 (citing *State v. Chandler*, 5 La. Ann. 489, 489–90 (1850); *Nunn v. State*, 1 Ga. 243, 250–51 (1846)).

228. See, e.g., John R. Lott Jr., More Guns, Less Crime: Understanding Crime and Gun-Control Laws (1998); John R. Lott Jr., Straight Shooting: Firearms, Economics and Public Policy (2006); John R. Lott Jr., The Bias against Guns: Why Almost Everything You've Heard about Gun Control Is Wrong (2003); John R. Lott Jr. & David B. Mustard, Crime, Deterrence, and Right-to-Carry Concealed Handguns, 26 J. Legal Stud. 1 (1997).

229. See Ian Ayres & John J. Donohue III, Shooting Down the "More Guns, Less Crime" Hypothesis, 55 Stan. L. Rev. 1193 (2003).

230. Stephen Teret, Critical Commentary on a Paper by Lott and Mustard, The Johns Hopkins Center for Gun Policy and Research (1996), www.asahi-net.or.jp/~zj5j-gttl/teret.htm. See also Mark Duggan, More Guns, More Crime, 109 J. Pol. Econ. 1086 (2001); Jens Ludwig, Concealed-Gun-Carrying Laws and Violent Crime: Evidence from State Panel Data, 18 Int'l Rev. L. & Econ. 239 (1998).

231. Jeffrey M. Drazen et al., Editorial, Guns and Health, 359 New Eng. J. Med. 517, 517 (2008).

232. Id. (citing David Hemenway, Private Guns, Public Health (2004); Matthew Miller et al., Household Firearm Ownership and Rates of Suicide across the 50 United States, 62 J. Trauma 1029–35 (2007)).

233. See *Planned Parenthood of S.E. Pa. v. Casey*, 505 U.S. 833, 991 n.6 (1992) (Scalia, J., concurring in the judgment in part and dissenting in part).

234. *City of Akron v. Akron Ctr. for Reprod. Health, Inc.*, 462 U.S. 416, 458 (1983) (O'Connor, J., dissenting).

235. See, e.g., Paul Duggan & Mary Beth Sheridan, D.C. Legislation Would Remove More Gun Limits, Wash. Post, Sept. 13, 2008, at A1 (explaining that legislators' proposed changes to the D.C. gun laws "result from a careful review of [*Heller*]" and would result in "a dramatic shift in public policy" from D.C.'s long-standing policies on gun restrictions).

236. NRA-ILA Website, Who We Are, and What We Do, www.nraila.org /About/.

237. See Coalition to Stop Gun Violence Website, About Us, www.csgv.org /site/c.pmL5JnO7KzE/b.3509221/.

238. Maurice Carroll, American Voters Oppose Same-Sex Marriage, 2008 Quinnipiac U. Polling Inst. 1, available at www.quinnipiac.edu/images/polling /us/us07172008.doc.

239. Mental Health Measures Broadly Backed, but Culture Gets More Blame Than Guns, http://abcnews.go.com/images/US/1037a1VaTechGuns.pdf.

240. *Romer v. Evans*, 517 U.S. 620, 636 (1996) (Scalia, J., dissenting).

241. Id. at 652.

242. See Drazen et al., supra note 231, at 517 (citing C. Loftin et al., Effects of Restrictive Licensing of Handguns on Homicide and Suicide in the District of Columbia, 325 New Eng. J. Med. 1615–20 (1991)).

243. See *Hill v. Colorado*, 530 U.S. 703, 741 (2000) (Scalia, J., dissenting) (quoting *Madsen v. Women's Health Ctr., Inc.*, 512 U.S. 753, 785 (1994) (Scalia, J., concurring in the judgment in part and dissenting in part)).

244. See Sunstein, supra note 128, at 16 (arguing that *Heller* can be understood as a recognition of a changing "national consensus" on firearms regulation).

245. See *Hill*, 530 U.S. at 741 (Scalia, J., dissenting).

246. See *Doe v. Bolton*, 410 U.S. 179, 222 (1973) (White, J., dissenting) ("[The abortion] issue, for the most part, should be left with the people and to the political processes the people have devised to govern their affairs.").

247. *Webster v. Reprod. Health Services*, 492 U.S. 490, 532 (1989) (Scalia, J., concurring in part and concurring in the judgment).

248. *Planned Parenthood of S.E. Pa. v. Casey*, 505 U.S. 833, 1002 (1992) (Scalia, J., concurring in the judgment in part and dissenting in part).

249. See, e.g., Wardle, supra note 104, at 232 (recognizing that abortion traditionally had been "the exclusive province of the states to regulate"); see also *Gonzales v. Raich*, 545 U.S. 1, 42 (2005) (O'Connor, J., dissenting) ("The States' core police powers have always included authority to define criminal law and to protect the health, safety, and welfare of their citizens.").

250. *Roe*, 410 U.S. at 174–75 (Rehnquist, J., dissenting); id. at 116 (majority opinion) ("The Texas statutes under attack here are typical of those that have been in effect in many States for approximately a century.").

251. Clarke D. Forsythe & Stephen B. Presser, Restoring Self-Government on Abortion: A Federalism Amendment, 10 Tex. Rev. L. & Pol. 301, 338 (2006) [hereinafter Forsythe & Presser, A Federalism Amendment]; see also Clarke D. Forsythe & Stephen B. Presser, The Tragic Failure of *Roe v. Wade:* Why Abortion Should Be Returned to the States, 10 Tex. Rev. L. & Pol. 85, 162 (2006) [hereinafter Forsythe & Presser, Tragic Failure] (noting that the states were actively enforcing, reaffirming, or re-forming their prohibitions on abortions in the years preceding *Roe*).

252. Terrance Sandalow, Federalism and Social Change, 43 Law & Contemp. Probs. 29, 35 (1980); Wardle, supra note 104, at 232.

253. Sandalow, supra note 252, at 33; id. at 35 (noting that the opinions in *Roe* did not "consider the relevance of federalism to the appropriate decision").

254. Michael W. McConnell, Federalism: Evaluating the Founders' Design, 54 U. Chi. L. Rev. 1484, 1487 (1987) (book review).

255. See *Roe*, 410 U.S. at 174–77 (Rehnquist, J., dissenting).

256. *Thornburgh v. Am. Coll. of Obstetricians & Gynecologists*, 476 U.S. 747, 793 (1986) (White, J., dissenting).

257. Id. at 793–94 & n.3 (White, J., dissenting).

258. See McConnell, supra note 254, at 1493–94. For general discussions of this benefit of federalism and those that follow, see, for example, *Gregory v. Ashcroft*, 501 U.S. 452, 458 (1991), and McConnell, supra note 254.

259. See Robert H. Bork, The Judge's Role in Law and Culture, 1 Ave Maria L. Rev. 19, 24 (2003) (arguing that abortion should have been left "to the moral choice of the American people expressed in the laws of their various states"); Earl M. Maltz, Individual Rights and State Autonomy, 12 Harv. J.L. & Pub. Pol'y 163, 184 (1989).

260. See Roderick M. Hills Jr., The Individual Right to Federalism in the Rehnquist Court, 74 Geo. Wash. L. Rev. 888, 900 (2006).

261. *Planned Parenthood of S.E. Pa. v. Casey*, 505 U.S. 833, 995 (1992) (Scalia, J., concurring in the judgment in part and dissenting in part); see also McConnell, supra note 200, at 1202 (observing that abortion policy—absent *Roe*—could exhibit "significant variations in the approaches taken from state to state").

262. Sandalow, supra note 252, at 36.

263. Lynn D. Wardle, "Time Enough": *Webster v. Reproductive Health Services* and the Prudent Pace of Justice, 41 Fla. L. Rev. 881, 936 (1989); see also *Casey*, 505 U.S. at 995 (Scalia, J., concurring in the judgment in part and dissenting in part) ("Roe's mandate for abortion on demand . . . required the entire issue to be resolved uniformly, at the national level."); *Doe v. Bolton*, 410 U.S. 179, 222 (1973) (White, J., dissenting) ("[*Roe*] impos[ed] . . . an order of priorities on the people and legislatures of the States."); Maltz, supra note 259, at 187 & n.110.

264. *New State Ice Co. v. Liebmann*, 285 U.S. 262, 311 (1932) (Brandeis, J., dissenting).

265. See, e.g., Forsythe & Presser, A Federalism Amendment, supra note 251, at 329 ("The states are in the best position to experiment and create the optimal policy with regard to abortion.").

266. *Roe*, 410 U.S. at 116; id. at 139–40 (acknowledging that four states recently had repealed their criminal penalties for abortions performed early in the pregnancy, and fourteen other states had adopted some form of the less stringent Model Penal Code abortion statute).

267. See *Maher v. Roe*, 432 U.S. 464 (1977).

268. See *Planned Parenthood of S.E. Pa. v. Casey*, 505 U.S. 833 (1992).

269. Id. at 877 (opinion of O'Connor, Kennedy, and Souter, JJ.).

270. See *Stenberg v. Carhart*, 530 U.S. 914, 978–79 (2000) (Kennedy, J., dissenting); Forsythe & Presser, Tragic Failure, supra note 251, at 159–60.

271. The Federalist No. 51, at 323 (James Madison) (Isaac Kramnick ed., 1987).

272. See, e.g., Maltz, supra note 259, at 173 (arguing that the Court's approach in *Roe* "exemplifies its general disregard for federalism concerns in individual rights cases"). Contra Laurence H. Tribe, American Constitutional Law 1351 (2d ed. 1988) (asserting that abortion is too fundamental a liberty to be left to the states).

273. See McConnell, supra note 254, at 1503.

274. "For example, in 1971, the second year New York's liberalized abortion law was in effect, 60% of the women having abortions in New York were non-residents." Ginsburg, supra note 39, at 380 n.36. Mobility is subject to financial and other constraints, of course. See Chemerinsky, supra note 42, at 117–18; Ely, supra note 37, at 936 n.94.

275. See McConnell, supra note 254, at 1503.

276. See, e.g., Forsythe & Presser, Tragic Failure, supra note 251, at 162–63 ("[*Roe*] made the abortion debate more divisive because it prevented resolution through the normal give and take of political and legislative discourse and decision."); Ginsburg, supra note 44, at 1208 ("*Roe* . . . halted a political process that was moving in a reform direction and thereby, I believe, prolonged divisiveness and deferred stable settlement of the issue."); Wardle, supra note 263, at 927, 936 (arguing that *Roe* terminated the process by which a national consensus might have emerged on abortion when the Court mandated a national abortion policy).

277. See *Roe*, 410 U.S. at 116 ("We forthwith acknowledge our awareness of the sensitive and emotional nature of the abortion controversy, of the vigorous opposing views, even among physicians, and of the deep and seemingly absolute convictions that the subject inspires. . . . Our task, of course, is to resolve the issue by constitutional measurement, free of emotion and of predilection."); *Planned Parenthood of S.E. Pa. v. Casey*, 505 U.S. 833, 867 (1992) (asserting that decisions like *Roe* "[call] the contending sides of a national controversy to end their national division by accepting a common mandate rooted in the Constitution").

278. *Casey*, 505 U.S. at 995 (Scalia, J., concurring in the judgment in part and dissenting in part).

279. See, e.g., *United States v. Morrison*, 529 U.S. 598 (2000); *City of Boerne v. Flores*, 521 U.S. 507 (1997); *United States v. Lopez*, 514 U.S. 549 (1995).

280. See, e.g., Chemerinsky, supra note 135; Robert A. Levy, *District of Columbia v. Heller: What's Next?* Lead Essay, July 14, 2008, www.cato-unbound.org /2008/07/14/robert-a-levy/district-of-columbia-v-heller-whats-next/ (agreeing that the Second Amendment "will no doubt be incorporated" against the states). With respect to the Court's jurisprudence on incorporating the Bill of Rights against the states, see, for example, *Duncan v. Louisiana*, 391 U.S. 145, 147–48 (1968).

281. *Heller*, 128 S.Ct. at 2813 n.23.

282. Id. at 2815; see also supra text accompanying notes 136–146.

283. *Heller*, 128 S.Ct. at 2816–17 & n.26.

284. *Lopez*, 514 U.S. at 566.

285. See *Heller*, 128 S.Ct. at 2813 ("States, we said, were free to restrict or protect the right under their police powers.") (citing *United States v. Cruikshank*, 92 U.S. 542, 553 (1875) (holding that the people must look to the states' powers of "internal police" to protect the right to keep and bear arms); *Kelley v. Johnson*, 425 U.S. 238, 247 (1976) ("The promotion of safety of persons and property is unquestionably at the core of the State's police power.")).

286. See *Heller*, 128 S.Ct. at 2793–94, 2802–3 (recognizing early state constitutional provisions protecting gun rights); id. at 2819–20 (early regulations).

287. But see, e.g., 18 U.S.C. §§921–930 (2006) (federal criminal statutes relating to firearms); 26 U.S.C. §§5801–5872 (2000) (federal statutes imposing excise taxes and registration requirements on limited categories of firearms); Legal Community against Violence, Federal Law Summary (2008), www.firearmslawcenter .org/content/Federallawsummary.asp#keycongressionalacts (describing federal firearms laws).

288. See *Lopez*, 514 U.S. at 567 (holding that the Commerce Clause did not empower Congress to regulate guns in schools and that the opposite holding would have granted to Congress a "general police power of the sort retained by the States").

289. See *Heller*, 128 S.Ct. at 2825–26 (Stevens, J., dissenting) (pointing out the difference in meanings between the state and federal provisions).

290. Id. at 2796 (majority opinion).

291. See id. at 2795–96; see also id. at 2828–30 (Stevens, J., dissenting) (responding to the majority's attack on this point).

292. See id. at 2819–20 (majority opinion); id. at 2848–50 (Breyer, J., dissenting) (discussing these regulations and questioning the majority's recognition of self-defense exceptions in the statutes).

293. See id. at 2827 (Stevens, J., dissenting) ("[T]he ultimate purpose of the [Second] Amendment was to protect the States' share of the divided sovereignty created by the Constitution."); id. at 2822, 2831–36 & n.27 (same); Brief for N.Y. et al. as Amici Curiae in Support of Petitioners at 4, *District of Columbia v. Heller*, 128 S.Ct. 2783 (2008) (No. 07-290) ("A principal purpose of the Second Amendment is to function as a bulwark against federal intrusion into state sovereignty over militias. That purpose would be undermined, rather than supported, by interpreting the Amendment to authorize federal judicial review of state laws regulating weapons.").

294. *Heller*, 128 S.Ct. at 2804.

295. See Posner, supra note 98, at 32; see also Drazen et al., supra note 231, at 517–18 ("Given the diversity of geography and population in the United States, lawmakers throughout the country need the freedom and flexibility to apply gun regulations that are appropriate to their jurisdictions.").

296. See Regulating Guns in America, supra note 162, at 20–21. Hawaii and Maryland ban assault pistols; the other five states ban assault weapons generally. The term "assault weapons" refers to "a class of semi-automatic firearms designed with military features to allow rapid and accurate spray firing." Id. at 19.

297. See Brady Campaign to Prevent Gun Violence, 2007 Brady Campaign State Scorecard Rankings, www.stategunlaws.org/xshare/pdf/scorecard/2007/2007 _scorecard_rankings.pdf; Brady Campaign to Prevent Gun Violence, New Brady Scorecard Shows Most States Lack Common Sense Gun Restrictions (January 31, 2008), www.stategunlaws.org/xshare/pdf/scorecard/2007/2007_national _release.pdf (describing the methodology of the state rankings and the categories of gun laws analyzed).

298. See Regulating Guns in America, supra note 162, at 259–64 (presenting a table summarizing the gun regulations in the states and certain cities).

299. See id.

300. See id.

301. Id. at 40.

302. Id. at 40 & nn.19, 21. San Francisco's handgun ban has been held to be preempted by state law, although that ruling appears to have an appeal pending. See id. at 40 n.21.

303. See id. at 206–8.

304. See id. at 212–13.

305. See, e.g., *Heller*, 128 S.Ct. at 2857 (Breyer, J., dissenting) (citing studies demonstrating these differences between urban and rural environments).

306. Id. at 2855 (discussing the crime statistics in the District that prompted the initial passage of the handgun ban).

307. Id. at 2860.

308. See id. at 2818 (majority opinion); but see id. at 2851 (Breyer, J., dissenting) (noting that the District's prohibition was tailored more narrowly than the examples cited by the majority).

309. See id. at 2861 (Breyer, J., dissenting) (arguing that cities "must be allowed a reasonable opportunity to experiment with solutions to admittedly serious problems" (quoting *Renton v. Playtime Theatres, Inc.*, 475 U.S. 41, 52 (1986))).

310. See supra text accompanying notes 213–48.

311. See *Heller*, 128 S.Ct. at 2859 (Breyer, J., dissenting) (noting the difficulty of the causation issue).

312. Cf. id. at 2858 (citing studies that analyzed the results of particular experiments, including "a substantial drop in the burglary rate in an Atlanta suburb that required heads of households to own guns," and a "decrease in sexual assaults in Orlando when women were trained in the use of guns").

313. Gary Fields, Going after Crimes—and Guns, Wall St. J., August 5, 2008, at A12 (describing Richmond's efforts to achieve 100 percent prosecution of gun crimes through cooperation between local, state, and federal officials, and noting that other jurisdictions had instituted similar efforts).

314. Id. ("Other cities, including Springfield and Peoria in Illinois[,] have visited to see what Richmond is doing.").

315. Regulating Guns in America, supra note 162, at 5 & n.16. While some of the beneficial effects of local innovation may be muted in the large number of states that preempt local gun regulation, such state preemption laws are simply another data-producing policy experiment, see id. at 11–16.

316. Winkler, supra note 216, at 702–3.

317. See *Heller*, 128 S.Ct. at 2822.

318. See *United States v. Lopez*, 514 U.S. 549, 581–83 (1995) (Kennedy, J., concurring).

319. *Heller*, 128 S.Ct. at 2868 (Breyer, J., dissenting) ("And litigation over the course of many years, or the mere specter of such litigation, threatens to leave cities without effective protection against gun violence and accidents during that time.").

320. See supra text accompanying notes 148–160.

321. *Planned Parenthood of S.E. Pa. v. Casey*, 505 U.S. 833, 995 (1992) (Scalia, J., concurring in the judgment in part and dissenting in part).

322. See, e.g., E. J. Dionne Jr., Originalism Goes Out the Window, Wash. Post, June 27, 2008, at A17 (statement of Paul Helmke, president of the Brady Campaign to Prevent Gun Violence) ("[*Heller*] will make gun control less of a 'wedge issue.'"); Henigan, The *Heller* Paradox, supra note 140 (predicting that *Heller* "may make it easier for advocates of stronger gun laws to ensure that gun control is viewed as the public safety issue that it is, rather than as a divisive, cultural issue.").

323. See *Home Bldg. & Loan Ass'n v. Blaisdell*, 290 U.S. 398, 483 (1934) (Sutherland, J., dissenting).

324. *Casey*, 505 U.S. at 1002 (1992) (Scalia, J., concurring in the judgment in part and dissenting in part).

325. See Learned Hand, The Contribution of an Independent Judiciary to Civilization, in The Spirit of Liberty 163–64 (3d ed. 1960).

* * * *

Second Amendment Minimalism

Heller as *Griswold*

Cass R. Sunstein

* * * *

I. INTRODUCTION

District of Columbia v. Heller[1] is the most explicitly and self-consciously originalist opinion in the history of the Supreme Court.[2] Well over two hundred years since the Framing, the Court has, for essentially the first time, interpreted a constitutional provision with explicit, careful, and detailed reference to its original public meaning.[3]

It would be possible, in this light, to see *Heller* as a modern incarnation of *Marbury v. Madison*,[4] at least as that case is understood by some contemporary scholars,[5] and to a considerable extent as Chief Justice John Marshall wrote it. In *Marbury,* the Court also spoke on behalf of what it took to be the text, structure, and original meaning of the Constitution.[6] On one view, *Heller* represents the full flowering of the approach that Chief Justice Marshall imperfectly inaugurated—one that has been abandoned at crucial periods in American history. To its defenders, *Heller* speaks honestly and neutrally on behalf of the original meaning, and it should be appreciated and applauded for that reason.[7]

But there is a radically different reading of *Heller*. The constitutional text is ambiguous, and many historians believe that the Second Amendment does not, in fact, create a right to use guns for nonmilitary purposes.[8] In their view, the Court's reading is untrue to the relevant materials. If they are right, then it is tempting to understand *Heller* not as *Marbury* but as a modern incarnation of *Lochner v. New York*,[9] in which the Court overrode democratic judgments in favor of a dubious understanding of the Constitution. On this view, it is no accident that the five-justice majority in *Heller* consisted of the most conservative members of the Court (who were all Republican appointees). Perhaps *Heller* is, in the relevant sense, a twenty-first-century version of *Lochner*-style substantive due process, and perhaps it marks the beginning of a long series of confrontations between the Supreme Court and the political branches.

On a third view, this characterization badly misses the mark. *Heller* is more properly characterized as a rerun of the minimalist ruling in *Griswold v. Connecticut*.[10] In *Griswold*, the Court struck down a Connecticut law banning the use of contraceptives by married couples, under circumstances in which the Connecticut law was plainly inconsistent with a national consensus. The Court worked hard to support its decision by reference to the standard legal materials,[11] but the national consensus probably provides the best explanation of what the Court did.[12] Perhaps *Heller* is closely analogous. The Court spoke confidently in terms of the original meaning, but perhaps its ruling is impossible to understand without attending to contemporary values, and in particular to the fact that the provisions that the Court invalidated were national outliers.

In this comment, I contend that the third view is largely correct, and that *Heller* will, in the fullness of time, be seen as embracing a kind of Second Amendment minimalism. Notwithstanding the Court's preoccupation with constitutional text and history, *Heller* cannot be adequately understood as an effort to channel the document's original public meaning. The Court may have been wrong on that issue, and even if it was right, a further question remains: Why was the robust individual right to possess guns recognized in 2008, rather than 1958, 1968, 1978, 1988, or 1998? And notwithstanding the possible inclinations of the Court's most conservative members, *Heller* is not best seen as a descendent of *Lochner*. In spite of its radically different methodology, *Heller* is far closer to *Griswold* than it is to *Marbury* or to *Lochner*.

No less than *Griswold*, *Heller* is a narrow ruling with strong minimalist features. And if this view is correct, then the development of the gun right, as it is specified over time, will have close parallels to the development of the privacy right. As the law emerges through case-by-case judgments, the scope of the right will have as much to do with contemporary understandings as with historical ones. This point has general implications for constitutional change in the United States, even when the Court contends, in good faith, that it is merely channeling the original meaning or other established sources of constitutional meaning.

II. *HELLER* AS *MARBURY*

A. ORIGINAL MEANING AND BLANK SLATES

For many years, Justice Scalia has contended that the Constitution should be interpreted so as to fit with the original public meaning of the relevant provisions.[13] In his view, the judge's duty is to track that meaning, not to take account of changing circumstances or new moral commitments. What Justice Scalia seeks is "a rock-solid, unchanging Constitution."[14] His interest in originalism is explicitly connected with his interest in rule-bound law and in constraining judicial discretion; on his account, originalism is uniquely capable of ensuring that constitutional law is not a matter of judicial will or ad hoc, case-by-case judgments.[15] Indeed, originalism and rule-bound law help to protect liberties by stiffening the judicial spine, ensuring respect for constitutional rights even when the political pressure is intense.[16] It is in part because of his enthusiasm for rule-bound law that Justice Scalia rejects the original intention in favor of the original meaning.[17] To assess intentions, courts need to ask something subjective, involving what lies inside particular people's heads; to ask about meaning, courts can undertake a more objective inquiry.

Notwithstanding the energy and clarity with which Justice Scalia has argued for his approach, *Heller* is unique; he has never been able to embed originalism so explicitly and directly in a majority opinion.[18] On the contrary, originalism has not been a significant theme on either the Rehnquist Court or the Roberts Court.[19] For this reason, it is stunning to see that *Heller* is a thoroughly originalist opinion—a significant development, and one that is at least potentially important for the future, certainly of the Second Amendment, and perhaps more generally.

To be sure, the Court's originalism is less surprising here than it would be in other domains. In the Second Amendment context, the Court had sparse precedents[20] with which to work; the cases were neither recent nor carefully reasoned, and it was clear that the Court did not much like what it found.[21] In a sense, the question in *Heller* was one of first impression, or at least it could be so taken. In answering that question, many judges might be drawn to the original understanding even if they would not consider it, or would not give it a great deal of weight, if they were writing on an unclean slate.

But we should be careful about this point, for it is hardly inevitable that the Court would be drawn to originalism even when it lacked doctrinal signposts. After all, circumstances have changed dramatically since the ratification of the Second Amendment, making it tempting to follow the text but not the original meaning. The twenty-first-century United States is radically different from the eighteenth-century United States, in a way that seems to complicate and perhaps even to confound any form of originalism.[22] Compare the First Amendment: in approaching the meaning of that amendment in the context of commercial advertising, the Court did not ask about the original under-standing, even though the precedents were sparse in that domain as well.[23] In its first serious encounter with the question of affirmative action, the Court's members spent essentially no time with the original meaning of the Equal Protection Clause.[24] The same is true of the pivotal cases involving discrim-ination on the basis of sex.[25] The Court's decisions involving sexually explicit materials were not originalist, even when the Court had few precedents with which to work.[26] In its first real encounter with the legitimacy of congressional grants of standing to citizens as such, the Court decided to invalidate such grants—and without saying even a word about the original understanding.[27] Originalism seems to have more appeal when doctrine is not developed, but the Court has rarely spoken in originalist terms even when doctrine barely exists.[28]

Moreover, judges who believe in some kind of "moral reading" of the Consti-tution might attempt to make best moral sense of the relevant provision, rather than to track the understandings of over two centuries ago.[29] What is note-worthy is that no opinion in *Heller* approached the constitutional question in these terms, at least not explicitly. Justice Scalia's thoroughly originalist opin-ion commanded a majority of the Court, and Justice Scalia's distinctive brand of originalism, involving the original public meaning, was clearly ascendant. Indeed, the dissenters spoke in largely originalist terms as well, although Jus-tice Breyer's plea for balancing had pragmatic as well as originalist elements.[30]

B. *MARBURY*, ORIGINALISM, AND TIMING

Taken as a full-scale vindication of originalist methodology, *Heller* has few clear precedents,[31] even in the Founding era.[32] An imperfect but highly salient analogy is *Marbury*.[33] In recognizing the power of judicial review,

Chief Justice Marshall placed a great deal of emphasis on the constitutional text and structure.[34] True, he did not speak directly in terms of the original public meaning. But some of the foundations of his approach were textualist, with his emphasis on the Supremacy Clause and the judicial oath.[35] Indeed, it would not be implausible to say that he was attempting to channel the original understanding of the text. Some modern defenses of *Marbury* contend that the Court's conclusion was fully consistent with originalist methodology.[36] *Marbury* could easily have been written in originalist terms, and any such opinion would overlap with Chief Justice Marshall's own.

I do not mean to say anything controversial about *Marbury* here. But perhaps *Heller* represents a far more thorough, careful, and sophisticated version of *Marbury's* approach—one that, well over two hundred years since the Founding, attempts humbly and faithfully to recover and to implement the original judgment of We the People.[37] In seeing *Heller* as *Marbury,* then, I am taking *Marbury* to be a reasonable rendering of that original judgment, in a case that has unique salience in the canon of constitutional law.

This understanding of *Heller* is not at all implausible. The Court's reading of text and history was hardly preposterous;[38] whether or not the Court's analysis was convincing,[39] it grappled with textual and historical arguments on all sides. But as a full account of what the Court did, the understanding runs into two serious problems.[40] The first is that the original meaning of the Second Amendment is greatly contested and many historians reject the Court's conclusion—an issue to which I will shortly turn.

The second problem is less straightforward but more interesting and equally fundamental: Even if the Court's understanding of the original public meaning is correct, why did the Court vindicate that understanding in 2008? Why not in 1958, 1968, 1978, 1988, or 1998? Between 1942[41] and 2001,[42] lower courts had been virtually unanimous in rejecting the view that the Second Amendment creates an individual right to use guns for nonmilitary purposes. A quiz question: When was the first time a lower federal court invoked the Second Amendment to invalidate a state or federal law? Answer: *Heller* itself, in 2007.[43] In well over a half-century, the Court had many opportunities to reject the established view within the lower federal courts; it never did so. Indeed, for many decades, no member of the Court showed the slightest inclination to hold that the Second Amendment protects the right to have a gun for nonmilitary uses. Why did the Court accept that view in 2008?

The answer has everything to do with the particular context in which the *Heller* Court wrote—the context that led the Court to be composed as it was and to have the inclinations that it did. In terms of judicial as well as public convictions, it would be a mistake to underrate the influence of a powerful and aggressive social movement promoting public and judicial recognition of an individual right to have guns for nonmilitary purposes.[44] In part as a result of the immense influence of that movement, strong national majorities have come to favor that right.[45] Indeed, national opposition to a ban on handguns has been larger and more consistent in recent years than in the 1950s, 1960s, 1970s, and 1980s.[46] Politicians of both parties strongly favor some kind of individual right to have guns,[47] and the central holding of *Heller* is thus fully consistent with the view of national leaders as well as that of most citizens. It is highly revealing in this regard that majorities of both houses of Congress supported a robust individual right in an amicus brief[48] and that both nominees for the presidency—John McCain and Barack Obama—greeted *Heller* with general enthusiasm.[49]

Indeed, judicial rejection of an individual right to have guns for nonmilitary purposes would have produced a high degree of public outrage, thus making the Court, and its rejection of that right, a salient part of national politics. Any ruling against an individual right to have guns for purposes of self-defense and hunting would have been wildly unpopular. Such a ruling would have polarized the nation. By contrast, *Heller* itself was met with widespread social approval. Far from creating a firestorm, it was mostly met with reactions ranging from relative indifference to enthusiasm.

Of course, the Court does not merely channel public opinion, and hence it is necessary to identify mechanisms that would link the Court's recognition of a robust individual right to a period in which most people support that right.[50] It is surely relevant here that the Court's composition is determined by the views of the president (and, through the power to advise and consent, the Senate), and the Republican presidents who appointed the five-member *Heller* majority were strong supporters of a broad Second Amendment right.[51] The fact that in 2008 the Court was willing to read the Constitution so as to safeguard that right had everything to do with the social and political context in which the Court wrote.

In short, I am suggesting that even if *Heller* accurately captured the original meaning, the Court's willingness to do so cannot be explained in terms that point only to historical accuracy. In any number of areas—affirmative action, sex equality, property rights, commercial advertising, standing to sue—the Court could choose, but has not chosen, to be originalist. We also need to ask: *Why originalism now, in particular? Why originalism here, in particular?* The most sensible answers point to context and culture, and both of these strongly favored the Court's conclusion.

III. *HELLER* AS *LOCHNER*

In *Lochner v. New York,* the Court struck down a maximum hour law.[52] The Court reasoned that freedom of contract is part of the "liberty" protected by the Due Process Clause, and it found that the state's police power did not extend to maximum hour regulation, which could not be justified as either a labor law or a health law.[53] In so ruling, the Court attempted, in good faith, to justify its conclusion by reference to the standard legal materials.[54] There is no reason to doubt that the Court's members genuinely believed that the legal sources justified their conclusion. But it is now widely agreed that *Lochner* was a mistake and even a disgrace, because the Court could not claim adequate legal support for its conclusion and actually entrenched its own, controversial view of public policy.[55] The general problem with the *Lochner* decision, thus understood, is captured in Justice Holmes's dissenting suggestion that "[t]he Fourteenth Amendment does not enact Mr. Herbert Spencer's Social Statics."[56] After *Heller,* does the Constitution enact the latest position paper of the National Rifle Association? The conclusions of the Republican Party on gun control?

At first glance, it seems reckless and insulting to ask such questions or to see *Heller* as a modern incarnation of *Lochner,* because the Court took such pains to attempt to justify its approach by reference to constitutional text, structure, and history. But Judge J. Harvie Wilkinson has objected that *Heller* suffers from the same defects as *Roe v. Wade,*[57] in an analysis that links *Heller* with *Lochner* as well.[58] In his view, the *Heller* Court allowed litigants to "bypass the ballot and seek to press their political agenda in the courts."[59] Rejecting this approach, Judge Wilkinson explicitly invokes Justice Holmes's dissenting opinion in *Lochner.*[60]

To know whether it is plausible to see *Heller* as *Lochner,* we need to know what the claim of analogy is meant to assert.[61] On one view, which should be congenial to those who approve of *Heller,* the vice of *Lochner* consisted in a departure from the original meaning of the relevant text. On a different view, the vice of *Lochner* consisted in invalidation of a statute when the constitutional text was ambiguous. Of course, there are other possibilities, most prominently the view that the vice of *Lochner* consisted in an aggressive judicial posture in a context in which there was no particular reason to think that the democratic process was malfunctioning.

A. Originalism and Lochnerism

The *Heller* Court purported to be originalist, but many historians have concluded and even insisted that the Second Amendment did not create an individual right to use guns for nonmilitary purposes. On this view, the understanding enshrined in *Heller* is a product of the nation's most recent decades, not the Founding period.

In one of the most elaborate and detailed studies, Saul Cornell concludes that the Second Amendment right did not extend to nonmilitary uses of guns.[62] He finds, for example, that the right did not cover the use of guns for purposes of hunting; in his account, the suggestion that it did cover such use was expressed on only one isolated occasion in the Founding era, and even that reference, in a dissent in the Pennsylvania ratifying convention, was obscure.[63] More generally, Cornell concludes that the "original understanding of the Second Amendment was neither an individual right of self-defense nor a collective right of the states, but rather a civic right that guaranteed that citizens would be able to keep and bear those arms needed to meet their legal obligation to participate in a well-regulated militia."[64] In Cornell's view, the understanding endorsed in *Heller* is simply wrong; the Second Amendment, as originally understood, did not create a right to have guns for nonmilitary purposes.

Similarly, Jack Rakove, a Pulitzer Prize winner and one of the most careful students of the period, concludes that the purpose of the Second Amendment was merely to affirm "the essential proposition—or commonplace—that liberty fared better when republican polities relied upon a militia of citizen soldiers for their defense, rather than risk the dire consequences of sustaining a permanent military establishment."[65] Rakove believes that the Second Amendment must be understood in the context of the effort to preserve state militias; he rejects a broader understanding of the right created by the amendment. Rakove flatly rejects the position adopted by the Court in *Heller*.[66]

In his dissenting opinion in *Heller*, Justice Stevens outlined the narrower reading of the Second Amendment, focused on military uses of firearms; he provided numerous and detailed references to the primary and secondary materials.[67] The much more important point is that many historians believe that he is right. The *Heller* Court itself relied on numerous academic writings by law professors, as did Justice Breyer's dissenting opinion,[68] but few members of that group are trained historians. More commonly, they are advocates with a rooting interest in one or another position. There is a marked difference (in my view) between the care, sensitivity to context, and relative neutrality generally shown by historians and the advocacy-oriented, conclusion-driven, and often tendentious treatments characteristic of academic lawyers on both sides of the Second Amendment debate. As Rakove writes: "[H]istorical operations in the Second Amendment theater of combat are often mounted by campaigners not intimately familiar with the terrain. These are raiders who know what they are looking for, and having found it, they care little about collateral damage to the surrounding countryside that historians better know as context."[69] Law office history plays a large role in the law reviews and, thanks to *Heller*, in the pages of the *United States Reports.* To be sure, the competing arguments by the Court and Justice Stevens are impressively detailed. But the subtlety, nuance, acknowledgment of counterarguments, and (above all) immersion in Founding era debates, characteristic of good historical work, cannot be found in *Heller.*

This should not be a surprise. No member of the Court is a historian. None can claim to be anything like a true specialist in the Founding period.[70] In these circumstances, it is more than a little disturbing to find that the most conservative members of the Court concluded, apparently with great confidence, that the Second Amendment creates an individual right to have guns for nonmilitary purposes, whereas the less conservative members of the Court concluded, apparently with equal confidence, that the Second Amendment does no such thing. *Heller* is plausibly taken as a great triumph less for historical recovery than for a social movement determined to create a robust individual right to have guns.[71]

At the same time, it must be acknowledged that the analogy to *Lochner* is highly imperfect, at least if we see *Lochner* as a case that was wrong because it so plainly defied the original meaning. The *Lochner* Court did not take pains to defend its decision in textual and historical terms, and it is most doubtful that the decision could be so defended. By contrast, *Heller* offers ample detail on the original meaning, and *Heller* could be so defended, notwithstanding the existence of intense debate. For this reason, the analogy to *Lochner* seems to fail if we understand the analogy to be based on a judgment that the twentieth-century Court flagrantly departed from originalist methodology, properly applied.

B. THAYERISM AND LOCHNERISM

It is not standard, however, to say that the flaw of *Lochner* was that it departed from originalism. Let us understand *Lochner* in a different way, one that invokes one of the greatest and most influential essays in the history of American law (and one that has received a prominent and powerful modern defense).[72] In that essay, James Bradley Thayer argues that courts should uphold national legislation unless it is plainly and unambiguously in violation of the Constitution.[73] Thayer notes that because the American Constitution is often ambiguous, those who decide on its meaning must inevitably exercise discretion. Laws that "will seem unconstitutional to one man, or body of men, may reasonably not seem so to another[, because] the constitution often admits of different interpretations; . . . there is often a range of choice and judgment."[74] In Thayer's view, "whatever choice is rational is constitutional."[75]

Thayer's argument, in brief, is that courts should strike down laws only "when those who have the right to make laws have not merely made a mistake, but have made a very clear one, —so clear that it is not open to rational question."[76] The question for courts "is not one of the mere and simple preponderance of reasons for or against, but of what is very plain and clear, clear beyond a reasonable doubt."[77] In so arguing, Thayer emphasizes two points. The first is the fallibility of federal judges. When judges conclude that a law is unconstitutional, they are of course relying on their own interpretation, and they might be wrong. Judges are learned in the law, certainly. But should we conclude that judicial interpretations are necessarily correct?

Thayer's second point is that a strong judiciary might harm democracy itself. He suggests that if judges become too aggressive, the moral vigilance of elected officials might weaken. Thayer laments that "our doctrine of constitutional law has had a tendency to drive out questions of justice and right, and to fill the minds of legislators with thoughts of mere legality, of what the constitution allows."[78] Indeed, things have often been worse, for "even in the matter of legality, they have felt little responsibility; if we are wrong, they say, the courts will correct it."[79] Thayer seeks to place the responsibility for justice on democracy, where it belongs. "Under no system can the power of courts go far to save a people from ruin; our chief protection lies elsewhere."[80] Modern Thayerians might well emphasize this point in the context of the Second Amendment as elsewhere, suggesting that regulation of guns raises complex moral and pragmatic considerations that should be engaged directly, not as a matter of "mere legality."

On a Thayerian view, the problem with the *Lochner* decision was that the Court invalidated legislation even though the constitutional infirmity was far from plain. On this view, *Heller* runs into exactly the same problem. We have seen that reasonable people, including reasonable historians, fiercely debate the meaning of the Second Amendment and that the view defended by Justice Stevens—that the right extends only to military uses of guns—is hardly without support.[81] In these circumstances, Thayerians will insist that the Court owed a duty of respect to a democratic judgment.

C. Guns, *Carolene Products*, and Politics

It is true that the Thayerian reading of *Lochner* cuts very broadly, and, for most observers, unacceptably so. If Thayer was right, *Heller* is surely wrong, but the same must be said about many other decisions accepted by most of *Heller*'s likely critics, including (for example) *Brown v. Board of Education*[82] (banning racial segregation), *Califano v. Goldfarb*[83] (striking down sex discrimination), and *Boumediene v. Bush*[84] (vindicating the right to habeas corpus). Almost no one is a universal Thayerian.[85] If *Heller* is to be treated as a modern incarnation of *Lochner* for less-than-universal Thayerians, then we must specify a less-than-universal domain for Thayerism, one that would reject both decisions but allow a more aggressive judicial approach in many areas. In the most famous footnote in all of constitutional law, the Court suggested such a possibility in *United States v. Carolene Products Co.*,[86] indicating that a more aggressive approach would be justified when there was some kind of defect in majoritarian processes.[87] John Hart Ely's *Democracy and Distrust*[88] elaborates an approach of this kind, which is supported by an illuminating footnote from Justice Stevens as well.[89]

On this understanding, the Thayerian view is generally correct, but a more intrusive approach from the Court is justified (only) when the democratic process is not functioning well, in the sense that certain rights and groups are at particular risk. Perhaps an aggressive approach can be justified in (for example) sorting out ambiguities in the Equal Protection Clause in *Brown*, but not in sorting out ambiguities in the Second Amendment in *Heller*. There is no special reason for an aggressive judicial role in protecting against gun control, in light of the fact that opponents of such control have considerable political power and do not seem to be at a systematic disadvantage in the democratic process. The *Carolene Products* approach offers no support for *Heller*. Indeed, the widespread commitment to an individual right to own guns itself operates as a safeguard against excessive or unjustified gun control laws.

The *Carolene Products* approach is of course controversial, especially to those who favor the originalist methodology of *Heller*. To those who embrace originalism, judges must follow that methodology, and considerations involving deference to the democratic process, or its limits, are irrelevant. At this point, we seem to have reached a dead end. On some accounts of what was wrong with *Lochner, Heller* is analogous. The question is whether those accounts are correct.

IV. *HELLER* AS *GRISWOLD*

In *Griswold,* the Court protected an individual right that enjoyed broad popular support, at the expense of a law that counted as a national outlier. In *Heller,* the Court did the same thing. In *Griswold,* the Court proceeded in minimalist fashion, with its holding focusing narrowly on the law before it. The same is true of the Court's approach in *Heller.* Just as *Griswold* reflected a kind of privacy minimalism, *Heller* signals the arrival of Second Amendment minimalism. These conclusions have strong implications for the future development of Second Amendment doctrine.

A. RATIONALIZING *GRISWOLD*

In *Griswold,* the Court struck down Connecticut's ban on the use of contraceptives by married couples.[90] The Court struggled mightily to find a textual source for its conclusion. It explored a range of provisions that might be seen to protect some kind of "privacy,"[91] and it urged that the right to use contraceptives fell within "penumbras" or "emanations" from the Bill of Rights.[92] But constitutional provisions have domains, not "penumbras" or "emanations," and hence almost no one defends *Griswold* as originally written. It is an understatement to say that the Court's analysis has not survived the test of time.[93]

Three other rationales for *Griswold* have received respectful attention. The first, drawing on the work of Alexander Bickel, emphasizes desuetude.[94] The Connecticut law at issue was enacted long before the Court's decision, it was not much enforced,[95] and under these circumstances, it might be taken to have "lapsed." To be sure, a great deal of work must be done to show how this idea can be made to justify *Griswold* on constitutional grounds; no constitutional provision declares statutes invalid because they are infrequently enforced, anachronistic, or both.[96] But perhaps the Due Process Clause, in its purely procedural sense, is sufficient. Perhaps it could be said that a law violates that clause if it is so wildly out of step with prevailing social norms that its enforcement is necessarily sporadic and therefore unpredictable, in a way that compromises the rule of law.[97]

The second rationale, pressed by Justice Harlan, emphasizes the grounding of substantive due process in tradition.[98] Perhaps the sanctity of marriage is honored by tradition, and perhaps the tradition, which should not be taken as static, is fatally inconsistent with the Connecticut law.[99] On this view, substantive due process is rooted in long-standing social understandings, and the tradition of respect for marital privacy requires a powerful justification for any intrusion. The underlying claim might be that courts should not be licensed to define "liberty" as they see fit, and that if a certain conception of liberty is sanctified by tradition, it has a kind of epistemic credential.[100]

A third rationale, prominently suggested by Judge Richard Posner, is that the Connecticut law was fatally out of step with the national consensus.[101] On this view, the *Griswold* Court was acting to vindicate that consensus against an outlier. Indeed, Justice Harlan himself invoked this point, urging that for him, the "conclusive" factor was "the utter novelty of [the state's] enactment. Although the Federal Government and many States have at one time or other had on their books statutes forbidding or regulating the distribution of contraceptives, none, so far as I can find, has made the use of contraceptives a crime."[102]

Here too, of course, a great deal of work would be necessary to demonstrate why and when the Due Process Clause should be construed to give authority to a national consensus or to raise serious doubts about national outliers. Perhaps the basic claim is that if a law is a genuine outlier, there is reason to doubt whether it is grounded on a firm foundation; an intrusion on liberty that lacks anything like broad support might lack epistemic credentials, simply because and to the extent that it is so unusual. On this view, Judge Posner's approach is a close cousin of Justice Harlan's, and it is no surprise that Justice Harlan invoked the point in the context of an opinion emphasizing the importance of tradition.

The Court itself has often rooted its analysis in Justice Harlan's approach,[103] but Judge Posner's understanding of *Griswold* fits well with a broader fact about the arc of constitutional law. The Court rarely points to the importance of a national consensus or suggests that it is in any sense responsive to what most people think. But the development of doctrine, over time, unquestionably shows that kind of responsiveness.[104] As a clear example, very much in line with this understanding of *Griswold,* consider *Lawrence v. Texas.*[105] In that case the Court was even willing to invoke "an emerging awareness that liberty gives substantial protection to adult persons in deciding how to conduct their private lives in matters pertaining to sex" in invalidating a ban on same-sex sexual relations.[106] Both historians[107] and political scientists[108] have shown that the connections between judicial rulings and public convictions are far more pervasive than is usually thought.

Consider *Brown v. Board of Education*,[109] invalidating racial segregation; *Loving v. Virginia*,[110] striking down bans on racial intermarriage; *Reed v. Reed*,[111] inaugurating the constitutional attack on laws discriminating on the basis of sex; *Craig v. Boren*[112] and *United States v. Virginia*,[113] cementing the ban on such laws; and *Romer v. Evans*,[114] striking down a highly unusual Colorado state constitutional amendment precluding state or local action banning measures forbidding discrimination on the basis of sexual orientation. In these cases, and many more, it would be reasonable to suggest that the Court's decision was, in an important sense, insisting that states must obey a national consensus.

Heller can be seen in the same light. As I have noted, a strong majority of Americans now supports the individual right to own guns for nonmilitary purposes.[115] At the same time, the law at issue in *Heller* was among the most draconian in the nation—a genuine national outlier.[116] The *Heller* Court might be understood as reacting to the District of Columbia law in the same way that the *Griswold* Court reacted to the Connecticut law, with skepticism about an intrusion that departs so radically from the general practice and hence the national consensus. Recall here that both presidential candidates—John McCain and Barack Obama—responded to the *Heller* decision with statements reflecting their support for the Court's conclusion.

To be sure, there are significant differences between the Connecticut law at issue in *Griswold* and the District of Columbia law at issue in *Heller*. The Connecticut provision was old,[117] making the claim of desuetude plausible. The *Griswold* Court could even have been said to have engaged in a project of "modernization," in a way that fits with some general tendencies in constitutional law.[118] By contrast, the District of Columbia provision was new, suggesting that the Court was not merely vindicating a national judgment but also challenging a departure from standard understandings of appropriate gun control legislation. A doctrine that would authorize challenges to recent departures and innovations raises quite different considerations from a doctrine that merely authorizes attacks on anachronistic laws. In this respect, Bickel's understanding of *Griswold* offers no help in *Heller*. What I am suggesting is a more general point: *Heller* is quite similar to *Griswold* in the critical sense that both decisions operated in accordance with a national consensus at the expense of a law that counted as a sharp deviation from it.

There is a possible response here. Whenever the Court begins a new area of constitutional doctrine, its initial step is likely to be analogous to *Griswold*. One reason is sensible litigation strategy; if the goal is to convince the Court to embark on a new path, the best strategy is usually to find an outlier and ask the Court to invalidate it in a way that leaves a door for future expansion. And if the Court itself is initiating a new avenue for potential invalidations, it is likely to begin narrowly and in a way that does not fit badly with public convictions, thus providing an analogy to *Griswold*. On this view, *Griswold* is likely to be the near-universal analogy whenever the Court embarks on a new path.

This response might be right, but it is not exactly an objection. If it is right, it suggests a general point of considerable interest. It is true that minimalism (at least in the sense of narrowness), alongside consistency with national commitments and invalidation of outliers, is a common starting point for doctrinal innovation. But if this point holds true for *Heller,* it suggests that despite its length and ambition, and its explicit originalism, the ruling fits with a number of decisions, most conspicuously *Griswold*, in which a new departure was drawn in narrow terms that fit well with public convictions.

It is also true that the District of Columbia law at issue in *Heller* could have been overridden by Congress at any time, unlike many state enactments. If Congress enacts a law that intrudes on privacy, or that regulates guns, it would be singularly odd to invalidate that law as a "national outlier." But there is a large difference between a national enactment from Congress and an enactment governing the District of Columbia. The latter reflects political pressures and dynamics that are not genuinely national but unique to the District. When Congress fails to override the law of the District, its inaction cannot plausibly be taken as a reflection of national will. In these circumstances, it is perfectly legitimate to treat legislation for the District as a kind of state law, and to conclude that for better or for worse, it may indeed count as a national outlier.

B. QUESTIONS AND PUZZLES

Of course, this understanding of the Court's role raises many questions and doubts. The first is empirical: What mechanisms link constitutional doctrine to a national consensus? The most obvious answer involves the appointments process. That process ensures that the views of the justices have some connection to political will.[119] Justices also live in society and are inevitably influenced by what other people in society think.[120] While judicial rulings are hardly a direct product of public opinion, there are clear links between what justices do and what the public believes.[121] Notwithstanding the Court's emphasis on what it took to be the original understanding of the Second Amendment, *Heller* is a clear example of these links.

There are also normative questions: Why does a national consensus matter? Why is it relevant to the Due Process Clause, the Equal Protection Clause, the Second Amendment, or anything else? Why and when should the Court strike down national outliers, rather than permitting them as a form of legitimate and even desirable experimentation? As I have suggested, the consensus may have epistemic value; if most people believe that X is true, X may well be true, certainly under favorable conditions. At least it might be said that if, in a democratic society, a national consensus supports some kind of individual right to own guns, the risks associated with recognition of that right are less likely to be terribly high. For purposes of law, the relevance of this point depends on the appropriate theory of constitutional interpretation.[122] Originalists will be puzzled about the idea that a national consensus matters unless the original understanding suggests that it does.

There are also legitimate questions about federalism, experimentation, and divergent norms. Certainly national outliers cannot be said to be invalid as such. Suppose that the District of Columbia seeks to embark on a path that differs from that of Montana and Georgia, or for that matter that is unique or nearly so. Should we not acknowledge the possibility (likelihood!) that it is responding to the distinctive values and information of its own citizens and representatives, in a way that deserves respect? Today's outlier is often tomorrow's norm. But prominent theories of interpretation do make a place for public will, most plausibly on the theory that at least in some domains, widespread social convictions convey information about the proper content of rights.[123] Indeed, judicial reliance on such convictions might even be counted as a form of "popular constitutionalism."[124] Both *Griswold* and *Heller* (and *Brown*, and *Lawrence*, and *Reed*, among many others) can be seen as reflections of popular constitutionalism, even if the *Heller* Court hardly spoke in those terms.

Even if it is correct to see *Heller* as a reflection of national convictions, a related problem remains: Could the Court have defended its opinion in the terms sketched here? Could it have done so in *Griswold*? Surely it is revealing that the Court did not attempt to do so in either case—and that it is unusual for the Court to acknowledge the relevance of the national consensus.[125] Suppose that we accept the publicity principle, in accordance with which public institutions should not root their judgments in considerations that they could not defend in public.[126] If so, the Court ought not to resolve cases by reference to arguments that it could not justify publicly. The only possible response to this objection is that in at least some variation, the approach I am sketching could indeed be offered by the Court.[127] In fact, I am willing to predict that in some domains, it will be offered in the future. And even when a national consensus is not explicitly invoked, it is often at work.

There is an important historical difference to be pondered as well. *Heller* is the product of a mature current of constitutional thought, spurred not only by private groups but also by committed academics. This current of thought has become prominent in national politics and culture and, by 2008, had established itself as thoroughly mainstream.[128] In sharp contrast, *Griswold* was the result of an early effort by an incipient movement for reproductive rights and sex equality, and this movement had yet to become highly visible on the nation's cultural viewscreen.[129] In this sense, *Heller* has far more in common with *Brown* than with *Griswold*—in the particular sense that *Brown*, like *Heller,* was the culmination of a long process of advocacy, in a self-conscious effort to entrench a certain understanding of the Constitution in the interest of social reform.[130] In short, *Heller* and *Griswold* have distinctive sociologies. While the two were both responsive to public convictions, their cultural backdrops were radically different.

Finally, there are questions of judicial competence: How will the Court identify the national consensus, if it is relevant? Ought the justices to consult opinion polls? To survey state law? I cannot answer such questions here. The goal is to understand *Heller,* not to defend it. My principal suggestion is that in its vindication of a national commitment against a provision that starkly departed from it, *Heller* is closely analogous to *Griswold.*

C. *Heller*'s Minimalism

Minimalists favor small steps, and they reject wide rulings and theoretical ambition. In the end, *Griswold* was a conspicuously minimalist opinion.[131] This is so in the sense that it did not adopt a theoretically ambitious understanding of privacy or offer a great deal of guidance about the scope of the right. Despite its rhetoric, the Court took a small step and narrowly focused on the particular provision at issue. The holding involved the right to use contraceptives within marriage. The Court did not resolve or even speak to the question of whether there is a right to purchase contraceptives within marriage, whether any right to use or purchase contraceptives applies outside of marriage, or whether any such right is part of a right to sexual activity as such. And notwithstanding its apparent sweep, the *Heller* Court's opinion had unmistakable minimalist elements. To be sure, the opinion displays a high degree of theoretical depth; with its explicitly originalist path, the Court adopted a particular method and did not seek an incompletely theorized agreement on its approach.[132] But the Court focused the key parts of its analysis on the particular provisions at issue.[133] Indeed, the ruling itself was exceedingly narrow. Moreover, the Court left numerous questions undecided.

Most obviously, the Court suggested that the Second Amendment right has clear limitations. In the Court's words, "nothing in our opinion should be taken to cast doubt on longstanding prohibitions on the possession of firearms by felons and the mentally ill, or laws forbidding the carrying of firearms in sensitive places such as schools and government buildings, or laws imposing conditions and qualifications on the commercial sale of arms."[134] To this the Court added that "the sorts of weapons protected [by the amendment] were those 'in common use at the time.'"[135] In its view, "that limitation is fairly supported by the historical tradition of prohibiting the carrying of 'dangerous and unusual weapons.'"[136] It follows that certain unusual or especially dangerous weapons, such as sawed-off shotguns, are also outside the domain of the Second Amendment. In these ways, the Court specified the validity of a number of actual or imaginable limitations on the right.

To be sure, these disclaimers are not, precisely, a form of minimalism; they do not leave the nature of the right unclear. They trim rather than refuse to decide.[137] But the Court acknowledged that its decision was, in some respects, quite narrow and that much remains to be resolved. After offering an account of measures on which it did not mean to cast doubt, the Court added an important footnote: "We identify these presumptively lawful regulatory measures only as examples; our list does not purport to be exhaustive."[138] In addition, the Court was sensitive to Justice Breyer's objection that its ruling left a great deal open: "[S]ince this case represents this Court's first in-depth examination of the Second Amendment, one should not expect it to clarify the entire field."[139] To support this point, the Court referred to its first decision involving religious liberty, *Reynolds v. United States*,[140] acknowledging, with understatement and an unmistakable dose of irony, that the Court's ruling there did not "[leave] that area in a state of utter certainty."[141]

Notwithstanding the Court's emphasis on historical markers, it is emphatically true that *Heller* leaves many questions open. To be sure, the Court squarely rejected the case-by-case interest-balancing urged by Justice Breyer.[142] But consider three fundamental issues that the Court did not resolve. First, the Court did not decide whether the Second Amendment is incorporated by the Fourteenth Amendment and thus made applicable to the states.[143] Second, the Court did not settle on a level of scrutiny for restrictions on the Second Amendment right.[144] Third, the Court did not come close to specifying the scope of the right. We know that "dangerous and unusual weapons" can be forbidden, and this idea undergirds the conclusion that "the sorts of weapons protected were those 'in common use at the time.'" But how, precisely, does this idea bear on modern questions, especially in light of the fact that the weapons at issue are necessarily modern ones?

The Court's answer here is opaque: "And there will be time enough to expound upon the historical justifications for the exceptions we have mentioned if and when those exceptions come before us."[145] Rejecting interest-balancing, the Court did say that the Second Amendment "elevates above all other interests the right of law-abiding, responsible citizens to use arms in defense of hearth and home."[146] But what exactly does that abstract phrase mean? How will it be specified in the future? Is interest-balancing appropriate or mandatory outside of the home? The Court did not say.

D. Evaluating *Heller* as *Griswold*

We have seen that on purely originalist grounds, the question resolved in *Heller* was not straightforward, and reasonable people believe that the Court was wrong.[147] In these circumstances, the Court might have used two tiebreakers. First, it might have emphasized the importance of respecting long-standing practices by federal and state legislatures and by federal courts, which seemed to suggest that the Second Amendment right is limited to military uses of guns. That understanding of the amendment was reflected in numerous lower federal court decisions, so much so as to represent an entrenched view.[148] The same view seems to fit with many legislative practices as well.[149] For followers of Edmund Burke, who believe less in the original meaning than in the need to follow social understandings over time,[150] the legislative and judicial practices might well have been invoked to reject a right to use guns for nonmilitary purposes.

Second, the Court might have concluded that, for Thayerian reasons, the democratic process should be given room to maneuver, at least in the face of reasonable doubt. Without any particular democratic malfunction specially justifying judicial intervention—for example, without any kind of claim on the basis of *Carolene Products*—a Thayerian approach would have had considerable appeal. Such an approach receives additional support from the fact that *Heller* will inevitably require federal courts, with limited guidance from *Heller* itself, to play an exceedingly difficult role in assessing the predictably numerous challenges to gun control legislation. Perhaps the Court should have adopted a militia-focused interpretation of the Second Amendment that was, at the least, textually and historically plausible, and that would prevent the federal judiciary from entering an unusual political thicket in which the democratic process does not seem to be working poorly.

There is, however, an important countervailing consideration. For the last decades, and perhaps for much longer, a robust individual right to use guns has become an entrenched part of American culture.[151] Many Americans believe that this right is both fundamental and essential—as much so, in its way, as the right to freedom of speech. They believe that the right to have guns is a crucial safeguard against private threats and even against government itself. Gun ownership is, for them, the ultimate form of security—an essential part of their identity and self-understanding.[152] About 40 million Americans—more than one in eight—are gun owners.[153] In these circumstances, it is no light thing for the Supreme Court to announce that tens of millions of Americans are simply mistaken, and that they hold their guns only at the government's sufferance.

Of course, it is legitimate to ask whether this consideration is important or even relevant. Should the Supreme Court interpret the Constitution to create rights simply because people understand the Constitution to create rights— and would be offended or worse if the Court failed to do so? After all, the Court did not recognize a right to Social Security benefits,[154] or to obscene materials,[155] or to certain kinds of property protection,[156] even though millions of Americans insist, with great conviction, that they have such rights. But the right to have guns is different. It has a unique status in contemporary American culture; it has been recognized as a right, and with great intensity, by citizens and politicians of both parties. An interpretation of the Founding document that denied the right would likely create forms of public outrage, political polarization, and social disruption that have not been seen in many decades. Out of respect for the intensely felt convictions of millions of Americans, and with concern for the risks of potential disruption, perhaps the Court should hesitate before denying the right.

In these circumstances, *Heller* starts to look even more like *Griswold;* recall that the latter case involved the right to marital intimacy, which (not to put too fine a point on it) is also understood to be fundamental by millions of Americans. In many ways, *Heller* may be no less defensible than *Griswold* on the ground I am exploring. As I have emphasized, it is certainly true that the Court did not write in these terms, and it would be speculative in the extreme to suggest that any member of the Court even thought about the Second Amendment question in this way. I am not contending that the explanation I am offering is ultimately sufficient. In the end, however, I believe that this explanation provides the strongest basis for understanding what made *Heller* possible—and it also offers a ground for seeing what makes *Heller* appealing.

V. A BRIEF NOTE ON IMPLICATIONS

What might be expected for the future? The three analogies offer competing answers. If *Marbury,* understood in originalist terms, provides the right analogy, then we should expect courts to follow an emphatically historicist course, in which the goal of judges, acting as amateur historians, is to transplant the original understanding to modern problems. This approach is consistent with the thrust of *Heller* itself, but it presents serious conceptual problems.[157] It is possible that the originalist inquiries, undertaken in radically different circumstances, will mask judgments that have a pragmatic component and that are driven by a sense of consequences and justifications. The more general point is that if *Marbury,* as understood here, is the analogy, the text, interpreted in light of the history, will be the actual as well as articulated foundation for future decisions, and the scope of the Second Amendment right will turn on history.

If *Heller* is to be a rerun of *Lochner,* then we should expect serious and continuing conflicts between the Court and the political process, with a series of politically controversial invalidations.[158] If the Court does not track but instead defies popular convictions, the *Lochner* analogy will be closer. To be sure, it is not imaginable that the Second Amendment will be taken to create the same kinds of obstacles to democratic initiatives as did the Due Process Clause in the *Lochner* era, if only because the scope of the Second Amendment is so much more limited. But it is at least imaginable that judicial invalidations of gun control laws will be frequent in the next decade and beyond.

If the analogy to *Griswold* holds, the path of the Second Amendment right will be similar to the path of the privacy right. Despite the *Heller* Court's emphatic rejection of interest-balancing, we should expect a long series of case-by-case judgments, highly sensitive to particulars. The law will follow a minimalist path. Many judges will speak in originalist terms, but contemporary reason and sense, as the judges understand them, will play crucial roles. If *Heller* is analogous to *Griswold,* the Court will not use the Second Amendment aggressively as a basis for striking down many gun control laws. Instead it will proceed cautiously, upholding most of the laws now on the books and invalidating only the most draconian limitations. It is very early, to be sure, but thus far, the lower courts are taking exactly this path.[159]

It should go without saying that, as with the right to privacy, judicial appointments will be crucial. After all, if *Bush v. Gore*[160] had been decided differently, it is most likely that *District of Columbia v. Heller* would have been decided differently as well.[161]

VI. CONCLUSION

Heller is the most explicitly and self-consciously originalist opinion in the history of the Supreme Court. Taken at face value, its oldest salient precursor seems to be *Marbury,* in which the Court also rested its decision on constitutional text and structure. I do not believe, however, that *Heller* can be adequately understood in this way. The relevant materials are ambiguous rather than clear; no member of the Court is a trained historian, and much of its opinion sounds like advocacy or law office history;[162] in the historical debate, the *Heller* opinion might have been wrong. In any event, it remains necessary to explain what made it possible for *Heller* to be issued in 2008, when it would not have been imaginable in 1958, 1968, 1978, or even 1988.

Skeptics will be tempted to see *Heller* as a triumph of politics and a defeat for law. On their view, the Court's detailed exploration of text and history is a smokescreen for a position that has been pressed hard by interest groups and political activists, that the Republican Party enthusiastically endorses, and that Republican appointees are likely to find congenial. If this view is correct, the most salient precursor is not *Marbury* but *Lochner.* This view can claim support from the fact that the Court was split along ideological lines; the most conservative members of the Court accepted the robust understanding of the Second Amendment right. But purely on the original understanding, *Heller* stands on plausible grounds—far more so than did *Lochner.* The Court did not, and could not, defend the invalidation of maximum hour laws by reference to text, structure, and history. At the very least, the *Heller* Court made a sustained effort to do so. If the flaw of *Lochner* consists in the Court's invocation of ambiguous constitutional text to strike down legislation, then *Heller* is indeed close to *Lochner*. But few people believe that it is always illegitimate for the Court to strike down legislation when the relevant provision of the Constitution is ambiguous. To be sure, *Lochner* and *Heller* will seem closely analogous to those who believe in a democracy-reinforcing approach to judicial review.

At first glance, it is jarring to suggest that *Heller* is a modern counterpart to *Griswold*. The two decisions seem to come from different jurisprudential universes. In originalist terms, there is nothing like a simple or clear defense of *Griswold*, and it would not be possible to produce a *Heller*-style opinion on its behalf. Nonetheless, the two rulings have a great deal in common. Both were made possible by a national consensus, which they simultaneously reflected. Both struck down a law that amounted to a national outlier. Despite their sweeping rhetoric, both had important minimalist features, ensuring that the content of the relevant right will be specified over time. It is clear that as it has developed, the right to privacy has had a great deal to do with contemporary convictions, not with the judgments of those long dead. Notwithstanding *Heller*'s barely qualified originalism,[163] I believe that the same will prove true of the right to bear arms. We have entered a period of Second Amendment minimalism.

NOTES

Source: Reprinted from 122 Harv. L. Rev. 246. Copyright © 2008 Harvard Law Review Association; Cass R. Sunstein.

1. 128 S. Ct. 2783 (2008).

2. Of course, there are other candidates. See, e.g., Printz v. United States, 521 U.S. 898 (1997); Plaut v. Spendthrift Farm, Inc., 514 U.S. 211 (1995). It is important to note as well that the Heller Court embraced a particular species of originalism, one that emphasizes the "original public meaning" of the Constitution rather than the "original intention" of its authors.

3. I do not mean to suggest that the Court was correct on the historical issue, a question explored below.

4. 5 U.S. (1 Cranch) 137 (1803).

5. See, e.g., ROBERT LOWRY CLINTON, MARBURY V. MADISON AND JUDICIAL REVIEW (1989).

6. 5 U.S. (1 Cranch) at 173–80.

7. For an early statement to this effect, see Randy E. Barnett, News Flash: The Constitution Means What It Says, WALL ST. J., June 27, 2008, at A13.

8. See, e.g., SAUL CORNELL, A WELL-REGULATED MILITIA: THE FOUNDING FATHERS AND THE ORIGINS OF GUN CONTROL IN AMERICA (2006); Jack N. Rakove, The Second Amendment: The Highest Stage of Originalism, 76 CHI.-KENT L. REV. 103, 158 (2000). See also the ambivalent treatment, showing that there are plausible views on both sides, in MARK V. TUSHNET, OUT OF RANGE: WHY THE CONSTITUTION CAN'T END THE BATTLE OVER GUNS (2007).

9. 198 U.S. 45 (1905).

10. 381 U.S. 479 (1965).

11. *Id.* at 484–85.

12. *See* RICHARD A. POSNER, SEX AND REASON 328–29 (1992).

13. *See, e.g.,* Antonin Scalia, *Common-Law Courts in a Civil-Law System: The Role of United States Federal Courts in Interpreting the Constitution and Laws,* *in* A MATTER OF INTERPRETATION: FEDERAL COURTS AND THE LAW 3 (Amy Gutmann ed., 1997) [hereinafter Scalia, *Common-Law Courts in a Civil-Law System*]; Antonin Scalia, *Originalism: The Lesser Evil,* 57 U. CIN. L. REV. 849 (1989).

14. Scalia, *Common-Law Courts in a Civil-Law System, supra* note 13, at 47.

15. *See* Antonin Scalia, *The Rule of Law as a Law of Rules,* 56 U. CHI. L. REV. 1175 (1989).

16. *See id.* at 1180. There is a clear connection between this claim and the Court's rejection of interest-balancing in *Heller. See* 128 S. Ct. at 2821 (citing *id.* at 2852 (Breyer, J., dissenting)).

17. Scalia, *Common-Law Courts in a Civil-Law System, supra* note 13, at 38.

18. In some cases, however, there have been unmistakable originalist features. *See, e.g., Crawford v. Washington,* 541 U.S. 36, 42–43 (2004). For a valuable discussion, see Stephanos Bibas, *Originalism and Formalism in Criminal Procedure: The Triumph of Justice Scalia, the Unlikely Friend of Criminal Defendants?* 94 GEO. L.J. 183, 201 (2005).

19. *See, e.g., Hein v. Freedom from Religion Found., Inc.,* 127 S. Ct. 2553 (2007) (nonoriginalist opinion by Justice Alito); *Lucas v. S.C. Coastal Council,* 505 U.S. 1003 (1992) (nonoriginalist opinion by Justice Scalia); *Lujan v. Defenders of Wildlife,* 504 U.S. 555 (1992) (same).

20. *See, e.g., United States v. Miller,* 307 U.S. 174 (1939); *United States v. Cruikshank,* 92 U.S. 542 (1876).

21. *Heller,* 128 S. Ct. at 2814–15.

22. *See* CORNELL, *supra* note 8; Rakove, *supra* note 8, at 158.

23. *See Va. State Bd. of Pharmacy v. Va. Citizens Consumer Council,* 425 U.S. 748 (1976).

24. *See Regents of the Univ. of Cal. v. Bakke,* 438 U.S. 265 (1978). For a detailed argument that affirmative action is unobjectionable on originalist grounds, see

Eric Schnapper, *Affirmative Action and the Legislative History of the Fourteenth Amendment*, 71 VA. L. REV. 753 (1985).

25. *See, e.g., Califano v. Goldfarb,* 430 U.S. 199 (1977); *Reed v. Reed,* 404 U.S. 71 (1971).

26. *See, e.g., Roth v. United States,* 354 U.S. 476 (1957).

27. *See Lujan v. Defenders of Wildlife,* 504 U.S. 555 (1992). For a critique on originalist grounds, see Cass R. Sunstein, *What's Standing after* Lujan? *Of Citizen Suits, "Injuries," and Article III,* 91 MICH. L. REV. 163 (1992).

28. For an illuminating discussion, see Adam M. Samaha, *Originalism's Expiration Date,* 30 CARDOZO L. REV. 102 (2008).

29. *See* RONALD DWORKIN, FREEDOM'S LAW: THE MORAL READING OF THE AMERICAN CONSTITUTION 7–15 (1996).

30. *See Heller,* 128 S. Ct. at 2851–53 (Breyer, J., dissenting). Note that Justice Stevens also emphasized judicial precedents, *id.* at 2823 (Stevens, J., dissenting), long-standing traditions, *id.* at 2842–45, and the need for judicial deference to reasonable legislative judgments, *id.* at 2846–47, 2846 n.39.

31. *But see supra* note 2.

32. The Court's clearest embrace of originalism, in its first century, can be found in *Dred Scott v. Sandford,* 60 U.S. (19 How.) 393, 405 (1857): "It is not the province of the court to decide upon the justice or injustice, the policy or impolicy, of these laws. The decision of that question belonged to the political or lawmaking power; to those who formed the sovereignty and framed the Constitution. The duty of the court is, to interpret the instrument they have framed, with the best lights we can obtain on the subject, and to administer it as we find it, according to its true intent and meaning when it was adopted." Note that in *Dred Scott,* the Court spoke in terms of original intentions, as well as original public meaning.

33. For an illuminating discussion of *Marbury,* with close reference to its context, see BRUCE ACKERMAN, THE FAILURE OF THE FOUNDING FATHERS: JEFFERSON, MARSHALL, AND THE RISE OF PRESIDENTIAL DEMOCRACY 182–88 (2005).

34. *Marbury v. Madison,* 5 U.S. (1 Cranch) 137, 180 (1803) ("Thus, the particular phraseology of the constitution of the United States confirms and strengthens the principle, supposed to be essential to all written constitutions, that a law repugnant to the constitution is void; and that *courts,* as well as other departments, are bound by that instrument.").

35. *Id.*

36. *See* CLINTON, *supra* note 5. For a very different understanding, see ACKERMAN, *supra* note 33, at 264–65.

37. For a brief suggestion to this effect, see Barnett, *supra* note 7.

38. *See* TUSHNET, *supra* note 8, at xv–xvi (suggesting that while the question is close, the original understanding is best read to create an individual right to have guns for nonmilitary purposes).

39. For some doubts on that score from one of the leading historians of the Founding period, see posting of Jack Rakove to Balkinization, http://balkin.blogspot .com/2008/06/thoughts-on-heller-from-real-historian.html (June 27, 2008, 20:02).

40. I put to one side some conceptual issues with attempting the originalist project under changed circumstances. *See* CASS R. SUNSTEIN, RADICALS IN ROBES: WHY EXTREME RIGHT-WING COURTS ARE WRONG FOR AMERICA 68–71 (2005).

41. *Cases v. United States,* 131 F.2d 916 (1st Cir. 1942).

42. *United States v. Emerson,* 270 F.3d 203 (5th Cir. 2001).

43. *Parker v. District of Columbia,* 478 F.3d 370 (D.C. Cir. 2007), *aff'd sub nom., Heller,* 128 S. Ct. 2783 (2008).

44. *See* Reva B. Siegel, *Dead or Alive: Originalism as Popular Constitutionalism in* Heller, reprinted in this volume.

45. *See* PollingReport.com, Guns, http://pollingreport.com/guns.htm; *see also* Jeffrey M. Jones, *Public Believes Americans Have Right to Own Guns,* GALLUP, March 27, 2008, www.gallup.com/poll/105721/Public-Believes-Americans -Right-Own-Guns.aspx.

46. Gallup Poll Editorial Staff, *Gallup Summary: Americans and Gun Control,* GALLUP, April 18, 2007, www.gallup.com/poll/27229/Gallup-Summary -Americans-Gun-Control.aspx.

47. Brief for Amici Curiae 55 Members of United States Senate et al. in Support of Respondent, *Heller* (No. 07-290), *available at* http://supreme.lp.findlaw.com /supreme_court/briefs/07-290/07-290.mer.ami.resp.cong.pdf.

48. *Id.*

49. Senator McCain responded as follows: "Today's decision is a landmark victory for Second Amendment freedom in the United States. . . . I applaud this decision as well as the overturning of the District of Columbia's ban on handguns and limitations on the ability to use firearms for self-defense." Posting of Tom Bevan to Real Clear Politics, http://time-blog.com/real_clear_politics/2008/06 /mccain_reacts_to_scotus_gun_de.html (June 26, 2008). Senator Obama stated: "I have always believed that the Second Amendment protects the right of individuals to bear arms. . . . Today's ruling, the first clear statement on this issue in 127 years, will provide much needed guidance to local jurisdictions across the country. As President, I will uphold the constitutional rights of law-abiding gun-owners, hunters, and sportsmen." *Id.*

50. For one account, see EDWARD H. LEVI, AN INTRODUCTION TO LEGAL REASONING 3–6 (1949).

51. Ronald Reagan was a member of the National Rifle Association, and he was committed to a broad individual right to have guns. *See* Chris Cox's Political Report—Ronald Wilson Reagan, www.nraila.org/issues/Articles/Read .aspx?ID=140. George H. W. Bush was also an NRA member for decades, although he resigned his membership in 1995. *See* John Minz, *Bush Resigns from NRA, Citing "Broadside" on Agents,* WASH. POST, May 11, 1995, at A1. George W. Bush has been strongly committed to a broad individual right. *See NRA Endorses George W. Bush for President,* NRA POLITICAL VICTORY FUND, Oct. 13, 2004, www.nrapvf.org/News/Read.aspx?ID=4614.

52. *Lochner v. New York,* 198 U.S. 45, 64 (1905).

53. *Id.* at 57–58.

54. *Id.* at 54–56.

55. For the Court's own recognition of this point, see, for example, *Ferguson v. Skrupa,* 372 U.S. 726, 728–29 (1963). For one discussion of the problems with the Court's entrenching its own policy views, see RONALD DWORKIN, TAKING RIGHTS SERIOUSLY (1977).

56. 198 U.S. at 75 (Holmes, J., dissenting).

57. 410 U.S. 113 (1973).

58. *See* J. Harvie Wilkinson III, *Of Guns, Abortions, and the Unraveling Rule of Law,* reprinted in this volume.

59. *Id.*

60. *Id.*

61. There are many different accounts of the vice of *Lochner;* I emphasize conventional ones here. For discussion of what might be wrong with *Lochner,* see JOHN HART ELY, DEMOCRACY AND DISTRUST: A THEORY OF JUDICIAL REVIEW 14–15 (1980); David A. Strauss, *Why Was Lochner Wrong?* 70 U. CHI. L. REV. 373 (2003); and Cass R. Sunstein, *Lochner's Legacy,* 87 COLUM. L. REV. 873 (1987).

62. CORNELL, *supra* note 8.

63. *Id.* at 51–52.

64. *Id.* at 2.

65. Rakove, *supra* note 8, at 158. In the process of supporting this argument, Rakove offers a sharp challenge to influential work by academic lawyers. *See id.* at 156–59.

66. *See id.*; *see also* Brief of Amici Curiae Jack N. Rakove et al. in Support of Petitioners, *Heller,* 128 S. Ct. 2783 (2008) (No. 07-290), reprinted in this volume; posting of the New York Times to Times Topics, http://topics.blogs.nytimes

.com/2008/06/26/qa-jack-rakove-on-heller-and-history (June 26, 2008 18:55); Rakove, *supra* note 39.

67. *Heller,* 128 S. Ct. at 2831–42 (Stevens, J., dissenting).

68. *See id.* at 2789, 2795, 2798–99, 2803, 2820 (majority opinion); *id.* at 2848–49, 2866 (Breyer, J., dissenting).

69. Rakove, *supra* note 8, at 105.

70. This point raises a general problem for originalism: if the Constitution is to be construed in accordance with the original public meaning, there is a serious question as to whether lawyers are competent for the task.

71. *See* Siegel, *supra* note 44.

72. *See* ADRIAN VERMEULE, JUDGING UNDER UNCERTAINTY: AN INSTITUTIONAL THEORY OF LEGAL INTERPRETATION (2006).

73. *See* James B. Thayer, *The Origin and Scope of the American Doctrine of Constitutional Law,* 7 HARV. L. REV. 129 (1893).

74. *Id.* at 144.

75. *Id.*

76. *Id.*

77. Id. at 151.

78. *Id.* at 155.

79. *Id.* at 155–56.

80. *Id.* at 156.

81. CORNELL, *supra* note 8; Rakove, *supra* note 8. The existence of ambiguity and reasonable disagreement underpins Judge Wilkinson's claim that *Heller* is closely analogous to *Roe. See* Wilkinson, *supra* note 58.

82. 347 U.S. 483 (1954).

83. 430 U.S. 199 (1977).

84. 128 S. Ct. 2229 (2008).

85. The word "almost" is necessary because of VERMEULE, *supra* note 72.

86. 304 U.S. 144 (1938).

87. *Id.* at 153 n.4 ("[P]rejudice against discrete and insular minorities may be a special condition, which tends seriously to curtail the operation of those political processes ordinarily to be relied upon to protect minorities, and which may call for a correspondingly more searching judicial inquiry.").

88. ELY, *supra* note 61.

89. *Heller,* 128 S. Ct. at 2846 n.39 (Stevens, J., dissenting) ("It was just a few years after the decision in *Miller* that Justice Frankfurter (by any measure a true judicial conservative) warned of the perils that would attend this Court's entry into the 'political thicket' of legislative districting. The equally controversial political thicket that the Court has decided to enter today is qualitatively different from the one that concerned Justice Frankfurter: While our entry into that

thicket was justified because the political process was manifestly unable to solve the problem of unequal districts, no one has suggested that the political process is not working exactly as it should in mediating the debate between the advocates and opponents of gun control. . . . It is, however, clear to me that adherence to a policy of judicial restraint would be far wiser than the bold decision announced today." (citations omitted) (quoting *Colegrove v. Green,* 328 U.S. 549, 556 (1946) (plurality opinion))).

90. *Griswold v. Connecticut,* 381 U.S. 479, 486 (1965).

91. *Id.* at 482–83.

92. *Id.* at 484.

93. *See, e.g., Lawrence v. Texas,* 539 U.S. 558 (2003) (understanding sexual privacy as part of liberty, and not stressing penumbras and emanations).

94. *See* Alexander M. Bickel, The Least Dangerous Branch: The Supreme Court at the Bar of Politics 148–56 (Yale Univ. Press, 2d ed. 1986) (1962).

95. *See* Posner, *supra* note 12, at 325–26.

96. See Cass R. Sunstein, *What Did* Lawrence *Hold? Of Autonomy, Desuetude, Sexuality, and Marriage,* 2003 Sup. Ct. Rev. 27, for one effort.

97. For discussion, see *id.*

98. *See Poe v. Ullman,* 367 U.S. 497, 542 (1961) (Harlan, J., dissenting).

99. *Id.* at 553.

100. *See* Cass R. Sunstein, *Due Process Traditionalism,* 106 Mich. L. Rev. 1543 (2008).

101. *See* Posner, *supra* note 12, at 329.

102. *Poe v. Ullman,* 367 U.S. 497, 554 (1961) (Harlan, J., dissenting), incorporated by reference in *Griswold v. Connecticut,* 381 U.S. 479, 500 (1965) (Harlan, J., concurring in the judgment).

103. *See, e.g., Washington v. Glucksberg,* 521 U.S. 702 (1997) (refusing to recognize a right to physician-assisted suicide owing to historical disapproval of the practice of assisting suicide). *But see, e.g., Lawrence v. Texas,* 539 U.S. 558 (2003) (rejecting limitation of due process clause to traditional mores).

104. *See* Michael J. Klarman, From Jim Crow to Civil Rights: The Supreme Court and the Struggle for Racial Equality 5 (2004); Robert A. Dahl, *Decision-Making in a Democracy: The Supreme Court as a National Policy-Maker,* 6 J. Pub. L. 279 (1957).

105. 539 U.S. 558.

106. *Id.* at 572.

107. *See, e.g., See,* Klarman, *supra* note 104.

108. *See, e.g.,* Dahl, *supra* note 104.

109. 347 U.S. 483 (1954).

110. 388 U.S. 1 (1967).

111. 404 U.S. 71 (1971).

112. 429 U.S. 190 (1976).

113. 518 U.S. 515 (1996).

114. 517 U.S. 620 (1996).

115. *See* sources cited *supra* note 45.

116. *Heller,* 128 S. Ct. at 2818 ("Few laws in the history of our Nation have come close to the severe restriction of the District's handgun ban.").

117. *See* Posner, *supra* note 12, at 325. Similarly, at the time of *Lawrence,* most state anti-sodomy laws were several decades old and rarely enforced. *See Lawrence v. Texas,* 539 U.S. 558, 570, 572 (2003).

118. *See* David A. Strauss, *Modernization and Representation Reinforcement: An Essay in Memory of John Hart Ely,* 57 Stan. L. Rev. 761, 762 (2004).

119. *See* Dahl, *supra* note 104, at 284–86.

120. *See* Cass R. Sunstein, A Constitution of Many Minds (forthcoming 2009).

121. *See* Dahl, supra note 104, at 284–85; *cf.* Public Opinion and Constitutional Controversy 8–9 (Nathaniel Persily et al. eds., 2008) (discussing the effects of Supreme Court decisions on public opinion).

122. Related issues are discussed in detail in Sunstein, *supra* note 120.

123. *See, e.g.,* Harry H. Wellington, *Common Law Rules and Constitutional Double Standards: Some Notes on Adjudication,* 83 Yale L.J. 221, 284 (1973) ("The Court's task is to ascertain the weight of the principle in conventional morality and to convert the moral principle into a legal one by connecting it with the body of constitutional law.").

124. *See* Larry D. Kramer, The People Themselves: Popular Constitutionalism and Judicial Review (2004).

125. The Court occasionally does refer to such a consensus in the Eighth Amendment context, *see, e.g., Kennedy v. Louisiana,* 128 S. Ct. 2641, 2650–53 (2008); *Roper v. Simmons,* 543 U.S. 551, 564 (2005), but the word "unusual" in the amendment provides a textual hook for that approach in these cases. *See also Lawrence v. Texas,* 539 U.S. 558 (2003) (considering the general practice of states in reaching the conclusion that the Texas anti-sodomy law was unconstitutional).

126. *See* John Rawls, A Theory of Justice 133, 453–54 (1971).

127. *Cf. Lawrence,* 539 U.S. at 571–72 ("[O]ur laws and traditions in the past half-century . . . show an emerging awareness that liberty gives substantial protection to adult persons in deciding how to conduct their private lives in matters pertaining to sex."); *Romer v. Evans,* 517 U.S. 620, 682–83 (1996) (emphasizing the unusual nature of the provision that the Court invalidated).

128. *See* Siegel, *supra* note 44.

129. *See* JOHN W. JOHNSON, GRISWOLD V. CONNECTICUT: BIRTH CONTROL AND THE CONSTITUTIONAL RIGHT OF PRIVACY (2005).

130. For a history of the social reform movement leading up to *Brown,* see RICHARD KLUGER, SIMPLE JUSTICE: THE HISTORY OF BROWN V. BOARD OF EDUCATION AND BLACK AMERICA'S STRUGGLE FOR EQUALITY (2d ed. 2006).

131. For a definition of minimalism, see CASS R. SUNSTEIN, ONE CASE AT A TIME: JUDICIAL MINIMALISM ON THE SUPREME COURT ix–xi (1999).

132. On the distinction between shallowness and narrowness, see *id.* at 16–19.

133. *Heller,* 128 S. Ct. at 2817–19.

134. *Id.* at 2816–17 (footnote omitted).

135. *Id.* at 2817 (quoting *United States v. Miller,* 307 U.S. 174, 179 (1939)).

136. *Id.* at 2817 (quoting 4 WILLIAM BLACKSTONE, COMMENTARIES *148–49).

137. *See* Cass R. Sunstein, *Trimming,* 122 HARV. L. REV. 1049 (February 2009).

138. *Heller,* 128 S. Ct. at 2817 n.26.

139. *Id.* at 2821.

140. 98 U.S. 145 (1879).

141. *Heller,* 128 S. Ct. at 2821.

142. *Id.* (citing *id.* at 2852 (Breyer, J., dissenting)).

143. In an opaque passage the Court said, "With respect to [the nineteenth-century case of *United States v.*] *Cruikshank*'s continuing validity on incorporation, a question not presented by this case, we note that *Cruikshank* also said that the First Amendment did not apply against the States and did not engage in the sort of Fourteenth Amendment inquiry required by our later cases. Our later decisions in *Presser v. Illinois,* 116 U.S. 252, 265 (1886), and *Miller v. Texas,* 153 U.S. 535, 538 (1894), reaffirmed that the Second Amendment applies only to the Federal Government." *Heller,* 128 S. Ct. at 2813 n.23 (parallel citations omitted).

144. *Id.* at 2817–18, 2821.

145. *Id.* at 2821.

146. *Id.*

147. *See* TUSHNET, *supra* note 8 (suggesting that reasonable arguments exist on both sides).

148. See the recitation in Justice Stevens's dissenting opinion. *Heller,* 128 S. Ct. at 2823 n.2 (Stevens, J., dissenting).

149. *See* TUSHNET, *supra* note 8, at 73–126.

150. *See* Cass R. Sunstein, *Burkean Minimalism,* 105 MICH. L. REV. 353 (2006).

151. For different but illuminating perspectives, see JOAN BURBICK, GUN SHOW NATION: GUN CULTURE AND AMERICAN DEMOCRACY (2006); and CORNELL, *supra* note 8.

152. *Cf.* Dan M. Kahan & Donald Braman, *More Statistics, Less Persuasion: A Cultural Theory of Gun-Risk Perceptions*, 151 U. PA. L. REV. 1291 (2003) (arguing that an individual's beliefs about gun control derive from her wider cultural worldview).

153. Christine Cadena, *Presidential Campaign Platforms 2008: The Issues of Gun Control*, ASSOCIATED CONTENT, July 2, 2007, www.associatedcontent.com /article/294410/presidential_campaign_platforms_2008.html.

154. *See Flemming v. Nestor*, 363 U.S. 603 (1960).

155. *See Miller v. California*, 413 U.S. 15 (1973).

156. *See Kelo v. City of New London*, 545 U.S. 469 (2005).

157. *See* SUNSTEIN, *supra* note 40, at 68–71.

158. I am greatly oversimplifying the *Lochner* era here. Although the Court did strike down important legislation, it also allowed considerable room for the police power. For discussion, see GEOFFREY R. STONE ET AL., CONSTITUTIONAL LAW 741–68 (5th ed. 2005).

159. *See, e.g.*, *United States v. Garnett*, No. 05-CR-20002-3, 2008 WL 2796098 (E.D. Mich. July 18, 2008); *Mullenix v. Bureau of Alcohol, Tobacco, Firearms & Explosives*, No. 5:07-CV-154-D, 2008 WL 2620175 (E.D.N.C. July 2, 2008); *United States v. Dorosan*, No. 08-042, 2008 WL 2622996 (E.D. La. June 30, 2008).

160. 531 U.S. 98 (2000).

161. If the arc of constitutional history is a guide, judicial appointments are only a part of the picture; perceived public convictions matter as well. *See* KLARMAN, *supra* note 104; Dahl, *supra* note 104.

162. Consider Jack Rakove's suggestion that "neither of the two main opinions in *Heller* would pass muster as serious historical writing." Rakove, *supra* note 39.

163. See the Court's notation: "Some have made the argument, bordering on the frivolous, that only those arms in existence in the 18th century are protected by the Second Amendment. We do not interpret constitutional rights that way. . . . [T]he Second Amendment extends, prima facie, to all instruments that constitute bearable arms, even those that were not in existence at the time of the founding." *Heller*, 128 S. Ct. at 2791–92. It is not clear, of course, that this passage is properly counted as a qualification of originalism.

Section IV

Historical Research after *Heller*

Originalism in a Digital Age

An Inquiry into the Right to Bear Arms

Nathan Kozuskanich

THE RECENT WASHINGTON, D.C., gun case *District of Columbia v. Heller* brought the question of the meaning of the Second Amendment before the U.S. Supreme Court for the first time in almost seventy years. At issue was whether the amendment protects an individual right to self-defense (an interpretation dubbed the Standard Model by those who adhere to it), or a collective right of arms-bearing so that states could regulate and men could participate in their own militias (the Collective Rights Model). Not surprisingly, the case touched off a firestorm of debate in editorials, scholarly articles, numerous amicus briefs, and even more blog postings. At the heart of most of these examinations of the meaning of the Second Amendment was a search for original intent. While originalism has generally focused on the intent of the Constitution's framers and ratifiers, there has been a more recent trend toward plain-meaning originalism, a method that emphasizes the original meaning that a rational listener would have placed on a constitutional provision. Such an approach, however, has been largely ahistorical because it operates under the notion that too much attention to "context may instead cloud what was otherwise a fairly clear meaning." While plain-meaning originalism may be unsatisfactory for historians, it has gained currency in the legal community. Indeed, in the majority opinion for the *Heller* case, Justice Scalia insisted that the "normal meaning" of words must be used to interpret the Second Amendment, not "secret or technical meanings that would not have been known to ordinary citizens in the founding generation." Thus the Court claimed that "the text and history [of the Second Amendment] demonstrate that it connotes an individual right to keep and bear arms," a right "unconnected with service in a militia." From a historical standpoint, Scalia's originalism is deeply flawed and unsubstantiated by the documentary record, and the evidence to refute him is just a few clicks of the mouse away.[1]

The digitization of historical documents into comprehensive archives with keyword search capabilities opens up a new avenue for scholars to recover the usage and meaning of key constitutional phrases, like "bear arms." Charles Evans's *American Bibliography,* the definitive collection of virtually every surviving book, pamphlet, and broadside in the colonies and United States from 1639 to 1800, has now been digitized by Readex, the company also responsible for the Early American Newspapers database, a searchable collection of over 120 American newspapers from 1690 to 1800. Together with the Library of Congress's online databases, these archives encompass most of the American newspapers, pamphlets, broadsides, and congressional proceedings published in the colonies and early republic, and provide an excellent way to tap into the common usage of words and phrases. A search of the exact phrase "bear arms" in all the text of documents dated 1750 to 1800 in the Evans collection returns 563 individual hits. If we discard reprints of the Bill of Rights and all references to the text of the Second Amendment in congressional debate, irrelevant foreign news, reprints of the Declaration of Independence, and all repeated or similar articles, 210 documents remain. All but eight of these articles use the phrase "bear arms" within an explicitly collective or military context to indicate military action. Likewise, the same search of the Early American Newspapers database yields 143 relevant hits, of which only three do not use the phrase to connote a military meaning. Finally, a keyword search of the Library of Congress's U.S. Congressional Documents and Debates database returns forty-one relevant hits. Only four of these documents do not use an explicitly military context when discussing bearing arms.[2]

While the evidence is very heavily weighted against an individual-rights interpretation, those looking for a complete vindication of the collective-rights view are bound to find disappointment as well. In fact, neither side in this debate has the story quite right. There is little doubt that Americans owned and used guns outside of the militia, and that they were firmly committed to the common law right of self-defense, a modification of the natural right to self-defense. What emerges clearly in these previously ignored texts is a civic conception of the right to bear arms. These digital databases reveal the limitations of the individual- and collective-rights paradigms, because both are unable to account for the civic responsibility of owning and bearing arms that is evident in the documents. Understanding that "bearing arms" meant fulfilling one's duty as a citizen to the common defense can account for personal firearm ownership while realizing that those arms were subject to robust regulation.[3]

Individual-rights scholars have not argued against the fact that "bear arms" was most often used in a military context; rather, they have asserted that such a context is irrelevant in determining original intent. In *Parker v. District of Columbia,* the decision that reversed the district court's ruling that D.C.'s gun control laws were constitutional because the Second Amendment applied only to the militia, Judge Silberman made this exact argument. Although the court agreed that the term "bear arms" is "obviously susceptible to a military construction," it argued that "it is not accurate to construe it exclusively so." In fact, Silberman argued that the word "bear" was "simply a more formal synonym for 'carry.' Looking at both the *Oxford* and *Webster's* dictionaries, the court acknowledged that the phrase "'bear arms' was sometimes used as an idiom signifying the use of weaponry in conjunction with military service" but that "these sources also confirm that the idiomatic usage was not absolute." Individual-rights scholars have maintained that *any* usage of "bear arms" outside of a military context is proof that the Founders meant to enshrine a nonmilitary right in the Second Amendment. "If 'bear arms' referred *only* to the military carrying or use of arms," Clayton Cramer and Joseph Olson argue, "then the right protected by the Second Amendment would not be an individual right." They are right on one level; not every single use of "bear arms" in the historical record is clearly military. The vast majority of uses are, however, and it is illogical to argue that a few idiosyncratic usages actually controlled the meaning of the Second Amendment. More important, no source from these archives makes the crucial link between a right to self-defense and a constitutional right to arms. Scalia agreed with Cramer and Olson, citing their work to make the inflated claim that "if one looks beyond legal sources, 'bear arms' was *frequently* used in nonmilitary contexts." Indeed, it is curious that a justice of the Supreme Court, especially a proclaimed originalist, would want to look outside legal sources to discover the meaning of a text drafted by a legislative body.[4]

Scalia has little use for relevant context. "The fact that the phrase [bear arms] was commonly used in a particular context," he argues, "does not show that it is limited to that context." Thus, he dismisses all congressional records, arguing that it is "unremarkable that the phrase was often used in a military context in the federal legal sources" because "those sources would have had little occasion to use it *except* in discussion about the standing army and the militia." It is baffling that Scalia willingly discards the military context of the Revolution and the very debates that Congress had up to the ratification of the Bill of Rights. This is particularly troubling because without considering these debates, he ignores the very reason the Second Amendment was proposed: to check congressional authority over the militia as outlined in Article I § 8 of the U.S. Constitution. As Woody Holton succinctly argues, "had there been no opposition to the Constitution, its supporters would not have felt the need to make concessions, and there would be no Bill of Rights." There is nothing in the surviving debates to indicate that Congress was concerned with anything but the militia while it discussed the right to keep and bear arms. To dismiss these sources as "unremarkable," and to ignore how the term "bear arms" was employed when Congress discussed the Second Amendment itself, is nothing short of reckless.[5]

Even if we do ignore all congressional records, the remaining sources show that Americans overwhelmingly used "bear arms" in a military sense both in times of war and in times of peace. Moreover, because these sources are newspapers, broadsides, and pamphlets, they allow us to determine the "normal meaning" of "bear arms" that the Court claims is so important. Rather than survey these sources, Scalia first dissects the phrase "bear arms" into two separate words. If the word "bear" has a nonmilitary meaning (such as a synonym for "to carry"), then "bear arms" must protect a nonmilitary right. Likewise, if the word "keep" could refer to possessing firearms that weren't connected with the militia, then the Second Amendment was meant to protect an individual right, or perhaps a dual right. He then argues that the phrase "bear arms" had an unequivocally military meaning only "when followed by the preposition 'against,' and that "every example given by the petitioner's *amici* for the idiomatic meaning of 'bear arms' from the founding period either includes the preposition 'against' or is not clearly idiomatic." The evidence from these digital databases easily proves this assertion to be false, because "bear arms" was used frequently in a military context without the preposition "against."[6]

In the years before the French and Indian War, the phrase "bear arms" appeared most often in military statutes. Under Scalia's reasoning, early lawmakers would have used "bear arms" in a nonidiomatic sense to draft these statutes because they do not also contain the preposition "against." His logic does not hold up in this case. Connecticut law demanded that all men aged sixteen to fifty "bear arms, and duly attend all musters, and military exercises." In 1699 the New York General Assembly tried to clamp down on privateers and pirates by enabling commissioned officers to "raise and levy such a number of well-armed men" to seize suspected pirates and put them in jail. The law they passed also allowed for fines and a possible court-martial for "those that refuse to bear arms under these officers." It is obvious that "bear arms" in all these examples had to do with using a firearm as part of a regulated militia.[7]

Virginia's militia law gives us valuable insight on the colonial regulation of arms for military purposes and the protection of military arms under the law. In 1738 the House of Burgesses proposed a new act "for the better regulation of the militia." Every eligible man was to be furnished with a gun, a bayonet or sword, a cartouche box, and three charges of powder, and was expected to "keep at his house one pound of powder, and four pounds of ball" and bring them to muster. Every man eligible for muster was given eighteen months to "provide himself with arms and ammunition," and all "furniture, arms, and ammunition" listed in the militia act were to be "exempted, at all times, from being impressed, upon any accounts whatsoever." Under the act, "free Mulattoes, Negroes, or *Indians*" were expected to appear "without arms," to be employed as "drummers, trumpeters, and pioneers." As the explanatory notes in the index succinctly stated, "free mulattoes, Negroes, and *Indians* shall not bear arms." Virginia's militia law points to the benefit of understanding the right to bear arms as being foremost a civic right. First, the militia law recognized private gun ownership and the fact that individual citizens were familiar with the upkeep of their firearms. However, those arms were subject to regulation and appropriation by the government.[8]

The other major usage of "bear arms" before the French and Indian War was in exemptions from military service for conscientious objectors. In Pennsylvania, the battle between the Quaker Assembly and numerous governors over a militia made bearing arms a perennial subject. In 1702 Governor Andrew Hamilton pleaded with "those of the Assembly, who profess themselves under a religious tye [*sic*] not to bear arms," to pass a militia law so that those who did not object to bearing arms could defend themselves. In response, the Assembly argued that to pass a law that would "compel others to bear arms" and exempt pacifists, especially those in the Assembly itself, "would be an inconsistency." Pacifists wanted guarantees that they would not be forced to bear arms, like the one granted in a 1747 act of Parliament assuring emigrating Moravians they would not "be summoned to bear arms, or do military service, in any of His Majesty's Colonies in *America*." These worries became even more salient as war with France broke out in the Ohio country and moved toward eastern Pennsylvania. In 1754, under instructions from the Proprietors, Governor Robert Hunter Morris implored the Assembly to establish a regular militia and provide "arms and stores of war," but to be sure "not to oblige persons to bear arms who are or may be conscientiously scrupulous against it." In 1755 the Assembly did pass a quasi-militia act allowing volunteers to be assembled into militia units. Critics pointed out that a militia law that did not compel service would be of no use. As one essayist argued, the law was "so loose, that nobody is obliged by it, who does not voluntarily engage," and asked for a law similar to those in other colonies that compelled "all sorts of persons to bear arms, or suffer heavy penalties."[9]

The war with France galvanized discussion of the militia and the importance of bearing arms for defense, as well as a concern for how many men in the colonies could be mustered to fight. Wary of creating a standing army, one essayist looked to the Roman Commonwealth, which had no standing army but "*Soldiers* as *Men* able to bear arms," who "learned the then art of war from their youth" and "inlisted as volunteers, whenever their country required their assistance." Colonial legislatures sought to regulate their militias through law in order to provide effective security against the French. For example, in 1758 Massachusetts passed a supplement to the existing laws regulating the militia, setting forth additional requirements for every man "liable to bear arms." It is worth noting that the law differentiated between bearing and carrying arms, stipulating that every man liable to bear arms, when ordered, "carry his arms and ammunition with him to the place of public worship, and to his labour in the field" or face a six shilling fine.[10]

As peace with France in 1763 and the end of Pontiac's War in 1764 gave way to increasing animosity between Britain and her American colonies, the militia and those who could bear arms in it remained a salient topic of public concern and discussion. Laws regulated those "liable to bear arms," and legislators sought to mobilize all those "capable to bear arms." Needless to say, both colonial and imperial leaders were interested in the number of men "fit" or "able to bear arms." By 1775, when political tension with Britain escalated into an armed military conflict, the colonists were preoccupied with mobilizing communities so that they could defend themselves. On July 18, 1775, John Dickinson proposed to the Continental Congress that it be "earnestly recommended to such of the inhabitants of these colonies, as have not already entered into associations for learning the military exercise, that all who are capable of bearing arms, do immediately associate themselves." Royal governors were also seeking out pockets of loyal supporters that they could arm against the growing patriot movement. As John Hancock reported to George Washington, Lord Dartmouth had written from Whitehall to North Carolina governor Josiah Martin, "recommending him to embody such of the men in four counties (which Governor Martin had represented as favourable to the views of administration) as are able to bear arms." It is clear from these documents and colonial militia laws that the ability to bear arms referred to meeting the legal requirements for participation in the militia, not the physical capacity to carry a firearm as Scalia suggests.[11]

After the Continental Congress issued the Declaration of Independence, Americans were faced with the task of actually securing that independence with a victory over the world's most formidable military power. Because the task before them was now primarily military in nature, it is perhaps no surprise that every mention of bearing arms in the newspapers from 1777 to 1784 refers to military action. Yet it would be a mistake to dismiss this crucial context to the formation of the American nation, because the idea of the republican militia was very powerful. "It is said the General Assembly of this state have enrolled in the militia list every person, able to bear arms, from 16 to 60," reported the *Norwich Packet*. As *rage militaire* swept the new states in the early years of the Revolution, pacifists once more asserted their right not to bear arms. Many states were willing to grant objectors an exemption from physical service, but they also felt that these men should fulfill their civic duty in other ways. One essayist proposed "a tax of two dollars . . . for every man able to bear arms and not actually in the Continental army." The Maryland Assembly rejected a petition from pacifist sects asking for an exemption from such fines, arguing "that every indulgence, consistent with the defence and security of the state, should be given to religious people, but that to release persons able to bear arms from military duty tends to weaken the defence of the state, and that such exemptions ought not to be granted till the war is ended."[12]

The debate over militia exemptions reveals that early Americans considered bearing arms for the state to be the obligation of every man who enjoyed the state's protection. This duty, or liability, is crucial to understanding bearing arms in the early years of U.S. nationhood. When the British declared any person taken "not in arms, but peaceably in their own houses" to be "prisoners of war on parole," South Carolina's governor, John Rutledge, proclaimed that all men were still "liable to bear arms in defence of the state." Likewise, in 1781 North Carolina's Assembly ordered "all persons who can be armed, and are able to bear arms, to assemble themselves under Major General Caswell to form an army." Of considerable concern were the British proclamations issued throughout the states calling all those on parole to swear allegiance to the king. In South Carolina, Henry Clinton discharged "from their paroles all who had taken them, and [required] their immediate attendance to swear allegiance and bear arms in favor" of the king. It is obvious that ideas of personal gun ownership and self-defense played no role in framing these proclamations and declarations. An American could not own or carry a gun "in favor" of the king any better than he could own or carry it "against" his country. He could, however, bear arms in a militia and fight alongside the British regulars.[13]

Even with the Peace of Paris in 1783, men were reminded that they still had a duty to serve in the militia. The captain-general of the New Hampshire militia hoped that his state's citizens, "so far from deeming it a *burthen* to bear arms," would "esteem it a *privilege,* which no person, worthy of the name of *freeman,* would willingly relinquish." Not surprisingly, pacifists again asserted their right not to bear arms. In Virginia, members of the Menonist Church petitioned the Assembly to be "exempted from militia duty" because it was "contrary to the principles of their church, that its members should upon any occasion bear arms." For Americans of the new republic, however, the refusal to bear arms was no small barrier to public service. As Massachusetts pastor David Parson preached, every subject had to "bear arms, i.e. he must pay due obedience to the powers of the state."[14]

The duty of men in securing the safety of the state was put to the test with the uprising of veterans of the Revolution in western Massachusetts in 1786. Indeed, when Daniel Shays and his band of rebels stormed the Northampton courthouse and eventually the Springfield armory in early 1787, it brought discussion of the extent of the right to bear arms to the fore. Some in Massachusetts feared that the Shaysites could "muster in all their united force . . . more than 2000 men, if they all turned out, who would bear arms" but that "their numbers would be less" if "there was a force against them." When the regular militia refused to muster against the men of their own state, leaders in Boston funded a private militia to suppress the rebellion. In the aftermath of the violence, the General Court passed an act "for the more speedy and effectual suppression of tumults and insurrections," which plainly stated in the first sentence that "the people have a right to bear arms for the common defense." Thus, all "virtuous citizens" needed to "hold themselves in readiness" and be prepared to ensure the "safety of the state." In the new republic, as during the Revolution, recognizing and fulfilling one's duty of militia service was an essential element of citizenship. Not only did the Shaysites not have the right to rebel against the government, but also the militia did not have the option to opt out of service despite any sympathy its members might have for the rebels.[15]

It seemed obvious after Shays's Rebellion that a more coherent system of defense was needed to guard the republic from internal and external threats. State militias were arguably ineffective, but the proposal of a new Constitution in 1787, with its Federalist focus on domestic tranquility, promised to solve this problem through congressional regulation. Of course, in light of the American Revolution, some were wary about such controls. To calm these fears, James Madison argued that "the highest number to which . . . a standing army can be carried in any country, does not exceed one hundredth part of the whole number of souls; or one twenty-fifth part of the number able to bear arms." Because such an army would "be opposed by a militia amounting to near a half a million citizens with arms in their hands," Madison asserted that "it may well be doubted whether a militia thus circumstanced could ever be conquered by such a proportion of regular troops." It is important to note that Madison used the phrase "bear arms" to connote military action, exactly the same way his contemporaries did. And it is no mistake that, as part of the founding generation, Madison also appealed to the ideal of the republican militia as the bulwark of liberty.[16]

Alongside concerns about the abuse of military power came revived worries from pacifists about forced military service. Federalists tried to calm fears that conscientious objectors would be compelled to duty by arguing that while Congress could call forth the militia, only the states could raise a militia. Because "men conscientiously scrupulous by sect or by profession are not forced to bear arms in any of the states," there was nothing to worry about. Indeed, forcing pacifists into service made little sense from a strategic point of view. As one Federalist essayist wrote, "there is not the least danger of the federal government compelling persons of a scrupulous conscience to bear arms, as the United States would be poorly defended by such." A Rhode Island Federalist assured his wary countrymen that "although the President of the United States is a man of defensive principles," he would never "suffer any man to be dragged into the field of battle who was fully convinced that it was not right for him to bear arms." Of course, mere lip service was not good enough, and pacifist anti-Federalists wanted an explicit provision incorporated into the proposed Constitution. "There is room to fear," wrote one such critic, "that a majority of those who composed the Convention were deists, or men of little or no religious principles—as they have made no provision for those who refuse to bear arms; especially the Society of Friends."[17]

The Bill of Rights emerged as a compromise to anti-Federalist opposition in states like New York and Virginia, and as a way to appease men who were not satisfied to let the separation of powers guarantee their liberties. The very "written-ness" of the amendments testifies to that fact that Federalists were bowing to pressure to detail explicitly the power reserved to the states. The Virginia convention asked that a lengthy Bill of Rights be added to the Constitution, including the provision "that the people have a right to keep and bear arms; that a well-regulated militia, composed of the body of the people trained to arms, is the proper, natural, and safe defence of a free state." Another proposed clause for the Bill of Rights sought an exemption for "any person religiously scrupulous of bearing arms," provided that that person "make payment of an equivalent to employ another to bear arms in his stead." These provisions clearly spell out the meaning of "bear arms." While one could be trained to use a firearm, and one could own a firearm, one could not be forced to bear that arm in a militia if one conscientiously objected.[18]

Attending to the concerns of conscientious objectors was no small matter, and Madison himself proposed a specific exemption to the militia bill for those conscientiously scrupulous of bearing arms. "The pride of the federal constitution [was that] the rights of man had been attended to," he argued, and although "it was possible to oppress their sect," no one had ever been able "to make [the Quakers] bear arms." Therefore, Congress would be wise to "make a virtue of necessity and grant them the privilege." To argue that Madison was proposing a general exemption for all those who opposed using arms for any violent purpose ignores the way "bear arms" had been employed up to 1790, as well as the fact that the ensuing congressional debate centered on militia service. Representative James Jackson of Georgia opposed the exemptions on the grounds that men would be tempted to evade militia duty "by a pretended attachment to religious principles." If Quakers were to be exempt from personal service, then they would have to pay a fine to contribute to the common defense. Representative William Giles also opposed the exemption, arguing that "personal service . . . was a debt every member owed to the protection of government, a debt which it was immoral not to pay." Representative Roger Sherman questioned if Congress could give an exemption to pacifists since the "state governments had [not] given out of their hands the command of the militia, or the right of declaring who should bear arms." He went on to argue that it was the

> privilege of every citizen, and one of his most essential rights, to bear arms, and to resist every attack made upon his liberty or property, by whomever made. The particular states, like private citizens, have a right to be armed, and to defend, by force of arms, their rights, when invaded. A militia existed in the United States, before the formation of the present constitution: and all that the people have granted to the general government is the power of organizing such a militia. The reason of this grant was evident; it was in order to collect the whole force of the union to a point, the better to repel foreign invasion, and the more successfully to defend themselves.

It is crucial to realize that Sherman's comments were made in discussing the militia. His assertion of the privilege to bear arms was directly tied to communal service. Indeed, the very mechanism by which Americans could defend themselves was in the collection of force, not individual action.[19]

The hesitance to grant military exemptions also highlights the civic element of bearing arms in the militia. Representative Aedanus Burke from South Carolina feared that such exemptions would "oblige the middling and poorer classes of citizens to the toils and dangers of military service" while the "wealthy, the potent, and influential" could escape service, leading to the "disgrace of the militia." Even so, he agreed that no man should be forced to bear arms against his conscience. Burke had no love for the Quakers, and during the Revolution had been in charge of imprisoning all Quakers in Charleston who "refused to bear arms" and disobeyed the governor's orders to "defend the town." The real issue at hand was which governing body should grant the exemptions, and most members felt that state governments, not Congress, should be entitled to give exemptions. Therefore, Madison's proposal was defeated. As the *Provincial Gazette* reported, "it was not, however, the sense of the House that [conscientious objectors] should be forced to bear arms."[20]

The need for men to contribute to the militia to ensure adequate and coherent defense was perhaps even more urgent on the westward fringe of the United States. When members of the Ohio Company decided to donate some of their landholdings to encourage westward migration, they stipulated that "proper defences" were to be built and maintained, and every settler on these donated lands was to be provided with arms and ammunition, as outlined in the militia law. Every "man able to bear arms" who complied with these requirements would receive an official deed to the land after five years. The Ohio Company's insistence that all men comply with militia law and contribute to securing and maintaining community security was an extension of the community militia responses of the American Revolution. Indeed, the right to bear arms continued to be understood as a civic responsibility to the community. "The right of the people to keep and bear arms has been recognized by the General Government," wrote one commentator, "but the best security of that right after all is, that military spirit, that taste for martial exercises, which has always distinguished the free citizens of these states: From various parts of the Continent the most pleasing accounts are published of reviews and parades in large and small assemblies of the militia."[21]

In South Carolina, the military spirit appeared to be alive and well. In October 1791 the governor organized a regimental muster and ordered every officer to "take the necessary steps for bringing all men liable to bear arms in their respective battalions into the field armed and accoutred according to law." Indeed, in 1791 "bearing arms" still maintained its collective and military meaning. When the Court of Enquiry sat to look into the personal conduct of Brigadier General Josiah Harmar in the 1790 expedition against the Miami Indians, one of the deponents, Major Ferguson, reported that the Kentucky militia's "arms were generally very bad, and unfit for service," and that "amongst the [Pennsylvania] militia were a great many hardly able to bear arms, such as old infirm men, and young boys." He was even further perplexed that there were "a great number of them . . . who probably had never fired a gun." Ferguson's musings show us that he expected the men to be proficient with firearms from their personal use of them on the frontier, but was curious why the militia was composed of men who barely made the age requirements. Not only were the men from Pennsylvania untrained, but also their youth or old age made them "hardly able to bear arms."[22]

While almost all of the documents from these online databases support a civic and military interpretation of bearing arms, a select few do not explicitly support such a reading. They are not, however, effective support for the so-called Standard Model. For example, the April 23, 1776, issue of the *Pennsylvania Evening Post* reported that one Peter Wikoff had reportedly been seen "bear[ing] arms about twelve months before in Philadelphia." It is unclear exactly what Wikoff was doing, but it was enough to prompt Governor William Shirley of Massachusetts to offer a £500 reward for his capture. It seems certain, though, that he was not simply carrying his gun. Perhaps somewhat less ambiguous but by no means more clear is a report of the settlement on the Genesee tract in New York in 1791. The *General Advertiser* printed that there were "upwards of six thousand persons already established in this new country, half of whom may be presumed able to bear arms, [which] gives the most perfect security to the settlers." While it is reasonable to assume this "perfect security" came from men banding together for the common defense, there is no explicit mention of any militias or military associations. And while it is plausible that the author was describing the measure of personal safety that came with owning a firearm on the frontier, it is unlikely, given the history of the phrase, that he meant for the term "able to bear arms" to be equated with "able to carry a gun."[23]

More illuminating are the writings of Scribble-Scrabble (Federalist judge George Thatcher) who examined the Massachusetts constitution in a series of newspaper essays. Of particular interest is his rejection of the idea that the constitution limited personal freedoms by placing negatives on rights not mentioned. In a state of nature, he argued, "individuals have a right to keep arms—say muskets," which they could use "to kill game, fowl, or in self-defence, or in defence of their fellow creatures." Although the constitution stated that "the people have a right to keep and bear arms in their common defence," this article did not deprive the people of their natural right "of using arms when they are attacked privately and not in common and together." As he argued, "who will say that if an honest farmer were to discharge his musket, ten times a day, at pigeons or other game, he thereby becomes an enemy to the Constitution?" Thatcher, as Scribble-Scrabble, highlights the key difference between having arms and bearing arms. While the constitution explicitly protected the right to bear arms communally, that did not negate the natural right to use arms for other purposes, even self-defense. This did not mean, though, that firearms were to escape state regulation, and Thatcher argued that the legislature should have the "power to control it [the right to keep and bear arms] in all cases, except the one mentioned in the bill of rights, whenever they think the good of the whole require it." In other words, only those firearms not used for militia duty could be restricted.[24]

The use of "bear arms" in documents from 1791 to 1800 continued to connote collective, military action. Debates over federal militia law, regulating state militias, defense on the frontier, and exemptions for pacifists all employed standard phrasing of men being "liable to bear arms," "competent to bear arms," "fit to bear arms," and "compelled to bear arms." Rather than list the many uses of "bear arms" in this period, it would be more fruitful to discuss the few cases where "bear arms" was not used in an explicit discussion of the militia. These usages are largely found in reprints of state constitutions drafted by 1800, containing the guarantee that citizens or people could "bear arms for the defense of themselves and the state." The one exception is Massachusetts, and scholars have largely agreed that its state constitution protected a communal right because it contained an explicit communal qualifier. Thus it comes as no surprise that in a 1797 speech Governor Samuel Adams extolled the virtue of a militia as "the most safe defense of a Republic," and reminded his listeners (quoting the state constitution) that "the people have a right to keep and bear arms for the common defense."[25]

While the case for Massachusetts seems fairly cut and dried, Standard Model scholars maintain that the phrase "bear arms" in fact had two meanings, and that if no explicit provision for the common defense was given, then the right granted was an individual one. This seems highly unlikely given the predominant usage of the phrase "bear arms," and it is curious that an individual right is assumed even when no explicit individual qualifier is given. The closest phrasing to an individual right is "bear arms for the defense of themselves and the state," which many have interpreted to mean a right both to self-defense and to participate in a militia. The phrase originated in Pennsylvania's 1776 constitution, and was slightly revised in the 1790 constitution, which, after declaring that "the freemen of this commonwealth shall be armed and disciplined for its defence," and providing an exemption for "those who conscientiously scruple to bear arms" (Article VI, sec. 2), recognized the "right of citizens to bear arms, in defence of themselves in the state" (Article IX, sec. 21). Individual-rights scholars have pointed to James Wilson, Pennsylvania Supreme Court justice and main author of the 1790 constitution, who wrote that Pennsylvania's provision of a right to bear arms supported "the great natural law of self preservation." Even though Wilson's lectures, delivered in late 1790 but never published, lean toward a more modern individual-rights construction, his perception of self-preservation was still tied into community mobilization. With regard to defending one's house, Wilson quoted Lord Coke: "Every man's house is his castle . . . and he ought to keep and defend it at his peril; and if any one be robbed in it, it shall be esteemed his own default and negligence." Therefore, Wilson argued, "one may assemble people together in order to protect and defend his house."[26]

Those familiar with the Fort Wilson incident will probably not be surprised that Wilson endorsed defending one's property by mustering collective force. With political tensions still inflamed from the debate over the 1776 Pennsylvania constitution, 1779 saw a group of disaffected militia roaming the streets of Philadelphia. After hearing that these men were headed to his house, Wilson (who opposed the constitution, even though it was popular among the militia) gathered up a group of friends and barricaded himself in his home. Undaunted by the calls to disperse, the militia rushed the house, smashing down the doors to gain entry. In the end, six men lay dead, and further deaths were prevented when the mob was stopped by Pennsylvania's president, Joseph Reed, and the City Troop of the Light Horse. Wilson was forced to leave the city. Of course, this episode is by no means proof that Wilson saw self-defense only as tied to military action, but it does show that Wilson's concept of self-defense was more complicated than a simple endorsement of what is now called the Standard Model.[27]

Despite Wilson's personal convictions or intentions, he did not control the meaning of Pennsylvania's right to bear arms. When Dr. James Reynolds stood trial in 1799 for assault with intent to murder, after brandishing a pistol at an angry mob, neither the prosecution nor the defense considered Reynolds's possession or use of his gun to be a matter of constitutional law. If the individual right to bear arms was constitutionally protected (i.e., defense of oneself), it is logical to assume that his lawyer would have appealed to that constitution. Even more important, Reynolds was never considered to have borne arms, despite the fact that he obviously carried his firearm with him. The debate that ensued only reaffirms the difference that existed between the natural right to self-defense and the constitutional right to bear arms. Reynolds's lawyer argued that because there was "no law in Pennsylvania to prevent it; every man has a right to carry arms who apprehends himself to be in danger." That right came not from the state constitution but from "the law of nature and the law of reason," which allowed deadly force "if necassary [*sic*] to [one's] own safety." Although the prosecution disagreed, arguing from

Blackstone that "the law says, if a man attack you by a sword, you have no right to kill him, till you have made every attempt to escape," the jury acquitted Reynolds. While Reynolds had indeed carried a gun for self-defense, he had not borne that arm.[28]

Further complicating the matter is the fact that other prominent Pennsylvanians clearly saw Pennsylvania's constitutional right to bear arms as tied to collective duty. During the Quasi-War with France, Congress proposed a bill that gave President Adams the power over a volunteer military corps that was neither militia nor regular army. The constitutional gray area surrounding this special force was a cause of much concern and debate. In light of the Alien and Sedition Bills, the Federalists' attempt to create "military associations of one part of the people, in order to suppress a supposed disaffection of the rest of the community" was highly suspect. Pennsylvanian Albert Gallatin opposed the bill, in part because wealthy Federalists would join the ranks of the volunteer corps and subvert the constitutional rights of poorer Republicans to participate in the militia. "Whether a man be rich or poor," Gallatin argued, "provided he has a common interest in the welfare, of the community, he had an equal reliance upon him. And this is a Constitutional idea; for the Constitution says, 'the rights of the people to bear arms shall not be questioned.'" In other words, the proposed corps would subvert citizens' constitutional right to bear arms in a militia.[29]

A collective right also had currency in Kentucky in the 1790s. Kentucky's 1792 constitution guaranteed that "that the right of the citizens to bear arms in defense of themselves and the State shall not be questioned." As in Pennsylvania and other states, local politics was fueled by bitter party animosity between the Federalists and emerging Democratic Republicans. The Federalists' attempts to suppress demonstrations against their policies only heightened paranoia and talk of waning American liberty. It is no surprise, then, that the use of arms to defend liberty became part of the public discussion. "The president calls out,—to arms—to arms—all the rest of America are putting themselves in a posture of defense; and yet it is unwarrantable in you to make any attempts of the same kind," complained one essayist to his fellow Republicans. The author considered arms to be essential to preserving liberty, arguing that only an armed people could "assert and defend" their constitutional rights, but considered the right to bear arms as essentially linked to militia service. "Standing armies are such dangerous foes to liberty," he argued, "that whenever one soldier is ordered to be raised ten muskets ought to be put in the hands of the militia." Thus, he continued, "the federal constitution declares that 'a well regulated militia being necessary for the security of a free state, the right of the people to keep and bear arms shall not be infringed:' and the state constitution says that 'The right of the citizens to bear arms in defense of themselves and the state, shall not be questioned.'"[30]

Perhaps the greatest trick individual-rights scholars have pulled off is convincing the courts that an amendment that begins "A well-regulated militia" actually has little to do with the militia. Their scholarship has made it possible for Supreme Court justices to declare American law and congressional records irrelevant when determining original intent, and to ignore crucial contexts that informed the meaning of words. The evidence clearly shows that in times of war and in times of peace, the term "bear arms" was used to connote military action. Defense, whether it was of the United States, the individual states, or the individuals in those states, was a perennial concern, but such a concern never translated into extended debates over the use of firearms for personal safety. Instead, the discussion revolved around men's civic obligation to the militia, the very mechanism that would provide safety for Americans. This should come as no surprise, because the Founders were trying to fight a Revolution and establish a new nation, not solve the problems of modern gun control. To ignore these debates that shaped America's transition from a British colonial possession to a new and independent nation is simply bad historical and originalist scholarship. Because history and historical documents have played such a central role in Second Amendment scholarship, we need to ensure that those sources are examined with a careful eye for context and that originalists conform to the standards of historical scholarship. Although digital research cannot be a substitute for traditional historical methods, it can give legal scholars access to a wealth of resources that have been relatively unused in constitutional research. Indeed, a historical focus on context and change over time can complement the legal focus on structure and precedent. Rather than move away from context, as the *Heller* decision encourages, digital research can restore originalist scholarship to its historical roots.

NOTES

Source: Reprinted from *Journal of the Early Republic* 29 (Winter 2009): 585–606. Copyright © 2009 Society for Historians of the Early American Republic. All rights reserved.

1. The last case to deal with the Second Amendment was *U.S. v. Miller* in 1939. The parameters of the modern debate are best charted in Stuart Banner, "The Second Amendment So Far," *Harvard Law Review* 117 (January 2004): 898– 917.

For differing interpretations of the republican origins of the Second Amendment, see Robert E. Shalhope, "The Armed Citizen in the Early Republic," and Lawrence Delbert Cress, "A Well-Regulated Militia: The Origins and Meaning of the Second Amendment," in *Whose Right to Bear Arms Did the Second Amendment Protect?* ed. Saul Cornell (Boston, 2000), 27–62. For a summary of the modern individual rights model, see Glenn Harlan Reynolds, "A Critical Guide to the Second Amendment," *Tennessee Law Review* 62 (Spring 1995): 461–512. For an overview of the legal debate over originalism, see Daniel A. Farber, "The Original-ism Debate: A Guide for the Perplexed," *Ohio State Law Journal* 49 (1989): 1085–1106. One of the best historical approaches to originalism is Jack Rakove's *Original Meanings: Politics and Ideas in the Making of the Constitution* (New York, 1996). For more on plain-meaning originalism, see Randy E. Barnett, "An Originalism for Nonoriginalists," *Loyola Law Review* 45 (Winter 1999): 612–54; Barnett, "The Original Meaning of the Commerce Clause," *University of Chicago Law Review* 68 (2001): 107; Majority Opinion, *District of Columbia v. Dick Anthony Heller*, No. 07-290 (June 26, 2008), 3, 1, available at www.supremecourtus.gov/opinions /07pdf/07-290.pdf (hereafter cited as *Heller* Decision).

2. It should be noted that some sources employ the phrase "bear arms" multiple times. The research in this article builds on my previous findings of the period 1750–1791 published in "Originalism, History, and the Second Amendment: What Did Bearing Arms Really Mean to the Founders?" *University of Pennsylvania Journal of Constitutional Law* 10 (March 2008): 413–46. My research also supplements David Yassky's work with the Library of Congress database. See David Yassky, "The Second Amendment: Structure, History, and Constitutional Change," *Michigan Law Review* 99 (December 2000): 588–668. A link to these archives can be found at http://infoweb.newsbank.com under the "Archive of Americana" link (subscription required). By "explicitly collective or military context," I mean that "bear arms" appears in an obvious discussion of the militia (and citizens' civic obligation to participate in the militia), the army, or people banding together to protect the community. I searched only the relevant databases on the LOC site (http://rs6.loc.gov/ammem/amlaw/): Letters of Delegates to Congress, Journals of the Continental Congress, Elliot's Debates, and the House and Senate Journals of the First Congress (1789–1791).

3. For a comprehensive history of the civic nature of the right to bear arms, see Saul Cornell, *A Well-Regulated Militia: The Founding Fathers and the Origins of Gun Control in America* (Oxford, 2006).

4. *Shelly Parker et al. v. District of Columbia*, No. 04-7041, U.S. App. LEXIS 5519 (2007), 24; Clayton Cramer and Joseph Olson, "What Did 'Bear Arms' Mean in the Second Amendment?" *Georgetown Journal of Law & Public Policy* 6 (Summer 2008): 511–29, quote 511; *Heller* Decision, 15 (emphasis added).

5. See *Heller* Decision, 15, 13. Article I, § 8 stipulates that Congress shall have the power "to provide for calling forth the militia to execute the laws of the union, suppress insurrections and repel invasions" and "to provide for organizing, arming, and disciplining, the militia, and for governing such part of them as may be employed in the service of the United States, reserving to the states respectively, the appointment of the officers, and the authority of training the militia according to the discipline prescribed by Congress." Woody Holton, *Unruly Americans and the Origins of the Constitution* (New York, 2007), xi.

6. See *Heller* Decision, 13, 12–13.

7. *Acts and Laws of His Majesty's* English *Colony of Connecticut in New England in America* (New London, 1750), 12; *Laws of New York, from the Year 1691, to 1751, Inclusive* (New York, 1752), 27 and marginalia.

8. *The Acts of Assembly, Now in Force, in the Colony of Virginia* (Williamsburg, 1752), 155; ibid., 158, 156, 439.

9. *Votes and Proceedings of the House of Representatives of the Province of Pennsylvania* (Philadelphia, 1752), 1:xx (appendix); *Votes and Proceedings of the House of Representatives of the Province of Pennsylvania* (Philadelphia, 1754), 3:362. See also *An Act for the Better Ordering Regulating Such as are Willing and Desirous to be United for Military Purposes Within This Province* (Philadelphia, 1756), 1; *An Act for Encouraging the People Known by Name of* Unitas Fratrum, *or* United Brethren, *to Settle in His Majesty's Colonies in America* (New London, 1751), 36. For responses to this act and its exemption from bearing arms, see *New-York Gazette*, December 17, 1750, and January 1, 1751; *Pennsylvania Gazette*, December 31, 1754, and December 18, 1755.

10. *Boston Evening Post*, August 9, 1756; *Boston Newsletter*, January 26, 1758.

11. For example, see *Acts Passed by the General Assembly of Georgia, at a Session Begun and Holden at Savannah, on Tuesday the 20th day of November, anno Domini 1764* (Savannah, 1765), 35; *Acts and Laws of His Majesty's Province of New Hampshire in New England* (Portsmouth, 1761), 86. The phrase "able to bear arms" appears most in newspapers from 1758 to 1775 (in fifteen of forty-four articles), followed by "fit [or unfit] to bear arms" (four articles), and "capable to bear arms (three articles). The remaining usages relate to conscientious objectors ("compelled to bear arms" and "cannot bear arms," for example), or other military matters; John Dickinson's Proposed Resolutions (July 18, 1775), in *Letters of Delegates to Congress, 1774–1789*, ed. Paul H. Smith et al., 25 vols. (Washington, D.C., 1976–2000), 1:633 (hereafter cited as *Letters*); July 24, 1775, in *Letters*, 1:663.

12. *Norwich Packet and Connecticut, Massachusetts, New-Hampshire, and Rhode-Island Weekly Advertiser*, January 20, 1777; *Independent Ledger, and American Advertiser* (Boston), May 15, 1780; *Votes and Proceedings of the House of Delegates of the State of Maryland. November Session, 1781* (Annapolis, 1782), 56.

13. *Pennsylvania Packet,* July 6, 1779; *Connecticut Courant,* March 27, 1781; July 26, 1780, *New Jersey Gazette,* July 26, 1780.

14. *Journal of the House of Delegates of Virginia* (Richmond, 1786); David Parsons, *A Sermon, Preached Before His Excellency John Hancock, Esq.* (Boston, 1788), 27.

15. *Independent Journal* (New York), December 23, 1786; *American Recorder* (Charlestown, Mass.), March 30, 1787.

16. *The Federalist: A Collection of Essays, Written in Favour of the New Constitution, as Agreed upon by the Federal Convention, September 17, 1787* (New York, 1788), 90.

17. *New York Journal,* November 21, 1787; *Federal Gazette* (Philadelphia), November 18, 1788; *Newport* (R.I.) *Herald,* February 25, 1790; *United States Chronicle* (Providence, R.I.), March 27, 1788.

18. June 27, 1788, in *The Debates in the Several State Conventions on the Adoption of the Federal Constitution,* ed. Jonathan Elliot, 5 vols. (Philadelphia and Washington, D.C., 1836–1859), 3:659. Hereafter cited as Elliot's *Debates.* The North Carolina convention used the same language. See July 21, 1788, in Elliot's *Debates,* 4:244.

19. *General Advertiser* (Philadelphia), December 27, 1790; see June 27, 1778, in Worthington C. Ford et al., eds., *Journals of the Continental Congress.* 34 vols. (Washington, DC, 1904–37), 11:671; *Pennsylvania Packet,* December 21, 1790.

20. *Federal Gazette* (Philadelphia), December 28, 1790; *Providence* (R.I.) *Gazette,* January 15, 1791.

21. *Daily Advertiser* (New York), May 23, 1789; *Gazette of the United States,* October 14, 1789.

22. *City Gazette and Daily Advertiser* (Charleston, S.C.), October 26, 1791; Josiah Harmar, *The Proceedings of a Court of Enquiry, Held at the Special Request of Brigadier General Josiah Harmar* (Philadelphia, 1791), 2.

23. *Pennsylvania Evening Post,* April 23, 1776; *General Advertiser* (Philadelphia), August 5, 1791; William Temple Franklin, *An Account of the Soil, Growing Timber, and other Productions, of the Lands in the Countries Situated in the Back Parts of the States of New-York and Pennsylvania* (London, 1791), 36.

24. *Cumberland Gazette* (Portland, Me.), March 16, 1787, and December 8, 1786.

25. *City Gazette and Daily Advertiser* (Charleston, S.C.), October 20, 1792; *Dunlap's American Advertiser* (Philadelphia), January 25, 1792; *The Diary* (New York), August 4, 1792; *American Minerva* (New York), May 20, 1794; *Columbian Centinel* (Boston), January 28, 1797.

26. For a detailed look at the impact of ideas of communal defense on the 1776 Pennsylvania constitution, see Nathan Kozuskanich, "Defending Themselves: The Original Understanding of the Right to Bear Arms," *Rutgers Law Journal*

38 (Summer 2007), 1041–70; *The Collected Works of James Wilson,* ed. Kermit L. Hall and Mark David Hall, 2 vols. (Indianapolis, 2007), 2:1142. Vermont's constitution also recognized a right of citizens to "bear arms for the defense of themselves and the state." When put into context with the rest of the clause, the meaning is decidedly military: "and as standing armies in time of peace are dangerous to liberty, they ought not to be kept up; and that the military should be kept under strict subordination to and governed by the civil power." See *Constitution of Vermont* (Windsor, 1793), 10.

27. For a detailed narrative on the Fort Wilson incident, see C. Page Smith, "The Attack on Fort Wilson," *Pennsylvania Magazine of History and Biography* 78 (April 1954): 177–88.

28. William Duane, *A Report of the Extraordinary Transactions Which Took Place at Philadelphia, in February 1799 in Consequence of Memorial from Certain Natives of Ireland to Congress, Praying Repeal of the Alien Bill* (Philadelphia, 1799), 33; ibid., 32; ibid., 45.

29. *Claypoole's American Daily Advertiser* (Philadelphia), June 4, 1798.

30. Kentucky Constitution, Article XLL, § 23; 1799 Kentucky Constitution, Art X, § 23; *Stewart's Kentucky Herald,* September 18, 1798.

Firearms, Militias, and the Second Amendment

Kevin M. Sweeney

★ ★ ★ ★

FEW IMAGES ARE more embedded in Americans' historical consciousness than that of the "embattled farmers" of Lexington and Concord who grabbed their guns and gathered to repel the British regulars on April 19, 1775. In particular, Daniel Chester French's 1875 sculpture of *The Minute Man* leaving his plow with musket firmly in hand has become iconic, literally so for the NRA. What limited military training these men had came from membership in the colonial militia, which is usually described as having included all males from sixteen to sixty. In spite of—or, as some believe, because of—their limited exposure to drill and martial discipline, these farmers succeeded in besting professional British soldiers. Familiarity with firearms from an early age and individual initiative are assumed to have trumped skills gained on parade grounds and European battlefields. The actions of these eighteenth-century Massachusetts minutemen have come to embody the American ideal of the citizen soldier, and to confirm a popular impression that most adult males in the American colonies possessed firearms and were skilled in their use in combat. But in reality, the performance of these militiamen was specific to a particular historical context and was not typical or representative of that more expansive and often mythic era that is today called "early America."[1]

The well-known image of *The Minute Man* is nevertheless a powerful one, as the majority opinion in *District of Columbia v. Heller* attests. The ruling by Justices Alito, Kennedy, Roberts, Scalia, and Thomas firmly locates its understanding of colonial militias, the uses of firearms during the colonial era, and the likely aims of the Second Amendment in a largely mythical time and place instead of actual eighteenth-century conditions and experiences. The majority opinion treats the use of the word "militia" in the Second Amendment as meaning "all able-bodied men"[2] or the "body of all citizens capable of military service,"[3] who constituted an unorganized "citizens' militia" or a "people's militia" which was primarily "a safeguard against tyranny."[4] It further assumes that the privately owned firearms of individuals were always the arms of the militia, maintaining that "the conception of the militia at the time of the Second Amendment's ratification was the body of all citizens capable of military service, who would bring the sorts of lawful weapons that they possessed at home to militia duty."[5] The handgun in particular is singled out as Americans' choice "to be the quintessential self-defense weapon," and is therefore most worthy of the Second Amendment's constitutional protection.[6]

This essay challenges these assumptions of the majority opinion by providing a historical overview of the colonial militias, the variable patterns of private gun ownership throughout the colonies, and the evolving understanding and use of what were seen as appropriate military firearms. Contrary to what the justices believe, there was no unorganized "citizens' militia" or a "people's militia."[7] In the 1600s and 1700s, militia service was compulsory, and militias existed only when and where governments passed laws specifying how they would be organized, armed, and disciplined.[8] To create and maintain militias, well over six hundred laws were passed by colonial and state governments during this period.[9] Despite these laws, not all able-bodied men wanted to or were required to serve in the militia: by the late 1600s, Virginia and Maryland had select militias; in a number of colonies, up to a third of their able-bodied white men from sixteen to sixty escaped militia service; and for most of the colonial period, Delaware and Pennsylvania did not have militias. Colonial militias decayed over the first half of the eighteenth century. During the War of Independence, state governments attempted to reverse this trend as demands on the militias increased and militia service expanded. At the same time, problems with organizing, disciplining, and arming the militias also increased dramatically and became a matter of concern and debate for military and political leaders.

Outside of the Delaware Valley (where militias were nonexistent or very weak), gun ownership appears to have been very common during the 1600s and remained widespread during the 1700s.[10] But there were still problems in arming the militias arising from costs and personal preferences. As a rule, colonists preferred guns better suited to hunting, pest control, and self-defense. As a rule these were smaller and lighter firearms, not necessarily well suited to military use in the field. By the third quarter of the eighteenth century, colonial governments and then revolutionary state governments wanted to arm both their regular forces and militiamen with heavy, large-caliber military muskets that fired a lead ball weighing about an ounce and accepted a bayonet. Weapons answering personal needs related to hunting, pest control, and self-defense were no longer considered desirable at muster nor appropriate on a battlefield. Pistols in particular had a limited military role at this time. This shift in expectations and standards created problems arming the militia during the War of Independence and in its immediate aftermath. Failure to arm, not a threat to disarm, endangered the survival of the state militias in the late 1700s and played a role in shaping provisions of the federal Constitution, informing the debate over its adoption and influencing provisions of the Second Amendment.

This essay's findings and arguments are rooted in recovering what could be called patterns of original experience. These patterns have emerged from a systematic examination of evidence gathered from probate inventories, militia returns, census data, and official and private correspondence. Each of these sources has its uses and its shortcomings. Probate inventories do not exist for every male decedent but disproportionately record the possessions of older men, especially in New England, and wealthier men, especially in the South. Still, they exist in great numbers throughout the colonies, making possible relative comparisons among regions and over time. They also provide details on the types and condition of privately owned firearms. Surviving militia returns that list weapons offer valuable, often detailed snapshots of the arms in the hands of actual militiamen, but they are specific to particular times and places, apply only to militiamen—not to the male population at large—and, unlike probate inventories, have not survived in large numbers. Even rarer and so far largely overlooked by scholars are certain census returns that list the number of males over age sixteen and the number of available firearms in private hands in a given colony or state at a particular point in time. All of the foregoing sources also dramatically broaden the pool of historically significant actors beyond the usual suspects and familiar documents. Finally,

TABLE 1. LISTINGS OF WEAPONS, VIRGINIA MUSTERS, 1620 AND 1625

Year	Number of males	Peeces, snaphances, matchlocks	Pistols	Total of firearms	Average number of firearms per male colonist	Swords, rapiers, hangers	Average number of swords per male colonist
1620	670	686	Not reported	686	1.02	516	.75
1625	814	1,010	61	1,071	1.23	435	.50

SOURCES:
1620: All information from William Thorndale, "The Virginia Census of 1619," *Magazine of Virginia Genealogy* 33 (1995): 168–70. Historians now believe that this census dates to 1620.
1625: For the numbers of firearms in 1625, see D. A. Tisdale, *Soldiers of Virginia Colony, 1607–1699* (n.p.: Dietz, 2000), 161. For an estimate of the number of males over fifteen in 1625, see Edmund S. Morgan, *American Slavery, American Freedom: The Ordeal of Colonial Virginia* (New York: Knopf, 1975), 402, 404 table 1.

these sources help one read and understand from new perspectives official and private correspondence, political tracts, and records of debates that still contain much information on organizing, arming, and disciplining the militia in the later 1700s.

The earliest colonial ventures often supplied their settlers with firearms. The Virginia Company shipped quantities of firearms to the colony when it was getting established.[11] A 1620 muster of the colony listed 670 "Able men" and 686 firearms of various sorts "besides pistols" (table 1). Not every individual owned a gun, but guns outnumbered the male colonists able to use them. In 1623 the company distributed its arms, which had been stored in several magazines, to the populace. A muster or census taken during the next two years reveals that the colony contained 1,010 muskets and 61 pistols for 814 males over age fifteen. Fifteen years later in 1640 the colony gave up on supplying its colonists with arms, and instead required masters to provide themselves and their white servants with guns at their own expense. In 1673 the assembly authorized county militia commissioners to purchase arms and ammunition that would be lent to militiamen on active duty. Not all counties appear to have complied: in Middlesex County in 1675, four companies of militia, no more than four hundred men, needed two hundred firearms and an equal number of swords and bandoliers.[12]

Most colonies relied primarily on colonists to arm themselves. The Massachusetts Bay Company did import firearms, which it appears to have sold to its residents. As late as 1644 the Massachusetts legislature "ordered the Surveyor General to import or otherwise obtain quality arms and to offer these arms at cost to all who might need decent guns."[13] From the beginning, New Haven Colony and the relatively poor Plymouth Colony required their militiamen to provide themselves with arms. Maryland did the same, placing the burden of arming its male population on individual settlers and the masters of servants, who had to furnish with "arms & munition" any able-bodied man between the ages of sixteen and fifty whom they transported to the colony.[14] In 1643 Maryland's council issued warrants to military commanders to go into colonists' houses and view all arms and ammunition.[15] Father Thomas Copley, the head of the Jesuits' mission in Maryland, owned thirty-six guns to arm twenty-one servants working on the order's plantation.[16] A Maryland law passed in 1649 required a master of a family to provide "every hired servant or other Sojourner also residing and dwelling in his house" with one fixed gun, two pounds of powder, and eight pounds of shot, for which the master could charge servants or "Soujourners."[17]

For most men, the cost of a firearm, which ranged between twenty and thirty shillings new (£1 to £1.5), was not prohibitive. These prices compared favorably to the cost of a yoke of oxen, which was about £11 to £12 (229 to 240 shillings); a cow, which was about £3 (60 shillings); and the cost of a joined oak chest, which could range between 10 and 15 shillings new. Even though a common sword or cutlass cost between 5 and 6 shillings, these less expensive edged weapons were present in smaller numbers than firearms in both of the Virginia censuses and in early probate inventories (tables 1 and 2).[18] References in probate inventories to pikes, which were in use at the time, were very rare; it appears that most pikes, unlike most firearms, were usually public, not private, arms.[19]

Evidence drawn from inventories dating to the mid-1600s suggests that the first English settlers in the Chesapeake region and in New England were probably more than adequately supplied with a variety of firearms (table 2). Firearms were found in approximately 60 percent of the probate inventories drawn from the Virginia counties of Accomack (the Eastern Shore) and York and the Maryland counties of St. Mary's (Western Shore) and Kent (Eastern Shore), which account for all of the surviving pre-1658 Maryland inventories. Most of these guns were shoulder arms: muskets or fowling pieces. Purely antipersonnel weapons such as pistols and swords were less common. Not all of these firearms were in working order. Between 1638 and 1658, takers of

TABLE 2. PROBATE INVENTORIES OF MALES CONTAINING GUNS, PISTOLS, AND SWORDS, NEW ENGLAND AND CHESAPEAKE COLONIES, MID-1600S

Location and dates	Number of inventories in sample	% inventories with firearm*	% inventories with pistol	% inventories with sword
Maine, 1659–1669	36	52.7	2.7	16.6
Essex County, Mass., 1641–1660	160	64.4	5.0	55.0
Plymouth Colony, 1633–1660	91	74.7	12.1	51.6
Hartford County, Conn., 1637–1660	91	74.7	7.0	45.1
New Haven Colony, 1647–1664	71	73.2	7.0	70.4
Maryland, 1638–1658	55	61.8	7.2	25.5
Accomack County, Va., 1634–1645	22	59.0	9.0	13.6
York County, Va., 1637–1660	54	66.7	9.3	16.6

*Includes inventories with pistols.

SOURCES:

Maine: *Province and Court Records of Maine*, vols. 1 and 2, ed. Charles Thornton Libby (Portland: Maine Historical Society, 1928, 1931).

Essex County: Frederick Dow, *The Probate Records of Essex County, Massachusetts*, vol. 1, 1635–1664 (Salem: Essex Institute, 1916).

Plymouth Colony: Plymouth Colony Probate Records (1620–1692), transcribed by Ann Yentsch, Catherine Marten, and Joy Stein, vol. 1, computer printout, Research Library, Plimoth Plantation, Plymouth, Mass.

Hartford County: "Wills and Inventories," in *Public Records of the Colony of Connecticut Prior to the Union with New Haven*, ed. J. Hammond Trumbull, vol. 1 (Hartford: Brown & Parsons, 1850), 442–508; Connecticut Colonial Records, Hartford District, vol. 2, microfilm, Historic Deerfield Library, Deerfield, Mass.

New Haven Colony: New Haven Probate Records, vol. 1, pt. 1, 1647–1666, microfilm, Historic Deerfield Library, Deerfield, Mass.

Maryland: *Archives of Maryland*, ed. William Hand Browne et al., 72 vols. (Baltimore: Maryland Historical Society, 1883–1972), vols. 4, 10, 41, 54.

Accomack County: *County Court Records of Accomack-Northampton*, 1632–1640, ed. Susie M. Ames (Washington, D.C.: American Historical Association, 1954); *County Court Records of Accomack-Northampton*, 1640–1645, ed. Susie M. Ames (Charlottesville: University Press of Virginia for the Virginia Historical Society, 1973).

York County: "York County Deeds, Orders, and Wills," vols. 1–3, typed transcriptions, Department of Historic Research, Colonial Williamsburg Foundation, Williamsburg, Va.

inventories in Maryland described about a third (31 percent) of the firearms they listed as being in parts or as "old," or "unfix," that is, in need of repair or adjustment and therefore unserviceable. In York County, Virginia, during the same period, the rate was 26 percent.

The frequency with which guns appeared in early New England inventories differed only slightly from that found in the Chesapeake. Inventories suggest that the residents of New England communities may have been better armed than those in the Chesapeake region. Over 70 percent of the inventories of males probated in the mid-1600s contained firearms in the colonies of Connecticut, New Haven, and Plymouth, which was "certainly by much the poorest colony"[20] (see table 2). A portion of these guns were not heavy matchlock muskets, which is what early militia laws usually specified, but lighter flintlock fowlers and birding pieces better suited to fowling and hunting.[21] Only in Maine and in Essex County, Massachusetts, did the percentages of inventories with firearms slip below 70 percent in New England. This difference can be attributed in part to the presence along the Maine coast and in the ports of Ipswich, Gloucester, Marblehead, and Salem, Massachusetts, of fishermen and mariners, who usually avoided or were excused from active participation in the militia and often did not own firearms. During this period, most male New Englanders from sixteen to sixty regularly drilled and mustered with their local militia companies.

The continuing fear of attack either by Natives or by the Dutch in New Netherland sustained widespread participation in the militias in most parts of New England into the later 1600s. Militia service remained a recognized public duty in the aftermath of King Philip's War (1675–1677) and with the commencement in 1688 of a continuing series of wars against the French in Canada and their Native allies. Outside of Maine, approximately two-thirds of the inventoried males sampled from parts of rural New England owned a firearm in the late 1600s (table 3). The quality of some of these firearms, which may have been hastily acquired during and in the immediate aftermath of King Philip's War, probably left something to be desired, for as the archaeologist Emerson Baker cautions, although these people were now "numerously armed . . . for they had lots of arms," they may not have been "well armed," for some of these firearms "were not particularly good."[22] Some of the firearms carried by Dorchester, Massachusetts, militiamen who participated in the 1690 attack on Quebec may have been "60 to 70 years old," and had been repaired and reworked.[23]

In Maryland and Virginia a very different pattern of militia service developed in the late 1600s and early 1700s as both of these colonies reconsidered

TABLE 3. PROBATE INVENTORIES OF MALES CONTAINING GUNS, PISTOLS, AND SWORDS, SELECTED AREAS OF NEW AND OLD COLONIES, LATER 1600s

Location and dates	Number in sample	% inventories with firearm*	% inventories with pistol	% inventories with sword
Maine, 1678–1692	82	56.8	2.5	23.2
Plymouth Colony, 1680–1691	225	68.0	2.2	27.6
Hampshire County, Mass., 1681–1700	168	71.4	6.5	29.8
New Haven County, Conn., 1692–1693	23	95.7	0.0	56.5
New York, rural counties, 1677–1700	91	60.4	8.8	23.1
New York City, 1677–1700	84	45.2	17.9	32.1
Salem County, West Jersey, 1679–1692	55	56.4	3.6	5.5
Rural Pennsylvania, 1692–1700	41	46.3	4.9	2.4
City of Philadelphia, 1692–1700	58	32.8	6.9	3.4
Maryland, 1687–1688	61	68.9	14.8	14.8
York County, Va., 1691–1700	59	71.2	35.6	44.1
South Carolina, 1693–1697	20	70.0	30.0	35.0

*Includes inventories with pistols.

SOURCES:

Maine: *York Deeds*, ed. William M. Sargent, bk. 5 (Portland: Brown Thurston & Company, 1889).

Plymouth Colony: Plymouth Colony Probate Records (1620–1692), transcribed by Ann Yentsch, Catherine Marten, and Joy Stein, vol. 2, computer printout, Research Library, Plimoth Plantation, Plymouth, Mass.

Hampshire County: Hampshire County Probate Records, vols. 1–3, microfilm, Historic Deerfield Library, Deerfield, Mass.

New Haven County: New Haven Records, vol. 2, 1688–1703, microfilm, Historic Deerfield Library, Deerfield, Mass.

New York rural counties and New York City: Inventories and Accounts, 1666–1822, New York (State), Court of Probates, microfilm, New York State Archives, Albany.

Salem County: Salem Wills and Administrations, 1679–1683; Salem Wills and Administrations, vol. 2, 1684–1687; Salem Wills and Administrations, vol. A, 1688–1698, Salem County, N.J., microfilm, Downs Library, Winterthur Museum, Winterthur, Del.

Rural Philadelphia and City of Philadelphia: Wills of the County of Philadelphia, Pennsylvania, vols. A–D, microfilm, Downs Library, Winterthur Museum, Winterthur, Del.

Maryland: Prerogative Court, Inventories and Accounts, 1674–1718, vol. 10:1688–1692, SM 13, roll 65, Maryland Archives, in author's possession.

York County: York County Deeds, Orders, and Wills, vols. 9–11, typed transcriptions, Department of Historic Research, Colonial Williamsburg Foundation, Williamsburg, Va.

South Carolina: Charleston Will Book, 1692–1693, microfilm, Downs Library, Winterthur Museum, Winterthur, Del.

their efforts to promote near-universal participation in the militia and a widespread ownership of firearms. Political turmoil unleashed during the 1640s and 1650s by England's Civil Wars, the execution of King Charles I, and the establishment of the republican Commonwealth disrupted the Catholic Calvert family's hold on Maryland and led to political coups, rebellions, and plundering. Private arms were impressed and stolen, and the political loyalties of militia units and their officers became a matter of concern.[24] In 1658 the Maryland assembly passed a law requiring each county to maintain a list of all able-bodied men between sixteen and sixty, and authorities were to select from the lists "such persons to be of theyr constant Trayned Band as they shall judge fittest both for theyr ability of Body, Estate & Courage."[25] Left unstated was the Protestant-controlled government's concern with the fitness of the political loyalties of the men selected for these trained bands.

When the Calvert family regained control of Maryland, they secured passage in 1661 of a new militia law that continued the practice of selecting the militia from among all men aged sixteen to sixty.[26] Now loyalty to the Catholic proprietary family was the overriding, if unstated, criterion for determining who was "fit" to be in the militia. As Lord Proprietor Cecilius Calvert made clear in 1671, he wanted measures taken "for preventing and suppressing of all and all manner of Riots and seditions and Rebellions, Riotous seditious and Rebellious assemblies and meetings within our said Province."[27] During the same decade, the assembly authorized a mounted militia with each member supplying himself with a sword, carbine, pistols, holsters and ammunition.[28] In seventeenth-century England, the mounted arm of the militia, which consisted of gentlemen and their retainers, was considered particularly useful for suppressing civil disturbances, rebellions, and military mutinies, not for defending individuals' liberty, which many writers of the era's political tracts and later scholars assume to have been the sole purpose of a militia.[29]

To further improve the effectiveness of its militia, Maryland's government established a public magazine for storing ammunition and began setting up county arsenals in which firearms for arming the militia were stored.[30] While evidence drawn from seventeenth-century Maryland probate inventories indicates that firearms were found in over two-thirds of the sampled estates of males (table 3), it was also the case that at any given time, more than 40 percent of the male population over sixteen were young servants, and obtaining a firearm does not appear to have been a top priority for young planters.[31] The condition of a good portion of the firearms owned by males whose estates were probated in the late 1600s also left something to be desired: four in ten of the firearms were old, unfixed, or in pieces. By 1678 the county arsenals in Ann Arundel, Calvert, Charles, and St. Mary's counties contained 463 muskets, 177 carbines, and 1 blunderbuss for the 3,616 tithables (males over sixteen) who resided in these four counties.[32] Other publicly owned firearms appear to have been in private hands.[33] In 1660 and again in 1676, Maryland's militia successfully faced down incipient rebellions.

Thirteen years later, in 1689, the colony's militia refused to stand by the Calvert family's proprietary government, and it was overthrown by rebels. After learning of William of Orange's successful invasion of England in 1688, Maryland officials sought to avoid trouble by calling in all publicly owned firearms, claiming that they had to be fixed. In a letter to Charles Calvert, the deputy governor made clear that the Catholic members of the governor's council had in fact recalled the public arms for repair and then intended "to distribute the same into such hands as shall faithfully serve the King [James II], your Lordship, and the Country."[34] Even without knowledge of the council's true intention, the action fanned fears of a "popish plot" and inspired a popular uprising. The victorious Protestant Association disarmed the colony's Catholics, whose arms were subsequently restored in 1694.[35] The Calvert family lost control of Maryland's government until 1715, by which time members of the family had joined the Church of England.[36]

In the aftermath of this rebellion, the 1696 Maryland assembly resolved once again that "the militia of this Province be modelled anew, it being deemed impossible that the present act in force about the same should be complied with by means of the poverty of the people."[37] This law required the arming and mustering of only "every fourth or fifth taxable," who would be chosen by their neighbors, whom the law "obligated to find a Trooper, Dragoon, or Footman, according as it shall be agreed upon with necessary arms."[38] Despite this new system, arming the Maryland militia remained a problem. In 1716 the assembly levied a tax of three pence per hogshead on all tobacco exports to purchase firearms for the colony's select militia, a practice that continued until 1745.[39] But in 1733, the legislature itself concluded that such efforts at reform "have not had the desired Effect in a proper Regulation of the Militia of this Province."[40] After political contention in the late 1600s had ended Maryland's inclusive, trained militia, decades of peace in the early 1700s sapped the military effectiveness of the remaining rump of a select militia.

In Virginia, Bacon's Rebellion in the summer of 1676 led to the destruction and eventual reorganization of its militia. In the later stages of this conflict, armed servants and slaves opposed Governor William Berkeley's efforts to reassert his authority. During the rebellion and in its immediate aftermath, private arms were impressed and stolen, hundreds of men were disarmed, and the organization of the militia disintegrated.[41] Residents protested the loss of their arms to the English commissioners sent over to investigate the causes of the rebellion. These losses were not made up by the king's shipment and the colony's distribution of "1200 snaphance Muskets [a type of flintlock] and Bandoliers," "300 Matchlocks and Bandoliers," "1000 Swords and Belts," and "300 Pikes."[42] Of Virginia's 8,568 militiamen in 1680, "scarce one half of them [were] armed, especially of the horse."[43] The historian William Shea has concluded that the "Virginia militia was never the same after 1676. It, too, was a victim of Bacon's Rebellion."[44]

This specter of servile rebellion in 1676 and tobacco-cutting riots in 1682 scared the colony's leaders and substantial planters, who rethought the wisdom of a broad-based militia and a widely armed populace.[45] In 1687 Virginia's government limited service in the militia to independent freemen who were householders and freeholders; freedmen without land and servants were no longer trained, and no special efforts were made to arm them.[46] The number of foot soldiers in the militia dropped from 7,268 in 1680 to 3,000 in 1689, plus 1,300 men in horse troops.[47] Governor Francis Nicholson's proposal in 1699 to enlarge the militia from 4,625 men and to restore all indentured servants to the ranks of the militia was opposed by members of the legislature who believed that controlling unarmed laborers was hard enough, but if they were armed and trained, they might rise up and kill their masters.[48]

During the later 1600s, publicly purchased firearms and accouterments continued to play an important role in arming Virginia's smaller select militia. This was true even though the legislature had encouraged private individuals to purchase their own militia weapons by guaranteeing that these private arms could not be "imprest" nor were they "lyable to be taken by any distress, seizure, attachment, or execution."[49] In fact, many of the colony's troopers probably obtained their "trooping arms" or "horse arms" from a shipment of seven hundred carbines and one thousand swords sent to the colony in the aftermath of Bacon's Rebellion and from subsequent purchases by the colonial and county governments.[50] In 1702 the royal government supplied Virginia with an additional one thousand muskets, four hundred carbines, and four hundred pairs of pistols with holsters.[51] County militia officers passed these arms on to their men, who in turn came to regard them as their private property.[52] The marked increase in the number of inventories listing both pistols and swords in the later 1600s in York County was probably due in part to the distribution of this government largesse (table 3). And even though the over-all percentage of inventories containing firearms in York County remained largely unchanged from the mid-1600s to the late 1600s, there appears to have been in Virginia a "relative decline in the number and distribution of firearms after mid-century."[53] In Surry County from 1690 to 1715, only 19 per-cent of the inventories of non-householders listed firearms; only 32 percent of those of the poorest householders mentioned guns.[54]

By the beginning of the eighteenth century, the efforts of colonies in both New England and the Chesapeake to create an armed populace and an inclu-sive body of organized and trained militiamen had begun to fall by the way-side. Both Maryland and Virginia had adopted militia systems in which only a minority of free white men between sixteen and sixty received regular train-ing and were required to be equipped with arms provided by themselves, or in some instances by neighbors or from public stores of firearms. The reduction in the militia's role was in part possible because local Indian tribes no lon-ger presented a military threat in the Chesapeake region. At the same time, there was also evidence of a growing concern about putting arms in the hands of all men, especially slaves, servants, and even free white men of uncertain disposition.

New England militias remained much more inclusive and better trained because of external threats. Still, by the later 1600s these colonies could also be quite selective when it became necessary to draft militiamen for active mili-tary service. During King Philip's War, town militia committees in Massachu-setts tried to spare yeoman farmers, church members, and heads of families, choosing single, unmarried militiamen, who were likely to be younger sons and marginal members of the community.[55] When Massachusetts raised and impressed troops for offensive operations during Queen Anne's War (1702–1713), Governor Joseph Dudley characterized these soldiers as the colony's "loose people."[56] Even with the movement away from relying on an inclusive militia for military operations, private ownership of firearms remained wide-spread in New England and in the Chesapeake, where guns were also used for fowling, hunting, and killing vermin or "noxious animals."[57]

Serviceable firearms and militias were less common in the new English col-onies that lay between Maryland and New England. The 1664 conquest of New Netherland had led to the creation of a series of English colonies in the area formerly occupied by the single Dutch colony that had controlled the coastline from Long Island to the Delaware Valley. New Amsterdam became

New York, and joined to it were Long Island, Staten Island, and the settlements along the Hudson River to create the English colony of New York. New Netherland had had burgher guards in New Amsterdam and Albany, and the Puritan New Englanders on Long Island had had their own local militia companies, but as a rule the Dutch had relied on professional soldiers, volunteers, and Native allies to defend the colony.[58] English and Dutch New Yorkers living around New York City and on Long Island appear to have been a little less likely to own firearms than residents of New England, Maryland, and Virginia (table 3). This difference was a reflection of the prior colonial regime, the urban environment of New York City, their distance from French and Indian enemies, and the presence after 1664 of two to four companies of red-coated British regulars. In the later 1660s, one observer reported of the New York City militia that he had "never seen anything worse," while Governor Edmund Andros rated the colony's militiamen as "indifferently armed, [but] good firemen."[59] A later governor also considered his colony's people "generally expert in the use of firearms," which may have been a legacy of the Dutch tradition of holding competitions in marksmanship known as "shooting the parrot."[60]

In lands abutting the Delaware River, Quaker proprietors controlled the new English colonies of West Jersey, Pennsylvania, and Delaware. William Penn saw exemption from militia service as a matter involving liberty of conscience and took no steps to establish a militia in Pennsylvania despite the fact that his charter authorized him to do so. Because of the pacifist principles of the colony's influential Quaker community, efforts to pass a mandatory militia act in 1693 failed, and efforts to recruit voluntary military companies were not successful either.[61]

For most of the colonial period Pennsylvania did not have a militia, and in part because of this fact, the ownership of firearms as documented in samples of estate inventories generally ranged between 34 and 38 percent of the male population throughout the colonial period (tables 3, 4, and 7). Pennsylvanians' ownership of these firearms had little to do with defense and nothing to do with the militia. Persistence of this low incidence of gun ownership in Pennsylvania probate inventories was not due simply to the presence of Quakers, for they constituted a declining percentage of the colony's population over the course of the eighteenth century, and some Quakers did in fact own firearms to hunt and kill vermin.[62] Other Pennsylvanians who were not Quakers also opposed the creation of a militia because the absence of a militia released men from military training and a government-mandated requirement to obtain a firearm.

A somewhat similar situation existed along the east bank of the Delaware River. Quaker proprietors did not create a militia when they established their colony of West Jersey in 1677. Despite this fact, guns were present in 56 percent of the inventories of males who died in Salem County, New Jersey (table 3), during the 1680s and 1690s. But over time, the failure of a militia system to take root in this region appears to have affected the levels of private gun ownership. When a unified colony was created in 1702, a militia regiment was established in the western part of New Jersey, but the institution never took root. Continued opposition in the region to the militia extended beyond the Quakers, who "laughed at those [who] did [train and muster]; this made others murmur who were oblig'd to trayne and muster, and encouraged their refusing to do so; they clayming as much right to an examption from trayning as the Quakers."[63] As a result, militia companies did not muster and train in western New Jersey, and when militia officers died, they were not replaced. By the 1740s, only 33.3 percent of the probate inventories of males who died in Salem County contained a firearm, and these inventories lacked pistols and swords (table 4). In the 1740s, Governor Lewis Morris found "in the Eastern Division of this Province [New Jersey] the case is somewhat better. They have tryn'd much oftner, tho' but seldom, there are five regiments there of Militia, & I am in hopes to get them into some better Order than they have been for many yeares; but, they have been so long and so much neglected, the Militia Act so deficient and Armes so much wanted, that it will require time to do it."[64] By the 1730s, the entire colony of New Jersey had, in the opinion of the historian Edwin Tanner, "attained something more than the usual colonial standard of ineffectiveness in her militia system."[65]

The influence of Quaker principles was also felt in the Penn family's proprietary colony of Delaware, which was then known as the Three Lower Counties of Newcastle, Kent, and Sussex. Here again, the ownership of firearms had as a rule nothing to do with serving in a militia. Despite the expressed desire of some residents, the government of the Three Lower Counties did not create a militia. Several voluntary military companies mustered during the 1690s and formed again during the War of the Spanish Succession (1702–1713), but it wasn't until 1740 that the colony's assembly passed a law mandating enrollment in a militia for all males (except Quakers) from seventeen to fifty.[66] As it turned out, this law expired three years later, and because of this the colony did not have a militia when the French and Indian War began in 1754.[67] Even without a militia, about two-thirds of a sample of mid-eighteenth-century probate inventories belonging to males who died in Kent County, Delaware, contained a firearm (tables 4 and 7).

TABLE 4. PROBATE INVENTORIES OF MALES CONTAINING GUNS, PISTOLS, AND SWORDS, SELECTED AREAS OF THE BRITISH MAINLAND COLONIES, MID-1700S

Location and dates	Number in sample	% inventories with firearm*	% inventories with pistol	% inventories with sword
Maine, 1740–1743	43	62.8	4.7	14.0
Plymouth County, Mass., 1741–42	35	57.1	2.9	8.6
Worcester County, Mass., 1741–1744	53	39.6	0.0	7.5
Hampshire County, Mass., 1741–1745	80	60.0	5.0	17.5
New Haven County, Conn., 1740–1742	36	61.1	2.8	16.7
New York, rural counties, 1741–1750	75	36.0	1.3	20.0
New York City, 1741–1750	16	37.5	6.3	25.0
Salem County, N.J., 1740–1744	60	33.3	0.0	6.7
Rural Philadelphia County, 1740–1744	64	37.5	1.6	1.6
City of Philadelphia, 1740–1744	40	22.5	7.5	5.0
Kent County, Del., 1741–1750	30	66.6	10.0	10.0
Maryland, 1741–42	65	66.2	9.2	9.2
York County, Va., 1741–1750	103	63.1	26.2	38.8
Lunenburg County, Va., 1746–1750	14	71.4	0.0	0.0
Augusta County, Va., 1746–1749	47	48.9	2.1	0.0
South Carolina, 1742–43	118	77.1	39.0	50.0

*Includes inventories with pistols.

SOURCES:

Maine: York County Probate Records, vol. 5, 1735–1742, and vol. 6, 1742–1746, microfilm, in author's possession, Amherst College.

Plymouth County: Plymouth County Probate Records, vol. 8, 1738–1742, microfilm, Massachusetts Archives, Boston.

Worcester County: Worcester County Probate Records, vol. 2, 1739–1748, microfilm, Historic Deerfield Library, Deerfield, Mass.

SOURCES (*CONTINUED*):
Hampshire County: Hampshire County Probate Records, vol. 6, 1739–1745, microfilm, Historic Deerfield Library, Deerfield, Mass.
New Haven County: New Haven County Probate Records, vol. 6, pt. 2, 1737–1745, microfilm, Downs Library, Winterthur Museum, Winterthur, Del.
Rural New York and New York City: New York (State), Court of Probates, microfilm J0301, New York State Archives, Albany.
Salem County: Salem County, N.J., Inventories, Wills, and Administrative Papers, 1740–1744, microfilm, Downs Library, Winterthur Museum, Winterthur, Del.
Rural Philadelphia County and Philadelphia: Wills of the County of Philadelphia, vol. W, microfilm, Downs Library, Winterthur Museum, Winterthur, Del.
Kent County: "A Random Sample of Kent County, Delaware, Estate Inventories, 1727–1775," complied by Richard L. Bushman and Anna L. Hawley (Newark, Del., 1987), in author's possession.
Maryland: Prerogative Court, Inventories, vol. 26, 1741–1742, and vol. 27, 1742–43, SR 4339, Maryland Archives, in author's possession.
York County: York County Deeds, Orders, and Wills, vols. 19–20, typed transcriptions, Department of Historic Research, Colonial Williamsburg Foundation, Williamsburg, Va.
Lunenburg County: Will Book no. 1, 1746–1762, microfilm, in author's possession, Amherst College.
August County: August County, Will Book no. 1, 1745–1753, microfilm, in author's possession, Amherst College.
South Carolina: Charleston County, Inventories, K-K, 1739–1743, microfilm, Historic Deerfield Library, Deerfield, Mass.

At the same time, the weakness or absence of colonial militias in the Middle Atlantic region does appear to have had a lasting impact on patterns of private gun ownership in much of the region. In Pennsylvania, the lack of a government mandate to arm oneself for militia service and the presence of Quakers were undoubtedly reflected in the lower percentages of inventories in which firearms were found from the time of the colony's establishment until the end of the eighteenth century. In neighboring Salem County, New Jersey, the absence of a strong militia tradition, the presence of Quakers, and the area's relative security can also be seen in the similarly low percentages of eighteenth-century inventories with firearms. The percentages of probate inventories with firearms in southern New York also declined over the course of the eighteenth century despite the presence of a somewhat more active militia. Still, the burden of the colony's defense did not fall on militiamen living around New York City and on Long Island, but was instead borne by warriors of the Iroquois League, British regulars, volunteers, impressed militiamen from New England, and those Dutchmen living around Albany, who may have been among the best bush fighters in the British colonies from the 1690s to the mid-1700s.

The militias that English proprietors and colonists established in the Carolinas in the late 1600s produced two rather different institutions as a result of differing social, economic, and strategic situations. These differences also appear to have influenced patterns of private gun ownership. South Carolina was a relatively wealthy colony threatened externally by Spanish and Native foes and internally by enslaved Africans, who outnumbered white colonists by the early 1700s. Evidence from surviving probate inventories of male decedents suggests that from the colony's first settlement, South Carolinians were well armed (tables 3 and 4). One resident bragged in 1710 that "everyone among us is versed in Arms, from the Governour to the meanest Servant, and are all so far from thinking it below them, that most People take Delight in Military Affairs."[68] To deal with the external threats, masters were actually obliged to arm slaves, some of whom trained with the militia, and several hundred armed slaves served in the war against the Yamasees from 1715 to 1717. The colony's practice of training and arming "trusted Negroes" was suspended, but not ended, when a group of slaves stole firearms and rebelled in 1739.[69] During the 1720s and 1730s, roughly a third to sometimes one-half of the colony's annual budget went to pay for soldiers who guarded the frontiers, volunteers raised for offensive operations, and militiamen who provided for local defense and maintained slave patrols.[70] Among the colony's outlays were regular purchases in England of hundreds of military-style muskets, usually with bayonets.[71] Until the late 1750s, these public arms appear to have remained in storage and were not as a rule distributed to militiamen, only to those called to active service.

Neighboring North Carolina, with its relatively poor, dispersed population, provided a striking contrast. The historian Wayne Lee has characterized its colonial militia as having been distinguished by "the chronic resistance or just plain apathy displayed by both officers and soldiers."[72] At the outbreak of the Tuscarora War (1711–1713), "neither the Province in general, nor the people themselves were sufficiently provided with powder, lead, and arms," and "some were to be ordered from elsewhere; but they did not know where to find the money."[73] The colony had to borrow guns from its well-armed southern neighbor to supply some of its militiamen, and in the end, only the intervention of volunteers from South Carolina with several hundred Native allies saved the colony.[74] Somewhat belatedly, North Carolina attempted to improve its defenses by passing its first militia law in 1712. But after this war ended, the colony's relatively secure location did little to sustain a viable militia. In 1744 a legislative committee discovered that the inhabitants of many counties had for years refused to choose militia officers, assuming that in their absence no musters could be held.[75] The militia's lack of arms also remained a problem in the mid-1700s.[76]

Even when they did not face external threats, the militiamen of these and other southern colonies had to mount slave patrols and presumably depended on private arms for this duty. Over the course of the 1700s, the governments of South Carolina (1704), Virginia (1727), North Carolina (1753), and eventually Georgia (1757) formalized and codified their militias' patrol activities.[77] The patrols, in which both slave owners and non-owners served, looked for slaves without passes from their masters, for unauthorized gatherings of slaves, and for any other suspicious activities involving slaves. In 1734 the South Carolina legislature required every person serving in a slave patrol to "provide himself and always keep, a good horse, one pistol, and a carbine or other guns, a cutlass [and] a cartridge box with at least 12 cartridges in it."[78]

The outbreak of war between Britain and Spain in 1739 and renewal of war with France in 1744 found most of the British mainland colonies unprepared militarily. This situation existed despite the fact that private gun ownership appears to have remained widespread outside the middle colonies (table 4). Even though it raised an expeditionary regiment of paid volunteers in 1740, South Carolina and the recently founded colony of Georgia relied primarily on the presence of the red-coated British regulars of James Oglethorpe's Forty-second Regiment of Foot to defend them from 1737 to 1748 and to undertake offensive operations against the Spanish in Florida.[79] The militia of underpopulated Georgia was inconsequential, while the larger and better-armed population and militia of South Carolina focused more on controlling the colony's black slaves in the aftermath of the 1739 Stono Rebellion.

The militias of Maryland, Virginia, and North Carolina never faced any real threats during the 1740s. In 1746 North Carolina passed a new militia law but stipulated that its provisions would expire in three years.[80] Maryland reenacted its tax on tobacco exports to purchase public arms for the militia, and Virginia passed legislation allowing in time of danger "to arm part of the militia, not otherwise sufficiently provided, out of his majesty's magazine and other stores with this colony."[81] Such steps were taken even though firearms continued to appear in over 60 percent of the inventories probated in the tidewater counties during this period (table 4). Still, these samples of inventories, and especially those from inland counties, suggest that gun ownership was not universal, and that a number of these privately owned firearms, particularly in Maryland, appear to have been "very bad and scarcely fit for use."[82] An English traveler passing through Maryland, Virginia, and the Carolinas lamented that "the Musters of their Militia, would induce a Man to nauseate a Sash and hold a Sword, for ever in Derision," because of the "diversity of Weapons and Dresses, Unsizeableness of the Men, and Want of the least Grain of Discipline in their Officers."[83]

In 1747 and 1748 Pennsylvania and Delaware established voluntary military units known as Associators.[84] Inspired by voluntary military associations formed in Britain in 1745 to oppose the Jacobite army of Charles Edward Stuart, the Pennsylvania Military Association was, in the assessment of the historian Joseph Seymour, "neither a militia, nor paid levies, nor professional soldiers."[85] The Associators saw it as a temporary measure "until some more effectual Provision be made to answer the same good Ends and Purposes or until Peace shall be established between Great Britian and France."[86] Each member agreed to provide himself with "a good Firelock, Cartouch Box, and at least twelve Charges of Powder and Ball, and . . . with a good Sword, cutlass or Hanger."[87] Benjamin Franklin, the organizer of the Philadelphia Associators, sought to profit from the situation by offering for sale "a parcel of good Muskets, all well fitted with Bayonets, Belts and Cartouche Boxes, and Buff slings to cast over the shoulder, very useful to have to such as have occasion to ride with their Arms."[88]

The New England colonies, and to a lesser extent New York and New Jersey, shouldered most of the burden for King George's War (1744–1748). Despite the vitality of New England's militias in the seventeenth and early eighteenth centuries and what inventories suggest was probably widespread private ownership of firearms (table 4), these colonies were also not prepared for war in 1744. Two decades of peace that followed the conclusion of Governor Dummer's War (the Third English-Abenaki War) in 1725 had led to a noticeable decrease in military preparedness, and for three decades the Massachusetts legislature had passed no laws regarding the militia.[89] Evidence from probate inventories also suggests that by the 1740s there was a relative decline in the levels of private gun ownership in New England (tables 3 and 4), even though the levels remained well above those found in contemporary probate inventories from the colonies of New York and New Jersey.

Massachusetts officials realized that the colony and its residents did not have enough firearms both to defend the colony's frontiers and to mount offensive military expeditions against targets in New France. In Worcester County, a return for Colonel John Chandler's militia regiment reveals that only three of his nineteen companies of foot were "well equipped" or "mostly equipped," while four were "intirely deficient as to arms," another was "greatly deficient," yet another was only "a quarter fitted," three were only half armed, one lacked a quarter of the arms needed, and another was short by one-fifth.[90] After reviewing his men, a chagrined militia captain in St. George's on the Maine frontier (then part of Massachusetts) reported, "I find them poorly provided in arms and amonisshon though they generally apeered on Training days under arms yet I find several of them was borrowed and now everyone must have their own."[91] Elsewhere in Maine another militia officer reported that of thirty-three recent German immigrants, "there is twenty foure of them that Have noe armes & there none of them has any amanishon."[92]

New England's colonial governments scrambled to address these conditions. To defend towns in the western part of the colony, Massachusetts constructed a line of forts just south of its northern border and garrisoned these posts with soldiers recruited, paid, and if necessary armed by the colony.[93] The colony also built and garrisoned posts along the Maine frontier. No longer was the first line of defense dependent on the men in local militia companies.

To undertake offensive operations against French targets such as Louisburg on Cape Breton Island and in Canada itself, the colonies also did not employ militia units but created provincial regiments of paid volunteers. As Benjamin Franklin explained to an English correspondent, these soldiers were "not militia, but what we call our provincial troops, being regularly enlisted to serve a term, and in the pay of the province." These units were authorized each year by colonial legislatures, the officers commissioned by royal governors or the legislatures, the enlisted men mustered into service during the spring and kept in pay until November, when they were usually discharged. Also, these provincial soldiers, unlike militiamen, were subject to regulations and punishments set forth in special laws enacted by colonial legislatures, and in 1754 Parliament extended the provisions of the Mutiny Act to include colonial troops raised for service with British forces in America.[94]

To arm those provincial soldiers who lacked firearms of their own, Massachusetts purchased "Five Hundred good Fire Arms Tower mark" from England and impressed guns from its residents, who were reimbursed. Connecticut faced similar shortages and took similar steps to respond to the problem.[95] To arm provincial troops in 1746, Connecticut and Rhode Island purchased firearms from their residents.[96] To avoid problems in a future conflict, the government of Massachusetts purchased an additional 2,500 military-style muskets from England in 1754.[97]

When fighting broke out again in 1754, most colonies and their residents were still not prepared for the scale of the fighting that lasted until 1763. Late in 1755, concerned British officials in London wrote to colonial governors in an effort to assess the state of the colonial militias. (A summary of the responses to these inquires that has been supplemented by information from other official sources can be found in table 6.) The overwhelming majority of men between the ages of sixteen and sixty were enrolled in the militias of New Hampshire and Massachusetts, and most appear to have been armed. In Connecticut there were some militiamen "too poor to buy sufficient arms."[98] At the same time, a smaller percentage of men over the age of sixteen were enrolled in Connecticut's militia because the colony limited militia service to men between sixteen and fifty, which was also the case in Rhode Island. In addition, the latter colony had a significant Quaker population, which accounted for perhaps one-eighth of its men over the age of sixteen and contributed to the large number of "men able to bear arms" but who were not required to join the militia. In Rhode Island there were 5,052 small arms in private hands, which would barely have provided a shoulder arm for each of the colony's militiamen even if they were all owned by just the men "enlisted" (that is, enrolled) in the militia, which of course they weren't (table 5).[99] Clearly, an indeterminate but not inconsequential minority of Rhode Island's militiamen who were required by law to own firearms did not, and this appears to have been the case elsewhere in New England, though probably to a lesser degree.

Increasingly, the suitability of the firearms owned by these militiamen was found wanting. Most of their guns were not muskets. Today, as a rule, all eighteenth-century muzzle-loading smooth-bore firearms are erroneously referred to as "muskets." But as Benjamin Franklin noted in 1747, "Musket" was "the Name of a particular Kind of Gun."[100] Specifically, a musket was a sturdy, large-caliber military firearm fitted to carry a bayonet.[101] The standard British military musket since the early eighteenth century, the Long Land Pattern Musket—popularly known as the Brown Bess—weighed about eleven pounds, had a .760- to .780-caliber barrel, and fired bullets weighing fourteen to the pound.[102]

Most New Englanders preferred a lighter firearm with a relatively smaller bore that could be used for hunting and killing vermin as well as military service.[103] Especially popular in New England were .60- to .65-caliber smoothbore fowlers and fusils made in New England or imported from England, which weighed six to seven pounds.[104] If they could obtain them, New Englanders also liked French hunting guns, which usually weighed six

TABLE 5. DATA FROM 1755 RHODE ISLAND CENSUS LISTING PRIVATE ARMS, PLUS PROBATE INVENTORY DATA FROM 1747–1754

Categories	Small arms in private hands	Pistols in private hands	Total guns in private hands	Swords in private hands
Number of weapons	5,052	624	5,676	2,418
Average number of weapons per white man over age 16 (number of men: 9,177)	.55	.07	.62	.26
Average number of weapons per white man capable of bearing arms (number of men: 8,262*)	.61	.09	.69	.29
Average number of weapons per enlisted militiamen (number of men: 5,265)	.96	.12	1.07	.46
Probate Inventory Data	Small arms	Pistols	Total firearms	Swords
Numbers of weapons found in 380 Rhode Island inventories, 1747–1754	196	35	231	55
Average number of weapons per inventory	.52	.09	.61	.15

* Total of men enlisted in the militia: 5,262, plus 2,997 "men able to bear arms exclusive of the militia."
SOURCES:
1755 census data: *Account of the people in the Colony of Rhode-Island, whites, blacks, together with the quantity of arms and ammunition in the hands of private persons*, Early American Imprints, no. 40794 (n.p., 1800).
Probate inventory data: Bristol, Wills and Inventories, vol. 1; East Greenwich, Probate Records, vol. 2; Gloucester, Probate Records, vol. 1; Little Compton, Town Council and Probate Records, vol. 1; Newport, Town Council Records, vol. 9; Providence, Town Council Records, vols. 4–5; Scituate, Probate and Council Records, vol. 1; Smithfield, Probate Records, vol. 2; South Kingston, Town Council Records, vols. 4–5; Warwick, Wills, vol. 2; West Greenwich, Town Council Records, vol. 1; Westerly, Town Council and Probate Records, vol. 3. All on microfilm, Rhode Island Historical Society, Providence.

and a half to seven and a half pounds, had a .597- to .630-caliber barrel, and used bullets that weighed twenty to twenty-four to the pound.[105] As a result the firearms of militiamen in New Hampshire were considered to be "in general of the meanest Sort," and those in Connecticut "which belong to private persons [were] mostly poor and undersized and unfit for an expedition."[106]

TABLE 6. CONDITION OF COLONIAL MILITIAS, 1754–1756

Colony	White males 16 and up	Enrolled militiamen	% in militia	Proportion armed	Quality of their arms	Number of public arms**
New Hampshire	7,000	6,000	85.7%	"most armed"	"in general of the meanest Sort"	none
Massachusetts	45,764	37,446	81.2%	—	—	2,500
Rhode Island	9,177	5,265	56.7%	5,052 small arms and 624 pistols in private hands	—	436
Connecticut	28,000	20,000	71.4%	—	"poor and undersize"	none
New York	19,825	12,000	60.1%	"some are . . . so indigent" that "they cannot purchase their proper arms"	"chiefly for the Indian Trade"	1,000 belonging to NYC
New Jersey	16,000	10,000	62.5%	—	—	none
Pennsylvania	25,0000	none	0.0%	—	—	—
Delaware	4,000 – 5,000	none	0.0%	—	—	—
Maryland	26,000	16,500	63.5%	two-thirds	"very bad and scarcely fit for use"	652
Virginia	45,000	28,000	62.2%	"not above one-half"	"are of different Bores"	2,500
North Carolina	12,000*	12,500*	104.2%*	"not half armed"	"very bad"	1,000
South Carolina	unknown	5,500	n.a.	"every person in the province capable of bearing arms"	"already furnished with a good gun"	2,000
Georgia	unknown	756	n.a.	"many being unable to purchase arms"	"very badly armed"	none

* Based on incomplete data which includes free blacks and mulattos.
** These public arms are all muskets.

SOURCES:

New Hampshire: White males sixteen and up: Evarts B. Greene and Virginia Harrington, *American Population before the Federal Census of 1790* (1981; New York: Columbia University Press, 1932), 72. Enrolled militiamen: "Population of the British Colonies," *Documents Relative to the Colonial History of the State of New York*, ed. E. B. O'Callaghan, 15 vols. (Albany: Weed, Parsons, 1853–1887), 6:993 (hereafter cited as *NYCD*). Proportion armed, quality of arms, number of public arms: "Blair Report on the State of the Colonies, July 20, 1756," in Louis K. Koontz, *The Virginia Frontier*, 1754–1763 (Baltimore: Johns Hopkins University Press, 1925), 170.

Massachusetts: White males sixteen and up and enrolled militiamen for 1758: Greene and Harrington, American Population, 16. Number of public arms: *Acts and Resolves, Public and Private, of the Province of Massachusetts Bay*, 21 vols. (Boston: Wright and Potter, 1869–1922), 15:722.

Rhode Island: White males sixteen and up, enrolled (enlisted) militiamen, and proportion armed: *Account of the people in the Colony of Rhode-Island, whites, blacks, together with the quantity of arms and ammunition in the hands of private persons*, Early American Imprints, no. 40794 (n.p., 1800). Number of public arms, June 1749: *General Assembly of the Governor and Company of the English Colony of Rhode-Island and Providence Plantations, in New England in America, held at Newport* [May 2, 1749–February 1750], Early American Imprints, no. 6411 [Newport, 1749–50].

Connecticut: White males sixteen and up: estimated from 1756 Connecticut Census; see Greene and Harrington, *American Population*, 50. Enrolled militiamen: Harold E. Selesky, *War and Society in Colonial Connecticut* (New Haven: Yale University Press, 1990), 166, n. 29. Quality of arms, number of public arms: Governor Thomas Fitch to Sir Thomas Robinson, Norwalk, August 1, 1755, in *Collections of the Connecticut Historical Society*, vol. 1 (Hartford: published for the Society, 1860), 267.

New York: White males sixteen and up from 1756 New York Census; see Greene and Harrington, *American Population*, 101. Enrolled militiamen: *NYCD*, 6:993. Proportion armed, quality of arms, number of public arms: "Blair Report," 171.

New Jersey: White males sixteen and up, number of public arms: "Blair Report," 171–72. Enrolled militiamen: NYCD, 6:993.

Pennsylvania: White males sixteen and up: 25,000 men capable of bearing arms, *NYCD*, 6:993.

Delaware: White males sixteen and up: estimate based on number of militia in 1757; see "An Address from the Assembly of the Lower Counties to the Governor," October 26, 1757, in *Pennsylvania Archives*, 1st. ser., ed. Samuel Hazard, vol. 3 (Philadelphia: Joseph Stevens & Co., 1853), 308–12.

Maryland: White males sixteen and up, enrolled militiamen, proportion armed, quality of arms: "Blaire Report," 168–69; number of public arms: *Archives of Maryland*, 50:510–11.

Virginia: White males sixteen and up, proportion armed, quality of arms, number of public arms: "Blair Report," 165–67. Enrolled militiamen, *NYCD*, 6:993.

North Carolina: White males sixteen and up, enrolled militiamen: Greene and Harrington, *American Population*, 157. Proportion armed, quality of arms, number of public arms: Governor Dobbs to Earl of Loudoun, New Bern, July 10, 1756, in *Colonial Records of North Carolina*, ed. William L. Saunders, vol. 5 (Raleigh: Josephus Daniels, printer to the State, 1887), 599. The number of militiamen appears to exceed the number of free white males sixteen and up because of tax evasion and because free blacks and mulattos served in the North Carolina militia.

South Carolina: Enrolled militiamen: Greene and Harrington, *American Population*, 175. Proportion armed, quality of arms, number of public arms: Lawrence Henry Gipson, *The Great War for Empire: The Years of Defeat, 1754–1757* (New York: Knopf, 1959), 50.

Georgia: Enrolled militiamen: Greene and Harrington, *American Population*, 181. Proportion armed, quality of arms, number of public arms: Governor John Reynolds to the Board of Trade, Georgia, January 5, 1756, in *Colonial Records of the State of Georgia: The Original Papers of Governor John Reynolds, 1754–1756*, ed. Kenneth Coleman and Milton Ready, vol. 27 (Athens: University of Georgia Press, 1977), 104.

Outside New England, most militias remained less inclusive and were, as a rule, inadequately armed in terms of quantity and quality, for here too men preferred firearms that were lighter than military muskets (table 6).[107] Pennsylvania and Delaware did not have militias in 1754, and the level of private gun ownership in Pennsylvania may have been lower than in any other colony.[108] After General Edward Braddock's defeat at the battle of the Monongahela in early July 1755, residents of Pennsylvania's Lancaster and Chester counties petitioned the colony's legislature to "furnish them with Arms and Amunition for Defence of their Houses and Families."[109] The Pennsylvania assembly responded by purchasing and distributing five hundred guns and a supply of ammunition to arm the exposed residents of Cumberland, York, and Lancaster counties.[110] Finally, in 1757 Pennsylvania's legislature passed a militia law that requited all males (except Quakers, like-minded individuals, and Catholics) to be listed by the sheriff, to arm themselves, and to be formed into militia companies.[111] Delaware passed new militia acts in 1756 and 1757 that reestablished a militia for the duration of the war.[112]

The militias of New York, New Jersey, Maryland, and Virginia contained fewer than two-thirds of their eligible men, many of whom lacked adequate arms. New York's governor reported that "the Arms which are in the Possession of private People are Chiefly for the Indian trade," and "some of them [the militiamen] are so indigent, that they cannot purchase their proper arms."[113] Firearms produced for the Indian trade often weighed as little as five and a half pounds and had bores of .57 to .62 caliber and barrels only thirty-six to forty inches long.[114] At least one-third of Maryland's militia were "entirely destitute of Arms & many of the Guns that are the property of the Rest are very bad & scarcely fit for use," characterizations that are confirmed by the descriptions of a majority of guns found in samples of Maryland probate inventories during the mid-1700s.[115] In neighboring Virginia, "not above half" the militiamen were armed with firearms, and these had "different Bores."[116] During the French and Indian War it was sometimes necessary to arm some Maryland and Virginia militia companies with muskets from public stores.[117] Given these circumstances, it is not surprising that in 1758 Colonel Henry Bouquet, a regular officer, discovered that among "new recruits and provincials," who came primarily from Delaware, Maryland, Pennsylvania, North Carolina, and Virginia, "a great number had never seen a musket," by which he meant a heavy, large-caliber military firearm.[118]

Farther south the situation appears to have been even worse (table 6). By 1754, North Carolina's organized militia "was fallen much to decay" and "not near half armed and those [arms] they have very bad."[119] The colony's new governor, Arthur Dobbs, brought with him one thousand muskets, which he used to arm militiamen living on "the sea coast" and in "the exposed western Counties on the Frontier."[120] Still, he believed that members of the militia needed an additional two thousand firearms.[121] Even though Georgia had been founded in 1733, its militia was not put on a legal footing until 1751, and its first militia act was not passed until 1755.[122] In that year, Georgia's militia included most of its adult white males, but it was tiny and "very badly Armed, many being unable to purchase Arms, according to the militia act."[123] To address the latter problem, in 1757 the British Board of Ordnance sent Georgia five hundred muskets to arm its militiamen.[124]

Among the southern colonies, only South Carolina's militia appears to have been a credible institution in 1755.[125] Its strength of approximately six thousand men probably represented a near-universal enrollment of white males aged sixteen to sixty. In 1754 the colony's governor, James Glen, claimed, "There is no a single Person in this Province Capable of bearing a Gun but has one and we allow of no Indian Trading Guns,"[126] though in 1757 an unimpressed Colonel Bouquet asserted that "the Militia of this Province amounts to about six thousand badly armed Men."[127] In addition, the colony had on hand two thousand publicly owned muskets in storage.[128]

As it was, the colonies' militias played only supporting roles during what would prove to be the last colonial war, known today as the French and Indian War or the Seven Years' War. At various times from 1754 to 1758, Maryland, Pennsylvania, and Virginia used companies of militiamen to assist in frontier defense.[129] Many more militiamen volunteered to join provincial regiments, while untold others were conscripted into the provincial forces by local militia companies acting in essence as draft boards. Some militiamen had their firearms pressed into provincial service, so even though they themselves didn't go to war, their guns did. In Maryland, Virginia, and South Carolina the vast majority of militiamen served primarily to keep an eye on enslaved African Americans. Governor Robert Dinwiddie of Virginia claimed that the colony's slave population "alarms our People much and [they] are afr'd of bad consequences if the Militia are order'd to any great Distance from the presn't Settlem'ts."[130] In 1757 militiamen were briefly mobilized in Connecticut, Massachusetts, New York, and Rhode Island and marched toward New York's frontier after the fall of Fort William Henry in August. During 1760, when Cherokees and Creeks threatened Georgia, one-third of the colony's "whole Militia" found itself "on actual duty" for several months.[131] But such activity by units of the colonial militias was unusual by the third quarter of the eighteenth century.

The burden of the fighting during the French and Indian War was borne not by militiamen but by units of provincial soldiers who came of age "as quasi-regular troops" during this conflict.[132] As a rule, colonial governments wanted their provincial soldiers to be equipped like British regulars.[133] The motley collection of fowlers, smaller-bore trade guns, and fusils that still armed most militiamen and had equipped many provincial soldiers in the 1740s were no longer considered appropriate for military service. As Governor Thomas Fitch of Connecticut observed, "these arms being all of the private property are very various in their sorts and sizes, according to the different occasions and humors of their owners and accordingly not at all adapted to the business of a campaign."[134] They were too light to hold up in the field. Musket balls fired by the smaller-caliber firearms lacked the stopping power of the heavier balls fired by muskets with larger bores, and they were usually not fitted to accept a bayonet.

Colonial authorities came to believe that an adequately armed soldier needed a heavy, large-caliber musket with a .70- to .80-inch bore, a bayonet, and a cartridge box.[135] Thus armed, a provincial soldier could, theoretically, fire devastating volleys and deliver a bayonet charge. Arming men with muskets of the same bore or caliber also reduced problems resulting from the need to supply troops with ammunition of varying sizes.[136] As a result, officials in all of the colonies attempted, with varying degrees of success, to obtain military muskets for their provincial forces[137]

The challenge of arming provincial soldiers was compounded by the fact that the men who joined provincial regiments came disproportionately from those segments of society least likely to own any kind of firearm. Governor Fitch of Connecticut had alluded to this problem in an earlier letter where he made the point that it was difficult to obtain firearms "for the use of such as, tho' able bodied effective men, are unprovided and unable to provide themselves."[138] Overwhelmingly, the men joining provincial regiments were in their late teens and early twenties, and not independent property owners. Outside of New England, a majority of enlistees in provincial forces—regardless of their ages—were laborers, immigrants, servants, and poorer men.[139] By way of contrast, Virginia's militia consisted of "chiefly Free-holders," who insisted "on th'r Privileges not to enlist [in the provincials] or serve but on imminent danger."[140] South Carolina only completed its provincial regiment raised in

1757 by empowering magistrates to enlist "all idle, lewd, disorderly men who have no visible means of support and all sturdy beggars."[141] Needless to say, such men were less likely to own any kind of firearm than those older, better-off men who have left behind most surviving probate inventories. Studies of colonial inventories suggest that, as a rule, only 40 percent of males under the age of twenty-five owned a gun, while among the poorest 20 percent who were probated and inventoried, regardless of their age, only 33 percent owned a firearm.[142]

Initially, existing colonial stores of public arms, though relatively small, played crucial roles in arming provincial regiments that took the field in 1755 in Rhode Island, Maryland, and Virginia.[143] In addition, Virginia lent firearms from its public stores to New Jersey and New York, and Maryland offered to lend arms to North Carolina.[144] In 1756 a shipment of ten thousand muskets from the Board of Ordnance provided two thousand firearms each to Connecticut and Massachusetts, three hundred each to Rhode Island and New Hampshire, six hundred to Pennsylvania, and one thousand each to New York and Virginia.[145] As a result, starting in 1756 if not before, Massachusetts, Connecticut, New York, and New Jersey also armed the majority of their provincial troops with public arms.[146] A second shipment of twelve thousand muskets and two hundred rounds of ammunition for each was sent from London in 1758 to help arm the 21,286 provincial troops raised in the colonies for the 1758 campaigning season. The arrival and distribution of this shipment of muskets helped overcome what historians have called the "Great Arms Crisis" of 1758, which had left colonial and British officials scrambling to find suitable firearms to equip provincial soldiers.[147] Almost all of the Pennsylvania provincials raised in 1758 had to be armed or rearmed with publicly owned muskets.[148] In the same year, British officers also had to call upon Maryland to help arm the provincial soldiers in the Second Virginia Regiment.[149]

In addition to these military muskets provided by the Board of Ordnance, colonial governments purchased 7,610 muskets between 1757 and 1760. New Jersey ordered two thousand stands of arms, each of which included musket, bayonet, and cartridge box.[150] Of the three thousand South Carolina bought, at least one thousand went to arm militiamen, not just provincial troops in the field. Private arms shipments, categorized as "For the Planters," during the years 1756 through 1763 still outstripped public purchases, designated "For the Province," since colonial merchants imported 36,592 shoulder arms and four thousand pairs of pistols.[151] Although some of these privately imported arms resembled the publicly purchased arms in that they were muskets and bayonets with cartridge boxes, the majority of these guns for private sale were presumably the lighter fowlers and trade guns that colonists favored.

The wars of the mid-1700s marked a watershed in the development of colonial military institutions and in the arming of colonial military forces. Increasingly, when governments raised provincial soldiers for offensive operations, and even when they posted men to garrisons along the frontier stretching from Pennsylvania to Georgia, it became necessary to supply them with publicly owned muskets. Except for colonial cities, parts of the Delaware Valley, and some parts of the rural South, private ownership of firearms appears to have remained widespread in the third quarter of the eighteenth century. But the quality of these privately owned weapons, including those in the hands of militiamen, could not sustain military forces in the field. So even though the number of public arms was still dwarfed by tens of thousands of privately owned firearms, the approximately thirty thousand muskets that the British Board of Ordnance and colonial governments distributed to provincial troops had assumed a central role in each colony's ability to wage war by the late 1750s. In the southern colonies, especially in North Carolina, South Carolina, and Georgia, but also to some degree in Pennsylvania, Maryland, and Virginia, publicly owned muskets had also come to play a limited role in arming militiamen.

With the defeat of the French, the establishment of British control over all of North America east of the Mississippi River created a sense of security in which the military role of colonial militias appeared unnecessary. Pennsylvania's and Delaware's militias disappeared with the war's end.[152] Some Associator companies re-formed in eastern Pennsylvania in 1763 to oppose the march on Philadelphia of the Paxton Boys, though civil authorities also called on British regulars. Similarly, when faced with unrest among armed tenants in Albany, Dutchess, and Westchester counties in 1765, New York authorities also called in British regulars. By 1770 most New York militia companies had not trained for several years.[153] In fact New York's legislature failed to enact a militia law between 1768 and 1772.[154] Only in North Carolina in 1771 at the battle of the Alamance did militiamen prove capable of putting down armed civilian protesters who called themselves Regulators.[155]

Lax regulation was evident in the organization and discipline of other colonies' militias. In New Hampshire, the militia regulations were so little observed in the early 1770s that the governor "was sure there was not four ounces of powder per man or one musket to every four men."[156] Even in neigh-boring Massachusetts there were signs that militia units had deteriorated and training had become infrequent.[157] Writing in 1773, Governor William Franklin of New Jersey confessed that of his colony's twenty thousand militia-men, "not above half that number are regularly mustered and trained accord-ing to the law."[158] In Virginia militia officers along the frontier had a hard time mobilizing and disciplining their men during Dunmore's War in 1774.[159] Georgia's militia law was not renewed in 1770 and lapsed until 1773, which led to confusion.[160]

Despite the continuing decay of the militia even in New England, patterns in the private ownership of firearms as indicated by their presence in samples of probate inventories of deceased males seem to have remained relatively consistent from the 1740s to the early 1770s (tables 4 and 7). The impressment and purchase of privately owned firearms during the war years were appar-ently offset by the movement of some publicly owned firearms into private hands and by the ongoing importation of firearms by merchants and their sale to private individuals. In western Massachusetts (Hampshire County), over 60 percent of inventories continued to list firearms, while in areas closer to the coast in Massachusetts—Plymouth, Essex, and rural Suffolk counties—and in Connecticut, levels of firearm ownership found in inventories ranged from one-half to two-thirds (tables 4 and 7). Probate inventories from inland Worcester County still recorded particularly low levels of firearm ownership. Inventories probated in ports such as Gloucester, Marblehead, Newburyport, and Salem in Essex County, which were home to fishermen, mariners, and transients, recorded even lower levels of firearm ownership in the mid-1770s (table 7).

Elsewhere in the mainland British colonies, the levels of private gun own-ership found in probate inventories on the eve of the American Revolution document the persistence of patterns established earlier in the 1700s (table 7). In rural New York, percentages of gun ownership in surviving probate inven-tories were higher than those found in the 1740s (table 7). To the south in the region stretching from the Hudson River to the Delaware River Valley, the legacy of the Quaker proprietors persisted. In Pennsylvania and Delaware, raising provincial troops and the temporary establishment of militias during the Seven Years' War did not produce significant changes in the patterns of private gun ownership, which overall remained lower than those found in inventories from New England and the southern colonies. The percentage of inventories containing firearms ranged from 30 to 38 percent in western

TABLE 7. PROBATE INVENTORIES OF MALES CONTAINING GUNS, PISTOLS, RIFLES, AND SWORDS
IN SELECTED AREAS OF THE BRITISH MAINLAND COLONIES ON THE EVE OF THE REVOLUTION.

Location	Number in sample	% inventories with firearm*	% inventories with rifles	% inventories with pistols	% inventories with swords
Rural Essex County, Mass.	50	64.0	0.0	8.0	24.0
Ports in Essex County, Mass.	42	30.9	0.0	0.0	16.7
Rural Suffolk County, Mass.	44	52.3	0.0	2.3	13.6
Boston, Mass.	50	43.1	0.0	12.0	18.0
Plymouth County, Mass.	31	58.1	0.0	3.2	19.4
Worcester County, Mass.	40	42.5	0.0	5.0	10.0
Hampshire County, Mass.	26	65.4	0.0	0.0	11.5
Connecticut	59	52.5	0.0	5.1	22.0
Rural New York	38	52.6	2.6	13.2	15.8
New York City	13	38.5	0.0	23.1	23.1
Burlington County, N.J.	21	33.3	0.0	0.0	0.0
Salem County N.J.	63	38.0	0.0	1.6	3.2
Rural Philadelphia County	67	40.0	0.0	3.0	4.6
Philadelphia	52	38.5	0.0	17.3	19.2
Frontier Pennsylvania	28	32.1	10.7	0.0	0.0
Kent County, Del.	25	64.0	4.0	8.0	0.0
Maryland	56	60.7	1.8	8.9	7.1
York County, Va.	55	56.4	1.8	16.3	16.3
Lunenburg County, Va.	15	80.0	20.0	6.7	13.4
Augusta County, Va.	30	70.0	13.3	6.7	0.0
Halifax County, N.C.	35	74.3	0.0	5.7	37.1
Orange County, N.C.	30	70.0	33.3	0.0	10.0
Lowlands S.C.	47	80.1	0.0	44.7	38.3
Charles Town, S.C.	25	48.0	0.0	24.0	28.0

* Includes pistols and rifles.

SOURCES:

Most of the data in this table are taken from inventories of male decedents, in American Colonial Wealth: Documents and Methods, ed. Alice Hanson Jones, 3 vols. (New York: Arno Press, 1977).

ADDITIONAL DATA HAVE BEEN OBTAINED FROM THE FOLLOWING SOURCES:

Rural New York and New York City, 1768–1774: Inventories of Estates from New York City and Vicinity, 1680–1844, microfilm, New York Historical Society; Inventories and Accounts, 1666–1822, New York (State), Court of Probates, microfilm, New York State Archives, Albany.

Salem County, 1770–1775: Salem County, N.J., "Inventories, Wills, and Administrative Papers," 1770–1775, microfilm, Downs Library, Winterthur Museum, Winterthur, Del.

York County, 1771–1775: York County Deeds, Orders and Wills, 22 vols., typed transcriptions, Department of Historic Research, Colonial Williamsburg Foundation, Williamsburg, Va.

Lunenburg County, 1770–1775: Will Book no. 2, 1762–1778, microfilm, in author's possession, Amherst College.

Augusta County, 1773–1774: Will Book no. 5, 1772–1778, microfilm, in author's possession, Amherst College.

New Jersey and from roughly 38 to 40 percent in eastern Pennsylvania. In frontier areas of Pennsylvania, which lacked significant Quaker populations, the percentage was actually lower, 32 percent. Most of these firearms were not military muskets but guns for fowling, hunting, and controlling vermin. Ironically, in Pennsylvania, only in the City of Brotherly Love does one find a noticeable minority of inventories with such antipersonnel weapons as pistols and swords.

The proportion of male decedents' estate inventories mentioning firearms in the tidewater region of the Chesapeake, in the Carolina lowlands, and in the uplands of the South ranged from 56 to 80 percent (table 7), comparable to the levels found in sampled inventories for most of the colonial period in this region. Evidence of gun ownership in probate inventories from Lunenburg and August counties in Virginia and Orange County, North Carolina (table 7), also provides some support for the historian Matthew Ward's suggestion that the Seven Years' War "may also have played a vital role in the 'arming' of the backcountry," whereas "before the war many backcountry settlers had no need for arms."[161] At the same time, the proportion of inventories listing guns dipped lower in more secure jurisdictions containing urban areas such as Charles Town, South Carolina, and York County, Virginia, which included Williamsburg, the colony's capital, and the river port of Yorktown.

Pistols were more likely to show up in inventories from southern cities such as Charles Town and Williamsburg and in those from the northern cities of Boston, New York, and Philadelphia (table 7). Of the 624 pistols listed in the

1755 Rhode Island census of private arms, 42.6 percent were found in New-port.[162] In urban environments, pistols, which had limited range and accuracy, could have provided their owners with some protection. In most rural areas of New England and the middle colonies, pistols usually appeared in less than 10 percent of the inventories. Probate inventories thus provide little support for the belief that "civilians commonly carried" pocket-sized pistols "for protection whenever traveling,"[163] or that handguns were in common use at the time even though they were less expensive than long arms. In southern colonies, pistols were found more frequently in rural regions than in the North, because southern militiamen rode on slave patrols. Militarily, the use of pistols was as a rule limited to horsemen and officers.[164] South Carolina did have a mounted militia regiment, which probably accounts for the unusually large percentage of this colony's rural probate inventories that contained pistols and swords.[165]

A personal firearm with a greater potential for military use was the long rifle, which could be found in inventories of upland areas such as Augusta, Lunenburg, and Orange counties (table 7). Originally based on heavier, shorter-barreled German hunting rifles, the longer-barreled, slender-stocked American long rifle evolved in Pennsylvania during the 1730s and 1740s as a firearm for hunting.[166] As a rule long rifles weighed between seven and eight pounds, had .58- to .62-inch bores, though some were even smaller, and fired balls, depending on the bore, that weighed from eighteen to thirty-six to the pound.[167] Because of the rifling of the barrel, these guns were more accurate than smoothbore muskets and outranged them as well, enabling a skilled marksman to hit a target at two to three hundred yards. But because of the barrel's rifling, the tight fit of its balls, and the use of a greased patch to enhance the ball's ability to grab the grooves in the rifled barrel, a long rifle took two to three times longer to load than a smoothbore musket. Rifles also could not be fitted with bayonets, and because of their slender stocks were more vulnerable to breakage on a battlefield. Despite their shortcomings as military arms, some of Pennsylvania's provincial soldiers carried rifles in the late 1750s.[168] Still, rifles, which were more expensive than smoothbore muskets, remained uncommon outside the backcountry of Pennsylvania and the southern colonies and were rare east of the Hudson River.

During the political agitation of the early 1770s, firearms and militias acquired a political importance that had previously been largely latent and unexpressed. Now it became overt as the mere display of guns came to embody the political demands and inherent power of an aroused populace. In the assessment of the historian Lawrence Cress, colonists had actually been slow "to inject the citizen-soldier ideal into the ideological context developing in prerevolutionary America."[169] This situation was in large measure a result of the fact that by the mid-eighteenth century, colonial militias had assumed such a secondary role in defending the colonies, particularly the middle and southern colonies. It was only after the March 5, 1770, Boston Massacre that the militia entered the mainstream of public debate even in New England. After the passage of the Coercive Acts in 1774, the militia and the ideal of the citizen soldier came to be regarded as centrally important to an American ideology of republicanism.[170] By 1774, patriot leaders and legislative assemblies throughout the colonies were giving expression to this recently rediscovered ideal that "a well regulated militia, Composed of gentlemen and yeomen, is the natural strength and only security of a free government."[171] Not for the first time during the revolutionary era, ideology trumped practicality and history in discussions of the militia.

To put this rediscovered ideal into practice, colonists took over existing units of the colonial militias, revived the Associator tradition in Pennsylvania, and in some instances created new volunteer military units. In Massachusetts and New Hampshire, patriot leaders assumed control of existing militias by replacing, where necessary, uncooperative officers who had been appointed by royal governors.[172] To characterize this process as "individuals banding together in militias of association," or as a "resort to quasi-private and extralegal militias of association," slights the close resemblance between the prerevolutionary militias and their immediate predecessors.[173] The resemblance between the colonial and revolutionary militias was even closer in Connecticut and Rhode Island, where popularly elected colonial governments and the existing militias transferred their allegiance and along with it their authority to the patriot cause. In the southern colonies, patriots and the colonial legislatures that they controlled took over and breathed new life into their militias, though the process was not without conflicts as yeoman farmers in Virginia and loyalists in the Carolinas and Georgia resisted these efforts.[174] Eventually militias loyal to revolutionary state governments were created, though Georgia's militia proved to be "highly ineffective in stopping the constant raids from Florida, did not fill the ranks of the Continental Line, and did very little to contain the native Americans."[175]

The reorganization of Maryland's militia and its transformation are particularly well documented. In December 1774 Maryland's Provincial Convention passed a new militia act that began by acknowledging that "a well regulated militia composed of the gentlemen, freeholders, and other freemen, is the natural strength, and only stable security of a free government."[176] This law was part of a conscious effort to create a military force that would be able to fight conventional set piece battles.[177] Responding to a call from the Continental Congress, Maryland passed a law in July 1775 that created forty companies of minutemen, who constituted a select militia of volunteers who were organized into separate units, armed by the state, and trained twice a week. Unlike the colonial militia, minutemen could be marched "to such places, either in this or the neighboring colonies and at such times as we shall be commanded by the Convention."[178] In January, yet another militia law reduced exemptions from service in the militia and set up a classing system that provided for calling out militiamen on a rotating basis for two-month periods of active service. Unlike its colonial predecessor, the resulting revolutionary militia was a "microcosm" of Maryland society in that exemptions no longer had a socioeconomic bias and the classing system distributed active service across all classes.[179] Those who did not enroll in the militia by March 1776 were systematically disarmed.[180]

Not surprisingly, patriot leaders and revolutionary governments in the colonies lying between Connecticut and Maryland faced greater challenges because of these colonies' lack of strong traditions of militia service and their current political divisions. Because of these divisions, popular actions in New York and New Jersey played prominent roles in forming voluntary military companies that initially stood outside the existing colonial militias.[181] Early in 1775, some residents of New York City "formed themselves into companies under officers of their own choosing [and] distributed the [public] arms."[182] At about the same time, a wary royal governor of New Jersey reported men "arming themselves, forming into companies, and taking uncommon pains to perfect themselves in Military Discipline."[183] During 1774 and 1775, patriots in Pennsylvania acting on their own revived the Associator tradition and created fifty-three battalions, which received legislative sanction in November 1775.[184] As a number of these units joined the Continental Army and the *rage militaire* that supported such voluntary efforts flagged, Pennsylvania passed a compulsory militia law early in 1777.[185] In 1775 Delaware's revolutionary legislature acknowledged, "We have for sometime past been carelessly negligent of military art and discipline, and are therefore the more exposed to the insult and ravages of our natural enemy."[186] Despite its best efforts, Delaware never really succeeded in overcoming these decades of neglect. In the assessment of one historian, "the Delaware militia displayed markedly little enthusiasm for the war effort, and the state's citizenry seemed more intent on avoiding, not confronting, the advancing redcoats and Germans."[187]

The rebelling colonists sought to equip their militias and Continental regulars with military firearms and in doing so set a high bar. In July of 1775, the Continental Congress recommended to the states that each militiaman "be furnished with a good musket, that will carry an ounce ball, with a bayonet, steel ramrod, worm, priming wire and brush fitted thereto, a cutting sword or tomahawk, a cartridge-box, that will contain 23 rounds of cartridges, twelve flints and a knapsack."[188] Steel or iron ramrods, which were a relatively recent refinement in military long arms, were seen as an improvement over wooden ramrods that speeded up the process of loading: New York's Committee of Safety concluded that the city's store of military muskets "at present fitted with ordinary wooden rammers . . . cannot be of much use in case of necessity."[189] Not all contracts for producing muskets conformed to these specifications; calibers varied from .67 to .90 and weights ranged from nine to twelve pounds.[190] But as a rule, provincial congresses, Committees of Safety, and other officials specified a stand of arms consisting of a heavy, large-caliber musket, bayonet, and cartridge box.

Just about everywhere, even in parts of New England, revolutionary officials encountered difficulties in obtaining such arms for their militias in 1774 and 1775. The problem was only compounded by the often competing efforts to raise and arm troops for the Continental Army starting in mid-1775. According to Governor Nicholas Cooke, Rhode Island's militiamen had by then "disposed of their arms so generally, that at the breaking out of the present war, the colony was in a manner disarmed." The state appointed twenty-nine men to take an account of all public and private "powder, arms, and ammunition" and "directed and empowered [them] to go to the house of each person in their respective towns; to take an account of the power, arms and ammunition."[191] In the end, reported Cooke, the state used "every method in our power, by purchasing, by employing manufacturers, and by importation, to procure a sufficient quantity, but are still deficient."[192] Governor Cooke's assessment appears to have exaggerated the situation. Fragmentary returns from a Rhode Island gun census conducted in late 1775 and early 1776 indicate that a little over 60 percent of the "Persons Able to Bear Arms" had some kind of firearm, which was actually somewhat better than the situation in Rhode Island in 1755 (table 5).[193] Still, in March 1776 the Rhode Island General Assembly voted to buy "two thousand stand of good fire-arms with bayonets, iron ramrods and cartouche boxes," stamp them with C.R., and distribute them to the individual towns, and empowered the towns' councils "to determine what persons in their respective towns shall have the benefit and use of the arms provided."[194]

In New Hampshire the availability of firearms appears to have been about the same as in Rhode Island, though the figures varied dramatically from town to town (table 8).[195] Incomplete returns from a 1775 New Hampshire census reported that eighty towns with 8,443 males over the age of sixteen (and 6,790 between sixteen and fifty) had a total of 4,189 firearms but lacked 3,173 firearms to arm completely their 7,362 militiamen, suggesting that 56.9 percent of the men between sixteen and sixty had firearms. Viewed another way, eighty-eight New Hampshire towns with 9,505 men over the age of sixteen (and 7,664 between sixteen and fifty) indicate that they lacked 3,610 firearms, suggesting that 47.1 percent of these towns' total of approximately 8,288 militiamen (estimated as 87.2 percent of the men over 16) lacked guns.[196] Petitions from concerned residents of the state's towns show a variation ranging from less than a fifth, to half, to three-quarters armed.[197]

The militias of Massachusetts and Connecticut appear to have been better armed at the outset of hostilities. Even before any fighting had occurred, both colonies took steps to make up for shortfalls in militia arms. In November 1774 the Massachusetts Provincial Congress ordered fifteen thousand muskets, which, with the aid of Benjamin Franklin, were shipped from France to Boston via Philadelphia.[198] Connecticut and Massachusetts also ordered militia officers and local officials to recover public arms that had passed into private hands during and after the Seven Years' War.[199] Finally, both colonies resorted to pressing arms and compensating owners.[200] By April 1775 the "Warlike Stores" in Massachusetts included 21,549 firearms and 10,108 bayonets.[201] Scattered strength returns for militia units and minute companies from Massachusetts for the years 1775 and 1776 suggest that over 80 percent of the state's militiamen were armed, though not all of these arms appear to have been military muskets, and bayonets were lacking.[202] Fragmentary militia returns from Connecticut suggest that the state could equip somewhere between 60 and 75 percent of its able-bodied men.[203]

Because of internal divisions, severe fighting in 1776 and 1777, and sustained military occupation by British forces in some areas, it is difficult to reconstruct the degrees to which the militias of New York and New Jersey were armed before fighting began in this area. Patriots had seized public and royal

TABLE 8. DISTRIBUTION OF FIREARMS, NEW HAMPSHIRE, 1769–1771, FROM 1775 CENSUS AND PROBATE INVENTORY DATA.

Number of towns	Number of males over 16	Number of males 16–50 not in army	Number of guns found in town or inventory	Average number of guns per male over 16	Average number of guns per male 16–50	Number of guns wanting in town	Average number of guns wanting per male 16–50
A. 27 towns with guns found	3,162	2,462	1,872	.59	.76	—	—
B. 80 towns with guns found and guns wanting	8,443	6,790	4,189	.50	.62	3,173	.47
C. 107 towns = total rows A and B	1,605	9,252	6,061	.52.	.66	—	—
D. 8 towns with guns wanting	1,062	874	—	—	—	437	.50
E. 88 towns = total rows B and D	9,505	7,664	—	—	—	3,610	.47
F. 18 towns with no returns for guns*	3,166	2,562	—	—	—	—	—
G. Inventories from rural New Hampshire. 1769–1773	88	—	60	.68**	—	—	—

* Portsmouth did not return data on guns and is included in this group of eighteen towns for which there are no useful returns. Because of this omission, Portsmouth probate inventories were excluded from the group of New Hampshire probate inventories 1769–1773.

**Average number of guns per probated male decedent, all of whom would have been over twenty-one. It is not surprisingly a higher average since it does not include males between sixteen and twenty, who were less likely to own firearms.

SOURCES:

1775 census data from "Census of New Hampshire, 1775," in *Provincial Papers: Documents and Records relating to the Province of New Hampshire*, comp. and ed. Nathaniel Bouton, vol. 7 (Nashua: Green C. Moore State Printer, 1873), 724–79.

Probate data from New Hampshire Probate Records, vol. 5, 1700–1773, and vol. 26, 1769–1771, microfilm, Historic Deerfield Library, Deerfield, Mass.

arms in New York City in April and May 1775.[204] Scattered regimental returns for New York from 1776 and 1777 indicate that three-quarters of their officers and men were armed. Still, in July 1776 New York authorized county authorities to arm militia levies drafted into the Continental Army but "hav[ing] no arms by taking them from those [militiamen] not drafted and such other persons in the districts as have arms," a solution that only worsened the situation in local militia companies.[205] The next year, the Supreme Executive Council of New York reported that the militias of Tryon, Albany, Charlotte, Gloucester, and Cumberland counties (the latter two located in what is today Vermont) remained improperly armed when reviewed in February 1777.[206] Four years later some militiamen in this area "were occasionally supplied from the Cont'l [Continental] armory in this place [Albany]."[207] And by 1780 Colonel Samuel Drake's Westchester County militia regiment of 446 men had only 212 guns, 146 bayonets, 167 cartridge boxes, no powder, and no lead.[208]

New Jersey began the conflict with "a very considerable number of muskets and bayonets" that had been distributed "to Court-Houses, or some other particular places in each County."[209] This attracted the attention of New York authorities, who wanted to use these weapons to arm their own Continentals. Early in 1776, both New Jersey and New York had begun disarming loyalists and transferring their weapons to patriot militias and Continental regiments.[210] Two regimental returns for New Jersey—one from 1779 and another from 1780—report that three-quarters of these militiamen were armed.[211] Given the date of these returns, it's possible that they include firearms seized from loyalists and firearms provided from state and possibly Continental stores.[212]

East of the Delaware River, firearms in general were harder to obtain.[213] In Pennsylvania, patriots initially took up subscriptions to arm poor Associators, and the assembly called upon the counties to supply their citizens with a total of six thousand firearms.[214] Eventually, the assembly voted to order five thousand muskets with bayonets. Maryland contracted for 5,600 stands of arms.[215] In July 1776 Pennsylvania also disarmed non-Associators and ordered that their arms be given to Associators or units of the Continental Line.[216] Both states committed themselves to obtaining enough public arms to equip two classes of their militias when they were mobilized.[217] Over the course of the war, "many thousands of arms had been distributed to the militia of Pennsylvania especially throughout the very extensive frontier counties."[218] Despite these efforts, mobilized militiamen from Pennsylvania and Maryland lacked the arms they needed to resist British troops in the late summer of 1777, when a British army under Sir William Howe invaded Pennsylvania.[219]

Farther south there is more evidence of serious shortfalls when it came to arming militiamen. Military arms were initially scarce in Virginia, where authorities refurbished seventeenth-century firearms, purchased rifles from men in the backcountry, and in one instance recovered some "eighty guns, some bayonets, swords, etc. from their slaves."[220] By late 1775 and early 1776, militia units in different parts of Virginia were reported as being "less than half armed," with "but few arms," "without arms," and "badly armed" because they had given their best arms "to the soldiers intended for their immediate protection."[221] Strength returns for regiments made up of mobilized militiamen from North Carolina and South Carolina taken in 1776 and 1778–79, respectively, suggest that over 80 percent of militiamen on active military service in the field were armed.[222] But evidence is lacking on the quantity and quality of arms found in units of militiamen in 1775 and early 1776 in the Carolinas. And according to James Biser Whisker, "Georgia's militiamen were poorly supplied, many being without blankets, canteens, knapsacks, shoes or firearms."[223]

These problems arose from the unprecedented mobilizations of manpower being attempted and because of the expanded military roles given to the organized militias. In recent years historians have tended to slight the militia's military role during the War of Independence, especially on the battlefield.[224] Instead they have emphasized the militia's political role in enforcing loyalty to the new state government and intimidating loyalists. Some have acknowledged the usefulness of the militia for preventing British forces from maneuvering, raiding, and, most important, foraging. Such activities by militiamen helped pen British forces in seaports, which created logistical nightmares for the government in London. But to make these efforts possible, militia call-ups and time spent on active service by mobilized militiamen expanded well beyond anything attempted since the late 1600s in New England, and in most other states exceeded anything ever attempted. Men enrolled in militia units were also called upon to serve outside their states and to face professional soldiers in battle, actions that were rarely if ever demanded of colonial militiamen.

The scale of the demands for manpower and the ages of those who enlisted or were called up placed strains on available supplies of firearms. In 1776 Connecticut called up 18,915 men, a figure that represented almost 70 percent of its militia strength that year, and approximately 45 percent of its entire male population between the ages of sixteen and fifty.[225] A similar proportion of the colony's males between these ages may have been mobilized and served over the entire course of the French and Indian War from 1755 to 1763, but not in just one year. During the War of Independence, around half of Virginia's white men over the age of sixteen saw active service in the Continental Army or as activated militiamen. Of these Virginians, those who saw duty only as mobilized militiamen and spent no time in the Continental Army still accumulated on average a total of over a year in active service.[226] In Virginia and Massachusetts, those who served as mobilized militiamen, not just as Continentals, tended to be in their late teens and early twenties.[227] As was the case earlier, these younger men were less likely to own firearms, and the deficiency had to be made up from other sources.

The performance in the field of units composed solely of mobilized militiamen during actual campaigns and in battle varied according to fairly predictable patterns. During the 1776 New York campaign and the 1777 Philadelphia campaign, some militia regiments from New England to Maryland distinguished themselves, if at all, only by the speed with which they fled and on occasion threw away their firearms. Washington's complaints about the performance of most militia units in these two campaigns are well known.[228] But the usefulness of the militiamen improved as Washington learned how to work with them. The sustained performance in the field by New Jersey's militia in 1777 earned it praise from both patriots and its foes.[229] The same year also saw over twenty thousand New England militiamen mobilized, with most of them serving out of state in Rhode Island, Vermont, and upstate New York, where they contributed significantly to the American victories at Bennington and Saratoga.

The contrast between these militiamen and the performance of the militias of the middle states in the 1777 campaign around Philadelphia was not lost on Washington. He observed with envy that "the states of New York and New England resolving to crush Burgoyne, continued pouring in their militia, till the surrender of that army, at which time not less than 14,000 militia ... were actually in General [Horatio] Gates's camp and those composed, for the most part, of the best yeomanry in the country, well armed, and in many instances, supplied with provisions of their own carrying."[230] Regimental returns support Washington's claims about the continued ability of a majority of New England's militiamen to arm themselves.[231]

The organized militias of the southern states saw less extended service during the early years of the War of Independence. North Carolina's militia defeated a gathering of partially armed loyalists at Moore's Creek Bridge in 1776, and militiamen in South Carolina had seen active service suppressing loyalists in 1775, campaigned against the Cherokees in 1776, and aided in repelling Henry Clinton's June 1776 attack on Charleston.[232] The situation changed abruptly in late 1778, when the British captured Savannah, and then in 1780, when they laid siege to Charleston. When the city fell on May 12, over six thousand Continentals and militiamen and their arms were lost. At Camden, South Carolina, on August 16, 1780, the British destroyed another newly created American army consisting of Maryland and Delaware Continentals, who fought valiantly, and of militiamen from North Carolina and Virginia, who threw down their guns and broke without firing a shot. Militiamen from the Carolinas and Virginia gave a better account of themselves in the American victories at King's Mountain and Cowpens in South Carolina and at the Battle of Guilford Court House in North Carolina. General Charles Cornwallis grudgingly acknowledged the effectiveness of some southern militiamen he had encountered, with qualified contempt: "I will not say much in praise of the Militia of the Southern Colonies but the list of British officers & Soldiers killed & wounded by them since last June [1780] proves but too fatally that they are not wholly contemptible."[233]

These battles in the Carolinas during 1780 and 1781 placed a great burden on Virginia and its militia. All of the state's Continental regiments and about a thousand of the state's muskets were captured at Charleston, and approximately four thousand more of Virginia's muskets had been sent to arm North Carolina's militia and were also lost.[234] During 1780 and 1781 British forces invaded Virginia three times, and for most of these years one-quarter of the state's militia was always in the field on active service.[235] Repeated calls to service exhausted the state's militiamen, and great quantities of both private and public firearms were lost.[236] To meet these demands, Governor Thomas Jefferson distributed public arms to militiamen and ordered militia officers to impress any usable firearms, which only compounded the problem.[237] By the spring of 1781 the situation had reached a crisis. Around Richmond, three hundred out of five hundred militiamen arrived unarmed, and another five hundred had to be discharged for "want of arms"; in the north along the Potomac River, only sixty of two hundred militiamen had arms; and along the North Carolina border, only fifty guns were reported in Brunswick County, which mustered "upwards of six hundred Militia."[238] In September 1781, on the eve of the siege at Yorktown, eight hundred militiamen drawn from six counties had only 220 guns, of which 120 were "small guns" (probably trade guns and light fowlers) and not muskets.[239]

The lack of arms and increasing war weariness, combined with the Royal Navy's superior mobility, allowed the British to move through Virginia unopposed, laying waste to the countryside and destroying arms and matériel.[240] Militiamen proved unable "to repel . . . ravaging Parties of the Enemy," who were "armed only with swords and Pistols."[241] Former lieutenant governor John Page found it "to our eternal disgrace to be unarmed and undisciplined after five years [of] war [as] are our militia."[242]

While the situation in Virginia may have been extreme, it appears that eight years of war had removed a lot of firearms from private hands by the early 1780s (table 9). In some areas the percentages of probate inventories of male decedents listing firearms remained largely unchanged from those found in the early 1770s or actually increased a bit. In particular, these levels of ownership could be found in areas close to the fighting, where men in militia units often played active roles but were spared the effects of catastrophic defeats. Militiamen from Plymouth and Worcester counties in Massachusetts had been mobilized to contain the British in Newport, Rhode Island, while militiamen from Dutchess and Ulster counties in New York had helped defend the Hudson Highlands, and militiamen armed with rifles from Augusta County, Virginia, had served in a number of campaigns but as a rule did not have their special weapons impressed (table 9). It is also possible that militiamen serving in these situations were more likely to have benefited from the flow of firearms primarily from public stores into private hands that was produced by the distribution of public arms and the inevitable pilferage that went on.

In most instances, firearms moved from private hands into state or Continental stores, where increasingly they were stamped to indicate public ownership, regardless of the source.[243] Loyalists had been disarmed in most areas controlled by revolutionaries.[244] Where loyalists asserted or British forces reasserted royal authority, revolutionaries were disarmed.[245] Occupied cities had been disarmed beginning early in 1775, when General Gage got Boston's residents to surrender 1,778 muskets, 634 pistols, 978 bayonets, and 38 blunderbusses.[246] The percentages of inventories with firearms in both New York City and Philadelphia were much lower in the early 1780s than they had been in the early 1770s (tables 7 and 9). Both American and British forces had plundered homes for arms in war zones such as Westchester County, New

York, and throughout the Carolinas,[247] where a significantly smaller percentages of inventories contained firearms by the early 1780s.

Elsewhere outside of war zones, some firearms had also apparently passed from private owners to Continental soldiers and activated militiamen. After the war the percentages of probate inventories containing firearms declined a bit in some areas that had experienced little or no fighting, such as western Massachusetts (Hampshire County), central Connecticut (Wethersfield), southern New Jersey (Salem County), and Lunenburg County, Virginia. Weapons had been lost in service elsewhere, and wastage had claimed other firearms. Preventing the wastage of weapons was a particular concern for Washington, who believed—somewhat counterintuitively—that a soldier or militiaman was harder on a privately owned firearm because "he is at liberty to use his own firelock as he pleases."[248] But decay and wastage were inevitable, especially in the field; the average life expectancy of an eighteenth-century British military musket is believed to have been eight to ten years.[249] During the economic downturn after the war, men may not have had the funds to purchase a new firearm or may not have seen a need to purchase one after independence had been secured.

The states were in no position to supply the militias' lack of arms during the 1780s. Writing during this period on the state of Virginia, former governor Jefferson explained that "the law requires every militia-man to provide himself with arms usual in regular service [i.e., Continental Army]. But this injunction was always indifferently complied with, and the arms they had have been so frequently called for to arm the regulars [the American Continentals], that in the lower parts of the country they are entirely disarmed. In the middle country a fourth or fifth part of them may have such firelocks as they had provided to destroy the noxious animals which infest their farms."[250] Near the end of the decade another former wartime governor, Patrick Henry, lamented, "We have learned by experience, that necessary as it is to have arms, and though our Assembly has, by a succession of laws for many years endeavored to have the militia completely armed, it is still far from being the case."[251] Militia returns confirm their assessment. By the early 1780s, only 37.2 percent of Virginia's militiamen carried private arms, another 9.2 percent had public arms, and the remaining 53.8 percent appear to have lacked the necessary firearms.[252]

Other state militias were probably in no better shape in the aftermath of the War of Independence. In Pennsylvania, some militiamen remained dependent on publicly supplied firearms and protested late in 1787 when the state

TABLE 9. PROBATE INVENTORIES OF MALES CONTAINING GUNS, RIFLES, PISTOLS, AND SWORDS, SELECTED AREAS, EARLY 1780S.

Locations and dates	Number of inventories in sample	Percentage of inventories with firearm*	Percentage of inventories with rifles	Percentage of inventories with pistols	Percentage of inventories with swords
Plymouth County, Mass., 1784–85	42	54.8	0.0	2.4	9.5
Worcester County, Mass., 1784–85	52	42.3	0.0	1.9	3.8
Hampshire County, Mass., 1784–85	78	48.7	0.0	3.8	5.1
Wethersfield, Conn., 1783–1785	26	30.8	0.0	0.0	23.1
Hudson Valley, N.Y., 1783–1786	25	80.0	0.0	8.0	16.0
Westchester County, N.Y., 1783–1786	37	21.6	0.0	0.0	2.7
Long Island, N.Y., 1783–1786	33	51.5	0.0	18.2	21.2
New York City, 1783–1786	37	24.3	0.0	5.4	5.4
Salem County, N.J., 1784–85	40	27.5	0.0	0.0	5.0
Rural Philadelphia County, 1784–85	78	32.1	1.3	3.8	3.8
Philadelphia, 1784–85	55	10.9	0.0	1.8	7.3
Maryland, 1784–85	59	54.2	0.0	0.0	5.1
York County, Va., 1783–1785	23	61.0	0.0	8.7	8.7
Lunenburg County, Va., 1783–1785	24	45.8	0.0	0.0	20.8
Augusta County, Va., 1784–85	27	66.7	30.0	3.7	7.4
South Carolina, 1784–85	77	44.2.	1.3	9.0	10.4

*Includes inventories with pistols and rifles.

SOURCES:
Plymouth County: Plymouth County Probate Records, vol. 29, microfilm, Massachusetts Archives, Boston.
Worcester County: Worcester County Probate Records, vols. 18–19, microfilm, Massachusetts Archives, Boston.
Hampshire County: Hampshire County Probate Records, vols. 14–16, microfilm, Historic Deerfield Library, Deerfield, Mass.
Wethersfield: Photocopies of Wethersfield Probate Inventories, Research Files, Webb-Deane-Stevens Museum, Wethersfield, Conn. Made from the originals at the Connecticut State Library, Hartford.
Hudson Valley, Westchester County, Long Island, and New York City: New York (State), Court of Probates, microfilm J0301, New York State Archives, Albany.
Salem County: Salem County Inventories, Wills, and Administrative Papers, 1784–85, microfilm, Downs Library, Winterthur Museum, Winterthur, Del.
Rural Philadelphia County and Philadelphia: Wills of the County of Philadelphia, Pennsylvania, 1784–85, microfilm, Downs Library, Winterthur Museum, Winterthur, Del.
Maryland: Queen Anne County, Inventories and Accounts, vol. RW, no. 1, 1784–1786, Maryland Archives; Ann Arundel County, vol. TG, no. 1, 1780–1787, Maryland Archives, both in author's possession.
York County: York County Deeds, Orders and Wills, vols. 19–20, typed transcriptions, Department of Historic Research, Colonial Williamsburg Foundation, Williamsburg, Va.
Lunenburg County: Will Book, no. 3, 1778–1791, microfilm, in author's possession, Amherst College.
August County: Will Book, no. 6, 1778–1787, microfilm, in author's possession, Amherst College.
South Carolina: Charleston County, Inventories A, 1783–1787, microfilm, Historic Deerfield Library, Deerfield, Mass.

called them in to clean them and possibly redistribute them to the state's exposed frontier counties.[253] Three years later Pennsylvania and Kentucky militiamen were mobilized to join General Josiah Harmar's expedition against Natives in the Ohio Country. Major William Ferguson, a regular army officer who inspected their arms, found those of the Kentucky militiamen to be "generally very bad, and unfit for service."[254] The Pennsylvania militiamen "were equipped nearly as the Kentucky, but were worse armed, several were without any [firearms]. The General [Harmar] ordered all the arms in store to be delivered to those who had none, and those whose guns could not be repaired."[255] The quality of men also left much to be desired, "a great number of them *substitutes*, who probably had never fired a gun . . . and were so awkward, that they could not take their gunlocks off to oil them, and put them on again, nor could they put in their flints."[256]

It is also telling that in the fall and winter of 1786–87, both sides in the confrontation in western Massachusetts that came to be known as Shays's Rebellion appear to have lacked adequate supplies of firearms, or at the very least supplies of adequate firearms. Historians David Szatmary and Leonard Richards both claim that when Shays's men approached the arsenal in Springfield, Massachusetts, they had only "old guns and wooden clubs" or "old muskets, some with only swords and bludgeons."[257] Things were not much better on the government side. Letters written by militia general William Shepard revealed his desperate situation: he claimed that his mobilized militiamen were "not more than half armed" and "half of the Militia which will be in the field for the defense of the public stores, will not have arms so good as clubs."[258] It is not clear if he was complaining that only half of his men had firearms or that half their guns were worthless, or possibly both. Fragmentary militia returns from the late 1780s suggest that somewhere between 25 and 60 percent of the militiamen in central Massachusetts appeared armed at musters; only about one-fifth had a bayonet.[259]

Given the apparent inadequacy of available firearms, both sides were drawn to the central government's arsenal, with its seven thousand military muskets with bayonets and supplies of powder. General Shepard implored Henry Knox, the Confederation's secretary of war, to give him permission to use the arsenal's stores to arm his state militiamen. In response, Knox claimed that although he was "restrained from authorizing any appropriation of Arms and Stores for state purposes," he was of the opinion "that propriety & necessity would justify the action of taking part of the arms and ammunition for the defense of the remainder."[260] Taking the hint, Shepard armed his militiamen from the Confederation's store of firearms, rolled out three canons, and repelled the insurgents. Once more, as they had in North Carolina in 1771 and would again during the Whiskey Rebellion in 1794, militiamen put down armed citizens protesting what they saw as government oppression.

During this period, some military and political leaders sought to address the problems involving the organization and arming of state militias by establishing national standards and creating a select militia.[261] The most ambitious and detailed proposal was first put forth by Secretary Knox. In 1786 he published a plan calling for the classing of militia into an Advanced Corps consisting of men aged eighteen to twenty, a Main or Active Corps of men aged twenty-one to forty-five, and a Reserve Corps of men from forty-six to sixty. Each state's Advanced Corps, which in its purpose, composition, and training resembled the minutemen of 1775, was to train forty-two days a year and be ready when called upon to march anywhere in the United States.[262] Each new member of the Advanced Corps was to be presented "his arms by the general in the name of the people of the state as indispensable appurtenances of his character as a free citizen."[263] These military muskets, which would conform to uniform specifications supplied by the United States government, would remain the "unalterable" property of the militiaman.[264] After receiving a favorable reception in the Confederation Congress, Knox's plan was not adopted.[265]

Still, other leaders also favored some system involving the creation of a select militia. George Mason of Virginia believed that "thirteen States will never concur in any one system if the disciplining of the Militia be left in their hands." He therefore proposed at the 1787 Constitutional Convention in Philadelphia that "if they [the states] will not give up the power over the whole, they probably will over part of a select militia," which he spoke in favor of.[266] Another delegate to the convention, Alexander Hamilton, agreed with Mason, arguing in Federalist No. 29 that "the scheme of disciplining the whole nation must be abandoned as mischievous or impractical," and therefore "the attention of the government ought particularly to be directed to the formation of a select corps of moderate size upon such principles as will really fit for service in case of need."[267] At the convention, Oliver Ellsworth of Connecticut argued against a select militia on practical, not ideological, grounds, fearing that it "would be followed by a ruinous declension of the great body of the Militia."[268]

Instead of providing for a select militia, the convention's Committee of Eleven reported a clause that empowered Congress "to make laws for organizing, arming & disciplining the Militia, and for governing such parts as may be employed in the service of the United States reserving to the States respectively, the appointment of officers, and the authority of training the militia according to the discipline prescribed."[269] A member of this committee, Rufus King of Massachusetts, offered by way of explanation that "by *organizing* the Committee meant, proportioning the officers & men—by *arming,* specifying the kind size and caliber of arms—& by *disciplining* prescribing the manual exercise evolutions &c."[270] An apparently concerned James Madison observed that "arming" as explained did not extend to furnishing arms, nor did the term "disciplining" to "penalties & Courts martial for enforcing them."[271] By way of reassurance, King "added, to his former explanation that *arming* meant not only to provide for uniformity of arms, but included authority to regulate the modes of furnishing, either by the militia themselves, the State Governments, or the National Treasury; that laws for *disciplining,* must involve penalties and every thing necessary for enforcing penalties." Madison emphasized that "the primary object is to secure an effectual discipline of the Militia," because he believed that "the States neglect their Militia now, and the more they are consolidated into one nation, the less each will rely on its own interior provisions for its safety & the less prepare its Militia for that purpose."[272] Another delegate from Virginia, Edmund Randolph, echoed Madison's sentiments, "observing that the Militia were every where neglected by the State Legislatures, the members of which courted popularity too much to enforce a proper discipline. Leaving the appointment of officers to the States protects the people agst. every apprehension that could produce murmur."[273]

Other delegates at the convention remained skeptical of granting these powers over the state militias to Congress. Delegate Elbridge Gerry of Massachusetts asserted that "he had as lief let the Citizens of Massachusetts be disarmed, as to take the command from the States, and subject them to the Genl Legislature. It would be regarded as a system of Despotism."[274] Oliver Ellsworth offered an alternative militia clause providing Congress with the power "to establish an uniformity of arms, exercise & organization for the Militia, and to provide for the Government of them when called into the service of the U. States." The object of his substitute wording was "to refer the plan for the Militia to the General Govt. but leave the execution of it to the State Govts."[275] Maryland delegate Luther Martin was also "confident that the States would never give up the power over the Militia; and that, if they were (to do so) the militia would be less attended to by the Genl. than by the State Governments."[276] Still, the proposal to give Congress the power to make laws for organizing, arming, and disciplining the militia passed by a vote of nine to two, with the delegations of Connecticut and Maryland in opposition.

The adoption of the Constitution's militia clause as written did leave several concerns unresolved. Did the clause enable Congress to organize the militia by creating a select militia as Mason advocated and Hamilton and others favored? Did the clause commit the new central government and its "National Treasury" to furnishing military muskets to arm the various state militias? Just what powers were retained by the states to organize, arm, discipline, and employ their militias, particularly in the absence of action by the central government? As delegate Abraham Baldwin of Georgia observed a few years after the Constitutional Convention, "the subject of the Militia" was one of those areas "left a little unsettled," believing that they could "without any great risk, be settled by practice or by amendments."[277]

These unsettled matters concerning the militia clause served to fuel the fears of some who opposed the proposed federal Constitution. At least one critic warned against the possible creation of a select militia by the central government. A New York Anti-Federalist (probably Melancton Smith) writing as Federal Farmer warned that "the constitution ought to secure a genuine and guard against a select militia, by providing that the militia shall always be kept well organized, armed, and disciplined and include, according to the past and general usage of the states, all men capable of bearing arms."[278] He was convinced that "the mind that aims at a select militia, must be influenced by a truly antirepublican principle."[279] In order "to preserve liberty," Federal Farmer argued," it is essential that the whole body of the people always possess arms, and be taught alike, especially when young how to use them."[280] But in Virginia, another prominent Anti-Federalist, William Grayson, praised England's "excellent militia law," which provided for "thirty thousand select militia," and he wanted to see something similar "established by the general government."[281] Not even all Anti-Federalists spoke with one voice on select militias.

More common were Anti-Federalist complaints about potential abuses of the militia clause that could arise from either overregulating or underregulating state militias. These warnings were all rooted in the claim that the proposed Constitution gave the central government exclusive power to organize, arm, and discipline the militia. William Grayson feared that "as the exclusive power of arming, organizing, &c. was given to Congress, they might entirely neglect them; or they might be armed in one part of the union, and totally neglected in another," which was the case in Great Britain, where Scotland and Ireland lacked militias.[282] Former convention delegate and Anti-Federalist Luther Martin also claimed that the central government could destroy the militia by deliberate inaction because it was granted "the powers by *which only* the militia can be organized and armed, and neglect of which they may be rendered utterly useless and insignificant, when it suits the ambitious purposes of government."[283] In almost the same breath, Martin suggested that this power could also be used to overdiscipline the militia "to improperly oppress and harass the militia, the better to reconcile them to the idea of regular troops, who might relieve them of the burden."[284] As Alexander Hamilton observed when discussing the constitution's militia clause in Federalist No. 29, "there is a striking incoherence in the objections which have appeared and sometimes from the same quarter, not much calculated to inspire a very favourable opinion of the sincerity or fair dealing of their authors."[285]

The most revealing exchanges on the possible threat to destroy the state militias by disarming them occurred at the Virginia ratifying convention during June 1788, for they clearly reflected in part concerns arising from its own militia's critical need to obtain military muskets. At the Philadelphia convention, George Mason had been the delegate who originally proposed giving the central government the power "to make laws for the regulation and discipline of the Militia of the several states,"[286] but now he saw the proposed Constitution's militia clause as giving the central government the "power to abolish our militia."[287] He argued that "the militia may be here destroyed by that method which has been practised in other parts of the world before: that is, by rendering them useless by disarming them."[288] How would they be disarmed? By failing to provide them with needed arms: "Under various pretenses, Congress may neglect to provide for arming and disciplining the militia; and the state governments cannot do it, for Congress has an exclusive right to arm them &c."[289] Mason therefore wished "that, in case the general government should neglect to arm and discipline the militia, there should be an express declaration, that the state governments might arm and discipline them."[290]

The responses to Mason's arguments by those who supported the proposed Constitution made clear that they too regarded public arming of the militia as necessary, but had more faith in the central government's role in the process. Convention delegate James Madison asked rhetorically, "Have we not found that, while the power of arming and governing the militia has been solely vested in the state legislature, they were neglected and rendered unfit for immediate service?" He was confident that "the general government can do it more effectively."[291] If the general government did fail to do so, George Nicholas sought to reassure his fellow Virginians with the argument that "the states would have the power to arm them. The power of arming them is concurrent between the general and state governments."[292] Supporting Nicholas's belief in concurrent power, another delegate to the Virginia ratifying convention, John Marshall, had no doubt that "if Congress neglect our militia, we can arm them ourselves. Cannot Virginia import arms? Cannot she put them into the hands of her militiamen?"[293] To reassure further those who remained unconvinced, the Virginia convention adopted twenty recommended amendments to the new federal Constitution, the eleventh of which provided "that each State respectively shall have the power to provide for organizing, arming and disciplining its own militia, whensoever Congress shall omit or neglect to provide the same."[294]

To respond to Anti-Federalist critics of the Constitution and honor his personal pledge to his constituents, Congressman James Madison introduced at the first session of Congress a series of proposed amendments to the recently adopted Constitution. Included among his proposed amendments was one providing that "the right of the people to keep and bear arms shall not be infringed; a well armed, and well regulated militia being the best security of a free country: but no person religiously scrupulous of bearing arms, shall be compelled to render military service in person."[295] The House reversed the order of the first and second clauses, dropped the reference to "a well armed militia," and after "bear arms" added "for the common defence."[296] The Senate dropped the clause about religious scruples and also the phrase "for the common defence," probably because this language, found in the Articles of Confederation, referred specifically to the collective defense of the United States and could possibly be misconstrued to interfere with the individual states' ability to preserve internal order and suppress insurrections.[297]

The Senate also apparently attempted to include in the amendment language banning or limiting the federal government's ability to supply arms to the militia. After observing the Senate's consideration of the proposed amendment, the Virginian John Randolph informed his stepfather, St. George Tucker, that "a Majority of the Senate were for not allowing the militia arms & if two thirds had agreed it would have been an amendment to the Constitution."[298] This unsuccessful effort may have been a preemptive strike by senators from states with relatively well-armed militias to secure constitutional language that would prevent or limit the federal government's ability to arm state militias, particularly the poorly armed southern militias. As finally approved and adopted, the Second Amendment did seek to address the concerns of those who feared that Congress would either overregulate the militia or alternatively neglect to organize, arm, or discipline the militia. But it left unresolved for the time being the question whether the "National Treasury" would actually supply the state militias with needed military arms. This fight with clear regional preferences for and against federal funding did arise during debates over the 1798 federal militia act and again over the 1808 militia act, when Congress finally voted to begin appropriating annually $200,000 to enable the states to arm their militias.[299]

The War of Independence had greatly expanded the demands placed on the various state militias, inflated their reputations in some quarters, and increased their ideological importance without really solving the problems associated with their ongoing decay and with the quantity and quality of their firearms.[300] Outside of New England and South Carolina, the reality and ideal of an inclusive militia of well-armed yeoman farmers either had disappeared by the early 1700s or had never even existed in practice. By the mid-1700s, all of the colonies needed considerable quantities of publicly supplied military muskets to arm their provincial soldiers in the field, and in some instances had to provide publicly owned firearms to some militiamen who lacked firearms. During this period the private ownership of firearms among adult males still appears to have remained widespread, though it was far from universal and in some areas may have been declining over the course of the eighteenth century. The problem of adequately arming troops in the field and in some instances arming militiamen became only more pronounced during the War of Independence, when the importation of over 100,000 military muskets—perhaps as many as 200,000—from France enabled the regiments of the Continental Army and many militiamen south of the Delaware River to carry on the fight.[301] The situation was if anything worse after the war ended because the quantities and quality of privately owned arms in the hands of militiamen had declined even further by the 1780s and 1790s.

So when most political leaders addressed questions about organizing, arming, and disciplining the militia during the 1780s and 1790s, they were more concerned with the arming or rearming of the existing state militias than with the possible disarming of some imaginary "citizens' militia" or "people's militia." And no one was threatening to take away people's rifles, squirrel guns, fowlers, and pistols.[302] Leaders were instead grappling with actual problems evident in the thirteen state militias, some of which no longer appeared to be capable of ensuring the "security of a free State" without improved organization, better training, and thousands of publicly supplied military muskets with bayonets. In 1798, a protest meeting in Kentucky captured this changed environment by resolving that "standing armies are dangerous to liberty and that a well regulated and well armed militia are the only natural and safe defenders of a republican government; that it was and is the duty of both the general and state government to provide arms for this purpose; that they have neglected to perform this duty; and that it is now incumbent on every freeman to furnish himself without delay, at his own expence."[303] Even on the American frontier in 1798, arming oneself for militia service was no longer regarded as the first and obvious choice.

Once one knows the real history of regulating and arming the militia that members of the founding generation knew, one appreciates the federal Constitution's concern "to provide for organizing, arming and disciplining" the state militias and understands the Second Amendment's effort to ensure that this was actually done. One also has to be aware that by the late 1700s, militia arms were not all privately owned, and not all privately owned firearms, particularly pistols, were militia arms, nor had they ever been. And the Second Amendment was not about protecting handguns for self defense, but securing muskets for national defense.

NOTES

The author thanks Saul Cornell, Jan Dizard, Clark Dougan, Evan Haefeli, Richard H. Kohn, Randoph Roth, Seanegan Scully, and John Servos for their comments and suggestions.

1. See David Hackett Fischer, *Paul Revere's Ride* (New York: Oxford University Press, 1994), for the best account and explanation of the performance of the Massachusetts minutemen and militiamen at Lexington and Concord on April 19, 1775. See also Charles Neimeyer, "'Town Born, Turn Out': Town Militias, Tories, and the Struggle for Control of the Massachusetts Backcountry," in *War and Society in the American Revolution: Mobilization and Home Fronts*, ed. John Resch and Walter Sargent (DeKalb: Northern Illinois University Press, 2007), 23–41.

2. *District of Columbia et al. v. Heller*, 554 U.S. (Prelim. Print 570), 596 (2008).

3. Ibid., 627.

4. Ibid., 599–600.

5. Ibid., 627.

6. Ibid., 629.

7. Until 1840 there was no such thing as the "unorganized" militia and, therefore, no distinction between the organized and the unorganized militia. After 1840 the states moved to militia systems that relied on voluntary uniformed militia companies, which became the only organized, active militias on the eve of the Civil War. All other men between the ages of eighteen and forty-five were enrolled in the inactive or "unorganized" militia, which did not train but could be called upon to defend the country during emergencies. See Lyle D. Brundage, "The Organization, Administration, and Training of the United States Ordinary and Volunteer Militia, 1792–1861" (Ph.D. diss., University of Michigan, 1958), ii, 88, 314–39.

8. Lt. Col. Marvin A. Kreidberg and 1st Lt. Merton G. Henry, *History of the Military Mobilization in the United States Army, 1775–1945* (Washington, D.C.: Department of the Army, 1955), 3. For two existing overviews of variations and changes in the colonial military institutions, see John Shy, *A People Numerous and Armed: Reflections on the Military Struggle for American Independence*, rev. ed. (Ann Arbor: University of Michigan Press, 1990), 29–41; and Don Higginbotham, "The Military Institutions of Colonial America: The Rhetoric and the Reality," in *Tools of War: Instruments, Ideas, and Institutions of Warfare, 1445–1871*, ed. John A. Lynn (Urbana: University of Illinois Press, 1990), 131–53.

9. Kreidberg and Henry, *History of the Military Mobilization*, 4.

10. For existing studies that suggest the variations in gun ownership over time and space, see James Lindgren and Justin Lee Heather, "Counting Guns in Early America," *William and Mary Law Review* 43 (2002): 1777–1842; Robert H. Churchill, "Gun Ownership in Early America: A Survey of Manuscript Militia Returns," *William and Mary Quarterly*, 3rd ser., 60.3 (July 2003): 615–42. Like these authors, I am critical of the approach and findings in Michael Bellesiles, *Arming America: The Origins of a National Gun Culture* (New York: Knopf, 2000).

11. For evidence of arms shipments for particular plantations, see *Records of the Virginia Company of London*, ed. Susan Myra Kingsbury, vol. 3 (Washington, D.C.: Government Printing Office, 1906–1935), 94–98, 178–79.

12. William L. Shea, *The Virginia Militia in the Seventeenth Century* (Baton Rouge: Louisiana State University Press, 1983), 31, 54, 75, 92–93; Warren M. Billings, *Sir William Berkeley and the Forging of Colonial Virginia* (Baton Rouge: Louisiana State University Press, 2004), 226–27. For additional evidence of militia companies that were incompletely armed in the 1670s, see Philip Alexander Bruce, *Institutional History of Virginia in the Seventeenth Century*, 2 vols. (New York: G. P. Putnam's Sons, 1910), 2:39–40.

13. *Records of the Governor and Company of Massachusetts Bay in New England*, ed. Nathaniel Shurtleff, 5 vols. (Boston: W. White printer to the Commonwealth, 1853–54), 2:67.

14. *Archives of Maryland*, ed. William Hand Browne et al., 72 vols. (Baltimore: Maryland Historical Society, 1883–1972), 3:99–101.

15. Ibid., 3:132–33.

16. Timothy B. Riordan, *The Plundering Time: Maryland and the English Civil War, 1645-1646* (Baltimore: Maryland Historical Society, 2004), 209.

17. *Archives of Maryland*, 1:254–55.

18. For the cost of new guns and swords see *The Inconveniencies that have happened to some Persons which have transported themselves from England to Virginia* . . . (London: Felix Kyngston, 1622), broadside, and Harold L. Peterson, *Arms and Armor in Colonial America, 1526-1783* (1956; Mineola, N.Y.: Dover Publications, 2000), 321. Basing his conclusion on the assumption that new firearms cost £4 to £5, Michael Bellesiles claims that they were too expensive; see Bellesiles, *Arming America*, 106. Another scholar characterized seventeenth-century matchlock muskets as "relatively inexpensive." See Patrick M. Malone, *The Skulking Kind of War: Technology and Tactics among the New England Indians* (1991; Baltimore: Johns Hopkins University Press, 1993), 39.

19. In Plymouth Colony, towns supplied pikes. The colonies of New Haven and Connecticut also maintained "a large number of pikes." See Peterson, *Arms and Armor in Colonial America*, 99.

20. This was the assessment of commissioners from England in 1665. See *Calendar of State Papers Colonial,* ed. William N. Sainsbury et al. (London: Public Record Office, 1860–1994), 1661–1668, no. 1000, 300.

21. James Deetz and Patricia Scott Deetz, *The Times of Their Lives: Life, Love, and Death in Plymouth Colony* (New York: Anchor Books, 2001), 2; Plymouth Archaeological Rediscovery Project, "Firearms in Plymouth Colony," 1–11, and table pages, 1–4, http://plymoutharch.tripod.com/id71.html and http://plymoutharch.tripod.com/id73.html.

22. Emerson Baker, "The Archaeology of 1690, the Year of Living Dangerously in New England," 5, manuscript in the author's possession.

23. R. James Ringer, "Phips's Fleet," *National Geographic* 198.2 (August 2000): 80. See also Charles Bradley, Phil Dunning, and Gerard Gusset, "Material Culture from the Elizabeth and Mary (1690): Individuality and Social Status in a Late Seventeenth-Century New England Assemblage," in *Archéologiques, Collection Hors-Série 1: Mer et Monde; Question d'archéologie Maritime,* Association des Archéologues du Québec (2003): 150–70.

24. *Archives of Maryland,* 10:24, 40–41, 425, 429.

25. Ibid., 3:345.

26. Ibid., 1:412.

27. Ibid., 15:13.

28. Ibid., 7:55.

29. Roger B. Manning, *Apprenticeship in Arms: The Origins of the British Army, 1585–1702* (New York: Oxford University Press, 2006), 132.

30. *Archives of Maryland,* 7:18.

31. For percentages of servants in the population, see Lois G. Carr and David William Jordan, *Maryland's Revolution of Government, 1689–1692* (Ithaca: Cornell University Press, 1974), 182–83. For information on firearms ownership, see Gloria L. Main, *Tobacco Colony Life in Early Maryland, 1650–1720* (Princeton: Princeton University Press, 1982), 176, 242.

32. *Archives of Maryland,* 7:30.

33. Ibid., 8:56–57.

34. Ibid., 8:65; 8:56–57, 62–65, 67.

35. Ibid., 20:224.

36. Carr and Jordan, *Maryland's Revolution of Government,* 17, 46–47, 52–60.

37. *Archives of Maryland,* 19:508, 557.

38. Ibid.

39. Ibid., 30:628.

40. Ibid., 39:113.

41. On the impressment of firearms, see "Causes of Discontent in Virginia, 1676: Gloster County Grievances and Surry County Grievances" *Virginia Magazine of*

History and Biography 2.2 (October 1894): 168, 171–72; "Causes of Discontent in Virginia, 1676: Isle of Wight Grievances," *Virginia Magazine of History and Biography* 2.4 (April–October 1895): 387.

42. Tisdale, *Soldiers of Virginia Colony*, 166–68.

43. "A Copie of a Letter to the 20 Colonels in Virginia touching the Militia," November 20, 1680, in Sainsbury, *Calendar of State Papers Colonial, 1677–1680*, no. 1600, 634.

44. Shea, *Virginia Militia in the Seventeenth Century*, 121. For evidence of inadequately armed militia companies during the 1680s, see Bruce, *Institutional History*, 2:39, 44.

45. Shea, *Virginia Militia in the Seventeenth Century*, 120–21, 125–26, 127–30, 138–39.

46. "Order of the Governor and Council of Virginia, October 24, 1687," in *Executive Journal of the Council of Colonial Virginia*, ed. H. R. McIlwaine, vol. 1 (Richmond, 1925), 85.

47. For 1680, see "A Copie of a Letter to the 20 Colonels in Virginia touching the Militia"; for 1689, see Evarts B. Greene and Virginia Harrington, *American Population before the Federal Census of 1790* (1981; New York: Columbia University Press, 1932), 137.

48. Bruce, *Institutional History*, 2:7.

49. William W. Hening, ed., *Statutes at Large: Being a Collection of All the Laws of Virginia, from the First Session of the Legislature, in the Year 1619*, 13 vols. (Richmond, 1810–1823), 3:13–14.

50. Shea, *Virginia Militia in the Seventeenth Century*, 119–20; Bruce, *Institutional History*, 2:44.

51. *Calendar of Virginia State Papers and Other Manuscripts, 1652–1781*, ed. William P. Palmer [et al.], 11 vols. (1875–1893; New York: Kraus Reprint, 1968), 1:81.

52. Governor Alexander Spotswood to the Council of Trade, Virginia, July 26, 1712, in *The Official Letters of Alexander Spotswood, Lieutenant-Governor of the Colony of Virginia, 1710–1722*, 2 vols. (Richmond: Virginia Historical Society, 1882–1885), 1:166–67.

53. Shea, *Virginia Militia in the Seventeenth Century*, 139.

54. Anna L. Hawley, "The Meaning of Absence: Household Inventories in Surry County, Virginia, 1690–1715," in *Early American Probate Inventories: The Dublin Seminar for New England Folklife, Annual Proceedings, 1987*, ed. Peter Benes (Boston: Boston University, 1989), 28, table 1.

55. Kyle F. Zelner, *A Rabble in Arms: Massachusetts Towns and Militiamen during King Philip's War* (New York: New York University Press, 2009), esp. 141–80.

56. Governor Joseph Dudley to Council of Trade and Plantations, November 15, 1710, in *Calendar of State Papers Colonial*, ed. Cecil Headlam (London: Printed for His Majesty's Stationary Office, 1924), 1710–1711, no. 491, 268.

57. On the nonmilitary uses of firearms see Randolph Roth, "Guns, Gun Culture, and Homicide: The Relationship between Firearms, the Uses of Firearms, and Interpersonal Violence," *William and Mary Quarterly*, 3rd ser., 59.1 (January 2002): 230–31.

58. Japp Jacobs, *New Netherland: A Dutch Colony in Seventeenth-Century America* (Leiden: Brill, 2005), 366–71.

59. *Journal of Jasper Danckaerts, 1670–1680*, ed. Bartlett B. James and J. Franklin Jameson (New York, 1913), 239; Edmund Andros, "Copy of the Proceeding Answers to Inquiries Concerning New York," April 1678, in *Calendar of State Papers Colonial, 1677–1680*, no. 660, 237. According to the *Oxford English Dictionary*, at this time "fireman" referred to one who uses firearms; it was not until the early 1700s that "fireman" referred to one who extinguishes fires.

60. Governor George Clark to the Board of Trade, June 2, 1738, in *Documents Relative to the Colonial History of the State of New York*, ed. Edmund B. O'Callaghan and Berthold Fernow, 15 vols. (Albany: Weed, Parsons, 1856–1887), 6:120. On the tradition of "shooting the parrot," or wooden *papegaai* that sat on a pole, see Donna Merwick, *Possessing Albany, 1630–1710: The Dutch and English Experiences* (New York Cambridge University Press, 1990), 79.

61. William J. Frost, "Religious Liberty in Pennsylvania," *Pennsylvania Magazine of History and Biography* 105 (1981): 427, 442.

62. Richard R. Beeman, *The Varieties of Political Experience in Eighteenth-Century America* (Philadelphia: University of Pennsylvania Press, 2004), 206.

63. Governor Morris to the Duke of Newcastle, Burlington, October 18, 1740, in *Archives of the State of New Jersey*, 1st ser., ed. William A. Whitehead et al., 10 vols. (Newark: State of New Jersey, 1880–1928), 6:104.

64. Ibid., 6:105.

65. Edwin Platt Tanner, *The Province of New Jersey, 1664–1738* (New York: Columbia University Press, 1908), 559.

66. *Laws of the Government of New-Castle, Kent and Suffolk Upon Delaware* (Philadelphia: Benjamin Franklin, 1742), 171–78.

67. The 1740 militia law was not included in the 1752 compilation of the laws of Delaware. *Laws of the Government of New-Castle, Kent and Suffolk Upon Delaware* (Philadelphia: Benjamin Franklin and D. Hall, 1752).

68. Thomas Nairne quoted in Peter Wood, *Black Majority: Negroes in Colonial South Carolina from 1670 through the Stono Rebellion* (New York: Knopf, 1974), 126, n. 116.

69. Ibid., 124–30; Fitzhugh McMaster, *Soldiers and Uniforms: South Carolina*

Military Affairs, 1670–1775 (Columbia: University of South Carolina Press for the South Carolina Tricentennial Commission, 1971), 17. Slaves continued to serve in the South Carolina militia into the early 1770s. See Clyde R. Ferguson, "Functions of the Partisan-Militia in the South during the American Revolution: An Interpretation," in *The Revolutionary War in the South: Power, Conflict, and Leadership*, ed. W. Robert Higgins (Durham, N.C.: Duke University Press, 1979), 241.

70. Theodore Harry Jabbs, "The South Carolina Militia, 1663–1733" (Ph.D. diss., University of North Carolina, Chapel Hill, 1973), 411–14.

71. De Witt Baily, *Small Arms of the British Forces in America, 1664–1815* (Woonsocket, R.I.: Mowbray Publishers, 2009), 110–11, 113; De Witt Baily, "The Wilsons: Gunmakers to the Empire, 1730–1832," *American Society of Arms Collectors Bulletin*, no. 85 (April 2002): 11; McMaster, *Soldiers and Uniforms*, 11.

72. Wayne E. Lee, *Crowds and Soldiers in Revolutionary North Carolina: The Culture of Violence in Riot and War* (Gainesville: University Press of Florida, 2001), 130.

73. "De Graffenried's Manuscript," in *Colonial Records of North Carolina*, ed. William L. Saunders, 10 vols. (Raleigh: State of North Carolina, 1886–1890), 1:953.

74. James Biser Whisker, *The American Colonial Militia*, 5 vols. (Lewiston, N.Y.: Edwin Mellen Press, 1997), 5:98–99.

75. *Colonial Records of North Carolina*, 4:745.

76. Mathew Rowan to My Lords [of Trade], Cape Fear, June 3, 1754, ibid., 5:124–25; Governor Dobbs to the Board of Trade, Newbern, March 15, 1756, ibid., 5:571; Governor Dobbs to Earl of Loudon, Newbern, July 10, 1756, ibid., 5:599.

77. Sally E. Hadden, *Slave Patrols: Law and Violence in Virginia and the Carolinas* (Cambridge: Harvard University Press, 2003), 14–40; James M. Johnson, *Militiamen, Rangers, and Redcoats: The Military in Georgia, 1754–1776* (Macon: Mercer University Press, 1992), 29.

78. Quoted in Whisker, *American Colonial Militia*, 5:141.

79. McMaster, *Soldiers and Uniforms*, 38–41; Johnson, *Militiamen, Rangers, and Redcoats*, 1–16.

80. *State Records of North Carolina*, ed. Walter Clark, 16 vols. (Raleigh: P. M. Hale, 1886–1907), 13:244–47.

81. *Archives of Maryland*, 46:32, 34–35, 80, 97; Henning, *Statutes*, 6:118.

82. *Archives of Maryland*, 6:353.

83. "Observations in Several Voyages and Travels in America: From the London Magazine, July 1746," *William and Mary Quarterly* 15.3 (January 1907): 5–6.

84. Samuel J. Newland, *Pennsylvania Militia: The Early Years, 1669–1792* (Annville: Pennsylvania National Guard Foundation, 1997), 29–47; Joseph

Seymour, *The Pennsylvania Associators, 1747–1777* (Yardley, Penn.: Westholme, 2012), 30–60; Leon de Valinger Jr., *Colonial Military Organization in Delaware, 1638–1776* (Wilmington: Delaware Tercentenary Commission, 1938), 41–42.

85. Seymour, *Pennsylvania Asssociators*, 45.

86. "Form of Association," in *The Papers of Benjamin Franklin*, ed. Leonard W. Labaree et al., 40 vols. to date (New Haven: Yale University Press, 1959–), 3:208.

87. Ibid.

88. *Philadelphia Gazette*, March 8, 1748.

89. From 1712 to 1738 Massachusetts passed no laws to revise or render more effective its militia act. *Acts and Resolves, Public and Private, of the Province of Massachusetts*, 21 vols. (Boston: State of Massachusetts, 1869–1922), 1:697, 2:939–41.

90. "A List of Officers & Soldiers in the First Regiment in the County of Worcester Where of John Chandler Esq. is Col.," taken May 1744, dated June 1, 1744, in Mass. Collections, box 3, folder 4, Militia Returns, Officers' Commissions, and Misc. Papers, 1629–ca. 1869, American Antiquarian Society, Worcester, Mass. Five of the companies are cited as being "intirely deficient as to ammunition" or "want half their ammunition," but no mention is made of deficiencies in firearms.

91. Thomas Procter to Samuel Waldo, St. Georges [Maine], May 25, 1744, in Samuel Waldo Papers, Massachusetts Historical Society, Boston.

92. John Ulmer to Col. Arthur Noable, Broadbay, May 18, 1744, Samuel Waldo Papers, Massachusetts Historical Society, Boston.

93. For the forts, see Michael Coe, "The Line of Forts: The Archeology of the Mid-Eighteenth Century on the Massachusetts Frontier," in *New England Historical Archeology: Dublin Seminar for New England Folklife*, ed. Peter Benes (Boston: Boston University, 1977), 44–55. For examples of arming province soldiers serving on the line of forts with firearms paid for by the province with "gun money" or borrowed, see Elijah Williams, Account Book 1746–1756, vol. 2, "Old Soldiers' Book," 46, and 44 in the second series of page numbers near the back of the account book, Pocumtuck Valley Memorial Association, Deerfield, Mass.

94. John K. Mahon, *History of the Militia and the National Guard* (New York: Macmillan, 1983), 5; David Richard Millar, "The Militia, the Army, and Independency in Colonial Massachusetts" (PhD. diss., Cornell University, 1967), 148–53.

95. *Acts and Resolves*, 13:370, 432–33, 563–64, 610, 665, 697, 706. The colony of Connecticut also impressed arms, finding that "a considerable number of the souldiers that have inlisted themselves to go on the intended expedition against Cape Breton are destitute of firearms and other accoutrements, and there not being a sufficient number to be purchased." See *Public Records of the Colony of Connecticut*, ed. Charles Hoadly, vol. 9 (Hartford: Case, Lockwood & Brainard,

1876), 95–96. At least 20 percent of the 516 men in the Connecticut regiment sent to Cape Breton had to be issued arms procured by the government. See *Collections of the Connecticut Historical Society*, vol. 13 (Hartford, 1911), 83–85.

96. Hezekiah Huntington's Accounts, 1746–47, ms. S-585, Massachusetts Historical Society, Boston; *Records of the Colony of Rhode Island and Providence Plantation in New England*, ed. John Russell Bartlett, 10 vols. (Providence: State of Rhode Island, 1856–1865), 5:172–73, 180, 236.

97. *Acts and Resolves*, 15:722. See also John R. Galvin, *The Minute Men: A Compact History of the Defenders of the American Colonies, 1645–1775* (New York: Hawthorne, 1967), 27. The colony of Connecticut had more difficulty arming its troops and had to impress arms. See Harold E. Selesky, *War and Society in Colonial Connecticut* (New Haven: Yale University Press, 1990), 152–53.

98. Governor Thomas Fitch to Sir Thomas Robinson, August 1, 1755, in *Collections of the Connecticut Historical Society*, vol. 1 (Hartford: published for the Society, 1860) 265–66.

99. *Account of the people in the Colony of Rhode-Island, whites, blacks, together with the quantity of arms and ammunition in the hands of private persons*, Early American Imprints, no. 40794 (n.p., 1800).

100. "Form of Association," *Franklin Papers*, 3:208.

101. Peterson, *Arms and Armor in Colonial America*, 14. See also George D. Moller, *American Military Shoulder Arms*, vol. 1: *Colonial and Revolutionary War Arms* (Boulder: University Press of Colorado, 1993), 99, 497.

102. Bill Ahearn, *Muskets of the Revolution and the French and Indian Wars* (Lincoln, R.I.: Andrew Mowbray, 2005), 176.

103. Baily, *Small Arms of the British Forces*, 123.

104. George C. Neumann, *Battle Weapons of the American Revolution: The Historian's Complete Reference* (Texarkana: Scurlock Publishing Company, 1998), 126, 142, 144, 145, 147; Tom Grinslade, *Flintlock Fowlers: The First Guns Made in America* (Texarkana: Scurlock Publishing Company, 2005), 16, 21, 27, 31.

105. Steven C. Eames, *Rustic Warriors: Warfare and the Provincial Soldier on the New England Frontier, 1689–1748* (New York: New York University Press, 2011), 121–22; Neumann, *Battle Weapons of the American Revolution*, 206–10.

106. "Blair Report on the State of the Colonies," reprinted in Louis K. Koontz, *The Virginia Frontier, 1754–1763* (Baltimore: Johns Hopkins University Press, 1925), 170, hereafter cited as "Blair Report"; Governor Thomas Fitch to Sir Thomas Robinson, August 1, 1755, in *Collections of the Connecticut Historical Society*, 1:265–66.

107. Governor Henry Ellis to the Board of Trade, Georgia, May 25, 1757, in *Colonial Records of the State of Georgia: Original Papers of Governors Reynolds, Ellis, Wright, and Others, 1757–1763*, ed. Kenneth Coleman and Milton Ready,

vol. 28, part 1 (Athens: University of Georgia Press, 1976), 29; Baily, *Small Arms of the British Forces*, 121.

108. The 1740 militia law was not included in the 1752 compilation of the laws of Delaware, *Laws of the Government of New-Castle, Kent and Suffolk Upon Delaware* (1752).There is in fact no militia law in this collection of the laws then in force in Delaware.

109. Quoted in William Hunter, *Forts on the Pennsylvania Frontier, 1753–1758* (Harrisburg: Pennsylvania Historical and Museum Commission, 1960), 173.

110. Ibid.

111. Newland, *Pennsylvania Militia*, 82–83.

112. *Laws of the Government of New-Castle, Kent and Suffolk Upon Delaware* (Philadelphia: Benjamin Franklin and D. Hall, 1763), 10, 11–12. See also John A. Munroe, *Colonial Delaware: A History* (Millwood, N.Y.: KTO Press, 1978), 220–23.

113. "Blair Report," 171.

114. M. L. Brown, *Firearms in Colonial America: The Impact on History and Technology, 1492–1792* (Washington, D.C.: Smithsonian Institution Press, 1980), 283; Neumann, *Battle Weapons of the American Revolution*, 203–5.

115. *Archives of Maryland*, 6:353. The sixty-five Maryland inventories included in Table 4 contained eighty-six firearms. Of these, fifty, or 58.1 percent, were old, broken, or in parts.

116. "Blair Report," 166.

117. René Chartrand, *Colonial American Troops, 1610–1774*, 3 vols. (Wellington, England: Osprey Publishing, 2002–2003), 1:34; Washington's Memoranda [Conegogee, June 13, 1758], in *Papers of Henry Bouquet*, vol. 2, *The Forbes Expedition*, ed. S. K. Stevens, Donald H. Kent, and Autumn L. Leonard (Harrisburg: Pennsylvania Historical and Museum Commission, 1951), 83.

118. Henry Bouquet to the Duke of Portland, Fort Du Quesne, December 3, 1758, in *Bouquet Papers*, 2:620.

119. Mathew Rowan to My Lords [of Trade], Cape Fear, June 3, 1754, in *Colonial Records of North Carolina*, 5:124–25; Governor Dobbs to Earl of Loudon, Newbern, July 10, 1756, ibid., 5:599. See also Governor James Glen to Governor Robert Dinwiddie, South Carolina, August 22, 1754, Colonial Records Office, British Archives, Kew, London, 5:14, 502.

120. Governor Dobbs to the Board of Trade, Newbern, March 15, 1756, in *Colonial Records of North Carolina*, 5:571.

121. Governor Dobbs to Earl of Loudoun, New Bern, July 10, 1756, ibid., 5:599.

122. Johnson, *Militiamen, Rangers, and Redcoats*, 17, 26–28.

123. Governor John Reynolds to the Board of Trade, Georgia, January 5, 1756, in *Colonial Records of the State of Georgia: The Original Papers of Governor John*

Reynolds, 1754–1756, ed. Kenneth Coleman and Milton Ready, vol. 27 (Athens: University of Georgia Press, 1977), 104.

124. Governor Henry Ellis to the Board of Trade, London, October 5, 1756, ibid., 27:121–22; Henry Ellis to the Board of Trade, Georgia, May 25, 1757, ibid., 28: pt. 1, 29.

125. For a similar assessment, see Lawrence Henry Gipson, *The British Empire before the American Revolution: The Great War for Empire; Years of Defeat,* vol. 6 (1946; New York: Knopf, 1959), 50.

126. Governor James Glen to Governor Robert Dinwiddie, South Carolina, August 22, 1754, Colonial Office Records, British Archives, Kew, London, 5:14, 503.

127. Col. Henry Bouquet to the Earl of Loudon, Charles Town, August 25, 1757, in *Papers of Henry Bouquet,* vol. 1, ed. S. K. Stevens, Donald H. Kent, and Autumn L Leonard (Harrisburg: Pennsylvania Historical and Museum Commission, 1972), 175.

128. Gipson, *The Great War for Empire,* 6:50.

129. Frederick Stoke Aldridge, "Organization and Administration of the Militia System of Colonial Virginia" (Ph.D. diss., American University, 1964), 159–67.

130. Governor Robert Dinwiddie to the Earl of Loudoun August 9, 1756, in *Official Records of Robert Dinwiddie, Lieutenant Governor of the Colonial of Virginia, 1751–1758,* ed. Robert Alonzo Brock, 2 vols. (Richmond: Virginia Historical Society, 1884), 2:474; see also Aldridge, "Organization and Administration of the Militia System," 115–27.

131. Johnson, *Militiamen, Rangers, and Redcoats,* 32–33.

132. For characterizing the provincials as "quasi-regulars," see Chartrand, *Colonial American Troops,* 3, 34. For characterizing them as "quasi-standing forces" see Mahon, *History of the Militia,* 26.

133. Don Higginbotham, "The Second Amendment in Historical Context," *Constitutional Commentary* 16.2 (Summer 1999): 267; Franklin Thayer Nicholas, "The Organization of Braddock's Army," *William and Mary Quarterly,* 3rd ser., 4.2 (April 1947): 133; J. Luther Sowers and Ross M. Kimmel, "The Maryland Forces, 1756–59," *Military Collector and Historian* 31.2 (Summer 1979): 81.

134. Governor Thomas Fitch to Lords of Trade, Hartford, March 30, 1756, in *Collections of the Connecticut Historical Society,* 1:283. See also Baily, *Small Arms of the British Forces,* 121.

135. Governor Robert Dinwiddie to Sir Thomas Robinson, October 25, 1754, in *Dinwiddie Papers,* 1:353; Dinwiddie to Governor James DeLancy, May 3, 1755, in *Dinwiddie Papers,* 2:22.

136. *Archives of Maryland,* 32:26; "Blair Report," 166; see also Baily, *Small Arms of the British Forces,* 121.

137. For an overview of these efforts see Jim Mullins, *"Of Sorts for Provincials"*: *American Weapons of the French and Indian War* (Elk River, Minn.: Track of the Wolf, 2008), 103–76.

138. Governor Thomas Fitch to Sir Thomas Robinson, August 1, 1755 in *Collections of the Connecticut Historical Society*, 1:267.

139. For Virginia, see James Titus, *The Old Dominion at War: Society, Politics, and Warfare in Late Colonial Virginia* (Columbia: University of South Carolina Press, 1981), 78–91, 176–77; for Pennsylvania, see R. S. Stephenson, "Pennsylvania's Provincial Soldiers in the Seven Years' War," *Pennsylvania History* 62 (1995): 204–9; for Delaware, see Munroe, *Colonial Delaware*, 223–25. For Virginia and Pennsylvania, see also Matthew C. Ward, *Breaking the Backcountry: The Seven Years' War in Virginia and Pennsylvania, 1754–1765* (Pittsburgh: University of Pittsburgh Press, 2003), 113–21.

140. Governor Robert Dinwiddie to Lord Halifax, February, 24, 1756, in *Dinwiddie Papers*, 2:346.

141. Quoted in McMaster, *Soldiers and Uniforms*, 42.

142. For gun ownership among the lowest 20 percent in terms of wealth, see Lindgren and Heather, "Counting Guns in Early America," chart 1, 1790; chart 7, 2002. For gun ownership among those under the age of twenty-five, see ibid., chart 4, 1802.

143. *Colonial Records of Rhode Island*, 5:420, 430–31.

144. "Blair Report," 166; *Archives of Maryland*, 50:534.

145. Governor William Shirley to Henry Fox, Boston, February 24, 1756, and Shirley to Fox, Boston, April 12, 1756, in *Correspondence of William Shirley, Governor of Massachusetts and Military Commander in America, 1731–1760*, ed. Charles Henry Lincoln, 2 vols. (New York: Macmillan, 1912), 2:401, 427; Baily, *Small Arms of the British Forces*, 120.

146. Brenton C. Kemmer, *Redcoats, Yankees, and Allies* (Bowie, Md.: Heritage Press, 1998), 57–58, 61–63, 67, 70–72, 73–76.

147. Baily, *Small Arms of the British Forces*, 121–23; John A. Schultz, "The Disaster of Fort Ticonderoga: The Shortage of Muskets during the Mobilization of 1758," *Huntington Library Quarterly* 14 (1951): 307–15.

148. Colonel Henry Bouquet to General John Forbes, Carlisle, May 25, 1758; Forbes to Bouquet, May 29, 1758; Bouquet to Forbes, Carlisle, May 30, 1758; and John St. Clair to Henry Bouquet, May 31, 1758, in *Papers of Henry Bouquet*, 1:361, 379, 395, 404; Bouquet to Forbes, [Carlisle, June 7, 1758], and Forbes to Bouquet [Philadelphia, June 6, 1758], ibid., 2:47, 103.

149. John St. Clair to Henry Bouquet, Winchester, June 9, 1758, ibid., 2:60.

150. Baily, *Small Arms of the British Forces*, 121.

151. Ibid., 215, 237, 303.

152. De Valinger, *Colonial Military Organization in Delaware*, 52.

153. Alan and Barbara Aimone, "New York's Provincial Militia," *Military Collector and Historian* 33.2 (Summer 1981): 60.

154. Arthur Vollmer, comp., *Backgrounds of Selective Service Military Obligation: The American Tradition; A Compilation of the Enactments of Compulsion from the Earliest Settlements of the Original Thirteen Colonies in 1607 through the Articles of Confederation, 1789*, Special Monograph no. 1, vol. 2 (Washington D.C.: Government Printing Office, 1947), pt. 1:54, pt. 9:340–41.

155. Lee, *Crowds and Soldiers*, 46–96.

156. Governor John Wentworth quoted in Hugh Jameson, "The Organization of the Militia of the Middle States during the American War for Independence, 1775-1781" (Ph.D. diss., University of Michigan, 1936), 160.

157. Hugh Jameson, "Equipment for the Militia of the Middle States," *Journal of the American Military Institute* 3.1 (Spring 1939): 29; John R. Galvin, *The Minutemen: The First Fight: Myths and Realities of the American Revolution* (1989; repr., Washington, D.C.: Brassey's, 1996), 60.

158. Quoted in Jameson, "Organization of the Militia of the Middle States," 161.

159. Albert A. Tilson, "The Militia and Popular Culture in the Upper Valley of Virginia, 1740–1775," *Virginia Magazine of History and Biography* 94.3 (July 1986): 285–306.

160. Johnson, *Militiamen, Rangers, and Redcoats*, 28, 82.

161. Ward, *Breaking the Backcountry*, 258.

162. *Account of the people in the Colony of Rhode-Island*.

163. Neumann, *Battle Weapons of the American Revolution*, 230.

164. Ibid.

165. McMaster, *Soldiers and Uniforms*, 26–33.

166. Brown, *Firearms in Colonial America*, 263–72.

167. John W. Wright, "The Rifle in the American Revolution," *American Historical Review* 29.2 (January 1924): 293–99; Neil L. York, "Pennsylvania Rifle: Revolutionary Weapon in a Conventional War?" *Pennsylvania Magazine of History and Biography* 103.3 (July 1979): 302–24; Neumann, *Battle Weapons of the American Revolution*, 215–25.

168. Archibald Blaine to Henry Bouquet, Ligonier, March 2, 1759, in *The Papers of Henry Bouquet*, vol. 3, ed. Donald H. Kent, Louis M. Waddell, and Autumn L. Leonard (Harrisburg: Pennsylvania Historical and Museum Commission, 1976), 166–67.

169. Lawrence D. Cress, *Citizens in Arms: The Army and the Militia in American Society to the War of 1812* (Chapel Hill: University of North Carolina Press, 1982), 41.

170. For the best discussion of this surprisingly late development, see ibid., 17–52. See also Higginbotham, "Military Institutions of Colonial America," 147–48.

171. Patrick Henry in *Patrick Henry: Life, Correspondence, and Speeches,* ed. William Wirt Henry, 3 vols. (New York: Charles Scribner's Sons, 1891), 1:257–58.

172. For Massachusetts, see Ray Raphael, *The First American Revolution: Before Lexington and Concord* (New York: New Press, 2002), 57–168. See also Ronald L. Boucher, "The Colonial Militia as a Social Institution: Salem, Massachusetts, 1764–1775," *Military Affairs: Journal of the American Military Institute* 37 (December 1973): 127–29. For New Hampshire, see Whisker, *The American Colonial Militia,* 2:124–28.

173. Robert H. Churchill, *To Shake Their Guns in the Tyrant's Face: Libertarian Political Violence and the Origins of the Militia Movement* (Ann Arbor: University of Michigan Press, 2009), 36, 37.

174. Barry Windsor Fowle, "The Maryland Militia during the Revolutionary War: A Revolutionary Organization" (Ph.D. diss., University of Maryland, 1982), 11–40; Michael A. McDonnell, *The Politics of War: Race, Class, and Conflict in Revolutionary Virginia* (Chapel Hill: University of North Carolina Press, 2007), 34–134; Lee, *Crowds and Soldiers,* 146–58; Ferguson, "Functions of the Partisan-Militia," 243–47; Johnson, *Militiamen, Rangers, and Redcoats,* 103–25.

175. Whisker, *American Colonial Militia,* 5:176.

176. Quoted in Fowle, "Maryland Militia," 15.

177. Ibid., 13.

178. Quoted ibid., 38, n. 20.

179. Ibid., 41–52.

180. Ibid., 29–31.

181. Churchill, *To Shake Their Guns in the Tyrant's Face,* 38–40.

182. *Lloyd's Evening Post and British Chronicle,* June 14, 1775, quoted in Whisker, *American Colonial Militia,* 4:26.

183. Governor William Franklin to the Earl of Dartmouth, May 6, 1775, in *Archives of New Jersey,* 10:591–92.

184. Newland, *Pennsylvania Militia,* 125–56. For the struggles surrounding the Associator movement and its political significance, see Steven Rosswurm, *Arms, Country, and Class: The Philadelphia Militia and the "Lower Sort" during the American Revolution* (New Brunswick: Rutgers University Press, 1987).

185. Newland, *Pennsylvania Militia,* 146.

186. *American Archives,* ed. Peter Force, 9 vols. (Washington, D.C.: M. St. Claire Clarke and Peter Force, 1837–1853), 4th ser., 2:45.

187. Stephen R. Taaffe, *The Philadelphia Campaign, 1777–1778* (Lawrence: University Press of Kansas, 2003), 60.

188. *Journals of the Continental Congress, 1774–1789,* ed. Worthington Chauncey Ford et al., 35 vols. (Washington, D.C.: U. S. Government Printing Office, 1904–1976), 2:188.

189. New York Committee of Safety, May 9, 1775, in *American Archives,* 4th ser., 2:530.

190. Brown, *Firearms in Colonial America,* 307–11; Ahearn, *Muskets of the American Revolution,* 148–61; Neumann, *Battle Weapons of the American Revolution,* 131, 135, 137, 139, 147.

191. *Records of the Colony of Rhode Island and Providence Plantations,* 7:477.

192. Governor Nicholas Cooke to General George Washington, January 25, 1776, ibid., 7:501.

193. Robert H. Churchill, "Gun Ownership in Early America," *William and Mary Quarterly,* 3rd. ser. 60.3 (July 2003): 631, table 2.

194. *Records of the Colony of Rhode Island,* 7:478.

195. *Provincial Papers, Documents and Records relating to the Province of New Hampshire from 1764 to 1776,* ed. Nathaniel Bouton, vol. 8 (Nashua: Orren C. Moore, State Printer, 1873), 724–79.

196. Using a slightly different approach to the same data, Robert Churchill estimates that 58 percent of New Hampshire's "men able to bear arms" were armed. See Churchill, "Gun Ownership in Early America," 631, table 2.

197. Ibid., 626, table 1.

198. Moller, *American Military Shoulder Arms,* 1, 206.

199. For examples, see John Reed, Colonel of the Fourth Regiment, Reading, May 5, 1775, Bound Manuscripts, Massachusetts Historical Society, Boston. See also Churchill, "Gun Ownership in Early America," 623.

200. On the government's search for firearms in Massachusetts in 1775 and the need to impress arms, see Richard M. Ketchum, *Decisive Day: The Battle of Bunker Hill* (1962; New York: Henry Holt, 1999), 61, 64, 81, 94, 194, 201; Allen French, *First Year of the American Revolution* (1934; New York: Octagon Books, 1968), 85.

201. For "Warlike Stores" in "almost all the towns of the several counties of Massachusetts and Maine, except Dukes and Nantucket, April 14, 1775," see *Journals of the Provincial Congress of Massachusetts in 1774 and 1775 and of the Committee of Public Safety* (Boston: Dutton and Wentworth, 1838), 756.

202. My calculation, based on data in Churchill, "Gun Ownership in Early America," 626, table 1.

203. For the lower estimate, see Richard Buel Jr., *Dear Liberty: Connecticut's Mobilization for the Revolutionary War* (Middletown: Wesleyan University

Press, 1980), 357, n. 224. For the higher estimate, see Churchill, "Gun Ownership in Early America," 631, table 2.

204. Ahearn, *Muskets of the Revolution,* 57; Alan and Barbara Aimone, "Organizing and Equipping Montgomery's New Yorkers in 1775," *Military Collector and Historian* 28.2 (Summer 1976): 56.

205. *New York in the Revolution, State Archives,* vol. 1 (*Documents Relating to the Colonial History of the State of New York,* vol. 15), ed. Berthold Fernow (Albany: Weed, Parsons and Company, 1887), 122–23.

206. Ibid., 146.

207. General Peter Gansevoort to Governor George Clinton, Albany, April 14, 1781 *Public Papers of George Clinton, First Governor of New York, 1775-1795, 1801-1804,* ed. Hugh Hastings, 10 vols. (New York, 1899–1914), 6:765.

208. Return of Colonel Drake's Regiment of Militia, August 5, 1780, Ibid., 6:104.

209. Jameson, "Equipment for the Militia of the Middle States," 34–35.

210. John Hancock to Thomas Cushing, Philadelphia, February 1, 1776, Miscellaneous Bound Manuscripts, Massachusetts Historical Society, Boston; *Documents Relating to the Colonial History of New York,* 15, 127–28; Mark V. Kwasny, *Washington's Partisan War, 1775-1783* (Kent: Kent State University Press, 1996), 32; Jeffrey M. Dorwart, *Invasion and Insurrection: Security, Defense, and War in the Delaware Valley, 1621-1815* (Newark: University of Delaware Press, 2008), 119; Adrian C. Leiby, *Revolutionary War in the Hackensack Valley: The Jersey Dutch and the Neutral Ground* (1962; New Brunswick: Rutgers University Press, 1980), 87–88, 90; Jameson, "Organization of the Militia of the Middle States," 171.

211. Churchill, "Gun Ownership in Early America," 631, table 2.

212. Jameson, "Equipment of the Militia of the Middle States," 34–35.

213. The divide at the Delaware River, which persisted into the early 1800s, is also noted in Churchill, "Gun Ownership in Early America," 630, 636, table 4, 639.

214. Rosswurm, *Arms, Country, and Class,* 50–53; Newland, *Pennsylvania Militia,* 128, n. 9.

215. Jameson, "Equipment of the Militia of the Middle States," 28.

216. *Pennsylvania Archives, Second Series,* ed. John B. Linn and William H. Eagle, 19 vols. (Harrisburg: Clarence M Busch, 1896), 1:658.

217. Jameson, "Organization of the Militia of the Middle States," 163–64.

218. William Finley, speech, April 15, 1808, in *Annals of Congress,* 10th Cong., 1st sess., 18:2182.

219. Taaffe, *Philadelphia Campaign,* 60.

220. Ivor Noel Hume, *James Geddy and Sons, Colonial Craftsmen* (Williamsburg: Colonial Williamsburg Foundation, 1970), 18–19; McDonnell, *Politics of*

War, 186; Philip D. Morgan and Andrew Jackson O'Shaugnessy, "Arming Slaves in the American Revolution," in *Arming Slaves: From Classical Times to the Modern Age*, ed. Christopher Leslie Brown and Philip D. Morgan (New Haven: Yale University Press, 2006), 185.

221. Richard Henry Lee to George Washington, December 6, 1775, in *Papers of George Washington, Revolutionary War Series*, ed. Philander D. Chase et. al,. 21 vols. to date (Charlottesville: University Press of Virginia, 1985–), 2:500; *A Man Apart: The Journal of Nicholas Cresswell, 1774–1781*, ed. Harold B. Gill Jr. and George M. Curtis III (Lanham, Md.: Lexington Books, 2009), 106 (March 21, 1776); John Page to Richard Henry Lee, February 19, 1776, quoted in McDonnell, *Politics of War*, 180.

222. Churchill, "Gun Ownership in Early America," 631–32, table 2.

223. Whisker, *American Colonial Militia*, 5:173.

224. For informed and thoughtful discussions of the roles of the militia during the American Revolution, see Shy, *A People Numerous and Armed*, 163–79, 213–44; Walter Sargent, "The Massachusetts Rank and File of 1777," and John Resch, "The Revolution as a People's War," in Resch and Sargent, *War and Society in the American Revolution*, 42–69, 70–102; Kwasny, *Washington's Partisan War*; Jameson, "Equipment for the Militia of the Middle States," 26–38; Robert C. Pugh, "The Revolutionary Militia in the Southern Campaign, 1780–81," *William and Mary Quarterly*, 3rd. ser. 14.2 (April 1957): 154–75.

225. Buel, *Dear Liberty*, 77–80.

226. Allan Kulikoff, "The Political Economy of Military Service in Revolutionary Virginia," in Kulikoff, *The Agrarian Origins of American Capitalism* (Charlottesville: University Press of Virginia, 1992), 163, 168, table 4.

227. Ibid.; Sargent, "The Massachusetts Rank and File of 1777," 57–58, table 2.3.

228. Kwasny, *Washington's Partisan War*, 79.

229. For praise from a foe, see Johann Conrad Dohla, November 25, 1777, in *A Hessian Diary of the American Revolution*, trans. and ed. Bruce E. Burgoyne (Norman: University Press of Oklahoma, 1990), 61. For praise from a patriot leader, see James Innes to Thomas Jefferson, October 21[?], 1780), in *The Papers of Thomas Jefferson*, ed. Julian P. Boyd, Lyman H. Butterfield et al., 38 vols. (Princeton: Princeton University Press, 1950–), 4:55.

230. George Washington to Patrick Henry, November 13, 1777, in *Patrick Henry*, 1:542–44.

231. See Churchill, "Gun Ownership in Early America," 630–32, table 2.

232. Ferguson, "Functions of the Partisan-Militia," 247–52.

233. Earl Cornwallis to Sir Henry Clinton, June 30, 1781, quoted in Richard H. Kohn, "The Murder of the Militia System in the Aftermath of the American Revolution," in *The Human Dimensions of Nation Making: Essays on Colonial and*

Revolutionary America, ed. James Kirby Martin (Madison: The State Historical Society of Wisconsin, 1976), 309–10.

234. Statement of Arms and Men in Service, February 29, 1781, in *Papers of Jefferson,* 4:470–71.

235. John David McBride, "The Virginian War Effort, 1775–1783: Manpower Policies and Practices" (Ph.D. diss, University of Virginia, 1977), 38.

236. For a concise discussion of the collapse of the Virginia militia in 1780–81, see Kulikoff, "Military Service in Virginia," 171–79. For a good discussion of the problems arming the Virginia militia, see McBride, "Virginian War Effort," 185–90.

237. Thomas Jefferson to Steuben, Richmond, February 15, 1780 [1781]; Steuben to Jefferson, Chesterfield, February 15, 1781; Steuben to Jefferson, Ch[esterfield] Co., February 23, 3 O'clock PM; and Jefferson to the County Lieutenants of Chesterfield and Dinwiddie, Richmond, February 18, 1871, all in *Papers of Jefferson,* 4:695, 621–22, 624, 646.

238. Thomas Jefferson to Steuben, Richmond, April 24, 1/2 after 7 AM; Isaac and Abraham Van Bibber & Co. to Jefferson, Baltimore, March 22, 1781; and Edmund Read to Jefferson, Boyds Hole, on Potomack, April 10, 1871, ibid., 5:549, 210, 349; John Jones to Governor Thomas Nelson, July 27, 1781, in *Calendar of Virginia Papers,* 2:261.

239. Benjamin Blunt to General John Peter Gabriel Muhlenberg, September 11, 1781, in *Calendar of Virginia Papers,* 2:413.

240. Elizabeth Cometti, "Depredations in Virginia during the Revolution," in *The Old Dominion: Essays for Thomas Perkins Abernethy,* ed. Darrett B. Rutman (Charlottesville: University of Virginia Press, 1964), 143.

241. Inhabitants of Amelia to Governor Thomas Nelson, [summer] 1781, in *Calendar of Virginia Papers,* 2:684.

242. John Page to Colonel Theodore Blank, December 10, 1780, *Virginia Historical Register* 4 (1895): 195–99.

243. Brown, *Firearms in Colonial America,* 325–26. For examples of firearms acquired from foreign sources, public purchases, and private sources that have received "supercharges" or stamps of the United States, individual states, and even counties, see Ahearn, *Muskets of the Revolution,* 45–47, 67, 129–30, 145–47, 174–81, 184, 193, 196–97.

244. Richard F. Upton, *Revolutionary New Hampshire: And an Account of the Social and Political Forces Underlying the Transition from Royal Province to American Commonwealth* (Hanover: Dartmouth College Productions, 1936), 124; Jameson, "Equipment for the Militia of the Middle States," 31; McDonnell, *Politics of War,* 279. See also sources cited in note 200.

245. Lee, *Crowds and Soldiers,* 182, 311.

246. Paul Lockhart, *The Whites of Their Eyes: Bunker Hill, the First American Army, and the Emergence of George Washington* (New York: Harper, 2011), 75.

247. Lee, *Crowds and Soldiers*, 200–201.

248. George Washington to Governor Jonathan Trumbull, Head Quarters, Morris Town, February 6, 1777, in *The Writings of George Washington from the Original Manuscript Sources, 1745–1799*, ed. John C. Fitzpatrick, vol. 7 (Washington, D.C.: United States Government Printing Office, 1932), 112–13.

249. John. A. Houlding, *Fit for Service: The Training of the British Army, 1715–1795* (New York: Oxford University Press, 1981), 140; Richard Holmes, *Redcoat: The British Soldier in the Age of Horse and Musket* (New York: Norton, 2001), 195.

250. Thomas Jefferson, *Notes on the State of Virginia*, ed. William Peden (New York: Norton, published for the Institute of Early American History and Culture, 1982), 88.

251. *The Debates in the Several State Conventions on the Adoption of the Federal Constitution as Recommended by the General Convention at Philadelphia in 1787*, ed. Jonathan Elliot, vol. 3 (Philadelphia: J. B. Lippincott, 1859), 386.

252. Computed from table 3 in Churchill, "Gun Ownership in Early America," 634.

253. *The Documentary History of the Ratification of the Constitution* (hereafter cited as *DHRC*), ed. Merrill Jensen, John Kaminski, Gaspare Saladino et al., 25 vols. (Madison: State Historical Society of Wisconsin, 1976–2012), 17:239, 242, n. 6, 253, n. 6.

254. Josiah Harmar, defendant, in *Proceedings of a Court of Enquiry, Held at the Special Request of Brigadier General Josiah Harmar* (Philadelphia: Fenno, 1791), 2, Evans no. 23905.

255. Ibid.

256. Ibid.

257. David P. Szatmary, *Shays' Rebellion: The Making of an Agrarian Insurrection* (Amherst: University of Massachusetts Press, 1980), 99; Leonard L. Richards, *Shays's Rebellion: The American Revolution's Final Battle* (Philadelphia: University of Pennsylvania Press, 2002), 28.

258. William Shepard to Benjamin Lincoln, January 18, 1787, and William Shepard to Henry Knox, Springfield, January 12, 1787, Shays' Rebellion Papers, Historic Deerfield Library, Deerfield, Mass.

259. Militia returns for 1788 from Charlton, Dudley, and Sturbridge, Massachusetts, in Massachusetts Collection, box 5, folder 5, American Antiquarian Society, Worcester, Mass. The Massachusetts adjutant general's statewide annual return for 1790 reported 35,818 muskets for 57,940 militiamen, indicating that 61.8 percent of the men brought firearms to their musters. See Churchill, "Gun Ownership in America," 635n52.

260. Copy of letter to Major General Sheppard from Henry Knox, New York, January 21, 1787, Henry Knox Papers, microfilm, Massachusetts Historical Society, Boston.

261. Don Higginbotham, "The Federalized Militia Debate: A Neglected Aspect of Second Amendment Scholarship," *William and Mary Quarterly*, 3rd ser., 55.1 (January 1998): 39–58.

262. War Office [Henry Knox], *A Plan for the General Arrangements of the Militia of the United States* (New York, 1786).

263. *A Plan for the General Arrangements of the Militia*, 15.

264. Ibid.

265. *Journals of Continental Congress, 1774–1789*, 31:642.

266. *Records of the Federal Convention of 1787*, ed. Max Farrand, 3 vols. (New Haven: Yale University Press, 1911), 2:236, 331.

267. *The Federalist Papers by Alexander Hamilton, James Madison, and John Jay*, ed. Garry Wills (Bantam Books: New York, 1982), 140.

268. *Records of the Federal Convention*, 2:332.

269. Ibid., 2:384–85.

270. Ibid., 2:385.

271. Ibid., 2:385.

272. Ibid., 2:386–87.

273. Ibid., 2:387.

274. Ibid., 2:385.

275. Ibid., 2:386.

276. Ibid.

277. Abraham Baldwin, "Speech in the House of Representatives," March 14, 1796, ibid., 3:369–70.

278. Federal Farmer XVIII, in *DHRC*, 17:362.

279. Ibid.

280. Ibid.

281. Elliot, *Debates*, 3:418.

282. Ibid.

283. Luther Martin, Address no. 1, *Maryland Journal*, March 18, 1788, in *DHRC* 16:419.

284. Ibid.

285. Hamilton No. 29, in *The Federalist Papers*, 139. See also The Landholder No. 10 to the Honourable Luther Martin, Esqu., *Maryland Journal*, February 29, 1788, in *DHRC*, 16:267.

286. *Records of the Federal Convention*, 3:330.

287. Elliot, *Debates*, 3:380.

288. Ibid., 3:379.

289. Ibid. Jack Rakove has also pointed to the fact that some Anti-Federalists feared that the militia could be disarmed by federal failure to arm it. See Rakove, "The Second Amendment: The Highest Stage of Originalism," *Chicago-Kent Law Review* 76 (2002): 138–42, and Rakove, "Words, Deeds, and Guns: *Arming America* and the Second Amendment," *William and Mary Quarterly*, 3rd ser., 59.1 (January 2002): 209–10.

290. Elliot, *Debates*, 3:380.

291. Ibid., 3:382.

292. Ibid., 3:390–91.

293. Ibid., 3:421.

294. Helen E. Veit, Kenneth R. Bowling, and Charlene Bangs Bickford, eds., *Creating the Bill of Rights: The Documentary Record from the First Federal Congress* (Baltimore: Johns Hopkins University Press, 1991), 20.

295. Veit, Bowling, and Bickford, *Creating the Bill of Rights*, 12.

296. Ibid., 38.

297. Ibid., 38–39, n. 13.

298. John Randolph to St. George Tucker, September 11, 1789, New York, ibid., 293. Later, as a member of the House of Representatives, Randolph led the fight in 1807 and 1808 to secure federal funds for arming the state militias. See *Annals of the Congress of the United States: The Debates and Proceedings of the Congress*, vol. 18 (Washington, D.C.: Gales and Seaton, 1852), 1020–21, 1025–26, 1049–50, 2176–77, 2183–84, 2186–87, 2195–96.

299. *Annals of the Congress of the United States: The Debates and Proceedings of the Congress*, vol. 7 (Washington, D.C.: Gales and Seaton, 1851), 1384–86, 1928–34; *Annals of the Congress*, 18:1019–56, 2175–96.

300. This is also the conclusion reached by Jameson, "Equipment for the Militia of the Middle States," 27.

301. Moller, *American Military Shoulder Arms*, 1:291, 484–85.

302. For similar assessments see Rakove, "The Second Amendment," 110–11, 113, 154.

303. *Boston Independent Chronicle*, October 1–4, 1798.

★ ★ ★ ★

Appendix A

The Scholarly Landscape since *Heller*

Saul Cornell and Nathan Kozuskanich

★ ★ ★ ★

DISTRICT OF COLUMBIA V. HELLER has triggered an avalanche of writing since the case was decided in 2008. Activists, law review student editors, scholars, and judges have all contributed to this burgeoning literature. Almost all of the commentary on *Heller* has appeared in law journals. Unencumbered by the often lengthy process of peer review which limits publication turnaround in other scholarly journals, law reviews have been particularly well suited to respond quickly to this landmark case. Law reviews are well positioned to evaluate the impact *Heller* has had in the great American gun debate.[1] With over a thousand law reviews now published in the United States, and many of the top law reviews publishing online supplements to deal with hot issues, one might have predicted an explosion in writing on this issue. Indeed, nearly six hundred articles published between 2008 and 2012 mentioned the *Heller* decision. One thing seems certain: courts will be wrestling with the consequences of *Heller* for some time to come. Given this fact, it also seems a foregone conclusion that students, scholars, judges, and activists will continue to publish on this issue at the same brisk pace.

Although there has been an unrelenting stream of law review articles on *Heller*, to date the case has not attracted much interest from book publishers.[2]

The one notable exception to this general lack of interest is Adam Winkler's 2011 book *Gun Fight: The Battle over the Right to Bear Arms in America*.[3] Aiming for a poplar audience, Winkler casts his story as a heroic battle of legal outsiders, primarily libertarians, who mounted an effective challenge to the District of Columbia's draconian handgun ban. If one digs beneath this Hollywood-style narrative framing device of little guys taking on the establishment and winning against all odds, Winkler's analysis is consistent with his earlier legal scholarship on *Heller*.[4] Winkler's effort to stake out a middle position in the gun debate—both pro-regulation and pro–individual rights— has made him a key player in the public debate over *Heller* and the future of gun regulation. *Gun Fight*'s unique contribution lies primarily in its behind-the-scenes look at *Heller* and its leading players. The information he obtained by interviewing many of the participants in the *Heller* litigation makes for fascinating reading.[5] As far as the future of gun control is concerned, Winkler concludes that *Heller*'s affirmation of an individual right to have guns in the home for purposes of self-defense poses no serious constitutional barriers to reasonable gun control.

It would be a monumental undertaking to survey comprehensively the entire body of *Heller* literature that encompasses a range of questions as esoteric as "can Martha Stewart have a gun?" to issues about race and the Second Amendment rights of Native Americans.[6] Three areas of inquiry within this vast literature are worth focusing on because they have generated some of the best scholarship to appear after *Heller,* and also because they touch on the most important legal issues raised by the case. The first question is empirical: did *Heller* get the history right? The second set of issues *Heller* raises deals with the legal implications of the theory of constitutional originalism. The third is the problem of deducing a workable judicial framework for evaluating future challenges to gun regulations.

OF HISTORY AND ORIGINALISM

Given the central role history played in the case, it is unsurprising that assessments of the Court's use of history and its originalist methods constitute a major focus of post-*Heller* scholarship. Joyce Lee Malcolm, one of the few historians to support the gun rights position prior to *Heller,* was also one of the few post-*Heller* commentators to endorse Scalia's majority opinion unequivocally as "a model of rigorous historical inquiry" and chastise Justice Stevens for disregarding "inconvenient facts."[7] By contrast, the historian David Konig argues that Scalia got his history badly wrong. A key issue in *Heller* was the proper way to interpret the amendment's preamble affirming the necessity of a well-regulated militia. Konig notes that Founding era interpretive practice does not support Scalia's claim that one might resort to the preamble only in cases of ambiguity.[8] In fact, the rule Scalia cites did not gain judicial support until decades after the adoption of the Second Amendment. The historian Paul Finkelman also offers a critical appraisal of the majority's history, pronouncing it to be "at best confused" and based "on an historical argument that is limited and wrongheaded."[9] In a harsher assessment, William G. Merkel calls Scalia's sense of originalism a "conscious fraud" and suggests that it demonstrates that "the originalist project . . . has failed—and failed colossally."[10]

Gun rights supporters and libertarians have generally applauded *Heller*.[11] Yet not all conservative legal thinkers have embraced the decision and its use of originalism. Indeed, some of the most critical commentary on *Heller* has been produced by conservatives.[12] Leading conservative critics of the opinion have excoriated the decision and attacked originalism as little more than a smokescreen for a type of judicial activism rivaling that of the Warren Court. For these critics, *Heller* starkly reveals the hypocrisy and intellectual incoherence of originalism. Richard A. Posner, a Reagan nominee on the Seventh Circuit, is highly critical of the decision. Although "the decision was the most noteworthy of the Court's recent term," he argues, "it is questionable in both method and result, and it is evidence that the Supreme Court, in deciding constitutional cases, exercises a freewheeling discretion strongly flavored with ideology."[13] Conservative luminary Charles Fried focuses on the problems of judges doing history. The justices in *Heller* "traveled a mistaken path," he argues, by following originalism, "a mistaken and sometimes incoherent doctrine that has time and again led the Court down the garden path to disastrous conclusions."[14] In Fried's view, *Heller*'s naïve reliance on history provided a fragile basis for such a sweeping decision. Finally, another respected conservative, Richard Epstein, attacks the historical foundations of the decision by focusing on Scalia's failure to recognize the centrality of federalism and the militia to the original understanding of the amendment. Scalia's private right of self defense ignores the most important contexts for understanding the original meaning of the Second Amendment: "the instability of the union, the risks of invasion, and the disruption by internal violence."[15]

Posner and Fried (as well as J. Harvie Wilkinson in the essay reprinted in this volume) all acknowledge that *Heller* mocks the notion that originalism can serve as a meaningful constraint on judicial activism.[16] Originalism has clearly entered a new phase in its history. Jamal Greene endorses these conclusions. In his view, *Heller's* version of originalism was an "interpretive methodology that has been radicalized and weaponized by conservative activists."[17]

Scalia's methodology in *Heller* embraced a variant of the "new originalism." One of the most vocal champions of this method, Lawrence B. Solum, describes *Heller* as the best judicial example of the recent turn away from original intent to public meaning in originalist theory. "Given the inevitable differences between judicial practice and constitutional theory," he writes, "it is hard to imagine finding a clearer example of original public meaning originalism in an actual judicial decision."[18] Solum applauds Scalia's approach, including his emphasis on public meaning and the decision to give greater weight to dictionaries than to the debates within the First Congress over the language of the amendment.[19] By contrast, Solum finds Stevens's dissent confused, describing it as "wide-ranging and argumentative, advancing a hodgepodge of critical arguments."[20]

John McGinnis and Michael Rappaport, supporters of a different strain of new originalism, also praise Scalia for using Founding era interpretive practices to resolve issues such as the role of preambles.[21] The fact that Scalia cites legal treatises from the nineteenth century, not the eighteenth century, to ascertain what those rules are does not trouble McGinnis and Rappaport. Indeed, the notion that interpretive practices might have changed in the period between the Founding era and the Civil War seems alien to many of originalism's leading champions.[22]

Historians have not been as generous in their assessments of new originalist assumptions and methodologies. The battle between opposing originalist theories in *Heller,* a conflict between the so-called new originalism (with its emphasis on public meaning) and traditional originalism (with its focus on intent), has produced a number of comments. Saul Cornell notes that the new originalism is nothing but "the latest incarnation of the old law office history."[23] He doubts that the new originalists' turn to public meaning, or their invocation of philosophy of language as a way around earlier historical critiques of originalism, can survive close scrutiny. Looking at old dictionaries might be a good starting point for historical research on what particular terms meant in the Founding era, but it is no substitute for genuine historical research. The earliest American dictionaries postdate the Second Amendment by several decades, and early lexicographical practices were radically different from modern ones. Early English dictionaries and the first American dictionaries were more prescriptive than descriptive. Another theoretical problem with "new originalist" methodology may be found in the way Scalia's opinion assesses various historical texts as evidence for the meaning of the right to bear arms. Scalia gives great weight to the Anti-Federalist "Dissent of the Pennsylvania Minority," which used the phrase "bear arms" in conjunction with hunting.[24] Virtually all of the historians who have written about *Heller* have noted not only that this text was atypical but also that its formulation of the right was never emulated by any other writer or ratification convention.[25] Given that the text was widely printed but was not copied or echoed in any other publication, most historians have concluded that it is not representative of American attitudes on this issue. Madison used a compilation of the various amendments suggested by the state ratification conventions which did not even include the Dissent, which was not an official document but a statement of a minority Anti-Federalist view from a single state convention. Yet, despite all of the historical arguments against making the Dissent the key to unlocking the public meaning of the Second Amendment, Scalia took the amendment's odd formulation as not simply probative, but actually dispositive of the amendment's public meaning.[26]

Mark Tushnet also finds Scalia's new originalism deeply flawed and ultimately unpersuasive as an interpretive method. "Give me an interesting term in a constitution," he writes, "and I will find a bunch of people at the time of its adoption who understood it to mean one thing, and a bunch of other people who understood it to mean something else."[27] Tushnet faults Scalia for searching for a univocal meaning for the right to bear arms. Equally problematic is the Court's implicit assumption that constitutional meanings are stable over long spans of time. Finally, Tushnet wonders why Justice Scalia's historical excursions mysteriously end in the late nineteenth century, just prior to the period when modern gun control emerged. In short, Scalia's use of history is highly selective and results-oriented.

Many other commentators are also puzzled by the way *Heller* dealt with the amendment's relationship to America's revolutionary origins and the militia's role in early American history. The legal scholar David C. Williams is baffled that Scalia "purged the Amendment of its revolutionary quality" by not recognizing the right to "keep and bear arms to resist tyranny."[28] Conversely, Carl T. Bogus finds aspects of Scalia's rhetoric too sympathetic to an insurrectionary view of the amendment.[29] The decision to cast aside the preamble and ignore the militia seems to some commentators to set the amendment adrift from its historical moorings. Elizabeth L. Hillman argues that the Court, in its exuberance to declare an individual right to bear arms for self-defense that was not tied to military service, neglected "the long-recognized link between citizenship and military service, and the changes—demographic, technological, and geopolitical—that have remade the United States military since the Constitution was drafted and ratified."[30]

The notion that *Heller* is more living constitution than originalist in spirit is shared by several commentators.[31] Adam Winkler argues that although *Heller* has been heralded as a victory for originalism, "the decision really hinges on a modern understanding of the right to keep and bear arms—that is, it relies on the 'living' Constitution."[32] Rory K. Little also has problems with Scalia's originalism, asserting that "the implications of the *Heller* majority opinion demonstrate that its purely originalist approach to constitutional interpretation, and indeed the majority opinion itself—as well as Justice Scalia personally—are moved by necessity toward a theory more akin to 'living constitutionalism' than originalism."[33]

The selective reading of evidence was an issue many commentators noted. Akhil Reed Amar finds fault with the majority opinion and the two dissents for ignoring his intratextualist methodology. Neither side "offered a sufficiently holistic account of certain important methodological and substantive issues," he argues, and they both "scanted various amendments [nine, fourteen, nineteen] beyond the Second . . . [that] are in fact key to a full understanding of what 'the right of the people to keep and bear arms' properly means in America today."[34]

LEGAL IMPLICATIONS

Whether motivated by originalism or living constitutionalism, *Heller*'s holding will necessarily have an impact on future court decisions on gun regulation. The first question *Heller* raised, and the one that proved to be the least controversial, was the incorporation of the right to bear arms against the states. There was broad agreement among legal scholars that the Second Amendment would be incorporated. The only issue that provoked any real scholarly interest was the method of incorporation.[35] A few law professors and activists hoped that the Supreme Court would use the right to bear arms as a test case to revisit the notion of incorporation through the privileges and immunities clause of the Fourteenth Amendment. In *McDonald v. City of Chicago* (2010), the Supreme Court rejected this route and instead incorporated the right through the more orthodox mechanism of substantive due process.[36]

Although *Heller* and *McDonald* guarantee an individual right to bear arms for self-defense that applies to both federal and state laws, the extent of that constitutional protection remains largely unclear. There has been an explosion of litigation on gun-related questions in the wake of *Heller,* but virtually all of these challenges have failed. Indeed, Adam Winkler believes that *"Heller's* bark is much worse than its right" and that it will not threaten America's already weak gun control regime.[37] Scholars sympathetic to gun control applaud this fact, while those supportive of gun rights bemoan it. At this writing, there have been over six hundred cases litigated on gun issues since *Heller* was decided. Apart from outright handgun bans, which are politically unpopular, most state and federal gun control laws seem likely to survive challenge. Indeed, as Sanford Levinson predicted, *Heller* "will have differential import to different audiences who will be consulting the case for decidedly various purposes."[38]

Glenn Harlan Reynolds and Brannon P. Denning believe (or at least believed in 2008, when they wrote their first post-*Heller* article) that "the reach of a case depends on lots of actors who often have tremendous discretion and little effective oversight when it comes to implementation."[39] *Heller's* impact will largely depend on future decisions by lower courts, which will have to implement a decision that provides little clear guidance. What *Heller* "amounts to" may well be determined by the "foot-dragging" in the lower courts (which Denning and Reynolds claim have been traditionally hostile to gun rights) and may limit *Heller's* reach.[40] In 2009 Reynolds and Denning assessed the various lower court decisions made since their first article was published and concluded, "Our [original] skepticism appears to have been warranted: courts have not rushed to overturn the federal gun laws that, hypothetically, were vulnerable following the Court's decision."[41] How one evaluates this legacy has much to do with the commentator's political stance on the issue of gun rights and gun control.

Mark Tushnet, who claims to hold no opinion on the "correct" way to interpret the Second Amendment, asks that gun rights advocates "temper their jubilation" and that gun control proponents "avoid despair," since the decision allows for some "presumptively constitutional" gun regulations.[42] While some elements of the majority opinion are originalist, when it comes to permissible regulations, Scalia appears to be content to leave most existing laws alone. Tushnet argues that if and when any substantive Second Amendment challenge reaches the Supreme Court again, the issue at hand will be either to give *Heller* a "respectful burial" or to "pretend that the Second Amendment protects an individual right while giving essentially no content to it except as a constitutional barrier to complete [handgun] prohibitions."[43]

Some have even argued that *Heller* could make moderate gun control more politically palatable. Allen Rostron believes that *Heller* will help rather than hinder sensible gun control since only outright handgun bans are unacceptable. In the final analysis, he argues, *Heller* may very well be "a victory for all Americans, having finally driven home to everyone that respecting gun rights and achieving sound gun control are not mutually exclusive endeavors."[44] Part of the reason *Heller* may not have much of a practical impact on the ground is that the law it overturned was a statistical outlier, far more restrictive than the vast majority of laws in place.

LOOKING TO THE FUTURE

Developing a workable firearms jurisprudence in the wake of *Heller* has left courts and scholars scrambling to make sense of the decision. The absence of a clear standard of review to apply has prompted considerable comment and confusion. One of the most comprehensive attempts to construct a coherent judicial paradigm for evaluating gun laws appears in Eugene Volokh's 107-page article devoted to fashioning a "workable constitutional doctrine." Volokh hopes that the courts will use more than just intuition to decide what is and what is not reasonable regulation, and will follow his advice to look closely "at the scope of the right, at the burden the regulation imposes, at evidence on whether the regulation will actually reduce danger of crime and injury . . . , and at any special role the government may be playing as proprietor."[45]

Andrew R. Gould believes that there is a "hidden" Second Amendment framework buried within *Heller*.[46] Sifting through the decision to consider how the Court defines the scope of the right to bear arms, Gould presents a two-pronged approach that considers whether the regulation being challenged falls within the core right and whether it can satisfy heightened scrutiny. Alan Brownstein is less optimistic that such a framework exists. In his view *Heller* "does not provide adequate answers to three critical questions . . . : (1) what is the nature and scope of the right, (2) what constitutes an infringement of the right, and (3) what constitutes an adequate justification of the right?"[47] This problem is compounded by the fact that the Court relied heavily on history to suggest exceptions to the scope of the right, even though contemporary fundamental rights doctrine (how we interpret freedom of speech, for example) has very little grounding in historical considerations. Likewise, Carlton F. W.

Larson argues that the Court's list of presumptively lawful limits on the right to bear arms "lack[s] the historical grounding that would normally justify an exception to a significant constitutional right."[48] The ruling is thus bereft of any coherent standard of review, leaving it to the lower courts to speculate as to what standard of scrutiny should be applied. Jason T. Anderson argues that "categorical exclusions and intermediate scrutiny could be used as they are for the First Amendment."[49] Nicholas J. Johnston suggests that the Court's rulings on abortion can inform the way future courts deal with the implications of the *Heller* decision on assault weapons. He seeks to prove how "assault weapons might be protected under *Heller* as a threshold matter."[50] Craig S. Lerner and Nelson Lund find more helpful guidance in *Kyllo v. United States* (in which police use of a thermal-imaging device was ruled in violation of the Fourth Amendment) in helping develop a new Second Amendment jurisprudence. The authors criticize *Heller*'s reliance on "a mechanical and insupportable version of *Kyllo*'s reasoning to justify legislative bans on weapons that are not currently in common civilian use," and propose instead a Second Amendment test that can account for emerging (and thus uncommon) technologies that may produce "nonlethal weapons that would be substantially superior to firearms for personal self-defense."[51]

Calvin Massey also offers a blueprint for future courts by suggesting five rules that should be followed since *Heller* "leaves us with the barest of guidelines for the formulation of constitutional decision rules."[52] Courts must precisely define the right, identify those who are entitled to that right, outline special situations that qualify the right, articulate all burdens upon that right, and employ a usable level of scrutiny. Michael P. O'Shea, while recognizing that *Heller* affirmed a right to personal self-defense as "the core lawful purpose" of the Second Amendment, argues that the right to keep and bear arms even for self-defense also serves a civic purpose (aiding crime reduction, for example).[53] Since *Heller* has replaced *Miller* by adopting a broad individual right to bear arms for self-defense, future courts will have to deal with the question of what weapons are protected and under what circumstances. O'Shea recommends that "in order to promote clarity and avoid circularity or obvious errors of omission, courts should rely as much as possible upon verifiable, external sources of evidence on this matter, especially the revealed judgments of citizens and police departments about which arms are worth obtaining today for defense."[54] Rather than fit *Heller* into the familiar framework of judicial scrutiny used to evaluate many other rights claims, Joseph Blocher examines Scalia's framework in terms of categoricalism (that is, does a particular regulation fit into one of the long list of categorical exceptions to *Heller*'s general claims about the right to bear arms?) and finds that "*Heller*'s categoricalism neither reflects nor enables a clear view of the Second Amendment's core values—whatever they may be—and that *Heller* therefore fails to justify the constitutional categories it creates." In short, post-*Heller* scholarship acknowledges that the decision left ample room for a wide variety of regulations. There is also general agreement that Scalia's opinion failed to lay out a coherent legal framework for evaluating future challenges to gun regulations.[55]

Some of the most interesting post-*Heller* scholarship has focused on Justice Breyer's dissent. Although Scalia rejected Breyer's freestanding balancing approach, a number of scholars have noted that in the absence of a clear framework for weighing Second Amendment claims, some type of informal balancing approach is likely to occur. To complicate matters further, *Heller*'s acceptance of a range of presumptively lawful regulations might itself be interpreted as an acceptance of a balancing grounded in historical practices and precedents, as opposed to choices made by contemporary judges engaging in a "freestanding" balancing test.[56] Richard Schragger looks more closely at Breyer's dissent, arguing that his approach is out of step with twentieth-century jurisprudential trends, particularly those that view rights as strong trumps against government interference. Although "Breyer's approach is both realist and optimistic," his insistence on judicial judgment "is a distinctly minority view."[57] Former *New York Times* Supreme Court correspondent Linda Greenhouse offers a different view of Breyer's dissent. She sees much merit in Breyer's approach but recognizes that "whether it will ever command a majority of the Court is a matter of conjecture."[58] After surveying the efforts of lower courts to apply *Heller*, Allen Rostron concludes that the balancing framework Breyer advocates may have emerged as a default solution in the absence of any coherent alternative. Rostron does not attribute this development to any conscious effort to substitute the dissent's model in place of the majority's views, but finds that the injunction to look to history for guidance has provided ample justification for upholding virtually every form of gun regulation challenged in the post-*Heller* era. While contemporary judges may not be engaging in balancing, it is perfectly consistent with *Heller* to ratify balancing decisions made in the past by an earlier generation of judges and legislators.[59]

One of the most pressing unresolved issues raised by *Heller* is the scope of the right outside the house. Michael C. Dorf explores the application of the right to keep and bear arms in public places in light of *Heller*'s explicit recognition of lawful gun possession in the home. He argues that the "home/public line can be defended" and hopes that "since the Court erred in *Heller,*" it would "[limit] the damage by holding that the home is different."[60] The notion of a homebound right also shapes the analysis of Darrell Miller, who argues that courts ought to limit the right to carry guns in public and offers the First Amendment's treatment of pornography as a model for how one might conceptualize such a limited right.[61] In his preliminary sketch of a framework for post-*Heller* gun regulation, Eugene Volokh urges the Court to recognize some type of right to carry outside the home. Mike O'Shea endorses this view and claims it is supported by Founding era history. Conversely, Patrick Charles challenges the historical foundation that the right to carry was well established by the Founding generation.[62] Refuting both O'Shea and Joyce Lee Malcolm, Charles argues that under English law there was no right to travel armed in public. New research by Saul Cornell on the right to travel armed in the nineteenth century identifies two radically different traditions in early American law regarding the scope of that right outside the house. In parts of the antebellum slave South an expansive conception of the right to travel armed developed in some places. According to this model, the state might ban concealed weapons but was obligated to allow open carry. A different and more limited model emerged in other parts of the United States. Beginning with Massachusetts in the 1830s, this alternative paradigm restricted this right to extraordinary occasions when an imminent threat existed. This model was emulated in more than half a dozen states in the Northeast, Midwest, and Pacific Northwest. Even Texas eventually embraced this limited right-to-carry model. The prohibition on the right to carry recognized a common law affirmative defense exception in cases where one faced an imminent threat. The mechanism for enforcing the ban on traveling armed drew on the common law model of peace bonds, a mechanism well suited to the predominantly rural, preindustrial face-to-face communities of early modern England. According to this model, any citizen or justice of the peace could request that a peace bond be posted as a method of preventing individuals from arming themselves wantonly. Adapting this model to the modern regulatory state and modern legal mechanisms will doubtless require some creative constitutional theorizing. Nor is it clear that courts will rush to embrace this type of historical model, given that peace bonds do not fit squarely into modern categories of analysis or contemporary legal practice. Still, the notion that modern courts would take their cues from the Slave South's model for regulating firearms seems hard to justify.[63]

Although *Heller* looked to history for guidance, the incorporation of the amendment against the states raises some fascinating questions about which moments in history ought to provide guidance for courts. Should the courts look to Founding era practices? The Age of Jackson? Gun regulations during the era of the Fourteenth Amendment? Or perhaps the entire span of American history?[64] These questions are difficult to answer because *Heller* approached the constitutional past in static terms and ignored the evolving meaning, changing technologies, and shifting historical practices that defined the right to bear arms in different periods of American history. To remedy this defect, future scholarship and rulings must recognize that gun regulation in America has consistently evolved in response to changing perceptions of the threat posed by firearms.[65] This will no doubt be an uphill battle, for some originalists reject the idea that the actual practices envisioned by the Founders or subsequent generations have any role to play in understanding the original meaning of the amendment. For these originalists, the expected application of the amendment is simply irrelevant to constitutional adjudication. Alternatively, Joseph Blocher argues that legal conceptions of the scope of the right to bear arms have always been shaped by a recognition of material factors. First Amendment theory has long recognized the legitimacy of time, place, and manner restrictions. The history of gun regulation presents an even more pronounced recognition of the spatial contours of the right. As Blocher observes, "from colonial Boston to 19th-century Tombstone to contemporary New York City, gun rights have always been more heavily regulated in cities—a degree of geographic variation that is hard to find with regard to any other constitutional right." Blocher argues that courts need to recognize that geography has always played a role in regulating firearms and as a result courts ought to give urban areas greater latitude in crafting laws to deal with the problems of gun violence.[66]

The turn to history enjoined by *Heller* has raised more questions than it has answered. The only claim one can make with any certainty is that scholarship on *Heller* and its implications will continue to keep law review editors busy for decades to come.[67]

NOTES

1. For a critique of legal scholarship and law reviews, see Robert J. Spitzer, "Why History Matters: Saul Cornell's Second Amendment and the Consequences of Law Reviews," *Albany Government Law Review* 1 (2008): 312–53.

2. A group of gun rights scholars and activists produced the first casebook on the Second Amendment, but the fact that no other legal publisher rushed to put out a competing volume suggests that the market is seen to be very small. Courses on the Second Amendment are not very common in American law schools and are generally taught by gun rights–oriented scholars teaching an audience that is typically pro-gun. See Nicholas Johnson et al., *Firearms Law and the Second Amendment: Regulation, Rights, and Policy* (New York: Aspen Publishers, 2012).

3. Adam Winkler, *Gun Fight: The Battle over the Right to Bear Arms in America* (New York: Norton, 2011). Winkler's earlier writing analyzed state court decisions on the right to bear arms and found that judges typically evaluated gun laws by using a reasonableness standard somewhere between rational basis review and strict scrutiny. See Winkler, "Scrutinizing the Second Amendment," *Michigan Law Review* 105 (2007): 683–733. The same standard appears to have emerged as the most common standard in post-Heller decisions, as discussed later in this essay.

4. Robert Levy, the millionaire libertarian who helped lead the charge in *Heller*, had close ties to the Cato Institute and the Federalist Society, connections that hardly qualify him for outsider status or even as a latter-day David fighting a legal Goliath. As an effective narrative framework, however, Winkler's choice was brilliant. See Mark Ames, "Independent and Principled? Behind the Cato Myth," *The Nation*, April 20, 2012. See also Stephen M. Teles, *The Rise of the Conservative Legal Movement* (Princeton: Princeton University Press, 2010); Adam Winkler, "*Heller*'s Catch-22," *UCLA Law Review* 56 (2009): 1552–53.

5. The argument that gun regulation and gun ownership are each deeply rooted in American history builds on earlier work by Saul Cornell, *A Well-Regulated Militia: The Founding Fathers and the Origins of Gun Control in America* (Oxford: Oxford University Press, 2006).

6. Kevin C. Marshall, "Why Can't Martha Stewart Have a Gun?" *Harvard Journal of Law & Public Policy* 32 (2009): 695–735; Angela R. Riley, "Indians and Guns," *Georgetown Law Journal* 100 (2012): 1675–1745. The former article deals with nonviolent felons and their access to firearms, and the latter deals with the complex history and constitutional significance of laws restricting Indians' access to firearms in American history.

7. Joyce Lee Malcolm, "The Supreme Court and the Uses of History: *District of Columbia v. Heller*," *UCLA Law Review* 56 (2009): 1377–98, quotations on 1377, 1378.

8. David T. Konig, "Why the Second Amendment Has a Preamble," *UCLA Law Review* 56 (2009): 1295–1342.

9. Paul Finkelman, "It Really Was about a Well-Regulated Militia," *Syracuse Law Review* 59 (2008): 267–81, quotation on 267.

10. William G. Merkel, "*The District of Columbia v. Heller* and Antonin Scalia's Perverse Sense of Originalism," *Lewis & Clark Law Review* 13 (2009): 349–81, quotations on 349, 381. Merkel's work is based, in part, on Nathan R. Kozuskanich, "Originalism in a Digital Age: An Inquiry into the Right to Bear Arms," reprinted in this volume.

11. Randy E. Barnett, "News Flash: The Constitution Means What It Says," *Wall Street Journal,* June 27, 2008; Glenn H. Reynolds and Brannon P. Denning, "*Heller*'s Future in the Lower Courts," *Northwestern University Law Review* 102 (2008): 2035–44; David B. Kopel, "The Natural Right of Self-Defense: *Heller*'s Lesson for the World," *Syracuse Law Review* 59 (2008): 235–52.

12. See Nelson Lund, "The Second Amendment, *Heller,* and Originalist Jurisprudence," reprinted in this volume, and Nelson Lund, "*Heller* and Second Amendment Precedent" *Lewis & Clark Law Review* 13 (2009): 335–47.

13. Richard A. Posner, "In Defense of Looseness: The Supreme Court and Gun Control," *New Republic,* August 27, 2008.

14. Charles Fried, "The Second Annual Kennedy Lecture: On Judgment," *Lewis & Clark Law Review* 15 (2011): 1025–46, quotation on 1033.

15. Richard A. Epstein, "A Structural Interpretation of the Second Amendment: Why *Heller* Is (Probably) Wrong on Originalist Grounds," *Syracuse Law Review* 59 (2008): 171–84, quotation on 174.

16. For a critique of Wilkinson from a libertarian perspective, see Nelson Lund and David B. Kopel, "Unraveling Judicial Restraint: Guns, Abortion, and the Faux Conservatism of J. Harvie Wilkinson III," *The Journal of Law and Politics* 25 (2009): 1–19.

17. Jamal Greene, "*Heller* High Water? The Future of Originalism," *Harvard Law and Policy Review* 3 (2009): 325– 45, quotation on 326. For a discussion of the relationship between *Heller,* originalism, and activism, see Thomas B. Colby, "The Sacrifice of the New Originalism," *Georgetown Law Journal* 99 (2011): 713–78.

18. Lawrence B. Solum "What Is Originalism? The Evolution of Contemporary Originalist Theory," in *The Challenge of Originalism: Theories of Constitutional Interpretation,* ed. Grant Huscroft and Bradley W. Miller (Cambridge: Cambridge University Press, 2011).

19. Lawrence B. Solum, "*District of Columbia v. Heller* and Originalism," *Northwestern University Law Review* 103 (2009): 923–82.

20. Ibid., 954, 959.

21. John O. McGinnis and Michael B. Rappaport, "Original Methods Originalism: A New Theory of Interpretation and the Case against Construction," *Northwestern University Law Review* 103 (2009); 751–802.

22. On Scalia's misuse of preambles, see Konig, "Why the Second Amendment Has a Preamble." For criticism of both these variants of new originalism, see Saul Cornell, "The People's Constitution vs. the Lawyer's Constitution: Popular Constitutionalism and the Original Debate over Originalism," *Yale Journal of Law & the Humanities* 23 (2011): 295–337.

23. Saul Cornell, "*Heller,* New Originalism, and Law Office History: 'Meet the New Boss, Same as the Old Boss,'" *UCLA Law Review* 56 (2009): 1097; on the problems with using old dictionaries in place of real historical research, see Cornell, "The People's Constitution vs. the Lawyers Constitution." See also Keith Whittington, "The New Originalism," *Georgetown Journal of Law & Public Policy* 2 (2004): 599–614; Randy Barnett, *Restoring the Lost Constitution: The Presumption of Liberty* (Princeton: Princeton University Press, 2005); and Randy E. Barnett, "An Originalism for Nonoriginalists," *Loyola Law Review* 45 (1999): 611–54.

24. The text states: "That the people have a right to bear arms for the defence of themselves and their own state, or the United States, or for the purpose of killing game." See "The Address and Reasons of Dissent of the Minority of the Convention, of the State of Pennsylvania, to their Constituents" (Philadelphia, 1787).

25. See Brief of Amici Curiae Jack N. Rakove, Saul Cornell, David T. Konig, William J. Novak, Lois G. Schwoerer et al. in Support of Petitioners, *District of Columbia v. Heller,* no. 07-290 (2008): 23–24; reprinted in this volume.

26. The Dissent reflected the views of Pennsylvania's Anti-Federalist minority, but there is no evidence that Madison consulted it in framing his own list of amendments. On the origins of the Bill of Rights, including the sources of Madison's own list of amendments, see Kenneth R. Bowling, "'A Tub to the Whale': The Founding Fathers and Adoption of the Federal Bill of Rights," *Journal of the Early Republic* 8 (Fall 1988): 223– 51, esp. 235–36.

27. Mark Tushnet, "*Heller* and the New Originalism," *Ohio State Law Journal* 69 (2008): 609–24, quotation on 611.

28. David C. Williams, "Death to Tyrants: *District of Columbia v. Heller* and the Uses of Guns," *Ohio State Law Journal* 69 (2008): 641–669, quotation on 641.

29. Carl T. Bogus, "*Heller* and Insurrectionism," *Syracuse Law Review* 59 (2008): 253–67.

30. Elizabeth L. Hillman, "*Heller,* Citizenship, and the Right to Serve in the Military," *Hastings Law Journal* 60 (2009): 1269–83, quotation on 1269.

31. See Reva B. Siegel, "Dead or Alive: Originalism as Popular Constitutionalism in *Heller,*" reprinted in this volume; Jamal Greene, "Guns, Originalism, and Cultural Cognition," *University of Pennsylvania Journal of Constitutional Law* 13 (2010): 511–28.

32. Winkler, "*Heller*'s Catch-22," 1552–53.

33. Rory K. Little, "*Heller* and Constitutional Interpretation: Originalism's Last Gasp," *Hastings Law Journal* 60 (2009): 1417–18.

34. Akhil Reed Amar, "*Heller, HLR*, and Holistic Legal Reasoning," *Harvard Law Review* 122 (2008): 145–90, quotation on 146.

35. Lawrence Rosenthal, "Second Amendment Plumbing after *Heller:* Of Standards of Scrutiny, Incorporation, Well-Regulated Militias, and Criminal Street Gangs," *Urban Lawyer* 41 (2009): 1–92; Michael O'Shea, "Federalism and the Implementation of the Right to Arms," *Syracuse Law Review* 59 (2008): 201–24; Nelson Lund, "Anticipating Second Amendment Incorporation: The Role of the Inferior Courts," *Syracuse Law Review* 59 (2008): 185–200; Patrick J. Charles, "'Arms for Their Defence?' An Historical, Legal, and Textual Analysis of the English Right to Have Arms and Whether the Second Amendment Should Be Incorporated in *McDonald v. City of Chicago*," *Cleveland State Law Review* 57 (2009): 351–460; Lawrence Rosenthal and Joyce Lee Malcolm, Colloquy Debate, "*McDonald v. Chicago:* Which Standard of Scrutiny Should Apply to Gun Control," *Northwestern University Law Review Colloquy* 105 (2010): 85–114.

36. 130 S. Ct. 3020, 3050 (2010).

37. Ibid., 1553.

38. Sanford Levinson, "For Whom Is the *Heller* Decision Important?" *Lewis & Clark Law Review* 13 (2009): 316–17. On the explosion of litigation, see Law Center to Prevent Gun Violence, "The Second Amendment Battleground: Victories in the Courts and Why They Matter," available at http://smartgunlaws .org/the-second-amendment-battleground-victories-in-the-courts/.

39. Brannon P. Denning and Glenn H. Reynolds, "Five Takes on *District of Columbia v. Heller*," *Ohio State Law Journal* 69 (2008): 671–99, quotation on 671.

40. Ibid., 699; Brannon P. Denning and Glenn H. Reynolds, "*Heller*'s Future in the Lower Courts," *Northwestern University Law Review* 102 (2008): 2035–44.

41. Brannon P. Denning and Glenn H. Reynolds, "*Heller*, High Water(mark)? Lower Courts and the New Right to Keep and Bear Arms," *Hastings Law Journal* 60 (2009): 1245–68, quotation on 1245.

42. Mark Tushnet, "Permissible Gun Regulations after *Heller:* Speculations about Method and Outcomes," *UCLA Law Review* 56 (2009): 1425–42, quotations on 1426; Mark Tushnet, "*Heller* and the Perils of Compromise," *Lewis & Clark Law Review* 13 (2009): 419–32, quotation on 419.

43. Tushnet, "Permissible Gun Regulations," 1441–42.

44. Allen Rostron, "Protecting Gun Rights and Improving Gun Control after *District of Columbia v. Heller*," *Lewis & Clark Law Review* 13 (2009): 383–418, quotation on 418.

45. Eugene Volokh, "Implementing the Right to Keep and Bear Arms for Self-Defense: An Analytical Framework and a Research Agenda," *UCLA Law Review* 56 (2009): 1443–1549, quotations on 1445, 1549.

46. Andrew R. Gould, "The Hidden Second Amendment Framework within *District of Columbia v. Heller,*" *Vanderbilt Law Review* 62 (2009): 1535–76, esp. 1538.

47. Alan Brownstein, "The Constitutionalization of Self-Defense in Tort and Criminal Law, Grammatically Correct Originalism, and Other Second Amendment Musings," *Hasting Law Journal* 60 (2009): 1205–44, quotation on 1207.

48. Carlton F. W. Larson, "Four Exceptions in Search of a Theory: *District of Columbia v. Heller* and Judicial *Ipse Dixit,*" *Hastings Law Journal* 60 (2009): 1371–86, quotation on 1372.

49. Jason T. Anderson, "Second Amendment Standards of Review: What the Supreme Court Left Unanswered in *District of Columbia v. Heller,*" *Southern California Law Review* 82 (2009): 547–94, quotation on 549.

50. Nicholas J. Johnson, "Supply Restrictions at the Margins of *Heller* and the Abortion Analogue: *Sternberg* Principles, Assault Weapons, and the Attitudinalist Critique," *Hasting Law Journal* 60 (2009): 1285–1338, quotation on 1289.

51. Craig S. Lerner and Nelson Lund, "*Heller* and Nonlethal Weapons," *Hasting Law Journal* 60 (2009): 1387–1414, quotations on 1388–89.

52. Calvin Massey, "Second Amendment Decision Rules," *Hasting Law Journal* 60 (2009): 1431–44, quotation on 1432.

53. Michael P. O'Shea, "The Right to Defensive Arms after *District of Columbia v. Heller,*" *West Virginia Law Review* 111 (2009): 349–93, quotation on 351 (citing *Heller,* 128 S. Ct. at 2818).

54. Ibid.

55. Joseph Blocher, "Categoricalism and Balancing in First and Second Amendment Analysis," *New York University Law Review* 84 (2009): 377–78. Blocher has also written a fascinating article on the "right not to bear arms," a neglected legacy of Founding era conceptions of arms bearing; see Joseph Blocher, "The Right Not to Keep or Bear Arms," *Stanford Law Review* 64 (2012): 1–54.

56. Darrell A. H. Miller, "Text, History, and Tradition: What the Seventh Amendment Can Teach Us about the Second," *Yale Law Journal* 122 (2013): 852–938.

57. Richard Schragger, "The Last Progressive: Justice Breyer, *Heller,* and 'Judicial Judgment,'" *Syracuse Law Review* 59 (2008): 283–97, quotations on 297.

58. Linda Greenhouse, "'Weighing Needs and Burdens': Justice Breyer's *Heller* Dissent," *Syracuse Law Review* 59 (2008): 299–308, quotation on 308.

59. Allen Rostron, "Justice Breyer's Triumph in the Third Battle over the Second Amendment," *George Washington Law Review* 80 (2012): 703–63.

60. Michael C. Dorf, "Does *Heller* Protect a Right to Carry Guns Outside the Home?" *Syracuse Law Review* 59 (2008): 225–34, quotation on 226.

61. Darrell A. H. Miller, "Guns as Smut: Defending the Home-Bound Second Amendment," *Columbia Law Review* 109 (2009): 1278–1356. For a criticism of Miller's model, see Eugene Volokh, "The First and Second Amendments," *Columbia Law Review,* Sidebar 109 (2009): 97–104.

62. Michael P. O'Shea, "Modeling the Second Amendment Right to Carry Arms (I): Judicial Tradition and the Scope of 'Bearing Arms' for Self-Defense," *American University Law Review* 61 (2012): 585–676; Patrick J. Charles, "The Faces of the Second Amendment Outside the Home: History versus Ahistorical Standards of Review," *Cleveland State Law Review* 60 (2012): 1–55.

63. Saul Cornell, "The Right to Carry Firearms Outside of the Home: Separating Historical Myths from Historical Realities" *Fordham Urban Law Journal* 39 (2012): 1695–1726.

64. Volokh, "Implementing the Right to Keep and Bear Arms for Self-Defense"; Rostron, "Justice Breyer's Truimph."

65. See Rostron, "Justice Breyer's Triumph," 736–43. On the expansion of gun regulation during the era of the Fourteenth Amendment, see Saul Cornell and Justin Florence, "The Right to Bear Arms in the Era of the Fourteenth Amendment: Gun Rights or Gun Regulation?" *Santa Clara Law Review* 50 (2010): 1043–71; and Winkler, *Gun Fight.*

66. Joseph Blocher, "Firearms Localism," *Yale Law Journal* 123 (2013; forthcoming).

67. In his effort to synthesize the theory of the living constitution and originalism, Yale legal scholar Jack Balkin draws a distinction between original meaning and original expected application. See Jack M. Balkin, *Living Originalism* (Cambridge: Cambridge University Press, 2011), esp. 6–8.

★ ★ ★ ★

Appendix B
A Summary of the Briefs Submitted in *Heller*

★ ★ ★ ★

Briefs for District of Columbia v. Heller

PETITIONERS:
DISTRICT OF COLUMBIA AND
ADRIAN M. FENTY, MAYOR OF THE DISTRICT OF COLUMBIA

RESPONDENT:
DICK ANTHONY HELLER

CERTIORARI STAGE

1. PETITION FOR A WRIT OF CERTIORARI

- *Question Presented:* Whether the Second Amendment forbids the District of Columbia from banning private possession of handguns while allowing possession of rifles and shotguns.
- *Summary:* The Petitioners sought a review of the appellate court's reversal of the D.C. District Court's decision in *Parker v. District*

of Columbia, noting that it was the first time in U.S. history that a federal appellate court had invoked the Second Amendment to strike down a gun law. They asked that their petition be granted because the court's decision directly conflicted with precedent by adopting a view that the Second Amendment protected a right to bear arms for self-defense unrelated to military service.

2. Brief in Response to Petition for Certiorari

- *Question Presented:* Whether the Second Amendment guarantees law-abiding, adult individuals a right to keep ordinary, functional firearms, including handguns, in their homes.
- *Summary:* The Respondent agreed that the Court should review the appellate court's decision, but reformulated the question that the Court should consider. He disagreed that the court of appeals had acted in a unprecedented manner, and argued that the Supreme Court had repeatedly indicated that the Second Amendment secures an individual right.

3. Petitioner's Reply to Brief in Response

- *Summary:* The petitioners asked the Court to disregard the Respondent's framing question. They again recognized that the central meaning of the Second Amendment was at issue, and again asked that the Court grant the petition.

4. Conditional Cross-Petition for a Writ of Certiorari

- *Question Presented:* Whether the court of appeals erred in holding, in acknowledged conflict with this Court's decisions in *Babbitt v. United Farm Workers National Union,* 442 U.S. 289 (1979), and *Virginia v. American Booksellers Ass'n,* 484 U.S. 383 (1988), that cross-petitioners cannot maintain a pre-enforcement constitutional challenge to a criminal law without showing that they "have been singled out or uniquely targeted by the D.C. government for prosecution." Petitioners' Appendix ("Pet. App.") at 7a.
- *Summary:* Cross-Petitioners Shelly Parker, Tom G. Palmer, Gillian St. Lawrence, Tracey Ambeau, and George Lyon were plaintiff-appellants

held to have no standing by U.S. Court of Appeals for the D.C. Circuit, thus leaving Anthony Heller as the only one able to contest the D.C. Circuit Court's dismissal of Parker et al.'s lawsuit challenging D.C's 1975 Firearms Control Regulations Act. The cross-petitioners asked that the Court clarify that pre-enforcement challenges under the United States Constitution may be heard in the nation's capital without demonstration of a personalized prosecutorial threat.

5. Cross-Respondent's Brief in Reply

- *Summary:* The Cross-Respondents argued that granting the cross-petition would complicate pending litigation on the meaning of the Second Amendment, and, since the Court had denied certiorari to *Seegars v. Ashcroft* (and the cross-petitioners could identify no reason why this case would obtain a different result), they asked that the cross-petition be denied.

6. Reply to Opposition to Cross-Petition for Writ of Certiorari

- *Summary:* The Cross-Petitioners countered that to deny the cross-petition would be to deprive the cross-petitioners of their right to access the courts, and that the appellate court's ruling conflicted with other Supreme Court and federal appellate court decisions.

7. Brief of the American Academy of Pediatrics, the Society for Adolescent Medicine, and the Children's Defense Fund as Amici Curiae in Support of the Petition for Certiorari

- *Summary:* Since handguns pose a unique danger to children, the amici considered the D.C. gun law to be a reasonable restriction and asked that the writ be granted.

8. Brief of the States of New York, Hawaii, Illinois, and Maryland as Amici Curiae in Support of the Petition for a Writ of Certiorari

- *Summary:* The lower court's decision was inconsistent with *Miller,* and its granting of absolute protection to all arms related to those in use during the Founding created an unmanageable standard.

9. Brief of Amici Curiae Russell Nordyke, Sallie Nordyke, T S Trade Shows, Madison Society, and Golden State Second Amendment Council on "Standing Issues" in Support of Cross-Petitioners' Conditions Cross-Petition

- *Summary:* Under *Seegars*, residents of D.C. will have to violate the District's ordinances to gain access to federal court, and violate state and federal law to persuade federally licensed firearms dealers (like some of the amici) to do the same.

MERITS STAGE

- *Question Presented:* Whether the following provisions—D.C. Code §§ 7-2502.02(a)(4), 22-4504(a), and 7-2507.02—violate the Second Amendment rights of individuals who are not affiliated with any state-regulated militia, but who wish to keep handguns and other firearms for private use in their homes.

1. Brief for Petitioners

- *Summary:* Declaring the decision below to be wrong because (a) D.C. had been regulating guns for two centuries; (b) the decision broke with precedent established in *Miller;* and (c) the Second Amendment is not implicated by local legislation governing only the Nation's capital, the petitioners argued that the text and history of the Second Amendment conclusively prove that it protects the possession and use of guns only in service of an organized militia, not the right of individuals to have guns for their own private purposes.

2. Respondent's Brief

- *Summary:* While some regulation of guns is permissible, an outright ban on the home possession of all functional firearms clearly violates the individual right of the people to keep and bear arms under the Second Amendment. The preamble of the Second Amendment ("A well-regulated militia . . .") is a non-exclusive justification for securing the right to bear arms, but does not limit or negate that right.

3. Reply Brief for Petitioners

- *Summary:* The Court should reverse the decision below because (a) the Second Amendment protects a militia-related right; (b) the Amendment was enacted to preserve state autonomy; (c) the Amendment does not confer a right to possess the weapons of one's choosing.

AMICUS BRIEFS

BRIEFS IN SUPPORT OF THE PETITIONER, OR NEITHER PARTY

1. Brief for Brady Center to Prevent Gun Violence, International Association of Chiefs of Police, Major Cities Chiefs, International Brotherhood of Police Officers, National Organization of Black Law Enforcement Executives, Hispanic American Police Command Officers Association, National Black Police Association, National Latino Peace Officers Association, School Safety Advocacy Council, and Police Executive Research Forum as Amici Curiae Supporting Petitioner

- *Summary:* The lower court denied the importance of the prefatory clause of the Second Amendment, and thus denied the militia-related purpose of the right to bear arms the Founders intended to protect. In so doing, the court broke with two hundred years of precedent and undermined the power of legislatures to deal with the problem of gun violence.

2. Brief for Professors of Linguistics and English Dennis E. Baron, Ph.D., Richard W. Bailey, Ph.D., and Jeffrey P. Kaplan, Ph.D. in Support of Petitioners

- *Summary:* The prefatory clause of the Second Amendment is an absolute clause which dictates the meaning of the right: to perpetuate a "well-regulated militia." The words of the amendment confirm its military meaning, since "bear arms" is an idiom that means to serve as a solider.
- *Cited in the Majority Opinion*
- *Cited in Justice Stevens's Dissent*

3. Brief of the American Academy of Pediatrics, the Society
for Adolescent Medicine, the Children's Defense Fund,
Women against Gun Violence, and Youth Alive! as Amici Curiae
in Support of Petitioners

- *Summary:* Handgun-related injuries and fatalities are significant
  public health problems exacerbated by the presence and easy
  availability of handguns. In the interest of preventing such injuries
  and deaths, and regardless of whether the Second Amendment
  protects the right to possess guns for private purposes, the Court
  should reverse the decision of the Court of Appeals.
- *Cited in Justice Breyer's Dissent*

4. Brief for American Public Health Association, American College
of Preventive Medicine, American Trauma Society, and American
Association of Suicidology as Amici Curiae in Support of Petitioners

- *Summary:* Firearms have a profound effect on the public's health in
  the United States, with handguns being responsible for the majority
  of all firearm-related homicides and suicides. Since there is evidence
  that statutes restricting access to handguns can help prevent such
  deaths, the Court should reverse the decision of the Court of Appeals.

5. Brief for New York, Hawaii, Maryland, Massachusetts, New Jersey,
and Puerto Rico as Amici Curiae in Support of Petitioners

- *Summary:* The Supreme Court, lower federal courts, and state courts
  have consistently ruled that the Second Amendment has no application to state laws. Since the Second Amendment protects state sovereignty by restricting the federal government's ability to regulate gun
  ownership in ways that would interfere with state militias, upholding
  the lower court's decision would reduce state autonomy. The amici
  note that they do not endorse D.C.'s handgun ban, but believe that the
  Second Amendment restricts only the federal government.

6. Brief of Amici Curiae National Network to End Domestic
Violence, National Network to End Domestic Violence Fund,
District of Columbia Coalition against Domestic Violence et al. in
Support of Petitioners

- *Summary:* Domestic violence accounts for over one-third of all
  female murders in the United States, and these murders are most

often committed with a handgun. Statutes like those enacted in D.C could help curb such violence, and thus the Court should reverse the decision of the Court of Appeals.

- *Cited in Justice Breyer's Dissent*

7. Brief Supporting Petitioners of Amici Curiae American Jewish Committee, Anti-Defamation League, Baptist Peace Fellowship of North America, Ceasefire N.J., Central Conference of American Rabbis et al.

- *Summary:* The lower court erred in viewing state and local authority as inconsistent with individual liberty and disregarded the prefatory clause of the Second Amendment to support that error. Since the States have long been able to enact and enforce laws necessary to ordered liberty, the Court must reverse the decision below and recognize that the Second Amendment is a structural protection for federalism meant to preserve the integrity of state militias.

8. Brief of the American Bar Association as Amicus Curiae Supporting Petitioners

- *Summary:* The decision below should be reversed because it improperly rejected the long and consistent line of precedent on which the United States has built its entire matrix of gun regulation. The Court has long recognized the tenet of stare decisis (respect for precedent), and must reverse the decision.

9. Brief for Amici Curiae D.C. Appleseed Center for Law and Justice, D.C. Chamber of Commerce, D.C. for Democracy, D.C. League of Women Voters, Federal City Council, and Washington Council of Lawyers in Support of Petitioners

- *Summary:* The amici, for the purpose of the brief, concede that an individual right to bear arms for self-defense exists, but ask the Court to accord substantial deference to the decisions of elected officials to regulate that right.

10. Brief of Law Professors Erwin Chemerinsky and Adam Winkler as Amici Curiae in Support of Petitioners

- *Summary:* If the Court recognizes an individual right to bear arms for self-defense, it will also have to determine an appropriate standard of review for firearms regulations. The amici argue that reasonableness review remains the appropriate standard.

11. Brief of the City of Chicago and the Board of Education of the City of Chicago as Amici Curiae in Support of Petitioners

- *Summary:* The central purpose of the Second Amendment is to protect States against the threat to their sovereignty posed by the power of the federal government.

12. Brief of Professors of Criminal Justice as Amici Curiae in Support of Petitioners

- *Summary:* D.C.'s handgun ban is an effective law enforcement tool that has promoted public health and safety by reducing the level of handgun violence in the District.

13. Amicus Curiae Brief of District Attorneys in Support of Petitioners

- *Summary:* The three D.C. Code provisions at issue do not violate the Second Amendment, and affirming the decision below could undermine the well-settled Second Amendment principles under which numerous state and local criminal firearms laws have been upheld by courts nationwide.

14. Brief for Former Department of Justice Officials as Amici Curiae in Support of Petitioners

- *Summary:* In opposing various Second Amendment challenges to federal firearms legislation, the government contended for more than sixty years that the Second Amendment did not protect an individual right to keep and bear arms for purposes unrelated to participation in a well-regulated militia. Disregarding this precedent, and that established in *Miller,* will make it more difficult for the government to defend present and future firearms laws.

15. Brief of Amici Curiae Major American Cities, the United States Conference of Mayors, and Legal Community against Violence in Support of Petitioners

- *Summary:* Gun violence poses a serious threat to American cities, and firearm regulation is a critical part of city governments' efforts to protect the health and safety of their residents. Since the Second Amendment does not constrain the ability of local elected officials to respond to local problem like gun violence, the lower decision must not be validated.

16. Brief of Amicus Curiae the NAACP Legal Defense and Educational Fund, Inc., in Support of Petitioners

- *Summary:* The language of the Second Amendment has historically been interpreted to permit Congress and various State legislatures to enact firearms regulations, and the Court has never invalidated such a statute under the Second Amendment. To uphold the decision below would constitute a radical and unwarranted departure from the Court's jurisprudence.

17. Brief of Amici Curiae Jack N. Rakove, Saul Cornell, David T. Konig, William J. Novak, Lois G. Schwoerer et al. in Support of Petitioners

- *Summary:* The context of the ratification of the Second Amendment establishes that the private keeping of firearms was not the right the Framers of the Bill of Rights guaranteed. Instead, the issue of the militia was in dispute in 1787–1789, and that is why the exceptional preamble to the Second Amendment is a true guide to its original meaning.
- *Cited in Justice Stevens's Dissent*

18. Brief for the United States as Amicus Curiae

- *Summary:* Although the court of appeals correctly recognized the individual right to keep and bear arms for self-defense, it applied the wrong standard for evaluating the respondent's Second Amendment claim. Nothing in the Second Amendment calls for the invalidation of the numerous federal laws regulating firearms, so the Court should remand the case for further proceedings.
- *Cited in the Majority Opinion*

19. Brief of Violence Policy Center and the Police Chiefs for the Cities of Los Angeles, Minneapolis, and Seattle as Amici Curiae in Support of Petitioners

- *Summary:* If the Court recognizes an individual right to bear arms outside of militia service, it should also recognize that such a right is subject to reasonable restrictions, and that D.C.'s handgun ban is an eminently reasonable restriction.

20. BRIEF OF MEMBERS OF CONGRESS AS AMICI CURIAE IN SUPPORT OF REVERSAL

- *Summary:* The decision below disregards the Court's settled precedent limiting the application of the Second Amendment to those situations where the preservation and efficiency of a well-regulated militia is potentially impaired, and fails to evaluate the D.C. statutes with the normally applied standards concerning constitutional rights.

BRIEFS IN SUPPORT OF THE RESPONDENT

1. BRIEF OF SECOND AMENDMENT FOUNDATION AS AMICUS CURIAE SUPPORTING RESPONDENT

- *Summary:* The purpose of the Second Amendment is to prevent the federal government from disarming citizens. The language, text, and history of the Second Amendment show that its protection is not limited to militia-related activities, and that the protected right does extend to having arms for self-defense against violent criminals.

2. BRIEF OF AMICI CURIAE SOUTHEASTERN LEGAL FOUNDATION, INC., SECOND AMENDMENT SISTERS, INC., WOMEN AGAINST GUN CONTROL, 60 PLUS ASSOCIATION, INC., ROBERT B. SMITH, J.D., CHRISTIE DAVIES, M.A., PH.D., JOE MICHAEL COBB, AND MRS. MINNIE LEE FAULKNER IN SUPPORT OF RESPONDENT

- *Summary:* The right to use a handgun for self-defense is especially important to women, the elderly, and the physically disabled because their physical characteristics make them the most vulnerable to attack. The Second Amendment embodies an individual right to self-defense that preexisted recognition in the Bill of Rights.
- *Cited in Justice Breyer's Dissent*

3. BRIEF OF THE ALASKA OUTDOOR COUNCIL, ALASKA FISH AND WILDLIFE CONSERVATION FUND, SITKA SPORTSMAN'S ASSOC., JUNEAU RIFLE AND PISTOL CLUB, JUNEAU GUN CLUB, AND ALASKA TERRITORIAL SPORTSMEN, INC., AS AMICI CURIAE SUPPORTING THE RESPONDENT

- *Summary:* The existence of a well-regulated militia rests on the prior existence of an armed citizenry, and the District's collective right theory undercuts the principal purpose of the Second Amendment to protect individuals' firearms.

4. Brief of Amicus Curiae Gun Owners of America, Inc., Gun Owners Foundation, Maryland Shall Issue, Inc., Virginia Citizens Defense League, Gun Owners of California, Inc., Lincoln Institute for Research and Education, and Conservative Legal Defense and Education Fund in Support of Respondent

- *Summary:* According to its text, context, and historic setting, the Second Amendment protects an individual right to private possession and use of handguns in one's home. D.C.'s handgun ban violates this right and discriminates against law-abiding citizens.

5. Brief of Major General John D. Altenburg Jr., Lieutenant General Charles E. Dominy, Lieutenant General Tom Fields, Lieutenant General Jay W. Garner, General Ronald H. Griffith, General William H. Hartzog, Lieutenant General Ronald V. Hite, Major General John G. Meyer Jr., Honorable Joe R. Reeder, Lieutenant General Dutch Shoffner, General John Tilelli, and the American Hunters and Shooters Association as Amici Curiae in Support of Respondent

- *Summary:* The Second Amendment is a cogent blend of both individual and community rights, with each depending on the other. D.C.'s handgun ban directly interferes with various Acts of Congress aimed at enhancing the national defense by promoting martial training amongst the citizenry.
- *Cited in Justice Breyer's Dissent*

6. Brief of the International Law Enforcement Educator and Trainers Association (ILEETA), the International Association of Law Enforcement Firearms Instructors (IALEFI), Maryland State Lodge, Fraternal Order of Police, Southern States Police Benevolent Association et al. as Amici Curiae in Support of Respondent

- *Summary:* Guns in the hands of law-abiding citizens provide very substantial public safety benefits. The Court's own precedent points to the unconstitutionality of D.C.'s handgun ban; therefore the decision below must be affirmed.
- *Cited in Justice Breyer's Dissent*

7. BRIEF OF THE STATES OF TEXAS, ALABAMA, ALASKA, ARKANSAS,
COLORADO, FLORIDA, GEORGIA, IDAHO, INDIANA, KANSAS, KENTUCKY,
LOUISIANA, MICHIGAN, MINNESOTA, MISSISSIPPI, MISSOURI, MONTANA,
NEBRASKA, NEW HAMPSHIRE, NEW MEXICO, NORTH DAKOTA, OHIO,
OKLAHOMA, PENNSYLVANIA, SOUTH CAROLINA, SOUTH DAKOTA, UTAH,
VIRGINIA, WASHINGTON, WEST VIRGINIA, AND WYOMING AS AMICI CURIAE
IN SUPPORT OF RESPONDENT

- *Summary:* The District misconstrues the prefatory clause by claiming
  it restricts the operative clause. The text and original understanding
  of the Second Amendment support an individual right to keep and
  bear arms with which the D.C. handgun ban cannot be reconciled.

8. BRIEF OF AMICI CURIAE 126 WOMEN STATE LEGISLATORS
AND ACADEMICS IN SUPPORT OF RESPONDENT

- *Summary:* D.C.'s prohibition against handguns effectively eliminates
  a woman's ability to defend her life and those of her children against
  violent attack, thus allowing gender-inspired violence free rein by
  ignoring the biological differences between men and women.

9. BRIEF FOR AMICUS CURIAE THE ASSOCIATION OF AMERICAN
PHYSICIANS AND SURGEONS, INC., IN SUPPORT OF RESPONDENT

- *Summary:* In response to the American Academy of Pediatrics (AAP)
  and American Public Health Association (APHA) briefs in support
  of the petitioner (see Briefs in Support of the Petitioner, nos. 3 and 4),
  the amici contend that medical professionals have no more qualifications or basis to opine about the Second Amendment than anyone
  else. The benefits of guns are undeniable, benefits that far outweigh
  the adverse effects.

10. BRIEF OF ACADEMICS AS AMICI CURIAE IN SUPPORT OF RESPONDENT

- *Summary:* There is no evidence that the District's gun ban has
  reduced murder rates since it was enacted in 1977.
- *Cited in Justice Breyer's Dissent*

11. AMICUS CURIAE BRIEF OF THE AMERICAN CENTER
FOR LAW AND JUSTICE IN SUPPORT OF RESPONDENT

- *Summary:* The Bill of Rights was created to ensure that the federal
  government did not act in a manner that would infringe on the fun-

damental rights of the people. Since the Second Amendment was drafted with the express purpose of protecting the right of individual citizens to arm themselves, the decision below should be upheld.

12. Amicus Curiae Brief of the American Civil Rights Union in Support of Respondent

- *Summary:* The Second Amendment's prefatory clause does not nullify the individual right to keep and bear arms in the operative clause. D.C.'s gun law violates the plain terms of the Second Amendment because it prevents citizens from effectively keeping and bearing arms for self-defense within the home.

13. Brief for Amicus Curiae American Legislative Exchange Council in Support of Respondent

- *Summary:* The right to keep and bear arms inside the home (and not outside the home) is deeply rooted in the United States' tradition and history. This history matches the modern national consensus that the Second Amendment is not restricted to the militia, and that handguns should not be banned.

14. Brief of Buckeye Firearms Foundation LLC, National Council for Investigation and Security Services, Ohio Association of Private Detectives Agencies, Inc., DBA Ohio Association of Security and Investigation Services (OASIS), Michigan Council of Private Investigators, Indiana Association of Professional Investigators, and Kentucky Professional Investigators Association as Amici Curiae Supporting Respondent

- *Summary:* The District of Columbia Metropolitan Police Department has failed to protect and serve the citizens under their jurisdiction, a problem compounded by laws that disarm law-abiding citizens.

15. Brief of the Cato Institute and History Professor Joyce Lee Malcolm as Amici Curiae in Support of Respondent

- *Summary:* The right to have and use arms, a right of individuals not conditioned on militia service, was established in English law by the time of the Founding, and Americans claimed and extended that right through the Second Amendment. D.C.'s handgun ban tramples this core right, and thus the Court must affirm the decision below.

16. Brief of Amicus Curiae the Congress of Racial Equality in Support of Respondent

- *Summary:* The history of gun control in America has been one of discrimination, disenfranchisement, and oppression of racial and ethnic minorities. While laws like those in D.C. purport to be neutral, they are often enforced in a discriminatory fashion.
- *Cited in Justice Breyer's Dissent*

17. Brief of Criminologists, Social Scientists, Other Distinguished Scholars, and the Claremont Institute as Amici Curiae in Support of Respondent

- *Summary:* D.C.'s handgun ban removes from law-abiding citizens the best means of protecting themselves from violent criminals.
- *Cited in Justice Breyer's Dissent*

18. Brief of Amicus Curiae the Center for Individual Freedom in Support of Respondent

- *Summary:* The Supreme Court has never settled the issue of whether the Second Amendment protects an individual right to keep and bear arms, nor has it held that the Second Amendment protects only the collective right of state governments to maintain and organize militias. Upholding the Second Amendment as a collective right would contradict other provisions in the Constitution, undermine numerous federal firearms laws, and question the structure of the U.S military and National Guard.

19. Brief of Dr. Suzanna Gratia Hupp, D.C., and Liberty Legal Institute as Amici Curiae in Support of Respondent

- *Summary:* Categorical bans on all gun ownership are per se unconstitutional.

20. Brief for Amici Curiae Disabled Veterans for Self-Defense and Kestra Childers in Support of Respondent

- *Summary:* The Second Amendment protects an individual right, a right based in the moral and common law recognized by the Founders.

21. Brief of Amicus Curiae Eagle Forum Education and Legal Defense Fund in Support of Respondent

- *Summary:* The plain language of the Second Amendment supports the conclusion that it guarantees an individual right to keep and bear arms.

22. Brief for Amici Curiae Former Senior Officials of the Department of Justice in Support of Respondent

- *Summary:* A response to the brief filed by former Department of Justice officials in support of the respondent (see Briefs in Support of the Petitioner, no. 14). Amici argue that the Executive Branch had long interpreted the Second Amendment to secure an individual right before *Miller;* that the Second Amendment secures the rights of law-abiding citizens only; and that the D.C. gun laws are unconstitutional.

23. Brief of the Foundation for Free Expression as Amicus Curiae Supporting Respondent

- *Summary:* The Declaration of Independence recognizes life and liberty as "inalienable" [*sic*] rights, and the Second Amendment safeguards the corresponding right to defend these rights.

24. Brief of Amicus Curiae the Foundation for Moral Law in Support of Respondent

- *Summary:* The common understanding of the Second Amendment at the time of its ratification is crucial to its meaning. The history and text of the Second Amendment supports the interpretation that it protects an individual right to self-defense.

25. Brief for GeorgiaCarry.org as Amicus Curiae Supporting Respondent

- *Summary:* The Petitioner's laws are deeply rooted in a racist attempt to keep arms out of the hands of the politically and economically disadvantaged.

26. Amicus Curiae Brief of the Goldwater Institute
in Support of Respondent

- *Summary:* A response to the United States' brief in support of the petitioner (see Briefs in Support of Petitioners, no. 18). The government correctly argues that the Second Amendment protects a personal right to keep and bear arms, but errs in recommending that the Court not apply the strict scrutiny that traditionally attaches to fundamental personal rights enumerated in the Constitution.

27. Brief of Amicus Curiae Grass Roots of South Carolina, Inc.,
in Support of Respondent

- *Summary:* The right to keep and bear arms in one's home, and unconnected with the militia, is a preexisting right that is unabridged by the Constitution.

28. Brief of Amicus Curiae the Heartland Institute
in Support of Respondent

- *Summary:* The Second Amendment's protections descended from the primary right of self-defense, and thus D.C.'s gun laws are unconstitutional since they completely ban handguns (the gun most commonly used for self-defense) instead of merely regulating them.

29. Brief for the Institute for Justice as Amicus Curiae
in Support of Respondent

- *Summary:* The history and adoption of the Fourteenth Amendment demonstrates the Framers' specific and repeated concern that freedmen were being disarmed in violation of the right to bear arms. The Framers of the Amendment intended for the Second Amendment to be incorporated, and the Court's decision on the reach of the Amendment will support incorporation.
- *Cited in the Majority Opinion*

30. Brief of Amicus Curiae Jews for the Preservation
of Firearms Ownership in Support of Respondent

- *Summary:* Since disarmament naturally and inextricably goes hand in hand with mass oppression and genocide, and because the Founders never intended that the people be stripped of their ability to defend themselves against tyranny, the Court must affirm the decision below.

31. Brief for Amici Curiae [Ohio Concealed Carry Permitholders and the U.S. Bill of Rights Foundation] in Support of Respondent

- *Summary:* The right to keep and bear arms is a fundamental right, and if such a right is undercut, "we start down a path that will lead to the tyranny of colonial England where our rights and freedoms are infringed upon."

32. Amicus Curiae Brief of the Libertarian National Committee, Inc., in Support of Respondent

- *Summary:* In his amicus brief, Solicitor General Paul D. Clement proposes a balancing test involving heightened scrutiny as a standard of review (see Briefs in Support of Petitioners, no. 18). The Solicitor General misinterprets the standard he proposes, and even if that standard were applicable, it would affirm the decision below.

33. Brief of Maricopa County Attorney's Office and Other Prosecutor Agencies as Amici Curiae in Support of Respondent

- *Summary:* The right to keep and bear arms belongs to the people, and speculation that recognizing this individual right will dismantle existing firearms regulations is unfounded.

34. Amicus Curiae Brief of Mountain States Legal Foundation in Support of Respondent

- *Summary:* The Founders' two primary motivations for drafting the Second Amendment were self-defense and protection from government tyranny. These goals can be realized only if individuals, not militias, are protected in their right to keep and bear arms.

35. Brief for the National Rifle Association and the NRA Civil Rights Defense Fund as Amici Curiae in Support of Respondent

- *Summary:* The individual right to keep and bear arms is a fundamental right, and one essential to a free state. The Second Amendment, like the First, should be subjected to strict scrutiny—a standard of review that does not challenge long-standing laws regulating the ownership and use of firearms.
- *Cited in Justice Breyer's Dissent*

36. Brief of the National Shooting Sports Foundation, Inc., as Amicus Curiae in Support of Respondent

- *Summary:* Firearms played a central role in Americans' lives before and during the Founding era, proving that the Framers intended to protect these important tools of survival.

37. Brief of Amici Curiae Organizations and Scholars Correcting Myths and Misrepresentations Commonly Deployed by Opponents of an Individual-Rights-Based Interpretation of the Second Amendment in Support of Respondent

- *Summary:* D.C. and various amici misstate and decontextualize history to perpetuate two common myths: (a) that the right to bear arms pertains only to the militia or National Guard; (b) that gun ownership is dangerous and gun owners are more likely to harm themselves than a potential attacker.

38. Brief of the Paragon Foundation, Inc., as Amicus Curiae in Support of Respondent

- *Summary:* The individual right to keep and bear arms guaranteed by the Second Amendment flows from the preexisting natural right to self-defense. The Court must affirm the decision below to be consistent with the Founding Fathers' vision of the Bill of Rights.

39. Brief for Amicus Curiae the President Pro Tempore of the Senate of Pennsylvania, Joseph B. Scarnati III, in Support of Respondent

- *Summary:* Pennsylvania has recognized an individual right to bear arms since 1776, and thus its history can inform any inquiry into the meaning of the Second Amendment.
- *Cited in Justice Breyer's Dissent*

40. Brief of Pink Pistols and Gays and Lesbians for Individual Liberty as Amici Curiae in Support of Respondent

- *Summary:* Laws that restrict personal firearms use disproportionately impact minority individuals who are targets of hate violence. The Petitioner's argument to limit the right to bear arms to those serving in militias would eradicate any Second Amendment rights for members of the LGBT community under the government's "Don't Ask, Don't Tell" policy.

41. Brief of Amici Curiae Retired Military Officers in Support of Respondent

- *Summary:* The Second Amendment enshrined the preexisting right to personal firearm ownership and assuaged the Anti-Federalists' fears of a large standing army by ensuring that the American people had the arms necessary to oppose a tyrannical government. Ensuring that this right is protected plays a key role in national security by creating a pool of talented recruits for the U.S. Army and deterring foreign aggressors from attacking the United States.
- *Cited in Justice Breyer's Dissent*

42. Brief of Amicus Curiae the Rutherford Institute in Support of Respondent

- *Summary:* The gun has long been a symbol of freedom in the United States. By removing the basic protection the Second Amendment affords individuals, an essential barrier against a potentially oppressive government would be eviscerated.

43. Brief for Amici Curiae 55 Members of the United States Senate, the President of the United States Senate, and 250 Members of United States House of Representatives in Support of Respondent

- *Summary:* Congress has a long history of protecting the right of the people to keep and bear arms. Congress's understanding of the Second Amendment is that it protects an individual right, and that the District's firearms prohibitions infringe upon that right.

44. Brief for State Firearm Associations as Amici Curiae in Support of Respondent

- *Summary:* Private firearm ownership is an essential element of the free society the Framers envisioned and remains integral today.

45. Brief of Virginia1774.org, Amicus Curiae, in Support of Respondent

- *Summary:* The Second Amendment preserves to the people both a well-regulated militia and the individual right to keep and bear arms for self-defense. The rights are separate and distinct, and one does not nullify the other.

46. Brief of the State of Wisconsin as Amicus Curiae
in Support of Respondent

- *Summary:* Affirming the decision below will protect Wisconsin citizens against possible federal infringement of the right to keep and bear arms, protected by the Wisconsin Constitution.

Appendix C
Articles Cited in Briefs

Listed here is all scholarship used in the *Heller* case (brief and opinions) that makes a significant historical argument about the Second Amendment. The number given for each article or book refers to the number of times that article or book was listed in the Table of Authorities for a brief or cited in the majority or dissenting opinions.

			Briefs		*Opinion*	
Author(s)	Title	Publication	Pet	Res	Ma	Dis
Amar, Akhil Reed	"The Bill of Rights and the Fourteenth Amendment"	101 Yale L..J. 1193 (1992)		7		
	"The Bill of Rights as a Constitution"	100 Yale L..J. 1131 (1991)		1		
	The Bill of Rights: Creation and Reconstruction	Yale University Press (2000)	1	4		

			Briefs		Opinion	
Author(s)	Title	Publication	Pet	Res	Ma	Dis
Barnett, Randy E.	"Was the Right to Keep and Bear Arms Conditioned on Service in an Organized Militia?"	83 Tex. L. Rev. 237 (2004)		3	1	
(and Don B. Kates)	"Under Fire: The New Consensus on the Second Amendment"	45 Emory L.J. 1259 (1996)		3		1
Barton, David	*The Second Amendment: Preserving the Inalienable Right of Individual Self-Protection*	WallBuilder Press (2000)		1		
Bellesiles, Michael	*Arming America, The Origins of a National Gun Culture*	Alfred A. Knopf (2000)		1		
Bogus, Carl T.	"The Hidden History of the Second Amendment"	31 U.C. Davis L. Rev. 309 (1998)	4			
	"The History and Politics of Second Amendment Scholarship: A Primer"	76 Chi.-Kent L. Rev. 3 (2000)	1			
	"What Does the Second Amendment Restrict? A Collective Rights Analysis"	18 Const. Comment. 485 (Winter 2001)	1			
Churchill, Robert	"Gun Ownership in Early America: A Survey of Manuscript Militia Returns"	60 Wm. & Mary Q. 615 (2003)		1		
	"Gun Regulation, the Police Power, and the Right to Keep Arms in Early America"	25 Law & Hist. Rev. 139, 162 (2007)		1		1
Cornell, Saul	"St. George Tucker and the Second Amendment: Original Understandings and Modern Misunderstandings"	47 Wm. & Mary L. Rev. 1123 (2006)	3			1
	"The Early American Origins of the Modern Gun Control Debate: The Right to Bear Arms, Firearms Regulation, and the Lessons of History"	17 Stan. L. & Pol'y. Rev. 571 (2006)	2			

Author(s)	Title	Publication	Briefs Pet	Briefs Res	Opinion Ma	Opinion Dis
	"The Original Meaning of Original Understanding: A Neo-Blackstonian Critique"	67 Md. L. Rev. 150 (2007)	2			
	A Well-Regulated Militia: The Founding Fathers and the Origins of Gun Control in America	Oxford Univ. Press (2006)	8			1
(and Nathan DeDino)	"A Well-Regulated Right: The Early American Origins of Gun Control"	73 Fordham L. Rev. 487 (2004)	7			
Cottrol, Robert, and Raymond Diamond	"Never Intended to Be Applied to the White Population: Firearms Regulation and Racial Disparity—The Redeemed South's Legacy"	70 Chi.-Kent L. Rev. 1307 (1995)		4		
	"The Second Amendment: Toward an Afro-Americanist Reconsideration"	80 Geo. L.J. 309 (1991)		6		
Cramer, Clayton E.	*Armed in America: The Remarkable Story of How and Why Guns Became as American as Apple Pie*	Thomas Nelson (2009)		2		
	For the Defense of Themselves and the State	Praeger (1994)		1		
(and Joseph Olson)	"Pistols, Crime, and Public Safety in Early America"	44 Willamette L. Rev. (2008)		1		
(and Joseph Olson)	"What Did 'Bear Arms' Mean in the Second Amendment?"	6 Geo. J. L. & Pub. Pol'y. (2008)		2	1	
Cress, Lawrence D.	"An Armed Community: The Origins and Meaning of the Right to Bear Arms"	71 J. Am. Hist. 22 (1984)	4			
Dorf, Michael C.	"What Does the Second Amendment Mean Today?"	76 Chi.-Kent L. Rev. 291 (2000)	1			
Dowlut, Robert, and Janet A. Knoop	"State Constitutions and the Right to Keep and Bear Arms"	7 Okl. City Univ. L. Rev. 177 (1982)		2		

Author(s)	Title	Publication	Briefs		Opinion	
			Pet	Res	Ma	Dis
Emery, Lucilius A.	"The Constitutional Right to Keep and Bear Arms"	28 Harv. L. Rev. 473 (1915)	1			
Feller, Peter B., and Karl L. Gotting	"The Second Amendment: A Second Look"	61 N.W. U. L. Rev. 46 (1966)	1			
Finkleman, Paul	"'A Well-Regulated Militia': The Second Amendment in Historical Perspective"	76 Chi.-Kent L. Rev. 195 (2000)	2			
Halbrook, Stephen P.	"Congress Interprets the Second Amendment: Declarations by a Co-Equal Branch on the Individual Right to Keep and Bear Arms"	62 Tenn. L. Rev. 597 (1995)		1		
	"Personal Security, Personal Liberty, and 'the Constitutional Right to Bear Arms': Visions of the Framers of the Fourteenth Amendment"	5 Seton Hall Const. L.J. 341 (1995)		1		
	"The Freedmen's Bureau Act and the Conundrum over Whether the Fourteenth Amendment Incorporates the Second Amendment"	29 N. Kentucky L. Rev. 683 (2002)		1		
	"The Original Understanding of the Second Amendment"	In *The Bill of Rights: Original Meaning and Current Understanding*, ed. Eugene Hickock Jr. (University of Va. Press, 1991)		1		
	"The Jurisprudence of the Second and Fourteenth Amendments"	4 Geo. Mason L. Rev. 1 (1981)		2		
	"The Right of the People or the Power of the State: Bearing Arms, Arming Militias, and the Second Amendment"	26 Val. U. L. Rev. 131 (1991)		1		
	"To Keep and Bear Their Private Arms: The Adoption of the Second Amendment, 1787–1791"	10 N. Ky. L. Rev. 13 (1982)		1		

Author(s)	Title	Publication	Briefs Pet	Briefs Res	Opinion Ma	Opinion Dis
	"What the Framers Intended: A Linguistic Analysis of the Right to 'Bear Arms'"	49 Law & Contemp. Probs. 151 (1986)		1		
	A Right to Bear Arms: State and Federal Bills of Rights and Constitutional Guarantees	Greenwood Press (1989)		2		
	Freedmen, the Fourteenth Amendment, and the Right to Bear Arms, 1866–1876	Praeger (1998)		6	1	
	That Every Man Be Armed: The Evolution of a Constitutional Right	Independence Institute (1984)		7		
	The Founders' Second Amendment: Origins of the Right to Bear Arms	Ivan R. Dee (2008)		2		
Hardaway, Robert	"The Inconvenient Militia Clause of the Second Amendment"	16 St. John's J. Legal Comment. 41 (2002)	1			
Hardy, David T.	"Armed Citizens, Citizen Armies"	9 Harv. J. of L. & Pub. Pol'y. 559 (1986)		1		
Henigan, Dennis A.	"Arms, Anarchy, and the Second Amendment"	26 Valparaiso L. Rev. 107 (1991)	1			
Heyman, Steven J.	"Natural Rights and the Second Amendment"	76 Chi.-Kent L. Rev. 237 (2000)	1		1	
Higginbotham, R. Don	"The Federalized Militia: A Neglected Aspect of Second Amendment Scholarship"	55 Wm. & Mary Q. 39 (1998)	4			
	"The Second Amendment in Historical Context"	16 Const. Comment. 221 (1999)	1			
Kates, Don	"Handgun Prohibition and the Original Meaning of the Second Amendment"	82 Mich. L. Rev. 204 (1983)		9	1	
Konig, David T.	"The Second Amendment: A Missing Transatlantic Context for the Historical Meaning of 'the Right of the People to Keep and Bear Arms'"	22 Law & Hist. Rev. 119 (2004)	5			

Author(s)	Title	Publication	Briefs		Opinion	
			Pet	Res	Ma	Dis
Kopel, David B.	"It Isn't about Duck Hunting: The British Origins of the Right to Arms"	93 Mich. L. Rev. 1333 (1995)		1		
	"The Second Amendment in the Nineteenth Century"	BYU L. Rev. 1359 (1998)		4		
	"The Supreme Court's Thirty-five Other Gun Cases: What the Supreme Court Has Said about the Second Amendment"	18 St. Louis U. Pub. L. Rev. (1999)	1			
	"What State Constitutions Teach about the Second Amendment"	29 N. Ky. L. Rev. 827 (2002)	1			
Kozuskanich, Nathan	"Defending Themselves: The Original Understanding of the Right to Bear Arms"	39 Rutgers L.J. 1041 (2008)	4			
	"Originalism, History, and the Second Amendment: What Did Bearing Arms Really Mean to the Founders?"	10 U. Pa. J. Const. L. 413 (2008)	1			
Levinson, Sanford	"The Embarrassing Second Amendment"	99 Yale L.J. 637 (1989)	1	7		
Lund, Nelson	"D.C.'s Handgun Ban and the Constitutional Right to Arms: One Hard Question?"	18 Geo. Mason U. Civ. Rts. L.J. 299	1	5		
	"Putting the Second Amendment to Sleep"	8 Green Bag 2d 101 (2004)		1		
	"The Ends of Second Amendment Jurisprudence: Firearms Disabilities and Domestic Violence Restraining Orders"	4 Tex. Rev. L. & Pol. 157 (1999)		1		
	"The Past and the Future of the Individual's Right to Bear Arms"	31 Ga. L. Rev. 35 (1996)	1	3		
	"The Second Amendment, Political Liberty, and the Right to Self-Preservation"	39 Ala. L. Rev. 103 (1987)		1		

			Briefs		Opinion	
Author(s)	Title	Publication	Pet	Res	Ma	Dis
Malcolm, Joyce Lee	"The Role of the Militia in the Development of the Englishman's Right to be Armed: Clarifying the Legacy"	5 J. Firearms & Pub. Pol'y. 139 (1993)		1		
	Guns and Violence: The English Experience	Harvard University Press (2002)		4		
	The Right of the People to Keep and Bear Arms: The Common Law Tradition	10 Hastings Const. L.Q. 285 (1983)		2		
	To Keep and Bear Arms: The Origins of an Anglo-American Right	Harvard University Press (1996)	1	6	1	
Merkel, William G.	"A Cultural Turn: Reflections on Recent Historical and Legal Writing on the Second Amendment	17 Stan. L. & Pol'y. Rev. 671 (2006)	1			
Nosanchuk, Mathew S.	"The Embarrassing Interpretation of the Second Amendment"	29 N. Ky. L. Rev. 705 (2002)	2			
Powe Jr., L.A.	"Guns, Words, and Constitutional Interpretation"	38 Wm. & Mary L. Rev. (1997)		1		
Rakove, Jack	*Original Meanings: Politics and Ideas in the Making of the Constitution*	Knopf (1996)	1			
	"The Second Amendment: The Highest Stage of Originalism"	76 Chi.-Kent L. Rev. 103 (2000)	5		1	
Reynolds, Glenn H.	"The Right to Keep and Bear Arms under the Tennessee Constitution: A Case Study in Civic Republican Thought"	61 Tenn. L. Rev. 647 (1994)		1		
(and Don B. Kates)	"The Second Amendment and States' Rights: A Thought Experiment"	36 Wm. & Mary L. Rev. 1737 (1995)		1		
Schwoerer, Lois G.	"To Hold and Bear Arms: The English Perspective"	76 Chi.-Kent L. Rev. 27 (2000)	5		1	
Shalhope, Robert E.	"The Ideological Origins of the Second Amendment"	69 J. Am. Hist. 599 (1982)		2		

			Briefs		Opinion	
Author(s)	Title	Publication	Pet	Res	Ma	Dis
Uviller, Richard H., and William G. Merkel	"The Second Amendment in Context: The Case of the Vanishing Predicate"	76 Chi.-Kent L. Rev. 403 (2000)	4	1		
	The Militia and the Right to Arms, or, How the Second Amendment Fell Silent	Duke University Press (2002)		1		
Van Alstyne, William	"The Second Amendment and the Personal Right to Arms"	43 Duke L.J. 1236 (1994)		2		
Volokh, Eugene	"Necessary to the Security of a Free State"	83 Notre Dame L. Rev. 1 (2007)		3	1	
	"State Constitutional Rights to Keep and Bear Arms"	11 Tex. Rev. L. & Pol. 191 (2006)	2	2	1	
	"The Commonplace Second Amendment"	73 NYU L. Rev. 793 (1998)	3	8	1	
Weatherup, Roy G.	"Standing Armies and Armed Citizens: An Historical Analysis of the Second Amendment"	2 Hastings Const. L.Q. 961 (1975)	5	2		
Wiener, Frederick B.	"The Militia Clause of the Constitution"	54 Harv. L. Rev. 181 (1940)	3			1
Williams, David C.	"Civic Republicanism and the Citizen Militia: The Terrifying Second Amendment"	101 Yale L.J. 551 (1991)		1		
Wills, Garry	"To Keep and Bear Arms"	N.Y. Rev. of Books, Sept. 21, 1995	3			
Yassky, David	"The Second Amendment: Structure, History, and Constitutional Change"	99 Mich. L. Rev. 588 (2000)	4			
Young, David E.	*The Founders' View of the Right to Bear Arms*	Golden Oak Books (2007)		3		

Appendix D
Briefs and Articles Cited in *Heller*

The numbers refer to the page(s) of the decision on which each brief was cited.
Diss (S) = Stevens dissent. Diss (B) = Breyer dissent.

Title of Brief	*Opinion*		
	Majority	Dis (S)	Dis (B)
Brief for Petitioners	3, 9, 22, 26, 58, 59		13, 31
Brief for Respondent	3		9, 13, 23, 37
Brief for Professors of Linguistics and English Dennis E. Baron, Ph.D., Richard W. Bailey, Ph.D., and Jeffrey P. Kaplan, Ph.D., in Support of Petitioners	3, 12, 13, 15	12	
Brief for the Institute for Justice as Amicus Curiae in Support of Respondent	41		
Brief of Amici Curiae Jack N. Rakove, Saul Cornell, David T. Konig, William J. Novak, Lois G. Schwoerer et al. in Support of Petitioners		30 (n. 31)	
Brief of Criminologists, Social Scientists, Other Distinguished Scholars, and the Claremont Institute as Amici Curiae in Support of Respondent			20, 21, 23, 25

| | Opinion | | |
Title of Brief	Majority	Dis (S)	Dis (B)
Brief of Amicus Curiae Congress of Racial Equality in Support of Respondent			20
Brief for the National Rifle Association and the NRA Civil Rights Defense Fund as Amici Curiae in Support of Respondent			20, 31
Brief of Academics as Amici Curiae in Support of Respondent			21
Brief of the International Law Enforcement Educator and Trainers Association (ILEETA), the International Association of Law Enforcement Firearms Instructors (IALEFI), Maryland State Lodge, Fraternal Order of Police, Southern States Police Benevolent Association et al. as Amici Curiae in Support of Respondent			21, 31
Brief for Amicus Curiae the President Pro Tempore of the Senate of Pennsylvania, Joseph B. Scarnati III, in Support of Respondent			22
Brief of Amicus Curiae the Heartland Institute in Support of Respondent			22
Brief of Amici Curiae the Southeastern Legal Foundation, Inc., Second Amendment Sisters, Inc., Women against Gun Control, 60 Plus Association, Inc., Robert B. Smith, J.D., Christie Davies, M.A., Ph.D., Joe Michael Cobb, and Mrs. Minnie Lee Faulkner in Support of Respondent			23, 25
Brief for American Public Health Association, American College of Preventive Medicine, American Trauma Society, and American Association of Suicidology as Amici Curiae in Support of Petitioners			25
Brief for Amicus Curiae the Association of American Physicians and Surgeons, Inc., in Support of Respondent			26
Brief of Amici Curiae Retired Military Officers in Support of Respondent			26
Brief of Major General John D. Altenburg Jr., Lieutenant General Charles E. Dominy, Lieutenant General Tom Fields, Lieutenant General Jay W. Garner, General Ronald H. Griffith, General William H. Hartzog, Lieutenant General Ronald V. Hite, Major General John G. Meyer Jr., Honorable Joe R. Reeder, Lieutenant General Dutch Shoffner, General John Tilelli, and the American Hunters and Shooters Association as Amici Curiae in Support of Respondent			29
Brief of the American Academy of Pediatrics, the Society for Adolescent Medicine, and the Children's Defense Fund as Amici Curiae in Support of the Petition for Certiorari			32
Brief of Amici Curiae the National Network to End Domestic Violence, National Network to End Domestic Violence Fund, District of Columbia Coalition against Domestic Violence et al. in Support of Petitioners			33

Index